1001 Things You Wanted To Know About Visual FoxPro

Marcia Akins
Andy Kramek
Rick Schummer

Hentzenwerke Publishing

Published by:
Hentzenwerke Publishing
980 East Circle Drive
Whitefish Bay WI 53217 USA

Hentzenwerke Publishing books are available through booksellers and directly from the
publisher. Contact Hentzenwerke Publishing at:
414.332.9876
414.332.9463 (fax)
www.hentzenwerke.com
books@hentzenwerke.com

1001 Things You Wanted to Know About Visual FoxPro
    By Marcia Akins, Andy Kramek and Rick Schummer
    Technical Editor: John Hosier
    Copy Editor: Julie A. Martin

ISBN: 0-9655093-3-8

Manufactured in the United States of America.

Dedications

Andy Kramek

This work is dedicated to my father, who was so proud when I began to have some of my writing published, but died shortly before completion of this, latest, book which I know would have made him even more happy.

Marcia Akins

To my sister Nancy who taught me that it's never too late to try and without whose help and support I would not have been able to do all that I have in the past year. Thank you, I would not have been able to write this book without you.

Rick Schummer

This book is dedicated to the memory of my Grandpa, Richard Holden. Grandpa gave me a pep talk on the darkest day of my college career. I was actually considering giving up my path to a degree in Computer Science from Oakland University. This man never finished high school, yet is one of the wisest people I have met in this lifetime. Had it not been for his perspective, I might not be the computer geek that I am today. For this direction I am eternally grateful.

List of Chapters

Table of Contents

Chapter 3: Design, Design and Nothing Else   55

Chapter 8: Data Buffering and Transactions   239

Chapter 9: Views in Particular, SQL in General   277

Chapter 10: Non-Visual Classes   313

Chapter 11: Forms and Other Visual Classes   363

Chapter 12: Developer Productivity Tools   391

Our Contract with You, The Reader

In which we, the folks that make up Hentzenwerke Publishing, describe what you, the reader, can expect from this book and from us.

Hi there!

I've been writing professionally (in other words, eventually getting a paycheck for my scribbles) since 1974 and writing about software development since 1992. As an author, I've worked with a half-dozen different publishers and corresponded with thousands of readers over the years. As a software developer and all-around geek, I've also acquired a library of over a hundred computer and software-related books.

Thus, when I donned the publisher's cap four years ago to produce the 1997 Developer's Guide, I had some pretty good ideas of what I liked (and didn't like) from publishers, what readers liked and didn't like and what I, as a reader, liked and didn't like.

Now, with our new titles for the spring and summer of 2000, we're entering our third season. (For those keeping track, the '97 DevGuide was our first, albeit abbreviated, season and the batch of six "Essentials" for Visual FoxPro 6.0 in 1999 was our second.)

John Wooden, the famed UCLA basketball coach, had posited that teams aren't consistent – they're always getting better – or worse. We'd like to get better… One of my goals for this season is to build a closer relationship with you, the reader.

In order to do this, you've got to know what you should expect from us.

- You have the right to expect that your order will be processed quickly and correctly and that your book will be delivered to you in new condition.
- You have the right to expect that the content of your book is technically accurate, up to date, that the explanations are clear and that the layout is easy to read and follow without a lot of fluff or nonsense.
- You have the right to expect access to source code, errata, FAQs and other information that's relevant to the book via our website.
- You have the right to expect an electronic version of your printed book (in compiled HTML Help format) to be available via our website.
- You have the right to expect that, if you report errors to us, your report will be responded to promptly and that the appropriate notice will be included in the errata and/or FAQs for the book.

Naturally, there are some limits that we bump up against. There are humans involved and they make mistakes. A book of 500 pages contains, on average, 150,000 words and several megabytes of source code. It's not possible to edit and re-edit multiple times to catch every last misspelling and typo, nor is it possible to test the source code on every permutation of development environment and operating system – and still price the book affordably.

Once printed, bindings break, ink gets smeared, signatures get missed during binding. On the delivery side, websites go down, packages get lost in the mail.

Nonetheless, we'll make our best effort to correct these problems – once you let us know about them.

And, thus, in return, when you have a question or run into a problem, we ask that you first consult the errata and/or FAQs for your book on our website. If you don't find the answer there, please email us at books@hentzenwerke.com with as much information and detail, including (1) the steps to reproduce the problem, (2) what happened and (3) what you expected to happen, together with (4) any other relevant information.

I'd like to stress that we need you to communicate questions and problems clearly. For example...

"Your downloads don't work" isn't enough information for us to help you. "I get a 404 error when I click on the **Download Source Code** link on www.hentzenwerke.com/book/downloads.html." is something we can help you with.

"The code in chapter 14 caused an error" again isn't enough information. "I performed the following steps to run the source code program DisplayTest.PRG in chapter 14 and receive an error that said "Variable m.liCounter" not found" is something we can help you with.

We'll do our best to get back to you within a couple of days either with an answer, or at least an acknowledgment that we've received your inquiry and that we're working on it.

On behalf of the authors, technical editors, copy editors, layout artists, graphic artists, indexers and all the other folks who have worked to put this book in your hands, I'd like to thank you for purchasing this book and hope that it will prove to be a valuable addition to your technical library. Please let us know what you think about this book – we're looking forward to hearing from you.

As Groucho Marx once observed, "Outside of a dog, a book is a man's best friend. Inside of a dog, it's too dark to read."

Whil Hentzen
Hentzenwerke Publishing
May, 2000

Acknowledgements

If we were to try and acknowledge, individually, all of those who had contributed, even indirectly, to this book we would have a list of acknowledgements longer than the book itself. But there are some whose contributions have been so significant that we must acknowledge specifically.

First, we'd like to recognize our Technical Editor, John Hosier. Without John the book would never have been in such good shape. Not only did he correct us when we were wrong but his suggestions and improvements were invaluable to us all. The job of Technical Editor is, in many ways, harder than actually writing (and even more thankless) but he has managed it wonderfully - thank you so much, John.

Next, of course, comes our friend and gallant publisher, Whil Hentzen. He was the inspiration behind this book, (though we are still not sure that what he got was what he originally wanted) and his support and assistance has been invaluable. Thanks are also due to all of the team at Hentzenwerke for taking our random scribblings and creating this wonderful book from them. We really appreciate it.

Now we must tackle the most difficult group, the FoxPro Community. We consider ourselves very fortunate to be members, however humble, of this wonderful, multi-national, community. Without you, this book could not have been written and certainly would never have sold a single copy.

The FoxPro Community really IS a community and it sustains itself physically through the many Fox-based User Groups in all parts of the world, electronically through the CompuServe Forums, News Groups, Universal Thread, FoxForum, the Wiki and so on. The comradeship and mutual support is, we believe, unrivalled and long may it continue to be so. Putting faces to names has always been part of the fun of attending DevCon, WhilFest, SoCal, Frankfurt, Amsterdam or any of the many other FoxPro conferences and meetings all over the world. That so many of those "faces" have also become friends is a wonderful bonus and we look forward to renewing old friendships and forging new ones over the years to come.

While it is true that everyone in the community has contributed, in some way, to this book, there are a few individuals whose contributions have been very direct and very specific and we want to take this opportunity to thank them publicly.

- *Steven Black* (for his "Share" and "MC" utilities)
- *Gary DeWitt* (for mining the Windows API constants)
- *Tamar Granor and Ted Roche* (for the indispensable "Hacker's Guide to Visual FoxPro 6.0")
- *Doug Hennig* (for sharing his work with the Visual FoxPro Builders)
- *Christof Lange* (for his method of making a FoxPro application "single instance")
- *John Petersen* (for his contribution of OptUtility)

Last, but by no means least, comes the most important person to us authors, *you*, our Reader. Thank you for buying the book. We hope that it both pleases you and is useful to you.

Maybe, if we are ever crazy enough to tackle another, you will remember us and give us a look then too.

Andy Kramek
Marcia Akins
Rick Schummer

February 2000

About Us

Andy Kramek

Andy is an independent consultant and long-standing FoxPro developer based, at the time of writing, in England. As well as being a Microsoft Most Valuable Professional, he is also a Microsoft Certified Professional for Visual FoxPro in both Desktop and Distributed applications. Andy is a long time member of the FoxPro support forums on CompuServe, where he is also a SysOp.

Andy's published work includes "The Revolutionary Guide to Visual FoxPro OOP" (Wrox Press, 1996) and, together with his friend and colleague Paul Maskens, the monthly "Kitbox" column in FoxTalk (Pinnacle Publications). Andy has spoken at conferences and user group meetings in England, mainland Europe and the USA.

In the little spare time that he has, Andy enjoys playing squash and golf (though not necessarily at the same time), traveling and listening to Marcia.
You can reach Andy at:
AndyKr@Compuserve.com

Marcia Akins

Marcia is an experienced developer in several languages who has been working mainly in Visual FoxPro for the past eight years. She is an independent consultant and, at the time of writing, had deserted her native Ohio to live and work (with Andy) for a year or so in England. She is a Microsoft Most Valuable Professional, and holds Microsoft Certified Professional qualifications for both Visual FoxPro Desktop and Distributed applications.

She has several articles in *FoxPro Advisor* to her credit and is widely, and at least half-seriously, known as the "Queen 'o' the Grids". She has spoken at conferences and user group meetings in the USA, England and mainland Europe and is a frequent contributor to CompuServe, the Universal Thread and FoxForum.com.

When she is not busy developing software, Marcia enjoys golfing, skiing, playing tennis, working out at the gym, traveling, and harassing Andy.
You can reach Marcia at:
MarciaGAkins@Compuserve.com

Rick Schummer

Rick is the Director of Development for Kirtland Associates, Inc. in Troy MI, USA. Kirtland Associates writes custom database applications for a rapidly expanding customer base. He not only directs the development of this fun organization, but also participates in the education of new and experienced Visual FoxPro developers. It is a great way to further your own skills. After hours he enjoys writing developer tools that improve his team's productivity and occasionally pens articles for *FoxTalk, FoxPro Advisor*, and several user group newsletters.

Rick recently became a Microsoft Certified Professional by passing both the VFP Desktop and Distributed exams.

He spends his free time with his family, cheers the kids as they play soccer, has a volunteer role with the Boy Scouts, and loves spending time camping, cycling, coin collecting, photographing and reading. Rick is a founding member and secretary of both the Detroit Area Fox User Group (DAFUG – http://www.dafug.org) and Sterling Heights Computer Club (http://member.apcug.org/shcc).

You can reach Rick at:

rschummer@compuserve.com
ras@kirtlandsys.com
http://my.voyager.net/rschummer

John Hosier

John has been active in the FoxPro community since 1987 and has been a developer, consultant, author, conference speaker and trainer. John was also a founding board member of the Mid-Atlantic FoxPro User Group and has served as its president and treasurer. As a consultant, John has worked with both large and small clients in Eastern and Western Europe, the Middle East, the Caribbean and all over the United States. John's publishing credits include FoxPro Advisor, FoxTalk, FoxPro User's Journal and a German magazine called "Data Base: Das Fachmagazin für Datenbankentwickler." No, John does not speak German, but he thinks it is pretty funny that he wrote an article that he was unable read in the final publication. As a Microsoft Certified Professional in Visual FoxPro, John has worked on a wide variety of projects including client server, internet/intranet (including an XML parser written in VFP) and distributed applications. John currently makes his home in the Chicago area.

You can reach John at:

JHosier@earthlink.net

How to Download the Files

There are two sets of files that accompany this book. The first is the source code referenced throughout the text, and noted by the spider web icon; the second is the e-book version of this book – the compiled HTML Help (.CHM) file. Here's how to get them.

Both the source code and the CHM file are available for download from the Hentzenwerke website. In order to do so, following these instructions:

1. Point your web browser to www.hentzenwerke.com.

2. Look for the link that says "Download Source Code & .CHM Files." (The text for this link may change over time – if it does, look for a link that references Books or Downloads.)

3. A page describing the download process will appear. This page has two sections.

Section 1: If you were issued a username/password from Hentzenwerke Publishing, you can enter them into this page.

Section 2: If you did not receive a username/password from Hentzenwerke Publishing, don't worry! Just enter your email alias and look for the question about your book. Note that you'll need your book when you answer the question.

4. A page that lists the hyperlinks for the appropriate downloads will appear.

Note that the .CHM file is covered by the same copyright laws as the printed book. Reproduction and/or distribution of the .CHM file is against the law.

If you have questions or problems, the fastest way to get a response is to email us at books@hentzenwerke.com.

Introduction

Thank you for buying this book. We hope that you have as much fun reading it as we did in writing it and that you manage to find as many useful things as we did when compiling it. The objectives behind this book underwent considerable change between its inception (at the Dutch User Group "Conference to the Max" held in Arnhem, Holland in May 1999) and the version of the text which you now hold in your hands. However, the paragraphs below describe what we finally hoped to achieve with the book.

What is this book?

First, it must be stated that this is not a book that will teach you how to use Visual FoxPro. Our primary objective has been to try and distill some of the (often painful) experiences which we, and many others, have accumulated over the years so that you can avoid falling into the same traps that we did and maybe even find some alternative ways of doing things. This is not to say that there is always a *'best'* or even a *'right'* way of doing things in FoxPro. The language is so rich and powerful that there are usually several ways of tackling any given problem, however, there are also many traps for the unwary, and many techniques that have proven useful. The problem which we have tried to tackle is to collect such tricks and traps together, to group them into some logical order and to try and provide the one thing that almost every developer we know has been asking for – concise and 'relevant' example code.

A word about the code in this book

The code samples in this book have been consciously written to make them easy to follow – at times this has meant that we have forgone some obvious optimizations. Thus you will find many places where you might say 'Why didn't they do it like this? It would have saved a dozen lines of code!' Please bear with us, and remember that not everyone is as perceptive as you are.

You will also note that, for similar reasons, we have not repeated, in every code snippet, method or function, the "standard" tests and error handling code that you would normally expect to find (like checking the type of parameters passed to a function). We have assumed that you know how to do this and, if you want to use the code from this book, will add it yourself where necessary.

So who is this book for?

As we have already said, this book will not teach you to use Visual FoxPro – it assumes you have a reasonable degree of comfort with the basic operation of the VFP Database and Command Language and with the basic principles of Object Oriented Programming. We would expect that you will have read and used such excellent and useful references as Whil Hentzen's *'Programming VFP,'* *'The Revolutionary Guide to VFP OOP'* by Will Phelps, Andy Kramek and Bob Grommes and, of course, the indispensable *'Hacker's Guide to VFP,'* by Tamar Granor and Ted Roche.

If you are looking for alternative ways of tackling problems, code improvement hints, workarounds for common traps and 'war stories' of those who have been there and done it (yes, we even have the tee-shirts), then this book is for you.

What is in this book?

This book includes tried and tested solutions to common problems in Visual FoxPro together with some basic techniques for building Visual FoxPro tools and components. The book is organized into chapters that attempt to group subjects under logical headings. Each chapter consists, essentially, of a series of 'How Do I ...?' questions. Each question includes a working example, and each chapter's example code may be downloaded individually.

All example code was written and tested using Visual FoxPro Version 6.0 (with Service Pack 3). While much of it should run in any version of Visual FoxPro, there are obviously some things that are version specific. (Each new version of Visual FoxPro has introduced some entirely new commands and functions to the language.)

What is not in this book?

An awful lot! In order to keep this book to a manageable size we have left out a lot of things. Since this is essentially a 'How To' book for Visual FoxPro, we have not even attempted to cover such topics as building COM components, or Internet web pages (there are excellent books on these subjects available). Nor have we covered ActiveX controls or Automation (another book would be needed for this topic alone). We recognise that there are significant omissions but felt that since we could not possibly cover everything, we should concentrate on the 'pure' Visual FoxPro issues – and we make no apology for doing so.

Where do you start?

The short answer is wherever you want to! While it has been one of our main concerns to make this a "readable" book, we recognize that you are probably looking at this book because you have a specific problem (or maybe more than one) to deal with and are looking for inspiration if not an actual solution. We cannot hope to provide "solutions" for everyone but if we can offer you a little inspiration, backed up with sample code to get you started, then we will have succeeded in our aims – and you can relax in the knowledge that your modest expenditure on this tome has already proven a worthwhile investment.

Chapter 1
Controlling the VFP
Environment

"To begin at the beginning" (Narrator, "Under Milk Wood" by Dylan Thomas)

One of the major benefits of developing in Visual FoxPro is that you have almost complete control over the environment in which your code will run. However, like many benefits this can be a double-edged sword and there are many things to be aware of when establishing and controlling both your development and production environments. In this chapter we will cover some of the techniques we have found to work well.

Starting Visual FoxPro

Visual FoxPro, like most applications, supports several 'command line switches'. Most of the time these tend to get forgotten, but they do exist and are all documented in the online Help files in the *'Customizing Visual FoxPro Startup Options'* topic. Probably the most useful ones to remember are:

- -C   which specifies the configuration file to use
- -T   which suppresses the VFP sign-on screen
- -R   which refreshes the VFP registry settings (Note, the settings that get refreshed are those relating to information about VFP, such as file associations. The –R switch does not update the settings controlled through Visual FoxPro's Options Dialog. This is only done when 'Set As Default' is used to exit the dialog).

So to start Visual FoxPro without the sign-on screen display and with a refresh of the registry settings the required command line would be:

```
G:\VFP60\VFP6.EXE -R -T
```

Configuration files

There are several ways of handling the initialization of Visual FoxPro, but the easiest, and most flexible, is still to use a configuration file. Visual FoxPro uses a simple formatted text file, called *"CONFIG.FPW"* by default, as the source for a number of environmental values which can be set as the system starts up.

How to specify a config.fpw file

The actual file name does not matter as you can specify the configuration file which Visual FoxPro is to use as a command line parameter by using the '-c' switch in the command line which is used to start Visual FoxPro. So to set up your own configuration file (for example for a specific application) use the following command line:

```
G:\VFP60\APPS\MYAPP.EXE -cG:\VFP60\myconfig.txt
```

How VFP locates its configuration file

The default behavior of Visual FoxPro, in the absence of a specific configuration file, is to search the following locations for a file named '*config.fpw*' in this order:

- The current working directory
- The directory from which Visual FoxPro is being started
- All directories in the DOS path

If you are using the '-c' switch to specify a file named other than the default, or in a specific location, you must include the fully qualified path and file name. This provides a simple method of handling the initialization of different applications installed on the same machine.

How VFP starts up when no configuration file is found

If no configuration file is found or specified, then Visual FoxPro will be started with only those settings that are specified in the Options Dialog (located on the TOOLS pad of the main Visual FoxPro menu).

Why *these* settings in particular?

The answer is simply that all of the settings from this dialog are actually stored in the Windows Registry and can be found under the Registry Key:

```
HKEY_CURRENT_USER\Software\Microsoft\VisualFoxPro\6.0\Options
```

Including a configuration file in the project

One little "trap" to watch out for – if you add a configuration file named '*config.fpw*' to your project as a text file, it will be *INCLUDED* in the project by default. When you build an .exe from the project, the *config.fpw* file will be built into the resulting file. Since Visual FoxPro looks for a file named '*config.fpw*' during startup, it will always find the built-in version first and will not look any further. This would apply even if you were to explicitly specify a different configuration file using the '-C' switch! Your specified file would be ignored, and the built-in congfiguration file would be executed. The best solution is NOT to add your configuration file to the project at all, but if you do, to make sure that it is marked as 'excluded' from the build.

How to suppress a configuration file
Starting Visual FoxPro with the command line parameter '-c' alone suppresses the default behavior and prevents any configuration file that may be found from being run. The result is that you can force Visual FoxPro to start up with its default settings only.

How to determine which configuration file is being used
One of the commonest problems with configuration files is failing to ensure that Visual FoxPro is reading the correct *CONFIG.FPW*. As noted above, if Visual FoxPro can't find a configuration file, it will search the DOS path and simply use the first one it finds. This could be anywhere on a network. The SYS(2019) function will return the full path and file name of the configuration file that Visual FoxPro actually used. If no configuration file was found, the function merely returns an empty string.

What goes into the configuration file?
Now that we know something about how the configuration file is used, the next question is what can we put into it? The answer is quite a lot! Essentially there are three categories of things that can be specified in the configuration file as follows:

Special settings
There are a number of settings that can **ONLY** be made in a configuration file. (For full details see the "Special Terms for Configuration Files" topic in the Visual FoxPro online Help and the entry under "Configuring Visual FoxPro" in the online documentation.) Notice that the ability to set the location for temporary files is also available in the Options Dialog. Specifying the TMPFILES location in the configuration file will override any setting that is made there and can be useful when you need to differentiate between development and run time locations for temporary files.

Table 1.1 Example of specific Configuration File terms

KeyWord	Description
MVCOUNT = nn	Sets the maximum number of variables that Visual FoxPro can maintain. This value can range from 128 to 65,000; default is 1024.
TMPFILES = *drive:*	Specifies where temporary EDITWORK, SORTWORK, and PROGWORK work files are stored if they have not been specified with any of the other options. Because work files can become very large, specify a location with plenty of free space. For faster performance, especially in a multiuser environment, specify a fast disk (such as a local disk). Default is the startup directory.
OUTSHOW = OFF	Disables the ability to hide all windows in front of the current output by pressing SHIFT+CTRL+ALT. Default is ON.

One other setting that can be used in the configuration file only, but which is **not** included in the Help file list is "SCREEN = OFF". This prevents the Visual FoxPro main screen from being displayed when your application starts and prevents the annoying 'flash' of the VFP screen that still occurs even if your startup program turns off the main screen with the command `_Screen.Visible = .F.` (which enables you to present your application's initial form, or a "splash" screen, without displaying the main VFP window first).

SET Commands

Virtually all of the standard SET commands can be issued in a configuration file. The only thing to watch out for is that some settings are actually scoped to the datasession. (See the "*Set DataSession*" topic in the online Help for a full listing.) So, there is little point in specifying them in the configuration file if you plan to use Private DataSessions for your forms. The syntax for specifying SET commands in the configuration file is a simple assignment in which the keyword 'SET' is omitted:

```
DEFAULT = C:\VFP60\TIPSBOOK
DATE = BRITISH
```

Commands

Well actually you can only specify one (count 'em!) command, and it must be the **last** line of the configuration file. Like other configuration file entries, it is entered as a simple assignment:

```
COMMAND = DO setupfox
```

What is the use of just ONE command? Well, quite a lot really because that one command can call a FoxPro program, and **that** can do a lot of things!

One of the main limitations of the configuration file is that you cannot actually set things that are internal to Visual FoxPro (e.g. system variables) because, when the configuration file runs, Visual FoxPro hasn't actually started. Using this setting allows you to specify a program file to run immediately after Visual FoxPro has started up – even before the command window is displayed.

This program can then be used to set up your development environment the way that you really want it. For example, here are some of the things that are in our standard setup file:

```
*** Standard 'SET' options (These could be entered directly into the Config
File)
SET TALK OFF
SET BELL OFF
SET SAFETY OFF
SET STATUS OFF
SET STATUS BAR ON
SET DATE BRITISH
SET CENTURY ON
*** Re-define Function Keys
SET FUNCTION 2 TO "CLOSE TABLES ALL;CLEAR WINDOWS;"
SET FUNCTION 3 TO "CANCEL;SET SYSMENU TO DEFA;ACTIVATE WINDOW COMMAND;"
SET FUNCTION 4 TO "CLEAR ALL;SET CLASSLIB TO;SET PROC TO;"
SET FUNCTION 5 TO "DISP STRU;"
SET FUNCTION 6 TO "DISP STAT;"
SET FUNCTION 7 TO "DISP MEMO LIKE *"
SET FUNCTION 8 TO "CLEAR;CLEAR WINDOWS;"
SET FUNCTION 9 TO "MODI FORM "
```

```
SET FUNCTION 10 TO "MODI COMM "
SET FUNCTION 11 TO "DO setpath WITH "
SET FUNCTION 12 TO "=CHGDEFA(); "
***Set up the Screen properties
_SCREEN.CAPTION = "VFP 6.0 (Development Mode)"
_SCREEN.CLOSABLE = .F.
_SCREEN.FONTNAME = "Arial"
_SCREEN.FONTSIZE = 10
_SCREEN.FONTBOLD = .F.
*** Run Cobb Editor Extensions
DO G:\VFP60\CEE6\CEE6.APP
*** Set up some On Key Labels
ON KEY LABEL CTRL+F10 suspend
ON KEY LABEL CTRL+F11 o=SYS(1270)
ON KEY LABEL CTRL+F12 RELEASE o
*** Set up any system variables required
_Include = HOME() + "Foxpro.h"
_Throttle = 0.1
*** Set up any standard "Public" variables
PUBLIC gcUserName, gcAppPath, gcDataPath
STORE "" TO gcUserName, gcAppPath, gcDataPath
*** Run Standard Path Set-up
DO setpath WITH 1
```

As you can see, apart from setting up the basic VFP system environment and handling our own particular requirements, this 'one' command available in the configuration file has now been used to run a couple of other programs (CEE and our own SetPath procedure) so we get three for the price of one. By putting these settings in a program, we also have a simple way of re-initialising the environment by re-running this program at any time.

Giving VFP a path

Visual FoxPro has the ability to use its own search path and, as a general rule, you should always specify a path for Visual FoxPro for both development and production environments - although they may be very different (see above for one way of handling this requirement). Setting a path for Visual FoxPro does not change the normal DOS search path but can significantly speed up your application by limiting the places that Visual FoxPro has to search in order to find its files – especially in a network environment.

How VFP looks for files

By default Visual FoxPro uses the current directory as its 'path' and you can always restore this setting by simply issuing: SET PATH TO

However for more sophisticated applications, and in development, you will normally have some sort of directory structure and you should always set a proper search path to include all required directories.

Setting the default directory

Normally you still will want to set a default (or "working") directory – this is where Visual FoxPro will look first for any file that it requires. This can be done in a number of ways, depending on your requirements:

- Specify a default in the Configuration File using DEFAULT = <path to directory>
- Set the default directly in code using SET DEFAULT TO <path to directory>
- Change to a directory using the CD <path to directory> and issue SET PATH TO

Note that using the Get, Put or Locate functions (e.g. GetDir()) does not change either the default directory or the path. To change the default directory interactively use: `SET DEFAULT TO ( GetDir() )`. (The '`CD`' (or '`CHDIR`') command can also be used to change both drive and directory to the specified location).

Using the SET PATH command

Setting the path is simplicity itself. Just issue the SET PATH command followed by a list of the directories that you wish to include. You do not need to fully qualify subdirectories – separating them with either commas or semi-colons is sufficient. The example shows a typical Visual FoxPro search path:

```
SET PATH TO G:\VFP60;C:\VFP60\TIPSBOOK\;DATA;FORMS;LIBS;PROGS;UTILS;
```

To retrieve the current path setting you can use the SET() function (which will work with most of the Visual FoxPro SET commands) as shown below. You can assign the result directly to a variable or, as shown below, directly to the clipboard so that you can then paste the current path into a program or documentation file:

```
_ClipText = SET( 'PATH' )
```

Visual FoxPro allows the use of both UNC path names, like:

```
\\SERVERNAME\DIRECTORYNAME\.
```

and allows the use of embedded spaces (when enclosed in quotation marks) in directory names like:

```
"..\COMMON DIRECTORY\"
```

However, while the latter may be allowed, we tend to subscribe to the principle that *'although you can use embedded spaces, arsenic is quicker.'* (The same, by the way, applies to file names with spaces!) While improving readability, spaces can also cause problems when trying to handle files and directories programmatically and we still feel that the best advice is to avoid them wherever possible in applications. For example, the following code works perfectly well for conventional directory names, but will fail if the selected directory contains embedded spaces:

```
LOCAL lcDir
lcDir = GETDIR()
IF ! EMPTY(lcDir)
  SET DEFAULT TO &lcDir
ENDIF
```

Where am I?

Fortunately, Visual FoxPro provides us with a number of functions that will help us locate where we are at any time:

- SYS(2004) returns the directory from which Visual FoxPro was started but in a distributed run time application, this will always be the location of the *VFP6R.DLL* (which is normally the appropriate version of the Windows 'System' directory)
- HOME() returns the directory from which Visual FoxPro was started by default, but has a number of additional useful options in VFP6 which return information about Visual Studio Components
- _VFP.FULLNAME accesses a property of the Visual FoxPro application object that contains the full path and file name which was used to start VFP
- FULLPATH('') or FULLPATH(CURDIR()) returns the full drive and directory of the current working directory (including the terminal "\").
- SYS(5) returns the default drive (including the ':')
- CD shows the current drive and directory in the current output window – but will also change drive and directory in one single command
- CHDIR will change to the specified Drive/Driectory (just like CD) but will not report the current status (and so does not mess up your forms)
- CURDIR() returns just the current directory (with terminal '\') but not the drive

How to set a path programmatically

As an alternative to hard coding the paths in your setup file, it is possible to derive the path (assuming that you use standard directory structures) using the native Visual FoxPro functions. The little function below shows how this might be done to account for both development and run time structures. It uses the PROGRAM() function to determine how it was called and returns a different path when called from a Form or a Program than when called from a compiled file:

```
****************************************************************************
* Program....: CalcPath.prg
* Version....: 1.0
* Author.....: Andy Kramek
* Date.......: August 16, 1999
* Compiler...: Visual FoxPro 06.00.8492.00 for Windows
* Abstract...: Sets a VFP Path based on the type of the calling program.
* ..........: Assumes standard directory structures - but could use lookups
****************************************************************************
FUNCTION CalcPath()
LOCAL lcSys16, lcProgram, lcPath, lcOldDir
  *** Get the name of program that called this one.
  lcSys16 = SYS(16, 1)
  *** Save current working directory
  lcOldDir = (SYS(5)+CURDIR())
  *** Make the directory from which it was run current
  lcProgram = SUBSTR(lcSys16, AT(":", lcSys16) - 1)
  CD LEFT(lcProgram, RAT("\", lcProgram))
  IF INLIST( JUSTEXT( lcProgram ), "FXP", "SCX" )
```

```
   *** If we are running a PRG/Form directly, then find the parent directory
   CD ..
   *** Set up path to include VFP Home plus the standard DEV directory tree
   lcPath = (HOME()+';'+SYS(5)+CURDIR()+";DATA;FORMS;LIBS;PROGS;UTILS")
ELSE
   *** We are using an EXE/APP! Adjust path for DISTRIBUTION directory tree
   lcPath = (HOME()+';'+SYS(5)+CURDIR()+";DATA")
ENDIF
*** Restore original directory
CD (lcOldDir)
*** Return the calculated path
RETURN lcPath
ENDFUNC
```

Making sure VFP is only started once

So far so good! We have managed to cover the process of starting VFP and setting up the basic environments for both development and production. At this point one of the things we all come across is the absent-minded user who minimizes an application and then, ten minutes later, starts a fresh copy from their desktop. Within the hour they have six copies of the application running and are complaining that their machine is slowing down. What to do? (Apart from shooting the user which, appealing though the idea may be, is generally frowned upon and, depending on their seniority, may also be a career-limiting move.) There are actually several approaches that can be taken, as described below.

Using a 'semaphore' file

This is probably the simplest approach of all. It relies on your application creating, on first launch, a zero-byte file whose sole purpose is to indicate that the application is running. Any time the application is launched, it looks for this file and, if it finds it, simply shuts down again:

```
****************************************************************************
* Program....: ChkSFile.prg
* Compiler...: Visual FoxPro 06.00.8492.00 for Windows
* Abstract...: Checks for a Semaphore File, creates one if not found and
* ..........: returns a flag
****************************************************************************
FUNCTION ChkSFile( tcAppName )
LOCAL lcAppName, lcFile, lnHnd, llRetVal

*** Default lcAppName if nothing passed
lcAppName = IIF( EMPTY(tcAppName) OR VARTYPE( tcAppName ) # "C", ;
                 'apprun', LOWER( ALLTRIM( tcAppName ) ) )

*** Force a TXT extension for the semaphore file in current directory
lcFile = (SYS(5) + CURDIR() + FORCEEXT( lcAppName, 'txt' ))

*** Now check for the file?
IF ! FILE( lcFile )
  *** File not found, so create it
  lnHnd = FCREATE( lcFile )
  IF lnHnd < 0
```

```
      *** Cannot create the file, some sort of error! Set Return Flag
      llRetVal = .T.
   ELSE
      *** Close the file
      FCLOSE( lnHnd )
   ENDIF
ELSE
   *** Set Return Flag
   llRetVal = .T.
ENDIF
*** Return Status Flag
RETURN llRetVal
```

The function returns a logical value that can be used to determine whether to allow the current application to continue, as the following snippet illustrates:

```
*** Check for a second instance of the application
IF ChkSFile()
   QUIT
ENDIF
```

Of course the catch with this approach is that your application **must** delete the file as part of its close-down routine (unless you *really want* a once-only application). That raises the question of what can you do if, heaven forbid, the application terminates abnormally (euphemism for 'crash') or the user makes an improper exit (disconnecting the power supply for example!). The answer is "Not much." Typically this will require the intervention of 'System Support' to physically delete the file.

But it is a nice, easy approach with no other real drawbacks providing that the semaphore file is always created on the end-user's machine, or in a specific user directory.

Using the Windows API

The function below makes use of three Windows API functions to look for a window that is named the same as the application (*FindWindow*), to make an existing window the uppermost window (*BringWindowToTop*) and to maximize it (*ShowWindow*):

```
****************************************************************************
* Program....: OnceOnly.prg
* Compiler...: Visual FoxPro 06.00.8492.00 for Windows
* Abstract...: Checks for an existing instance of the application window
* ..........: and, if found, activates the original and returns a flag.
****************************************************************************
FUNCTION OnceOnly
LOCAL lnHWND, lcTitle, llRetVal

*** Set UP API Calls
Declare Integer FindWindow IN Win32Api AS FindApp String, String
Declare BringWindowToTop   IN Win32APi AS MakeTop Integer
Declare ShowWindow         IN Win32Api AS ShowWin Integer, Integer

*** Get the current Screen Caption
lcTitle = _Screen.Caption
```

```
*** Change it to avoid finding the current instance
_Screen.Caption = SYS(3)

*** Now locate another instance
lnHWND = FindApp( NULL, lcTitle )

*** And restore the original caption
_Screen.Caption = lcTitle

*** Check the results
IF lnHWND > 0
   *** We have found something!
   *** So make it uppermost and maximize it (ShowWin => 3)
   MakeTop( lnHWND )
   ShowWin( lnHWND, 3 )
   *** Set the Return Value
   llRetVal = .T.
ENDIF

*** Return Status for action
RETURN llRetVal
```

The function returns a logical value that can be used to determine whether to allow the current application to continue, as the following snippet illustrates:

```
*** Check for a second instance of the application
IF OnceOnly()
   QUIT
ENDIF
```

There is one major drawback to watch out for here. The API functions used check for the *name* of a window – in this case we are using `_Screen.Caption`. If your application changes the Caption of the screen at run time (as many do), this approach will not work.

Combination of semaphore and Windows API

The last example here shows how combining the principles of the other two examples gives a better all-round approach:

```
*****************************************************************************
* Program....: IsAppRun.prg
* Compiler...: Visual FoxPro 06.00.8492.00 for Windows
* Abstract...: Checks for a window which is created with a Unique ID by and
* ..........: in  the application. Combination of Semaphore and API.
* ..........: Based on code originally posted into the Public Domain
* ..........: by Christof Lange
*****************************************************************************
FUNCTION IsAppRun( tcUniqueID )
LOCAL llRetVal, lcUniqueID

*** MUST pass an application ID to this function!
IF EMPTY(tcUniqueID) OR VARTYPE( tcUniqueID ) # "C"
    MESSAGEBOX( 'An Application Specific Character ID is mandatory' + CHR(13) ;
              + 'when calling the IsAppRun() function', 16, 'Developer Error' )
    RETURN .T.
```

```
ELSE
   *** Strip out any spaces
  lcUniqueID = STRTRAN( tcUniqueID, " " )
ENDIF
*** First check for the existence of the Semaphore window
IF WEXIST("_Semaphore_")
  RETURN .T.
ENDIF
*** Look for an occurrence of this ID as a Window Name
DECLARE INTEGER FindWindow IN Win32Api AS FindApp String, String
IF FindApp( NULL, lcUniqueID ) > 0
   *** We found one!  Set Return Value
  llRetVal = .T.
ELSE
   *** Create a new window with this ID
  DEFINE WINDOW _Semaphore_ IN DESKTOP FROM 1,1 TO 2,2 TITLE lcUniqueID
ENDIF
*** Return Status Flag
RETURN llRetVal
```

To use this function, it is simplest to include a #DEFINE in your standard startup file so that you can specify a new unique ID for each application:

```
#DEFINE APPID "App0001-99"
IF IsAppRun( APPID )
  QUIT
ENDIF
```

This very neat solution avoids both the problem of 'dangling files' in the semaphore method and that of changing the caption in the API method because the window can only be created and maintained within an instance of the application. As soon as it terminates in any way – even as a result of a crash - the window is destroyed and there is nothing to clean up. Since the window gets its name explicitly from the application, it does not rely on the caption being constant either. Cool stuff Christof, thank you!

SET Commands and DataSessions

OK – we've got Visual FoxPro up and running (and made sure that we can only start one instance of our application) so now what? There are, in case you hadn't noticed, an awful lot of SET commands in Visual FoxPro that allow you to configure the environment in detail. Many of these affect the environment globally, but some are scoped to the currently active datasession (see the "*Set DataSession*" topic in the on-line help for a full listing of these). When you start Visual FoxPro you are always in the *DEFAULT* datasession.

What exactly does "Default DataSession" mean?

The Oxford English Dictionary (Ninth Edition) offers a definition of "default" as:
   "A pre-selected option adopted by a computer program when no alternative is specified by the user or programmer"
   Unfortunately Visual FoxPro seems to prefer to define the word according to the rules proffered by Humpty-Dumpty in Lewis Carroll's '*Alice Through the Looking Glass*':

"When I use a word," Humpty Dumpty said in rather a scornful tone, "it means just what I choose it to mean – neither more nor less."

In fact the Default DataSession is actually DataSession #1 – neither more nor less. It has no special significance other than that when you start Visual FoxPro, it is selected (just as Work Area #1 is always selected as the first available work area in any DataSession). This is easily demonstrated using the SET DATASESSION window and the command window.

When you open the DataSession window, it will display the name of the current DataSession as 'Default(1)', however the command:

```
SET DATASESSION TO DEFAULT
```

results in a *'Variable Default Not Found'* error, while

```
SET DATASESSION TO 1
```

is accepted without comment.

However, when you run a form whose DataSession property is set to "*1 Default Data Session*", VFP interprets the term "default" as meaning 'CURRENT' – in other words, a Form which is designed using this setting will use whichever data session is active when the form is initialized. This does not appear very logical at first sight since one might reasonably expect that because Data Session #1 is named 'Default', setting a form's DataSession property to '1 Default Data Session' would ensure that the form would actually use that Data Session and no other. Not so!

The actual behavior makes sense when you wish forms to share a data session. By setting the child form's DataSession property to 1 (Default Data Session), it will use whatever DataSession its parent form was using – whether that DataSession is Private or not.

So can I have a "public" Datasession?

The short answer is NO! Visual FoxPro does support the concept of a truly 'default' (or 'public') DataSession. In other words, if a specified table is not found in the current Data Session VFP will not look for it elsewhere. All DataSessions are effectively "Private" – even Data Session #1.

How can I ensure SET commands apply to a private data session?

This is actually a complex question and the answer, as so often in VFP, is 'it depends.' Normally you will be using data sessions that are being created by a form (or formset) as 'Private'. It also matters whether you are using the Form's native DataEnvironment or not. In any case it is important to understand the order in which things happen – the sequence below shows how a form with a Private DataSession, and a table in its native DE, is initialized:

```
METHOD: DATAENVIRONMENT.OPENTABLES()
DATASESSION: 2
ALIAS(): <None>


METHOD: DATAENVIRONMENT.BEFOREOPENTABLES()
DATASESSION: 2
```

```
ALIAS(): <None>

METHOD(): FORM.LOAD()
DATASESSION: 2
ALIAS():  <TableName>

METHOD: DATAENVIRONMENT.INIT()
DATASESSION: 2
ALIAS():  <TableName>
```

Notice that the DataSession is always 2, the new Private DataSession, and that the table is already available in that DataSession when the form Load() event fires.

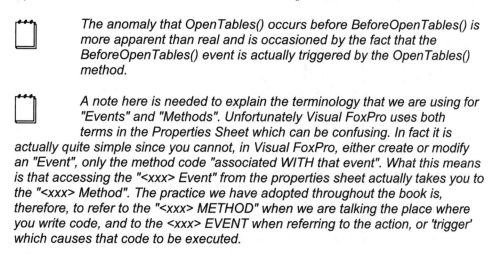

The anomaly that OpenTables() occurs before BeforeOpenTables() is more apparent than real and is occasioned by the fact that the BeforeOpenTables() event is actually triggered by the OpenTables() method.

A note here is needed to explain the terminology that we are using for "Events" and "Methods". Unfortunately Visual FoxPro uses both terms in the Properties Sheet which can be confusing. In fact it is actually quite simple since you cannot, in Visual FoxPro, either create or modify an "Event", only the method code "associated WITH that event". What this means is that accessing the "<xxx> Event" from the properties sheet actually takes you to the "<xxx> Method". The practice we have adopted throughout the book is, therefore, to refer to the "<xxx> METHOD" when we are talking the place where you write code, and to the <xxx> EVENT when referring to the action, or 'trigger' which causes that code to be executed.

So if you need to explicitly change settings that apply to the way in which tables are handled (e.g. *MultiLocks*) you really need to do it in the DataEnvironment's *BeforeOpenTables()* code – anything else is just too late because the DataSession is already present, with tables open, by the time the first form based method (*Load()*) fires.

This presents a problem because a VFP Form **class** doesn't have a DataEnvironment, so you cannot just add code to the class from which you create your forms. There are really only two solutions if you have to use the form's DataEnvironment, and both require code, or more specifically some action in every instance of a form:

- Add the relevant code (or a call to a Procedure) to every form's BeforeOpenTables() event
- Don't allow the native DataEnvironment to open your tables automatically. Set AutoOpenTables = .F. and call the OpenTables() method explicitly from within the Form Load()

Adding code to BeforeOpenTables()

This is very simple, but must be done in every instance of the form. Simply open the Form DataEnvironment in the designer and add whatever environmental settings you require directly to the *BeforeOpenTables* method. Alternatively you could place the relevant code in a procedure and call it from the method or create an environment setting class (see below) and instantiate it using the Form's *AddObject()* method. (A DataEnvironment does have an *AddObject()* of its own, but you can only add objects based on Cursor and Relation classes directly to the DataEnvironment.)

One additional suggestion, if you adopt this methodology, is to place code in the Load() event of your form class which checks for a specific setting and if it is not found displays a MessageBox. Thus:

```
IF This.DataSessionId # 1
  *** We have a Private DataSession
  IF SET( 'MULTILOCKS' ) = 'OFF'
    *** Or whatever setting you ALWAYS set!
    lcText = "You have not set the BeforeOpenTables() Code Up"
    MESSAGEBOX( lcText, 16, 'Developer Blunder!' )
  ENDIF
ENDIF
```

Suppressing auto-open tables

If you wish to use the Form's *Load* method to set options for a DataSession, you must first suppress the default behavior of the DataEnvironment that is to automatically open tables. This is a simple matter of setting the *AutoOpenTables* property to false in the DataEnvironment, but again it must be done explicitly in each instance of the form. Once you have suppressed this property you can put code into the form's load method to either call a procedure, or a form method, which will handle the setting of the environment. Our preferred method is to use an environment setting class and simply instantiate an object based on that class directly in the form's *Load* method as illustrated in the next section.

Creating an environment setting class

We think that the best method of setting up your own environment in a Private DataSession is to use a class. By placing all of the necessary SET commands in a method which is called by the *Init* method of the class, merely instantiating an object based on this class will set things up the way you want them. The code to do this can then be placed in the *Load* method of your form class so that every time the form is instantiated, the correct settings are applied. The only limitation of this methodology is that, as noted above, you cannot allow the DataEnvironment to automatically handle the opening of tables. The following code shows how such a class may be defined programmatically (although there is no reason why such a class should not be created in the visual class designer):

```
*****************************************************************************
* Program....: EnvSet.prg
* Compiler...: Visual FoxPro 06.00.8492.00 for Windows
```

```
* Abstract...: Class definition for setting environmental options.
Instantiating
* ..........: the class sets the required options. The GetOption() method
shows
* ..........: how the object can be used to retrieve settings as well.
***************************************************************************
DEFINE CLASS cusEnvSet AS custom
   ***********************************************************************
   *** Init merely calls the SetOptions() method
   ***********************************************************************
   PROCEDURE Init
     This.SetOptions()
   ENDPROC
   ***********************************************************************
   *** Sets Required Environmental options
   ***********************************************************************
   PROCEDURE SetOptions
     *** Locking and Environment
     SET TALK OFF
     SET MULTILOCKS ON
     SET REPROCESS TO AUTOMATIC
     SET DELETED ON
     SET SAFETY OFF
     SET BELL OFF
     SET ECHO OFF
     SET NOTIFY OFF
     SET CONFIRM OFF
     SET EXACT OFF
     SET REFRESH TO 60,60
     SET STATUS BAR ON
     *** Path

     *** Date and Currency
     SET CENTURY ON
     SET CENTURY TO 19 ROLLOVER 75
     SET DATE TO BRITISH
     SET CURRENCY LEFT
     SET CURRENCY TO "£"
   ENDPROC
   ***********************************************************************
   *** Returns current setting of an environment option
   ***********************************************************************
   PROCEDURE GetOption( tcOption )
     LOCAL luRetVal, lcOption
     STORE "" TO luRetVal
     lcOption = UPPER(ALLTRIM( tcOption ))
     *** If we were given a setting, get its current status
     *** NOTE: If really needed this method would require more checking
     *** and options because not every setting can simply be returned
     *** by the SET() function - but this illustrates the point!
     IF VARTYPE( lcOption ) = "C" AND ! EMPTY( lcOption )
       luRetVal = SET( lcOption )
     ENDIF
     RETURN luRetVal
   ENDPROC
ENDDEFINE
```

To use this class, simply add the following code to the *Load* method of your Form class:

```
*** Add object to set environment (suppress any display explicitly)
SET TALK OFF
IF ! "ENVSET" $ UPPER( SET( 'PROCEDURE' ))
  SET PROCEDURE TO envset ADDITIVE
ENDIF
This.AddObject( "oCusEnv", "CusEnvSet" )
```

This will instantiate the object, thereby setting the defined options, and at the same time creates a reference on the form so that any additional methods that you may have defined (e.g. the *GetOption()* method outlined above) can be accessed.

How do I get rid of the system toolbars?

When you start Visual FoxPro, one or more of the system toolbars will normally be visible. (The actual toolbar status is stored in the Resource File.) Fortunately all of the system toolbars can be addressed using their window names (which are actually the same as their Captions) and so manipulating them is relatively simple.

The simplest way of ensuring that only those toolbars that you require are visible is to create an array of all the toolbar names, then loop through it, testing to see if each is visible and hiding those that are not required. The following code will hide all visible system toolbars:

```
DIMENSION laTbState[11]
laTbState[ 1]="Color Palette"
laTbState[ 2]="Database Designer"
laTbState[ 3]="Form Controls"
laTbState[ 4]="Form Designer"
laTbState[ 5]="Layout"
laTbState[ 6]="Print Preview"
laTbState[ 7]="Query Designer"
laTbState[ 8]="Report Controls"
laTbState[ 9]="Report Designer"
laTbState[10]="Standard"
laTbState[11]="View Designer"
FOR lnCnt = 1 TO 11
  IF WEXIST(laTbState[lnCnt])
    HIDE WINDOW ( laTbState[lnCnt] )
  ENDIF
NEXT
```

Of course, this raises the issue of what happens if you then wish to re-display a system toolbar. Perhaps unsurprisingly, the SHOW WINDOW command can be used to re-display a previously hidden system toolbar, while RELEASE WINDOW will actually release the specified toolbar.

The system toolbar "Gotcha!"

But there is a catch! In order to use Show Window, the named window must have been defined to VFP and even though the System Toolbars are generated by VFP, there is no way of actually defining or activating the toolbars programmatically. The consequence is that unless a toolbar is first activated by VFP itself, you cannot later make it visible. The only toolbars that can be made visible by default are the 'Standard', 'Layout' and 'Form Designer' but there does not seem to be any reliable way of programmatically forcing any of the other system toolbars to be made visible at startup.

Can I make use of keyboard macros in VFP?

The short answer is yes. In fact, one of the often-forgotten capabilities of Visual FoxPro is its ability to use keyboard macros. These can, with a little thought, make your life as a developer much easier when you assign your own particular keystrokes to a simple key combination. For example instead of running a 'reset' program to close tables and databases, release class libraries and restore the default FoxPro menu, you can program the necessary commands on to the '*F2*' function key like this:

```
SET FUNCTION F2 TO "CLEAR ALL ;" ;
  + "SET CLASSLIB TO ;" ;
  + "SET PROC TO ;" ;
  + "CLOSE ALL ;" ;
  + "SET SYSMENU TO DEFAULT ;" ;
  + "ACTIVATE WINDOW COMMAND;"
```

Of course you can also use the Macro Editor (invoked from the *Tools|Macros* option of the main menu) to create your macros. The macro created by the above command is visible, and editable, in the Macro Editor as:

```
CLEAR{SPACEBAR}ALL{SPACEBAR}{ENTER}
SET{SPACEBAR}CLASSLIB{SPACEBAR}TO{SPACEBAR}{ENTER}
SET{SPACEBAR}PROC{SPACEBAR}TO{SPACEBAR}{ENTER}
CLOSE{SPACEBAR}ALL{SPACEBAR}{ENTER}
SET{SPACEBAR}SYSMENU{SPACEBAR}TO{SPACEBAR}DEFAULT{SPACEBAR}{ENTER}
ACTIVATE{SPACEBAR}WINDOW{SPACEBAR}COMMAND{ENTER}
```

How can I construct a more complex macro?

You can use the macro "record" facility (yes, just like in Word or Excel!) to save yourself the grief of working out exactly how to write the necessary keyboard commands. We normally use an empty program file to do this sort of thing, as the following steps illustrate:

- Open a PRG file (MODIFY COMMAND)
- Choose Tools, Macros, Record from the Main System menu
- Write your code as normal
- Choose Tools, Macros to stop recording
- Test your macro!

Using this technique, the following code to write a simple Yes/No Messagebox handler (and leave the cursor positioned between the first set of quotes in the MessageBox function call) was assigned to the F9 key. The code written was:

```
LOCAL lnOpt
lnOpt = MessageBox( '', 36, '' )
```

```
IF lnOpt = 6    && YES

ENDIF
```

And the resulting macro was:

```
LOCAL{ SPACEBAR}lnOpt{ENTER}
lnOpt{SPACEBAR}={SPACEBAR}MessageBox({SPACEBAR}'',
{SPACEBAR}36,{SPACEBAR}''{SPACEBAR}){ENTER}
IF{SHIFT+SPACEBAR}lnOpt{SPACEBAR}={SPACEBAR}6
{TAB}&&{SPACEBAR}YES{ENTER}
{ENTER}
ENDIF{UPARROW}{UPARROW}{UPARROW}{END}{LEFTARROW}{LEFTARROW}{LEFTARROW}
{LEFTARROW}{LEFTARROW}{LEFTARROW}{LEFTARROW}{LEFTARROW}{LEFTARROW}
{LEFTARROW}{LEFTARROW}
```

What is a "Macro Set"?

Visual FoxPro allows you define and save 'sets' of macros. These are stored in a special file format with a default extension of '.*FKY*' (the Help file has a topic devoted to FKY file structure). You can create multiple sets of macros and save them to files that can be loaded and unloaded through the macro editor. You can also specify a set of 'developer' macros as defaults to be loaded automatically when Visual FoxPro starts up. (Although if you adopt this approach, we advise you to include a CLEAR MACROS command in all application start-up programs.) Some 'developer' macros that we have found useful are:

- Insert WITH This...ENDWITH (ALT+T)
  ```
  WITH{ SPACEBAR}This{ENTER}
  {ENTER}
  ENDWITH{UPARROW}{TAB}
  ```
- Insert WITH ThisForm...ENDWITH (ALT+F)
  ```
  WITH{ SPACEBAR}ThisForm{ENTER}
  {ENTER}
  ENDWITH{UPARROW}{TAB}
  ```
- Insert Quoted Parentheses ("") (ALT+B)
  ```
  ("") {LEFTARROW}{LEFTARROW}
  ```
- Insert a WAIT "" WINDOW NOWAIT command (ALT+W)
  ```
  WAIT{ SPACEBAR}""{SPACEBAR}WINDOW{ SPACEBAR}NOWAIT
  {LEFTARROW}{LEFTARROW}{LEFTARROW}{LEFTARROW}{LEFTARROW}{LEFTARROW}
  {LEFTARROW}{LEFTARROW}{LEFTARROW}{LEFTARROW}{LEFTARROW}{LEFTARROW}
  {LEFTARROW}{LEFTARROW}{LEFTARROW}{LEFTARROW}{LEFTARROW}
  ```
- Open 'Find Next' Window and paste in highlighted text (SHIFT+ALT+F)
  ```
  {CTRL+C}{CTRL+HOME}{CTRL+F}{CTRL+V}{TAB}{BACKSPACE}{CTRL+ENTER}
  ```

The scope for creating custom shortcuts like these is limited only by your imagination but can greatly enhance your productivity when writing code or even when working interactively through the command window.

Finally, also check out the PLAY MACROS command, which allows you to run macros programmatically (for creating self-running demos, or even simple test scripts), although the behavior of this command has some quirks all of its own.

What's the difference between a macro and an On Key Label?

The key difference is that a macro is just a Visual FoxPro program which streams keyboard entry. In this sense it is no different than any other program and runs within the normal Visual FoxPro event loop. An On Key Label, on the other hand, operates outside of the normal event processing and allows a specific command to be executed even when VFP is ostensibly engaged in some other task. This can be very useful, but is also potentially dangerous! The following little program illustrates the difference in behavior clearly. The On Key Label will interrupt the pending READ command immediately and suspend the program, while the Keyboard Macro is simply ignored:

```
**************************************************************************
* Program....: MACOKL.prg
* Compiler...: Visual FoxPro 06.00.8492.00 for Windows
* Abstract...: Illustrate the difference between a keyboard macro
* ..........: and an On Key Label command. Enter '99' to exit from either loop
* ..........: and continue with the program!
**************************************************************************
*** Define an On Key Label
ON KEY LABEL F10 SUSPEND
CLEAR
*** Initialise Key Buffer
LOCAL lnKey
lnKey = 0
*** Start Loop - Use 99 to exit
DO WHILE .T.
    *** Check for 'x' to exit
    ? "Inside an OKL loop"
    @ 10,10 GET lnKey PICT "99"
    READ
    IF lnKey = 99
        EXIT
    ENDIF
ENDDO
*** Clear the OKL
ON KEY LABEL F10
CLEAR

*** Now define a Function Key Macro
SET FUNCTION 10 TO "SUSPEND;"
*** Initialise Key Buffer
lnKey = 0
*** Start Loop - Use 99 to exit
DO WHILE .T.
    *** Check for 'x' to exit
    ? "Inside a F10 loop"
    @ 10,10 GET lnKey PICT "99"
    READ
    IF lnKey = 99
        EXIT
    ENDIF
ENDDO
*** Clear the macro
SET FUNCTION 10 TO ""
```

Clearly, because On Key Labels can operate outside of the normal event handling mechanisms, their impact on code already executing can be unpredictable. Moreover On Key Labels can be called repeatedly unless you include the `PUSH KEY CLEAR/POP KEY CLEAR` commands to disable the OnKey Label itself while the routine it calls is processing.

For these reasons we strongly advise against their indiscriminate use in applications especially since there is almost always an alternative way (typically by using code in the *KeyPress* method) of handling special keystrokes.

How do I create a 'Splash' screen?

This is one of the tasks which Visual FoxPro Version 6.0 handles a little better than its predecessors. The first thing that is needed is a form that is devoid of a title bar and the normal form controls. In version 6.0 the *TitleBar* property was added to the Form class and simply setting `TitleBar = .F.` gives you a plain form. In earlier versions of VFP there are a number of properties that must all be set to achieve the same result:

```
Caption = ""
ControlBox = .F.
Closable = .F.
MaxButton = .F.
MinButton = .F.
Movable = .F.
```

The form should also be set up as a Top-Level form (`ShowWindow = 2, AlwaysOnTop = .T.`). What goes into the form is dependent upon your requirements, but typically it will include a graphic of some sort and probably some text. You may also want to add either a timer or code for allowing the user to explicitly clear the splash screen.

How do I run my splash screen?

The most effective way of running a splash screen is:

- Include 'SCREEN = OFF' in your Configuration File
- Run your splash form as the first line of your application start-up
- Do whatever set-up is needed – including your initial menu
- Restore the main VFP Window and remove the Splash Screen
- Start the Application Event Loop

The code snippet below shows how the start-up program would look in practice:

```
*** Show the splash screen

DO FORM splash NAME splash LINKED
*** Do Any Set-up Stuff here
*** On completion
*** Restore VFP Screen/Menu if required
DO <mainmenu.mpr>
_SCREEN.WINDOWSTATE = 2
_SCREEN.VISIBLE = .T.
_
```

```
*** Remove Splash Screen when ready
RELEASE splash
*** Start Application Event Loop
READ EVENTS
```

An alternative to the splash screen

If your application is going to be using the main Visual FoxPro window as its desktop, then rather than using a form as a splash screen, it is simpler to add an object directly to the VFP Screen and remove it when ready. The Visual FoxPro _Screen object has both *AddObject()* and *RemoveObject()* methods which can be called from within your programs.

All that is needed is to create a container class that includes the graphic, and any other controls, and add it directly to the screen. Once your application set up is completed, the object can simply be removed. This is simpler to implement since it does not require that the screen be turned off on start up, as the following code snippet shows:

```
*** Maximise the Screen
WITH _Screen
  .WINDOWSTATE = 2
  *** Add the Container
  SET CLASSLIB TO splashfiles
  .AddObject( 'cntSplash', 'xCntSplash' )
  *** Report Progress
  WITH .cntSplash.txtProcess
    .Value = 'Loading Class Libraries'
    *** Load Application Libs
    .Value = 'Initialising Data'
    *** Set up DBC
    *** Set up Menus and so on...
  ENDWITH
  .RemoveObject( 'cntSplash' )
ENDWITH
*** Start Application Event Loop
READ EVENTS
```

(Note: We are assuming that the class definition includes the Top/Left settings and a `This.Visible = .T.` command in the container's *Init()* method so there is no need to explicitly make the object visible, or re-position it, in the application code.)

How to wallpaper your desktop

Adding a background (for example a company logo) to your application's desktop can add a 'professional' look and feel to your VFP application. However it is not always as easy as it first appears. The basic principle is easy enough – simply set the *Picture* property of Visual FoxPro's _Screen object to the required bitmap.

The catch is that the default behavior is to 'tile' the bitmap if its dimensions do not exactly match the size of the available screen area in the currently selected resolution. The result is that what works at, say 800 x 600 resolution will not look right at either higher or lower resolutions. Moreover the available area depends on whether you have the status bar on or off, whether you have a menu displayed and whether you have toolbars docked or not. So in order to get it right it seems that you need to know the actual size of the desktop at various resolutions and to create an appropriately sized bitmap for each possibility.

So how can I get the size of the current _Screen area?

The Visual FoxPro's *SCOLS()* and *SROWS()* functions return the number of columns and rows in the current screen area (based on the selected display font). So to determine, in pixels, the size of the display area you also need to use the *Fontmetric()* function, as follows:

```
lnScreenHeight = SROWS()* FONTMETRIC(1, _screen.fontname, _screen.fontsize)
lnScreenWidth  = SCOLS()* FONTMETRIC(6, _screen.fontname, _screen.fontsize)
```

Using these formulae we get the following results with a single line menu visible:

Table 1.2. Available Screen Heights at various resolutions with Screen Font set to Arial 10pt

Screen	Status Bar = ON		Status Bar = OFF	
Resolution	Docked Tbar	UnDocked Tbar	Docked Tbar	UnDocked Tbar
1024 x 768	646	678	670	702
800 x 600	478	510	502	534
640 x 480	358	390	382	414

The screen width is (unless toolbars are docked at the side of the screen) always the same as the horizontal resolution. When designing your application you will, of course, only need to use one set of values since you will always start the application in the same way (in respect of menus, toolbars and status bars).

If you were now to create a series of bitmaps, sized correctly for each resolution, you can simply set the *_Screen.Picture* property to the appropriate one in the application start-up.

Do I really need to create all these bitmaps?

Well, actually, the answer is possibly not! There is an alternative strategy, although its success will depend on the nature of the picture you wish to display. You could simply create a class (based on the **IMAGE** baseclass, named, for example, *aImgWallPaper*) which has its *Picture* property set to a single bitmap, and its *Stretch* property set to 2 (expand to fill the control). Add a method named '*AdjustSize*' and call it from the *Init method* of this class. It should be coded like this:

```
WITH This
    .Height  = FONTMETRIC(1, _SCREEN.FONTNAME, _SCREEN.FONTSIZE) * SROWS()
    .Width   = FONTMETRIC(6, _SCREEN.FONTNAME, _SCREEN.FONTSIZE) * SCOLS()
    .Visible = .T.
ENDWITH
```

Now in your application start-up you simply add an object based on this class directly to the screen immediately before you execute your **DO EVENTS** as follows:

```
_Screen.AddObject( 'oWallPaper', 'aImgWallPaper')
```

The image will then auto-size itself to fill the available screen area giving a really professional look to your application. The only thing to watch for is that if your bitmap is not symmetrical, setting the image's `Stretch = 2` may give a distorted image. A possible solution is to use `Stretch = 1` (Isometric) which will keep the relative proportion of the original bitmap, but this may not entirely fill the screen when it is re-sized. The best advice here is to experiment.

A toolbar 'gotcha!'

One problem with using wallpapers in conjunction with toolbars is that docking and undocking a toolbar alters the visible screen area, but not the size of the image. Handling the docking of a toolbar is quite straightforward since the _Screen.Resize()_ event is fired <u>after</u> the toolbar's *BeforeDock() event* but <u>before</u> the *AfterDock()* event. Actually the event tracker indicates that the Resize event fires twice! (Presumably this is so that the screen resizes when the toolbar is moved from the main screen area to the title bar, and again after it is actually docked). So your image class '*AdjustSize*' method can be called from the toolbar's *AfterDock()* event to handle docking cleanly, thus:

```
IF VARTYPE( _Screen.oWallPaper ) = 'O'
   WITH _Screen
      .LockScreen = .T.
      .oWallPaper.AdjustSize()
      .LockScreen = .F.
   ENDWITH
ENDIF
```

Unfortunately it would appear that undocking a toolbar does not fire the _Screen.Resize() event at all! Although the screen actually does re-size when a toolbar is undocked, the new size is not available to any method that can be called from within the toolbar. We think this must be a bug because an explicit call to the image *AdjustSize* method (from outside the toolbar) after undocking is completed, recalculates the size correctly and adjusts the image appropriately. We do not have a satisfactory solution to this problem other than to avoid movable toolbars when using desktop wallpapers that are not defined directly in the *Picture* property.

Tidying up your development environment

One of the hazards that you may occasionally encounter when developing in Visual FoxPro is that one of your programs will crash. (We know that this is extremely rare but are assured that it really does happen to some other people from time to time.) In such a situation it is useful to have a simple way of cleaning up and getting back to your starting point. We like to use a little program called '*ClearAll*' to handle this for us which makes sure that everything is properly closed down and cleaned up.

The first thing that this program does is to turn off any error handling. This will allow us to force through any anomalous commands (such as selecting a datasession that does not exist) without interruption – after all since we clearing up we do not really care about errors any more!

```
*********************************************************************
* Program....: ClearAll.PRG
* Compiler...: Visual FoxPro 06.00.8492.00 for Windows
* Abstract...: Cleans up the Development environment
*********************************************************************
LOCAL lnCnt, lnCntUsed
LOCAL ARRAY laUsed[1]
*** Turn off error handling for now
ON ERROR *
```

Next we just clear the screen and post a wait window, before rolling back any open transactions:

```
*** Clear Screen
CLEAR
WAIT WINDOW 'Clearing... please wait...' NOWAIT
*** Roll Back Any Transactions
IF TXNLEVEL() > 0
  DO WHILE TXNLEVEL() > 0
    ROLLBACK
  ENDDO
ENDIF
```

Now we need to handle any uncommitted changes. Of course we cannot know how many forms there may be open, or what datasession each form is actually using. The solution is to use the Forms collection and to work through each form's datasession reverting all tables in that datasession and closing them before releasing the form itself.

```
*** Revert Tables and Close Them
FOR EACH loForm IN _Screen.Forms
  *** Find out what Datasession it is in
  lnDS = loForm.DataSessionID
  *** Has it any tables open?
  lnCntUsed = AUSED(laUsed, lnDS)
  IF lnCntUsed > 0
     SET DATASESSION TO (lnDS)
     *** If so, revert all uncommitted changes
     FOR lnCnt = 1 TO lnCntUsed
       SELECT (laUsed[lnCnt,2])
       IF CURSORGETPROP('Buffering') > 1
         =TABLEREVERT( .T. )
       ENDIF
       USE
     NEXT
  ENDIF
  *** And release the form
  loForm.Release()
NEXT
```

Having got rid of the forms we can now close any remaining tables and their associated databases, and clear out any programs in memory, memory variables and libraries:

```
*** Now Close other tables and databases
CLOSE TABLES ALL
```

```
CLOSE DATA ALL
*** Release Memory Variables, Procedures
*** and Class Libraries
CLEAR MEMORY
CLEAR ALL
SET PROCEDURE TO
SET CLASSLIB TO
```

With all of this gone we can safely restore the command window and the default system menu and clear out any global settings defined using the ON commands:

```
*** Get the command window and system menu back
ACTIVATE WINDOW COMMAND
SET SYSMENU TO DEFAULT
*** Clear global settings
ON SHUTDOWN
ON ERROR
ON KEY
ON ESCAPE
WAIT CLEAR
```

The final step is to cancel any open programs (including this one). This is needed to ensure that any forms that have called modal dialogs are properly released:

```
*** Cancel any open programs
CANCEL
```

Closing VFP down

Thus far we have been concentrating on setting up and managing the Visual FoxPro environment, however, the way in which you close down Visual FoxPro is just as important. In the run-time environment there are two ways of initiating the closing down process. Firstly through the use of the CLEAR EVENTS command, either within a menu or in the *Release* method of a form. Secondly through the standard windows close button of the main Visual FoxPro window. Fortunately, Visual FoxPro provides us with a global handler for the close down process, irrespective if how it is initiated – the ON SHUTDOWN command.

What is an On ShutDown procedure?

Like other ON commands, the ON SHUTDOWN command is implemented by a special handler that is outside of the normal Visual FoxPro event processing loop. When invoked, control is immediately transferred to whatever command, or function, has been specified as the target. This is by far the best way (if not the *only* way) to ensure that Visual FoxPro closes down cleanly without the irritating the *'Cannot Quit Visual FoxPro'* message.

What triggers an On Shutdown procedure?

The command specified in ON SHUTDOWN is executed if you try to exit Visual FoxPro by clicking the 'Close' button in the main Visual FoxPro screen, by choosing Exit from the FoxPro control menu, or by issuing the QUIT command in a program (or the command window!). Additionally it will be triggered if you try to exit Windows while Visual FoxPro is open. (Control is returned to Visual FoxPro and the specified ON SHUTDOWN procedure is executed.)

What goes into an On Shutdown procedure?

The procedure called by an ON SHUTDOWN command contains anything that you can legally place into a Visual FoxPro program, with the exception of SUSPEND or CANCEL commands (both of which will cause an error), but at a minimum it must handle the following issues:

- Close any Open Transactions
- Commit or Revert any pending changes in tables or views
- Close all forms (an open Modal Form is one cause of the 'Cannot Quit' message)
- Issue a Clear Events (an active *READ EVENTS* is another cause of the 'Cannot Quit' message)
- Restore the Development Environment (if not running an *APP* or *.exe* file) OR
- Quit Visual FoxPro (if running an *APP* or *.exe* file)

> *The behavior in VFP3.0 was that a QUIT command would close open Modal forms and cancel any existing READ EVENTS. This is not the case in either Version 5.0 or 6.0.*

You will notice that these elements are almost identical to those which we placed in our 'ClearAll.prg' for cleaning up the development environment and the code which was used there can, with minor modifications, be used as the basis for your shut down procedure.

One such modification is to include a test to determine whether the currently executing program was actually called from the development or run-time environments. This is one of the few things for which we advocate the use of a Public variable. In our application startup program we include the following code:

```
*** Check for Run Mode
RELEASE glExeRunning
PUBLIC glExeRunning
glExeRunning = "EXE" $ UPPER( SYS(16) ) OR 'APP' $ UPPER( SYS(16) )
IF glExeRunning
  *** Do the full start-up, Splash screen, log-in etc
ELSE
  *** Start up in development mode
ENDIF
```

While you do not actually need a public variable (a normal Private variable would actually work here) we like to define such 'system' variables explicitly and to treat them as exceptions to the general rules. Having defined the variable we can now use it in our shutdown routine to detemine whether to actually quit Visual FoxPro or simply to cancel the current program as follows:

```
IF glExeRunning
    QUIT
ELSE
```

```
      CANCEL
ENDIF
```

Some people also advocate placing an 'Are You Sure' message box in the shutdown procedure – while this is a matter of style, we do not like it! It seems to us that there can be nothing more irritating to a user who has just specifically chosen 'Quit' than to be asked if they really meant to do it. If your user interface is designed in such a way that a user can "accidentally" shut down your application then we would, very respectfully, suggest that you may need to re-visit the UI design.

Chapter 2
Functions and Procedures

"We can forgive a man for making a useful thing as long as he does not admire it. The only excuse for making a useless thing is that one admires it intensely." ("The Picture of Dorian Gray" by Oscar Wilde)

How many times have you inherited an application from another developer who used twenty lines of code when one or two would have been sufficient? How often have you plowed through miles of code and wondered why it wasn't broken up into separate methods to handle discrete functionality? A well-stocked library of re-usable functions reduces the number of lines of code required to accomplish a given task. In addition to reducing method code at the instance level, descriptive function and procedure names make your code more self-documenting. In this chapter we will share some of the cool functions we have discovered over the years as well as some gotchas to watch out for. All of the code in this chapter is contained in the CH02.PRG procedure file in the subdirectory of the same name.

How shall we proceed?

In prior versions of FoxPro, applications were limited to a single active procedure file at any time. This meant that all user-defined functions and commonly used procedures were kept in a single file. With Visual FoxPro, the ability to have multiple procedure files active at any given time provides much more flexibility. Such procedures can now be grouped logically, by functionality, into different procedure files that can be loaded incrementally as needed. The downside, of course, is that procedure files are loaded into memory by Visual FoxPro and held until explicitly released. This may not be the best use of that precious resource.

Fortunately, it is also possible to define procedure classes. The individual functions that would previously have been kept in a procedure file can now become methods of a class. This approach has the benefit that, when defined visually in the Class Designer, all the functions in the procedure can be neatly viewed under the methods tab of the property sheet. Procedure classes containing specific functionality can be dropped onto forms that require this functionality. A second major benefit is that a procedure class can be sub-classed - for those special situations when standard functionality must be augmented.

The approach that we like is a combination of these two approaches. We recommend using a procedure file for truly generic functions (i.e. those that are used, unchanged, by many different applications). For example, our procedure file contains a *NewID* function for generating surrogate primary keys, a *SetPath* function to set the path for the application and a few key functions that Visual FoxPro should have, but doesn't. Two examples of such functions are the *Str2Exp* and *Exp2Str* functions (used later in this chapter These functions, as the names imply, are used to convert character strings into the values of another specified data type and vice versa.

Separate *Procedure Classes* contain application specific functionality. For example, an accounting application might require several functions to calculate tax and invoice totals. The *Accounting Procedures Class* can be dropped onto any form that requires these functions – or can be instantiated as an Application Level object. Clearly, such functions are not generic, nor are they even required by the entire application. By grouping them into a single procedure class, we can make this functionality available at the specific parts of the application that require it without compromising the rest of the application.

Parameters (an aside)

We have all used parameters extensively in FoxPro but in Visual FoxPro's object oriented environment, parameters have taken on a new importance as the principle means of implementing *messaging* – the very lifeblood of an OO application! (We have more to say on this subject later!)

By reference, by value?

Parameters are passed either by reference or by value. When a parameter is passed to a function or procedure by reference, any changes made to its value in the called code are reflected in the original value in the calling program. Conversely when a parameter is passed by value, the called code can change that value but the value in the calling program remains unchanged.

Visual FoxPro interprets the code being called by the mechanism by which parameters are passed. So when the calling syntax looks like this:

```
luRetVal = CallMyFunction( param1, param2 )
```

Visual FoxPro treats this as a *Function Call* and passes the parameters by value. However if the same code is called like this:

```
DO CallMyFunction WITH param1, param2
```

then Visual FoxPro treats this as a *Procedure Call* and passes the parameters by reference. The old coding rule that a "*Function must always return a value*" is not really true in Visual FoxPro, but it does make sense when the calling syntax is considered.

You can change this default behavior in two ways. One way is to:

```
SET UDFPARMS TO REFERENCE or SET UDFPARMS TO VALUE
```

However, we do not consider this a good idea because it affects the way all functions in your entire application handle the parameters they are passed. (It is *never* a good idea to use a global solution to solve a local problem). In this case there is a simple solution because parameters can be passed by value explicitly just by enclosing them in parentheses. Thus:

```
DO CallMyFunction WITH (param1), (param2)
```

passes the parameters by value, even though the syntax used would normally cause them to be passed by reference. To pass parameters explicitly by reference, simply preface the parameter with the "@" symbol. (This is, by the way, the only way to pass an entire array to a procedure, function or method). So we could also make our function call and pass its parameters by reference like this:

```
luRetVal = CallMyFunction( @param1, @param2 )
```

How do I know what was passed?

There are two ways for a function to determine how many parameters were passed to it. The *PARAMETERS*() function returns the number of parameters that were passed to the most recently called function or procedure. This can give unexpected results since it is reset each time a function or procedure is called. Most importantly, it is also reset by functions that are not called explicitly, such as *ON KEY LABEL* routines.

A better way of determining how many parameters were passed to a function is to use the *PCOUNT()* function. This always returns the number of parameters that were passed to the currently executing code. Save yourself a lot of grief and unnecessary hair pulling by always using *PCOUNT()* for determining the number of parameters passed.

How should I position my parameters?

The best advice is that if a function takes optional parameters, you should place these at the end of the parameter list. *PCOUNT()* can then be used in the function to determine whether or not the optional parameters were passed allowing the function to take the appropriate action.

You can take advantage of the fact that Visual FoxPro always initializes parameters as logical false. By setting up your function to expect a logical false as its default, you can invoke the function without passing it any parameters. Then, in those cases where you want an alternative behavior, just invoke the function by passing it a logical true.

How can I return multiple values from a function?

Of course, returning values is simply the reverse of passing parameters - with one gotcha!. While you can easily pass multiple parameters to a function, there is no obvious mechanism for returning multiple values! The RETURN command only allows a single value to be passed back to the calling program.

One solution is to pass multiple values as a comma-delimited string. This is a little messy, however, as you will need to convert your values into character format to build the return string and then parse out the individual values again in the receiving code.

Another possibility is to define all the values you want populated by the function as *Private* variables in the calling program. As such, they will be available to any function or procedure that is called subsequently and they can be populated directly. However, this is neither specific nor easy to maintain and is not really a good solution.

A better possibility is to create an array in the calling code for the return values and then pass that array by reference. The called function can then simply populate the array and the values will also be available in the calling program. This is workable, at the very least, and was probably the most common method of handling the issue prior to the introduction of Visual FoxPro.

Once again Visual FoxPro has made life a lot easier. Returning multiple values from a UDF is easy if you create, and use, a parameter class. Ours is based on the *Line* baseclass and is named *xParameters*. You can find it in the CH02.VCX class library. All it needs is one custom array property, *aParameters,* to hold the return values and this line of code in its *INIT()*:

```
LPARAMETERS taArray
ACOPY(taArray, This.aParameters)
```

The user-defined function can then simply populate its own local array with the values it needs to return and create the parameter object on the fly — and populate the object's array property with a single line of code:

```
RETURN CREATOBJECT( 'xParameters', @laArray )
```

What about using *named* parameters?

The parameter object discussed above passes parameters by position, in much the same way as Visual FoxPro. Although Visual FoxPro does not actually support the concept of named parameters, you can, in Version 6.0, use the *AddProperty()* method to add named parameters to your object by creating a property for each parameter or value that you want to transfer

Even when using this approach, there is no need to create a special class for the parameter object. It can be created on the fly using a lightweight baseclass such as *Line* or *Separator* as the following code snippet shows:

```
LOCAL oParam
oParam = CREATEOBJECT( 'line' )
WITH oParam
  .AddProperty( "Name", "Christine Johannson" )
  .AddProperty( "Age", 34 )
  .AddProperty( "Sex", "Female" )
ENDWITH
RETURN oParam
```

To retrieve values in this fashion your calling code would simply assign the return value of the called function to an object reference and read off its properties locally:

```
LOCAL oRetVal
oRetVal = CallMyFunction()
lcName = oRetVal.Name
lnAge  = oRetVal.Age
lcSex  = oRetVal.Sex
```

Of all the possibilities discussed so far, we like this the best!

Passing parameters optionally

There is an important side benefit to the ability to use named parameters. This becomes especially important when a function accepts a large number of parameters, many of which are optional. For example, a function to set fonts might have many parameters (name, size, bold, italic, underline, strikethrough and so on). A simple check for:

```
PEMSTATUS( toParameterObject,  'FontName',  5 )
```

determines unambiguously whether or not a specific parameter was passed. This approach removes the tedious task of counting commas in the calling program (as well as the necessity to remember the specific order in which parameters are expected by the called function). The elapsed time function below shows how an object employing named parameters can be used to return multiple values.

Date and time functions

Visual FoxPro has several handy dandy, built in functions for manipulating dates. The functions below illustrate how they can be used to perform a few of the most common tasks required when dealing with dates in your applications.

Elapsed time

Simply subtracting one DateTime expression from another gives you the elapsed time – this is good. Unfortunately Visual FoxPro gives you this result as the number of seconds between the two – this is bad. This value is seldom directly useful! You can use this little set of functions, which rely on the Modulus operator (%), to calculate the components of elapsed time in days, hours, minutes and seconds.

```
FUNCTION GetDays( tnElapsedSeconds )
RETURN INT(tnElapsedSeconds / 86400)

FUNCTION GetHours( tnElapsedSeconds )
RETURN INT(( tnElapsedSeconds % 86400 ) / 3600 )

FUNCTION GetMinutes( tnElapsedSeconds )
RETURN INT(( tnElapsedSeconds % 3600 ) / 60 )

FUNCTION GetSeconds( tnElapsedSeconds )
RETURN INT( tnElapsedSeconds % 60 )
```

Of course, there is more than one way to skin the fox. You can also use a single function to return an array containing the elapsed time positionally, with days as its first element through to seconds as its fourth like so:

```
FUNCTION GetElapsedTime( tnElapsedSeconds )
LOCAL laTime[4]
laTime[1] = INT( tnElapsedSeconds / 86400 )
laTime[2] = INT(( tnElapsedSeconds % 86400 ) / 3600 )
laTime[3] = INT(( tnElapsedSeconds % 3600 ) / 60 )
laTime[4] = INT( tnElapsedSeconds % 60 )
RETURN CREATEOBJECT( 'xParameters', @laTime )
```

If you prefer named parameters to the positional variety, the following code accomplishes the task:

```
FUNCTION GetElapsedTime( tnElapsedSeconds )
LOCAL loObject
loObject = CREATEOBJECT( 'Line' )
WITH loObject
  .AddProperty( 'nDays', INT( tnElapsedSeconds / 86400 ) )
  .AddProperty( 'nHours', INT(( tnElapsedSeconds % 86400 ) / 3600 ) )
  .AddProperty( 'nMins', INT(( tnElapsedSeconds % 3600 ) / 60 ) )
  .AddProperty( 'nSecs', INT( tnElapsedSeconds % 60 ) )
ENDWITH
RETURN loObject
```

Alternatively, if you merely require a string that contains the elapsed time in words, you can just reduce it to a single line of code!

```
FUNCTION GetElapsedTime( tnElapsedSeconds )
RETURN PADL( INT( tnElapsedSeconds / 86400 ), 3 )+' Days ';
  + PADL( INT(( tnElapsedSeconds % 86400 ) / 3600 ), 2, '0' )+' Hrs ' ;
  + PADL( INT(( tnElapsedSeconds % 3600 ) / 60 ), 2, '0')+' Min ' ;
  + PADL( INT( tnElapsedSeconds % 60 ), 2, '0' )+' Sec '
```

Date in words

Converting a value from date format into text can be a tricky business, especially when you are writing international applications. Visual FoxPro makes this task a lot easier with its native MDY(), CMONTH(), CDOW(), MONTH(), DAY() and YEAR() functions, to name but a few. Version 6.0, with its ability to use strict dates, makes this task even easier. The following function provides one example of how to use these functions.

```
FUNCTION DateInWords( tdDate )
RETURN CDOW( tdDate ) + ', ' + MDY( tdDate )
```

However, the function listed above will not attach the ordinal suffix to the day portion of the date. If your application requires these suffixes when formatting the date in words, use the longer form of the function listed below. You could even extract the portion that calculates the suffix and place it in a function called *MakeOrdinal*. It can then be invoked any time you need to format a given number *n* as *nth*.

```
FUNCTION DateInWords( tdDate )
LOCAL lnDay, lnNdx, lcSuffix[31]
*** Initialize suffix for day
lnDay = DAY( tdDate )
lnNdx = lnDay % 10
IF NOT BETWEEN( lnNdx, 1, 3 )
  lcSuffix = 'th'
ELSE
  IF INT( lnDay / 10 ) = 1
    lcSuffix = 'th'
  ELSE
```

```
    lcSuffix = SUBSTR( 'stndrd', ( 2 * lnNdx ) - 1, 2 )
  ENDIF
ENDIF
RETURN CDOW( tdDate ) + ', ' + CMONTH( tdDate ) + ;
  ' ' + ALLTRIM( STR( lnDay )) + lcSuffix + ;
  ', ' + ALLTRIM( STR( YEAR( tdDate )))
```

Calculating Age

Calculating age is even trickier than calculating elapsed time. This is because months do not contain the same number of days and every fourth year is a leap year. The function below calculates age on a given date and returns the value as a formatted string containing the number of years and months. It can easily be modified to return the values in a parameters object like the *ElapsedTime()* function listed above.

```
FUNCTION CalcAge( tdDob, tdBaseDate )
*** Default Base Date to Today if empty
IF TYPE( "tdBaseDate" ) # "D" OR EMPTY(tdBaseDate)
  tdBaseDate = DATE()
ENDIF

LOCAL lnYrs, lnMth, lcRetVal, lnBaseYear, lnBaseMnth
lnYrs = YEAR( tdBaseDate ) - YEAR( tdDob )

*** Calculate this year's Birthday
ldCurBdy = CTOD('^' + STR( YEAR( tdBaseDate )) + '-' + ;
  PADL( MONTH( tdDob ), 2, '0' ) + '-' + ;
  PADL( DAY( tdDob ), 2, '0'))

*** Calculate Age
IF ldCurBdy > tdBaseDate
  lnYrs = lnYrs - 1
  lnMth = 12 - (MONTH( tdBaseDate ) - MONTH( tdDob )) - 1
ELSE
  lnMth = MONTH( tdBaseDate ) - MONTH( tdDob )
ENDIF

*** Format Output String
lcRetVal = PADL( lnYrs, 4 ) + " Years, " + PADL( lnMth, 2, '0' ) + " Month" + ;
  IIF( lnMth = 1, "", "s" )
RETURN ALLTRIM( lcRetVal )
```

What date is the second Tuesday in October of 2000?

This is a handy little function that can be used to calculate the exact date of holidays in a given year. For example, in the United States, Thanksgiving always falls on the fourth Thursday in November. Another example we encountered recently was that the academic year for schools and universities always begins on the first Monday in August. The ability to calculate the actual dates for such defined days is essential in any application that requires planning an annual schedule.

```
************************************************************************
* Program....: nthSomeDayOfMonth
* Compiler...: Visual FoxPro 06.00.8492.00 for Windows
* Abstract...: Returns the date of a specific type of day; e.g., the
* ...........: second Tuesday in November of the year 2001
* ...........: nthSomedayOfMonth( 4, 3, 7, 2000 ) returns the date of
* ...........: the 3rd Wednesday in July of the year 2000
* Parameters.: tnDayNum: Day number 1=Sunday 7=Saturday
* ...........: tnWhich : Which one to find; 1st, 2nd, etc.
* ...........:           If tnwhich > the number of this kind of day
* ...........:           in the month, the last one is returned
* ...........: tnMonth : Month Number in which to find the day
* ...........: tnYear  : Year in which to find the day
************************************************************************
FUNCTION nthSomedayOfMonth( tnDayNum, tnWhich, tnMonth, tnYear )
LOCAL ldDate, lnCnt

*** Start at the first day of the specified month
ldDate = DATE( tnYear, tnMonth, 01 )

*** Find the first one of the specified day of the week
DO WHILE DOW( ldDate ) # tnDayNum
  ldDate = ldDate + 1
ENDDO

*** Find the specified one of these...e.g, 2nd, 3rd, or last
IF tnWhich > 1
  lnCnt = 1
  DO WHILE lnCnt < tnWhich
    lnCnt = lnCnt + 1
    *** Move forward one week to get the next one of these in the month
    ldDate = ldDate + 7
    *** Are we are still in the correct month?
    IF MONTH( ldDate ) # tnMonth
      *** If not, jump back to the last one of these we found and exit
      ldDate = ldDate - 7
      EXIT
    ENDIF
  ENDDO
ENDIF

RETURN ldDate
```

Setting up a payment schedule

Another interesting problem is that of setting up a monthly schedule. Take, for example, a schedule of monthly payments to be collected via direct debit of a debtor's checking account. Obviously these payments cannot be collected on Sundays or holidays. They also cannot be collected earlier than the day specified when the schedule is first set up. This poses some interesting problems if the initial seed date for the schedule is between the 28th and the 31st of the month. So, in this case, simply using the *GOMONTH()* function may return an unacceptable date.

This function handles weekends, holidays, and *GOMONTH()* and assumes that you have created your holiday table with two columns: one for the date and one for the name of the holiday. An index on the holiday date is also desirable. Also keep in mind that to be useful, this holiday table must contain, at the very least, the holidays for both this year and next year.

```
FUNCTION MonthlySchedule ( tdStartDate, tnNumberOfMonths )
LOCAL laDates[1], lnCnt, ldDate, llOK, llUsed

*** Make sure we have the class library loaded
IF 'CH02' $ SET( 'CLASSLIB' )
*** Do nothing...class library is loaded
ELSE
  SET CLASSLIB TO CH02 ADDITIVE
ENDIF

*** Make sure we have the Holidays table available
IF !USED( 'Holidays' )
  USE Holidays In 0
  llUsed = .F.
ELSE
  llUsed = .T.
ENDIF
SELECT Holidays
SET ORDER TO dHoliday

FOR lnCnt = 1 TO tnNumberOfMonths
  *** we want to return the passed date as date[1]
  IF lnCnt > 1
    ldDate = GOMONTH( tdStartDate, lnCnt-1 )
  ELSE
    ldDate = tdStartDate
  ENDIF
  *** Now we have to check to be sure that GoMonth didn't give us back a day
  *** that is earlier than the seed date...can't do a direct debit BEFORE the
  *** specified date i.e., the 28th of the month
  IF DAY(tdStartDate) > 28
    IF BETWEEN( DAY( ldDate ),  28, DAY( tdStartDate ) - 1 )
      ldDate = ldDate + 1
    ENDIF
  ENDIF
  llOK = .F.
  DO WHILE !llOK
    *** If current date is a Saturday, go to Monday
    IF DOW( ldDate ) = 7
      ldDate = ldDate + 2
    ELSE
      *** If current date is a Sunday, go to Monday
      IF DOW( ldDate ) = 1
        ldDate = ldDate + 1
      ENDIF
    ENDIF
    *** OK, now check for Holidays
    IF !SEEK( ldDate, 'Holidays', 'dHoliday' )
      llOK = .T.
    ELSE
      ldDate = ldDate + 1
    ENDIF
  ENDDO
  DIMENSION laDates[lnCnt]
  laDates[lnCnt] = ldDate
```

```
ENDFOR

IF !llUsed
  USE IN Holidays
ENDIF

RETURN CREATEOBJECT( 'xParameters', @laDates )
```

What date is ten business days from today?

A somewhat similar problem is how to calculate a date that is a specified number of business days from a given date. As with the previous example, this assumes the existence of a holiday table that is both region and application specific.

```
FUNCTION BusinessDays ( tdStartDate, tnNumberOfDays )
LOCAL lnCnt, ldDate, llOK, llUsed

*** Make sure we have the Holidays table available
IF !USED( 'Holidays' )
  USE Holidays In 0
  llUsed = .F.
ELSE
  llUsed = .T.
ENDIF
SELECT Holidays
SET ORDER TO dHoliday

ldDate = tdStartDate
FOR lnCnt = 1 TO tnNumberOfDays
  ldDate = ldDate + 1
  llOK = .F.
  DO WHILE !llOK
    *** If current date is a Saturday, go to Monday
    IF DOW( ldDate ) = 7
      ldDate = ldDate + 2
    ELSE
      *** If current date is a Sunday, go to Monday
      IF DOW( ldDate ) = 1
        ldDate = ldDate + 1
      ENDIF
    ENDIF
    *** OK, now check for Holidays
    IF !SEEK( ldDate, 'Holidays', 'dHoliday' )
      llOK = .T.
    ELSE
      ldDate = ldDate + 1
    ENDIF
  ENDDO
ENDFOR

IF !llUsed
  USE IN Holidays
ENDIF

RETURN ldDate
```

Gotcha! Strict date format and parameterized views

Visual FoxPro's StrictDate format is especially comforting with the specter of the millennium bug looming large in front of us. At least it is as we are writing this. There, is however, one small bug that you should be aware of. If you have **SET STRICTDATE TO 2** and try to open a parameterized view that takes a date as its parameter, you will be in for trouble. If the view parameter is not defined or is not in scope when you open or re-query the view, the friendly little dialog box prompting for the view parameter will not accept anything you enter. It will keep saying you have entered an ambiguous date/datetime constant.

The workaround is to ensure your view parameter is defined and in scope before trying to open or re-query the view. This means that, if your view is part of a form's data environment, its **NoDataOnLoad** property must be set to avoid getting the dialog as the form loads.

The other workaround, setting StrictDate to 0 and then back to 2, is not recommended. As we have already mentioned, using a global solution for a local problem is a little bit like swatting flies with a sledgehammer.

Working with numbers

Mathematical calculations have been handled fairly well since the days of *Eniac* and *Maniac*, except for the notable bug in the Pentium math co-processor. The most common problems arise because many calculations produce irrational results such as numbers that carry on for an infinite number of decimal places. Rounding errors are impossible to avoid because computing demands these numbers be represented in a finite form. The study of numerical analysis deals with how to minimize these errors by changing the order in which mathematical operations are performed as well as providing methods such as the trapezoidal method for calculating the area under the curve. A discussion of this topic is beyond the scope of this book, but we can give you some tips and gotchas to watch out for when working with numbers in your application.

Converting numbers to strings

Converting integers to strings is fairly straightforward. **ALLTRIM(STR(lnSomeNumber))** will handle the conversion if the integer contains ten digits or less. If the integer contains more than ten digits, this function will produce a string in scientific notation format unless you specify the length of the string result as the second parameter. When converting numeric values containing decimal points or currency values, it is probably better to use another function. Although it can be accomplished using the *STR()* function, it is difficult to write a generic conversion routine. In order to convert the entire number you must specify both the total length of the number (including the decimal point) and the number of digits to the right of the decimal point. Thus **STR(1234.5678)** will produce '1235' as its result, and to get the correct conversion you must specify **STR(1234.5678, 9, 4)**.

In Visual FoxPro 6.0, the *TRANSFORM()* function has been extended so that when called without any formatting parameters, it simply returns the passed value as its equivalent character string. Thus **TRANSFORM(1234.5678)** will correctly return '1234.5678'.

In all versions of Visual FoxPro you can use **ALLTRIM(PADL (lnSomeNumber, 32))** to get the same result (providing that the total length of *lnSomeNumber* is less than thirty-two digits).

Gotcha! calculations that involve money

This one can bite if you are not careful. Try this in the command window and you will see what we mean.

```
? ( $1000 / 3 )
```

returns the expected result of 333.3333 since currency values are always calculated to a precision of four decimal places. However,

```
? ( $1000 * ( 1/3 ) )
```

returns 333.3000, which is not a very accurate result! Especially when you consider the result of the equivalent numeric calculation:

```
SET DECIMALS TO 4
? ( 1000 * ( 1/3 ) )
```

returns 333.3333. The actual precision of the displayed result depends on the setting of *SET DECIMALS,* although the result is actually calculated to 8 places by default.

The moral of this story is that currency values should always be converted to numeric prior to using them in arithmetic operations. The functions *MTON()* and *NTOM()* are essential in this scenario, although watch out for unexpected results if you do not convert both ways!

```
? ( MTON( $1000 ) * ( 1/3 ) )
```

displays 333.333333 even with decimals set to 2. While

```
? NTOM( ( MTON( $1000 ) * ( 1/3 ) ) )
```

finally gets the expected result of 333.3333.

String functions

Visual FoxPro has several native string manipulation functions to handle almost everything you could ever need. *ALLTRIM()* to remove leading and trailing spaces, *PADL()* and *PADR()* to left and right pad, and *STRTRAN()* and *CHRTRAN()* to replace individual characters within a string. But did you know that you can use this line of code:

```
cString1 - cString2 - cString3
```

to accomplish the same thing as this one?

```
RTRIM( cString1 ) + RTRIM( cString2 ) + RTRIM( cString3 )
```

Gotcha! string concatenation

Even if the tables in your application do not allow null values, you may still need to deal with them. Very often, SQL statements using outer joins result in one or more columns that contain null values. This can be troublesome in cases where you may want to display a concatenated value from a result set, for example, in a drop down list. Try this in the command window:

```
c1 = 'Yada Yada Yada'
c2 = .NULL.
? c1 + c2
```

As you might expect, Visual FoxPro complains about an operator/operand type mismatch. If, however, you do this instead:

```
? c1 + ALLTRIM( c2 )
```

you will see .**NULL**. displayed on the Visual FoxPro screen.

No error, just .NULL. If you do not cater for null values by using *NVL()* to trap for them, you may find this behavior a little difficult to debug when it occurs in your application. We sure did the first time we encountered this behavior!

Converting between strings and data

The following are examples of functions that Visual FoxPro doesn't have, but in our opinion definitely should have. We keep these in our general all-purpose procedure file because we use them so frequently.

Combo and List boxes store their internal lists as string values. So when you need to use these to update or seek values of other data types, you need to convert these strings to the appropriate data type before you are able to use them. The first of these functions is used to do just that:

```
FUNCTION Str2Exp( tcExp, tcType )
*** Convert the passed string to the passed data type
LOCAL luRetVal, lcType

*** Remove double quotes (if any)
tcExp = STRTRAN( ALLTRIM( tcExp ), CHR( 34 ), "" )
*** If no type passed -- map to expression type
lcType = IIF( TYPE( 'tcType' ) = 'C', UPPER(ALLTRIM( tcType )), TYPE( tcExp ) )
*** Convert from Character to the correct type
DO CASE
   CASE INLIST( lcType, 'I', 'N' ) AND ;
     INT( VAL( tcExp ) ) == VAL( tcExp )            && Integer
     luRetVal = INT( VAL( tcExp ) )
   CASE INLIST( lcType, 'N', 'Y', 'B' )             && Numeric or Currency
     luRetVal = VAL( tcExp )
   CASE INLIST( lcType, 'C', 'M' )                  && Character or memo
     luRetVal = tcExp
   CASE lcType = 'L'                                && Logical
     luRetVal = IIF( !EMPTY( tcExp ), .T., .F.)
   CASE lcType = 'D'                                && Date
     luRetVal = CTOD( tcExp )
   CASE lcType = 'T'                                && DateTime
     luRetVal = CTOT( tcExp )
   OTHERWISE
     *** There is no otherwise unless, of course, Visual FoxPro adds
     *** a new data type. In this case, the function must be modified
ENDCASE
*** Return value as Data Type
RETURN luRetVal
```

If you write client/server applications, you already know that you must convert all expressions to strings before using them within a *SQLEXEC()*. Even if you are not doing client/server development, you will require this functionality in order to build any kind of SQL on the fly.

The following function not only converts the passed parameter to a character value, it also wraps the result in quotation marks where appropriate. This is especially useful when invoking the function from an onthefly SQL generator. It is even easier in Visual FoxPro 6.0 because you can use the *TRANSFORM* function without a format string to convert the first argument to character. TRANSFORM(1234.56) produces the same result as ALLTRIM(PADL(1234.56, 32)).

```
FUNCTION Exp2Str( tuExp, tcType )
*** Convert the passed expression to string
LOCAL lcRetVal, lcType
*** If no type passed -- map to expression type
lcType=IIF( TYPE('tcType' )='C', UPPER( ALLTRIM( tcType ) ), TYPE( 'tuExp' ) )
*** Convert from type to char
DO CASE
   CASE INLIST( lcType, 'I', 'N' ) AND INT( tuExp ) = tuExp       && Integer
      lcRetVal = ALLTRIM( STR( tuExp, 16, 0 ) )
   CASE INLIST( lcType, 'N', 'Y', 'B' )                 && Numeric or Currency
      lcRetVal = ALLTRIM( PADL( tuExp, 32 ) )
   CASE lcType = 'C'                                    && Character
      lcRetVal = '"' + ALLTRIM( tuExp ) + '"'
   CASE lcType = 'L'                                    && Logical
      lcRetVal = IIF( !EMPTY( tuExp ), '.T.', '.F.')
   CASE lcType = 'D'                                    && Date
      lcRetVal = '"' + ALLTRIM( DTOC( tuExp ) ) + '"'
   CASE lcType = 'T'                                    && DateTime
      lcRetVal = '"' + ALLTRIM( TTOC( tuExp ) ) + '"'
   OTHERWISE
      *** There is no otherwise unless, of course, Visual FoxPro adds
      *** a new data type. In this case, the function must be modified
ENDCASE
*** Return value as character
RETURN lcRetVal
```

Other useful functions

There are several other generic functions that can live in your general procedure file or base procedure class. One obvious example is the *SetPath()* function (presented in Chapter One). We find the following functions particularly useful and hope you will too.

How do I determine if a tag exists?

Wouldn't it be nice if Visual FoxPro had a native function that returned true if a tag existed? This would be especially useful, for example, when creating a custom grid class that allows the user to click on a column header to sort the grid by the tag on that column. It would also be useful to test for the existence of an index if it must be created programmatically. This code provides that functionality.

```
FUNCTION ISTAG( tcTagName, tcTable )
LOCAL lnCnt, llRetVal, lnSelect

IF TYPE( 'tcTagName' ) # 'C'
  *** Error - must pass a Tag Name
  ERROR '9000: Must Pass a Tag Name when calling ISTAG()'
  RETURN .F.
ENDIF

*** Save Work Area Number
lnSelect = SELECT()
IF TYPE( 'tcTable' ) = 'C' AND ! EMPTY( tcTable )
  *** If a table specified, select it
  SELECT lcTable
ENDIF
*** Check Tags
FOR lnCnt = 1 TO TAGCOUNT()
  IF UPPER(ALLTRIM( tcTagName ) ) == UPPER( ALLTRIM( TAG( lnCnt ) ) )
    llRetVal = .T.
    EXIT
  ENDIF
NEXT
*** Restore Work Area
SELECT (lnSelect)
*** Return Whether Tag Found
RETURN llRetVal
```

By the way, notice the use of the **ERROR** command in this function. Rather than simply displaying a message when a parameter fails validation, this function raises an application error that can be trapped by an error handler, just like a normal Visual FoxPro error.

How do I determine if a string contains at least one alphabetic character?

The Visual FoxPro *ISALPHA()* returns .T. if the string passed to it begins with a letter. Similarly, *ISDIGIT()* will do the same if the string begins with a number. But what if you need to know if the string contains any alphabetic characters? Code like this would work, but it is slow and bulky:

```
FUNCTION ContainsAlpha( tcString )
LOCAL lnChar, llRetVal
llRetVal = .F.
*** Loop through the string and test each character
FOR lnChar = 1 TO LEN( tcString )
  IF ISALPHA( SUBSTR( tcString, lnChar, 1 )
    llRetVal = .T.
    EXIT
  ENDIF
ENDFOR
RETURN llRetVal
```

However, why write ten lines of code when two will do the same job?

```
FUNCTION ContainsAlpha( tcString )
RETURN LEN( CHRTRAN( UPPER( tcString ), "ABCDEFGHIJKLMNOPQRSTUVWXYZ", "" ) );
  # LEN( tcString )
```

Obviously, a similar methodology can be used to determine if a string contains any digits. However, we refuse to insult our readers' intelligence by listing it here. After all, you were all smart enough to buy this book, weren't you?

How to convert numbers to words

One common problem is that of converting numbers into character strings, for printing checks, or as confirmation of an invoice or order total. There have been many solutions proposed for this over the years, but we still like this one the best because it handles large numbers, negative numbers and adopts an innovative approach to decimals too.

```
***********************************************************************
* Program....: NumToStr
* Compiler...: Visual FoxPro 06.00.8492.00 for Windows
* Abstract...: Convert number into a text string
* Notes......: Handles Numbers up to 99,999,999 and will accommodate
* ..........: negative numbers.  Decimals are rounded to Two Places
* ..........: And returned as 'and xxxx hundredths'
***********************************************************************
FUNCTION NumToStr
LPARAMETERS tnvalue
LOCAL lnHund, lnThou, lnHTho, lnMill, lnInt, lnDec
LOCAL llDecFlag, llHFlag, llTFlag, llMFlag, llNegFlag
LOCAL lcRetVal

*** Evaluate Parameters
DO CASE
  CASE TYPE('tnValue') # 'N'
    RETURN('')
  CASE tnvalue = 0
    RETURN 'Zero'
  CASE tnvalue < 0
    *** Set the Negative Flag and convert value to positive
    llNegFlag = .T.
    tnvalue = ABS(tnvalue)
  OTHERWISE
    llNegFlag = .F.
ENDCASE

*** Initialise Variables
STORE .F. TO llHFlag,llTFlag,llMFlag
STORE 0 TO lnHund, lnThou, lnMill
STORE "" TO lcRetVal
*** Get the Integer portion
lnInt = INT(tnvalue)
*** Check for Decimals
IF MOD( tnValue, 1) # 0
  lnDec = ROUND(MOD(tnvalue,1),2)
  llDecFlag = .T.
ELSE
  llDecFlag = .F.
ENDIF
```

```
*** Do the Integer Portion first
DO WHILE .T.
  DO CASE
    CASE lnInt < 100        && TENS
      IF EMPTY(lcRetVal)
        lcRetVal = lcRetVal + ALLTRIM(con_tens(lnInt))
      ELSE
        IF RIGHT(lcRetVal,5)#" and "
          lcRetVal = lcRetVal+' and '
        ENDIF
        lcRetVal = lcRetVal + ALLTRIM(con_tens(lnInt))
      ENDIF
    CASE lnInt < 1000       && HUNDREDS
      lnHund = INT(lnInt/100)
      lnInt = lnInt - (lnHund*100)
      lcRetVal = lcRetVal + ALLTRIM(con_tens(lnHund)) + " Hundred"
      IF lnInt # 0
        lcRetVal = lcRetVal+" and "
        LOOP
      ENDIF
    CASE lnInt < 100000     && THOUSANDS
      lnThou = INT(lnInt/1000)
      lnInt = lnInt - (lnThou*1000)
      lcRetVal = lcRetVal + ALLTRIM(con_tens(lnThou)) + " Thousand"
      IF lnInt # 0
        lcRetVal = lcRetVal + " "
        LOOP
      ENDIF
    CASE lnInt < 1000000    && Hundred Thousands
      lnHTho = INT(lnInt/100000)
      lnInt = lnInt - (lnHTho * 100000)
      lcRetVal = lcRetVal + ALLTRIM(con_tens(lnHTho)) + " Hundred"
      IF lnInt # 0
        lcRetVal = lcRetVal + " and "
        LOOP
      ELSE
        lcRetVal = lcRetVal + " Thousand"
      ENDIF
    CASE lnInt < 100000000  && Millions
      lnMill = INT(lnInt/1000000)
      lnInt = lnInt - (lnMill * 1000000)
      lcRetVal = lcRetVal + ALLTRIM(con_tens(lnMill)) + " Million"
      IF lnInt # 0
        lcRetVal = lcRetVal + ", "
        LOOP
      ENDIF
  ENDCASE
  EXIT
ENDDO
*** Now Handle any Decimals
IF llDecFlag
  lnDec = lnDec * 100
  lcRetVal = lcRetVal + " and " + ALLTRIM(con_tens(lnDec)) + ' Hundredths'
ENDIF
*** Finally Handle the Negative Flag
IF llNegFlag
  lcRetVal = "[MINUS " + ALLTRIM(lcRetVal) + "]"
ENDIF
*** Return the finished string
```

```
RETURN lcRetVal
***********************************************
*** Handle the TENS conversion
***********************************************
FUNCTION con_tens
LPARAMETERS tndvalue
LOCAL lcStrVal, lcStrTeen
STORE '' TO lcStrVal,lcStrTeen
DO CASE
  CASE tnDValue < 20
    RETURN(con_teens(tnDValue))
  CASE tnDValue < 30
    lcStrVal = 'Twenty'
    tnDValue = tnDValue - 20
  CASE tnDValue < 40
    lcStrVal = 'Thirty'
    tnDValue = tnDValue - 30
  CASE tnDValue < 50
    lcStrVal = 'Forty'
    tnDValue = tnDValue - 40
  CASE tnDValue < 60
    lcStrVal = 'Fifty'
    tnDValue = tnDValue - 50
  CASE tnDValue < 70
    lcStrVal = 'Sixty'
    tnDValue = tnDValue - 60
  CASE tnDValue < 80
    lcStrVal = 'Seventy'
    tnDValue = tnDValue - 70
  CASE tnDValue < 90
    lcStrVal = 'Eighty'
    tnDValue = tnDValue - 80
  CASE tnDValue < 100
    lcStrVal = 'Ninety'
    tnDValue = tnDValue - 90
ENDCASE
*** Now convert any remaining portion
lcStrTeen = con_teens(tnDValue)
IF LEN(lcStrTeen) # 0
  *** Add on the relevant text
  lcStrVal = lcStrVal + '-' + lcStrTeen
ENDIF
RETURN TRIM(lcStrVal)

***********************************************
*** Handle the Units/Teens Conversion
***********************************************
FUNCTION con_teens
LPARAMETERS tntvalue
DO CASE
  CASE tntvalue = 0
    RETURN('')
  CASE tntvalue = 1
    RETURN('One ')
  CASE tntvalue = 2
    RETURN('Two ')
  CASE tntvalue = 3
    RETURN('Three ')
  CASE tntvalue = 4
```

```
      RETURN('Four ')
CASE tntvalue = 5
  RETURN('Five ')
CASE tntvalue = 6
  RETURN('Six ')
CASE tntvalue = 7
  RETURN('Seven ')
CASE tntvalue = 8
  RETURN('Eight ')
CASE tntvalue = 9
  RETURN('Nine ')
CASE tntvalue = 10
  RETURN('Ten ')
CASE tntvalue = 11
  RETURN('Eleven ')
CASE tntvalue = 12
  RETURN('Twelve ')
CASE tntvalue = 13
  RETURN('Thirteen ')
CASE tntvalue = 14
  RETURN('Fourteen ')
CASE tntvalue = 15
  RETURN('Fifteen ')
CASE tntvalue = 16
  RETURN('Sixteen ')
CASE tntvalue = 17
  RETURN('Seventeen ')
CASE tntvalue = 18
  RETURN('Eighteen ')
CASE tntvalue = 19
  RETURN('Nineteen ')
ENDCASE
```

The design here is interesting in itself. The problem has been tackled by reducing the various components of a number to a minimum, and the result is a useful function that can be used as a single line call as follows:

```
lcOutStr = NumToStr(1372.23) + " Dollars"
Returns: "One Thousand Three Hundred and Seventy-Two and Twenty-Three
Hundredths Dollars"
```

How to extract a specified item from a list

More and more often we need to be able to accept and interpret data that is supplied in a *separated list* format. This may be a simple, comma-delimited file or possibly the result of a more complex data transfer mechanism or just some data we need to pass around internally. The construction of a string that contains data in a *separated* format is simple enough. Retrieving the data from such a string, however, can be a little more problematic. Enter the *GetItem()* function.

This function parses the string it is given, looking for the specified occurrence of the separator and extracting the item it finds. It assumes that, unless specified otherwise, you want the first item and the separator is a comma. However, both elements can be specified. Here it is:

```
**********************************************************************
* Program....: GetItem.PRG
* Compiler...: Visual FoxPro 06.00.8492.00 for Windows
* Abstract...: Extracts the specified element from a list
**********************************************************************
FUNCTION GetItem( tcList, tnItem, tcSepBy )
LOCAL lcRetVal, lnStPos, lnEnPos, lcSepBy
lcRetVal = ""
*** Default to Comma Separator if none specified
lcSep = IIF( VARTYPE(tcSepBy) # 'C' OR EMPTY( tcSepBy ), ',', tcSepBy )
*** Default to First Item if nothing specified
tnItem = IIF( TYPE( 'tnItem' ) # "N" OR EMPTY( tnItem ), 1, tnItem)
*** Add terminal separator to list to simplify search
tcList = ALLTRIM( tcList ) + lcSep
*** Determine the length of the required string
IF tnItem = 1
  lnStPos = 1
ELSE
  lnStPos = AT( lcSep, tcList, tnItem - 1 ) + 1
ENDIF
*** Find next separator
lnEnPos = AT( lcSep, tcList, tnItem )
IF lnEnPos = 0 OR (lnEnPos - lnStPos) = 0
  *** End of String
  lcRetVal = NULL
ELSE
    *** Extract the relevant item
  lcRetVal = SUBSTR( tcList, lnStPos, lnEnPos - lnStPos )
ENDIF
*** Return result
RETURN ALLTRIM(lcRetVal)
```

Typically we use this function inside a loop to retrieve the items from a separated list in the order in which it was constructed, as follows:

```
lcStr = "David|Jones|12 The Street|Someplace|"
lnCnt = 0
DO WHILE .T.
  lnCnt = lnCnt + 1
  lcItem = GetItem( lcStr, lnCnt, "|" )
  IF ! ISNULL(lcItem)
    *** Do whatever with it
  ELSE
    *** End of the string - exit
    EXIT
  ENDIF
ENDDO
```

Is there a simple way of encrypting passwords?

The answer (and since we asked the question, you would expect nothing less) is **Yes!** The next pair of functions provide an easy way to add a reasonable level of password security. The encryption process is based on converting each character in the plain string to its ASCII number and then adding a constant. We have used 17 in this example but suggest that if you adopt these functions you use a different number, plus a random seed number, plus the position of the letter in the string to that value. The character represented by this new number is then returned as the encrypted version. The returned string includes the seed number used in its generation as the first character so it can always be decoded. This methodology has several benefits:

- The same string will, within the limits of Visual FoxPro's *RAND()* function, produce different encrypted strings each time it is passed through the function
- There is no easy way to translate an encrypted character since the result for any given character depends on the seed number and its position in the string
- The encrypted password is always one character longer than the original because of the seed value
- There is no restriction on the number of characters (i.e. it will handle 6, 8 or 12 character passwords equally well)
- The password can include numbers and special characters
- While by no means foolproof, it is actually quite difficult to hack since although the plain string is always converted to upper case, the encrypted string can contain any combination of characters
- Since the password contains its seed, an administrator can always decode passwords

Anyway, here are both the Encode and Decode functions:

```
*****************************************************************
* Program....: AEnCode.PRG
* Compiler...: Visual FoxPro 06.00.8492.00 for Windows
* Abstract...: Encrypt a Password
*****************************************************************
FUNCTION aencode(tcKeyWord)
LOCAL lcRaw, lnVar, lcEnc
IF TYPE('tcKeyWord') # "C" OR EMPTY(tcKeyWord)
   *** Must pass a character key to this process
     ERROR( "9000: A Character string is the required parameter for AEnCode" )
   RETURN ""
ENDIF
lcRaw = UPPER(ALLTRIM(tcKeyWord))    && Keyword
lnVar = INT(RAND() * 10)       && Random Number Key: 0 - 9
lcEnc = ALLTRIM(STR(lnVar))       && Encrypted string starts with key #
*** Parse the Keyword and encrypt each character
*** Using its ASCII code + 17 + Random Key + Position in Keyword
FOR lnCnt = 1 TO LEN(lcRaw)
  lcChar = SUBSTR(lcRaw, lnCnt,1)
  lcEnc = lcEnc + CHR( ASC(lcChar) + 17 + lnVar + lnCnt + 1)
NEXT
RETURN lcEnc


*****************************************************************
* Program....: ADeCode.PRG
* Compiler...: Visual FoxPro 06.00.8492.00 for Windows
* Abstract...: Decodes a password encrypted with AEnCode()
*****************************************************************
FUNCTION adecode(tcKeyWord)
LOCAL lcRaw, lnVar, lcEnc
```

```
IF TYPE('tcKeyWord') # "C" OR EMPTY(tcKeyWord)
  *** Must pass a character key to this process
    ERROR( "9000: An Encrypted string is the required parameter for ADeCode" )
  RETURN ""
ENDIF
lcEnc = ALLTRIM(tcKeyWord)        && Keyword
lnVar = VAL(LEFT(lcEnc,1))        && Encryption Key
lcRaw = ""                && Decoded Password
*** Parse the Keyword and decrypt each character
*** Using its ASCII code + 17 + Random Key + Position in Keyword
FOR lnCnt = 2 TO LEN(lcEnc)
  lcChar = SUBSTR(lcEnc, lnCnt, 1)
  lcRaw = lcRaw + CHR( ASC(lcChar) - (17 + lnVar + lnCnt) )
NEXT
RETURN lcRaw
```

And here are some samples of the encrypted output:

Pass 1	? AEnCode('Andy%Kr#02')	8\jawDksESV
Pass 2	? AEnCode('Andy%Kr#02')	6Zh_uBiqCQT
Pass 3	? AEnCode('Andy%Kr#02')	3We\r?fn@NQ

Each of which decodes back to the same original string:

Pass 1	? ADeCode('8\jawDksESV')	ANDY%KR#02
Pass 2	? ADeCode('6Zh_uBiqCQT')	ANDY%KR#02
Pass 3	? ADeCode('3We\r?fn@NQ')	ANDY%KR#02

We are sure you will find ways of improving or adapting these functions, but they have served us well for several years now and we hope you like them.

Where do you want to GOTO?

We all use the GOTO <nn> command from time to time, but one of a Visual FoxPro programmer's little annoyances is that GOTO does not do any error checking of its own. If you tell Visual FoxPro to GOTO a specific record number it just tries to go there. Of course if the record number you have specified is not in the table, or if you inadvertently have the wrong work area selected you get an ugly error.

The problem of the work area selection has been largely resolved with the introduction of the *IN* clause for many commands – including GOTO. However that does not resolve the problem of other errors. We got tired of putting checks around every GOTO statement in our code so we devised a little function to wrap the GOTO command and make it safer and friendlier. We named it GOSAFE() and here it is:

```
*******************************************************************
* Program....: GoSafe.PRG
* Compiler...: Visual FoxPro 06.00.8492.00 for Windows
* Abstract...: Wrapper around the GOTO command
*******************************************************************
FUNCTION GoSafe( tnRecNum, tcAlias )
LOCAL ARRAY laErrs[1]
LOCAL lcAlias, lnCount, lnCurRec, lnErrCnt, lLRetVal
```

```
*** Check parameter is numeric and valid
IF VARTYPE( tnRecNum ) # "N" OR EMPTY( tnRecNum )
    ERROR "9000: A valid numeric parameter must be passed to GoSafe()"
    RETURN .F.
ENDIF
*** Default alias to current alias if not specified
IF VARTYPE( tcAlias) #"C" OR EMPTY( tcAlias )
    lcAlias = ALIAS()
ELSE
    lcAlias = UPPER( ALLTRIM( tcAlias ))
ENDIF
*** Check that we have got the specified Alias
IF EMPTY( lcAlias ) OR ! USED( lcAlias )
    ERROR "9000: No table was specified or the specified table is not open"
    RETURN .F.
ENDIF
*** Get Max No records and the currently selected
*** record number in the specified alias
lnCount = RECCOUNT( lcAlias )
lnCurRec = RECNO( lcAlias )
*** Save Error handling and turn off error trapping for now
lcOldError = ON("ERROR")
ON ERROR *
*** Now try and GO to the required record
GOTO tnRecNum IN (lcAlias)
*** Did we succeed?
IF RECNO( lcAlias ) # tnRecNum
    *** Check for Errors
    lnErrCnt = AERROR( laErrs )
    IF lnErrCnt > 0
        DO CASE
            CASE laErrs[1,1] = 5
                *** Record Out of Range
                lcErrTxt = 'Record Number ' + ALLTRIM(PADL(tnRecNum, 32)) ;
                        + ' Is not available in Alias: ' + lcAlias
            CASE laErrs[1,1] = 20
                *** Record Not in Index
                lcErrTxt = 'Record Number ' + ALLTRIM(PADL(tnRecNum, 32)) ;
                        + ' Is not in the Index for Alias: ' + lcAlias ;
                        + CHR(13) + 'Table needs to be Re-Indexed'
            OTHERWISE
                *** An unexpected error
                lcErrTxt = 'An unexpected error prevented the GOTO succeeding'
        ENDCASE
        MESSAGEBOX( lcErrTxt, 16, 'Command Failed' )
    ENDIF
    *** Restore the original record
    GOTO lnCurRec IN (lcAlias)
    llRetVal = .F.
ELSE
    llRetVal = .T.
ENDIF
*** Restore Error Handler
ON ERROR &lcOldError
RETURN llRetVal
```

One thing to notice in this program is the use of the ON("ERROR") function to save off the current error handler so that we can safely suppress the normal error handling with ON ERROR * and restore things at the end of the function.

This is a very important point and is all too easily forgotten in the heat of battle. Any procedure or function should save environmental settings before changing any of them (well, maybe we should state that it is best to validate parameters first. After all, if they are incorrect, the function is not going to do anything anyway.) On completion, your procedure or function absolutely must reset everything exactly as it was before the function was called.

Chapter 3
Design, Design and Nothing Else

"It's by design." (Anonymous, but often associated with Microsoft Corporation)

Can you guess what this chapter is all about? Correct, it's about the three most important things to consider when working with Visual FoxPro's object oriented environment. We are not strictly certain that this chapter comprises 'Tips', but it is certainly full of advice – most of it hard-won over the years that we have been working with Visual FoxPro. We will cover quite a range of topics, starting with some basic reminders of what OOP is all about.

So why all the fuss about OOP anyway?

It's always difficult to know where to start. In this case we felt it was probably worth beginning with a few words about why on earth you should bother with all this OOP stuff – and what adopting the OOP paradigm will mean to you as a developer.

The first point to make about OOP is that it is not, of itself, a new programming language, but is actually a different way of looking at the way you design and build computer programs. In terms of VFP this is the good news – it means that you don't actually have to learn a whole new language – just a different way of doing things. The bad news is that the new way of doing things is so radically different that you'll probably wish you just had to learn a new language. Like so many aspects of programming, doing OOP is easy, doing it well is much harder!

Two of the most basic benefits that programmers have long striven for are re-usability (write a piece of code once, debug it once and use it many times) and extensibility (make changes to one part of a system without bringing the rest of it crashing down around you). Properly implemented, OOP has the capability to deliver both of these benefits. The only question is how?

Firstly, as implied by its name, Object Orientation is focused on 'Objects' that are designed and created independently of applications. The key thing to remember about an object is that it should know HOW to do what it is meant to do. In other words, an object must have a function. Whether that function is entirely self contained, or merely a link in a chain, is irrelevant providing that the function is clearly defined as being the responsibility of a particular object.

In terms of an application, or a system, the overall functionality is achieved by manipulating the characteristics and interactions of the objects that make up the system. It follows then that modifications to the system's functionality will be made by adding or removing objects, rather than by altering the code within an existing object.

There are, of course, consequences inherent in adopting this approach to system development. First it will mean a change in the emphasis of the development cycle. Much more time will have to be spent in the design, creation and testing of the objects required by an application. Fortunately, less time will actually be needed to develop the system. By the time you have a stock of properly tested objects, you will also have the majority of the functionality needed by an application and all you need to do is to link things properly. (Sounds pretty good so far.)

Of course, there is also a learning curve. Not just in terms of the mechanics of programming in Visual FoxPro's OOP environment (that's the easy bit) but also learning to change the way you think about your development work. The bad news is that while there has never been a substitute for good software design, in the OOP world design is not only critical, it is everything! Get your original design right and everything is simple. Get it wrong and life rapidly becomes a misery.

The final bit of bad news is that not only is the design critical, but so is documentation. Since your objective is to write a piece of code once, and once only, and then lock it away forever, it is imperative that you document what each object does, what information it needs and what functionality it delivers. (Notice that we don't need to know how it does whatever it does – that is the object's responsibility.)

So, just what does all this OOP jargon mean?

As with any new technology, the advent of Object Orientation has introduced a lot of new words and phrases into the FoxPro development language. While most of the jargon is 'standard' in the object oriented world, it is not always immediately obvious to those of us who come from a FoxPro background. Working with objects requires an understanding of *PEMs* (Properties, Events and Methods). Just what do these terms actually mean?

Property

A property of an object is a variable that defines some characteristic of that object. All objects have a default 'Set' of properties (derived initially from the class definition) which describe the object's state.

For example a text box object has properties for:

- Size and location (e.g. Height, Width, Top, Left)
- Appearance (e.g. FontName, FontSize)
- Status (e.g. ReadOnly)
- Contents (e.g. Controlsource, Value)

The property set of an object may be extended in Visual FoxPro by the addition of "custom properties" to the class definition from which the object is derived.

Properties answer the question: "What is the state of the object?"

Method

A method of an object is a procedure associated with that object. All objects have a default 'Set' of methods (derived initially from the class definition) which define how an object behaves. For example a text box object has methods for:

- Updating itself (Refresh)
- Making an object current (SetFocus)
- Changing its position (Move)

The method set of an object may be extended in Visual FoxPro by the addition of "custom methods" to the class definition.

Methods answer the question: "What does the object do?"

Event

An event is an action that an object can recognize, and to which it can respond. All objects have a default 'Set' of events which they inherit from the FoxPro Base Class. Thus, for example, a text box object can recognize events like:

- Mouse or keyboard actions
- Changes to its current value
- Receiving or losing focus

The action that an object takes when an event occurs is determined by the content of a method associated with the event. However, calling such a method directly does NOT cause the event to fire, it merely executes the method. Certain events have default actions in their methods which are defined by the FoxPro Base Class (e.g. GotFocus) while others do not (e.g. Click).

The event set of an object cannot be extended - you cannot create "custom events". However, code can be added to the method associated with an event to call another method.

Events answer the question: "When does the object do something?"

Messages

A message is the result of an object's action and is the mechanism by which it communicates with its environment. In Visual FoxPro messages are handled by passing parameters/returning values or by setting properties/calling methods.

Messages answer the question "How do we know an object has done something?"

Classes and Objects

Understanding the difference between a Class and an Object is crucial to OOP. A class is the template from which objects are created. However, objects are not "copies" of a class definition, they are references to it. The consequence is that when a class definition is changed, any object derived from that class will reflect that change. This is what is meant by *'Inheritance'*.

The relationship between an Object and its Class is similar to that between a recipe for a cake and the actual cake – the recipe tells you how to make the cake, but you cannot actually eat the recipe! In the same way a class does not actually DO anything. It is only when an object is created as an "*INSTANCE*" of that class (the process is therefore called *'Instantiation'*) that anything useful can actually be done.

In Visual FoxPro Classes may be defined hierarchically, and objects may be instantiated from any level of the hierarchy. It is important, therefore, that the definition of classes is undertaken using a logical and consistent methodology – referred to as '*Abstraction*'. The principle behind abstraction is to identify the key characteristics appropriate to the level of hierarchy under consideration.

This sounds more complex than it actually is – we all do it every day without thinking about it. For example, if someone stated "Hand me a pen," we would not normally hesitate to consider just what a 'pen' actually is – we just *"know what a pen is."*

In fact there is no such thing as 'a pen' – the term is actually an abstraction which describes a class of physical objects which share certain characteristics and which differ from other classes of physical objects. We wouldn't normally confuse a pen and a pencil – even though both are clearly writing implements.

This basic principle translates directly in the construction of classes within VFP. Starting with the VFP base classes we can construct our own class hierarchies by adding to the functionality (Augmentation) or changing the functionality (Specialization) in subclasses which then form the Class Hierarchy.

Inheritance

Inheritance is the term used to describe the way in which an object (an '*Instance*' of a class) derives its functionality from its parent class. In Visual FoxPro whenever you use an object, you are actually creating a reference back to that parent class definition. This reference is not static and is re-evaluated every time the object is instantiated. The result is that if you change the definition in the parent class, any object based on that class will exhibit the result of the change the next time it is instantiated.

> *This is why, when working in Visual FoxPro, you will occasionally get an error message saying 'Cannot modify a class that is in use'. What this is telling you is that you actually have one or more definitions in memory that are required by the object that you are trying to edit. Issuing a* '**CLEAR ALL**' *command will usually resolve this problem for you.*

How VFP implements inheritance

Visual FoxPro implements inheritance in a bottom upward fashion. When an event occurs which requires that an object takes some action, Visual FoxPro begins by executing any code that has been defined in the method associated with that event in the object (such code is, therefore, referred to as "Instance Level" and it will override any inherited code unless an explicit '**DODEFAULT ()**' function call is included at some point).

If there is no code in the object (or a *DoDefault()* has been specified), VFP continues by executing any code defined in the same method in the class identified in the object's *ParentClass* property. This process continues up the hierarchy defined by successive *ParentClass* references until either a method containing code without an explicit *DoDefault()* or a class where the *ParentClass* property points directly to a Visual FoxPro baseclass, is found. Either condition identifies the 'Top' of the class hierarchy for that object and no further references are searched for.

On completion of any instance level code, and any inherited code, Visual FoxPro finally runs any code that is defined in the relevant native baseclass method. (Any such code will **always** be executed unless you include an explicit **NODEFAULT** command somewhere in the inheritance chain.) Unfortunately there is no documentation to tell you which baseclass methods actually do have executable code, although some are obvious. *KeyPress*, *GotFocus* and *LostFocus* are all examples of events that require native behavior and which, therefore, have code in the baseclasses. Conversely there are events that obviously do not have any native behavior – *Click*, *When* and *Valid* are all examples of baseclass methods which simply return the default value (a logical **.T.**).

The inheritance 'trap'

Inheritance seems, at first sight, to embody the very essence of working in an object oriented manner. By defining a class, and then creating subclasses that are either augmented or specialized, it would appear that we can greatly simplify the task of building an application. However, there is a subtle trap in relying too much on inheritance as the following simple example illustrates.

Let us suppose that we wish to create a standard Form class that we will use in all of our applications. We decide that one thing every form will need is an '*Exit*' button and so we add a suitably captioned command button to our form class and in its *Click* method, we place a '*ThisForm.Release()*' call. This is just fine, and every time we create a new form it comes complete with an "Exit" button which *works*, although there is no code in the button's *Click* method. (Of course there really *is* code, but instead of being in every form it exists only once - in the button that we defined as part of the Form class and to which the button on each instance of our form class always refers). So far, so good. Over time we add more "standard" functionality to our form class by creating custom properties and methods to handle our needs.

Then one day we get asked to create a new form which, instead of an 'Exit' button, has two buttons '*OK*' and '*Cancel*'. The first must "save changes and exit the form" and the second must "discard changes and exit the form". We immediately have a problem because we cannot simply create a subclass of our standard form! Any subclass will *ALWAYS* have an 'Exit' button that simply releases the form, and we cannot delete that button in a subclass because Visual FoxPro will complain that it '*Cannot delete objects because some are members of a parent class*'. Of course we could simply create a new subclass of the form base class, but that would not have any of our other custom properties and methods! We would have to add them all again and copy and paste code into our new form class, thereby creating two sets of code to maintain forever more and losing one of the main benefits of using Object Orientation at all.

One solution we have seen to this dilemma is to go ahead and create the subclass anyway. Then, in that subclass, the inherited Exit button's *Enabled* and *Visible* properties are set to FALSE and the required new buttons are added! OK, this **will** work but, we are sure you will agree, it is not exactly the best way of doing things.

The correct approach is, as we explain in the "So how do you go about designing a class" section later in this chapter, is to design your classes properly and instead of relying entirely on inheritance, to use composition to add specific functionality when it is needed.

Composition

Composition is a term used to describe the technique in which a class is given access to specific behavior (or functionality) by adding an object which already has that behavior, rather than by adding code directly to the class. This is actually a far better way of constructing complex objects than relying directly on inheritance because it allows you to define functionality in discrete units that can be re-used in many different situations. (It is also the best way of avoiding the 'inheritance trap' outlined in the preceding section.)

Most importantly you are not limited to using composition only at design time. All Visual FoxPro containers (i.e. those classes which can 'contain' other objects - including Forms and Toolbars, PageFrames and Pages, Grids and Columns, as well as both the Container and Custom classes)) have native *AddObject* and *RemoveObject* methods which make using composition at run time a relatively straightforward matter. (For a diagrammatic representation of the categorization of base classes see "Chapter 3: Object-Oriented Programming" in the Programmer's Guide or online documentation.)

The result of using composition, whether at design or run time, is always that the added object becomes a "child" (or "member") of the object to which it is being added. This ensures that the child object shares the same lifetime as its parent - when the parent is destroyed, so are all of its children.

Finally, note that composition is not limited to particular types of classes - it is perfectly possible (and permissible) to mix Visual and Non-Visual classes in the same composite object. The only restriction is that the intended parent object must be based on a class that is capable of containing the type of object to be added. In other words you cannot add an object based on a Visual FoxPro *"column"* class to anything other than a grid, no matter how you define it.

Aggregation

Aggregation is the term used to describe the technique in which a class is given access to specific behavior (or functionality) by creating a reference to an object which already has that behavior, rather than by adding code directly to the class. If this sounds similar to composition, it is, since composition is actually a special case of Aggregation. The difference is that aggregation is based on creating a reference to an object as a member of the class, while composition requires that the child object itself be created as a member of the class. The consequence is that aggregation is not limited to container classes and there is no requirement for the aggregated object to share the same lifetime as the object that refers to it.

It is precisely because Aggregation relies on "loose coupling" between objects that it is both more flexible than composition and potentially more hazardous. It is more flexible because it does not require direct containership (so that, for example, an object based on a text box class could be given a direct reference to another object based on a DataEnvironment class). It is more hazardous because the lifetimes of the object that owns the reference and the referenced object are not directly linked. You must ensure that any references are properly resolved when releasing either object and this can be difficult in Visual FoxPro because there is no way for an object to know what external references to it may exist at any time.

The simplest form of aggregation (and therefore the safest) is when an object actually creates the target object itself and assigns that object's reference directly to one of its own properties. The more complex form is when one object either passes a reference to itself to another object, or acquires a reference to an existing object.

Delegation

Delegation is the term used to describe the situation in which one object instructs another to perform an action on its behalf. It is, effectively, a form of classless inheritance because it allows functionality that actually belongs to objects of a specific class to be accessed by objects that do not inherit from that class. This is an extremely powerful tool in the developer's armory because it allows us to centralize our code and call on it when needed.

The power of delegation can be seen when you consider the situation in which you need controls for a form to be implemented either as contained objects (e.g. Command Buttons) or as stand-alone objects (e.g. a Toolbar). Obviously the situation with buttons on a form is fairly easy – the buttons belong to the form after all so code can be placed in their own methods. However, a toolbar is more difficult.

To provide different toolbars for every type of form would be both time-consuming and wasteful of resources, not to say difficult to maintain. By adding code directly to standard form methods it is possible to code both toolbars and buttons generically so that a single button set or toolbar (or both) may be used with any form. Each individual button, wherever it is situated, can delegate its function to a method of the currently active form – which, by the way, is entirely in keeping with our earlier definition of objects needing to know how to get something done, without actually needing to know how it is implemented.

Encapsulation

There are two aspects to encapsulation. The first is that an object must be self-contained, and that no dependencies on the way in which an object works may exist outside of the object itself. Clearly if such dependencies were permitted, inheritance would not work properly since a change to the way in which a class was defined would affect not only those objects which derived from that class but also objects which depended on derived objects functioning in a particular way.

The second is the requirement to protect an object's inner workings from its environment. This is necessary to ensure that an object can perform its allotted function reliably in all situations and follows from the first.

The mechanism for defining the interaction of an object with its environment is referred to as its 'Public Interface'. Many of the so called 'pure' OOP languages demand total encapsulation of an object and limit the Public Interface to a few specific "Get and Set" methods. Visual FoxPro (for better or worse) is more open, and by default an object exposes all of its PEMs in its Public Interface unless specifically instructed otherwise. The "Access" and "Assign" methods, introduced in Visual FoxPro Version 6.0, correspond in many ways to the Get and Set methods referred to above, although the implementation is different.

Polymorphism

Polymorphism is a characteristic of object oriented languages that arises out of the requirement that, when calling a method of an object, the reference to the object must be included as part of the call. The consequence is that it's perfectly possible to have methods which have the same *name* in several different objects but which actually *do different things* in different objects. The call to a method is only meaningful in the context of a specific object and there is therefore no possibility of confusion.

This is a very powerful tool in the context of application development and maintenance because it allows objects to be added or swapped for one another without the necessity of actually changing the working application's code.

Hierarchies

When working within Visual FoxPro it is important to remember that there are two distinct hierarchies with which you are interacting:

- The first is the "Class" (or "Inheritance") hierarchy that is defined by the relationships of the various classes that you create. It is the relationship of an object (through its parent class) to this hierarchy that determines what PEMs it will inherit. *The construction and management of the Class Hierarchy is, therefore, essentially a 'design time' issue.*
- The second is the "Object" (or "Containership") hierarchy. This is determined by the relationships between objects (irrespective of their Class) and the containers in which they reside. It is the position of an object in this hierarchy that determines how you must manage its interactions with other objects. *Whilst the construction of the Object Hierarchy may be initiated at design time, the management of it is, essentially, a 'run time' issue.*

Practical object oriented programming (POOP)

So much for the theory, now lets get down to some more practical issues. The key question is how can we turn all this theory into practice? That is what POOP is all about! (We have, by the way, noticed that *'Rules of Three'* play an important role in the POOP world).

When should you define a class?

Right away we hit our first 'Rule of Three', which defines the criteria for deciding that a new class (or a new subclass of an existing class) is required. These, we suggest, are:

- Is the object going to be re-used?
- Will it ease the management of complexity?
- Is it worth the effort?

Re-usability

This is probably the most common reason for creating a class and the achievement of re-usability is, after all, one of the primary goals of OOP. At its simplest level this can mean as little as setting up your own personal preferences for objects – Font, Color and Style for example, so that all objects of your class are created with the correct settings in place.

Things get a little trickier when you consider functionality. How often, in practice, do you do exactly the same thing, in exactly the same way, to achieve exactly the same results, in exactly the same environment? The answer is probably "not very often" and you may even begin to wonder whether re-usability is so valuable after all. This leads us neatly to the second criterion.

Managing complexity

As we hinted in the preceding section, it is actually very rare that anything other than the simplest of functional classes can simply be re-used 'as-is'. There are almost always differences in the environment, the input or the output requirements and sometimes all of them. This apparent complexity can sometimes obscure the issue, which is that the desired functionality remains constant, although the implementation may differ in detail between applications.

By applying the rules for designing classes outlined in the next section, you should find it easier to decide whether using a class will ease the management of this complexity or not. Even if the creation of a class *could* ease the management of the complexity, we still have to consider our third criterion.

Is it worth the effort?

You will recall we stated above that an object should be encapsulated so that it contains within itself all of the information needed to complete its task, and that no object should ever rely on the internal implementation of another object.

Clearly this can make life extremely difficult. It could mean that your class will have to check dozens of possible conditions to determine (for itself) exactly what the state of the system is before it can perform its allotted function. When considering the creation of a new class, it is important to be sure that it is actually worth the effort of doing so.

So how do you go about designing a class?

The first and most basic requirement is to be sure that you know what the class is actually going to do. This may sound obvious, but there is a subtle trap here. It is very easy to build so much into every class you design that before you realize it, you have built classes that are not re-usable because they do too much! The solution is always to be sure that you have identified the 'Responsibilities' of your class, and have categorized them before you start writing code.

A responsibility can be defined simply here as "*some element of functionality that has to be completed*". This categorization, in keeping with our 'Rules of Three', can be done by assigning each identified responsibility to one of three pigeonholes as follows:

- Must Do
- Could Do
- Should Be Done

Actions which fall into the first 'Must Do' category are those things which an object derived from the class would have to do in **every** situation and are, therefore, clearly the direct and sole responsibilities of the class. These must form part of the class definition.

Things which come in the 'Could Do' category are normally indicators that the class may itself require either one or more subclasses (or, more rarely, the cooperation of objects of another class). In other words these are the things that it would be possible for the class to do, but which would not actually be required in every situation. It is the inclusion of such 'Could Do' items in a class definition that can actually prevent that definition from being properly re-usable.

The final category is very important indeed. This is the category that defines the 'assumptions' that a class must have fulfilled in order to function properly. Items listed here are definitely not the sole responsibility of the class in question but must, nonetheless, be done somehow.

Having defined and categorized the Responsibilities of the new class, you must define its Public Interface by deciding what Properties and Methods it will require, and how it will reveal itself to other objects with which it will interact.

At last you can code the class definition, instantiate an object from it and test it (thoroughly). But when all is done, you have still not finished because you MUST thoroughly document the new class and any subclasses.

This all sounds very good but what does it mean in practice?

Consider a simple example. The creation of a standard table navigation bar that might look something like this:

Figure 3.1 A standard Table Navigation Bar

Do we need a class for this at all?

Following the steps outlined above we can assess the need for the class as follows:

- *Is it going to be re-usable?* While this will, to some extent, depend on the type of applications you are building, navigation through a table (or cursor, or view) is a fundamental requirement and so this really should be re-usable in many different situations.
- *Will it help us to manage complexity?* The answer here is also "yes." The actual task of navigating between records in a table, cursor or view is not particularly difficult in Visual FoxPro. But there are still issues that need to be handled (like what to do at the beginning or end of a file for example).
- *Is it worth the effort of creating the class?* Given the answers to the first two questions, this one is a no-brainer – it is quite clear that we really do need a class for this task.

So what are the responsibilities of the class going to be?

This is an easy one - it's going to handle the navigation between records in a table, cursor or view! Unfortunately while this describes the intention, it does not really tell us what the 'responsibilities' of the class actually *are*. The best way we have found of doing this is to write down all the things that we can think of – as they occur to us – like this (this is by no means a complete listing):

- Display Message to Re-Cycle at BOF()/EOF()
- Ensure Data Table is open
- Ensure Records are available
- Handle BOF()/EOF() Errors
- Move Record Pointer
- Refresh Parent Form
- Select Correct Work Area
- Selectively Enable/Disable Buttons
- Select Specific Field on Completion

Having created our list, we then apply the "*Must-Could-Should*" rule to each item in order to refine our definition – the result might look something like:

Table 3.1 Refined list of responsibilities

Responsibility	Category
Display Message to Re-Cycle at BOF()/EOF()	Could
Ensure Data Table is open	Should
Ensure Records are available	Should
Handle BOF()/EOF() Errors	Must
Move Record Pointer	Must
Refresh Parent Form	Must
Select Correct Work Area	Should
Selectively Enable/Disable Buttons	Must
Select Specific Field on Completion	Could

From this list we can immediately see that we have four 'Must-Do' items. These will be required in all situations and must form the basis of the class definition. The two 'Could-Do' items clearly would apply only in special situations and are therefore candidates for sub-classes since we would not want either of these behaviors in **all** situations.

The three 'Should Do' items are more interesting. Clearly our class will not work if no table is available, or if it is open but contains no records, but then neither (presumably) would anything else on the form which houses the control. As for selecting the 'correct' area, why should the navigation bar care which table it navigates in? None of these are tasks that relate solely to the navigation bar class – all have wider ramifications and should be addressed *outside* of this class.

Put simply, the function of the navigation bar class is to move the record pointer, handle any errors that might arise from that movement and update its parent form when it has finished. No other class could handle any of these tasks, and there are no tasks here that do not relate solely to the class in question.

This now looks like a working definition and we can progress to the next stage.

How do you go about building your classes?

Here is another 'Rule of Three' – this time related to the way in which you design and construct your class libraries and the classes in them.

- Design your class structure as a whole before coding anything
- Look for Patterns when defining classes
- Code in Methods, not Events

Class Library Structure

There are no hard and fast rules about this. In fact Visual FoxPro is remarkably flexible in this respect (a class library is only a table after all) and makes no assumptions whatsoever about class libraries. If you wished, you could keep all your classes and all their sub classes in one single library. However, this would probably get a bit unwieldy after a while so it is recommended that you work within a logical library structure. Another consideration to bear in mind is that when working in a team environment, under source control, keeping all of your classes in one library can make maintenance very difficult indeed!

Essentially you can differentiate classes into three groups (yet another "Rule of Three"):

- Root (Abstract) Classes
- Generic Classes
- Application Specific Classes

The Root classes are your personal sub classes of the VFP Base Classes on which all the remainder of your classes are built. These should never be used to instantiate objects directly and so are "abstract" classes. Generic Classes are those that are not specific to any particular application and would normally consist of your standard controls. The application specific classes are, of course, those created for an application and will be subclasses of either your Root classes or one (or more) of the Generic Classes.

Whether you choose to further sub-divide you libraries is, of course, entirely up to you. We do keep all of our form classes in a separate library. We also create individual libraries for groups of classes which are related to specific functionality. (Our 'Graphics.vcx' is an example of a functional library. All the classes in this library are concerned with displaying various types of information graphically on screen. This allows exclusion of the entire library from an application if not needed).

Look for patterns

Design patterns are a way of communicating design experience and knowledge because problems always need solutions. Naturally similar problems tend to engender similar solutions and the reason that the solutions are similar is that they share a common core, or approach, to resolving the problem. A design pattern is simply a recognition of such a core and a description of that core in such a way that it can be used in many different scenarios. It is, in short, a generic description of how to solve a problem. Note however, that a Design Pattern is *not* a solution to a problem. Patterns are just as relevant in the context of designing classes as they are to application design. When designing your own classes it is important to look for patterns in your requirements so that your classes themselves can reflect the patterns that you will use when they are deployed.

By far the best reference we have found so far for learning about patterns is the excellent 'Design Patterns, Elements of Reusable Object-Oriented Software,' by Gamma, Helm, Johnson and Vlissides published by Addison-Wesley. We *strongly* recommend you get a copy of this book, either in paper form (ISBN 0-201-63361-2) so you can scribble in the margins, or in the newer CD format (ISBN 0-201-63498-8) so you can carry it around, search it and quote from it more easily.

Code in methods, not events

This is not really a rule, but we think it is good practice. When coding your classes try to avoid placing code directly in Visual FoxPro's native methods and events. Instead create custom methods and call those from the native methods. There is, admittedly, no requirement to do things this way, but it will make your life easier for (yet again) three reasons:

- Firstly it will allow you to give meaningful names to your method code. This may sound trivial, but it makes maintenance a lot easier when the code that actually 'calculates the tax' is called by `'ThisForm.CalcTax()'` rather than `'ThisForm.CmdButton1.Click()'`
- Secondly it allows you change the interface, if necessary, by simply re-locating the single line of code which calls the method instead of having to cut and paste functional code (with all the attendant possibilities for error that this entails).
- Finally it allows you to break complex code up into multiple, (and potentially re-usable) methods. The code in the method associated with the event merely acts as the initiator for your code.

But does all this design stuff really work in practice?

Well we certainly think so! The accompanying files for this chapter, in the CH03 directory, include a project which implements the design concepts discussed above. **Figure 3.2** (below) shows the Classes Tab of the project at an early stage in the development of the class libraries. Even though only partially built, the basic structure is already clear.

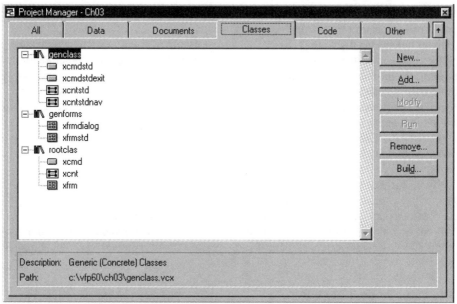

Figure 3.2 *Example class structure*

We will have more to say about the naming convention later. For the moment let's look at the class structure here. What you see is the beginnings of our 'generic' class libraries. As the name implies these libraries contain classes which do not contain any application specific functionality and are effectively the 'standard' controls that we have created.

The RootClas.vcx library

The first (lowest level) library in our structure is named *RootClas.vcx* and this contains the first level subclasses of the VFP Base Class controls. It is an abstract library (the sole function of these classes is to be the parent for other classes) and classes from this library are, therefore, never instantiated directly. By the same token the only classes that are ever added to this library are 'first level' abstract classes. This rule serves two functions:

- It provides an "insulating" layer between our classes and the VFP Base Classes. Should a new release of VFP change base class defaults or behavior, existing code can be corrected simply by changing the appropriate root class.
- It ensures that standard settings (and any custom properties and methods which are added to the root class) are available to all descendant classes. Changes in the root class will, by definition, be reflected in all classes based on them.

The GenForms.vcx library

The next library is a functional library, used to contain our form classes. The reason for splitting them out into a library of their own is simply so that we do not get form classes cluttering up the Controls ToolBar. One of the many developer-friendly enhancements, which VFP 6.0 introduced, was an extension to the `CREATE FORM` command which allows you to specify the class from which the new form is to be created. When developing, there is no longer any need to tinker with the "Form Options" setting, or create a formset, add a form of the required class and delete the base class that is supplied by default and so on. This command now does the job:

```
CREATE FORM mynewForm AS xFrmStd FROM genforms
```

All of the classes in this library ultimately descend from the 'xFrm' root class. By the way, in our naming convention the name of a class always indicates its lineage (this is achieved by naming it with a suffix to the name of the class from which it derives). We like this because it ensures that when a library is listed in alphabetical order (as in the project manager, or the Modify Class dialog) they are also in inheritance order. So, if we were to add a new 'Data' form class to this library based on the 'standard' form class, it would be named "*xFrmStdData*" and would appear in the listing immediately below the 'xFrmStd' class.

This is an important point because there is no reason why all classes in a library should be at the same level of inheritance, but it is useful to be able to distinguish, at a glance, just where a given class sits in its hierarchy.

The GenClass.vcx library

This library contains all of our 'generic' classes and is the library which, by default, is loaded into the Form Controls toolbar by VFP at startup (See below for details on how to make this happen). It is the classes in this library that we use to create our objects. Our convention is that every control in the Root Class library has a 'Std' version in the GenClass library that is the basis for all further sub classes and is the 'standard' version of the control that we use when creating composite controls.

In some cases the standard class is actually a simple copy of the root class, while in others the standard class may introduce additional functionality which we have designed as applicable to all future classes. For example our standard command button class has a new custom method added to it named '*OnClick*'. The native VFP Click Method has been amended so that, by default, it simply calls the OnClick method that is where all of our instance level code will be placed.

Even if we later change our mind and find that we need a class that does not include such additional functionality, we are not totally lost because we can simply use our root class as the parent for a new inheritance hierarchy.

How does the design actually translate into code?

If you look at the Navigation bar class (yes, finally we get back to it) you will see that we have constructed it so that all that the command buttons do is to call up to the parent container's *Navigate* method from their *OnClick* method. This conforms to the principle that an object only needs to know **how** to get something done without actually knowing what code is being implemented which, in this case, has been implemented by using delegation. All buttons can now have the same code in their *OnClick* method (and it is just one line) though they each pass a different parameter as shown:

First Button:	`This.Parent.Navigate( 'FIRST' )`
Prev Button:	`This.Parent.Navigate( 'PREV' )`
Next Button:	`This.Parent.Navigate( 'NEXT' )`
Last Button:	`This.Parent.Navigate( 'LAST' )`

The Container's *Navigate* method is where most of the work is done and is where the actual code that moves the record pointer is located. Although this is a method of the navigation bar class, the code does not depend upon anything other than being passed a parameter indicating the type of navigation required and so will work equally well whether it is called from one of the contained buttons or another, external, object:

```
LPARAMETERS tcMoveTo
LOCAL lcMoveTo, lcNewPos, lnRec
IF VARTYPE( tcMoveTo ) # "C" OR EMPTY( tcMoveTo )
  RETURN .F.
ENDIF
lcMoveTo = UPPER(ALLTRIM(tcMoveTo))
lcNewPos = 'MID'
*** Now we can process the parameter
DO CASE
    CASE lcMoveTo = "NEXT"
        *** Go to the next record
        SKIP
        IF EOF()
            *** We were on the last record anyway
            GO BOTTOM
            *** Set Position Flag accordingly
            lcNewPos = "LAST"
        ELSE
            *** Did we move TO the last record
            lnRec = RECNO()
            SKIP
            IF EOF()
                *** Yes we did, set position flag
                lcNewPos = "LAST"
            ENDIF
            GO lnRec
        ENDIF
    CASE lcMoveTo = "PREV"
        *** Go to the previous record
        SKIP -1
        IF BOF()
            *** We were on the First record anyway
            GO TOP
            *** Set Position Flag accordingly
            lcNewPos = "FIRST"
        ELSE
            *** Did we move TO the First record
            lnRec = RECNO()
```

```
            SKIP -1
            IF BOF()
                *** Yes we did, set position flag
                lcNewPos = "FIRST"
            ENDIF
            GO lnRec
        ENDIF
    CASE lcMoveTo = "LAST"
        *** Going to last record, so do it and set flag
        GO BOTTOM
        lcNewPos = "LAST"
    CASE lcMoveTo = "FIRST"
        *** Going to First Record, so do it and set flag
        GO TOP
        lcNewPos = "FIRST"
    OTHERWISE
        *** We have an invalid parameter! In this example
        *** we will just ignore it and abandon the move
        *** but return a ".F." in case this method is being
        *** called externally!
        RETURN .F.
ENDCASE
```

Notice that the case statement is ordered so that the Next/Prior methods come before the Last/First. In Visual FoxPro the speed of execution of a DO CASE statement depends upon the relative position of the statement which will be executed. It is likely that this code will be called most often for single step navigation than for jumps, so these options are placed first. It is, in this example, a small point but worth getting into the habit of doing.

We have also adopted a strategy of assigning a local variable indicating the placement of the record pointer within the table after navigation (*lcNewPos*). This has been initialized to '*MID*' – the middle of the table being the most likely result in a running application. This value is then passed to another container method that handles the enabling and disabling of the buttons based on the value it receives:

```
*** Call the SetButtons Method for Enabling/Disabling
*** But disable the screen first!
ThisForm.LockScreen = .T.
This.SetButtons( lcNewPos )
*** Call the RefreshParent Method to Update the display
This.RefreshParent()
*** Re-Enable the screen
ThisForm.LockScreen = .F.
*** Any method returns .T. by default, so this is not really needed
*** but is useful when stepping through code since it allows for a
*** breakpoint to be set to check values
RETURN .T.
```

The final responsibility (refreshing the parent form) is handled by another container method, the *RefreshParent* method. By splitting up the functionality like this we can handle different methods of navigation (calling form methods instead, for example) by simply overriding the *Navigate* method when necessary. Similarly we can change the button behavior or refresh behavior, without affecting anything else.

This last point is very important. If you examine the *RefreshParent* method you will notice that it refers explicitly to *ThisForm*:

```
*** This Method refreshes the parent form for the Navigation Bar
*** If we have a RefreshForm Method, call it, otherwise use native Refresh
IF PEMSTATUS( ThisForm, 'RefreshForm', 5 )
  ThisForm.RefreshForm()
ELSE
  ThisForm.Refresh()
ENDIF
```

This is not an unreasonable assumption because to make an object visible in Visual FoxPro it must be contained in either a Form or a Toolbar and the visual appearance of this control as we have it right now makes it unsuitable for a toolbar in its current format.

Creating a sub-class for use in a toolbar

To create a navigation bar that would be suitable for a toolbar we can simply sub-class this control and override the *RefreshParent* method in the subclass to utilize the form of referencing more appropriate to a toolbar (i.e. *_Screen.ActiveForm*, instead of *ThisForm*). Such a subclass is included in the CH03 project, and you will note that apart from changing the appearance of the class, the only code that has had to change is the single method which deals with the refresh which now looks like this:

```
*** This Method overrides the parent class behavior which refreshes the form
*** And uses _Screen.ActiveForm instead
WITH _Screen.ActiveForm
    IF PEMSTATUS( _Screen.ActiveForm, 'RefreshForm', 5 )
      .RefreshForm()
    ELSE
      .Refresh()
    ENDIF
ENDWITH
```

One possible 'gotcha' here occurs when you are using forms with Private DataSessions. Any toolbar that is relying on _Screen.ActiveForm to access data associated with that form must ensure that it first switches itself into the same datasession. This is not as simple as it might appear at first glance because a toolbar cannot receive focus. However you can use the following code in the *MouseMove* method to handle the problem:

```
IF TYPE( "_Screen.ActiveForm" ) = "O" AND ! ISNULL(_Screen.ActiveForm)
  This.DataSessionId = _Screen.ActiveForm.DataSessionId
ENDIF
```

Further extensions to the class

Another useful extension to this class would be to add behavior so that it automatically adjusts the button settings when it is initialized and perhaps whenever the form on which it resides is reactivated. To do this we would add another custom method (perhaps *CheckRecPointer* would be a suitable name). This would determine whether the record pointer is at the first, last or an intermediate record and call the *SetButtons* method with the appropriate parameter. The new method could then be called from the *Init* of the container itself to handle initialization and by an external event such as a form *Activate* or a toolbar *MouseMove* to force a status update.

Conclusion

This example, while trivial in detail, shows how important design is in the object oriented environment. The final design of this control is a long way from the "traditional" approach where the code for moving the record pointer would have been placed directly in the buttons. The secret of good design actually lies in determining what each component in the class is *really* responsible for. Thus in the navigation bar example above, the real responsibility of the buttons is to recognize that the user wishes to navigate in a particular fashion and to communicate that fact to the appropriate handler. These buttons do **not** need to be responsible for doing anything else and therefore should not **DO** anything else!

Working with your classes

Once you have defined your classes you will, of course, want to start using them in your daily work instead of merely hacking the Visual FoxPro base classes on an 'as needed' basis. To do this effectively you need to be able to instruct FoxPro when to use your classes instead of the standard defaults provided with the product.

How do I get my classes into the form controls toolbar?

The Form Controls toolbar shows the contents of one class library at any time, and by default opens the VFP Base Classes as 'Standard'. To change what is displayed, select the library icon from the Form Controls toolbar (**Figure 3.3**).

Figure 3.3 The "Library" Icon from the Form Control toolbar

This will bring up a pop-up menu which shows all the libraries currently available, which you can select and make current, and which also allows you to add an additional library to the toolbar.

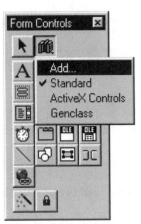

Figure 3.4 *The Add Class Library pop-up*

The entries for 'Standard' and 'ActiveX Controls' are always present. You can add one, or more, libraries to this list as part of Visual FoxPro's startup procedure by specifying the required library files in the Controls tab of the VFP Options dialog. Any libraries defined here are stored in the Registry under the key:

HKEY_CURRENT_USER\Software\Microsoft\VisualFoxPro\6.0\Options\VCXList

While the list of libraries to *load* is stored in the Registry, the library that you were using last is actually stored in the resource file. So if you want to preserve your setting between FoxPro sessions, you must have SET RESOURCE ON.

To change the library that will be displayed, simply open either the form or class designer, select the library that you want to make current, and then save your change when you close the designer. The next time you open the designer the last used library will be on the toolbar for you.

While we're at it, how can I identify my custom classes in the toolbar?

All classes have two properties (which can be accessed through the Class Info dialog by selecting the Class pad from the menu while in the Class Designer) named 'Container Icon' and 'Toolbar Icon'. The first refers to the icon that appears next to the class name in the Project Manager. The second refers to the icon which will be displayed in the Form Controls toolbar. VFP is expecting a 16 x 16 pixel image size for these icons, and despite referred to them to as 'icons', will accept either Icon or BMP format for display.

The Navigation bar in the CH03.vcx class library has been assigned separate bitmaps for the two properties. The reason for needing two is that the background for the toolbar icon is light gray but for the container icon must be white.

So, it is easy enough to do, but creating sufficiently distinctive and memorable pictures has proved rather more difficult, and we confess that we tend to stick with the standard VFP Icons unless there is an overwhelmingly good reason to do otherwise. After all, the class name is automatically displayed in the tooltip for each button in the form controls toolbar and we find that this is usually sufficient for our needs. (Although one of our wish-list items is that the tooltip would display the class description, rather than the name, if one is available.)

> *In Visual FoxPro Version 5.0 and later the display of a class's 'Container Icon' in the project manager is controlled by the setting of a check box on the Project tab of the global Options dialog. The entry in the Help files about Container Icons fails to mention this rather vital piece of information.*

But whenever I want white in my bitmaps it shows up gray!

One of Windows' irritating little quirks is that it interprets white in a bitmap or icon file as transparent and displays, instead, its default background color. To prevent this from happening, you need to create a "**mask**" file for each bitmap that uses white, in which all of the areas that you wish to see as white in the presented bitmap are colored black. This is best done by modifying your original bitmap and saving it with a '.*MSK*' extension into the same directory. **Figure 3.5** shows how the bitmaps and mask files we used for our navigation bar example actually look.

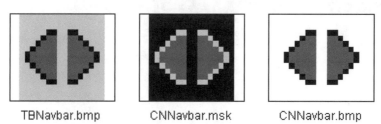

TBNavbar.bmp   CNNavbar.msk   CNNavbar.bmp

Figure 3.5 *Using a MSK file to display white in bitmaps*

Without the mask file, the 'CNNavbar' bitmap would look exactly the same as the "TBNavbar" bitmap, but with the mask file it will be displayed correctly. You can see the result in the CH03 project Class tab.

How do I make Visual FoxPro use my classes instead of base classes?

Visual FoxPro 5.0 introduced the "*intellidrop*" functionality which allows you define which classes are used for controls that are created when a data field is dragged onto a form from either the DataEnvironment or the Project Manager data tab. There are two ways of setting up this information.

The default information that VFP uses is stored in the Registry in the key:

```
HKEY_CURRENT_USER\Software\Microsoft\VisualFoxPro\6.0\Options\IntelliDrop
```

If there is nothing in this key, then the VFP Base Classes are used. To set up your own classes as defaults you can use the 'Field Mapping' tab of the Options Dialog. This allows you to define which class, from which library, to use for controls based on the data type of the field (see **Figure 3.6** below). Any settings you define here will be saved to the registry and used for all tables by default.

If you are using a database container, you have another way of setting up intellidrop that will override any default settings on a field by field basis. In the Table designer for bound tables there is a "Map field type to classes" section where you can define the class and library to be used whenever a specific field is dragged onto a form. This overrides any default setting and is useful when you have a field where the class to be used depends upon the actual *content* rather than the data type (for example, you might have a special ZipCode text box class which should be used any time a ZipCode is required).

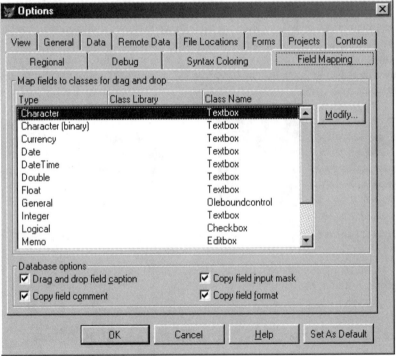

Figure 3.6 *Field Mapping Dialog for setting the default IntelliDrop classes*

How do I change the caption of the label that VFP adds?

When dragging a field onto a form (or in the class designer) from either the data environment, or from the project manager, the default behavior of intellidrop is to add a label whose caption is the name of the field. This is the only option that is available for a free table, but for tables which are part of a database there are some additional settings that can be made.

Again the Field Mapping tab of the Options dialog provides the mechanism for setting default behaviors. Notice the check boxes at the foot of this dialog – there are four of them.

- **Drag and drop field caption:** When checked, Visual FoxPro will add a label (of whatever class you have defined) to each field when it is dragged and set its caption to the "Caption" defined in the table designer for that field. If there is no caption defined, or the table is a 'free' table, the field name will be inserted instead. To prevent the automatic addition of a label, just un-check this box.
- **Copy field comment:** Each control has a 'Comment' property. When this option is checked the contents of the field's "Comment" property are inserted into the 'Comment' property of the target control.
- **Copy field input mask:** Ensures that any input mask that has been defined in the database is copied to the *InputMask* property of the inserted control.
- **Copy field format:** Ensures that any format that has been defined in the database is copied to the *Format* property of the inserted control.

When working with bound tables (those which are part of a database container) the Table Designer provides the ability to set all of the above items at individual field level. These are extremely useful and, in our experience anyway, woefully under-utilized by developers. As part of your database design you should always set the Caption and Comment properties as a minimum.

The only drawback is that the Caption is also used by Visual FoxPro for Grid Header (which is useful) and in Browse windows (which if you, like us, tend to use a command line BROWSE to check field names is not so useful). It may be the latter behavior, for which there is no override, which explains why so many developers seem reluctant to use the field level capabilities provided.

So can I get a browse to show the field name when a caption is set?

Well actually you can because in Visual FoxPro, the Browse window happens to be a grid object! Try this code from the command line:

```
USE clients
BROWSE NAME oBrowse NOWAIT
*** Minimise the browse window (so you can see the screen)
DISPLAY MEMORY LIKE oB*
```

The result will be:

```
OBROWSE              Pub          O    GRID
```

So if you need to be able to browse a table, and see the field names, all you need is a little 'decorator' program to enhance the standard BROWSE command. The following program does just that and could be a candidate for your 'Development Environment' Procedure file (we hope it would have no value at run time!):

```
**********************************************************************
* Program....: BrowExt.prg
* Compiler...: Visual FoxPro 06.00.8492.00 for Windows
* Abstract...: Decorator for standard Browse Command that restores the
* ..........: field name in place of the Caption in the Browse Window
**********************************************************************
*** This Version only works in VFP5 or later
LOCAL lnCnt
BROWSE NAME oBrowse NOWAIT
FOR EACH loCol IN oBrowse.Columns
  loCol.Header1.Caption = PROPER( SUBSTR(loCol.ControlSource, ;
                                  RAT('.',loCol.ControlSource)+1 ))
NEXT
```

User interface design

Thus far we have been concentrating on some of the key issues in designing and working with classes. However the design of your user interface is, ultimately, even more important if only because to your end users the UI actually *is* the application. In fact, users resemble objects in that they rarely, if ever, need to know **how** something is done, only where to go to get it done! The principles governing your UI design are, therefore, not dissimilar to those we have already expounded for designing classes.

In this section we are not going to dwell on such basic issues as using fonts, colors and the placement of labels, text boxes and other controls. We assume that you either already have, or will adopt, a set of standards for deciding such matters. Instead we want to try and cover some of the less obvious issues which, all too often, are implemented badly, if not incorrectly.

Perception governs acceptance

The first, and probably the most important issue, is that more often than not end users will judge your application by its perceived performance. If an application is intuitive and easy to use, and looks and feels quick and responsive, then it is likely to be well accepted even if it does not do things in exactly the way that people originally expected. Conversely, if your application is seen as being 'difficult' to use, sluggish or unresponsive, then users are less likely to accept it - even if it does exactly what was wanted in precisely the way that was requested. So how can you ensure that your application does not impart the wrong perception?

Make something happen immediately!

The first, golden rule is to ensure that *something* happens as soon as your user interacts with your application. The Microsoft Windows 95/98 interface has an excellent example of this principle. Clicking on the "Start" button will, in almost every situation, immediately display the entire first level "start menu". Of course it can then take several seconds, depending on what the system is doing, for a selection from that menu to be executed - but that is not the point. The key is that there is an instant response.

Alas, all too often we have seen applications in which a user clicks on a button and after a few seconds a message window pops up saying 'Working…Please Wait'. Of course, by this time the user has usually clicked the button several more times and has now locked up the entire application for several hours by causing the same lengthy process to run half a dozen times in succession. (Do users *really* think the system sometimes doesn't 'hear' the click?) The usual solution then appears to be to "*Ctrl+Alt+Delete!*"

Of course there are situations, especially in networked or client/server applications, when there will be a delay while data is retrieved, but this is no reason for not providing the user with some immediate feedback. One neat solution to this particular problem is to make the command button disable itself immediately after a click. This achieves two things – it provides a visual cue that something has happened, and more importantly it stops the user from inadvertently firing off the process multiple times by re-clicking on the button. The 'xCmdStdDisable' class in the CH03.VCX library is based on our standard command button class but overrides the click method to add this functionality:

```
WITH This
    .Enabled = .F.
    DODEFAULT()
    .Enabled = .T.
ENDWITH
```

Of course, if you use graphics on your command buttons you can even specify different pictures for each of the three states of the button simply by setting properties.

Table 3.2 Command Button Picture Properties

Property	Function
Picture	Displayed when the button is active but not selected
DownPicture	Displayed when the button is clicked, and held down
DisabledPicture	Displayed when the button is disabled

Keep the user informed of progress

The second important rule is keep users informed of what the system is doing – especially if the application is running a process which takes a significant amount of time.. How much time is significant? The only real answer is that 'it depends'. We would normally recommend that anything over five seconds requires some sort of information, even if only a wait window, and anything that runs over one minute should have some sort of progress display.

This begs the question of what sort of progress display should you use? The standard Windows approach is to use a "thermometer bar". We have included a sample class (*ThermBar.VCX*) and demonstration program (*ShoTherm.PRG*) in the sample code for this chapter. However, it is not the only mechanism for displaying progress, and in some circumstances, is not even the best. For example, when you have a very long or multi-stage process that does not necessarily progress linearly with time, a thermometer bar is not very helpful.

In such situations we like to use a list box because it has the major benefit that a user can scroll up and see what has been done, and thus gain an idea of how the process is progressing. Again we have included an example class (*ListProg.VCX*) and demonstration program (*ShoList.PRG*) in the code for this chapter.

Don't overdo progress reporting!

There is one caveat in respect to progress reporting. You must ensure that the process of reporting progress does not, of itself, significantly impact the process being reported. Too much is as bad as too little in this respect and while 'cute' methods for showing progress can be fun to program, they can rapidly become irritating for the end user. Again Microsoft has provided a classic example – when copying files in Windows Explorer, the little fluttering pages are amusing the first time you see them but it doesn't take long to realize that if you use a DOS Copy command, you can copy files much faster than Explorer. Why so? The answer is that continuously updating the progress display significantly slows the copying process.

Keep your users focussed

One of the most common flaws that we see in user interfaces are screens that are stuffed full of controls with hardly a square pixel free. This usually means that the screens are slow to load and almost impossible to work with unless you happen to have eyes like a hawk to spot the cursor amongst the mass of controls. Normally the reason given is that users need to see all the information at once and this can present some serious problems for the developer. There are, however, some steps you can take to help your users.

Make your controls select-on-entry

Editable controls in Visual FoxPro have a SelectOnEntry property that you might think would ensure that whenever a control is selected, (i.e. receives focus) the entire contents of the control will be highlighted as 'selected'. This is obviously a useful thing to do, especially on cluttered screens, since it makes it clear to the user where the focus currently resides. The Help file for SelectOnEntry states that it:

> *Specifies whether text in a column cell, edit box, or text box is selected when the user moves to it. Available at design time and run time.*

It also notes that only controls contained in grid columns will exhibit this behavior by default. Notice however that the text uses the phrase 'when the user moves to it'. In other words, it only works when a control receives focus by virtue of its position – it does *NOT* work when the user just clicks into a control with the mouse (neither does the alternate solution of setting the Format property = 'K'). So you need to write some code if you want a true 'Select On Entry' capability.

The best solution we have found is to use the *GotFocus* method and, (in your class) add the following code:

```
TextBox::GotFocus()
This.SelStart = 0
This.SelLength = 999
NODEFAULT
```

This purpose of this code may not be obvious until you remember that *GotFocus* is one of the native events that does have some behavior defined. Part of this native behavior is, apparently, to set both SelStart and SelLength to 0!

So to make our code work in all circumstances, we must first force VFP to execute the base class behavior 'out of sequence'. (Normally the base class code runs after any custom code and we DO need it because without it, the control will not get focus at all!) Once that has been done, we can set the properties to position the cursor (SelStart) and to add the highlight (SelLength) to highlight the entire contents of the control. Finally we must stop the base class code from executing in its normal place, so we add a **NODEFAULT** command. The *xTxtStdSel* text box class (see *GenClass.VCX* library in the code for this chapter) has this behavior and will properly select all text, however the user gives focus to a control.

Use tooltips to help your users work with the form

One of the nicest features of Visual FoxPro is that all controls have a ToolTipText property that behaves like all other tooltips in Windows. When you hover the mouse over a control, the tip is displayed after a couple of seconds. This is non-intrusive and only appears when the user actually 'asks' for it. More importantly, it appears at the location of the mouse pointer as opposed to the text specified by the StatusBarText property that only appears on the status bar. (This then requires that your application use a status bar and so is useless unless your application runs inside the main VFP screen.)

Remember – although the ability to **have** a tooltip is a property of an object, the ability to **display** it is a property of the Form (or Toolbar) on which it resides. To enable tooltips you should, set the ShowTips property to **TRUE** in your root class for both Form and Toolbar classes.

But tooltips are *NOT* a substitute for context sensitive help! The maximum length allowed is 127 characters (and even that is really too long!). We do recommend using tooltips for:

- Warning the user that an entry in a field is required
- Specifying that the control is limited to a particular type of entry
- Reminding users when additional options exist (e.g. Right-Click menus)

Use the right control for the job

This may sound obvious, but is amazing how many times we have heard people say something like "I'm trying to load a combo box with 13,000 rows and it's slow." Well, there's a surprise! By the way, just *how* is a user supposed to work with a combo box that, in all versions of VFP prior to Version 6.0, is limited to a 7 row display but contains 13,000 rows of data? Even with incremental search, that's a pretty daunting combo. Worse yet, a combo box is not an easy control to manipulate at the best of times - one slip of the mouse and you have to start all over again.

Use a grid for long lists

We will have a lot more to say about the mechanics of handing list controls in the chapter devoted specifically to them, for now we want to concentrate on the 'when' rather than the 'how' we should use them. So here is our ideal guideline, though we recognize that, in practice, you may *have* to break it:

For lists containing a few TENS of rows, a combo (or list box) is fine, but for anything more than that you should really consider using a read-only grid.

Why use a read-only grid? The reason is that a grid will load data sequentially, as needed, rather than having to retrieve all data on initialization, which a list or combo box must do. The trick here is to set up a grid class that looks like an ordinary list box. This is simple enough, just set a few properties for the grid (see *xGrdStdList* class in the *GenClass.VCX* library):

```
ColumnCount = 1
AllowHeaderSizing = .F.
AllowRowSizing = .F.
DeleteMark = .F.
GridLines = 0
HeaderHeight = 0
ReadOnly = .T.
RecordMark = .F.
ScrollBars = 2
SplitBar = .F.
```

Then set the Movable property to .F. for the column.

A couple of refinements have been added. First we have added a nRows property to the class to define how many rows should be visible. This is used, in the *Init* method of the class, to set the grid height exactly and to avoid the unsightly 'partial rows' that all too often mar the appearance of grids. Secondly, we also size the visible column to fill the entire width of the display area (less the width of vertical scroll bar of course):

```
*** Set Height to the exact number of rows specified in nRows property
This.Height = This.RowHeight * This.nRows
*** Force Column to fill the available width
This.Columns[1].Width = This.Width - SYSMETRIC(7)
```

Finally the grid's text box includes the select-on-entry code, which we explained earlier, to ensure that when a user clicks into the grid the 'row' is properly highlighted. However, because the text box is in a grid, instead of placing the code in the text box *GotFocus* method, it must go in the *Click* method!

Depending on your use for a long list class you will need to add any necessary code, and maybe some custom properties and methods, but the basic behavior is already provided. Since scrolling in a grid will move the record pointer in its recordsource, getting the selected item is not an issue – just grab the record number (or contents of whichever field you want).

Most importantly, because the grid can use all fields in the table you are searching, you do not even have to specify which fields you need. You can even use a cursor (or view) to create a subset of data from multiple tables.

The only problem is that you may need to use a combo box, rather than a list box, to conserve space on a form. To address this issue we have created a "combo-grid" class which mimics the behavior of a combo but uses a grid instead of the standard drop down list – see the chapter on Combos and Lists for details.

An example using a modal form to return a selected client ID is included in the sample code for this chapter. Note that to set the initial highlight, we simply locate the desired record in the form's *Init* method and set focus to the grid. To run this form, simply do the following from the command window (109 is simply a key value for the table):

```
DO FORM frmGList WITH 109 TO lcSelection
? lcSelection
```

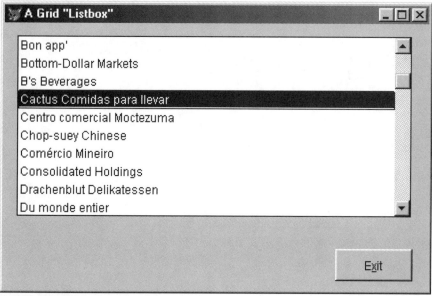

Figure 3.7 *The grdList class in use*

Chapter 4
Basic Controls

"There is a great satisfaction in building good tools for other people to use."
("Disturbing the Universe" by Freeman Dyson)

The majority of time required to design and develop an application is spent creating the interface. A well-designed library of reusable control classes will greatly reduce the amount of work required to create this interface. Inheritance allows common functionality to be built into your classes once at the higher levels of the class hierarchy leaving you free to concentrate on the complex logical processes of your specific application. In this chapter, we will share some cool features we have built into our set of base classes. You will find all of the classes described in the CH04.VCX library.

What do we mean by 'basic'?

You may wonder what we mean by "basic" controls. For the purpose of this chapter we are referring to controls that form the majority of any user interface. This typically includes text boxes, edit boxes, spinners, command buttons and the like. All of the custom controls presented in this chapter will work when dropped on a form, page, or when placed inside a container. However, they are not guaranteed to work when placed in a grid as grids impose different requirements on the construction of their controls. Custom controls for use inside grids, therefore, will be covered in chapter 6 "Grids: The Misunderstood Controls". Grids, especially data entry grids, are sufficiently complex that we have devoted an entire section exclusively to them.

Text boxes *(Example: CH04.VCX::txtBase)*

Most of the controls in your interface will probably be based on either text boxes or edit boxes. They are unambiguous, understood by even novice users. They can be used as they come out of the box but do not possess anything more than the most basic functionality. For example, to make a text box select its entire contents when it receives focus, you might just set the *SelectOnEntry* property to .T. (or set the Format property to "*K*"). In fact either of these will only work when the control receives focus by movement from another control and will not do anything when the user mouse-clicks into the text box. Fortunately, it is easy enough to give all text boxes this basic functionality by putting this code in the *GotFocus* method of your standard text box class:

```
TextBox::GetFocus()
.SelStart  = 0
.SelLength = 999
NODEFAULT
```

Since this is a root class, you may wonder why we use the line `Textbox::GotFocus()` instead of just issuing a *DODEFAULT()*. The reason is that in Visual FoxPro 5.0a, there was a bug in *DODEFAULT()* that caused the Visual FoxPro base class behavior to be executed after executing the code in the parent class. This meant that, unless you had a *NODEFAULT* at the end of the method in the sub class, the base class code would be executed twice. (This is because, by default, Visual FoxPro runs any custom code that you have put into a method and then runs the base class code afterward.) In Visual FoxPro 6.0, *DODEFAULT()* no longer runs the base class code unless, of course, the subclass is directly descended from Visual FoxPro's base class. So in Visual FoxPro 6.0, base class behavior is guaranteed to execute when calling it directly with the scope resolution operator.

As usual, there is more than one way to skin a fox. This single line of code in the text box's *GotFocus()* method accomplishes the same thing as the four lines listed above:

```
This.SetFocus()
```

We like our text boxes to be selected on entry by default. You, however, may prefer different behavior. In order to provide flexibility, we conditionally execute the code above only if the text box's *SelectOnEntry* property is set to true.

We have also added a custom *SetInputMask* method to our text box root class, as follows:

```
LOCAL lcAlias, lcField, lcType, laFields[1], ;
      lnElement, lnRow, lcIntegerPart, lcDecimalPart
WITH This
   IF ! EMPTY( .ControlSource )
     IF EMPTY( .InputMask )
       *** Only set the inputmask for numeric and character fields
       *** and check the data type of the underlying field so we
       *** can set it appropriately
       lcType = TYPE( This.ControlSource )
       IF INLIST( lcType, 'C', 'N' )
         *** Parse the alias and the field name from the ControlSource
         lcAlias    = JUSTSTEM( .ControlSource )
         lcField    = JUSTEXT ( .ControlSource )
         *** Don't attempt to check the properties of the underlying
         *** field if we are bound to a form property
         IF UPPER( lcAlias ) # 'THISFORM'
           *** format the field if it is character
           IF lcType = 'C'
             InputMask = REPLICATE( 'X', FSIZE( lcField, lcAlias ) )
           ELSE
             AFIELDS(laFields, lcAlias)
             lnElement = ASCAN(laFields, UPPER(lcField))
             IF lnElement > 0
               lnRow = ASUBSCRIPT(laFields, lnElement, 1)
               lcIntegerPart = REPLICATE('9', laFields[lnRow, 3] - ;
                            laFields[lnRow, 4] - 1)
               lcDecimalPart = REPLICATE('9', laFields[lnRow, 4])
               .InputMask = lcIntegerPart + '.' + lcDecimalPart
             ENDIF
           ENDIF
         ENDIF
       ENDIF
     ENDIF
   ENDIF
ENDIF
```

```
ENDWITH
```

This code simply sets up a default input mask for bound controls that have no input mask specified if the control is bound to character and numeric data. In the case of character data, users are prevented from typing in more characters than could be saved into the underlying field without restricting, what those characters may be. For numeric fields, it prevents numeric overflow errors.

Text box gotchas

You probably know that you cannot issue a call to a control's *SetFocus* method from the *Valid* method of any control in Visual FoxPro version 5.0 and higher. This makes perfect sense when you consider that the sole purpose of the *Valid* method is to determine whether or not the control should be allowed to lose focus. To retain focus in a control when your validation fails, you can simply issue a RETURN 0, which tells VFP that focus must remain in the current control. The best way to explicitly pass focus to another control is to use code like this in the *LostFocus* method:

```
This.Parent.SomeControl.SetFocus()
NODEFAULT
```

This works well, but you should also be aware that when you put this code in the *LostFocus* method of a text box, its *Valid* method will be fired again whenever it executes. This is not a problem unless you have code in the *Valid* method that relies on a single execution before the text box loses focus (for example, incrementing a counter or displaying a message box).

Text box label class *(Example: CH04.VCX::txtLabel)*

When you need to have a label that can be bound to some data, we find it handy to have a text box class that looks and acts like a label. Because a label does not have a refresh and a text box does, it's easy to change the display when the form is refreshed. We also like our labels to be right justified so we set up our *txtLabel* class to do this by default. (You can just as easily set yours up to be left or center justified.) The only minor limitation to our *txtLabel* class is that while it is easy enough to provide for hotkeys (by adding code to the *Keypress* method), there is simply no way to indicate what the hot key actually is. Setting up a text box to look and act like a label is a simple matter and involves changing the default values of the following properties:

```
Alignment      = 1 - Right
BackStyle      = 0 - Transparent
BorderStyle    = 0 - None
IntegralHeight = .T.
SpecialEffect  = 1 - Plain
StrictDateEntry = 0 - Loose
TabStop        = .F.
```

To perfectly mimic the behavior of a label, we also need to ensure that our altered text box class cannot receive focus. This is achieved by adding a single line of code to its *When* method so that it always returns a logical *FALSE* value:

```
RETURN .F.
```

Date text box *(Example: CH04.VCX::txtDate)*

The date entry text box is a very simple yet effective control. It makes use of the *Format* property to display the date in whatever format is specified by the user's Windows Long Date setting (*Format = "YL"*). Some simple code called from *GotFocus* and *LostFocus* forces the Century and Rollover settings to values that are set as class properties and ensures that users who insist on entering dates with a last-two-digit century do not cause invalid data to be committed to your tables. (We also like this form of display for dates.)

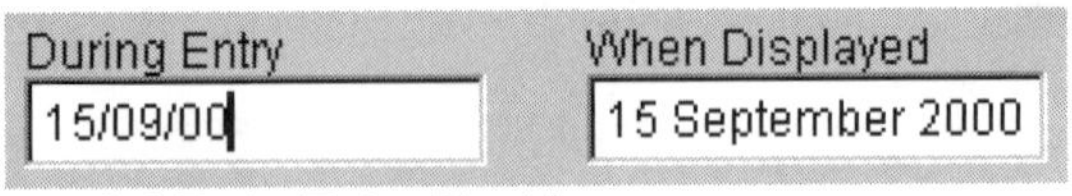

During Entry	When Displayed
15/09/00	15 September 2000

Figure 4.1 *Date Entry Text box*

Table 4.1 *Custom properties of the date text box*

Custom Property	Purpose
nRollYear	Set at design time and used by the custom *SetCent* method to set the rollover year
nCentury	Set at design time and used by the custom *SetCent* method to set the century
cCentWas	Used internally by the custom *SetCent* method to save the current values of SET ('CENTURY'), SET('CENTURY', 1) and SET('CENTURY' , 2)

SetCent is called from the text box's *GotFocus* method to save the current century settings and reset them using the control's *nRollYear* and *nCentury* properties The original century settings are restored in the *RestCent* method that is called from the *LostFocus* method. This code from the control's *SetCent* method shows you how we save the original settings before using the custom properties to reset them:

```
LOCAL lcCentWas, lcCentury, lcRollOn, lnRollYear, lnCentury
WITH This
   *** Save Current settings
   STORE '' TO lcCentWas, lcCent, lcRollOn
   *** Century On/OFF
   lcCentWas = PADL( SET('Century'), 3)
   *** Base Century
   lcCentury = PADL( SET('Century',1), 2, '0' )
   *** Rollover Year
   lcRollOn  = PADL( SET('Century',2), 2, '0' )
   *** Save off as character string
   .cCentWas = lcCentWas + lcCentury + lcRollOn
   *** If we have a specific RollOver Year use it, else default to current
   lnRollYear = IIF( !EMPTY( .nRollYear), .nRollYear, INT( VAL( lcRollOn )) )
   *** If we have a specific Century use it, else default to current
```

```
lnCentury = IIF( !EMPTY( .nCentury ), .nCentury, INT( VAL( lcCentury )) )
*** Set Century and Rollover
SET CENTURY TO (lnCentury) ROLLOVER (lnRollYear)
*** Force Century On
SET CENTURY ON
ENDWITH
```

This simply saves whatever settings are currently in force for the Century and sets up new settings based on the control's properties. This is useful because SET CENTURY is one of the many settings that is scoped to a DataSession and can be overlooked. Furthermore, because each control handles its own version of the century, you can set up several controls with different base centuries and different rollover years to handle such things as birth dates and insurance policy maturation dates on the same form. The *RestCent* method restores the original settings on the way out of the control:

```
LOCAL lcCentWas, lnCentury, lnRollOn
STORE '' TO lcCentWas
WITH This
   *** Read back the saved settings
   IF ! EMPTY( .cCentWas )
      lcCentWas = ALLTRIM( SUBSTR(  .cCentWas, 1, 3) )
      lnCentury = INT( VAL( SUBSTR( .cCentWas, 4, 2) ))
      lnRollOn  = INT( VAL( SUBSTR( .cCentWas, 6, 2) ))
      *** Set Century to default
      SET CENTURY &lcCentWas
      *** Restore Original Settings
      SET CENTURY TO (lnCentury) ROLLOVER (lnRollOn)
   ENDIF
ENDWITH
```

Incremental search text box *(Example: CH04.VCX::txtSearch)*

An incremental search text box is an extremely useful tool. Not only can it be used as is to find specific items of data in a form, it can also be made into a subclass for use in incremental search grids and other composite controls that require this functionality. For example, you can use this class to build a control that acts like the Help File index (you type into a text box and a list box displays the closest match).

Most of the incremental search text boxes we have seen use the *KeyPress* method to call custom methods that handle the keystrokes, manipulate the text box's *SelStart* and *SelLength* properties and do the searching. In our version of the class we call these methods from the *InteractiveChange* method instead. Since *InteractiveChange* fires **after** *KeyPress* it is easier (and requires less code) to let *KeyPress* handle the actual input as it always does and then do what we want to do afterward. As a matter of fact, our incremental search text box has no custom code at all in its *KeyPress* method. The only code is in *InteractiveChange*, which merely calls the custom *HandleKey* method when necessary as follows:

```
*** If the key pressed was a printable character, a backspace, or delete
*** handle the keystroke and search
IF This.SelStart > 0
  IF ( LASTKEY() > 31 AND LASTKEY() < 128 ) OR ( LASTKEY() = 7 )
    This.HandleKey()
  ENDIF
ENDIF
```

So what functionality does an incremental search text box require? Obviously, it should search the specified table for a match on the specified field as the user is typing it in. Also, it should optimize the search by using an index tag, if available. To meet these requirements we add some custom properties to our incremental search text box class:

```
cAlias = The table to search
cField = The field to search
cTag   = The index tag (if any) to use when searching
```

The text box should also *auto-complete* the text box entry (just like Quicken's *quick fill* does). But should it also refresh the controls in its parent container after repositioning the record pointer in the specified table? Maybe, but then again not always. Since this last feature is required only in specific circumstances, we need to add a logical property to determine when this behavior should occur. The property *lRefreshParent* is added to the class and set to true by default to provide this flexibility. Only when *lRefreshParent* is true, will our *HandleKey* method call the text box's *RefreshParent* method:

```
LOCAL loControl
FOR EACH loControl IN This.Parent.Controls
  IF loControl.name # This.name
    *** Make sure the control has a refresh method!!!
    *** Remember, labels don't have a refresh method!
    IF PEMSTATUS( loControl, 'Refresh', 5 )
      loControl.Refresh()
    ENDIF
  ENDIF
ENDFOR
```

Finally, an incremental search text box must, by definition, be an *unbound* control. (If it were bound, the value specified by its *Controlsource* would be changed with each keystroke.) So, we need a way to refresh the initial value when the user navigates to a new record. Therefore, a single *Synchronize* method has been added and is called from the *Refresh* method. This does all the necessary work:

```
LOCAL lnSelStart
WITH This
   *** Save the insertion point
   lnSelStart = .SelStart
   *** Update the value of the text box with the underlying field
   .Value = EVAL( .cAlias + '.' + .cField )
   *** Reset the insertion point and select the remainder of the text
   .SelStart = lnSelStart
   .SelLength = LEN( ALLTRIM( .Value ) ) - lnSelStart
ENDWITH
```

The rest of the code in our incremental search text box class resides in the *HandleKey* method. Despite the fact that it actually does most of the work, the amount of code is surprisingly small. We **strongly** recommend that methods be highly focussed in terms of their functionality. It allows you to keep the code short, making the tasks of debugging and maintaining the class much simpler. So now, without further ado, here is the code you've been dying to see:

```
LOCAL lcSofar, lnSelect, lnSelStart, lnSelLength
WITH This
   *** Save the insertion point
   lnSelStart = IIF( LASTKEY() # 127, .SelStart, .SelStart - 1 )
```

Here we make sure we do not display erroneous values in the text box if, for example, the user backspaces past the first character in the text box, leaving it empty. You may prefer to have the text box display the value for the first record in the table being searched. If so, this is where to change our standard behavior:

```
   *** Handle an empty value in the text box
   IF lnSelStart = 0
      .Value = ''
      .SelStart = 0
      GO BOTTOM IN ( .cAlias )
      SKIP IN ( .cAlias )
   ELSE
```

Now for the important stuff! We need to ensure the cursor is positioned at the end of the character string typed thus far by the user. So we must obtain that string and search the table specified by the text box's *cAlias* property for a match. The search uses the index tag indicated in the *cTag* property if one was specified. Otherwise, it must use **LOCATE** to attempt to find a matching record. Since the **LOCATE** command is scoped to the current work area (and cannot reference any other), we must make sure we save the current work area before selecting *cAlias* so we can restore the *status quo* afterward:

```
   *** Get the value typed in so far
   lcSofar = LEFT( .Value, lnSelStart )
   .Value = lcSoFar
   *** Use seek to find the record if a tag was provided
   IF ! EMPTY( .cTag )
     IF SEEK( UPPER( lcSoFar ), .cAlias, .cTag )
```

```
         .Value = EVAL( .cAlias + '.' + .cField )
      ENDIF
   ELSE
      *** Otherwise, save the current work area
      *** before switching to the specified table
      lnSelect = SELECT()
      SELECT ( .cAlias )
      *** And locate the specified record
      LOCATE FOR UPPER( ALLTRIM( EVAL (.cField ) ) ) = UPPER( lcSoFar )
      IF FOUND()
         .Value = EVAL( .cAlias + '.' + .cField )
      ENDIF
      *** Restore the original work area
      SELECT ( lnSelect )
   ENDIF
ENDIF
```

At this point we have either found the desired record in *cAlias* or we are at the end of the file. All that remains to be done is to reset the highlighted portion of the text box correctly and refresh the controls in the parent container (if this was specified by setting .lRefreshParent = .T.):

```
*** If we need to refresh the parent container do it here
IF .lRefreshParent
   .RefreshParent()
ENDIF
*** Highlight the portion of the value after the insertion point
.SelStart = lnSelStart
lnSelLength = LEN( .Value ) - lnSelStart
IF lnSelLength > 0
   .SelLength =  lnSelLength
ENDIF
*** If we have refreshed the controls in the parent container,
*** there are timing issues to overcome
*** Even though .SelStart and .SelLength have the correct values,
*** the search box does not appear highlighted correctly without this delay
=INKEY( .1, 'H' )
ENDWITH
```

Notice the **INKEY()** command here, and take some time to read the comment above if you haven't already. This problem is not specific to our incremental search text box and timing issues like this are not uncommon in Visual FoxPro. (We have also run into it when displaying multi-select list boxes in which the previous selections are highlighted. In that case, using **INKEY()** in the form's refresh allows the list box to be highlighted correctly.) It is interesting to note that the **INKEY()** command is not required in the code above when *lRefreshParent* = .F. This lends support to the assumption that this is nothing more than a timing issue. The short pause allows Visual FoxPro to catch up.

Numeric text box *(Example: CH04.VCX::txtNum and txtNumeric)*
Visual FoxPro has inherited some serious shortcomings with respect to entering numeric data from its FoxPro ancestors. It's not too bad when the entire field is selected, and the number is not formatted with separators. However, problems begin to occur when the insertion point is

not at the beginning of the displayed value. Sometimes the user is trying to type the number 10, but all he can type is 1 and, with confirm set off, the value of the text box becomes 1 and the cursor moves on to the next field. We have also seen the opposite problem. The user wants to enter 3 but after typing 3 and exiting the control, the number 30 is displayed instead of the intended 3. So what can a Visual FoxPro developer do to help?

There are a few workarounds to this problem. You could create a numeric text box to select the entire field and remove any separators used to format the number. This code in the text box's *GotFocus* method allows the number to be entered correctly:

```
WITH This
   *** Save the input mask
   .cOldInputMask = .InputMask
   *** Remove separators from input mask
   .InputMask = STRTRAN( .cOldInputMask, ',', '' )
   *** Perform Visual FoxPro native GotFocus()
   TextBox::GotFocus()
   *** Select the entire field
   .SelStart = 0
   .SelLength = LEN( .cOldInputMask )
   *** Don't let base class behavior reset SelStart/SelLength
   NODEFAULT
ENDWITH
```

Since we need to change the text box's *inputMask* to accomplish this, we add a custom property called *cOldInputMask* to hold the original *inputMask* assigned to the control. We will need this property in the text box's *LostFocus* method in order to restore the formatting like so:

```
This.InputMask = This.cOldInputMask
```

Of course, we already have a text box class that correctly selects the entire field where you tab into it or mouse-click on it. Our base class text box does this when *SelectOnEntry* = .T. So all we have to do is base our numeric text box on our base class text box, set *SelectOnEntry* to true, and put this code in its *GotFocus* method:

```
WITH This
*** Save the original input mask
   .cOldInputMask = .InputMask
   *** Remove separators from input mask
   .InputMask = STRTRAN( .cOldInputMask, ',', '' )
   *** Perform the parent class behavior
   DODEFAULT()
ENDWITH
```

The numeric text box described above may be sufficient for you. It's easy to create, doesn't contain a lot of code and works around the problems involved in entering numeric data correctly. But wouldn't it be nicer to have a numeric text box that does *calculator style* entry from right to left? We have seen several examples of such text boxes and, in our opinion, they all suffer from the same shortcoming. Either the cursor can be seen flashing to the left as characters appear from the right or there is no cursor at all. Both of these solutions tend to make things confusing for the user. So we set out to create the ultimate Visual FoxPro numeric text box. And we very quickly discovered why none currently exists. It was **HARD**! So we hope you find this useful as it is the result of entirely too many hours and too much blood, sweat, and tears. Not only does it do calculator style entry, the cursor is also positioned on the correct character. When the value in the text box is not selected, you can even delete or insert individual digits in the middle of the number displayed in the text box.

The numeric text box is a simple control to use. Just drop it on a form, page or container and set its *ControlSource* property. That's all! You don't even need to set its *InputMask* unless you want the control to be unbound because it is capable of formatting itself when bound. The way most numeric text boxes work is by changing the value into a character string, manipulating the string and the *InputMask* and then re-converting the string to a numeric value. However, our numeric text box is actually an unbound control (even though you can set it up as if it were bound) and works because its value actually **is** a character string and is manipulated as such. It uses custom code to update its *ControlSource* with the numeric equivalent of the character string which is its value.

This example is designed to work either unbound or bound to a field in a table, cursor or view. If you need to bind to a form property, the code will need a little modification to account for it. An example of how to do this can be found in the *UpdateControlSource* method of the *spnTime* class described later in this chapter.

The following, eight custom properties were added to our custom numeric text box. They are all used internally by the control and you do not need to do anything with them explicitly.

Table 4.2 *Custom properties of the numeric text box*

Property	Description
CcontrolSource	Saves the controlSource if this is a bound control before it is unbound in the Init method
Cfield	Field name portion of ControlSource if it is bound
CinputMask	Stores original inputMask when it is specified, otherwise stores the inputMask constructed by the control
ColdConfirm	Original setting of SET('CONFIRM') saved in GotFocus so it can be restored in LostFocus.
ColdBell	Original setting of SET('BELL') saved in GotFocus so it can be restored in LostFocus
Cpoint	Character returned by SET('POINT')
Cseparator	Character returned by SET('SEPARATOR')
Ctable	Table name portion of ControlSource if it is bound
LchangingFocus	Flag set to suppress KEYBOARD '{END}' which is used to position the cursor at the rightmost position in the text box. If we do this when the control is losing focus, it messes up the tab order
NmaxVal	Maximum value allowed in the control

The *SetUp* method, called by the TextBox's *Init* method, saves the content of the *ControlSource* property to the custom *cControlSource* property before unbinding the control from its *ControlSource*. It also determines, and sets up, the *InputMask* for the control. Even though this code is executed only once when the text box is instantiated, we have put it in a custom method to avoid coding explicitly in events whenever possible. Notice that we use

SET ('POINT') and **SET ('SEPARATOR')** to specify the characters used as the decimal point and separator instead of hard-coding a specific character. This allows the control to be used just as easily in Europe as it is in the United States without the necessity of modifying code:

```
LOCAL laFields[1], lnElement, lnRow, lcIntegerPart, lcDecimalPart, lcMsg
WITH This
  *** Save the decimal point and separator characters so we can use this
  *** class in either the USA or Europe
  .cPoint    = SET( 'POINT' )
  .cSeparator = SET( 'SEPARATOR' )
  *** Save the controlSource
  IF EMPTY( .cControlSource )
    .cControlSource = .ControlSource
  ENDIF
```

Next we parse the table name and field name out of the *controlSource*. It may seem redundant to store these two properties since they can easily be obtained by executing this section of code. However, because there are various sections of code that refer to one or the other, it's much faster to save them as localized properties when the text box is instantiated. You may wonder then why we have bothered to have a *cControlSource* property when we could just as easily have referred to This.cTable + '.' + This.cField. We believe this is more self-documenting and makes the code more readable. This is just as important as performance considerations. Be nice to the developer who inherits your work. You never know when you may wind up working for her! This code from the text box's *Setup* method makes its purpose very clear:

```
IF ! EMPTY( .cControlSource )
  *** If This is a bound control, save table and field bound to
  *** Parse out the name of the table if ControlSource is prefixed by an alias
  IF AT( '.', .cControlSource ) > 0
    .cTable = LEFT( .cControlSource, AT( '.', .cControlSource ) - 1 )
    .cField = SUBSTR( .cControlSource, AT( '.', .cControlSource ) + 1 )
  ELSE
    .cField = .cControlSource
    *** No alias in ControlSource
    *** assume the table is the one in the currently selected work area
    .ctable = ALIAS()
  ENDIF
```

The setup routine also saves any specified *InputMask* to the *cInputMask* property. If this is a bound control, you do not need to specify an *InputMask*, although you can do so if you wish. This section of the code will do it for you by getting the structure of the underlying field. It also sets the control's *nMaxVal* property, required during data entry to ensure the user cannot enter a number that is too large, causing a numeric overflow error:

```
*** Find out how the field should be formatted if no InputMask specified
IF EMPTY(.InputMask)
  AFIELDS(laFields, .cTable)
  lnElement = ASCAN(laFields, UPPER(.cField))
```

```
  IF lnElement > 0
    *** If the field is of integer or currency type
    *** and no InputMask is specified, set it up for
    *** the largest value the field will accommodate
    DO CASE
      CASE laFields[ lnRow, 2 ] = 'I'
        .cInputMask = "9999999999"
        .nMaxVal = 2147483647

      CASE laFields[ lnRow, 2 ] = 'Y'
        .cInputMask = "999999999999999.9999"
        .nMaxVal = 922337203685477.5807

      CASE laFields[ lnRow, 2 ] = 'N'
        lcIntegerPart = REPLICATE('9', laFields[lnRow, 3] - ;
                        laFields[lnRow, 4] - 1)
        lcDecimalPart = REPLICATE('9', laFields[lnRow, 4])
        .cInputMask = lcIntegerPart + '.' + lcDecimalPart
        .nMaxVal = VAL( .cInputMask )

      OTHERWISE
        lcMsg = IIF( INLIST( laFields[ lnRow, 2 ], 'B', 'F' ), ;
        'You must specify an input mask for double and float data types', ;
        'Invalid data type for this control' ) + ': ' + This.Name
        MESSAGEBOX( lcMsg, 16, 'Developer Error!' )
        RETURN .F.
    ENDCASE
  ENDIF
ELSE
  .cInputMask = STRTRAN( .InputMask, ',', '' )
  .nMaxVal = VAL( .cInputMask )
ENDIF
ELSE
  .cInputMask = STRTRAN( .InputMask, ',', '' )
  .nMaxVal = VAL( .cInputMask )
ENDIF
```

Now that we have saved the Control Source to our internal *cControlSource* property, we can safely unbind the control. We also set the *lChangingFocus* flag to true. This ensures our numeric text box will keep the focus if it's the first object in the tab order when SET('CONFIRM') = 'OFF'. This is essential because our text box positions the cursor by using a KEYBOARD '{END}'. This would immediately set focus to the second object in the tab order when the form is instantiated because we cannot force a SET CONFIRM OFF until our text box actually has focus:

```
.ControlSource = ''
*** This keeps us from KEYBOARDing an '{END}' and moving to the next control
*** if this is the first one in the tab order
.lChangingFocus = .T.
.FormatValue()
ENDWITH
```

The *FormatValue* method performs the same function that the native Visual FoxPro refresh method does for bound controls. It updates the control's value from its *ControlSource*. Actually, in this case, it updates the control's value from its *cControlSource*. Since *cControlSource* evaluates to a numeric value, the first thing we must do is convert this value to a string. We then format the string nicely with separators and position the cursor at the end of the string:

```
WITH This
  *** cControlSource is numeric, so convert it to string
  IF ! EMPTY ( .cControlSource )
    IF ! EMPTY ( EVAL( .cControlSource ) )
      .Value = ALLTRIM( PADL ( EVAL( .cControlSource ), 32 ) )
    ELSE
      .Value = ' '
    ENDIF
    *** And format it nicely with separators
    .AddSeparators()
  ELSE
    .Value = ' '
    .InputMask = '#'
  ENDIF
  *** Position the cursor at the right end of the textbox
  IF .lChangingFocus
    .lChangingFocus = .F.
  ELSE
    KEYBOARD '{END}'
  ENDIF
ENDWITH
```

The *AddSeparators* method is used to display the formatted value of the text box. The first step is to calculate the length of the integer and decimal portions of the current string:

```
LOCAL lcInputMask, lnPointPos, lnIntLen, lnDecLen, lnCnt
*** Reset the InputMask with separators for the current value of the text box
lcInputMask = ''
WITH This
  *** Find the length of the integer portion of the number
  lnPointPos = AT( .cPoint, ALLTRIM( .Value ) )
  IF lnPointPos = 0
    lnIntLen = LEN( .Value )
  ELSE
    lnIntLen = LEN( LEFT(.Value, lnPointPos - 1 ) )
  ENDIF
  *** Find the length of the decimal portion of the number
  IF AT( .cPoint, .cInputMask ) > 0
    lnDecLen = LEN( SUBSTR( .cInputMask, AT( .cPoint, .cInputMask ) + 1 ) )
  ELSE
    lnDecLen = 0
  ENDIF
```

Once we have calculated these lengths, we can reconstruct the *inputMask,* inserting commas where appropriate. The easy way is to count characters beginning with the rightmost character of the integer portion of the string. We can then insert a comma after the format character if the current character is in the thousands position (*lnCnt* = 4), the millions position (*lnCnt* = 7) and so on. However, if the text box contains a negative value, this could possibly result in "-,123,456" being displayed as the formatted value. We check for this possibility after the commas are inserted:

```
*** Insert the separator at the appropriate interval
lcInputMask = ''
FOR lnCnt = lnIntLen TO 1 STEP -1
  IF INLIST( lnCnt, 4, 7, 10, 13, 16, 19, 21, 24 )
    lcInputMask = lcInputMask + "#" + .cSeparator
  ELSE
    lcInputMask = lcInputMask + "#"
  ENDIF
ENDFOR
*** Make sure that negative numbers are formatted correctly
IF LEFT( ALLTRIM( .Value ), 1 ) = '-'
  IF LEN( lcInputMask ) > 3
    IF LEFT( lcInputMask, 2 ) = '#,'
      lcInputMask = '#' + SUBSTR( lcInputMask, 3 )
    ENDIF
  ENDIF
ENDIF
```

We finish up by adding a placeholder for the decimal point and any placeholders that are needed to represent the decimal portion of the number:

```
IF lnPointPos > 0
  *** Allow for the decimal point in the input mask
  lcInputMask = lcInputMask + '#'
  *** Add to the input mask if there is a decimal portion
  IF lnDecLen > 0
    lcInputMask = lcInputMask + REPLICATE( '#', lnDecLen )
  ENDIF
ENDIF
.InputMask = lcInputMask
ENDWITH
```

In order for the user to enter data, the control must receive focus. This requires that a number of things be done in the *GotFocus* method. The first is to make sure that SET ('CONFIRM') = 'ON' and that the bell is silenced, otherwise we will have problems when we KEYBOARD '{END}' to position the cursor at the end of the field. Next we have to strip the separators out of the *InputMask*, and finally we want to execute the default *SelectOnEntry* behavior of our base class text box. So the inherited 'Select on Entry' code in the *GotFocus* method has to be modified to handle these additional requirements, as follows:

```
This.cOldConfirm = SET('CONFIRM')
This.cOldBell = SET( 'BELL' )
SET CONFIRM ON
SET BELL OFF
This.SetInputMask()
DODEFAULT()
```

Note that the *SetInputMask* method is also called from the *HandleKey* method to adjust the *InputMask* as the user enters data. Here it is:

```
LOCAL lcInputMask, lnChar
*** Reset the InputMask for the current value of the text box
```

```
lcInputMask = ''
FOR lnChar = 1 to LEN( This.Value )
  lcInputMask = lcInputMask + '#'
ENDFOR
lcInputMask = lcInputMask + '#'
This.InputMask = lcInputMask
```

Like our incremental search text box, the numeric text box handles the keystroke in the *HandleKey* method that is called from *InteractiveChange* after *KeyPress* has processed the keystroke. The incremental search text box does not require any code in the *KeyPress* method because all characters are potentially valid. In the numeric text box, however, only a subset of the keystrokes are valid. We need to trap any illegal keystrokes in the control's *KeyPress* method and when one is detected, issue a **NODEFAULT** to suppress the input. We do this by passing the current keystroke to the *OK2Continue* method. If it's an invalid character, this method returns false to the *KeyPress* method, which issues the required **NODEFAULT** command:

```
LPARAMETERS tnKeyCode
LOCAL lcCheckVal, llretVal
llRetVal = .T.
WITH This
```

Since the current character does not become a part of the text box's value until **after** the *InteractiveChange* method has completed, we can prevent multiple decimal points by checking for them here:

```
DO CASE
  *** Make sure we only allow one decimal point in the entry
  CASE CHR( tnKeyCode ) = .cPoint          && decimal point
    IF AT( .cPoint, .Value ) > 0
      llRetVal = .F.
    ENDIF
```

Likewise, we will not allow a minus sign to be typed in unless it is the first character in the string:

```
  *** Make sure we only have a minus sign at the beginning of the number
  CASE tnKeyCode = 45
    IF .SelStart > 0
      llRetVal = .F.
    ENDIF
```

The most complex task handled by the *OK2Continue* method is the check for numeric overflow. We do this by determining what the value will be if we allow the current keystroke and compare this value to the one stored in the control's *nMaxVal* property:

```
  *** Guard against numeric overflow!!!!
  OTHERWISE
    IF ! EMPTY( .cInputMask )
      IF .SelLength = 0
        IF tnKeyCode > 47 AND tnKeyCode < 58
          DO CASE
```

```
         CASE .SelStart = 0
            lcCheckVal = CHR( tnKeyCode ) + ALLTRIM( .Value )
         CASE .SelStart = LEN( ALLTRIM( .Value ) )

            lcCheckVal = ALLTRIM( .Value ) + CHR( tnKeyCode )
         OTHERWISE
            lcCheckVal = LEFT( .Value, .SelStart ) + CHR( tnKeyCode ) + ;
                         ALLTRIM( SUBSTR( .Value, .SelStart + 1 ) )
      ENDCASE
      IF ABS( VAL( lcCheckVal ) ) > .nMaxVal
         llRetVal = .F.
      ENDIF
      *** Make sure that if the input mask specifies a
      *** certain number of decimals, we don't allow more
      *** than the number of decimal places specified
      IF AT( '.', lcCheckVal ) > 0
         IF AT( '.', .cInputMask ) > 0
            IF LEN( JUSTEXT( lcCheckVal ) ) > LEN( JUSTEXT( .cInputMask ) )
               llretVal = .F.
            ENDIF
         ENDIF
      ENDIF
    ENDIF     && tnKeyCode > 47 AND tnKeyCode < 58
  ENDIF     && .SelLength = 0
 ENDIF     && ! EMPTY( .cInputMask )
 ENDCASE
ENDWITH

RETURN llRetVal
```

This code may look rather ugly, but in fact it executes extremely quickly because the nested IF structure ensures that various checks are performed sequentially and that if any one fails, the rest are never processed at all.

Like our incremental search text box, a lot of work is done using a little bit of code in our *HandleKey* method. We can handle the positioning of the cursor and formatting of the value here because *InteractiveChange* will only fire after *KeyPress* has succeeded. Therefore, handling the keystrokes here requires less code than handling them directly in *KeyPress:*

```
LOCAL lcInputMask, lnSelStart, lnEnd
*** Save the cursor's insertion point and length of the value typed in so far
lnSelStart = This.SelStart
lnEnd = LEN( This.Value ) - 1
WITH This
   *** Get rid of any trailing spaces so we can Right justify the value
   .Value  = ALLTRIM(.Value)
   *** We need special handling to remove the decimal point
   IF LASTKEY() = 127                               && backspace
     IF .Value = .cPoint
        .Value = ' '
        .InputMask = '#'
     ENDIF
   ENDIF
   .SetInputMask()
```

If the character just entered was in the middle of the text box, we leave the cursor where it was. Otherwise we position it explicitly at the end of the value currently being entered:

```
IF lnSelStart >= lnEnd
  KEYBOARD '{END}'
ELSE
  .SelStart = lnSelStart
ENDIF
ENDWITH
```

Nearly there now! If this was originally a bound control, we must update the field specified by the *cControlSource* property. The *Valid* method is the appropriate place for this, so we use it:

```
WITH This
  IF ! EMPTY( .cControlSource )
    REPLACE ( .cField ) WITH VAL( .Value ) IN ( .cTable )
  ENDIF
ENDWITH
```

Finally, we need a little bit of code in the text box's *LostFocus* method to reset CONFIRM to its original value and to format the displayed value with the appropriate separators:

```
WITH This
  *** Set flag so we don't keyboard an end and mess up the tab order
  .lChangingFocus = .T.
  .Refresh()
  IF .cOldConfirm = 'OFF'
    SET CONFIRM OFF
  ENDIF
ENDWITH
```

Handling time

One of the perennial problems when constructing a user interface is how to handle the entry of time. Many applications require this support and we have seen varied approaches, often based on spinner controls. We feel there are actually two types of time entry that need to be considered, and their differences require different controls.

First there is the direct entry of an actual time. Typically this will be used in a time recording situation when the user needs to enter, for example, a start and a finish time for a task. This is a pure data entry scenario and a text box is the best tool for the job, but there are some issues that need to be addressed.

Second there is the entry of time as an interval or setting. Typically this type will be used in a planning situation when the user needs to enter, for example, the estimated duration for a task. In this case, a spinner is well suited to the task since users can easily adjust the value up or down and can see the impact of their changes.

A time entry text box *(Example: CH04.VCX::txtTime)*

The basic assumption here is that a time value will always be stored as a character string in the form *hh:mm*. We do not expect to handle seconds in this type of direct entry situation. Actually this is not unreasonable, since most time manipulation only requires a precision of hours and minutes. This is easiest when the value is already in character form. (If you truly need to enter seconds, it would be a simple matter to make this control into a subclass to handle them.) Also we have decided to work on a 24-hour clock. Again this simplifies the interface by removing the necessity to add the familiar concept of an AM/PM designator.

These decisions make the class' user interface simple to build because Visual FoxPro provides us with both an *InputMask* and a *Format* property. The former specifies how data entered into the control should be interpreted, while the latter defines how it should be displayed. In our *txtTime* class (based on our *txtbase* class) these properties are defined as follows:

```
InputMask = 99:99
Format = R
```

The 'R' in the format tells Visual FoxPro to use the input mask defined but not to include the formatting characters as part of the value to be stored. Although it can only be used with character and numeric data, it is very useful indeed. In this case the separator ':' is always visible but is not actually stored with the value. It is, therefore, always a four-character string.

We have some additional code in both the *GotFocus* and *LostFocus* methods to save and restore the current setting of CONFIRM and to force it to ON while the time entry text box has focus. While not absolutely necessary, we believe it's good practice when limiting entry lengths to ensure that confirm is on to prevent users from inadvertently typing through the field.

All of the remaining code in the class is in the *Valid* method of the text box and this is where we need to address the issues alluded to above about how users will use this control. The key issue is how to handle partial times. For example, if a user enters the string: '011' do they actually mean '01:10' (ten minutes past one in the morning) or '00:11' (eleven minutes past midnight)? How about an entry of '09'?

In fact there is no absolute way of knowing. All we can do is define and implement some reasonable rulesfor this class as follows:

Table 4.3 *Rules for entering a time value*

User Enters	Interpret as	Result
1	A specific hour, no minutes	01:00
11	Hours only, no minutes	11:00
111	Hours and minutes, leading zero omitted	01:11
1111	Exact time	11:11

The code implementing these rules is quite straightforward:

```
LOCAL luHrs, luMins, lcTime, lnLen
*** Note: we have to assume that a user only omits leading or trailing
*** zeroes.  We cannot guess at the intended result otherwise!!!
lcTime = ALLTRIM(This.Value)
lnLen = LEN(lcTime)
DO CASE
    CASE lnLen = 4
        *** We have 4 digits so we have a complete time!
        *** Do nothing else
    CASE lnLen = 3
        *** Assume minutes are correct, hours leading zero was omitted
        lcTime = PADL( lcTime, 4, '0' )
    CASE lnLen = 2
        *** Assume we have just got hours, no minutes
        lcTime = PADR( lcTime, 4, '0' )
    OTHERWISE
        *** A single number must be an hour!
        lcTime = "0" + lcTime + "00"
ENDCASE
*** Get the Hours and minutes components
luHrs  = LEFT( lcTime, 2 )
luMins = RIGHT( lcTime, 2 )
*** Check that we have not gone over 23:59, or less than 00:00
IF ! BETWEEN( INT(VAL(luMins)), 0, 59) OR ! BETWEEN( INT(VAL(luHrs)), 0, 23)
  WAIT "Invalid Time Entered" WINDOW NOWAIT
  This.Value = ""
  RETURN 0
ELSE
  This.Value = luHrs + luMins
  RETURN 1
ENDIF
```

A time entry composite class *(Example: CH04.VCX::cntTime)*

As noted in the introduction to this section, a spinner control is useful when you need to give the user the ability to change times, as opposed to entering them directly. However, one significant difference between using a spinner and a text box to enter time is that a spinner requires a numeric value. This means if we still want to store our time value as a character string, we need to convert from character to numeric and back again. For simplicity, this control is set up to always display a time in *hh:mm:ss* format and expects that, if bound, it will be bound to a Character (6) field. (The purpose here is to show the basic techniques. Modifying the control for other scenarios is left as an exercise for the reader.)

The next issue is how to get the time to be meaningful as a numeric value to display properly. Fortunately we can again make use of the *Format* and *InputMask* properties to resolve this dilemma. By setting the Spinner's InputMask = 99:99:99, and the Format = "RL" we can display a six digit numeric value with leading zeroes. (The '*L*' option only works with numeric values, so we could not use it in the preceding example.)

The final issue we need to address is how to determine which portion of our six-digit number will be changed when the spinner's up/down buttons are clicked. The solution is to create a composite class that is based on a container with a spinner and a three-button option group. The Option group is used to determine which portion of the spinner gets incremented (i.e. hours, minutes or seconds) and the Spinner's *UpClick* and *DownClick* methods are coded to act appropriately. Here is the class in use:

Figure 4.2 *Time Spinner Control*

The time spinner's container

The container is a subclass of our standard *cntBase* class, with a single custom property (*cControlSource*) and one custom method (*SetSpinValue*). These handle the requirement to convert between a character data source for our class and the numeric value required by the spinner. The *cControlSource* property is populated at design time with the name of the control source for the spinner. Code has been added to the *Refresh* method of the container to call the *SetSpinValue* method to perform the conversion when the control is bound. The *Refresh* code is simply:

```
WITH This
    IF !EMPTY( .cControlSource )
        This.SetSpinValue()
    ENDIF
ENDWITH
```

The code in *SetSpinValue* is equally simple, it merely converts the control source's value to a six-digit number padded with zeroes. However, there is one gotcha here – notice the use of the *INT()* function in this conversion. We must ensure our numeric value is actually an integer at all times. Whether we are dealing with hours, minutes or seconds is based on the positions of the digits in the numeric value and decimal places would interfere when using the *PADx()* functions:

```
WITH This
    IF !EMPTY( .cControlSource )
        .spnTime.Value = INT( VAL( PADL( EVAL( .cControlSource ), 6, "0" )))
    ENDIF
ENDWITH
```

The time spinner's option group

This is the simplest part of the class. It has no custom code whatsoever other than the change of its name from the Visual FoxPro default to *OptPick*. The native behavior of an option group is to record, in the *Value* property of the group itself, the number of the option button selected. Since we only need to know which button is selected, we don't need to do anything else.

The time spinner's spinner

This is, unsurprisingly, where most of the work in the class is done. Three properties have been set – the *InputMask* and *Format* (to handle the display issues) and the *Increment*. This has been set to 0 to suppress the native behavior of the spinner since we need to handle the value change in a more sophisticated manner.

The *GotFocus* and *LostFocus* methods are used to turn the cursor off and back on again, since this control is not intended for direct typing, eliminating the need to show the cursor.

The *Valid* method handles the conversion of the spinner's numeric value back into a character string and, if the control is bound, handles the **REPLACE** to update the control source. This code is also quite straightforward:

```
WITH This.Parent
    IF !EMPTY( .cControlSource )
        REPLACE (.cControlSource) WITH PADL( INT( This.Value ), 6, "0" )
    ENDIF
ENDWITH
```

The tricky bits are handled in the *UpClick* and *DownClick* methods. While this code may look a little daunting at first glance, it's really quite straightforward and relies on interpreting the position of the digits in the numeric value and handling them accordingly. The *UpClick* method checks the setting of the option group and increments the relevant portion of the numeric value:

```
LOCAL lnPick, lnNewVal, lnHrs, lnMins, lnSecs
lnPick = This.Parent.optPick.Value
DO CASE
   CASE lnPick = 1    && Hrs
      *** Get the next Hours value
      lnNewVal = This.Value + 10000
      *** If 24 or more, reset to 0 by subtracting
      This.Value = IIF( lnNewVal >= 240000, lnNewVal - 240000, lnNewVal )
   CASE lnPick = 2    && Mins
         *** Get the next value as a character string
      lcNewVal = PADL(INT(This.Value) + 100, 6, '0' )
         *** Extract hours as a value multiplied by 10000
      lnHrs = VAL(LEFT(lcNewVal,2)) * 10000
         *** Get the minutes as a character string
      lnMins = SUBSTR( lcNewVal, 3, 2)
         *** Check the value of this string, and either multiply up by 100
         *** or, if above 59, roll it over to 00
      lnMins = VAL(IIF( VAL(lnMins) > 59, "00", lnMins )) * 100
         *** Extract the seconds portion
      lnSecs = VAL(RIGHT(lcNewVal, 2 ))
      *** Reconstruct the Numeric Value
      This.Value = lnHrs + lnMins + lnSecs
   CASE lnPick = 3    && Secs
         *** Get the next value as a character string
      lcNewVal = PADL(INT(This.Value) + 1, 6, '0' )
         *** Extract hours as a value multiplied by 10000
      lnHrs = VAL(LEFT(lcNewVal,2)) * 10000
         *** Extract minutes as a value multiplied by 100
      lnMins = VAL(SUBSTR( lcNewVal, 3, 2)) * 100
         *** Get the seconds as a character string
```

```
    lnSecs = RIGHT( lcNewVal, 2)
       *** Check the value of this string,
       *** If above 59, roll it over to 00
    lnSecs = VAL(IIF( VAL(lnSecs) > 59, "00", lnSecs ))
    *** Reconstruct the Numeric Value
    This.Value = lnHrs + lnMins + lnSecs
ENDCASE
```

For hours the increment is 10000, for minutes it is 100 and for seconds it is just 1.

The control is designed so that if the user tries to increment the hours portion above '23', it rolls over to '00' by simply subtracting the value 240000 from the spinner's new value. Both the minutes and seconds are rolled over from '59' to '00', but in this case we need to actually strip out each component of the time to check the relevant portion before re-building the value by adding up the individual parts.

A similar approach has been taken in the *DownClick* method, which decrements the control's value. In this case we need to store the current value and use it to maintain the settings of the parts of the control that are not being affected. Otherwise the principles are the same as for the *UpClick* method:

```
LOCAL lnPick, lcNewVal, lnHrs, lnMins, lnSecs, lcOldVal
*** Get the Current value of the control as a string
lcOldVal = PADL(INT(This.Value), 6, '0' )
lnPick = This.Parent.optPick.Value
DO CASE
  CASE lnPick = 1    && Hrs
     *** Decrement the hours portion
    lnHrs = VAL( LEFT( lcOldVal, 2 ) ) - 1
    *** If it is in the desired range, use it, otherwise set to 0
    lnHrs = IIF( BETWEEN(lnHrs, 0, 23), lnHrs, 23 ) * 10000
       *** Extract the minutes
    lnMins = VAL(SUBSTR( lcOldVal, 3, 2)) * 100
    *** Extract the seconds
    lnSecs = VAL(RIGHT( lcOldVal, 2))
  CASE lnPick = 2    && Mins
       *** Determine the new, decremented, value
    lcNewVal = PADL(INT(This.Value) - 100, 6, '0' )
       *** Retrieve the current Hours portion
    lnHrs = VAL(LEFT(lcOldVal,2)) * 10000
    *** Get the minutes portion from the new value
    lnMins = VAL(SUBSTR( lcNewVal, 3, 2))
       *** Check for validity with the range, set to 0 if invalid
    lnMins = IIF( BETWEEN( lnMins, 0, 59), lnMins, 59 ) * 100
    *** Retrieve the current Seconds portion
    lnSecs = VAL(RIGHT(lcOldVal, 2 ))
  CASE lnPick = 3    && Secs
       *** Determine the new, decremented, value
    lcNewVal = PADL(INT(This.Value) - 1, 6, '0' )
       *** Retrieve the current Hours portion
    lnHrs = VAL(LEFT(lcOldVal,2)) * 10000
       *** Retrieve the current Minutes portion
    lnMins = VAL(SUBSTR( lcOldVal, 3, 2)) * 100
    *** Get the Seconds portion from the new value
    lnSecs = VAL(RIGHT( lcNewVal, 2))
       *** Check for validity with the range, set to 0 if invalid
    lnSecs = IIF( BETWEEN(lnSecs, 0, 59), lnSecs, 59 )
```

```
ENDCASE
*** Set the Value to the new, decremented, result
This.Value = lnHrs + lnMins + lnSecs
```

Conclusion

This time spinner is somewhat restricted in its ability to handle more than the simple environment that we defined for it. While clear to the end user, the mechanism for selecting which part of the time needs to be incremented or decremented is a bit cumbersome. A more elegant solution is offered in the final control in this section.

The true time spinner *(Example: CH04.VCX::spnTime)*

This control looks and acts just like the time spinner you see when using the Date/Time Picker ActiveX control that ships with Visual Studio. However, it has several features that make it more generally useful than the ActiveX control. First, this control does not require that it be bound to a field of the DateTime data type. As we have said, the best format for storing user entered time is in a character field formatted to include the universal ':' time separator. The control can be configured to display and recognize either a 5-character '*hh:mm*' format or a full 8-character '*hh:mm:ss*' format and update either appropriately. This is controlled by a single property, *lShowSeconds*. Finally, because this is a native Visual FoxPro control it does not suffer from the inherent problems that haunt ActiveX controls with respect to the multiple versions of specific windows DLLs, nor are there any problems associated with registering the control.

As with the container-based spinner, this control uses a *cControlSource* property for binding to an external data source and has associated methods (*RefreshSpinner* and *UpdateControlSource*) to handle the issue of converting between character (source) and numeric (internal) values and back. Unlike the container-based spinner, this control can also handle being bound to a form property, as well as to a data source. The *UpdateControlSource* method, called from the spinner's *Valid* method, allows the time spinner, which is really an unbound control, to behave just like one that is bound when its *cControlSource* property is set:

```
LOCAL lcTable, lcField, lcValue, lcTemp
WITH This
   *** Parse out the name of the table and the field in cControlSource
   IF ! EMPTY( .cControlSource )
     *** Get the name of the table if the ControlSource is prefaced by an alias
     IF '.' $ .cControlSource
       lcTable = LEFT( .cControlSource, AT( '.', .cControlSource ) - 1 )
       lcField = SUBSTR( .cControlSource, AT( '.', .cControlSource ) + 1 )
     ELSE
       *** Assume the alias is the current selected alias if none is specified.
       *** This is a little dangerous, but if it is a bad assumption, the
       *** program will blow up very quickly in development mode giving
       *** the developer a very clear indication of what is wrong once he checks
       *** out the problem in the debugger.
       lcTable = ALIAS()
       lcField = .cControlSource
     ENDIF
```

We must now convert the numeric value of the spinner to the character value required by the field or form property specified in *cControlSource* if this is a *bound* control. We must also format this character string with colons and take into account whether we are using *hh:mm* or *hh:mm:ss* format:

```
lcTemp = IIF( .lShowSeconds, PADL( INT ( .Value ), 6, '0' ), ;
                             PADL( INT ( .Value ), 4, '0' ) )
lcValue = LEFT( lcTemp, 2 ) + ':' + SUBSTR( lcTemp, 3, 2 ) + ;
          IIF( .lShowSeconds, ':' + RIGHT( lcTemp, 2 ), '' )
*** Check here to see if our alias is ThisForm. If it is,
*** we will assume that we are bound to a form property
IF UPPER( lcTable ) = 'THISFORM'
  STORE lcValue TO ( .cControlSource )
ELSE
  REPLACE ( lcField ) WITH lcValue IN ( lcTable )
ENDIF
  ENDIF
ENDWITH
```

Conversely, the *RefreshSpinner* method updates the spinner's value from its *cControlSource*. In true bound controls, this function is handled automatically whenever the control is refreshed. Our *RefreshSpinner* method is called from the spinner's *Refresh* to provide this functionality:

```
WITH This
  IF ! EMPTY( .cControlSource )
    .Value = IIF( .lSHowSeconds, ;
            VAL( STRTRAN( EVAL( .cControlSource ), ':', '' ) ), ;
            VAL( STRTRAN( LEFT ( EVAL( .cControlSource ), 5 ), ':', '' ) ) )
  ELSE
    .Value = IIF( .lSHowSeconds, VAL( STRTRAN( TIME(), ':', '' ) ), ;
              VAL( STRTRAN( LEFT( TIME(), 5), ':', '' ) ) )
  ENDIF
ENDWITH
```

To change the time, a user merely has to click on the hour, minutes or seconds displayed and then increment or decrement that value. Alternatively, the time can be entered by typing directly into the control and the cursor left and right keys can be used to navigate within the control. The hours are limited to the range 0 – 23, and minutes and seconds to the 0 – 59 range. Each unit of time acts independently and rolls over from its upper to lower limit and vice versa (just like setting a digital alarm clock).

At first we thought we would implement a continuous scroll function with our time spinner. It didn't take long before we gave up on the idea. We quickly discovered there was no convenient way to implement this functionality because of the order in which the spinner events fire. As you might expect, the *MouseDown* event happens first. This, however, is followed by the *MouseUp* event followed by either the *UpClick* or *DownClick* method. You can see this behavior yourself by keeping the down arrow of the spinner depressed. The spinner does not increment or decrement its value until you release the mouse!

The logic used to increment and decrement the different time segments is similar to that discussed previously. The primary difference between this control and the container discussed above is the methodology used to determine which time segment to increment or decrement. Since clicking on the up arrow or down arrow of the spinner causes the control's *SelStart* property to be reset to zero, this value is saved to the custom spinner property *nSelStart* whenever a particular time segment is selected. The control uses two custom methods, *SetHighlight* and *MoveHighlight* to select the appropriate time segment and store the cursor position to this property. The *SetHightlight* method below is used to select the appropriate time segment whenever the user clicks in the spinner with the mouse:

```
WITH This
  DO CASE
    *** Hightlight Hours
    CASE BETWEEN( .SelStart, 0, 2 )
      .SelStart = 0
    *** Highlight minutes
    CASE BETWEEN( .SelStart, 3, 5 )
      .SelStart = 3
    OTHERWISE
    *** Hightlight seconds if applicable
      .SelStart = IIF( .lShowSeconds, 6, 0 )
  ENDCASE
  .SelLength = 2
  *** Save insertion point
  .nSelStart = .SelStart
ENDWITH
```

The *MoveHighlight* method handles moving the highlight to the appropriate segment of the spinner when the user presses either the right (keycode = 4) or left (keycode = 19) cursor keys. It is called from the spinner's *KeyPress* method if the current time segment contains a valid value. When the user types a time segment directly into the control, the *ValidateSegment* method is called to make sure it is in the correct range. If it isn't, the time spinner's *lSegmentIsValid* property is set to false. This prevents the user from moving to either a different segment within the control or to any other object on the form without first correcting the input:

```
LOCAL llDecrement
WITH This
  DO CASE
    CASE nKeyCode = 19 OR nKeyCode = 4
      IF .lSegmentIsValid
        .MoveHighlight( nKeyCode )
      ENDIF
      NODEFAULT

    CASE nKeyCode = 5 OR nKeyCode = 24      && Up or down arrow
      IF nKeyCode = 24
        llDecrement = .T.
      ENDIF
      ChangeTime( llDecrement )
      SelStart = .nSelStart
      SelLength = 2
      NODEFAULT

    OTHERWISE
```

```
      *** So we don't mess up the formatted time
      *** If we start typing numbers and Part of the value is selected,
      *** we lose digits and the remaining ones shift
      .SelLength = 0
      *** If we are typing a number directly into the control,
      *** make sure it is a valid hours, minutes, or seconds value
      IF BETWEEN( nKeyCode, 48, 57 )
        Spinner::KeyPress( nKeyCode, nShiftAltCtrl )
        .ValidateSegment()
        IF ! .lSegmentIsValid
          .SelStart  = .nSelStart
          .SelLength = 2
        ENDIF
        NODEFAULT
      ENDIF
  ENDCASE
ENDWITH
```

The *MoveHighlight* method is somewhat similar to the *SetHighlight* method above. Based on the current location of the cursor and the key that was just pressed, it decides which time segment to select:

```
WITH This
  DO CASE
    CASE BETWEEN( .SelStart, 0, 2 )
      IF .lShowSeconds
        .SelStart = IIF( nKeyCode = 19, 6, 3 )
      ELSE
        .SelStart = 3
      ENDIF
    CASE BETWEEN( .SelStart, 3, 5 )
      IF .lShowSeconds
        .SelStart = IIF( nKeyCode = 19, 0, 6 )
      ELSE
        .SelStart = 0
      ENDIF
    OTHERWISE
      .SelStart = IIF( nKeyCode = 19, 3, 0 )
  ENDCASE
  .SelLength = 2
  .nSelStart = .SelStart
ENDWITH
```

Incrementing and decrementing the time segments is handled by the *ChangeTime* method. This is an overloaded method that is called from both the *UpClick* and *DownClick* spinner methods. A single logical parameter passed to this function tells it whether or not to increment or decrement the specified segment. The *ChangeTime* method then invokes the appropriate method to handle the hours and minutes calculations. Since the manipulation of the seconds value is so straightforward, it is handled directly in the *ChangeTime* method:

```
LPARAMETERS tlDecrement
*** when tlDecrement is true, we are decrementing the time, otherwise we are
*** incrementing. First, we must select which segment is being adjusted by
*** examining the previously saved value of nselstart
WITH This
```

```
DO CASE
  CASE BETWEEN( .nSelStart, 0, 2 )
    .IncrementHours( tlDecrement )

  CASE BETWEEN( .nSelStart, 3, 5 )
    .IncrementMinutes( tlDecrement )

  OTHERWISE
    IF tlDecrement
      .Value = IIF( INT( .Value % 100 ) = 0 OR INT( .Value % 100 > 59 ), ;
                    INT( .Value / 100 ) * 100 + 59, .Value - 1 )
    ELSE
      .Value = IIF( INT( .Value % 100 ) > 58, ;
                INT( .Value / 100 ) * 100, .Value + 1 )
    ENDIF
ENDCASE
.lSegmentIsValid = .T.
ENDWITH
```

Blinking labels *(Example: CH04.VCX::cntLblBlink)*

Even though some of this writing team is British, this is not a derisive comment about labels. Back in the days of FoxPro for DOS and FoxPro for Windows, we could specify blinking text by setting a format code of *'B'*. Unfortunately this no longer works in Visual FoxPro. However if you need a blinking label on occasion, creating this class is very simple.

All you need is a container with its *backStyle* set to 0-transparent and *borderwidth* set to 0. Drop a label and a timer into the container. Set the timer's interval to 300 and add the following line of code to its timer method:

```
WITH This.Parent.lblBase
  .Visible = !.Visible
ENDWITH
```

Voila! Blinking labels!

The expanding edit box *(Example: CH04.VCX::edtBase)*

One of the shortcomings of the Visual FoxPro base class edit box is that it may be too small to allow the user to see all the text in the memo field being displayed. We can solve this problem easily enough by adding a few properties to our base class edit box and a couple of methods to shrink and expand it.

At first glance one may be tempted to automatically expand the edit box when it gets focus and shrink it again when it loses focus. However, on reflection you will probably agree this would not make a good interface design and would, at the very least, be somewhat disconcerting for the end user. Therefore we have opted to allow the user to expand and shrink the edit box by creating a shortcut menu called from the edit box *RightClick* method. This menu also gives the user the ability to change the font of the text displayed in the edit box. (Your end users will appreciate the ability to ease the strain on their eyes by enlarging the font, especially when the memo fields to be edited are lengthy.)

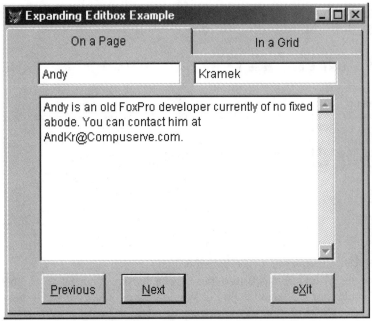

Figure 4.3 The expanding edit box at instantiation

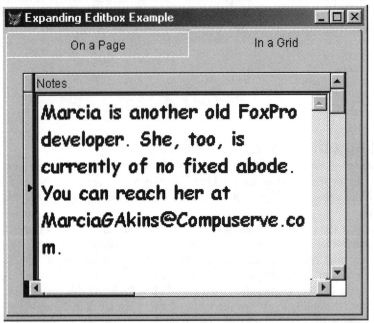

Figure 4.4 The expanding edit box when maximized with altered font

Our expanding edit box class uses nine custom properties, of which only the first three require any direct manipulation – but only if you want to change the default behavior.

Table 4.4 *Custom properties of the expanding edit box*

Property	Description
lCleanUpOnExit	Set to true to strip unprintable characters off the end of the memo
lPositionAtEnd	When true, positions the cursor at the end of existing text when the edit box gets focus
lResize	When true, enables the option to expand and shrink the edit box when the user right mouse clicks in the edit box to display the shortcut menu
lMaximized	Set to true when the edit box is maximized and false when it isn't
nOrigColWidths	Saves original column widths of all the columns in the grid that contains this edit box so we can expand the edit box to take up the space of the entire visible portion of the grid
nOrigHeight	Height of the edit box at instantiation
nOrigLeft	Left of the edit box at instantiation
nOrigRowHeight	Original RowHeight of the grid containing the edit box (if the edit box is contained in a grid)
nOrigTop	Top of the edit box at instantiation
nOrigWidth	Width of the edit box at instantiation

By the way, this particular control will work as is, even when inside a grid despite the caution at the start of this chapter. So how does it work? When the control is instantiated, a call from its *Init* method runs the custom *SaveOriginalDimensions* method, which does exactly what its name implies:

```
LOCAL lnCol
WITH This
   *** Save the editbox's original dimensions and position
   .nOrigHeight = .Height
   .nOrigWidth  = .Width
   .nOrigTop    = .Top
   .nOrigLeft   = .Left
   *** If it is in a grid, save the grid's rowheight and columnwidths
   IF UPPER( .Parent.BaseClass ) = 'COLUMN'
     .nOrigRowHeight = .Parent.Parent.RowHeight
     FOR lnCol = 1 TO .Parent.Parent.ColumnCount
       DIMENSION .nOrigColWidths[lnCol]
       .nOrigColWidths[lnCol] = .Parent.Parent.Columns[lnCol].Width
     ENDFOR
   ENDIF
ENDWITH
```

As with our text box classes, we like to be able to select all contents when the edit box gets focus, so we check if *SelectOnEntry* = .T. and select all text if required. In addition, we position the cursor at the end of the selected text using a **KEYBOARD** '{CTRL+END}', if our *lPositionAtEnd* property is set:

```
WITH This
  IF .SelectOnEntry
    .SelStart  = 0
    .SelLength = LEN( .Value )
  ENLSE
    IF .lPositionAtEnd
      KEYBOARD '{CTRL + END}'
    ENDIF
  ENDIF
ENDWITH
NODEFAULT
```

The edit box's *RightClick* method calls its *ShowMenu* method if its *lResize* property is set to true. The *ShowMenu* method then displays the shortcut menu (*mnuEditBox*) and takes the appropriate action based on what was chosen from the menu:

```
LOCAL lcFontString, lcFontStyle, lcFontName, lcFontSize, llBold, llItalic, ;
      lnComma1Pos, lnComma2Pos
PRIVATE pnMenuChoice
pnMenuChoice = 0
DO mnuEditbox.mpr
WITH This
  DO CASE
    *** If enlarge was selected, expand the edit box unless it is
    *** already expanded
    CASE pnMenuChoice = 1
      IF !.lMaximized
        .Enlarge()
      ENDIF

    *** If shrink was selected, shrink the edit box if it is expanded
    CASE pnMenuChoice = 2
      IF .lMaximized
        .Shrink()
      ENDIF

    CASE pnMenuChoice = 3
    lcFontStyle = IIF( .FontBold, 'B', '' ) + IIF( .FontItalic, 'I', '' )
      *** Get the user's choice of font to use
      lcFontString = GETFONT(.FontName, .FontSize, lcFontStyle )
      *** parse out the font properties from the returned string
      *** after checking to make sure that the user selected something
    IF ! EMPTY ( lcFontString )
        lnComma1Pos = AT( ',', lcFontString )
        lcFontName = LEFT( lcFontString, lnComma1Pos - 1 )
        lnComma2Pos = RAT( ',', lcFontString )
        lnFontSize = VAL( SUBSTR( lcFontString, lnComma1Pos + 1, ;
                    lnComma2Pos - lnComma1Pos - 1 ) )
        lcFontStyle = SUBSTR( lcFontString, lnComma2Pos + 1 )
        llBold = IIF( 'B' $ lcFontStyle, .T., .F. )
        llItalic = IIF( 'I' $ lcFontStyle, .T., .F. )
        .FontName = lcFontName
        .FontSize = lnFontSize
        .FontBold = llBold
        .FontItalic = llItalic
      ENDIF
```

```
ENDCASE
ENDWITH
```

The **GETFONT**() function returns a string in the form FontName, FontSize, FontStyle (where Fontstyle is 'B' if it is bold, 'I' if it is Italic and 'BI' if it is both). After parsing this font string, we convert the FontStyle characters, if any, to the logical values expected by the corresponding properties of the edit box.

The *Enlarge* method is used to expand the edit box, but the way in which the control is actually expanded has to take account of the various types of container in which it can be placed.

> *We could have called the method 'expand', but this is the sort of descriptive name that may well become a reserved word in some later version of Visual FoxPro. To program defensively we tend to shy away from using potential reserved words as method and field names. This has been a problem in the past as various versions of FoxPro have introduced new commands and functions. This holds true for Visual FoxPro too, as new properties, events and methods have been introduced. For example, many developers once used variables named OldVal or CurVal in FoxPro V2.x – only to have their code break when run in Visual FoxPro where both names refer to native functions.*

The code is, therefore, somewhat complex:

```
WITH This
  DO CASE
    CASE UPPER( .Parent.BaseClass ) = 'COLUMN'
```

If this is the *CurrentControl* in a grid column, we must expand the current grid cell before expanding the edit box. Then we can adjust the size of the edit box to fill the entire grid:

```
    .ExpandGridCell()
    .Height = .Parent.Parent.RowHeight
    .Width  = .Parent.Width

  CASE UPPER( .Parent.BaseClass ) = 'PAGE'
```

This is also a special case because pages do not have a height property. Instead the *PageFrame* itself has a *PageHeight* property, so we have to use that to expand the edit box:

```
    .Top    = 0
    .Left   = 0
    .Height = .Parent.Parent.PageHeight
    .Width  = .Parent.Parent.PageWidth
```

Then we must make sure the edit box appears on top of all the other controls on the page. Calling its *ZOrder* method with a parameter of 0 will do this:

```
.zOrder(0)
```

That takes care of the special cases. All other situations can be handled in the `Otherwise` clause as follows:

```
OTHERWISE
  .Top    = 0
  .Left   = 0
  .Height = .Parent.Height
  .Width  = .Parent.Width
  .zOrder(0)
ENDCASE
```

Finally, we must set the flag to indicate that the edit box is now in a maximized state:

```
.lMaximized = .T.
ENDWITH
```

If the edit box is in a grid, the handling requires a separate method to adjust both the column widths and the grid's *RowHeight* property before the edit box can be expanded. The *expandGridCell* method accomplishes this with just a few lines of code:

```
LOCAL lnCol
WITH This.Parent
```

First, we set the *ColumnWidth* property of all the columns in the grid to zero:

```
FOR lnCol = 1 TO .Parent.ColumnCount
  .Parent.Columns[lnCol].Width = 0
ENDFOR
```

Then we resize the *ColumnWidth* of the column containing the edit box to the same width as the grid. We also set the grid's *RowHeight* to the height of the grid itself (minus the *HeaderHeight* of the grid):

```
.Width             = .Parent.Width
.Parent.RowHeight  = .Parent.Height - .Parent.HeaderHeight
```

Finally, we must scroll the grid down until the current row is in the visible portion of the grid. The code below works because the visible portion of the grid, after it is resized, contains only a single row:

```
DO WHILE .Parent.RelativeRow # 1
  .Parent.DoScroll(1)
  ENDDO
ENDWITH
```

The *Shrink* method of the edit box, as its name implies, resizes the edit box to its original dimensions and contains similar code to that of the *Enlarge* method. In fact a good optimization for this control would be to add a '*SetParent*' method that would evaluate the parent container, make any adjustments required, and return the height and width to which the edit box should now be set. However, such a method would have to be *overloaded* to cope with both expanding and contracting the edit box. The approach we have taken is both simpler and clearer. As always we try to code with maintenance in mind.

Finally, we place a little code in the edit box's *Valid* method to shrink it in case the user decides to navigate to a new record while it is maximized. Most developers use some kind of *WriteBuffer* method that is called when the user clicks on a navigation button in a toolbar. This method, in its simplest form, contains code similar to this:

```
IF TYPE( '_Screen.ActiveForm.ActiveControl.Name' ) = 'C'
   *** For grid's you must drill down and set focus to the contained control
   IF UPPER( _Screen.ActiveForm.ActiveControl.BaseClass ) # 'GRID'
     _Screen.ActiveForm.ActiveControl.SetFocus()
   ENDIF
ENDIF
```

This will cause the *Valid* of the *ActiveControl* to fire. Obviously, it will also fire if the user clicks on a command button in order to navigate to a new record. So the code in the edit box's *Valid* method ensures that the control cleans up after itself even when the user forgets. It also strips any unprintable characters off the end of the memo field if the user has repeatedly pressed the **ENTER** key in an attempt to exit the field. This functionality is invoked when the edit box's *lCleanUpOnExit* property is set:

```
WITH This
   IF .lCleanUpOnExit
     .CleanUp()
   ENDIF
   IF .lMaximized
     .Shrink()
   ENDIF
ENDWITH
```

The Cleanup method works backwards from the last character in the field and removes any character whose ASCII value is less than 33 (the first printable, non-space character in the ASCII character set):

```
LOCAL lcMemoFld, lnChar
*** This will get rid of the empty lines which occur when the user presses
<Enter>
*** or other strange keys instead of <Tab> to exit the edit box
WITH This
   lcMemoFld = IIF( EMPTY( .Value ), '', ALLTRIM( .Value ) )
   *** Strip off invalid chars at the end of the MEMO-field.
   *** Loop backwards through the field and get the position of the
   *** first byte which is not a space, TAB or CR/LF or any other
   *** character with an ASCII-value smaller then 33:
   FOR lnChar = LEN( lcMemoFld ) TO 1 STEP -1
     IF ASC( SUBSTR( lcMemoFld, lnChar, 1 ) ) > 32
       EXIT
     ENDIF
   ENDFOR
   IF lnChar > 1
```

```
    lcMemoFld = LEFT( lcMemoFld, lnChar )
  ENDIF
  .Value = lcMemoFld
ENDWITH
```

Calendar combo *(Example: CH04.VCX::cntCalendar)*

This class is actually a composite designed to mimic the behavior of a drop-down list for entering dates. We have included it in our basic controls set because most applications require the entry/update of date fields.

The first step in creating this control was to create a subclass of Visual FoxPro's native container class as our own *cntBase* class. We based our *cntDate* class on this container rather than directly on the Visual FoxPro base class. To our new class we added a text box, a command button and finally an OLE Container object. (We used the *Insert Control* option of the OLE Container's native *Insert Object* dialog to select the calendar control that ships with Visual FoxPro and add it to the container.)

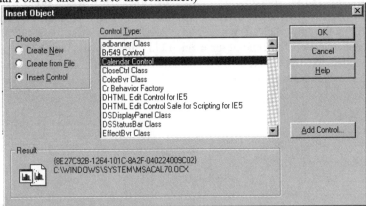

Figure 4.5 Insert object dialog

We generally design our composite classes so the member objects call container methods to perform their functions. For example, we could have just set the *ControlSource* of the text box in the container to bind to the underlying data source. Instead, we added a *cControlSource* property to *cntDate* as well as a *SetControlSource* method. The reason is so that at design time, we do not need to drill down into the container to set individual properties of the contained objects. Thus, to set up the contained text box we need only set the exposed *cControlSource* property on the container and leave the rest to the *SetControlSource* method, which is called from the container's *Init* method. The same method also initializes the caption of the command button so that it begins life as a *down* arrow.

We might have made this the default in the button and, indeed we tried to do so. However, testing the control after it was dropped on a form yielded inconsistent results. Sometimes it would display the desired down arrow while at other times it would display an up arrow when the form was instantiated. We found no obvious explanation for the behavior but did establish that the only way to prevent this inconsistency was to initialize the button's caption upon instantiation:

```
WITH This
  .txtDate.ControlSource = .cControlSource
  .CmdDrop.Caption = CHR( 25 )
ENDWITH
```

The drop-down functionality is implemented through three custom methods; *DropCalendar*, *PopCalendar* and *SetCalendar*.

DropCalendar makes the calendar visible and changes the caption on the command button from a down arrow to an up arrow. It is called from the click method of the command button and the *KeyPress* method of the text box. Since we want this control to behave like a combo, the calendar is opened whenever the user presses either **F4** or **ALT+DNARROW**:

```
WITH This
  .OleCalendar.Visible = .T.
  .cmdDrop.Caption = CHR( 24 )
ENDWITH
```

PopCalendar hides the opened calendar when either the command button is clicked or an entry is made from the calendar. It also updates the value of the text box with the value selected from the calendar. Finally, it changes the icon on the command button from an up arrow to a down arrow:

```
WITH This
  .txtDate.Value = TTOD( .OleCalendar.Object.Value )
  .OleCalendar.Visible = .F.
  .cmdDrop.Caption = CHR( 25 )
ENDWITH
```

SetCalendar synchronizes the date display of the calendar with the value contained in the text box. It is called from the *LostFocus* method of the text box in case the calendar is visible when the user types a new date in the text box. It is also called from the *Refresh* method to take care of the possibility that the user has navigated to a new record while the calendar is visible by ensuring that both the text box and the calendar display the same date. Finally, we call the *SetCalendar* directly from the container's *DropCalendar* method to ensure the correct date is always displayed when the calendar is made visible:

```
WITH This
  .OleCalendar.Object.Value = .txtDate.Value
  .OleCalendar.Refresh()
ENDWITH
```

We also need some code to mimic the native behavior of drop-down lists, which can be opened using **F4** or **<ALT>+<DNARROW>**. We trap these keys in the *Keypress* method of the text box so we can make the calendar visible when they are detected:

```
*** Check for F4 and ALT+DNARROW
IF ( nKeyCode = -3 ) OR ( nKeyCode = 160 )
  WITH This.Parent
    *** Make the calendar visible if it isn't
    IF ! .OleCalendar.Visible
      .DropCalendar()
      NODEFAULT
    ENDIF
  ENDWITH
ENDIF
```

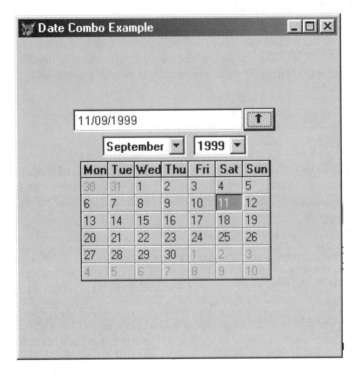

Figure 4.6 *Calendar Combo*

The only other code in this class is in the *AfterUpdate* method of the calendar control itself. It simply calls the container's *PopCalendar* method to update the text box with the value that was selected and make the calendar invisible.

Command buttons *(Example: CH04.VCX::cmdBase)*

Besides allowing the user to enter data, most applications also allow the user to take some sort of action. This is where command buttons, or some variation like toolbar buttons, enter the picture. As we discussed in the chapter on design, clicking a command button should give the user instant feedback that something has occurred. You can easily do this by disabling it, preventing the user from clicking it repeatedly and perhaps locking up the system. We put this functionality in our command button base class. Of course, you may not want every command button in all of your applications to exhibit this type of behavior. We planned ahead and added the property *lDisableOnClick* to the class. This way, clicking the command button only disables it when this property is set to true. We also added a custom *OnClick* method to this class. The command button's click calls its *onClick* method. Any instance specific code always goes in this *onClick* method.

The only code in our command button base class resides in its click method:

```
WITH This
  *** Disable the button if specified
  IF .lDisableOnClick
    .Enabled = .F.
  ENDIF
  *** Execute the custom code
  .OnClick()
  *** Re-enable the button
  IF ! .lDisableOnClick
    .Enabled = .T.
  ENDIF
ENDWITH
```

Notice that this approach allows us to disable a button and leave it disabled by changing its *lDisAbleOnClick* property in an instance's *OnClick* method. This is useful for buttons that should only be used once and are only enabled when some external condition is met (e.g. a 'Save' or 'Revert' button).

Gotcha! Programming the logical controls

Check boxes are designed primarily to handle logical data (i.e. Yes/No, On/Off etc). The *Style* property determines whether the checkbox is displayed conventionally or as a button. When using the mouse, there are only two possible values for a checkbox, a logical .T. (or numeric 1) and logical .F. (numeric 0).

The value property can accept either logical or numeric values and can even interchange between the two types providing that the control is not bound. However, setting the value programmatically to anything other than .T. or .F. or to any numeric value other than 0 or 1 gives a strange result, as **Figure 4.7** shows:

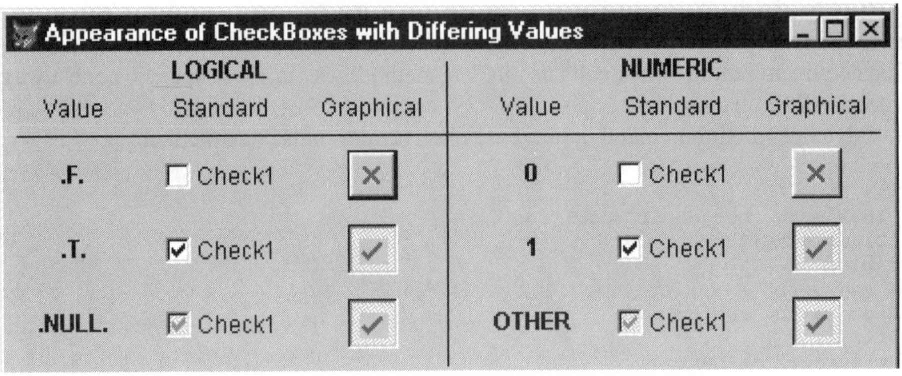

Figure 4.7 Check box programmatic behavior

Notice that the conventional check box appears to be both checked *and* disabled at the same time when an invalid value is specified. Worse, for the graphical style check box, there is no apparent difference between a valid positive and an invalid value! However, the saving grace is that in all cases and despite the visual appearance, the Value property *does* return the actual value.

Pages and page frames   *(Example: CH04.VCX::pgfBase and CH04.PRG)*
You can subclass Visual FoxPro's *pageframe* base class visually in the class designer. There is only one small problem – all of the contained pages are Visual FoxPro base class pages and there is no way of subclassing the *Page* base class visually. Worse yet, if you make a subclass for the *pageframe* and give it, for example, three pages, you cannot later use it on a form and remove one of the pages in the form designer. You will also find that if you use this type of subclassed page frame, you cannot even change the names of the pages in an instance of it.

This is because you cannot delete or change the names of contained objects that belong to a parent class. For this reason it is best, when subclassing the page frame, to set its *PageCount* property to 0 in the subclass. However, there may be situations in which you need to add methods directly to pages rather than to the page frame, something you can only do if you create a custom page class.

Actually you can subclass the page base class. You just can't do it visually in the class designer. It must be done in code. The good news is this is an easy task. Now for the bad news – the only way we found to use our custom pages was by adding them to our custom page frame at run time. The page frame does not have any accessible property to store to the class on which to base its pages and always instantiates the number of required pages from the Visual FoxPro Page base class. This means that custom pages are virtually useless unless you intend to use *delayed instantiation*.

Aside: what is 'delayed instantiation'?

Delayed instantiation is a technique in which an object is only instantiated when it is actually required. In the context of a page frame this means that when you have designed a page, you select all its controls (CTRL+A will do this) and then choose 'Save As Class' from the File menu. This will copy all the controls into a Visual FoxPro container class and save it as a new class. Now you can delete all the controls from the page and add them back by dropping your new container class on to the page and positioning it. Make a note of the *Top* and *Left* property values for the new container – you will need these later when you add the container at run time! Finally you can delete the entire page contents, leaving it blank and repeat the process for all pages in your page frame.

Note that you must plan your page's object hierarchy properly in order for this to work. Adding the controls to a container also adds an extra layer of referencing because the container now sits between the controls it contains and the page. So any references to the page as:

```
This.Parent.<something>
```

Must be replaced with:

```
This.Parent.Parent.<something>
```

to account for this. Another possibility is to use a constant if you are prototyping and then save the container class. So, instead of referring to This.Parent.<something>, you could #DEFINE Mom This.Parent and refer to the other objects as Mom.<Something>. Then you only need to change the way the constant is defined after the container is saved as a class. Finally you just add code directly to each page's *Activate* method like this:

```
IF This.ControlCount = 0
 This.AddObject( 'pagctrls', <controlclass> )
 WITH This.pagctrls
  .Top = <saved top position>
  .Left = <saved left position>
  .Visible = .T.
 ENDWITH
ENDIF
```

Now when you run the form containing this page frame, each page will be empty when the form instantiates, so the form will appear much quicker than normal (after all Visual FoxPro does not now have to instantiate and bind all of the controls on the 'invisible' pages). When the user clicks on a page for the first time, the appropriate container, with all the controls, is instantiated. While there is obviously a small delay upon first clicking a page, it is rarely noticeable to the users who will normally be very happy that their forms appear so much faster!

Now back to custom pages

In order to make use of custom pages we created a custom page frame class (*pgfBase*) in the class designer and set its *PageCount* and *ActivePage* properties to 0. It has one custom method named *SetPages* that is called from the *Init* method and whose sole purpose is to remove Visual FoxPro's base class pages and add our custom pages at run time. Here it is:

```
LOCAL lnPageCount, lnCnt
*** Make sure we can find the prg that defines the custom pages
SET PROC TO CH04 ADDITIVE
*** Remove base class pages and add our custom pages
WITH This
  lnPageCount = .PageCount
  .PageCount = 0
  .ActivePage = 0

  FOR lnCnt = 1 TO lnPageCount
  *** Add new one
    .AddObject( 'PgBase'+ALLTRIM( STR( lnCnt ) ), 'PgBase' )
  ENDFOR
  .PageCount = lnPageCount
  .ActivePage = 1
ENDWITH
```

However, we couldn't think of any other custom property or method which our new page frame class needed. Communication between pages could be handled by custom methods of the page frame that contains them. Typically this type of communication is handled by custom form methods. Arguably the page frame would actually be the more appropriate mediator.

Next, we defined our custom page class in code. We gave it a custom property called *lRefreshOnActivate*. When set to true, the page is refreshed when it becomes active and we added a custom method called *RefreshPage* that is used to wrap the page's refresh method in the same way that our *RefreshForm* method wraps the form's refresh method. We also added the property *lReadOnly* to allow our page frame to contain a combination of editable and view only pages. Our custom page checks this property in its *Activate* and sets its contained controls appropriately using a single line of code:

```
WITH This
  .SetAll( 'Enabled', !.lReadOnly )
ENDWITH
```

Just to be flexible, we also added this code to our *RefreshPage* method in case some action taken by the user (clicking on a toolbar button, for example) could possibly change the state of the current page. Finally, we gave it a *cPrimaryTable* property to be used for those forms that update multiple tables. In forms of this type, most developers tend to display the individual tables on separate pages. This addition of this property to the page enables the code that is written to be more generic:

```
DEFINE CLASS PgBase AS Page

lRefreshOnActivate = .T.
lReadOnly = .F.
cPrimaryTable = ''

FUNCTION Activate
  WITH This
    .SetAll( 'Enabled', !.lReadOnly )
  ENDWITH
ENDFUNC
```

```
FUNCTION RefreshPage
  *** This is a template method akin to RefreshForm
  *** If you need to refresh this page, put code here instead of in Refresh
  WITH This
    .SetAll( 'Enabled', !.lReadOnly )
  ENDWITH
ENDFUNC


ENDDEFINE
```

It seems that the class definition of the page frame is intrinsically linked to its contained pages at instantiation. We created a little page frame builder (*pgfbuild.prg*) in an attempt to add our custom pages to the page frame at design time. It appeared to work until we tried to run the form. Then, to our surprise, the snazzy new custom pages we had just added had been replaced by Visual FoxPro base class pages for no apparent reason!

The reason becomes apparent if you open an *SCX* file containing a page frame as a table and browse it. There is no record for any of the pages in the page frame and therefore no means for the page frame to determine which class to base its pages on. Instead, the properties field for the page frame object defines all the properties for its contained pages. Another interesting point is that after running our builder, the properties field of the page frame referenced those pages by the names that we had given them and showed them as being our custom pages! But when we looked at this same form in the form designer, the property sheet listed the pages as base class pages with the default names 'Page1', 'Page2', and so on. (Incidentally, the same appears to be true for Grids and their Columns. While you can specify custom headers for columns, and any control you like for inclusion in a column, grids always instantiate the actual columns directly from the Visual FoxPro base class.)

If you would like to see this behavior for yourself, just run the program *pages.prg* that is included with the sample code for this chapter. Set the number of pages in the page frame to some number greater than zero and run the builder. When the browse window appears, fill in the names and captions of your choice. Close and save the form. When you do, *pages.prg* runs the form that was just saved.

The conclusion is, therefore, that although you **can** define a custom page class and use a builder to add pages based on that class to a page frame at design time, the changes you make are lost when the page frame is instantiated. To use pages based on a custom class you must add them at run time, which means they must either be defined with all necessary controls, or you must add the controls individually (using the *AddObject* method) or use the deferred instantiation technique referred to above.

Our intention here was to give you an easy and convenient way to add custom pages to your own custom page frame in the form designer. Much to our disappointment, we discovered that it just couldn't be done. But at least we now know.

Chapter 5
Combos and Lists

"Why can't somebody give us a list of things that everybody thinks and nobody says, and another list of things that everybody says and nobody thinks."
("The Professor at the Breakfast-Table" by Oliver Wendell Holmes, Sr.)

Combos and lists are two very powerful controls that allow the user to select from a predetermined set of values. Used properly, they provide a valuable means of ensuring data validity. Used improperly, they can be your worst nightmare. If you use a combo box to present the user with thousands of items, you are asking for trouble! In this chapter, we present some handy combo and lists classes that can be used to provide a polished, professional interface while significantly reducing your development time. All the classes presented in this chapter can be found in the CH05 class library.

Combo and list box basics

One look at the properties and methods of combo and list boxes, and you can see they function internally in much the same way. Although a drop-down combo allows you to add items to its *RowSource*, you can't do this with a drop-down or scrolling list – or rather not with native base class controls. With no less than ten possible *RowSourceTypes* and two different ways of handling their internal lists (*ListItemID* and *ListIndex*), these classes provide the developer with almost too much flexibility. Of the ten *RowSourceTypes*, *0-None, 1-Value, 2-Alias, 3-SQL Statement, 5-Array and 6-Fields* are the most useful. This chapter contains examples using these six *RowSourceTypes*.

The remaining four, *4-Query (.QPR), 7-Files, 8-Structure* and *9-Popup* are not covered because they are either very specific in their nature (*7-Files* and *8-Structure*) or are included to provide backward compatibility (*4-Query* and *9-Popup*) and do not fit in the context of a Visual FoxPro application.

List and ListItem collections

These two collections allow you to access the items in the control's internal list without having to know anything about its specific *RowSource* or *RowSourceType*. Because of this, these collections and their associated properties and methods can be used to write some very generic code. The *List* collection references the items contained in the list in the same order in which they are displayed. The *ListItem* collection references these same items by their *ItemID's*. The *ItemID* is a unique number, analogous to a primary key that is assigned to items when they are added to the list. Initially, the *Index* and the *ItemID* of a specific item in the list are identical. But as items are sorted, removed and added, these numbers are not necessarily the same anymore.

Table 5.1 *Properties and methods associated with the List collection*

Property or method	What does it do?
List	Contains a character string used to access the items in the list by index. Not available at design time. Read only at run time.
ListIndex	Contains the index of the selected item in the list or 0 if nothing is selected
NewIndex	Contains the index of the item most recently added to the list. It is very useful when adding items to a sorted list. Not available at design time. Read only at run time.
TopIndex	Contains the index of the item that appears at the top of the list. Not available at design time. Read only at run time.
AddItem	Adds an item to a list with RowSourceType 0-none or 1-value
IndexToItemID	Returns the ItemID for an item in the list when you know its index
RemoveItem	Removes an item from a list with RowSourceType 0-none or 1-value

Table 5.2 *Properties and methods associated with the ListItem collection*

Property or method	What does it do?
ListItem	Contains a character string used to access the items in the list by ItemID. Not available at design time. Read only at run time.
ListItemID	Contains the ItemID of the selected item in the list or -1 if nothing is selected
NewItemID	Contains the ItemID of the item most recently added to the list. It is very useful when adding items to a sorted list. Not available at design time. Read only at run time.
TopItemID	Contains the ItemID of the item that appears at the top of the list. Not available at design time. Read only at run time.
AddListItem	Adds an item to a list with RowSourceType 0-none or 1-value
IItemIDToIndex	Returns the Index for an item in the list when you know its itemID
RemoveListItem	Removes an item from a list with RowSourceType 0-none or 1-value

Gotcha! AddItem

The online help states that the syntax for this command is `Control.AddItem(cItem [, nIndex] [, nColumn])`. It goes on to say that when you specify the optional nIndex and nColumn parameters, the new item is added to that row and column in the control. If you specify a row that already exists, the new item is inserted at that row and the remaining items are moved down a row. Sounds good! Unfortunately, it doesn't work quite like that.

The *AddItem* method really adds an entire row to the list. If the list has multiple columns and you use this syntax to add items to each column, the result is not what you would expect. When using the *AddItem* method to populate a combo or list, add the new item to the first column of each row using the syntax `Control.AddItem( 'MyNewValue' )`. Assign values to the remaining columns in that row using the syntax `Control.List[Control.NewIndex, nColumn] = 'MyOtherNewValue'`. The *AddListItem* method, however, does work as advertised. This gotcha! is clearly illustrated in the form ListAndListItem, included with the sample code for this chapter.

When do the events fire?

The answer to that, as usual, is "it depends." The events fire a little differently depending on the style of the combo box. The order in which they fire also depends on whether the user is navigating and selecting items with the mouse or with the keyboard. It is a gross understatement to say understanding the event model is important when one is programming in an object-oriented environment. This is absolutely critical when creating reusable classes, especially complex classes like combo and list boxes.

As expected, the first events that fire when the control gets focus are *When* and *GotFocus*. This is true for combo boxes of both styles as well as list boxes. And these events occur in this order whether you tab into the control or click on it with the mouse. Once small peculiarity about the drop-down combo is that the next event to fire is *Combo.Text1.GotFocus*! Text1 is not accessible to the developer. Visual FoxPro responds to any attempt to access it in code with "Unknown member: TEXT1." We assume that text1 is a protected member of Visual FoxPro's base class combo when it's style is set to 0 – DropDown Combo.

The following list contains the events that you will most often be concerned with when dealing with combo and list boxes. It is by no means a comprehensive list, but all the significant events are there. For example, the MouseDown and MouseUp events fire before the object's Click event. For the sake of simplicity and clarity, the mouse events are omitted.

Table 5.3 *Combo and list box event sequence*

Action	DropDown Combo	DropDown List	ListBox
Scroll through list using the down arrow (without dropping the combo's list first)	Not applicable	KeyPress(24, 0) InteractiveChange Click Valid When	KeyPress(24, 0) InteractiveChange Click When
Use the mouse to drop the list	DropDown	DropDown	Not Applicable
Use ALT+DNARROW to drop the list	KeyPress(160, 4) DropDown	KeyPress(160, 4) DropDown	Not Applicable
Scroll through dropped-down list using the down arrow	KeyPress(24, 0) InteractiveChange	KeyPress(24, 0) InteractiveChange	KeyPress(24, 0) InteractiveChange Click When
Select an item in the list using the mouse	InteractiveChange Click Valid When	InteractiveChange Click Valid When	InteractiveChange Click When
Select an item in the list by pressing the <ENTER> key	KeyPress(13, 0) Click Valid	KeyPress(13, 0) Click Valid	KeyPress(13, 0) DblClick Valid
Exit the control by clicking elsewhere with the mouse	Valid LostFocus Text1.LostFocus	LostFocus	LostFocus
Exit the control using the <TAB> key	KeyPress(9, 0) Valid LostFocus Text1.LostFocus	KeyPress(9, 0) LostFocus	KeyPress(9, 0) LostFocus

It is interesting to note that the *Valid* event does **not** fire when the control loses focus for either the DropDown List or the ListBox. One consequence of this behavior is that any code called from the *Valid* method will not get executed when the user merely tabs through a DropDown List or a ListBox. In our opinion, this is a good thing. It means that we can place code that updates underlying data sources in methods called from the *Valid* method of these controls and not worry about dirtying the buffers if the user hasn't changed anything.

It is also worth noting that for ComboBoxes, the *Valid* event fires whenever the user selects an item from the list. (However, if the user selects an item in the list by clicking on it with the mouse, the *When* event also fires.) Conversely for ListBoxes, the *Valid* event only fires when the user selects an item by pressing the ENTER key or by double clicking on it. It is interesting to note that selecting an item with the ENTER key also fires the *dblClick* event.

Another anomaly worth noting is that the *Click* event of the ListBox fires inconsistently depending on which key is used to navigate the list! When the user presses the up arrow and down arrow keys, the *Click* event fires. When the page up and page down keys are used, it doesn't.

How do I bind my combo and list boxes?

Obviously, you bind your combo and list boxes by setting the *ControlSource* property to the name of a field in a table, cursor, or view or to a form property. One gotcha! to be aware of is that you can only bind these controls to character, numeric, or null data sources. If you try to bind a combo or list box to a Date or DateTime field, Visual FoxPro will complain and display the following error at run time:

Error with <ComboName>-Value: Data Type Mismatch.
  Unbinding object <ComboName>

If you must bind a combo or list box to a Date or DateTime field, you will have to resort to a little trickery. In this case you cannot use *RowSourceTypes* of 2-Alias or 6-Fields. You can, for example, set the *RowSourceType* to 3-SQL Statement and use a SQL statement similar to this as the *RowSource:*

```
SELECT DTOC( DateField ) AS DisplayDate, yada, nada, blah FROM MyTable ;
    ORDER BY MyTable.DateField INTO CURSOR MyCursor
```

Leave the *ControlSource* blank and add this code to its *Valid* method to update the date field in the underlying table:

```
REPLACE DateField WITH CTOD( This.Value ) IN MyTable
```

You will also need to write some code to manually update the control's *Value* from its *ControlSource* to mimic the behavior of a bound control when you *Refresh* it. This code in the combo or list box's *Refresh* method does the trick:

```
This.Value = DTOC( MyTable.DateField )
```

Another gotcha! that may bite you occurs when the *ControlSource* of your combo box refers to a numeric value that contains negative numbers. This appears to be a problem that only occurs when the *RowSourceType* of the control is 3-SQL Statement and may actually be a bug in Visual FoxPro. The result is that nothing at all is displayed in the text portion of the control for any negative values. However, even though the control's *DisplayValue* is blank, its *Value* is correct. The easy workaround is to use a *RowSourceType,* other than 3-SQL Statement, when the control is bound to a data source that can contain negative values. It's not as if there are a lack of alternatives.

So what are BoundTo and BoundColumn used for?

These properties determine how the control gets its value. The value of a combo or list box is taken from the column of its internal list that is specified by its *BoundColumn.* A combo box's *DisplayValue*, the value that is displayed in the text portion of the control, **always comes from column one!** Its value, on the other hand, can be taken from any column of its internal list. This means you can display meaningful text, such as the description from a lookup table, at the same time the control gets its value from the associated key. You do not even have to display this associated key in the list to have access to it.

For example, suppose the user must assign a particular contact type to each contact when it is entered. The appropriate contact type can be selected from a DropDown List with its *RowSourceType* set to 6-Fields, its *RowSource* set to "`ContactType.CT_Type, CT_Key`" where `CT_Type` is the description and `CT_Key` is its associated key in the *ContactType* table. To set up the control, first set the DropDown List's *ColumnCount* to 2 and its *ColumnWidths* to 150, 0. Then set the *BoundColumn* to 2 to update the bound field in the *Contacts* table from the key value instead of the description.

The setting of *BoundTo* specifies whether the value property of a combo or list box is determined by its *List* or its *ListIndex* property. The setting of *BoundTo* only matters when the control is bound to a numeric data source. If the *ControlSource* of the combo or list box refers to numeric data, setting the control's *BoundTo* property to true tells Visual FoxPro to update the *ControlSource* using the data from the bound column of the control's internal list. Leaving *BoundTo* set to false here causes the *ControlSource* to be updated with the control's *ListIndex*, that is, the row number of the currently selected item.

The easiest way to illustrate how this works is by using a little code that simulates how the setting of the *BoundTo* property affects the way in which the control's *Value* property is updated:

```
WITH This
  IF .BoundTo
    .Value = VAL( .List[.ListIndex, .BoundColumn] )
  ELSE
    .Value = .ListIndex
  ENDIF
ENDIF
```

How do I refer to the items in my combo and list boxes?

As discussed earlier, you can use either the *List* or *ListItem* collection to refer to the items in your combo or list box. The big advantage to using these collections to access the items in the control's *RowSource* is that it is not necessary to know anything about that *RowSource*. You can use either *ListIndex* or *ListItemID* property to refer to the currently selected row. If nothing in the list is selected, the control's *ListIndex* property is 0 and its *ListItemID* property is –1. So in the *Valid* method of the combo box or the *LostFocus* method of the list box, you can check to see if the user selected something like this:

```
WITH This
  IF .ListIndex = 0    && You can also use .ListItemID = -1 here
    MESSAGEBOX( 'You must select an item from the list', 16, ;
                'Please make a selection' )
    IF LOWER( .BaseClass ) = 'combobox'
      RETURN 0          && If this code is in the valid of a combo box
    ELSE
      NODEFAULT         && If this code is in the LostFocus of a ListBox
    ENDIF
  ENDIF
ENDWITH
```

There are also several ways to refer to the value of a combo or list box. The simplest of them all is `Control.Value`. When nothing is selected, the control's value is empty. This is something to be considered if the *RowSource* for the control permits empty values. It means you cannot determine whether the user has made a selection merely by checking for an empty value property.

Because the *List* and *ListItem* collections are arrays, you can address them as you would any other array. (However, although you can address these collections as arrays, you cannot actually manipulate them directly using the native Visual FoxPro array functions such as `ASCAN()`, `ADEL()` or `ALEN()`.)

To access the selected item in the control's internal list when its *ListIndex* is greater than zero you can use:

```
Control.List[Control.ListIndex, Control.BoundColumn]
```

while this does exactly the same thing when its *ListItemID* is not –1:

```
Control.ListItem[Control.ListItemID, Control.BoundColumn]
```

You can also access the items in the other columns of the selected row of the control by referring to Control.List[Control.ListIndex, 1], Control.List[Control.ListIndex, 2], and so on all the way up to and including Control.List[Control.ListIndex, Control.ColumnCount].

Remember that, when using the control's *List* and *ListItem* collections in this manner, all the items in the control's internal list are stored as character strings. If the control's *RowSource* contains numeric, date, or datetime values, these items will **always** be represented internally as character strings. This means that if you want to perform some "behind the scenes" updates using the items in the currently selected row of the list, you will need to convert these items to the appropriate data type first. Otherwise, Visual FoxPro will complain, giving you a data type mismatch error.

List boxes with *MultiSelect* set to true behave a little bit differently. Its *ListIndex* and *ListItemID* properties point to the last row in the control that was selected. To do something with all of the control's selected items, it is necessary to loop through its internal list and check the *Selected* property of each item like so:

```
WITH Thisform.LstMultiSelect
  FOR lnCnt = 1 TO .ListCount
    IF .Selected[lnCnt]
      *** The item is selected, take the appropriate action
    ELSE
      *** It isn't selected, do something else if necessary
    ENDIF
  ENDFOR
ENDWITH
```

What is the difference between DisplayValue and Value?

Combo boxes are particularly powerful controls because they enable you to display descriptive text from a lookup table while binding the control to its associated key value. This is possible only because the combo box has these two properties. Understanding the role each of them plays can be confusing, to say the least.

DisplayValue is the descriptive text that is displayed in the textbox portion of the control. This is what you see when the combo box is "closed". The combo's *DisplayValue* always comes from the first column of its *RowSource*. On the other hand, the combo's *Value* comes from whichever column is specified as its *BoundColumn*. If the *BoundColumn* of the combo box is column one, its *Value* and *DisplayValue* are the same when the user picks an item from the list. When the control's *BoundColumn* is not column one, these two properties are not the same. See **Table 5.4** below for the differences between these two properties in different situations.

Table 5.4 *Combo and list box event sequence*

Bound Column	Action	DisplayValue	Value
1	Select an item in the list	Column 1 of selected row	Column 1 of selected row
1	Type item not in list	Typed text	Empty
N # 1	Select an item in the list	Column 1 of selected row	Column n of selected row
N # 1	Type item not in list	Typed text	Empty

What's the difference between RowSourceTypes "alias" and "fields"?

The basic difference is that *RowSourceType* "2-Alias" allows the *RowSource* property to contain just an Alias name. The control fills the number of columns it has available (defined by the *ColumnCount* property) by reading the data from the fields in the specified alias in the order in which they are defined. You may, however, specify a list of fields that are to be used even when the *RowSourceType* is set to "2-Alias." In this case there is no practical difference between the *Fields* and the *Alias* settings.

When using RowSourceType "6-Fields" the RowSource property **must** be filled in using the following format:

```
<Alias Name>.<first field>,<second field>,…….<last field>
```

When using either *RowSourceType* "2-Alias" or "6-Fields," you can still access **any** of the fields in the underlying data source - even if they are not specifically included in the *RowSource*. It is also worth remembering that whenever a selection is made, the record pointer in the underlying data source is automatically moved to the appropriate record. However if no valid selection is made, the record pointer is left at the last record in the data source - not, as you might expect, at `EOF()`.

> By the way, when using RowSourceType of "3-SQL", always select
> INTO a destination cursor when specifying the RowSource. Failing to
> specify a target cursor will result in a browse window being displayed!
> The behavior of the cursor is the same as when using a table or view directly - all
> fields in the cursor are available, and selecting an item in the list moves the record
> pointer in the cursor.

How do I make my combo and list boxes point to a particular item?

When these are bound controls, they automatically display the selection specified by their *ControlSources* so you don't need to do anything at all. But what if the control isn't bound or you want to display some default value when adding a new record? As usual, there is more than one way to skin a fox. Perhaps the easiest way to accomplish this is:

```
Thisform.MyList.ListIndex = 1
```

This statement, either in the form's *Init* method or immediately after adding a new record, selects the first item in the list. You can also initialize a combo or list box by directly setting its value. However, when initializing combos and lists that are bound to buffered data, the act of doing so will dirty the buffers. This means that if you have a routine that checks for changes to the current record using GETFLDSTATE(), the function will detect the "change" in the current record even though the user hasn't touched a single key. To avoid undesirable side effects, such as the user being prompted to save changes when he thinks he hasn't made any, use SETFLDSTATE() to reset any affected fields after initializing the value of your bound combo or list box.

One thing that will **not** initialize the value of a combo or list box is setting the selected property of one of its list items to true in the *Init* method of a form. The statement:

```
Thisform.MyList.Selected[1]
```

in the form's *Init* method, does **not** select an item in a combo or list box. This same statement in the form's *Activate* method will, however, achieve the desired result so we suspect the failure of the statement when used in the form's *Init* method might actually be a bug.

Quickfill combos *(Example: CH05.VCX::cboQFill)*

One example of quickfill methodology (and a more detailed explanation of just what "quickfill" is) was presented in Chapter 4 in the incremental search TextBox. This methodology is even easier to implement for the ComboBox class. Quickfill combo boxes give your forms a polished and professional look. They also make the task of selecting an item in the list much easier for the end user. Just type the letter 'S' in the text portion of the combo, and 'Samuel' is displayed. Next type the letter 'm' and the *DisplayValue* changes to 'Smith.' Very cool stuff!

Our quickfill combo can be used no matter what the *RowSource* of the ComboBox happens to be because it operates on the control's internal list. For this reason, it should only be used for controls that display, at most, a few dozen items. If you require this functionality, but need to display hundreds of items, we refer you to Tamar Granor's article on the subject in the September 1998 issue of *FoxPro Advisor*.

The quickfill combo has one custom property called *cOldExact*. Because we are looking for the first item that matches what has been typed in so far, we want to SET EXACT OFF. In the control's *GotFocus* method, the original value of SET('EXACT') is saved so it can be restored when the control loses focus. When SET('EXACT') = 'OFF', there is no need to use the *LEFT()* function to compare what the user has typed so far to find the closest match in the list. This improves the performance of the search.

Just as in the incremental search TextBox described earlier, the *HandleKey* method is invoked from the control's *InteractiveChange* method after the keystrokes have already been processed. In fact, there is no code at all in the ComboBox's *KeyPress* method. The *InteractiveChange* method contains only the code necessary to determine if the key must be handled:

```
IF This.SelStart > 0
  *** Handle printable character, backspace, and delete keys
  IF ( LASTKEY() > 31 AND LASTKEY() < 128 ) OR ( LASTKEY() = 7 )
    This.HandleKey()
  ENDIF
ENDIF
```

Most of the work is accomplished in the *HandleKey* method. It iterates through the combo's internal list to find a match for what the user has typed in so far:

```
LOCAL lcSofar, lnSelStart, lnSelLength, lnRow

WITH This
  *** Handle backspace key
  IF LASTKEY() = 127
      .SelStart = .SelStart - 1
  ENDIF

  *** Save the insertion point and extract what the user has typed so far
  lnSelStart = .SelStart
  lcSofar = LEFT( .DisplayValue, lnSelStart )

  *** Find a match in the first column of the combo's internal list
  FOR lnRow = 1 TO .ListCount
      IF UPPER( .List[ lnRow, 1 ] ) = UPPER( lcSoFar )
          .ListIndex = lnRow
          EXIT
      ENDIF
  ENDFOR

  *** Highlight the portion of the value after the insertion point
  .SelStart = lnSelStart
  lnSelLength = LEN( ALLTRIM( .DisplayValue ) ) - lnSelStart
  IF lnSelLength > 0
      .SelLength =  lnSelLength
```

```
    ENDIF
    ENDWITH
```

This is all that is required for a quickfill combo that works with any *RowSourceType*. Just drop it on a form and set its *RowSourceType, RowSource* and *ControlSource* (if it is to be a bound control). Nothing could be easier. The form Quickfill.scx, provided with the sample code for this chapter, illustrates the use of this class with several different *RowSourceTypes*.

How do I add new items to my combo and list boxes?
(Example: CH05.VCX::cboAddNew and lstAddNew)

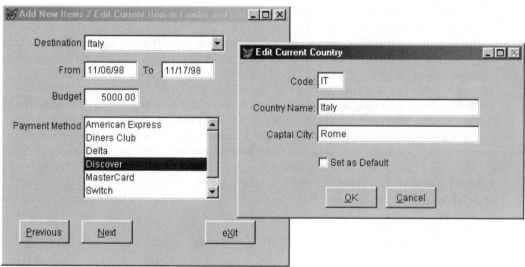

Figure 5.1 *Add new items and edit existing items in combo and list boxes*

Adding a new item to a ComboBox with style = 0-DropDown Combo is a pretty straightforward process because the control's *Valid* event fires whenever a selection is made from the list and again before it loses focus. When a user has typed something that is not in the current list, the control's *DisplayValue* property will hold the newly entered data but the *Value* property will be empty. A little code in the *Valid* method of the control allows you to determine whether the user selected an item in the list or typed a value not in the list. For example the following code could be used:

```
IF  NOT( EMPTY( This.DisplayValue ) ) AND EMPTY( This.Value )
   *** The user has typed in a value not in the list
```

However, this will not be reliable if the *RowSource* allows for empty values so a better solution is to use either:

```
IF  NOT( EMPTY( This.DisplayValue ) ) AND This.ListIndex = 0
```

OR

```
If  NOT( EMPTY( This.DisplayValue ) ) AND This.ListItemID = -1
```

You must then take action to add the new item to the control's *RowSource*. The code used to do this will be instance specific, depending on how the control is populated. If the combo's *RowSourceType* is "0-None" or "1-Value," use the *AddItem* or *AddListItem* method to add the new value to the list. If the *RowSourceType* is "2-Alias," "3-SQL Statement" or "6-Fields," the new item must be added to the underlying table and the combo or list box requeried to refresh its internal list. For *RowSourceType* "5-Array," add the item to the array and requery the control.

Although it is simple enough to add a new item to a DropDown Combo, this simplistic solution may not be adequate. If the only requirement is to add a new description along with its primary key to a lookup table, the methodology discussed above is up to the task. Much of the time, however, a lookup table contains more than two columns. (For example, the lookup table provided with the sample code for this chapter has a column for a user-defined code.) Additional fields may also need to be populated when a new item is added to the combo box.

We must also consider the fact that there is no quick and easy way to add new items to a ListBox. Considering how similar the ComboBox and ListBox classes are, we think it is appropriate that they share a common interface for adding new items. If the end-users add new items in the same manner, they have one thing to remember instead of two. The *cboAddNew* and *lstAddNew* classes provide this functionality through a shortcut menu invoked by right clicking the control. This shortcut menu also provides edit functionality. More often than not, if an item in a combo or list is misspelled, the user will realize it when he is selecting an item from the list. It is much more convenient to fix the mistake at this point, than having to use a separate maintenance form.

We created *cboAddNew* as a subclass of *cboQuickfill* to achieve a more consistent user interface. All of our custom combo box classes inherit from our quickfill combo class, so all behave in a similar manner. This type of consistency helps make an application feel intuitive to end users.

The "Add New" combo and list box classes have three additional properties. The *cForm2Call* property contains the name of the maintenance form to instantiate when the user wants to add or edit an item. The settings of the *lAllowNew* and *lAllowEdit* properties determine whether new items can be added or existing items edited. They are, by default, set to true because the object of this exercise is to allow new items to be added and current items to be edited. However, when designing the class we did our best to build in maximum flexibility, so these properties can be set to override this behavior at the instance level.

The code that does most of the work resides in the custom *ShowMenu* method and is called from the *RightClick* method of both. In this example, the combo's *BoundColumn* contains the primary key associated with the underlying data. It is assumed that the maintenance form will return the primary key after it adds a new item (If you need different functionality, code it accordingly.):

```
LOCAL lnRetVal, loparameters
PRIVATE pnMenuChoice
```

```
WITH This
  *** Don't display the menu if we can't add or edit
  IF .lAllowNew OR .lAllowEdit
    *** Display the shortcut menu
    pnMenuChoice = 0
    DO mnuCombo.mpr
    IF pnMenuChoice > 0
      *** Create the parameter object and populate it
      loParameters = CREATEOBJECT( 'Line' )
      loParameters.AddProperty('cAction', IIF( pnMenuChoice = 1, 'ADD', 'EDIT'
) )
      loParameters.AddProperty('uValue', .Value )
      *** Add any optional parameters if needed
      .AddOptionalParameters( @loParameters )
      *** Now call the maintenance form
      DO FORM ( .cForm2Call ) WITH loParameters TO lnRetVal
      lnValue = IIF(lnRetVal = 0, This.Value, lnRetVal )
      .Requery()
      .Value = lnValue
    ENDIF
  ENDIF
ENDWITH
```

The specifics of the maintenance form obviously depend upon the table being updated. However, any maintenance form called from the combo or list box's *ShowMenu* method will need to accept the parameter object passed to its *Init* method and use the passed information to do its job. It will also need to return to the required primary key after it has successfully added a new entry. While the specific fields to be updated by this process will vary depending on the table being updated, the process itself is fairly generic. All the forms used to add and edit entries are based on the *frmAddOrEdit* form class provided with the sample code for this chapter. This class clearly illustrates how the process works, and you can check out *Itineraries.scx* to see how this maintenance form is called by the *lstAddNew* and *cboAddNew* objects.

How do I filter the items displayed in a second combo or list box based on the selection made in the first? *(Example: FilterList.SCX)*

This is a lot easier than you may think. FilterList.scx, in the sample code for this chapter, not only filters a ListBox depending on what is selected in a ComboBox, it also filters the ComboBox depending on what is selected in the OptionGroup.

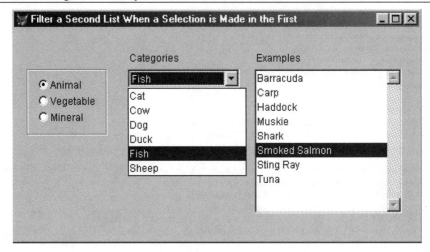

Figure 5.2 *Dynamically filter the contents of a combo or list box*

Our preferred *RowSourceType* for filtered controls is "3-SQL Statement" because it makes setting up the dependency easy. We just specify `WHERE Somefield = (` `Thisform.MasterControl.Value )` in the *WHERE* clause of the dependent control's *RowSource*. Then, each time the dependent control is requeried, it gets populated with the appropriate values.

There are two little snags here. First, if we use the expression *ThisForm* in the dependent control's *RowSource* directly in the property sheet, Visual FoxPro kicks up a fuss at run time. It tells us that ThisForm can only be used within a method. Secondly, although we could set the dependent control's *RowSource* in its *Init* method, this may also result in some rather unpleasant run-time surprises. If the dependent control is instantiated before the master control, Visual FoxPro will complain that ThisForm.MasterControl is not an object.

The trick to making this work properly is to put the code initializing the *RowSources* of the dependent controls in the right place. Since the form's controls are instantiated before the form's *Init* fires, a custom method called from the form's *Init* method is a **good** place to put this sort of code. This is exactly what we have done in our sample form's *SetForm* method:

```
LOCAL lcRowSource

*** Select only the items that have a Cat_No equal to the option selected
*** in the option group
```

All the controls on the sample form are bound to form properties. The OptionGroup is bound to Thisform.nType. Because this property is initialized to 1 in the property sheet, all the controls contain a value when the form displays for the first time:

```
lcRowSource = 'SELECT Cat_Desc, Cat_Key, UPPER( Categories.Cat_Desc ) AS '
lcRowSource = lcRowSource + 'UpperDesc FROM Categories '
lcRowSOurce = lcRowSOurce + 'WHERE Categories.Cat_No = ( Thisform.nType ) '
lcRowSource = lcRowSource + 'INTO CURSOR csrCategories ORDER BY UpperDesc'

*** Now set up the combo's properties
```

```
WITH Thisform.cboCategories
  .RowSourceType = 3
  .RowSource = lcRowSource
  *** Don't forget to repopulate the control's internal list
  .Requery()
  *** Inialize it to display the first item
  .ListIndex = 1
ENDWITH
```

Now that we have initialized the categories combo box, we can set up the SQL statement to use as the *RowSource* for the detail list box. We want to select only the items that match the Item selected in the combo box:

```
lcRowSource = 'SELECT Det_Desc, Det_Key, UPPER( Details.Det_Desc ) AS '
lcRowSource = lcRowSOurce + 'UpperDesc FROM Details '
lcRowSource = lcRowSource + 'WHERE Details.De_Cat_Key = ( Thisform.nCategory )
'
lcRowSOurce = lcRowSOurce + 'INTO CURSOR csrDetails ORDER BY UpperDesc'

*** Now set up the list box's properties
WITH Thisform.lstDetails
  .RowSourceType = 3
  .RowSource = lcRowSource
  *** Don't forget to repopulate the control's internal list
  .Requery()
  *** Initialize it to display the first item
  .ListIndex = 1
ENDWITH
```

This code, in the *Valid* method of the OptionGroup, updates the contents of the ComboBox when a new selection is made. It also updates the contents of the ListBox so all three controls stay in synch:

```
WITH Thisform
  .cboCategories.Requery()
  .cboCategories.ListIndex = 1
  .lstDetails.Requery()
  .lstDetails.ListIndex = 1
ENDWITH
```

Finally, this code in the ComboBox's *Valid* method updates the contents of the ListBox each time a selection is made from the combo. This code will work just as well if placed in the ComboBox's *InteractiveChange* method. The choice of method, in this case, is a matter of personal preference:

```
WITH Thisform
  .lstDetails.Requery()
  .lstDetails.ListIndex = 1
ENDWITH
```

A word about lookup tables

It is inevitable that a discussion about combo and list boxes should turn to the subject of lookup tables. After all, combos and lists are most commonly used to allow the user to select among a set of values kept in such a table. Generally speaking, the descriptive text from the lookup table is displayed in a control that is bound to the foreign key value in a data file. But what is the best way to structure a lookup table? Should there be one, all-purpose lookup table? Or should the application use many specialized lookup tables? Once again, the answer is "It depends." You need to pick the most appropriate solution for your particular application. Of course to make an informed decision, it helps to know the advantages and disadvantages of each approach. So here we go…

There are two major advantages to using a single, consolidated lookup table. The first is that by using a single structure, you can create generic, reusable combo and list box lookup classes that are capable of populating themselves. This minimizes the amount of code needed at the instance level, and less code means less debugging. The second advantage to this approach is that your application requires only one data entry form for maintaining the various lookups. A two-page lookup maintenance form accomplishes this task quite nicely. The user can select the lookup category from a list on the first page. The second page then displays the appropriate items for the selected category. An edit button on page two can then be used to launch a modal form for editing the current item. The big disadvantage to this approach is that all lookups share a common structure. This means that if you have a lookup category requiring more information for each item, you must either create a separate lookup table for that category or add extra columns to your consolidated table that will seldom be used.

Using a separate table for each type of lookup in your application provides more flexibility than the previous approach. Increased flexibility also brings increased overhead. It is more difficult to create generic, reusable lookup classes. This solution also requires multiple lookup table maintenance forms.

We use a combination of the two approaches. A single, all-purpose lookup table works for simple items that are likely to be reused across applications. We use separate tables for specialized lookups that are likely to have a unique structure. Our standard lookup table is actually two tables: a lookup header table containing the lookup categories and an associated lookup detail table that holds the items for each category.

Table 5.5 Structure of the Lookup Header table

Field Name	Data Type	Field Length	Purpose
Lh_Key	Integer		Primary Key – uniquely identify record
Lh_Desc	Character	30	Lookup Category Description
Lh_Default	Integer		Default Value (if any) to use from Lookup Details Table

Table 5.6 Data contained in the Lookup Header table

Lh_Key	Lh_Desc	Lh_Default
1	Contact Types	1
2	Telephone Types	5
3	Countries	10
4	Business Types	23
5	Relationships	63
6	Colors	

Table 5.7 Structure of the Lookup Details table

Field Name	Data Type	Field Length	Purpose
Ld_Lh_Key	Integer		Foreign key from Lookup Header Table
Ld_Key	Integer		Primary Key – uniquely identify record
Ld_Code	Character	3	User defined code (if any) for item
Ld_Desc	Character	30	Lookup detail item description

Table 5.8 Partial listing of data contained in the Lookup Details table

Ld_lh_key	Ld_Key	Ld_Code	Ld_Desc
1	1		Client
1	2		Prospect
1	3		Competitor
1	4		Personal
2	5		Home
2	6		Business
2	7		Fax
2	8		Cellular
2	9		Pager
3	10	USA	United States
3	11	UK	United Kingdom
3	12	CAN	Canada
3	13	GER	Germany

As you can see from the listings, it is quite easy to extract data from the detail table for any category. Since each item in the detail table has its own unique key, there is no ambiguity even if the same description is used in different "categories."

Generic lookup combos and lists *(Example: CH05.VCX::cboLookUp and lstLookUp)*

Generic, reusable combo and list box lookup classes allow you to implement your all-purpose lookup table with very little effort. Because of the way the lookup table is structured, it lends itself very well to *RowSourceType* = "3-SQL Statement." All that's required is a couple custom properties and a little code to initialize the control.

The *cCursorName* property is used to specify the cursor that holds the result of the SQL select. This is required in case there are multiple instances of the control on a single form. Each instance requires its own cursor to hold the result of the SQL statement in its *RowSource*. If the same name is used in every case, the cursor will be overwritten as each control instantiates. You will end up with all controls referring to the version of the cursor created by the control instantiated last.

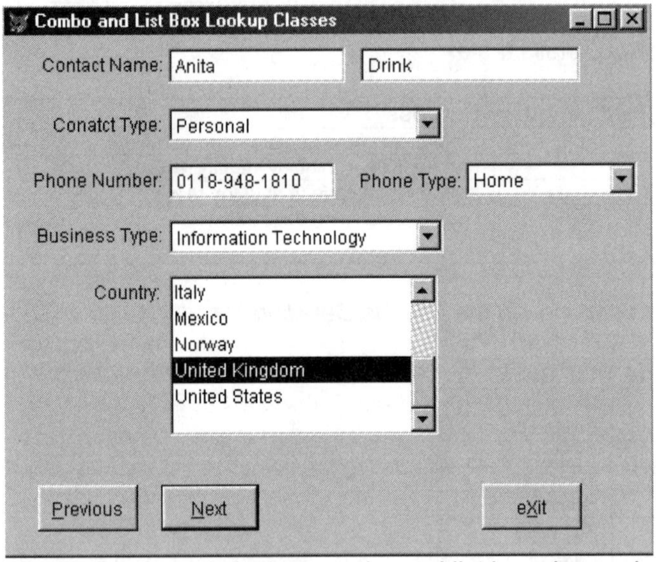

Figure 5.3 *Generic lookup combo and list box classes in action*

The *nHeaderKey* property is used to limit the contents of the control's list to a single category in the Lookup Header table. It contains the value of the primary key of the desired category and is used to construct the *WHERE* clause for the control's *RowSource*.

The control's *Setup* method, invoked upon instantiation, populates its *RowSource* using the properties specified above:

```
LOCAL lcRowSource

*** Make sure the developer set up the required properties
ASSERT !EMPTY( This.cCursorName ) MESSAGE ;
  'cCursorName MUST contain the name of the result cursor for the SQL SELECT!'
ASSERT !EMPTY( This.nHeaderKey ) MESSAGE ;
  'nHeaderKey MUST contain the PK of an item in LookupHeader.dbf!'

*** Set up the combo's RowSource
lcRowSource = 'SELECT ld_Desc, ld_Key FROM LookUpDetail WHERE '
lcRowSource = lcRowSource + 'LookUpDetail.ld_lh_key = ( This.nHeaderKey ) '
lcRowSource = lcRowSource + 'INTO CURSOR ( This.cCursorName ) '
lcRowSource = lcRowSource + 'ORDER BY ld_Desc'
```

```
*** Set up the combo's properties
WITH This
  .RowSourceType = 3
  .RowSource = lcRowSource
  .ColumnWidths = ALLTRIM( STR( .Width ) ) + ',0'
  .Requery()
ENDWITH
```

Using the lookup combo is very easy. Just drop it on a form, set its *ControlSource*, and fill in the *cCursorName* and *nHeaderKey* properties. Since it inherits from the cboAddNew class, it is also possible to add new entries to the lookup table and edit existing items on the fly. Since all instances of our generic lookup combo and list boxes populate their lists from the same generic lookup table, we can even put the name of the lookup maintenance form in the class's *cForm2Call* property. What could be easier? Lookups.scx, which is included with the sample code for this chapter, illustrates just how easy it is.

So what if I want to bind my combo to a value that isn't in the list? *(Example: CH05.VCX::cboSpecial and CH05.VCX::cboNotInList)*

The first question that leaps to mind here is "Then why are you using a combo box?" Combo and list boxes are used to limit data entry to a set of predefined selections. Permitting the user to enter an item that isn't in the list defeats the purpose of using a combo box in the first place. Having said that, we realize there may be occasions where this sort of functionality is required. For example, let's suppose a particular field in a table is usually populated from a set of standard selections. However, occasionally none of the standard selections are suitable and the end user needs to enter something that is not in the list. Clearly, if the non-standard items were regularly added to the underlying lookup table, the table would grow quickly with seldom used entries. In this instance, the field bound to the combo box must contain the description of the item in the lookup table and not its key value. Obviously, if we allow the field to be bound to items that are not in the list, we must store the information in this non-normalized manner. The only place to "look up" such ad hoc items is in the bound field itself!

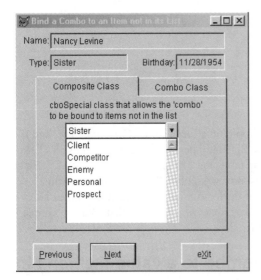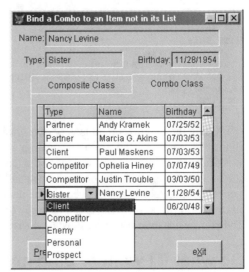

Figure 5.4 *Special combo class that binds to items not in the list*

Since such a combo can only be used when the table to which it is bound is not normalized, we are tempted to use a combo box with RowSourceType = 1-None and its *Sorted* property set to true. This code, in the combo's *Init* method, populates it with the types that currently exist in our "People" table:

```
LOCAL lnSelect
LnSelect = SELECT()
SELECT DISTINCT cType FROM People ORDER BY cType INTO CURSOR csrTypes
IF _TALLY > 0
  SELECT csrTypes
  SCAN
    This.AddItem( csrTypes.cType )
  ENDSCAN
ENDIF
SELECT ( lnSelect )
```

Then in the combo's *Valid* method, we could check to see if the user typed a value not in the list and add it:

```
WITH This
  IF !( UPPER( ALLTRIM( .DisplayValue ) ) == UPPER( ALLTRIM( .Value ) ) )
    .AddItem ( .DisplayValue )
  ENDIF
ENDWITH
```

While it's true this code works, there are a few fundamental problems. First, if the source table has a large number of records, the initial query could cause significant delay when the form is instantiated. Second, this will not solve the original problem. If new items are always added to the list, the list will continue to grow, making it difficult for the user to select an entry. This illustration also does not allow the user to distinguish which items are the "standard" selections in the list and which are merely ad hoc entries.

Our cboSpecial class, consisting of a text box, list box, and command button inside a container, solves the problem. The text box is the bound control. The list box is left unbound and its *RowSource* and *RowSourceType* are populated to display the standard selections. The class contains code to provide the text box with "quick fill" functionality and to synchronize the display in its contained controls.

The text box portion of the class uses this code in its *KeyPress* method to make the list portion visible when the user presses ALT+DNARROW or F4. It also makes sure the list becomes invisible when the TAB or ESC keys are pressed:

```
*** <ALT>+<DNARROW> OR <F4> were pressed
IF nKeyCode = 160 OR nKeyCode = -3
  This.Parent.DropList()
  NODEFAULT
ENDIF

*** <TAB> or <ESC> were pressed
IF nKeyCode = 9 OR nKeyCode = 27
  This.Parent.lstSearch.Visible = .F.
ENDIF
```

The only other code in the text box resides in its *InteractiveChange* method and its only purpose is to invoke the container's *Search* method:

```
*** If a valid character was entered, let the parent's search method handle it
IF This.SelStart > 0
  IF ( LASTKEY() > 31 AND LASTKEY() < 128 ) OR ( LASTKEY() = 7 )
    This.Parent.Search()
  ENDIF
ENDIF
```

The container's *Search* method then does the required work:

```
LOCAL lcSofar, lnSelStart, lnSelLength, lnRow

WITH This
  WITH .txtqFill
    *** Handle backspace key
    IF LASTKEY() = 127
      .SelStart = .SelStart - 1
    ENDIF
    *** Get the value typed in so far
    lnSelStart = .SelStart
    lcSofar =  LEFT( .Value, lnSelStart )
  ENDWITH
  *** Find a match in column #1 of the list portion of this control
  WITH .lstSearch
    *** Reset the list index in case we have type ion something that is not
    *** in the list
    .ListIndex = 0
    FOR lnRow = 1 TO .ListCount
      IF UPPER( .List[ lnRow, 1 ] ) = UPPER( lcSoFar )
```

```
      .ListIndex = lnRow
      *** Synchronize the contents of the textbox with what is selected
      *** in the list
      This.txtQfill.Value = .Value
      EXIT
    ENDIF
  ENDFOR
ENDWITH

WITH .txtqFill
  *** Highlight the portion of the value after the insertion point
  .SelStart = lnSelStart
  lnSelLength = LEN( ALLTRIM( .Value ) ) - lnSelStart
  IF lnSelLength > 0
    .SelLength =  lnSelLength
  ENDIF
ENDWITH
ENDWITH
```

The control's list box portion contains code in its *KeyPress* and *InteractiveChange* methods to update the text box's value with its value when the user selects from the list. This code is required in both methods because pressing either the **ENTER** key or the **SPACE BAR** to select a list item will cause its *KeyPress* event to fire but will not fire its *InteractiveChange* event. Selecting an item with the mouse fires the *InteractiveChange* event but does not fire the *KeyPress,* even though **LASTKEY()** returns the value 13 whether the mouse or the **ENTER** key is used. This code, from the list box's *InteractiveChange* method, is similar but not identical to the code in its *KeyPress* method:

```
IF LASTKEY() # 27
  This.Parent.TxtQFill.Value = This.Value
  *** a mouse click gives a LASTKEY() value of 13 (just like pressing enter)
  IF LASTKEY() = 13
    This.Visible = .F.
    This.Parent.txtQfill.SetFocus()
  ENDIF
ENDIF
```

The only other code in the list box portion of the class resides in its *GotFocus* method. This code simply invokes the container's *RefreshList* method to ensure the selected list box item is synchronized with the text box's value when the list box is made visible:

```
LOCAL lnRow
WITH This.lstSearch
  .ListIndex = 0
  FOR lnRow = 1 to .Listcount
    IF UPPER( ALLTRIM( .List[ lnRow ] ) ) = ;
       UPPER( ALLTRIM( This.txtQFill.Value ) )
      .ListIndex = lnRow
      EXIT
    ENDIF
  ENDFOR
ENDWITH
```

One of the shortcomings of the container class is that is cannot easily be used in a grid. To fulfill this requirement, we created the cboNotInList combo class. As you can see in **Figure 5.4**, when the list in the grid is dropped, the first item is highlighted when the *DisplayValue* is not in the list. That is why we prefer to use the cboSpecial class when it does not need to be placed in a grid. When *DisplayValue* is not in the list, notice no selection of the composite class is highlighted.

The cboNotInList combo class uses the same trick that we used when constructing the numeric textbox in Chapter 4. Although it may be a bound control, we unbind it behind the scenes in its *Init* method and save its *ControlSource* to the custom *cControlSource* property:

```
IF DODEFAULT()
  WITH This
    .cControlSource = .ControlSource
    .ControlSource = ''
  ENDWITH
ENDIF
```

The combo's *RefreshDisplayValue* method is called from both its *Refresh* and *GotFocus* methods to update its *DisplayValue* with the value of the field to which it is bound. It is interesting to note that it is only necessary to invoke this method from the combo's *GotFocus* when the combo is in a grid:

```
LOCAL lcControlSource
WITH This
  IF ! EMPTY( .cControlSource )
    lcControlSource = .cControlSource
      .DisplayValue = &lcControlSource
  ENDIF
ENDWITH
```

Finally, the combo's *UpdateControlSource* method is called from its *Valid* to (you guessed it) update its control source from its *DisplayValue:*

```
LOCAL lcAlias, lcControlSource
WITH This
  IF ! EMPTY( .cControlSource )
    lcAlias = JUSTSTEM( .cControlSource )
    IF UPPER( ALLTRIM( lcAlias ) ) = 'THISFORM'
      lcControlSource = .cControlSource
      STORE .DisplayValue TO &lcControlSource
    ELSE
      REPLACE ( .cControlSource ) WITH .DisplayValue IN ( lcAlias )
    ENDIF
  ENDIF
ENDWITH
```

See NotInList.scx in the sample code for this chapter to see both these classes in action.

How do I disable individual items in a combo or list?

Our first reaction is "Why are you displaying items in a combo box that the user is not allowed to select?" It certainly seems to be at odds with the basic reasoning for using a combo box in the first place: to allow the user to choose from a pre-defined list of allowable entries. If the user is not allowed to select an item, what the heck is it doing in the combo or list box to begin with? Again we realize there may be valid scenarios that require such functionality. For example, the CPT codes used in medical applications to define various transactions and the ICD-9 code used to define standard diagnoses may change over time. One cannot merely delete codes that are no longer used because historical detail may be linked to these obsolete codes. When displaying this historical data, it would be useful to display the inactive code as disabled. This way, a combo box bound to the ICD-9 code would not "lose" its display value because the code could not be found in the control's list. Nor would the user be permitted to select it for a current entry since it would be disabled.

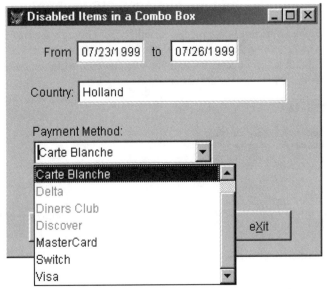

Figure 5.5 *Disabled items in a combo box*

To disable an item in a combo or list box, just add a back slash to the beginning of the string that defines the content of the first column in the control's *RowSource*. However, this only works for *RowSourceTypes* "0-None", "1-Value", and "5-Array". The form DisabledItems.scx, provided with the sample code for this chapter, provides an example for a combo with *RowSourceType* "5-Array". This code in the combo box's *Init* method populates the array and disables items only if the date in the underlying table indicates this item is inactive. This type of logic can be also used to disable specific items based on the value of a logical field that determines if the item is still active:

```
SELECT IIF( !EMPTY( PmtMethods.pm_dStop ), '\'+pm_Desc, pm_Desc ) AS pm_Desc, ;
    pm_Key FROM PmtMethods ORDER BY pm_Desc INTO ARRAY This.aContents
```

```
This.Requery()
```

We could just as easily set the combo box up with a *RowSourceType* of "0-None", set its *Sorted* property to true and populated it like this instead:

```
LOCAL lcItem

SELECT PmtMethods
SCAN
  lcItem = IIF( EMPTY( dStop ), dStop, '\' + dStop )
  This.AddItem( lcItem )
ENDSCAN
```

How do I create a list box with check boxes like the one displayed by Visual FoxPro when I select "View Toolbars" from the menu? *(Example: CH05.VCX::lstChkBox)*

Did you ever notice that list boxes have a *Picture* property? You can find this property listed under the layout tab of the property sheet. Technically speaking, the picture property really belongs to the list box's *items* rather than to the list box as an object. Essentially, you can manipulate the *Picture* property of the current *ListItem* and set it to a checked box if it is selected and to a plain box if it is not.

Figure 5.6 *Multiselect list box using check boxes*

List boxes of this type exhibit other nonstandard behavior that requires special programming. For example, clicking on a selected item in this list box de-selects it. Pressing the space bar also acts like a toggle for selecting and de-selecting items. This is much more convenient than the standard CTRL+CLICK and CTRL+SPACE BAR combinations normally used for selecting multiple items in a list box.

This list box class requires a custom array property to track the selected items. We can't just use the native *Selected* property because it is not always set in the expected way. For example, pressing the space bar selects the current item. But the item's *Selected* property isn't set to true until after the *KeyPress* method completes. Suppose we want to manipulate this property in the list box's *KeyPress* method. This.Selected[This.ListIndex] would return false even if we had just pressed the space bar to select the current item! You can see the dilemma. And it becomes even more complicated when trying to use the key to toggle the item's *Selected* property. The simple and straightforward solution is to maintain our own list of current selections over which we have total control. This is implemented using a custom array property (*aSelected*), initialized in the control's *Reset* method, which is called from its *Init:*

```
WITH This
    *** clear all selections
    *** If other behavior is required by default, put it here and call this
    *** method from any place that the list box's contents must be reset
    .ListIndex = 0
    DIMENSION .aSelected[.ListCount]
    .aSelected = .F.
ENDWITH
```

The *SetListItem* method is called from the list box's *Click* and *KeyPress* methods. Since the *Click* event fires so frequently (every time the user scrolls through the list using the cursor keys) we must make sure we only call the *SetListItem* method when the user actually clicks on an item. We do this by checking for LASTKEY() = 13. Likewise, it is only invoked from the *KeyPress* method when the user presses either the ENTER key or the SPACE BAR. This method sets the specified row in the custom array that tracks the list box selections and sets the item's *Picture* property to the appropriate picture for its current state:

```
WITH This
  IF .ListIndex > 0
    *** The item is currently selected so de-select it
    IF .aSelected[.ListIndex]
      .Picture[.ListIndex] = 'Box.bmp'
      .aSelected[.ListIndex] = .F.
    ELSE
      *** The item is not selected yet, so select it
      .Picture[.ListIndex] = 'CheckBx.bmp'
      .aSelected[.ListIndex] = .T.
    ENDIF
  ENDIF
ENDWITH
```

Visual FoxPro's standard behavior is to de-select all list box items when it gets focus. It seems that this default behavior also resets all of the pictures in the list. Because we do not want our multi-select list box to exhibit this type of amnesia, we call our its custom *RefreshList* method from its *GotFocus* method:

```
LOCAL lnItem
WITH This
  FOR lnItem = 1 TO .ListCount
    .Picture[ lnItem ] = IIF( .aSelected[ lnItem ], 'CheckBx.bmp', 'Box.bmp' )
  ENDFOR
ENDWITH
```

A mover list class *(Example: CH05.VCX::cntMover)*

Mover lists, like the "check box" list box class discussed above, are more user-friendly than the multi-select list box. Although they appear to be complex controls, it is relatively simple to create a generic, reusable, mover list class. Our mover list class consists of a container with one list box to hold the set of items from which the user may choose and another that will be populated with the selected items. It also contains four command buttons to move items between the two lists. The mover bars on the destination list are enabled to provide maximum flexibility. If the order of the selected items is critical to the mover list's functionality, this provides a mechanism for the user to order his selections. The container's *ResetList* method, which initially populates the lists, is the only method that is instance specific. The form MoverList.scx, provided with the sample code for this chapter, uses this method to populate the mover's source list from our "PmtMethods" table:

```
WITH This
  .lstSource.Clear()
  .lstDestination.Clear()
  SELECT Countries
  SCAN
    .lstSource.AddItem( c_Desc )
  ENDSCAN
ENDWITH
```

Our mover list class is by no means the last word in movers, but it will give you something to build upon.

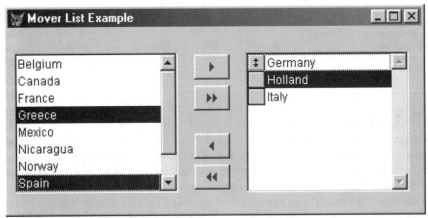

Figure 5.7 *Simple mover list*

The command buttons are not the only way to move items between the two lists. Double clicking on an item removes it from the current list and adds it to the other. Selected items may also be dragged from one list and dropped into the other. In fact, it doesn't matter how the items are moved between the lists. All movement is accomplished by invoking the container's *MoveItem* method and passing it a reference to the source list for the move. There is a call to this method from the *DblClick* and *DragDrop* methods of each of the list boxes as well as in the *OnClick* method of the two command buttons, *cmdMove* and *cmdRemove*:

```
LPARAMETERS toSource
LOCAL lnItem, toDestination
```

Since this method is passed an object reference to the source list, we can use this reference to determine which is the destination list:

```
WITH This
  IF toSource = .lstSource
    toDestination = .lstDestination
  ELSE
    toDestination = .lstSource
  ENDIF
ENDWITH

*** Lock the screen so to avoid the distracting visual side-effects
*** that result from moving the item(s)
THISFORM.LockScreen = .T.
```

We now loop through the source list to add each selected item to the destination list and remove it from the source list afterward. As items are removed from the source list, their *ListCount* properties are decreased by one. So we use a DO WHILE loop instead of a FOR loop to have more control over when the index into the source list is incremented. We increment it only when the current item in the list is not selected to move on to the next:

```
lnItem = 1
WITH toSource
  DO WHILE lnItem <= .ListCount
    IF .Selected[ lnItem ]
      toDestination.AddItem( .List[ lnItem ] )
      .RemoveItem( lnItem )
    ELSE
      lnItem = lnItem + 1
    ENDIF
  ENDDO
ENDWITH

*** Don't forget to unlock the screen!
THISFORM.LockScreen = .F.
```

Implementing drag and drop functionality requires a little more code. To accomplish this, we have added the n*MouseX*, n*MouseY* and *nDragThreshold* properties to the container. The *MouseDown* method of the contained list boxes sets the *nMouseX* and *nMouseY* properties to the current coordinates when the left mouse button is depressed. This is done to prevent dragging an item when the user has just clicked to select it. The drag operation does not begin unless the mouse has moved at least the number of pixels specified by the *nDragTheshold* property. The container's *StartDrag* method, called from the list boxes' *MouseMove* method, checks to see if the mouse has been moved sufficiently to start the *Drag* operation. The calling list passes an object reference to itself and the current coordinates of the mouse to this method:

```
LPARAMETERS toList, tnX, tnY

WITH This
  *** Only begin the drag operation if the mouse has moved
  *** at least the minumun number pixels
  IF ABS( tnX - .nMouseX ) > .nDragThreshold OR ;
    ABS( tnY - .nMouseY ) > .nDragThreshold
    toList.Drag()
  ENDIF
ENDWITH
```

Finally, the list's *DragIcon* property from which the drag operation originated, needs to be changed to the appropriate icon. When the cursor is on a portion of the screen that does not permit the item to be dropped, we want to display the familiar circle with a slash inside it that universally means "NO!" We do this by calling the container's *ChangeIcon* method from the list's *DragOver* method. This method, as the name implies, merely changes the drag icon to the appropriate icon:

```
LPARAMETERS toSource, tnState

IF tnState = 0
  *** allowed to drop
  toSource.DragIcon = THIS.cDropIcon
ELSE
  IF tnState = 1
    *** not allowed to drop
    toSource.DragIcon = THIS.cNoDropIcon
```

```
ENDIF
ENDIF
```

Not only is the mover list a lot easier to use than the multi-select list box, it also gives the application a more professional look and feel – without a lot of extra effort.

What if I need to display hundreds of items in my combo box?

In this case, a combo box is too slow because it must always populate its internal list with all items from the underlying data source. If we were able to combine the efficiency of a grid (which can load data as needed) with the incremental search capability of our quickfill combo box, we would have the prefect solution. Fortunately, using composition, we can do exactly that and we created a class for this "*ComboGrid*" control that uses a textbox, a command button and a grid as its main components.

The construction is similar to that described for our "*cboSpecial*" class - used to permit binding a control to a value not contained in the internal list. The main difference is that instead of the list box used in the earlier control, we now use a grid for the drop-down functionality. Some special handling is required at the container level to ensure that everything operates smoothly but the techniques are the same.

This control was originally written and posted as a "*FreeHelp*" contribution to the CompuServe Visual FoxPro forum, and later was used as the basis for an article in *FoxTalk* magazine. For a full discussion of the design and implementation of this control see "*Now you see it, now you don't*" an article in the July 1999 edition of *FoxTalk*. Figures 5.8 and 5.9 show the two incarnations of the combo grid:

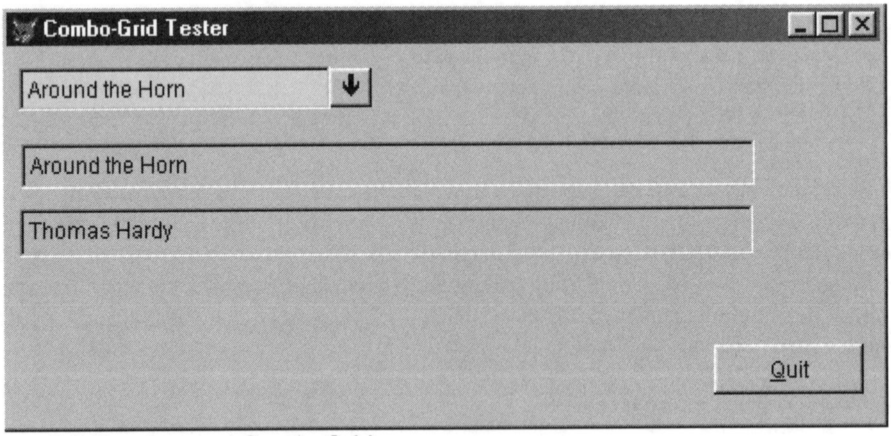

Figure 5.8 *The dormant ComboGrid*

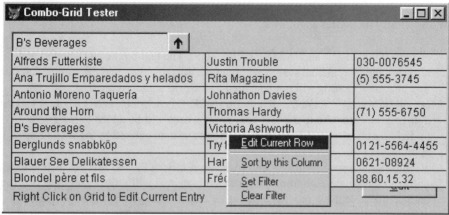

Figure 5.9 *The active ComboGrid*

Release Notes for the ComboGrid Class (*Class: CboGrid.vcx, Example Form: FrmCGrd.scx*)
Created By: Marcia G. Akins and Andy Kramek, and placed in the Public Domain in February 1999.
This class is designed to use a grid in place of a standard VFP Combobox for a large data volume or to enter data into more than one lookup table field, used to populate the dropdown. The class consists of a Textbox, a Command Button and a Grid inside a Container. The grid is normally invisible and the class looks and behaves just like a standard VFP combo box.

The class is controlled by 7 properties, as follows:

Table 5.9 *ComboGrid Custom Properties*

Property	Function
CAlias	Name of the Table to use as the RecordSource for the Grid
CColSource	Comma separated list of field names for columns in the Grid
CControlSource	Data Source for the Textbox (if required to be bound)
CkeyField	Field to use to set the Value of the TextBox
CtagName	Tag to use in cAlias
LAddNewEntry	Determines whether new entries are added to the Grid Table as well as to the textbox controlsource
NColCount	Number of columns to display in the grid

A single Instance level method is available so data can be read from the grid after a selection is made, for example, to populate other fields on the form:

Table 5.10 *ComboGrid custom methods*

Method	Function
RefreshControls	Instance Level Method called by Grid AfterRowColChange() and by KeyPress in the QuickFill TextBox

There are four ways of using this control depending on the setting of the cControlSource and lAddNewEntry properties as follows:

- cControlSource:= "" and lAddNewEntry = .F. The text box is NOT bound and although the incremental search will operate, and new data may be entered into the text box, new records will not be added to the grid's underlying table.
- cControlSource:= "" and lAddNewEntry = .T. The text box is NOT bound and new data may be entered into the text box, new records will be added to the grid's underlying table. Additional columns may have data entered by right clicking in the appropriate cell.
- cControlSource:= <Specified> and lAddNewEntry = .F. The text box is bound and will read its initial value from the specified table and will write changes to that field back to the table. New records will not be added to the grid's underlying table.
- cControlSource:= <Specified> and lAddNewEntry = .T. The text box is bound and will read its initial value from the specified table and will write changes to that field back to the table. Additional columns may have data entered by right clicking in the appropriate cell.

Acknowledgements
Thanks are due to Tamar Granor for the QuickFill methodology that she published in the September 1998 issue of *FoxPro Advisor* and to Paul Maskens who provided the inspiration for the self-sizing container and grid.

Following a suggestion by Dick Beebe, the ComboGrid was enhanced to incorporate a right-click menu in the drop-down grid. Depending on the settings, you can either sort by the selected column or edit the currently selected row. If neither is appropriate the menu does not appear.

To enable editing, the Container's lAddNewEntry property must be set. To enable sorting the grid's data source, you must have an index tag named exactly the same as the field used as the controlsource for the column. If this is not your normal practice, you should probably consider it anyway.

Author's disclaimer
As always we have tried to make the ComboGrid foolproof, but we have placed this control class in the Public Domain "as is," with no warranty implied or given. We cannot accept liability for any loss or damage resulting from its use (proper or improper). All source code is included in the CboGrid sub-directory of this chapter's sample code, so feel free to modify, change or enhance it to meet your specific needs.

Chapter 6
Grids: The Misunderstood Controls

"To be great is to be misunderstood." (Essays, *"Self-Reliance"* by Ralph Waldo Emerson)

The grid is the most maligned control in Visual FoxPro. Many experts have publicly expressed the opinion that they never, under any circumstances use a grid for data entry. Although it's difficult to tame, the grid can be used very effectively for this purpose in the right situation. A grid is also the best choice when it comes to displaying large amounts of data very quickly. In this chapter we will present you with some tried and tested techniques that you can use to get more from your grids.

When working with grids, the first thing to remember is that a grid is not a spreadsheet, although it may look like one. There is really only one row in a grid. The rest is done with smoke and mirrors. You can't refer to the cell in the third column of the tenth row of the grid. But you can refer to the third field in the tenth record of the grid's *RecordSource*. Generally speaking, if you need to access values in a particular grid cell, your best bet is to get that information from the field in the underlying data source.

A grid usually displays data from the data source that you specify in its *RecordSource* property. However even if you don't specify a *RecordSource*, you can still display data in the grid. If there is a cursor open in the currently selected work area, the grid will pull its data from there! The grid's *RecordSourceType* property specifies how to open the data source that populates the grid control. We usually choose the default, "2-Alias" as it's the most generally useful.

When do the events fire? *(Example: GridEvents.scx)*

Being able to use grids effectively relies on understanding when the events fire. There are also some *gotchas!* to note before you start. This is what happens when the grid first gets focus:

- The grid's *When* event fires
- The *When* event of the *CurrentControl* in the first column fires
- The *GotFocus* event of the *CurrentControl* in the *ActiveColumn* fires
- The grid's *AfterRowColChange* event fires

This alone has some important implications. If you place code in the grid's *AfterRowColChange* method thinking that it only fires after you move off the current cell, think again! It fires whenever the grid gets focus. Speaking of which, have you noticed that the grid is missing a *GotFocus* method although it has a *SetFocus* method?

Keep in mind that when the grid gets focus, its *ActiveColumn* is going to be the same column that was active when the grid previously lost focus. The first time you tab into a grid, the *CurrentControl* in the first column will become the *ActiveCell*. Suppose you then navigate to the third grid column before clicking on another form object. The next time the grid gets focus, the *ActiveColumn*, by default, will be the third column.

Things happen a little differently when the grid loses focus. And by the way, even though the grid loses focus, it has no *LostFocus* method. Interesting isn't it?

- The grid's *Valid* event fires
- The Grid's *BeforeRowColChange* event fires
- The *Valid* event of the *CurrentControl* in the *ActiveColumn* fires
- The *LostFocus* event of the active cell in the grid fires

Once the grid has focus and you use the keyboard to navigate between cells in the grid, the events fire like this:

- The *KeyPress* event of the *CurrentControl* in the *ActiveColumn* fires
- The grid's *BeforeRowColChange* event fires
- The *Valid* event of the *CurrentControl* in the *ActiveColumn* fires
- The *LostFocus* event of the active cell fires
- The *When* event of the *CurrentControl* in the column that you move to fires
- The *GotFocus* event of the new active cell fires
- The grid's *AfterRowColChange* event fires

When you use the mouse to navigate between the cells in a grid, obviously the *KeyPress* event does not fire. The remaining events fire in exactly the same order as they do when using the keyboard to navigate. However when using the mouse, the *Click* event of the newly active cell fires immediately after the grid's *AfterRowColChange*. This sequence is the same even when the *CurrentControl* in the grid's *ActiveColumn* is a combo box instead of a text box.

Gotcha! Grid's valid fires before the valid of the current control

Notice that when moving from a grid to another object on the form, the grid's *Valid* fires **before** the V*alid* of the active cell. This is a bug. Normally you would expect to use the control's *Valid* method to determine whether that control can lose focus. However, when a control is contained within a grid, there are two levels at which focus operates. First, between the control and other controls that are also within the grid. In this context things behave normally.

Second there is the issue of which form object has focus. This bug will bite you when focus is being moved between the grid and another object. It is, as you would expect, the grid's *Valid* method that determines whether the grid can lose focus. However, because the grid's *Valid* is called before that of any contained control, a contained control cannot prevent the grid from losing focus even though its own validation has failed.

This can and will allow bad data to be entered into the grid. Fortunately, there is an easy workaround, which ensures that the grid's *Valid* explicitly calls and returns the result of any contained control's validation. So if the text box in the first column of the grid has code in its *Valid*, this line in the grid's *Valid* method takes care of the problem:

```
RETURN This.Column1.Text1.Valid()
```

What is the difference between ActiveRow and RelativeRow? *(Example: ActiveRow&RelativeRow.scx)*

A grid has two sets of properties that can be used to refer to its current row and column. The *ActiveRow* and *ActiveColumn* properties contain "absolute" values. Suppose the grid is being used to display all the fields in all the records of its *RecordSource* in natural order. In this situation, the grid's *ActiveRow* is the same as the record number and *ActiveColumn* is the same as the field number. However, if the *RecordSource* is not in natural order, *ActiveRow* holds the *offset* of the current record from the first record in the current order. If a subset of fields is displayed in the grid, *ActiveColumn* holds the positional offset of the current field from the first field in this subset.

On the other hand, the *RelativeRow* and *RelativeColumn* properties refer to the position of the current row and column with respect to the visible portion of the grid. Seems pretty straightforward, doesn't it?

Well, not exactly. The above holds true only as long as the grid is the active control. When another form object is the active control, these properties are reset to zero. Furthermore, their values are reliable only when the active cell is in the visible portion of the grid. If a cell in the grid has focus and the vertical scroll bars are used to scroll the grid so the active cell is no longer visible, both *ActiveRow* and *RelativeRow* are set to zero! When this cell reappears in the grid, the *RelativeRow* and *ActiveRow* are reset to their correct values. The value held by the grid's *ActiveColumn* does not change, even when the active cell is scrolled out of sight. In this situation, the grid's *RelativeColumn* contains the correct values if you interpret this value as being the offset from the first column in the visible portion of the grid. In other words, the first "invisible" column immediately to the left of the first visible column in the grid is at offset 0. The column immediately to the left of the one at offset 0, is at offset −1, and so on.

So what does all this mean? Not a lot, really. The anomalies are interesting but will not have any effect on the way we use these properties. *ActiveRow* and *RelativeRow* properties are very useful when we want to provide our grid with special behavior. For example, the default behavior of the **TAB** key is to move focus to the next column in the current row of the grid. Suppose you want to move focus to the same column in the next row instead. You cannot do this just by incrementing the grid's *ActiveRow*. Instead, you need to make use of the grid's *RelativeRow* property to determine when to invoke its *DoScroll* method. The sample code to accomplish this task appears later in this chapter. We have also included a grid combo box class that allows the cursor keys to traverse the grid when the combo is "closed." This behavior is also implemented by making use of these properties.

Gotcha! ActiveColumn does not really tell you which is the active column

The *ActiveColumn* property sounds as though it should tell us which grid column is the one being accessed by the user and, after a fashion, it does. However, this is not very useful because it merely tells us the *position* of the currently active column in the grid, not *which* of the columns is currently active.

Personally, we think that if the grid's *ActiveColumn* is 1, it would be useful if this meant that Grid.Columns[1] was the active column. This is, in fact, true only if the grid's columns are not movable and if the developer did not rearrange the columns in the form designer before setting the column's *movable* property to false.

Take, for example, a grid containing five movable columns. If the columns are rearranged so they are in this order:

```
.Columns[4]     .Columns[5]     .Columns[1]     .Columns[2]     .Columns[3]
```

and the user tabs into the textbox contained in .Columns[5], the grid's *ActiveColumn* is 2. This is the same value as the *ColumnOrder* property of .Columns[5]. In order to do anything meaningful with the grid's *ActiveColumn*, we must write code to find out which is the active column:

```
FOR EACH loColumn IN This.Columns
  IF loColumn.ColumnOrder = This.ActiveColumn

    *** This is the active column
    *** Get a reference or do whatever needs to be done with it here
    EXIT
  ENDIF
ENDFOR
```

How do I highlight the current grid row? *(Example:*
CH06.VCX::grdBase)

When you look at the grid's property sheet, you'll see a property called *HighlightRow* under the layout tab. The first time you saw it, you probably thought that leaving this property at its default setting would highlight the current grid row. Wrong! At first glance, it appears that setting this property to either true or false does nothing. This is also incorrect. If you set *HighlightRow* to true, you'll notice the border of the current grid row is highlighted. Not very useful, is it? We suggest you set this property to false in your base grid class because leaving it set to true degrades performance.

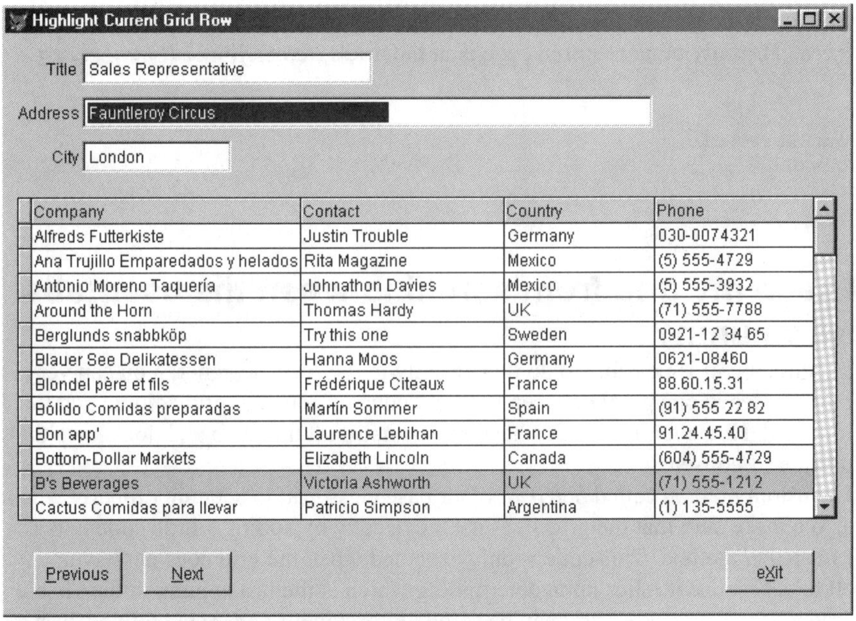

Figure 6.1 *Highlight the current grid row*

Fortunately, it is a fairly simple matter to add this functionality to your base class grid. The grid requires two custom properties to accomplish this. The first, initialized to zero, is *nRecNo*. It will hold the number of the record currently in the grid's *ActiveRow*. The second, initialized to false, is *lAbout2LeaveGrid*. It is used to reset the highlight properly when we are navigating in the grid and to make sure the grid stays highlighted when focus moves on to another form object. This code, in the grid's *Init* method, will highlight the current grid row in cyan:

```
LOCAL lcForeColor, lcBackColor

lcForeColor = 'IIF( RECNO( This.RecordSource ) = This.nRecNo, '
lcForeColor = lcForeColor + 'RGB( 0, 0, 128 ), RGB( 0, 0, 0 ) )'
lcBackColor = 'IIF( RECNO( This.RecordSource ) = This.nRecNo, '
lcBackColor = lcBackColor + 'RGB( 0, 255, 255 ), RGB( 255, 255, 255 ) )'

WITH This
  .nRecNo = RECNO( .RecordSource )
  .SetAll( 'DynamicForeColor', lcForeColor, 'COLUMN' )
  .SetAll( 'DynamicBackColor', lcBackColor, 'COLUMN' )
```

To change the highlight when the current grid row changes, this code is needed in the *When* method of each control in every column of the grid:

```
WITH This.Parent.Parent
  .nRecNo = RECNO( .RecordSource )
ENDWITH
```

We also need to set the grid's lAbout2LeaveGrid property to true in its *Valid* method and to false in its *When*. The only other required code is in the grid's *BeforeRowColChange* method:

```
IF !This.lAbout2LeaveGrid
  This.nRecNo = 0
ENDIF
```

How do I keep my grid from scrolling when the user tabs off the last column?

If you are the patient type, it is possible to do this visually in the form designer. You can very carefully make sure to leave one pixel between the right edge of your last grid column and the right edge of your grid. However, most of us have more important things to and don't have the patience for this kind of nonsense.

We added a custom method called *SetGrid* to our base class grid to set it up properly when it's instantiated. We make sure that the grid sizes itself correctly by adding a little code to our base class grid's *SetGrid* method. This code is only executed when the grid does not have horizontal scroll bars because it relies upon determining which is the last column in the visible portion of the grid. Clearly, when the grid can be scrolled horizontally, there is no fixed "last column."

This brings up another point. Grids that scroll horizontally demonstrate bad interface design. We believe all information presented in a grid should be immediately visible to the end user. This is especially important with data entry grids. In heads down data entry situations, it is difficult for end users to keep their place and is distracting when information is scrolling on and off the screen. It also requires fiddling around to view relevant information when it is hidden from view in a grid that scrolls horizontally:

```
*** If the grid does not scroll horizontally, make sure the columns are sized
*** properly so the grid doesn't scroll when you tab off the last column
WITH This
  IF INLIST( .ScrollBars, 0, 2 )

    *** Calculate the total width of all columns
    lnTotColWidth = 0
    FOR lnCnt = 1 TO .ColumnCount
      *** Add-on the width of this column
      lnTotColWidth = lnTotColWidth + .Columns[ lnCnt ].Width + 1

      *** work out if this is the last column
      IF .Columns[ lnCnt ].ColumnOrder = .ColumnCount
        lnLastColumn = lnCnt
      ENDIF
    ENDFOR

    *** Add-on the width of the scroll bar (if required)
    lnTotColWidth = lnTotColWidth + IIF( .ScrollBars = 2, ;
                SYSMETRIC( 5 ), 0 ) + 2

    *** Add-on the delete mark (if required)
```

```
lnTotColWidth = lnTotColWidth + IIF( .DeleteMark, 8, 0 )

*** Add-on the record mark (if required)
lnTotColWidth = lnTotColWidth + IIF( .RecordMark, 10, 0 )

*** Resize last column to ensure grid is completely filled
.Columns[ lnLastColumn ].Width = .Columns[ lnLastColumn ].Width + ;
                                   ( .Width - lnTotColWidth )
   ENDIF
ENDWITH
```

How do I create multiline headers? *(Example:*
CH06.VCX::grdBigHeaders and grdMLHeaders)
Personally, we think multiline headers are too much trouble and are far too restrictive. Having said this, we created a grid class that uses them. In order to use this class, all grid columns must have their *resizable* and *movable* properties set to false. This is because the class sets the grid's *HeaderHeight* property to zero and replaces the header with labels that sit above the grid. Because these labels do not resize or move, the grid class does not allow horizontal scrolling.

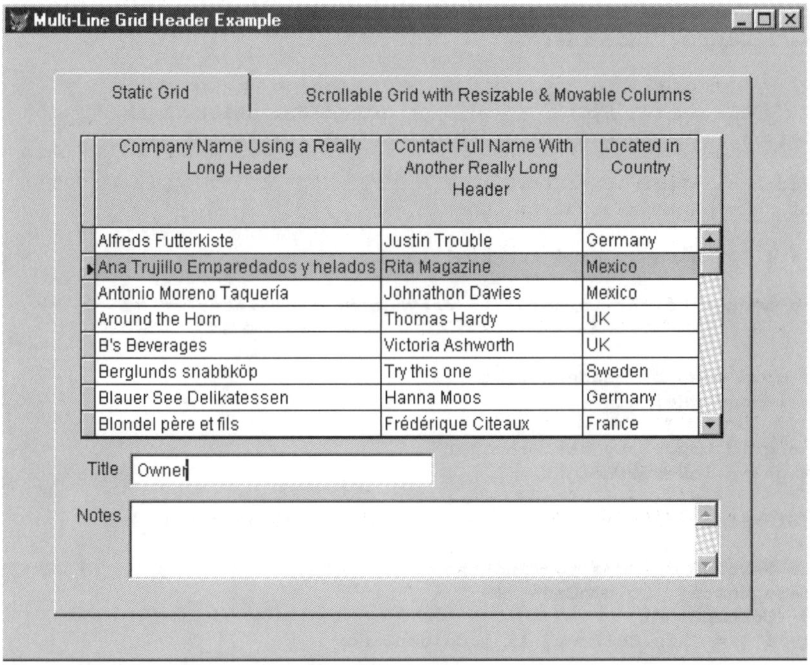

Figure 6.2 *Multiline grid headers in a static grid*

Our multiline header grid class has two new methods: *ReplaceHeaders*, which creates the labels above the grid, and *WhiteShadow*, which creates the visual effects to make these labels

look more like native Visual FoxPro headers. We also added some code to our *SetGrid* method
to ensure the columns in this grid class cannot be moved or resized:

```
LOCAL lnCnt

DODEFAULT()

WITH This
  FOR lnCnt = 1 TO .ColumnCount
    .Columns[ lnCnt ].Movable = .F.
    .Columns[ lnCnt ].Resizable = .F.
  ENDFOR

  *** Set up the multi-line headers
  .ReplaceHeaders()
ENDWITH
```

The *ReplaceHeaders* method, as the name implies, replaces the grid's column header with
labels. Keep in mind that the grid's *HeaderHeight* must be set high enough in the form designer
to accommodate the multiline caption. This value is used to set the label's height in the
ReplaceHeaders method:

```
LOCAL lnLeft, li, lnVSBWidth, lcName, lnDelRecBlobWidth, ;
    lnTop, lnHeaderHeight, lnOrdinal

WITH This
  LnLeft  = IIF (.DeleteMark, 8,0)          && Offset for delete mark
  LnLeft  = lnLeft + IIF (.RecordMark,10,0)  && Offset for record mark

  lnDelRecBlobWidth = lnLeft
  lnHeaderHeight    = .HeaderHeight

  lnTop = .Top + 1      && save Grid top position

  *** Reset grid header height to zero, to prevent it from interfering
  .HeaderHeight = 0

  *** Shift the grid down by headerheight
  .Top = .Top + lnHeaderHeight

  *** Adjust the grid height by headerheight
  .Height = .Height - lnHeaderHeight

  lnVSBWidth = SYSMETRIC (5) + 1      && Get width of vertical scroll bar

  *** quick scan through columns to find the column order
  LOCAL ARRAY laSequence[ .ColumnCount ]
  FOR li = 1 TO .ColumnCount
    laSequence[ li ] = This.Columns[ li ].ColumnOrder
  ENDFOR

  FOR li = 1 TO .ColumnCount
    *** find the ordinal column reference from the column order sequence number
    lnOrdinal = ASCAN( laSequence, li )
    lcName = "dHeader" + LTRIM( STR( lnOrdinal ) )
```

```
   This.Parent.Addobject(lcName, "Label")

   WITH EVAL("This.Parent." + lcName)
     .BackStyle   = 1
     .BorderStyle = 1
     .WordWrap    = .T.
     .Visible     = .T.
     .Alignment   = 2       && Center alignment looks best
     .Caption     = This.Columns[ lnOrdinal ].Controls[ 1 ].Caption
     .BackColor   = This.Columns[ lnOrdinal ].Controls[ 1 ].BackColor
     .FontName    = This.Columns[ lnOrdinal ].Controls[ 1 ].Fontname
     .FontSize    = This.Columns[ lnOrdinal ].Controls[ 1 ].FontSize
     .FontBold    = This.Columns[ lnOrdinal ].Controls[ 1 ].FontBold
     .Height      = lnHeaderHeight
     .Width       = This.Columns[ lnOrdinal ].Width + 2
     .Left        = This.Left + lnLeft
     .Top         = lnTop

     This.Columns[ lnOrdinal ].Controls[ 1 ].Caption = SPACE(0)
     This.WhiteShadow (.Left, .Top, .Height, .Width)

     lnLeft = lnLeft + This.Columns[ lnOrdinal ].Width + 1
   ENDWITH
ENDFOR

*** Add blob above record / delete mark
IF lnDelRecBlobWidth > 0
  WITH .Parent
    .Addobject ('shpDelRecBlob', "Shape")
    .shpDelRecBlob.Backcolor  = RGB (192,192,192)
    .shpDelRecBlob.Height     = lnHeaderHeight
    .shpDelRecBlob.Width      = lnDelRecBlobWidth + 1
    .shpDelRecBlob.Left       = This.Left
    .shpDelRecBlob.Top        = lnTop
    .shpDelRecBlob.Visible    = .T.

    WITH .shpDelRecBlob
      This.WhiteShadow (.Left, .Top, .Height, .Width)
    ENDWITH
  ENDWITH
ENDIF

*** Add blob above vertical scroll bar
IF .Scrollbars = 2
  WITH .Parent
    .Addobject ('cmdScrollBlob', "CommandButton")
    WITH .cmdScrollBlob
      .Enabled = .F.
      .Height  = lnHeaderHeight
      .Width   = lnVSBWidth
      .Left    = This.Left + This.Width - lnVSBWidth
      .Top     = lnTop
      .Caption = SPACE (0)
      .Visible = .T.
    ENDWITH
  ENDWITH
ENDIF
ENDWITH
```

This class is reusable and does not require a lot of instance specific code. It is, however, limited to static grids. We realize that once in a blue moon you may need a grid with multiline headers that also supports horizontal scrolling and columns that are both resizable and movable, so we created a class to do this. The function that makes this possible is OBJTOCLIENT(). This function returns the *Top, Left, Height* or *Width* property of an object relative to its form. Since neither grid columns nor grid headers have a *Left* property, this position must either be calculated by adding the width of each column to an accumulator, as in the previous example, or by using the OBJTOCLIENT function.

The result looks very cool and will impress all your geek buddies. However, there's no such thing as a free lunch. The price for this functionality is a large increase in the amount of instance specific code required to support it.

Instead of the *ReplaceHeaders* method used in the previous example, this grid class has a *SetHeaders* method because the headers are not actually replaced. The *SetHeaders* method creates transparent labels that float above the grid's existing headers with a margin sufficient to allow the end user to click on the header below in order to move or resize the column.

This grid class has two new custom properties:

- *nHdrMargin:* specifies the number of pixels to leave between the edges of the label and the grid header – the default is five pixels
- *nRight:* stores the x coordinate of the rightmost position in the visible portion of the grid so if we have columns that are not visible, we don't make the labels for their headers visible

We have also added the *RefreshHeaders* method to reposition the labels every time the grid is scrolled or the columns are moved or resized. *RefreshHeaders* is called from the grid class's *SetHeaders* and *Scrolled* methods. It must also be called from each column's *Moved* and *Resize* methods. The last two calls must be placed in every instance of this grid class, a task that can be made less tedious by creating a builder for this class. We will discuss such a builder later in the chapter on developer productivity tools.

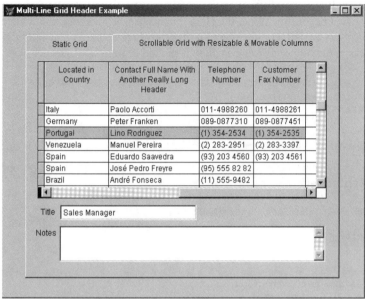

Figure 6.3 *Grid with multiline headers supporting horizontal scrolling and movable columns*

Gotcha! Scrolled event does not fire when cursor keys scroll the grid

We may just be quibbling about semantics here, but the Visual FoxPro Help file says the *Scrolled* event occurs in a grid control or form when the horizontal or vertical scroll bars are clicked or a scroll box is moved. The parameter *nDirection* specifies how the user scrolled though the contents of a grid control or form. It then goes on to list the following possible values for *nDirection*:

Table 6.1 *Possible values for nDirection parameter in the grid's scrolled method*

Value	User scrolled using...
0	UP ARROW Key
1	DOWN ARROW Key
2	Vertical scroll bar in the area above the scroll box
3	Vertical scroll bar in the area below the scroll box
4	LEFT ARROW key
5	RIGHT ARROW key
6	Horizontal scroll bar in the area to the left of the scroll bar
7	Horizontal scroll bar in the area to the right of the scroll bar

We think the reference to **LEFT ARROW** and **RIGHT ARROW** keys implies that the use of these cursor keys to scroll the grid horizontally fires the *Scrolled* method and passes a value of either

4 or 5 for *nDirection*. It does not. Even though the grid may scroll as a result of using these keys, its *Scrolled* event never fires. What the Help file meant when it spoke about **LEFT ARROW** and **RIGHT ARROW** keys was, in fact, the left and right arrows on the horizontal scroll bar.

This is the reason that the *AfterRowColChange* method of the grdMLHeader class contains the following lines of code:

```
Grid::AfterRowColChange( nColIndex )
This.RefreshHeaders()
NODEFAULT
```

The key to the functionality of this grid class can be found in its *RefreshHeaders* method. This method ensures that each column in the visible portion of the grid has the appropriate label positioned correctly above its header:

```
LOCAL lnCol, lcName, lnHdrLeft, lnHdrWidth

Thisform.LockScreen = .T.
WITH This

  *** Loop through each column and make sure that the label's Left and Width
  *** properties are set correctly
  FOR lnCol = 1 TO .ColumnCount
    lcName = "dHeader" + LTRIM( STR( lnCol ) )
    WITH EVAL("This.Parent." + lcName)
      lnHdrWidth = This.Columns[ lnCol ].Width - ( 2 * This.nHdrMargin )
      .Width = IIF( lnHdrWidth > 0, lnHdrWidth, 0 )
      lnHdrLeft = OBJTOCLIENT( This.Columns[ lnCol ].Controls[ 1 ], 2 )

      *** If we are in a container, find out the offset from the form
      *** and adjust the left value
      IF UPPER( This.Parent.BaseClass ) # 'FORM'
        lnHdrLeft = lnHdrLeft - OBJTOCLIENT( This.Parent, 2 )
      ENDIF
```

If the column is not in the visible portion of the grid, the first call to **OBJTOCLIENT** returns zero. If the grid is on a page or in another container, lnHdrLeft will contain a negative value after the second call. So if lnHdrLeft is greater than zero, the current column must be in the visible portion of the grid:

```
      *** Only set the left and visible properties if this column in the
      *** visible portion of the grid.
      IF lnHdrLeft > 0
        .Left = lnHdrLeft + This.nHdrMargin
        .Visible = .T.

        *** make sure that the width doesn't overflow the visible
        *** portion of the grid
        IF .Left + .Width > This.nRight
          lnHdrWidth = This.nRight - .Left - ( 2 * This.nHdrMargin )
          .Width = IIF( lnHdrWidth > 0, lnHdrWidth, 0 )
        ENDIF
      ELSE
        .Visible = .F.
```

```
      ENDIF
    ENDWITH
  ENDFOR
ENDWITH
Thisform.LockScreen = .F.
```

The grid class contains another method called *KeepHeadersVisible*. This method, as its name implies, keeps the labels that float above the grid headers visible when the grid loses focus. Whenever the grid loses focus, the multiline headers disappear because the grid's headers move to the front of the z-order and hide the labels. The only way we found to keep this from happening was by invoking the grid's *KeepHeadersVisible* method in the *GotFocus* method of every object on the form as well as in the form's *LostFocus*. As we stated earlier, the increased functionality of this grid class carries a high price tag.

Using tool tip text instead of multiline headers

A simple solution for providing verbose descriptions for grid column headers is providing tool tips for the user. This is can be accomplished quickly even though headers do not have a *ToolTipText* property. The header can make use of the grid's *ToolTipText*. A single line of code, in the header's *MouseMove* method, sets the grid's *ToolTipText* appropriately. Just remember to set the form's *ShowTips* property to true, since it is set to false by default:

```
This.Parent.Parent.ToolTipText = 'This is a long header description for the
column'
```

Of course, there is always the possibility that once your end users see these nifty tool tips, they will clamor to have them on every grid in the application. In that case, you will probably want to create a custom header class containing the code to set the grid's *ToolTipText* property in its *MouseMove* method. It is easy to define custom headers, but it cannot be done visually. It has to be defined with code:

```
DEFINE CLASS HdrBase AS Header

FUNCTION MouseMove
  LPARAMETERS nButton, nShift, nXCoord, nYCoord
  WITH This
    .Parent.Parent.ToolTipText = .Tag
  ENDWITH
ENDFUNC

ENDDEFINE
```

The last requirement is a custom grid builder that, among other things, automatically replaces Visual FoxPro's base class headers with your custom headers at design time. After running the builder, you can place the *ToolTipText* into the custom header's tag property. For our industrial strength grid builder, see the chapter on developer productivity tools.

How do I change the grid's display order? *(Example: Ch06.VCX::grdSetOrder)*

As usual, the answer is "it depends." The Combo-Grid in the last chapter used a shortcut menu selection to accomplish this. The same functionality can be obtained by calling a custom grid method from the header's *Click*. Like the previous example, if all of your grids need this is functionality you should enhance your custom header class by adding some code to its *Click* method.

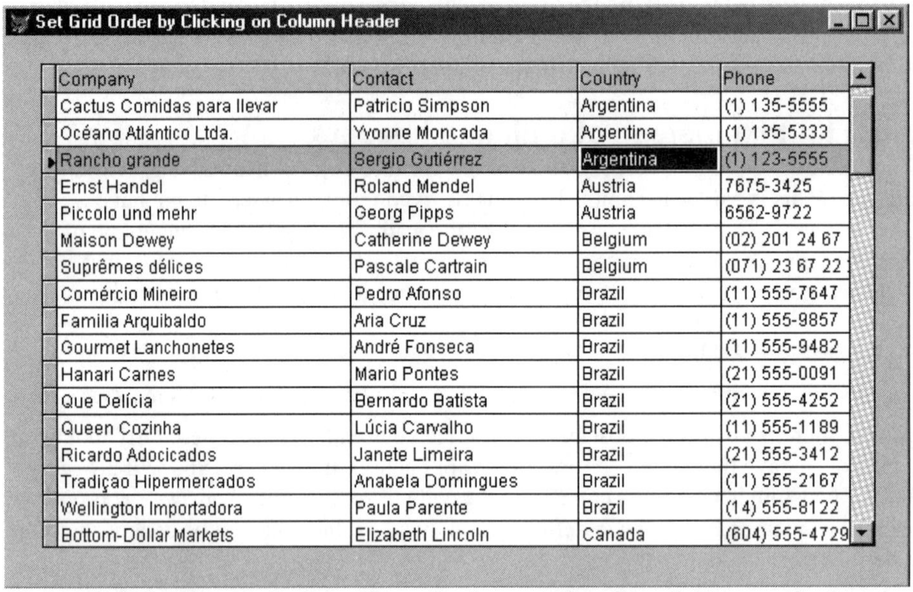

Company	Contact	Country	Phone
Cactus Comidas para llevar	Patricio Simpson	Argentina	(1) 135-5555
Océano Atlántico Ltda.	Yvonne Moncada	Argentina	(1) 135-5333
Rancho grande	Sergio Gutiérrez	Argentina	(1) 123-5555
Ernst Handel	Roland Mendel	Austria	7675-3425
Piccolo und mehr	Georg Pipps	Austria	6562-9722
Maison Dewey	Catherine Dewey	Belgium	(02) 201 24 67
Suprêmes délices	Pascale Cartrain	Belgium	(071) 23 67 22
Comércio Mineiro	Pedro Afonso	Brazil	(11) 555-7647
Familia Arquibaldo	Aria Cruz	Brazil	(11) 555-9857
Gourmet Lanchonetes	André Fonseca	Brazil	(11) 555-9482
Hanari Carnes	Mario Pontes	Brazil	(21) 555-0091
Que Delícia	Bernardo Batista	Brazil	(21) 555-4252
Queen Cozinha	Lúcia Carvalho	Brazil	(11) 555-1189
Ricardo Adocicados	Janete Limeira	Brazil	(21) 555-3412
Tradiçao Hipermercados	Anabela Domingues	Brazil	(11) 555-2167
Wellington Importadora	Paula Parente	Brazil	(14) 555-8122
Bottom-Dollar Markets	Elizabeth Lincoln	Canada	(604) 555-4729

***Figure 6.4** Grid items displayed in order by country after clicking on the header*

Here is the code that goes in the header's *Click* method:

```
WITH This.Parent
   .Parent.SetOrder( JUSTEXT( .ControlSource ) )
ENDWITH
```

There is a hidden assumption here – that you, like us, follow the convention of giving single field index tags the same name as the fields on which they are based. The *SetOrder* method of this grid class, which is called from the header's *Click* method, depends on this being true:

```
LPARAMETERS tcTag

*** Make sure a valid tag name was passed
IF ! EMPTY( tcTag )

  *** Make sure we have the procedure file loaded so we can access the
```

```
*** IsTag() function
SET PROCEDURE TO Ch06 ADDITIVE
WITH This
   *** Make sure it really is a tag for the grid's RecordSource
   IF IsTag( tcTag, .RecordSource )

      *** Go ahead and set the order for the table
      SELECT ( .RecordSource )
      SET ORDER TO ( tcTag )
      .SetFocus()
   ENDIF
ENDWITH
ENDIF
```

How do I control the cursor? *(Example: NxtGridRow.scx)*

When the user presses the **TAB** or **ENTER** key to navigate to the next cell, the grid's default behavior is to move to the next column in the same row. You may require your grid to behave a little differently, especially if it's being used to display mathematical calculations. Although a grid is not a spreadsheet, your end users may find it easier to learn if its keystrokes behave in a familiar way, perhaps like Microsoft Excel. It is a simple task to build grids that navigate vertically instead of horizontally when the user presses **TAB** or **ENTER** and because you can create it as a class, it only has to be done once. The *txtGrdNextRow* text box class provided with the sample code for this chapter provides this functionality. It has a single custom method called Move2NextRow and is called from the text box's *KeyPress* method when the **ENTER** or **TAB** key is detected:

```
LOCAL lnMaxRows

lnMaxRows = INT( ( .Height - .HeaderHeight - ;
   IIF( INLIST( .ScrollBars, 1, 3 ), SYSMETRIC( 8 ), 0 ) ) / .RowHeight )

WITH This.Parent.Parent
   IF RelativeRow >= lnMaxRows

      *** This means we are on the last row in the visible portion of the grid
      *** So we have to scroll the grid down one line

      .DoScroll( 1 )
   ENDIF
   .ActivateCell( .RelativeRow + 1, .RelativeColumn )
ENDWITH
```

How do I display the last full page of a grid? *(Example: EndofGrid.scx)*

Generally speaking, when a form containing a grid is instantiated, the first record displayed in the grid is the first record in its *RecordSource*. Obviously, if you have code in the grid's *Init* method that moves the record pointer, this is not going to be true. But there are situations in which you want to display a fully populated grid where the last available record is displayed as the last line of the grid. This can be done, but it is not a trivial exercise.

At first you may think "Oh, this is a piece of cake! All I have to do is something like this:"

```
WITH This
  GO BOTTOM IN ( .RecordSource )
  SKIP - <Number of rows - 1> IN ( .RecordSource )
  .SetFocus()
ENDWITH
```

But if you actually test this approach, you will quickly discover that it doesn't perform correctly. Even though the grid is positioned on the correct record, this record is in the middle of the page and you must use the **PAGE DOWN** key to see the last record. If this is a common requirement for your grids, this sample code in the *Init* method of EndOfGrid.scx is generic and can easily be put in a custom method of your grid class:

```
LOCAL lnKey, lnMaxRows, lcKeyField

*** Make sure procedure file is loaded
SET PROCEDURE TO Ch06.prg ADDITIVE

*** Display the last page of the grid when the form instantiates
IF DODEFAULT()
  WITH Thisform.GrdCustomer

    *** Calculate the maximum number of rows per grid page
    lnMaxRows = INT( ( .Height - .HeaderHeight - ;
      IIF( INLIST( .ScrollBars, 1, 3 ), SYSMETRIC( 8 ), 0 ) ) / .RowHeight )

    *** Get the name of the primary key field in the grid's RecordSource
    *** GetPKFieldName is a function defined in the procedure file for this
    *** Chapter (Ch06.prg)
    lcKeyField = GetPKFieldName( .RecordSource )

    *** Get the primary or candidate key of the first record to be displayed
    *** on the last page of the grid since the goal is to have the grid filled
    *** when the form opens
    GO BOTTOM IN ( .RecordSource )
    SKIP -( lnMaxRows - 1 ) IN ( .RecordSource )

    *** Save the primary or candidate key of this record if it has one
    IF ! EMPTY( lcKeyField )
      lnKey = EVAL( .RecordSource + '.' + lcKeyField )
      GO BOTTOM IN ( .RecordSource )
      .Refresh()

      *** Scroll up one record until we are on the one we want
      DO WHILE .T.
        .ActivateCell( 1, 1 )
        IF EVAL( .RecordSource + '.' + lcKeyField ) = lnKey
          EXIT
        ELSE
          .DoScroll( 0 )
        ENDIF
      ENDDO
```

```
      ENDIF
    ENDWITH
ENDIF
```

How do I use a grid to select one or more rows? *(Example: SelGrid.scx)*

A multiselect grid is the perfect solution when you must present the user with a large list of items from which multiple selections may be made. The only requirement is that the table used as the grid's *RecordSource* must have a logical field that can be set to true when that row is selected. If the base table does not have a logical field, it's a simple matter to provide one by either creating a local view from the table or by using it to construct an updateable cursor. See Chapter 9 for details on how to construct a *RecordSource* for the grid containing this selection flag.

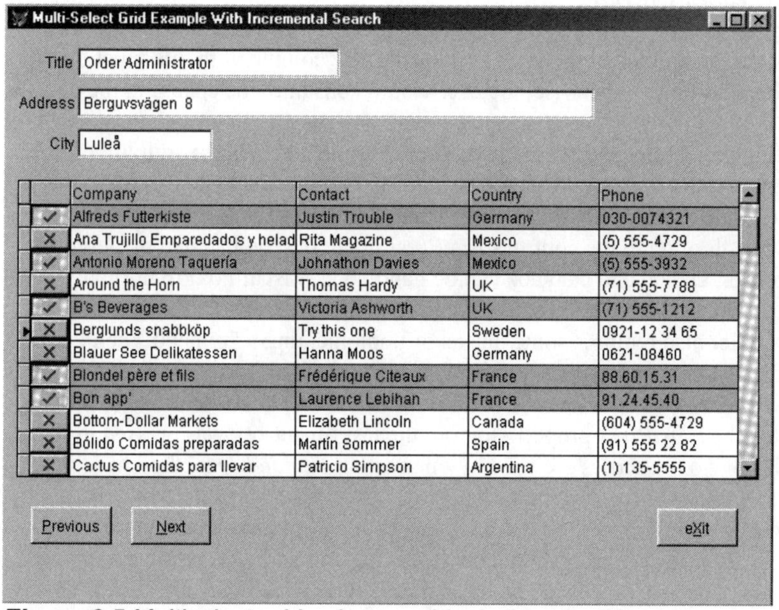

Figure 6.5 *Multiselect grid using graphical style checkboxes*

Setting up this grid is so easy it doesn't even require a custom grid class. In the example above, we merely dropped one of our base class grids (Ch06::grdBase) onto our form and added three lines of code to its *SetGrid* method:

```
DODEFAULT()

*** Set up for highlighting ALL Selected Rows
This.SetAll( 'DynamicBackColor', ;
  'IIF( lSelected, RGB( 0, 0, 128 ), RGB( 0, 0, 0 ) )', 'COLUMN' )
This.SetAll( 'DynamicBackColor', ;
  'IIF( lSelected, RGB( 0,255,255 ), RGB( 255, 255, 255 ) )', 'COLUMN' )
```

All that remains is to add a graphical style check box to the grid's first column and put two lines of code in its *Click* method:

```
DODEFAULT()
KEYBOARD '{DNARROW}'
```

This code moves the cursor to the next row in the grid. More importantly, it correctly highlights the current row depending on whether or not the user selected it. This is because the SETALL method that is used to highlight selected rows, does not change the grid's appearance until either a *Grid.SetFocus()* or a *Grid.Refresh()* is issued. Constantly refreshing the grid will degrade performance and moving to the next row accomplishes the same objective and makes the grid more convenient for the end user.

How do I give my multiselect grid incremental search capability?
(Example: Ch06.VCX::txtSearchGrid)
Technically speaking, this is accomplished by dropping a text box with incremental search capability into one or more columns of the grid. Obviously, any column with this functionality must, by definition, be read-only. Otherwise, the user would constantly be changing the data as he was searching!

The key to creating an incremental search text box for use in a grid is the addition of the *cSearchString* property to hold the current search string. This implies that all keystrokes are intercepted and passed to a custom keystroke handler that either uses the key to build the search string or passes it through to the control's *KeyPress* method to be handled by default. (Navigation keys like TAB, ENTER, and DNARROW can be handled as Visual FoxPro normally handles such keystrokes.)

The keystroke handler also requires some means of implementing a "time out" condition to reset the search string. The custom property, *nTimeOut*, holds the maximum number of seconds that may elapse between keystrokes before the control times out and its *cSearchString* property is reset. We also added the *tLastPress* property to hold the last time a key was pressed in DateTime format. These two properties are used by our custom *Handlekey* method to accomplish this task.

We gave the text box a *SetTag* method that includes code to optimize searching by using index tags if they are available. It runs when the control is instantiated. We assume, as always, that all single field index tags have the same name as the field on which they are based. This is how the *SetTag* method initializes the text box's custom *cTag* property:

```
WITH This.Parent

   *** If the column is bound, see if there is a tag in the grid's RecordSource
   *** that has the same name as the field the column is bound to
   IF ! EMPTY( .ControlSource )

      *** Make sure the procedure file is loaded
      SET PROCEDURE TO Ch06.Prg ADDITIVE
      IF IsTag( JUSTEXT( .ControlSource ), .Parent.RecordSource )
         This.cTag = JUSTEXT( .ControlSource )
      ENDIF
   ENDIF
ENDIF
```

```
ENDWITH
```

Most of the work is done in the control's *HandleKey* method, which is called from its *KeyPress* method. If the keystroke is handled successfully by this method, `.T.` is returned to the *KeyPress* method, which then issues a **NODEFAULT**. If the keystroke is not handled by this method, `.F.` is returned and the default Visual FoxPro *KeyPress* behavior occurs:

```
LPARAMETERS tnKeyCode

*** First check to see if we have a key that we can handle
*** A 'printable' character, backspace or <DEL> are good candidates
IF BETWEEN( tnKeyCode, 32, 128 ) OR tnKeyCode = 7
  WITH This

    *** First check to see if we have timed out
    *** and reset the search string if we have
    IF DATETIME() - .tLastPress > .nTimeOut
      .cSearchString = ''
    ENDIF

    *** So now handle the key
    DO CASE
      CASE tnKeyCode = 7

        *** If the delete key was pressed, reset the search string
        *** and exit stage left
        .cSearchString = ''
        RETURN .T.
      CASE tnKeyCode = 127
        *** Backspace: Remove the last character from the Search string
        IF LEN( .cSearchString ) . 1
          .cSearchString = LEFT( .cSearchString, LEN( .cSearchString ) - 1 )
        ELSE
          .cSearchString = ''
          RETURN .T.
        ENDIF
      OTHERWISE

        *** A garden variety printable character
        *** add it to the search string
        .cSearchString = .cSearchString + CHR( tnKeyCode )
    ENDCASE

    *** Search for the closest match in the grid's recordsource
    .Search()

    *** Update value for KeyPress interval timer
    .tLastPress = DATETIME()
  ENDWITH
ELSE

  *** Not a key we can handle. Let VFP handle it by default
  This.cSearchString = ''
  RETURN .F.
ENDIF
```

The *Search* method tries to find the closest match to the search string in the grid's *RecordSource*. If no match is found, it restores the record pointer to its current position:

```
LOCAL lnSelect, lnCurRec, lcAlias

*** Save Current work area
lnSelect = SELECT()

*** Get the grid's RecordSource
lcAlias = This.Parent.Parent.RecordSource

Thisform.LockScreen = .T.

*** Search for the closes match to the Search string
WITH This

   *** Save the current record
   lnCurRec = RECNO( lcAlias )
   IF ! EMPTY( .cTag )
     *** Use an index tag if one exists
     IF SEEK( UPPER( .cSearchString ), lcAlias, .cTag )
       *** Do nothing...we found a record
     ELSE

       *** Restore the record pointer
       GO lnCurRec IN ( lcAlias )
     ENDIF
   ELSE

     *** No Tag...have to use LOCATE
     SELECT ( lcAlias )
     LOCATE FOR UPPER( EVAL( JUSTEXT( .Parent.ControlSource ) ) ) = ;
       UPPER( .cSearchString )
     IF ! FOUND()
       GO lnCurRec
     ENDIF
     SELECT ( lnSelect )
   ENDIF
ENDWITH

Thisform.LockScreen = .F.
```

How do I use DynamicCurrentControl? *(Example: DCCGrid.scx)*

Use this property to choose which of several possible controls in single grid column is displayed at any time. Like other dynamic properties such as *DynamicBackColor* and *DynamicForeColor*, you can specify a condition that is evaluated each time the grid is refreshed.

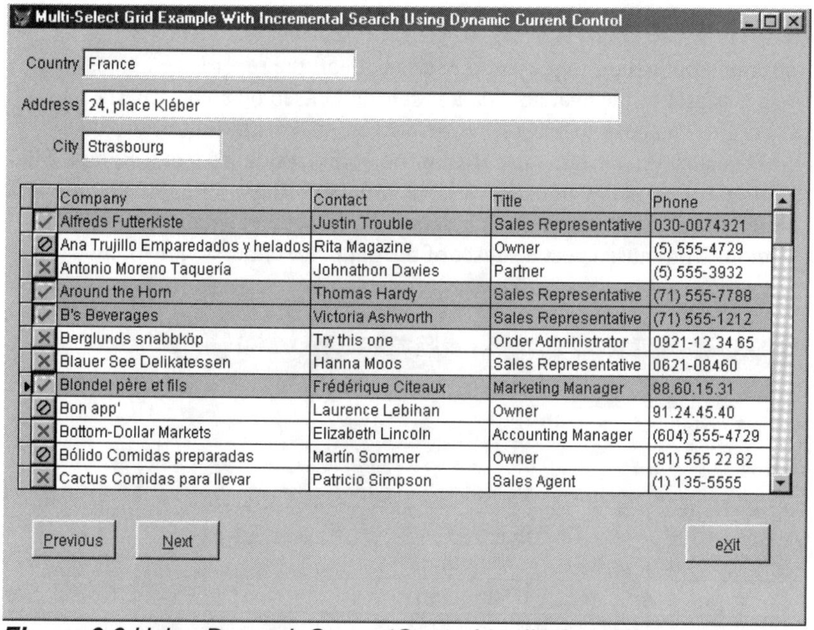

Figure 6.6 Using DynamicCurrentControl to display different controls

This example uses *DynamicCurrentControl* to selectively enable the graphical style check box in the first column of the grid. This is the only way to accomplish this as using the column's *SetAll* method to selectively enable the check boxes does not work. This code, in the grid's *SetGrid* method, causes any check box in the column to become disabled when an attempt is made to set focus to it:

```
This.collSelected.setall( "Enabled", ;
  IIF( UPPER( ALLTRIM( lv_Customer.Title ) ) = 'OWNER', .F., .T. ), ;
  "CHECKBOX" )
```

To take advantage of the column's *DynamicCurrentControl,* make sure the column contains all the controls to be displayed. For this to work, the column's *Sparse* property must also be set to false. The first column in the above grid contains two controls. The first is a base class graphical style check box. The second is a custom "disabled check box" class. After adding the controls to the column, the only other requirement is this line of code in the grid's *SetGrid* method:

```
This.collSelected.DynamicCurrentControl = ;
  "IIF( UPPER( ALLTRIM( lv_Customer.Title ) ) = 'OWNER', ;
  'chkDisabled', 'chkSelected' )"
```

When you run the example, you will see you cannot select any row where the contact's title is 'Owner.'

How do I filter the contents of a grid? *(Example: FilterGrid.scx)*

These days, it is rare for an application to present the user with all the records contained in a table. Most of the time, a subset of the available data is selected based on some criteria. The traditional method in FoxPro has been to use a filter. However, it's a bad idea to filter data being displayed in grid because grids cannot use Rushmore optimization. In fact, setting a filter on the *RecordSource* of your grid is the quickest way we know to bring your application to its knees. Moreover, as soon as you start working with data from a backend database, setting a filter is not even an option. You must select a subset of the data into either a view or an updateable cursor.

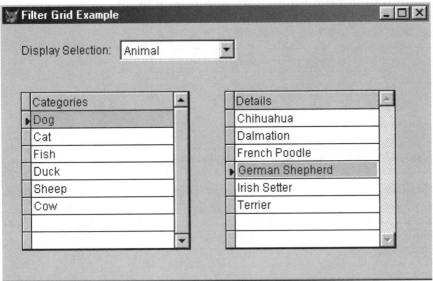

Figure 6.7 *Filtered grids using updateable cursor and parameterized view*

The code populating the *RecordSources* for the grids pictured above can be found in their respective *Reset* methods. The *Reset* method is a template method that was added to our base class grid for this purpose. Since the contents of the details grid depends on which row is the *ActiveRow* in the categories grid, and the contents of the categories grid depends on what is selected in the combo box, a *ResetGrids* method was added to the form. The method is called from the combo box's *Valid* method and merely calls each grid's *Reset* method.

The *RecordSource* of the categories grid is an updateable cursor. This cursor, csrCategory, is defined in the form's *Load* method using the CREATE CURSOR command. The cursor is populated in the grid's *Reset* method by ZAPping csrCategory, SELECTing the appropriate records into a temporary cursor and then appending the records from the temporary cursor into csrCategory. *Reset* is a custom method we added to our grid class to consistently populate or re-populate all grids using a common method. Here is the code from the categories grid's *Reset* method:

```
SELECT csrCategory
ZAP
SELECT * FROM Categories ;
   WHERE Categories.Cat_No = This.Parent.cboSections.Value ;
      INTO CURSOR Temp NOFILTER
SELECT csrCategory
APPEND FROM DBF( 'Temp' )
USE IN Temp
GO TOP IN csrCategory
This.nRecNo = 1
This.Refresh()
```

There are a few reasons for doing it like this. First, we can set the categories grid up visually in the form designer since its *RecordSource* exists prior to instantiation. More important is the fact that a grid does not like having its *RecordSource* ripped out from under it. If the grid's *RecordSource* were updated by SELECTing into it directly, it would appear as a blank grey blob on the screen. This is because the SELECT closes the cursor and effectively leaves the grid hanging in mid air, so to speak. ZAPping it, on the other hand, does not.

One way to avoid having the grid turn into a blank grey blob is to set its *RecordSource* to an empty string before running the SELECT and then resetting it afterward. Although this will work in the simplest of cases, it is not a solution we recommend. While it will keep your grid from losing its mind, the grid's columns still lose their *ControlSources* and any embedded controls. So, this works if your grid uses base class headers, base class text boxes, and displays the fields from the cursor in exactly the same order as they are SELECTed. Otherwise, you have to write a lot more code to restore all the things that get lost when the grid is re-initialized.

Another way to display a filtered subset in a grid is to use a parameterized view as its *RecordSource*. This is how it is accomplished in the details grid. It's *Reset* method uses the following code to change what is displayed. This method is called from the *AfterRowColChange* method of the categories grid to keep the two in synch:

```
LOCAL vp_Cat_Key

vp_Cat_Key = csrCategory.Cat_Key
REQUERY( 'lv_Details' )
GO TOP IN lv_Details
This.nRecNo = 1
This.Refresh()
```

The view to which it is bound is in the form's data environment and has its *NoDataOnLoad* property set to true. We do this because we don't know which details will be displayed in the grid initially and we do not want Visual FoxPro to prompt the user for a view parameter when the form opens. For more detailed information on parameterized views, see Chapter 9.

So what about data entry grids? *(Example: Ch06.VCX::grdDataEntry and DataEntryGrid.scx)*

So what about them? They are definitely not for the timid. If you try to force them to do things they don't handle well, they will be your worst nightmare! For example, in some accounting applications it makes sense to provide a grid for data entry. In this case, the end user is probably going to be most comfortable using this type of interface since most accountants seem to love spreadsheets. We have been able to use data entry grids without tearing out our hair in the process. This is because we have taken time to understand how grids work and have found some techniques that work consistently and reliably. We are sharing them with you so your experience with data entry grids can be less painful than it seems to be for most.

A word of caution is in order here. If you examine the code in our sample data entry grid form, you will be struck by the number of work-arounds (kludges, if you want to be blunt about it) required to implement functionality within the grid itself. We left it in the sample to show you that it **can** be done. However, you pay a high price if you try to get too cute with your data entry grids. The more functionality you try to include within the grid, the more problems you will have because of the complex interaction between grid events and those of the contained controls. For example, if you have code in the *LostFocus* method of a text box in a grid column that causes the grid's *BeforeRowColChange* event to fire, and there is code in that method that should not execute in this situation, you must use a flag to determine when it should be executed. This can get ugly very quickly. Keep it simple, and you will keep your headaches to a minimum.

How do I add new records to my grid?

The *AllowAddNew* property was added to the grid in Visual FoxPro version 5.0. When this property is set to true, a new record is added to the grid automatically if the user presses the DOWN ARROW key while the cursor is positioned on the grid's last row. Setting this property to true to add new records to the grid is not ideal because you have no control over when and how records are added.

There are a couple of different ways to add new records to the grid. We prefer using a NEW button next to the grid. A command button displayed next to the grid with the caption "New <Something or Other>" is unambiguous. Even a novice end-user can figure out that clicking on a "New" button adds a new record to the grid (although we **did** wonder if someone would mistakenly think it meant "New Grid"). You can also simulate what Visual FoxPro does when *AllowAddNew* is set to true. For example, check to see if the user pressed the ENTER, TAB, or DOWN ARROW key in the grid's last column and add a record if the cursor is positioned on the last row of the grid.

Most users seem to prefer to add new records to the bottom of the grid. This is the default behavior when the grid's *RecordSource* is displayed in natural order. However, if the grid's *RecordSource* has a controlling index tag in effect, the newly appended record appears at the top of the grid. This is why our custom *AddNewRecord* method of the data entry grid class saves the current order and turns off the indexes before adding the new record. After the new record has focus, the original order is restored, leaving the newly appended record as the last one in the grid:

```
LOCAL lcOrder, loColumn
WITH This

   *** First check to see if we have an index order set on the table
   *** because we want add the new record to the bottom of the grid
   *** and not in index order
   lcOrder = ORDER( .RecordSource )
   Thisform.LockScreen = .T.
   SELECT ( .RecordSource )
   SET ORDER TO
   APPEND BLANK IN ( .RecordSource )

   *** Find out which column is the first column
   FOR EACH loColumn IN .Columns
     IF loColumn.ColumnOrder = 1
       loColumn.SetFocus()
       EXIT
     ENDIF
   ENDFOR

   *** Reset the previous order
   IF ! EMPTY( lcOrder )
     SET ORDER TO ( lcOrder ) IN ( .RecordSource )
   ENDIF
   .RefreshControls()
   ThisForm.LockScreen = .F.
ENDWITH
```

This method can be called from the custom *OnClick* method of a command button, or it can be called conditionally from the *KeyPress* method of a control contained in a grid column. This code in the *LostFocus* method of the text box in the last grid column can be used to automatically add a new record in the grid when the cursor is positioned on its last row. Take note of the code that explicitly sets focus to a different object on the form. Attempting to add a record to the grid's *RecordSource* when the grid is the *ActiveControl*, causes Visual FoxPro to raise error 109 ("Record in use by another").

```
*** Check to see if TAB, ENTER, or DNARROW was pressed
IF INLIST( LASTKEY(), 9, 13, 24 )
  WITH This.Parent.Parent

     *** Check for EOF so if we are at end of file we can add a new record if
     *** TAB, ENTER, OR DownArrow was hit
     SKIP IN ( .RecordSource )
     IF ! EOF( .RecordSource )
       SKIP -1 IN ( .RecordSource )
     ELSE

       *** Set focus elsewhere to avoid Error 109 - 'Record in use by another'
       *** We may as well set focus to the page temporarily
       *** Also, if we do NOT set focus elsewhere, even though the AddNewRecord
       *** method DOES indeed add a new record, the cursor moves to the first
       *** column of the last row and does NOT move to the first column of the
       *** newly added record. We must also set the lAdding flag so validation
       *** doesn't occur on the record before it is displayed in the grid
       .lAdding = .T.
       .Parent.SetFocus()
```

```
      .AddNewRecord()
      .lAdding = .F.
      NODEFAULT
    ENDIF
  ENDWITH
ENDIF
```

Once the new record has been added and the user begins editing, what should happen? If the grid is displayed in indexed order, the newly added record should move to its proper position as soon as the relevant field is populated. In order to display the record in its proper position, you could just move the record pointer, move it back, and refresh the grid. This works but may have some unpleasant visual side effects. A better solution can be found in the *txtOrderGrid* text box class. It can be used in grid columns that are bound to the key field of the grid's controlling index tag in order to change the grid's display order as soon as the text box loses focus:

```
LOCAL lnrecno

*** If the grid's RecordSource has its order set to the index tag
*** on this field, we want make sure that as soon as we change its contents,
*** the grid's display order reflects this change.
*** First, check to see if we have changed this field
IF INLIST( GETFLDSTATE( JUSTEXT( This.ControlSource ), ;
  This.Parent.Parent.RecordSource ), 2, 4 )
  Thisform.LockScreen = .T.
  WITH This.Parent.Parent
    lnRecno = RECNO( .RecordSource )

    *** Scroll Up one Page
    GO TOP IN ( .RecordSource )
    .DoScroll(2)

    *** Scroll back down one page
    GO BOTTOM IN ( .RecordSource )
    .DoScroll(3)

    *** Finally, go back to the original record
    GO lnRecno IN ( .RecordSource )
  ENDWITH
  Thisform.LockScreen = .f.
ENDIF
```

How do I handle row level validation in my data entry grid?

As usual, there are several ways to handle record level validation. If the data entry grid is bound to a Visual FoxPro table, a rule can be defined in the DBC (see Chapter 7 for more information on table rules). If the grid's *RecordSource* is a view, DBSETPROP() can be used to define a row level rule. Any time the user attempts to move to a different row in the grid, the rule will fire and validate the current row. Seems pretty simple, doesn't it? Well, not exactly. Table rules do not provide complete row level validation in all situations and code is still required to ensure this validation is performed where required. For example, the user can exit the grid and close the form, leaving an invalid record in the grid's *RecordSource*. In this case, the table rule does not fire because the record pointer hasn't moved. And what if you decide to use an updateable cursor as the *RecordSource* for your grid? Technically speaking, you are then scientifically out of luck.

Our data entry grid class contains generic code to handle record level validation. The actual validation is handled in the template method called *ValidateCurrentRow* that we added to our data entry grid class for just this purpose. The code in this method is instance specific and can be used to validate the current row in the grid's *RecordSource* even if it is an updateable cursor. If you have chosen to define a record level rule for your table or view, the method can be left empty with no problem. The result is a generic data entry grid class that can be used with any type of *RecordSource* and perform row level validation when necessary. The only requirement is that the grid's *RecordSource* be table buffered.

The basic methodology used here is to save the current record number in the grid's *BeforeRowColChange* method. Then, in its *AfterRowColChange* method, this saved value is compared to the current record number. If they are different, the user has moved to a different row in the grid. In this case, the record pointer is moved back to the record that the user just left, and the contents of that record are validated. If the record is valid, the intended movement to the new record is allowed to proceed.

The only problem is that moving the record pointer programmatically in the grid's *RecordSource* causes its *BeforeRowColChange* event to fire. That's why we check to see if we are in the middle of the validation process in this method:

```
WITH This
   IF .lValidatingRow
     NODEFAULT
   ELSE

     *** Save current record number to grid property
     .nRec2Validate = RECNO(.RecordSource)

     *** This code handles highlighting the current row
     IF !.lAbout2LeaveGrid
       .nRecNo = 0
     ENDIF
   ENDIF
ENDWITH
```

The grid's *lValidatingRow* property is set to true in its *AfterRowColChange* method when the validation process begins. Here is the code that initiates the process and handles the movement between grid rows:

```
LOCAL lnRec2GoTo
WITH This

   *** If there is no record to validate, exit stage left
   IF .nRec2Validate = 0
     RETURN
   ENDIF

   *** Save the current record number in case we have changed rows
   lnRec2GoTo = RECNO( .RecordSource )
```

```
*** Check to see if the row has changed
IF .nRec2Validate # lnRec2GoTo

   *** We are validating the row we are attempting to leave...set the flag
   .lValidatingRow = .T.

   *** Return to the record we just left
   GOTO .nRec2Validate IN ( .RecordSource )

   *** If it checks out, let the user move to the new row
   IF .ValidateCurrentRow()
     GOTO lnRec2GoTo IN ( .RecordSource )
     .RefreshControls()
   ENDIF

   *** Finished with validation...reset flag
   .lValidatingRow = .F.
 ENDIF
ENDWITH
```

Finally, we add a little code to the data entry grid class's *Valid* method. This prevents the user from leaving the grid if the current row contains invalid information:

```
*** Make sure the current row stays highlighted when focus leaves the grid
This.LAbout2LeaveGrid = .T.

*** Make sure the current grid row is valid before leaving the grid
IF ! This.ValidateCurrentRow()
   RETURN 0
ENDIF
```

The code in the grid's *ValidateCurrentRow* method is instance specific. Since it is called whenever the user attempts to move off the current row, changes to this record can be committed if they pass validation. However, there is a small problem when this method is called from the Grid's *Valid* method. Because the grid's *Valid* fires before the *Valid* of the *CurrentControl* in the grid, this method must also ensure that the *ControlSource* of the active grid cell has been updated from its value **before** it attempts to validate the current record. Trying to explain this reasoning is difficult, so we are going to attempt to clarify this using an example.

Suppose a new record has been added to the grid and the information is being entered. After entering the telephone number, the user clicks on the form's close button to exit. In this case, the grid's *Valid* fires, calling its *ValidateCurrentRow* method. At this point, the *Valid* event of the text box, bound to the telephone number field, has not yet fired. Therefore, the text box in the grid contains the value that was just entered by the user, but its *ControlSource* (i.e.; the telephone number in the record buffer) is still empty. Attempting to run the record level validation at this point, before forcing the *Valid* of the text box to fire, would produce erroneous results. The validation would correctly display a message informing the user that the telephone number field could not be blank even though the user could see a telephone number on the screen!

To take care of this problem, we added code to the *ValidateCurrentRow* method, forcing the *Valid* method of the grid's active cell to fire before attempting to validate the current row.

The following code, from the sample form's *ValidateCurrentRow* method, illustrates the technique:

```
LOCAL lnRelativeColumn

*** Sneaky way to update data source from buffer
*** Otherwise, if this is called from the grid's valid when the user
*** tries to close the form by clicking on the close button or tries
*** to activate page 2, the error message will fire even if we have just
*** added a phone number but not tabbed off the cell yet
WITH This
  lnRelativeColumn = .RelativeColumn
  Thisform.LockScreen = .T.
  IF lnRelativeColumn = 1
    .ActivateCell( .RelativeRow, 2 )
  ELSE
    .ActivateCell( .RelativeRow, 1 )
  ENDIF
  .ActivateCell( .RelativeRow, lnRelativeColumn )
  Thisform.LockScreen = .F.
  SELECT ( .RecordSource )

  *** Company, contact, and phone are required fields
  IF EMPTY( Company ) OR EMPTY( Contact ) OR EMPTY( Phone )
    MESSAGEBOX( 'Company, contact and telephone are required.', 48, ;
      'Please fix your entry' )
    RETURN .F.
  ELSE

    *** All is valid...go ahead and update the grid's record source
    IF !TABLEUPDATE( 0, .F., .RecordSource )
      MESSAGEBOX( 'Problem updating customer table', 64, 'So Sorry' )
    ENDIF
  ENDIF
ENDWITH
```

How do I delete records in my data entry grid?

A grid's *DeleteMark* property determines whether the delete flag is displayed for each row in the grid. When it is displayed, the user may toggle the deleted status of a record by clicking on the *DeleteMark*. However, allowing users to delete records in this fashion is not a good idea because is does not allow control over when and how the records are deleted. A better solution is to present the user with a command button that provides this functionality. Since there is no "right" answer, we have presented both approaches in the sample code.

As stated earlier, code volume and headaches are directly proportional to the amount of functionality you try to implement within your data entry grid. This is especially true when you allow users to delete and recall records in the grid by clicking on its *DeleteMark*. This is why the *DeleteRecord* method that we have added to the grdDataEntry class assumes it is being called from an object outside the grid.

The biggest problem when deleting grid records is making the record disappear from the grid. This problem is solved quite easily by moving the record pointer in the grids *RecordSource* and refreshing the grid, either by explicitly calling its *Refresh* method or by setting focus to it. Obviously, in order for this to work, DELETED must be set ON. Remember, SET DELETED is one of a long list of settings that is scoped to the current data session! This code from the *DeleteRecord* method of our data entry grid class illustrates how to make the deleted record disappear from the grid after it is deleted:

```
LOCAL loColumn

*** Make sure the user REALLY wants to delete the current record
*** Display Yes and No buttons, the exclamation point icon
*** and make the second button (NO) the default button
IF MESSAGEBOX( 'Are you ABSOLUTELY POSITIVELY Without a Doubt SURE' + ;
   CHR(13) + 'You Want to Delete This Record?', 4+48+256, ;
   'Are you REALLY Sure?' ) = 6
   WITH This

      *** If we are in the process of adding a record and decide to delete it
      *** Just revert it instead
      IF '3' $ GETFLDSTATE( -1, .RecordSource ) OR ;
         '4' $ GETFLDSTATE( -1, .RecordSource )
         TABLEREVERT( .F., .RecordSource )
         GO TOP IN ( .RecordSource )
      ELSE
         DELETE IN ( .RecordSource )
         SKIP IN ( .RecordSource )
         IF EOF()
            GO BOTTOM IN ( .RecordSource )
         ENDIF
      ENDIF

      *** Find out which column is the first column
      FOR EACH loColumn IN .Columns
         IF loColumn.ColumnOrder = 1
            loColumn.SetFocus()
            EXIT
         ENDIF
      ENDFOR
   ENDWITH
ENDIF
```

You can obtain enhanced functionality by setting the grid's *DeleteMark* property to true and calling *DeleteRecord* from the grid's *Deleted* method. It is much easier to allow the user to cancel out of an add operation without having to go through all the validation that takes place when he tries to click the delete button. It also allows the user to recall a record if he deleted one by accident. OK, so what's the downside? It is expensive because more code is required. This is also not a good solution if the grid's *RecordSource* is involved in persistent relationships. Recalling and deleting records in this situation could have some interesting consequences if you are using triggers to maintain referential integrity. Here is the code called from the grid's *Deleted* method that deletes and recalls records:

```
LPARAMETERS nRecNo

LOCAL llOK2Continue, loColumn
llOK2Continue = .T.
WITH This
```

Before taking action, we must verify we are positioned on the record to be deleted. It is possible to click on the delete mark in any row of the grid. The record pointer in the grid's *RecordSource* does not move until the *Deleted* method has completed. This means that, at this point in time, it's possible that nRecNo, the parameter passed to the *Deleted* method, is not the same as the RECNO() of the current record. However, moving the record pointer unconditionally to nRecNo causes the grid's AfterRowColChange to fire. Setting focus to the grid afterward to refresh it causes the grid's *Valid* to fire. Both these events cause the row level validation to take place. If the user is trying to delete a record that he just mistakenly added, we don't want this validation to occur. We just want to revert the record. And just to make things interesting, the record number of the newly appended record is a negative number while nRecNo is positive:

```
SELECT Cust_ID from Customer WHERE nRecNo = RECNO( ) INTO CURSOR Temp
IF _TALLY > 0

   *** Not the same record...so move the record pointer.
   IF Temp.Cust_ID # Customer.Cust_ID

      *** Make sure we are not in the middle of adding one record and trying to
      *** delete or recall one in a different one
      IF .ValidateCurrentRow()
        .Parent.SetFocus()
         GO nRecNo IN ( .RecordSource )
        .SetFocus()
      ELSE
         llOK2Continue = .F.
      ENDIF
   ENDIF
ENDIF

*** Since the record is not actually deleted yet
*** This will work to decide if we are actually recalling a record
IF llOK2Continue
   IF DELETED( .RecordSource )
      RECALL IN ( .RecordSource )

      *** Move record pointer to refresh grid
      SKIP IN ( .RecordSource )
      SKIP -1 IN ( .RecordSource )
   ELSE

      *** Check here to see if we were in the middle of adding this record

      *** when we turned around and decided to delete it instead.
      *** In this case, just revert the add to avoid PK violations later
      *** if we decide to recall it
      IF '3' $ GETFLDSTATE( -1, .RecordSource ) OR ;
         '4' $ GETFLDSTATE( -1, .RecordSource )
         TABLEREVERT( .F., .RecordSource )
         GO TOP IN ( .RecordSource )
      ELSE
         DELETE IN ( .RecordSource )

         *** Must do a TableUpdate as soon as the record is deleted.
         *** Otherwise, when it is recalled, you will get a PK violation
```

```
        IF ! TABLEUPDATE ( 0, .F., .RecordSource )
          MESSAGEBOX( 'Unable to Update Customer Table', 48, 'So Sorry!' )
        ENDIF

        *** Need to move record pointer to refresh display
        SKIP IN ( .RecordSource )
        IF EOF( .RecordSource )
          GO BOTTOM IN ( .RecordSource )
        ENDIF
      ENDIF
    ENDIF

    *** Refresh the grid by setting focus to it
    *** Find out which column is the first column
    FOR EACH loColumn IN .Columns
      IF loColumn.ColumnOrder = 1
        loColumn.SetFocus()
        EXIT
      ENDIF
    ENDFOR
  ENDIF
ENDWITH
```

How do I add a combo box to my grid? *(Example: cboGrid::Ch06.vcx and cboInGrid.scx)*

The mechanics of adding a combo box to a grid are exactly the same as any other control. However, a combo box is quite complex in its own right (see Chapter 5 for combo box details) and integrating its native functionality with a grid can be tricky. The biggest problem involves binding the grid column to a foreign key in its *RecordSource* while displaying the descriptive text associated with it. Secondary issues include controlling the grid's appearance and providing keyboard navigation. This section presents a classy solution to these issues. The sample code included with this chapter illustrates this solution using a drop down combo (Business Type) as well as a drop down list (Locations).

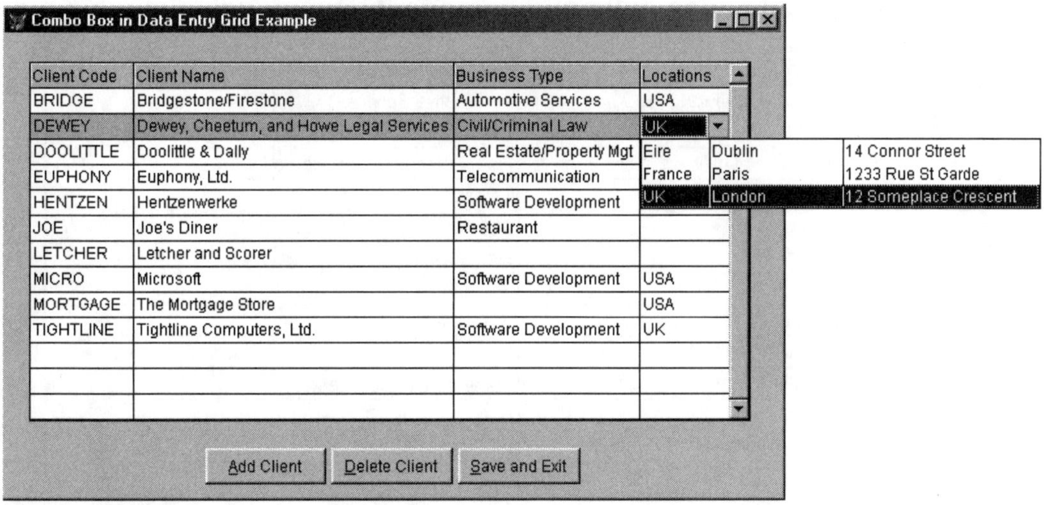

Figure 6.8 *Combo box in a grid*

The most common approach used when adding a combo box to a grid is to set the column's *Sparse* property to false. While this takes care of the problem of displaying descriptive text when the column is bound to a foreign key value, it's not a good solution. When combo boxes are displayed in every row, the grid looks cluttered. Apart from the unsightly appearance (see **Figure 6.9** below), there is a *Gotcha!* associated with using this technique to manage combos inside grids. The combo's *DisplayValue* may be truncated because the default *InputMask* for the grid column is calculated based on the width of its *ControlSource*. Fortunately, the workaround is simple. Just specify an *InputMask* for the column wide enough to accommodate the combo's *DisplayValue*. Unfortunately, there is no easy way to put this functionality into a class, so it is yet another task that must be performed at the instance level.

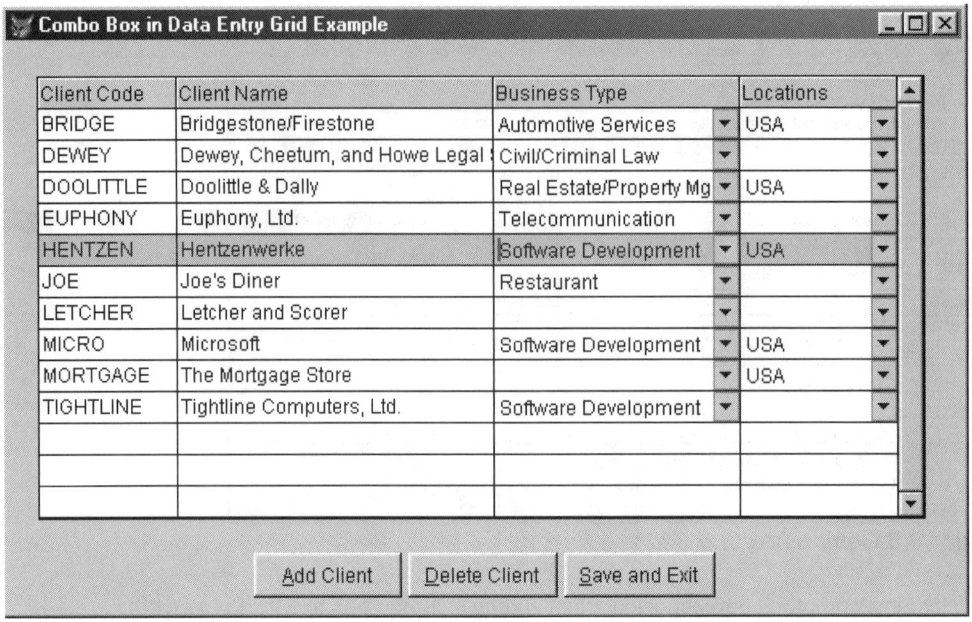

Figure 6.9 *Combos in every row appear cluttered*

When a combo box is required in a grid, we bind the grid to a local view or an updateable cursor. We make sure the descriptive text associated with the foreign key is present in the view or cursor so we can bind the column to that instead. You may wonder how we update the foreign key value in the grid's *RecordSource*. We use a special combo box class designed to address this issue. The code is generic, so it can be implemented with little additional overhead. There are just a few properties the developer must set.

The combo's *cFkField* property contains the name of the foreign key field in the grid's *RecordSource* that is associated with the descriptive text bound to the column. Its *nFkColumn* property specifies the column number containing the key value. The optional *lAllowAddNew* property, when set to true, allows the user to add entries to the combo's *RowSource* on the fly.

We added four custom methods to our grid combo box class: *ProcessSelection*, *UpdateGridRecordSource*, *AddNewEntry* and *HandleKey*. The combo's *ProcessSelection* method, called from its *Valid* method, calls its *UpdateGridRecordSource* method when the user selects a new value from the combo. If the combo's value hasn't changed, there is no need to update the grid's *RecordSource* and dirty the buffers. This method also invokes the *AddNewEntry* method when appropriate. *AddNewEntry* is a template method and code to insert a record into the lookup table must be added at the instance level, when the user is permitted to add new entries on the fly. All this activity is coordinated in the following *ProcessSelection* method:

```
WITH This

   *** Check to see if we have selected a valid entry in the combo
```

```
IF .ListIndex > 0

  *** If we haven't changed values, do not update the grid's recordSource
  *** We don't want to dirty the buffers if nothing has changed
  IF .uOriginalValue # .Value
    .UpdateGridRecordSource()
  ENDIF
ELSE

  *** If not, see if we typed something in the combo box
  *** that is not in the list
  IF ! EMPTY( .DisplayValue )

    *** add the new entry to the combo's RowSource
    *** if we are allowing the user to add new entries on the fly
    IF .lAllowAddNew
      .AddNewEntry( )
    ELSE
      MESSAGEBOX( 'Please select a valid entry in the list', 48, ;
        'Invalid Selection' )
      .Value = .uOriginalValue
    ENDIF
  ENDIF
ENDIF
ENDWITH
```

The *UpdateGridRecordSource* method replaces the Foreign key in the Grid's *RecordSource* with the primary key in the combo's *RowSource*. Because items in the combo's internal list are always stored as character data, we must first convert the list item to the correct data type using the *Str2Exp* function introduced in Chapter 2:

```
LOCAL lcField, lcTable

IF !EMPTY( .cFKField ) AND !EMPTY( .nFKColumn )
  lcTable = IIF( EMPTY( .cPrimaryTable ), ;
    .Parent.Parent.RecordSource, .cPrimaryTable)
  IF EMPTY( lcTable )
    MESSAGEBOX ;
      ( "You MUST set either This.cPrimaryTable OR the grid's RecordSource!", ;
      16, 'Developer Error!' )
  ELSE
    lcField = lcTable + "." + .cFKField
    REPLACE ( .cFKField ) WITH ;
      Str2Exp( .List[ .ListIndex, .nFKColumn ], ;
        TYPE( lcField ) ) IN ( lcTable )
  ENDIF
ENDIF
```

What other special functionality should a combo box have when inside a grid? We think the **UP ARROW** and **DOWN ARROW** keys should allow the user to navigate in the grid when the combo is closed but should also allow the user to traverse the list when it is dropped. The combo's custom *HandleKey* method is called from its *KeyPress* method to provide this functionality:

```
LPARAMETERS nKeyCode
LOCAL lnMaxRows, llRetVal

WITH This

  *** If escape or enter pressed, the list is not dropped down anymore
  IF nKeyCode = 27 OR nKeyCode = 13
    .lDroppedDown = .F.
  ENDIF

  *** If the list is not dropped down, traverse the grid with cursor keys
  IF !.lDroppedDown
    WITH .Parent.Parent

    *** Calculate the maximum number of rows in the visible portion of the grid
    lnMaxRows = INT( ( .Height - .HeaderHeight - ;
      IIF( INLIST( .ScrollBars, 1, 3 ), SYSMETRIC( 8 ), 0 ) ) / .RowHeight )

    *** Move up a row in the grid
    IF nKeyCode = 5 THEN

        *** If we are on the top row in the visible portion of the grid,
        *** Scroll the grid up a row in case there is a previous record

        IF .RelativeRow = 1
          .DoScroll( 0 )
        ENDIF
        .ActivateCell( .RelativeRow - 1, .RelativeColumn )
        ENDIF
        *** Let KeyPress know we have handled the keystroke
        llRetVal = .T.
      ELSE

        *** If we are on the bottom row in the visible portion of the grid,
        *** Scroll the grid down a row in case there is a next record

        IF nKeyCode = 24 THEN
          IF .RelativeRow >= lnMaxRows
            .DoScroll( 1 )
          ENDIF
          .ActivateCell( .RelativeRow + 1, .RelativeColumn )
          llRetVal = .T.
        ENDIF
      ENDIF
    ENDWITH
  ENDIF
ENDWITH

RETURN llRetVal
```

Is there anything else we might want a combo box in a grid to do? An obvious enhancement is to make each grid row display a different set of values. Take, for example, the grid pictured in **Figure 6.8**. It is possible for each client to have multiple locations. If screen real estate is at a premium, these locations can be displayed in a combo box. Just create a parameterized local view of locations by client. Set the combo box's *RowSourceType* to 6-Fields and select the required fields for the combo box's *RowSource*. A little code in the combo box's *GotFocus* method changes the contents of its *RowSource* to display the correct information for each grid row:

```
LOCAL lcGridAlias, vp_cl_key

DODEFAULT()
WITH This

  *** Requery the locations view to obtain all the locations for
  *** The client displayed in the current grid row
  WITH .Parent.Parent
    .nRecNo = RECNO(.RecordSource)
    lcGridAlias = .RecordSource
  ENDWITH
  vp_cl_Key = &lcGridAlias..Cl_Key
  REQUERY( 'lv_location' )

  *** Refresh the combo
  .Requery()
  .Refresh()
ENDWITH
```

Conclusion

Hopefully grids are now a little less misunderstood than when you started this chapter. We cannot hope to provide all the answers but have tried to offer as many pointers and hints as we can.

Chapter 7
Working with Data

"It is a capital mistake to theorize before one has data."
("The Adventures of Sherlock Holmes" by Sir Arthur Conan Doyle)

Visual FoxPro is, first and foremost, a relational database management system (RDMS). It has always had the fastest and most powerful data engine available on a PC platform. However, like all powerful development tools, Visual FoxPro can still prove awkward if you don't do things the way it expects. In this chapter we will cover some of the techniques and tips that we have learned from working with data in Visual FoxPro.

Tables in Visual FoxPro

Some basics

The basic unit of data storage in Visual FoxPro is still the '*DBF*' file, and its associated '*FPT*' (memo field) file. These files have their roots in the history of the xBase language and their format is still recognized as one of the standard structures by many applications. The DBF file format defines a record in terms of a number of fixed length fields whose data type is also defined. In what is now considered standard nomenclature, fields are referred to as the '*Columns*' and records as the '*Rows,*' while the DBF file itself is the '*Table.*'

Tables in Visual FoxPro are always stored as individual files (unlike Microsoft Access, for example, where the tables exist only inside the database [.*MDB*] file) and can exist as either "*free*" tables or be "*bound*" to a database container. A table can only be bound to a single database container at any time and, while it is bound to a database container, gains access to additional attributes and functionality which are not available when it is free (see the section on the database container in this chapter for more details). However, un-binding a table from a database container causes the irretrievable loss of these attributes and can result in major problems if it happens in an application environment.

The Visual FoxPro language has many commands and functions, which are concerned with the creation, modification and management of tables (and their close cousins, Cursors and Views). Part 2 of the Visual FoxPro Programmer's Guide (Chapters 5 through 8) is devoted to working with data and covers the basics pretty well. Additional information about the way the individual data management commands *actually* work can be found in 'The Hackers Guide to Visual FoxPro 6.0' (Granor and Roche, Hentzenwerke Publishing, 1998).

How to open the specific table you want to use

When working with the visual form designer, there is no real problem about identifying a table. You simply select the table through the 'Add' dialog called from the form's data environment. However when you need to refer to a table programmatically, things are more difficult.

The basic `USE <table>` command will open the first table with the specified name that it finds, according to the following rules:

- If a database is open, and is defined as the current database, it is searched first.
- If no database is open, or none is defined as current, the normal FoxPro search path is used

This has some implications for the programmer. If a table with the same name exists in more than one database, you must include a reference to the database when opening that table. The following code shows how this works:

```
CLOSE ALL
OPEN  DATABASE C:\VFP60\CH03\ch03
? SET( 'DATABASE' )    && Returns 'CH03'
OPEN DATABASE C:\VFP60\TIPSBOOK\DATA\tipsbook
? SET( 'DATABASE' )    && Returns 'TIPSBOOK'
USE clients            && Error - file does not exist!
USE ch03!clients       && Opens the correct table
```

By the way, notice that *opening* a database also sets it as the current database! Notice also that opening multiple databases makes the *last* one to be opened current. This needs watching when accessing stored procedures or using functions that operate on the *currently* set database (e.g. *DBGETPROP()*)

However if the database is not already open, and is not on the current search path, then even specifying the database will not be sufficient. You will need the full path as well. Thus to be certain of opening the '*Clients*' table in our "*CH03*" database we need to use a command like this:

```
CLOSE ALL
OPEN DATABASE C:\VFP60\TIPSBOOK\DATA\tipsbook
? SET( 'DATABASE' )           && Returns 'Tipsbook'
USE clients                   && Error - file does not exist!
USE ch03!clients              && Error - file does not exist
USE C:VFP60\CH03\ch03!clients && Opens the correct table
```

These search rules also mean that if a table name is used twice, once for a table in an open database container and again for a free table then opening the free table presents a problem unless you specify a hard-coded path as part of the `USE` command. By the way, we do not recommended this practice, it really is poor design. There is simply no mechanism, other than using an explicit path, to tell Visual FoxPro that the table being requested is a free table and Visual FoxPro will *always* search the open database container first. The only solution that we have found to this problem is to save the current database setting, then close the database, open the free table and, finally, restore the database setting, like this:

```
lcDBC = SET('DATABASE')
SET DATABASE TO
USE <free table name>
SET DATABASE TO (lcDBC)
```

How to get the structure of a table

The introduction of the database container finally allowed us to use long field names in Visual FoxPro (up to 128 characters, although the old 10 character limit remains applicable to free tables). While this isn't necessarily a good thing (after all, we also have both a Caption property and a Comment for fields in bound tables!) the use of long field names has proven popular with many people. The big snag is that the old FoxPro commands that list table structure have not caught up – even in Version 6.0a. Both the LIST and DISPLAY STRUCTURE commands are limited to 12 character output to leading to annoying displays like the following:

```
Structure for table:    C:\VFP60\CH07\JUNK.DBF
Number of data records: 0
Date of last update:    02/10/1999
Code Page:              1252
Field  Field Name      Type            Width   Dec   Index   Collate Nulls
    1  THISISALONGF..  Character         10                              No
    2  THISISALONGF..  Character         10                              No
** Total **                             21
```

You can use the COPY STRUCTURE EXTENDED TO <table> command to get the full structure of the table but this creates problems. First, you must output the results to a table – meaning that you have to remember to delete the table when finished. Secondly, the output table uses memo fields for much of the data so you also have an *FPT* file to deal with, and this makes reviewing the information more difficult. The benefit is that it's easy to modify the structure and you can use the output table directly to create a new table.

However for getting a simple listing, the best solution is to use the AFIELDS() function (which will get the full field name) and to write a little function to replace the old, and now inadequate, structure listing commands. An example of such a function is included in the sample code for this chapter (see *getStru1.prg*) which produces, for the same table, the output below by writing a text file and then opening the file in a MODIFY FILE window. (Of course you now have a text file to get rid of but this, in our opinion, is less of a bother than a table and is less likely to cause concern than deleting *DBF* and *FPT* files from your data directory):

```
Structure For: C:\VFP60\CH07\JUNK.DBF
=======================================
Long Name: A LONG TABLE NAME CAN BE USED HERE
Comment:   This is a junk table to illustrate the use of Long Field Names

Field Definitions
=================
  THISISALONGFIELDNAME                  C ( 10,0 )   NOT NULL
    Default: "something"
    (Error Message: VFP Default)
    Valid: .NOT.EMPTY(thisisalongfieldname)
    (Error Message: "This field may not be left empty")
  THISISALONGFIELDNAMETHATISDIFFERENT  C ( 10,0 )   NOT NULL
```

However, there is much more information that would be useful in a listing. For example, the name of the DBC from which the table comes would be useful, as would the names of any associated files. Most importantly it would be very nice to know what indexes were defined for the table too. The second variant (*GetStru2.prg*) produces the following result:

```
Structure For: C:\VFP60\CH07\JUNK.DBF
=======================================
DBC  : CH07.DBC
CDX  : JUNK.CDX
Memo : No Memo File

Associated Indexes
==================
  F02REG: THISISALONGFIELDNAMETHATISDIFFERENT
  ISDEL: DELETED()
  (Candidate): F03CAN: THISISALONGFIELDNAME+THISISALONGFIELDNAMETHATISDIFFERENT
  *** PRIMARY KEY: F01PRIME: THISISALONGFIELDNAME

Table Information
=================
Long Name: A LONG TABLE NAME CAN BE USED HERE
Comment: This is a junk table to illustrate the use of Long Field Names
No Table Rule
  On Insert: on_insert()
  On Update: on_update()
  On Delete: on_delete()

Field Details
=============
  THISISALONGFIELDNAME                 C ( 10,0 )      NOT NULL
      Default: "something"
      (Error Message: VFP Default)
      Valid: .NOT.EMPTY(thisisalongfieldname)
      (Error Message: "This field may not be left empty")
  THISISALONGFIELDNAMETHATISDIFFERENT C ( 10,0 )      NOT NULL
```

This function can be called in a couple of ways. First with no parameters, in which case the currently selected table (if there is one) is assumed. This method **will** work with both cursors and views in addition to tables! Second, you can pass a *FILE* name (include the extension if not simply the default '*DBF*') and it will try and find the file, open it if it isn't already open, return the structure and then close any table that it opened itself. Finally you can call it interactively using:

```
GetStru2( GETFILE() )
```

– which will bring up the file location dialog for you as well.

How to compare the structures of two tables?

Sometimes it's necessary to know whether two tables are actually identical in structure particularly when you are copying data using the APPEND FROM command which works on fields that are *named* the same irrespective of their data type or size. Perhaps oddly for a database system, Visual FoxPro does not have any direct way of comparing the structure of two tables, so we have to create our own. The following program (*CompStru.prg*) does just this and in the form presented here returns a simple logical value indicating whether or not the two tables are actually identical. However, it would be a simple matter to make this function display a list of the mismatched fields if that were necessary.

This function must be called with two *FILE* names. Just passing in *ALIAS* names is not sufficient because we will want to use the `FILE()` function to determine whether the physical file exists and can be found. We cannot assume that all files will actually have a 'DBF' extension. (For an example of forcing an extension see the program *"GetStru2"* in this chapter's code.):

```
**********************************************************************
* Program....: CompStru
* Compiler...: Visual FoxPro 06.00.8492.00 for Windows
* Abstract...: Compares the structure of two tables
**********************************************************************
LPARAMETERS tcFile1, tcFile2
LOCAL ARRAY laFields[1]
LOCAL lnSelect, lnCnt, lcFile, llRetVal

*** Did we get two parameters
IF NOT ( ( VARTYPE( tcFile1 ) = "C" AND ! EMPTY( tcFile1 ) ) ;
         AND ( VARTYPE( tcFile2 ) = "C" AND ! EMPTY( tcFile2 ) ) )
    ERROR "9000: Must pass two valid file names to CompStru()"
    RETURN .F.
ENDIF

*** Check Parameters to see if the files specified exist
IF NOT ( FILE( tcFile1 ) AND FILE ( tcFile2 ) )
    ERROR "9000: Must pass two valid file names to CompStru()"
    RETURN .F.
ENDIF

*** Now make sure they are both usable tables
*** (ISDBF() is a function in this program)
IF ! ISDBF( tcFile1 )
    ERROR "9000: File " + tcFile1 + " is not a usable FoxPro Table"
    RETURN .F.
ENDIF
IF ! ISDBF( tcFile2 )
    ERROR "9000: File " + tcFile2 + " is not a usable FoxPro Table"
    RETURN .F.
ENDIF

*** Save current work area
lnSelect = SELECT()
SELECT 0

*** Create a temporary cursor for comparing structures
CREATE CURSOR tmpstru ( ;
    fname C(10), ftype C(1), flen N(3,0), fdec N(3,0), fnul L(1) )

*** Open the files to compare and get their structures into the cursor
FOR lnCnt = 1 TO 2
    lcFile = ("tcFile" + PADL(lnCnt,1))
    USE (&lcFile) AGAIN IN 0 SHARED ALIAS TestFile
    AFIELDS( laFields, 'TestFile' )
    APPEND FROM ARRAY laFields
    USE IN TestFile
```

```
NEXT

*** Now see if the fields are identical
SELECT *, COUNT(*) cnt ;
  FROM tmpstru ;
  GROUP BY fname, ftype, flen, fdec, fnul ;
  HAVING cnt # 2 ;
  INTO ARRAY junk

*** Return Logical T/F if structure is identical
SELECT (lnSelect)
USE IN tmpstru
llRetVal = ( _TALLY = 0)
RETURN llRetVal


*******************************************************************
***   Check to see if a file can be opened as a table
*******************************************************************
FUNCTION ISDBF( tcFile )
LOCAL lcErrWas, llRetVal
*** Disable Error handling temporarily
lcErrWas = ON("ERROR")
ON ERROR *
*** Open the specified file as a DBF
USE (tcFile) IN 0 AGAIN ALIAS testopen
*** If successful it WAS a valid table
IF USED( 'TestOpen' )
    llRetVal = .T.
    USE IN TestOpen
ENDIF
*** Restore Error Handling and Work
ON ERROR &lcErrWas
RETURN llRetVal
```

Here, by the way, is another "oddity". Visual FoxPro does not include a function to determine whether a file is actually a usable table. So again we have had to create one (the ISDBF() function). This relies on disabling any error handling and trying to open the file – if successful then we can assume that the file is usable as a table.

How to test for the presence of a field in a table
This is a tricky one! Again it seems odd there is no native function to do this for us, but there are (as usual in Visual FoxPro) several possible solutions. However, all suffer from potential problems. Here are some suggestions:

Test for FSIZE()
The theory here is that if you ask Visual FoxPro for the size of a non-existent field, it will return 0. The code is very simple indeed:

```
IF FSIZE( 'myfield' ) > 0
    *** The field exists in the table, do something
ENDIF
```

However, note that the FSIZE() function (according to the Help file):

"Returns the size in bytes of a specified field or file."

Note the *"OR"* at the end of that sentence. We normally think of FSIZE() as returning the field width, but it doesn't always do so! The setting of SET COMPATIBLE determines which size gets returned (field or file) and if COMPATIBLE is ON, then you will either get the size of the file or an error if no file exists with the name you specify.

Use TYPE()
This function will return a value of "U" if the specified field does not exist. However, you do need to add the alias name to ensure that VFP actually looks at the field in the table, and not at a variable named the same as the field if the field does not exist.

```
IF TYPE( "junk.myfield" ) # "U"
    *** The field exists in the table, do something
ENDIF
```

There is, however, a real danger here. The same syntax of *<alias.field>* is used to reference *<object.property>* and the TYPE() function will handle both with equal facility and may well give you a totally wrong answer. It is not, therefore, a good solution!

> *Incidentally, the fact that the same syntax style is used for both <object.property> and <table.field> can be very useful. The functions JUSTSTEM() and JUSTEXT() were designed for extracting the table name and extension from a file name, but work just as well with object.property strings - or indeed ANY string which contains a "." Separator. (The fact that the Help file states that JUSTEXT() returns a "three letter extension" is simply inaccurate, it actually returns all characters to the right of the rightmost period in a string, irrespective of length. Similarly JUSTSTEM() returns all characters to the left of the rightmost period in a string).*

Use VARTYPE()
What about using VARTYPE() instead? This new function was introduced in Version 6.0 , but in this case it will not do at all. If you specify the field name without an alias there is the same possibility of a false positive if a variable exists and the field doesn't – even though Visual FoxPro will always return the field type if *both* exist. However if you also specify the alias (to force VFP to ignore variables) you will get a '*Variable <name> is not found*' error because VARTYPE() does not evaluate things the same way as TYPE().

Use AFIELDS() and ASCAN()
This approach makes use of the AFIELDS() function to get a list of all the field names (plus, as we have already seen, a lot more information) in a table. Then ASCAN() is used to find the field you are looking for. If you get a match, the field exists:

```
lnFieldCnt = AFIELDS(laFields, 'MyAlias')
IF ASCAN(laFields, 'MYFIELD') > 0
```

```
    *** The field exists in the table, do something
ENDIF
```

This has the benefit of simplicity but suffers from two possible *gotcha!*'. First make sure that SET EXACT is ON, and also format the string you are searching for to upper case, otherwise VFP might find "CLINICAL" when you are actually searching for "CLINIC." Also, because ASCAN() searches all columns, make sure the item you found is in the *first* (i.e. the field name) column. Otherwise you might have found only part of the validation code, comment or an error message. You can obviously make this approach work without these potential flaws, but it does require more code than would first seem necessary.

For example, a safer although slower method would be to use AFIELDS() and then loop through the array comparing the first column in each row with the field name you are searching for using a "==" for comparison. Thus,

```
lnFieldCnt = AFIELDS(laFields, 'MyAlias')
FOR lnCnt = 1 TO lnFieldCnt
    IF laFields[ lnCnt, 1 ] == 'MYFIELD'
       *** The field exists in the table, do something
       EXIT
    ENDIF
NEXT
```

The unambiguous solution
The most reliable solution is to use FCOUNT() to control a loop and check the name of each field as returned by the FIELD() function, using the double "=" to force an exact comparison, as follows:

```
FOR lnCnt = 1 TO FCOUNT()
   IF UPPER( FIELD( lnCnt) ) == 'MYFIELD'
      *** The field exists in the table, do something
      EXIT
   ENDIF
NEXT
```

While this may not be the fastest method, or the least amount of code, it does use only functions, which refer specifically to fields in a table and will reliably return whether or not the specified field really exists.

How to check if a table is being used by another user
Visual FoxPro does not provide this native functionality so we must resort to trickery to ensure the table we choose is not already in use by someone else. Why is this important to know? Typically this is needed when writing maintenance routines that will require exclusive use of a table. The solution is based on gaining exclusive use of the specified table, on the basis that if you *can* get such it then the table is not in use by anyone else. The only possible snag is that if you already have the table open with uncommitted changes pending you will lose them, and depending on the buffer mode, you may also get an error. However, we feel this must be your

own responsibility and that to add checks for this situation is unnecessarily complicating the function. Here is our *IsInUse* function:

```
***********************************************************************
* Program....: IsInUse.prg
* Compiler...: Visual FoxPro 06.00.8492.00 for Windows
* Abstract...: Tries to gain exclusive use of a table to see if the table
* ...........: is used by someone else
***********************************************************************
LPARAMETERS tcTable
LOCAL lcTable, lcOldError, llRetVal, lnWasUsedIn, lnWasOrder
*** Check parameters and ensure a table is available
IF EMPTY( tcTable ) OR VARTYPE( tcTable ) # 'C'
  MESSAGEBOX('No Table Passed to IsInUse()', 16, 'Aborting...')
  RETURN
ELSE
    lcTable = UPPER( ALLTRIM( tcTable ))
ENDIF
*** If we have the table in use already, close it and note the fact!
llWasUsedHere = USED( lcTable )
IF llWasUsedHere
    *** We were using it, so find out where and save it
    lnWasUsedIn = SELECT( lcTable )
    lnWasOrder = ORDER( lcTable )
    lnWasRec = IIF( RECNO( lcTable ) > RECCOUNT( lcTable ), ;
                        RECCOUNT( lcTable ), RECNO( lcTable ) )
    USE IN ( lcTable )
ELSE
    lnWasUsedIn = 0
    lnWasOrder = 0
    lnWasRec = 0
ENDIF
*** Save current error handling and disable it temporarily
lcOldError = ON( "ERROR" )
ON ERROR llRetVal = .T.
*** Try and use the table exlusively
USE ( lcTable ) IN 0 EXCLUSIVE
*** If we succeeded, close it again
IF ! llRetVal
    USE IN ( lcTable )
ENDIF
*** Restore the Error Handler
ON ERROR &lcOldError
*** If it was open, then reset it properly
IF llWasUsedHere
    USE ( lcTable ) AGAIN IN ( lnWasUsedIn ) ORDER ( lnWasOrder )
    IF lnWasRec # 0
        *** It was on a specific record
        GOTO ( lnWasRec ) IN ( lcTable )
    ELSE
        *** Just go to the first available record
        GO TOP IN ( lcTable )
    ENDIF
ENDIF
*** Return the result
RETURN llRetVal
```

Notice that if we already have the table open in our own session we restore it on completion. This may not actually be valid because presumably the usage of this function would be immediately prior to a USE EXCLUSIVE command, which would then fail anyway because we still have the table open. However, it provides a suitable opportunity to show how to restore a table so we have left this functionality in place. If you do not want it, just remove it!

One problem arises when the required table is already open in another work area under a *different* alias, or when a SQL generated cursor exists which is actually a filtered view of a table opened with a different alias on the current workstation. The function relies on the native Visual FoxPro *USED()* function which only tests the specified "alias". In either situation, the function will return *False* (correctly indicating that the table is already in use) but subsequent attempts to find the alias will fail with an 'Alias not found' error as the following code snippets illustrate:

```
*** Open Table under different Alias
USE clients ALIAS fred
? ISINUSE( 'clients' ) && RETURNS .T.
SELECT clients          && ERROR: 'Alias CLIENTS is not found'

*** Create filtered view from table with different alias
USE clients ALIAS fred
SELECT * FROM fred WHERE clisid = 96 INTO CURSOR joe  && Creates a filtered
view
USE IN fred             && Closes 'clients'
? ISINUSE( 'clients' ) && RETURNS .T.
SELECT clients          && ERROR: 'Alias CLIENTS is not found'
```

This could be an issue under some circumstances but we must look at the intended use for this function – which is to determine whether the specified table is in use by another user. The scenario outlined above could be resolved on a single workstation using the *AUSED()* function to get an array of all aliases in use in the current DataSession. Each alias could then be tested using the *DBF()* function to get the underlying table name, and the whole operation enclosed in a loop to test all open data sessions. But this could not be applied to another user's workstation anyway so we see little value in increasing the function's complexity. After all, it doesn't matter how the table is used, this function is intended to tell us it is in use *somewhere*.

What is exactly is a cursor?

The term *"cursor"* is an acronym derived from the phrase *"CURrent Set Of Records."* In Visual FoxPro a cursor is implemented as a temporary file which is created in whatever directory is pointed to by the TMPFILES system variable (if no TMPFILES setting has been specified, the VFP startup directory is used by default). Cursors are, therefore, very useful indeed for holding transient data because Visual FoxPro will clean them up for you.

A cursor can be created in two ways – first by executing a SQL Select statement, which includes the INTO CURSOR <name> clause. In all versions of FoxPro up to and including Version 6.0 this always creates a read-only cursor, and we will have more to say about SQL generated cursors in the chapter devoted to SQL. For now, we will simply note that creating a cursor in this way also opens the source table in a free work area if it's not already in use.

Secondly by using one of the variants of the CREATE CURSOR command. This produces a read/write cursor which is for all practical purposes, indistinguishable from a standard table. It is on this cursor type that we shall concentrate in this section. (Note that irrespective of how a cursor is created, it is always created explicitly on the user's local system and is always exclusive to that user.)

How to create a cursor based on an existing table

Probably the simplest way to create a cursor is to base it on an existing table. We have already used the AFIELDS() function several times in this chapter (and, no doubt, will be using it again!) to get the details of a table's structure into an array. The array it produces can be used directly to create a cursor (and yes, although a cursor is actually a 'free' table, it **can** accommodate long field names) using the command:

```
CREATE CURSOR <aliasname> FROM ARRAY <arrayname>
```

However there is one *gotcha*! in this! If the table being used as the source for the AFIELDS() function is bound to a database, then *ALL* information gathered about that table is transferred to the target cursor – including details like the long table name, triggers and default values. This will cause problems so we have created a little function to make a cursor based on a table that only gets the actual structural information needed (*CreCur.prg*). This function requires that a valid table name for the source be passed but will generate a default cursor name ('Cur_' + table name) if you do not specify a cursor name:

```
***********************************************************************
* Program....: CreCur.prg
* Compiler...: Visual FoxPro 06.00.8492.00 for Windows
* Abstract...: Creates a cursor based on the structure of the named table
* ..........: Removes anything but the basic structural information
***********************************************************************
LPARAMETERS tcSceTable, tcCursorName
LOCAL laFields[1]
LOCAL lcTable, lcTgtCur, lnSelect, llWasOpen, llRetVal, lnFields
LOCAL lnRow, lnCol
STORE .T. TO llWasOpen, llRetVal

*** Clean parameters and ensure a table is available
IF EMPTY(tcSceTable) OR VARTYPE(tcSceTable)#'C'
    lcTable = ALIAS()
ELSE
    lcTable = UPPER(ALLTRIM(tcSceTable))
ENDIF
IF EMPTY(lcTable)
  MESSAGEBOX('No Table Passed or Open', 16, 'Aborting...')
  RETURN
ENDIF
*** Save current work area (the create cursor command will change it!)
lnSelect = SELECT()
*** Open the table if necessary and note the fact!
IF ! USED( lcTable )
    USE (lcTable) IN 0
    llWasOpen = .F.
ENDIF
```

```
*** Default the cursor name if none passed
IF EMPTY(tcCursorName) OR VARTYPE(tcCursorName)#'C'
    lcTgtCur = "CUR_" + UPPER(ALLTRIM(lcTable))
ELSE
    lcTgtCur = UPPER(ALLTRIM(tcCursorName))
ENDIF
*** Get the structure of the table
lnFields = AFIELDS( laFields, lcTable )
*** Now blank out everything after Column 6 of the array
FOR lnRow = 1 TO lnFields
    FOR lnCol = 7 TO ALEN( laFields, 2 )
        laFields[ lnRow, lnCol ] = ""
    NEXT
NEXT
*** Create the Cursor
CREATE CURSOR (lcTgtCur) FROM ARRAY laFields
*** Get the Return value
llRetVal = USED( lcTgtCur )
*** Tidy Up
IF ! llWasOpen
    USE IN ( tcSceTable )
ENDIF
SELECT ( lnSelect )
RETURN lLRetVal
```

When can a cursor be used?

Once your cursor has been created, you can use it as if it were actually a table. It can be indexed, used as the source for an SQL **Select**, the *RecordSource* for a grid or the *RowSource* for a list or combo box. The only thing to remember is that certain operations require the actual file name instead of the *alias* and in those cases you need to use the DBF() function to ensure Visual FoxPro reads the cursor correctly. For example, to append from a cursor into a physical table you need to use the syntax:

APPEND FROM DBF('<CursorName>') instead of APPEND FROM <CursorName>

The most common use for a cursor is in situations where you would otherwise require a temporary table. The advantage of a cursor is that it will not remain on your system once Visual FoxPro has closed down and you do not have to worry about deleting it or having your data directory filled up with temporary tables. The only exception to this is when Visual FoxPro terminates abnormally (another euphemism for "crashes"). Under these circumstances the cursors will not be deleted automatically. It is easy to find them though, by checking the creation date and time, and then simply deleting them manually.

For example, if you have to import data from an external source, validate it and then append only the valid records to a physical table, a cursor is the ideal intermediary precisely because it can be handled as if it were the "real" table.

Indexes in Visual FoxPro

To say that indexes are important when working with data in Visual FoxPro is a "mild understatement". The speed and flexibility of working with data is governed, to a large extent, by the way you set up and use your indexes. It is precisely because indexes are so important that there is often a temptation to index everything in a table. As with most things, however, too much is as bad as too little. We are confining our remarks here specifically to the use of structural indexes and have included a note about some of the problems associated with stand-alone indexes later in this chapter.

First we need to remind ourselves of some the basic rules governing indexes.

Types of indexes

Visual FoxPro provides for four basic types of indexes as illustrated by the following table:

Table 7.1 Visual FoxPro index types

Type	Characteristics	Comments
Primary	Only applies to bound tables Only one Primary index per table Index enforces uniqueness of keys	Used by Visual FoxPro to handle persistent relationships between tables Identify the 'one' end of a one-to-many relationship
Candidate	Applies to both Free and Bound tables May define multiple candidate indexes Index enforces uniqueness of keys	So called because such indexes are 'candidates' to be made into primary keys Identify the 'one' end of a one-to-many relationship
Regular	Apply to both Free and Bound tables May define multiple regular indexes Any key value may be indexed whether unique or not	The standard Visual FoxPro index Identify the 'many' end of a one-to-many relationship
Unique	Apply to both Free and Bound tables May define multiple unique indexes Only the first occurrence of a key value is indexed, whether unique or not	Essentially a "legacy" from xBase – has no real function in Visual FoxPro and should be avoided

There are some rules that apply to the creation of all index types, as follows:

- The maximum number of bytes in an index key for compact indexes is 240, for non-compact indexes the limit is reduced to 100 bytes per key.
- Filtered indexes (i.e. those whose keys include expressions with **FOR** or **NOT** clauses) cannot be used to optimize operations that utilize Rushmore technology.
- If the table supports **NULL** values, an additional byte per key value is required, reducing the maximum length of the key string.
- **SET COLLATE** affects how index keys are stored. If the default ("**MACHINE**") setting is used, each character in the key requires one byte. All other settings require two bytes per character.
- The setting of **SET COLLATE** determines the sort order Visual FoxPro uses.

How to get information about an index

Visual FoxPro provides a number of functions that return information about the indexes associated with a table, as illustrated in the following table:

Table 7.2 *Functions that return information about indexes*

Function	Returns
KEY()	The index key expression for a specified tag, or current controlling tag if none specified
TAG()	The name of the tag corresponding to the specified number, or current controlling tag if none specified
TAGNO()	The number of the tag whose name has been specified, or current controlling tag if none specified
TAGCOUNT()	The number of index tags in the compound index associated with the table
CANDIDATE()	Returns logical value indicating whether the specified tag number is a candidate key
PRIMARY()	Returns logical value indicating whether the specified tag number is a primary key
ORDER()	The name of the currently controlling index tag
SYS(14)	The name for the specified tag number (equivalent to KEY())
SYS(21)	The number of the currently controlling index tag (equivalent to TAGNO())
SYS(22)	The name of the currently controlling index tag (equivalent to ORDER())
SYS(2021)	The filter expression for the specified tag number (if any)

As you can see, about the only information you cannot obtain is whether an index was created in *Ascending* or *Descending* order, and this does not really matter anyway since *any* index can be inverted by specifically adding the **ASCENDING** or **DESCENDING** keyword to the **SET ORDER** command. Consider the following:

```
USE clients ORDER TAG clisid ASCENDING
GO TOP
LIST NEXT 3 clisid            && Returns 96, 97, 98
USE clients ORDER TAG clisid DESCENDING
GO TOP
LIST NEXT 3 clisid            && Returns 186, 185, 184
```

How to test for the existence of an index tag

The simplest situation here is when you know the name of the tag that you need to test for. In this case you can simply use the **TAGNO()** function to return the index number of the name. If the return value is greater than 0, the tag exists otherwise it doesn't. Thus:

```
IF TAGNO( 'mytag', 'mytable' ) > 0
   *** The tag exists for the specified table
ENDIF
```

Things get more complex if you do not know the tag name but need to know if an index on a specific expression exists. In this case you need to loop through all of the tags, and check the KEY() expression using code like this:

```
lcTagName = ""
FOR lnCnt = 1 TO TAGCOUNT()
  IF UPPER( ALLTRIM( KEY(lnCnt) ) ) == <expression to find>
```

```
      lcTagName = TAG( lnCnt )
      EXIT
   ENDIF
NEXT
RETURN lcTagName
```

Using candidate (and primary) keys

The essential feature of all indexes that have been defined as candidate (including the one candidate key that can be defined, for a bound table, as 'primary') is that the responsibility for ensuring uniqueness of keys is handled by the indexing process itself. This sounds wonderful – no more code to check that a key does not already exist. There is, of course, a catch – after all, what can Visual FoxPro do if it finds that the index key is a duplicate while adding a new record? The answer is to do exactly what it does – raise an error and reject the addition. The consequence is that as developers, we need to ensure that the key we offer to VFP is unique when using candidate indexes. This raises two issues, first how to handle keys that are system generated (usually as "*surrogate*" keys) and second how to handle keys that are entered directly by a user.

What is a "surrogate key"?

A surrogate key has no business significance whatsoever and is simply a value stored in a specific field for the sole purpose of uniquely identifying that row in the table. Usually it's simply an integer value generated automatically by the system itself when a new record is added to a table. You may be wondering, at this point, why we do not simply use the record number, since that already uniquely identifies a record. (We obviously cannot have **two** records with the **same** record number in the same table.)

The reason is that the record number in Visual FoxPro is "positional" (i.e. it identifies the physical location in the file) and is not related to the actual record content. Certain commands in Visual FoxPro change the physical location of records within a table (e.g. PACK and SORT), while if you extract data from the file into a cursor or view the record number generated for the result set will not match the record number in the original table. These issues are avoided if the key is actually *part* of the data contained by the record.

Surrogate keys have two functions, both related to the fact that they uniquely identify records. First they can be used as the key for the primary index for tables that are acting as the parent in persistent relationships and as foreign keys in related tables. Secondly they can be used for joining tables when constructing SQL statements.

How should I implement surrogate keys?

Firstly your table structures must include fields for the keys. The simplest (and most usual) implementation uses an *INTEGER* data type. This data type requires only 4 bytes of storage per record, and allows for values in the range –2,147,483,647 to 2,147,483,647 (a range of just about 4 *billion*) - which should be enough for most practical purposes.

When designing tables that will use surrogate keys to maintain relationships you will need at least two additional fields. One in the parent table to store the actual record ID (the '*Primary key*') and one in each child table for the corresponding parent table record ID (the '*Foreign key'*). Various proposals have been put forward for *naming* such fields, and there is no "*right*" answer. The one we like uses "*xxxSID*" for a primary key (where "*xxx*" is the identifier for the table, and "*SID"* stands for 'System ID') and, in each related table includes a field named "*xxxKey*" (where the "*xxx"* again refers to the table that owns the system ID, and the "*KEY"* indicates this is a foreign key to that table). Other conventions suggest adding the suffix "PK" or "FK" to the field name as appropriate. It really doesn't matter how you name your keys but it is important to adopt a convention and be consistent in its use. **Figure 7.1** shows a typical relational structure using Primary/Foreign keys named in our preferred way:

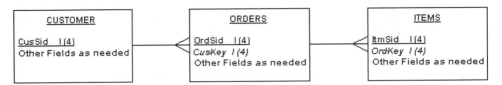

Figure 7.1 *Relational structure using surrogate keys*

You can see from the diagram that to get a list of all orders for a given customer a SQL statement like this can be constructed:

```
SELECT <fieldList> ;
  FROM Customer CU JOIN Orders OR ;
    ON OR.cuskey = CU.cussid ;
 WHERE CU.cussid = <value> ;
  INTO CURSOR cur_OrdList
```

Not only does this make joining the tables quite straightforward, but by including the *SID* fields from each table in the result set, you have an immediate and unambiguous route back to the source data at all levels, at all times. This is extremely useful in situations where you provide the user with lists of data to select a specific item for further work. The surrogate key points directly to the records required.

Finally you should also define an index on your surrogate key as the `primary` key for each table. This has several benefits:

- It avoids the necessity for compound keys. The surrogate key always identifies one, and only one, record
- You can use an auto-generated key, which will always be unique and so avoid the need to check for duplicate keys when adding a record.
- The key field doesn't need to be seen by the user and certainly never needs to be editable, simplifying the code needed to maintain referential integrity between tables.

How do I generate surrogate keys?
We think that the best solution is to use integer keys and use the field level *Default* for the key field to call a procedure to generate the next number in sequence. The procedure can either be a stand-alone procedure, included in a procedure file, or a stored procedure in a database

container. We prefer keeping the procedure as a stored procedure in a database container (if only because if a table is opened outside the application, and a new record is inserted, the presence of the DBC will ensure the correct new key value is inserted). So what should this procedure look like, and how should it be called?

The setting for the default value in the table designer is very simple indeed. All that's required is a call to a function that will return the value to be inserted. We have included a table named "*Clients*" in the CH07 database that has a surrogate key field "*clisid,*" which is used as the primary key for the table. (We always try to name our index tags so they indicate the field on which they are based. It makes it easier to remember the name of the key!) This field has a default defined that calls the *NEWID()* stored procedure to return the next available key when a new record is inserted. Notice that the function call includes the name of the table for which the key is required:

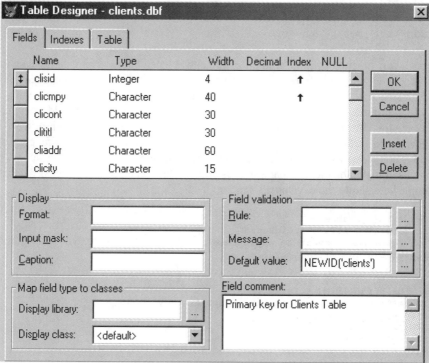

Figure 7.2 *How to set up a default value for a sequential primary key*

The actual procedure relies on the presence of a table that maintains a list of all tables in the database and the last primary key value that was assigned to each. We call this table "*SYSTABLE*" and it has the following structure (Actually we usually include a lot more table–related information in our *systable*, but this is all that's required for generating primary keys.):

```
Structure For: C:\VFP60\CH07\SYSTABLE.DBF
==========================================
DBC  : CH07.DBC
CDX  : SYSTABLE.CDX
Memo : No Memo File

Associated Indexes
==================
  *** PRIMARY KEY: CTABLE: CTABLE

Table Information
=================
Long Name: SYSTABLE
Comment: System Table for recording Primary Key Usage

Field Details
=============
  CTABLE    C ( 8,0 )   NOT NULL
  ILASTKEY  I ( 4,0 )   NOT NULL
```

The *NewId()* function is quite straightforward and is listed below. Points to note are that *systable* is opened without buffering (thereby avoiding the need to use a `TableUpdate()`) and is explicitly locked before the new key value is obtained (so that it will work reliably in a multi-user environment). Also the function is self-correcting. If you forget to add a new table to the list, the first time a record is inserted into that table, a new record will be inserted automatically into *systable*. However, while useful in development, making this function self-correcting is not necessarily a good thing in an application environment. The very act of correcting itself may hide the fact that a serious problem has occurred in a system's database! The example here shows the developer's version:

```
FUNCTION newid( tcTable )
LOCAL lcTable, lnNextVal, lnOldRepro
*** Check Param and convert to upper case
IF EMPTY(tcTable) OR TYPE( "tcTable" ) # "C"
  RETURN 0
ENDIF
lcTable = UPPER(ALLTRIM( tcTable ))
*** Save Settings and Open Systable if not already open
lnOldRepro = SET('REPROCESS')
IF ! USED('systable')
  USE systable IN 0
  *** Make sure that the table is not buffered
  =CURSORSETPROP( 'Buffering', 1, 'systable' )
ENDIF
*** Now find the required table
IF SEEK( lcTable, 'systable', 'cTable' )
  *** Found the required table
  *** Get a Lock on systable
  SET REPROCESS TO AUTOMATIC
  IF RLOCK( 'systable' )
    *** Get next value and update systable
    lnNextVal = systable.iLastKey + 1
    REPLACE iLastKey with lnNextVal IN systable
    UNLOCK IN systable
```

```
   ELSE
     *** This should NEVER happen!
     lnNextVal = 0
   ENDIF
ELSE
   *** Table Not Found!
   *** Needs a new entry in systable
   lnNextVal = 1
   INSERT INTO systable (cTable, iLastKey) VALUES ( lcTable, lnNextVal )
ENDIF
*** Return New ID
SET REPROCESS TO (lnOldRepro)
RETURN lnNextVal
ENDFUNC
```

That's all that there is to it. This function can be found as a stored procedure in the *CH07* database. Whenever a record is appended to the *Clients* table it will be automatically assigned the next ID in sequence.

What do I do if a user reverts an addition?

The short answer is "Nothing at all!" You'll have realized this approach means that a new ID is added to a record as soon as that record is appended to the table. If you do not commit that new record, the ID is "wasted" – there is no functionality to recover the used ID, nor is such functionality desirable. In a multi-user environment trying to recoup a lost ID is the very stuff of which nightmares are made and, if as we have suggested, you use an integer key you have nearly 2 billion values to play with (even if you ignore the values less than 0).

More importantly because the ID you are assigning is a *surrogate* ID it just does not matter if the numbers are out of sequence, or if there are gaps in the sequence. Remember, the only function of the key is to identify its record!

Managing user-entered keys

As already indicated, we strongly advocate using surrogate keys for managing referential integrity and as the basis for referencing data in SQL queries and statements. However there are still situations in which users need to be able to enter unique values (order and invoice numbers spring to mind). For these, the candidate index is ideal if we can ensure such values are in fact unique when we try to commit changes to the tables.

Of course, there is no absolute way of preventing users from *ever* entering duplicate values because we are dealing with data that is perfectly *valid* – it's just in that context it happens to be *wrong*. It is axiomatic that there is no *software* solution to the problem of *valid but wrong* data! You will still, therefore, need to handle the inevitable errors that will arise when you try to commit changes, but you can take steps to minimize the occurrence of 'Trigger Failed,' 'Update Conflict' or 'Uniqueness of Key Violated' errors by doing a little pre-save validation.

The SQL solution

The simplest solution is to use a SQL query to check the underlying table and see if the newly entered value already exists. There are two points to note here. First, a SQL query always refers to the physical database, so it cannot be "confused" by what is in any buffered entry.

Second, because the SQL always refers to the data on disk it will detect changes made (and saved) by other users. (In fact there is no way to detect other user's uncommitted changes anyway - they can only ever exist in the buffers on a user's machine.)

A big benefit of using SQL is that it does not move the record pointer in the table and so can be used even when a table is row-buffered. Here is a simple example that will check to see if an 'invoice number' already exists in the 'payments' table:

```
lcInvNum = ThisForm.txtInvNum.Value
SELECT invoice_number ;
  FROM payments ;
 WHERE invoice_number = lcInvNum ;
 INTO ARRAY results
IF _TALLY > 0
   *** Invoice number already exists
   *** So take appropriate action
ENDIF
```

The only drawback with this approach is that it may be quite slow when tables are very large unless you have all the necessary fields indexed. However as we have already pointed out, too many indexes can cause other problems, especially on large tables..

Other solutions

There are a couple of alternatives that do not use SQL and that may be better in some situations. If the table has the relevant indexes you can use the INDEXSEEK() function (introduced in VFP 6.0). This function will return a logical value depending on whether the value specified already exists in the index for the table. Unlike SEEK() the default behavior of INDEXSEEK() is not to move the record pointer to the matching record, although it can take an additional parameter (in the second position) to force the record pointer to be moved when necessary. This means it will not interfere with row-buffered tables, although it still requires that the table be indexed on the relevant field. The same results as illustrated above could be achieved using INDEXSEEK() like this:

```
lcInvNum = ThisForm.txtInvNum.Value
IF INDEXSEEK( 'lcInvNum', .F., 'payments', 'invoice_number' )
   *** Invoice number already exists
   *** So take appropriate action
ENDIF
```

There is one problem with using INDEXSEEK() with buffered tables. As soon as the record pointer is moved off the newly added row, the index is updated to include the new value - even if table buffering is in force. So the INDEXSEEK() solution is only valid if it is applied immediately upon adding a new record.

Another alternative is to make use of Visual FoxPro's ability to use the same table multiple times and simply scan the entire table. Surprisingly, Visual FoxPro is very good at this sort of manipulation, which doesn't require any indexes and is often faster than executing the equivalent SQL statement - even when the table has the relevant indexes. The code is very simple and the same results for our example can be achieved with the following few lines (which could even be parameterized and called in a form method):

```
lcInvNum = ThisForm.txtInvNum.Value
lnSelect = SELECT()
USE payments AGAIN SHARED IN 0 ALIAS schfile NOUPDATE
SELECT schfile
llRetVal = .F.
SCAN
  IF invoice_number = lcInvnum
    llRetVal = .T.
    EXIT
  ENDIF
ENDSCAN
USE IN schfile
SELECT (lnSelect)
RETURN llRetVal
```

Using indexes with bound tables

To create or delete a tag in the *structural* index for a table which is a part of a DBC (i.e. one which is bound) you must first have the table opened exclusively. This may seem restrictive, but it makes sense in the context of maintaining the integrity of the DBC's information about its tables. (This restriction does not apply to free tables or cursors, nor to the creation and modification of *CDX* files which are not structural for bound tables.) So at first sight it would seem that the best approach is to index everything that could possibly require an index when creating tables that are part of a DBC.

However, a major problem with maintaining large numbers of index tags in structural indexes is that updating the table can take a long time because of the necessity to maintain all the tags. (We did say that too much is as bad as too little in the context of indexes.) We strongly recommend, therefore, that you keep the number of index tags on your tables to the absolute minimum required at all times.

There is, of course, a *gotcha* here! To optimize the queries (and other commands that make use of indexes) you may need several indexes that are used only infrequently in an application. If you were using free tables you could simply create temporary indexes and delete them after use but for bound tables you need to adopt a different strategy.

One option is to use non-structural CDX files because you do not need to have exclusive use of the table in order to create them. While this will work, we do not generally recommend it because such indexes must be kept up to date. Visual FoxPro always maintains a structural index but non-structural indexes are only maintained as long as they are open. Unless you specifically re-index (or re-create the tags) on each use, there is always the danger of the index getting out of synchronization with its parent table.

A preferable alternative is to use an indexed cursor instead of accessing the bound table directly. While this may involve more thought when it comes to creating and populating the cursor or updating the underlying data, it ensures the structural index on the base table can be kept small. This helps reduce the overhead when updating the table and avoids having to maintain or re-build non-structural indexes, which can be lengthy for large tables.

How to index mixed data types when creating a compound key

We must say up front that we don't like compound keys – especially when they are included in the structural index of a table. However, we also recognize there may be special circumstances when a compound key is absolutely the only thing that will allow you to achieve your requirements. This raises two immediate questions.

First, how can we create an index using a mixture of data types? The answer is simply to create a single concatenated key in which each component is of the same data type. Normally this requires conversion of each component to its character equivalent. So to create an index on a character field and a numeric field the index expression would be:

```
INDEX ON <charfield> + STR( <numfield> ) TAG <name>
```

While the equivalent involving a date would be:

```
INDEX ON DTOS( <datefield> ) + <charfield> TAG <name>
```

Second, how can we create an index involving one element sorted in ascending order, with another element sorted in descending order? The ASCENDING/DESCENDING clauses apply to the expression as a whole, and only one can be applied in any index expression in any case. The solution is to create an expression that reverses the natural order for the element which must be inverted. For example:

```
INDEX ON acctref + STR( 10000000 - VAL( SYS( 11, invoicedate )) ) TAG
lastinvoice
```

would generate an index in which the ""*acctref*"" field is in ascending order, while the "*invoicedate*" field is in descending order, thereby placing the last invoice received for each customer at the top of the sort order. The SYS(11) function is being used here to convert the date field into a Julian Day (in numeric format) which is then subtracted from a very large number to invert the order before being converted to a string. As you may imagine, this would not be a good index to create, or maintain, on a large table that has a high level of update activity and is a case where one of the solutions outlined in the preceding section would be more applicable!

How to index a buffered table

The short answer here is that you cannot index a table for which *Table* buffering is enabled, Visual FoxPro will generate an error if you try. However, if you have no buffering, or Row buffering, an index can be created in the usual way. So all that is needed is to ensure that all tables are forced into a low level of buffering before indexing, or re-indexing.

The only catch is that you must also ensure that any pending changes are either committed or reverted before changing the buffer mode of the table. You can use the CURSORGETPROP('buffering') function to return the current buffering setting for a table and, if the result is either 4 or 5 (i.e. table buffered) check for pending changes, and either commit or revert them as appropriate. Code like this will be required:

```
lnOldBuffMode = CURSORGETPROP( 'buffering' )
IF lnOldBuffMode > 3
   *** You have table Buffering
   IF GETNEXTMODIFIED(0) > 0
      *** There are uncommitted changes
      *** Handle them here
   ENDIF
ELSE
   IF lnOldBuffMode > 1
      *** You have Row Buffering
      lcStatus = GETFIELDSTATE( -1 )
      IF '2' $ lcStatus OR '4' $ lcStatus
         *** The current row has uncommitted changes
         *** Handle them here
      ENDIF
   ENDIF
ENDIF
*** Force to Row Buffering if necessary
IF lnOldBuffMode > 1
   CURSORSETPROP( ' Buffering', 3 )
ENDIF
*** Now Build Indexes
INDEX ON <whatever> TAG <newtag>
*** Restore Buffering
CURSORSETPROP( 'Buffering', lnOldBuffMode )
RETURN
```

Some words of explanation about stand-alone indexes

In the introduction to this section, we stated that using stand-alone indexes does not fit comfortably with the Visual FoxPro model of using buffered tables and data sessions but did not explain any further. In fact using stand-alone (IDX) files (to create a temporary index for example) can cause some very strange things to happen.

This is because an IDX file is available in *all* data sessions, irrespective of where it was created. This behavior leads to some very peculiar results if you try use the index in one data session while the table to which it relates is opened in table buffered mode in another. The good news is that Visual FoxPro will trap for this situation, but the bad news is that it reports it with error number 1579 which states that:

"Command cannot be issued on a table with cursors in table buffering mode"

This can be disconcerting when the command is SET INDEX TO <file> and the table for which you are trying to set the index is definitely NOT using table buffering! Furthermore, if you are using multiple data sessions and a table is opened using table buffering in any of them, you cannot even create a stand-alone index on that table. You will get the same error!

If you realize what is going on and cheat by forcing buffering to either none or row mode in the offending data session, create the index and set it and then re-set the buffering you will find that you cannot then *close* the index file without getting Error #1579.

Don't even *try* and do the same thing while you have a transaction in force. If you manage to create the index (by playing around with the buffer modes) Visual FoxPro will not allow you to close the transaction while this index is in use. However, you will then find you cannot close the index while the transaction is open! We had to re-boot Visual FoxPro to get out of this one! The bottom line is, therefore, stay away from stand-alone indexes when using buffered tables.

Working with the database container

The advent of the database container in Visual FoxPro 3.0 provided some long-overdue functionality. While retaining the classical *DBF* format for tables, the DBC added many features that are standard in modern relational database management systems but which had to be developed individually in previous versions of FoxPro. The DBC provides support for:

- Data dictionary
- Persistent relationships
- Built-in referential integrity (RI)
- Insert, Update and Delete triggers for tables
- Long table names and record validation rules
- Long field names and field validation rules
- Default value and Comments for fields
- Field **InputMask** and **Format** properties
- Mapping of UI control classes to table fields
- Connections to remote data sources
- Local and Remote Views

The price for this was a modification to the header of the *DBF* file to include a 'backlink' to indicate the database container in which all this information was stored. The consequence is that bound VFP Tables cannot be read by older versions of FoxPro. However unless you absolutely **MUST** have your tables readable directly in both VFP and FP2.x there is absolutely no reason not to use the database container.

The limitation is that a table can only ever belong to one database container at a time. While Visual FoxPro can cope with multiple database containers being opened, the code to do so can get messy. So there is still a place for 'Free' tables in Visual FoxPro – especially for lookup data which is shared across several applications – even though a free table cannot share in the benefits that are available to its bound cousins.

Using long table names

When creating a table that is linked to a database container, you may specify a table name that is different from the file name and can contain up to 128 characters (must begin with a letter or an underscore!) and can include spaces.

The default behavior of FoxPro has always been to open a table with the same alias name as the file name unless an alias was explicitly supplied. When bound tables are opened, a reference is made back to the database container and, if a table name has been specified, it is used as the alias instead of the file name (although if the table name you specified contains spaces – horror! – underscores are inserted). The result is that you can define standard 'Aliases' for your tables.

However, because the long table name is stored in the database container, freeing a table from the database container means that its long name will be lost. Note that the standard COPY TO command will, by default, create a free table and will therefore not preserve any long table names (or any other DBC-related information). To avoid this you must always use the DATABASE clause and copy the table to another database container (which **must** already exist, Visual FoxPro will not create a new DBC "on the fly"), thus:

```
SELECT mytable
COPY TO newtable        && Creates a FREE table, but loses DBC-related
information
COPY TO newtable DATABASE newdbc     && Copies the table and all data to the
new DBC
```

Using long field names – don't!!!

The DBC also allows you to use long field names in your tables (again, up to 128 characters). However, in our opinion, this is **not** a good thing! There is a real and present danger in the use of long field names, in addition to the difficulty of merely typing correctly them into controls and in code. As with the long table name, the actual data for long field names is stored in the database container. The limit for field names in a free table is exactly the same as it always has been in FoxPro – 10 characters. The consequence is that if you free a bound table which uses long field names, the long name is lost and Visual FoxPro substitutes a 10-character field name. If the shortened field names are not unique, FoxPro makes them so by taking the first <n> characters and adding a numeric suffix – thus:

Table 7.3 *Truncating long field names*

Long Name	Short Name
THISISALONGFIELDNAME	THISISALON
THISISALONGFIELDNAMETHATISDIFFERENT	THISISALO2

This will break code and is very nasty indeed – although it is hard to see what else Visual FoxPro can do given this situation. So, you may say, we just won't free up tables that use long names…problem solved.

Alas, this is not the only situation in which field names get truncated. Cursors DO support long field names, so a SQL select out of a table that uses them will preserve the field name intact. However, if you then wish to preserve your cursor (we do this a lot when testing code that acts on large tables) and try to copy the result set to a temporary table – you end up with a free table, with shortened field names and code that will not run. Of course you could create another DBC, or create the table with a new name in the existing DBC – but neither solution will allow your existing code to run without modification!

So we think that the question that you must ask yourself is why you need long field names at all?

Every field in a bound table has a *Caption* property that is used, by default, instead of the field name in every place that a field name would normally be displayed by Visual FoxPro. This includes in the header of a grid, as the caption of the label that Visual FoxPro adds to your textbox control when dragging a field from the DE on to a form and in a BROWSE window. In fact the only places that you cannot directly display a field's caption property are in a structure listing or when using AFIELDS() (because the information is in the DBC and not in the table itself).

In any environment the field caption can always be retrieved from the DBC (which must be available, even if not already set as current, if the table is in use) using the DBGETPROP() function so it seems to us that although long field names are supported, there is not really a good case for using them.

Using database containers

When using the Visual FoxPro database container it is important to recognize that Visual FoxPro differentiates between a DBC which is merely *open* and the DBC which is *current*. Most database-related commands and functions only operate on the *current* DBC (e.g. DBGETPROP(), DBSETPROP(), ADBOBJECTS() and INDBC()). The CREATE command also behaves differently when a DBC is defined as current. The table created will be automatically added to that DBC, otherwise a free table is created.

Opening a table that is bound to a DBC also opens (but does NOT make current) the associated DBC while opening a DBC explicitly (OPEN DATABASE <name>) also makes that the current database container but does not open any of its tables.

To make an open DBC as the current database you must use the SET DATABASE TO <name> command. The database that is current remains current until either another OPEN DATABASE, or SET DATABASE TO, command is encountered. This allows Visual FoxPro to handle multiple database containers simultaneously, but using multiple DBCs can also make life tricky for the developer, particularly when both contain stored procedures as the ShoStPro.prg program illustrates:

```
***************************************************************
* Program....: ShoStPro.prg
* Compiler...: Visual FoxPro 06.00.8492.00 for Windows
* Abstract...: Illustrate the problems when using multiple DBCs
***************************************************************
*** Open up two database containers
CLEAR
OPEN DATA bCH07
OPEN DATA aCH07
*** Call the Store Procs
? "Current DBC = " + SET("DATABASE")
DO CheckStProc
*** Now make aCH07 current
SET DATA TO aCH07
? "Current DBC = " + SET("DATABASE")
DO CheckStProc
*** Now make bCH07 current
SET DATA TO bCH07
? "Current DBC = " + SET("DATABASE")
DO CheckStProc
*** Now make NO DBC current
SET DATABASE TO
? "Current DBC = " + SET("DATABASE")
DO CheckStProc
```

```
CLOSE ALL
RETURN

PROCEDURE CheckStProc
DO dummy
DO OnlyaCH07
DO OnlybCH07
```

If you run this program from the command line you will see that with multiple DBCs open, calling a stored procedure which exists only in **one** DBC is fine.It does not matter which DBC is current, the correct procedure is located. However, if **both** DBCs contain a stored procedure that is named the same, then the setting of the DBC is vitally important since Visual FoxPro will always search the current database first and only then will it search any other open databases.

Finally if NO DBC is defined as current, then Visual FoxPro executes the first procedure it finds – in this example it is always the '*dummy'* procedure in the aCH07 database container. Reversing the order in which the two DBCs are opened in the *ShoStPro* program changes the result for the last test. This suggests that Visual FoxPro is maintaining an internal collection of open databases, in which the last database to be opened is at the head of the list, and is searched first, when no database is set as current.

How to validate a database container
Visual FoxPro provides a **VALIDATE DATABASE** command that will run an internal consistency check on the currently open database. Currently (Version 6.0a) this command can *ONLY* be issued from the command window and by default its results are output to the main FoxPro screen. Attempting to use it within an application causes an error.

You can validate a database without first gaining exclusive use, but the DBC index will not be re-built, nor will you be able to fix any errors that the process may find. With exclusive use you may choose either to rebuild the index (a plain **VALIDATE DATABASE** command will do just that) or to invoke the repair mechanism by adding the '**RECOVER**' clause to the command.

While not very sophisticated, the recovery option at least highlights anything that VFP feels is wrong with your DBC and offers you options to either locate or delete a missing item and to delete or re-build missing indexes (providing that the necessary information is available in the DBC itself). The best way to avoid problems in the DBC is to ensure you always make changes to its tables (or views) *through* the DBC's own mechanisms. Avoid actions like building temporary indexes outside the DBC or programmatically changing view or table definitions without first getting exclusive use of the DBC.

In short, while not exactly fragile, the DBC relies heavily on its own internal consistency and errors (real or imagined) will inevitably cause you problems sooner or later.

How to pack a database container
The Visual FoxPro database container is, itself, a normal Visual FoxPro table in which each row contains the stored information for one object in the database. Like all Visual FoxPro tables, deleting a record only marks that record for deletion and the physical record is not

removed from the DBC. This means, over time, that a database can get large, even though it actually contains very few current items.

The **PACK DATABASE** command is the only method that you should use to clean up a DBC. Simply opening the DBC as a table and issuing a standard **PACK** command is not sufficient because the DBC maintains an internal numbering system for its objects that will not be updated unless the **PACK DATABASE** command is used. Using this command requires that you gain exclusive use to the database.

Moving a database container

We mentioned earlier in this section that the only price for gaining all the functionality that a database container provides is a minor modification to the header of the table to include a backlink to the DBC. This is, indeed, a trivial thing *UNTIL* you try to move a database container. Then its significance can assume monstrous proportions. The reason is that Visual FoxPro stores the *relative path* from the table back to the owning DBC directly in the table header. Providing that you always keep the DBC and all of its data tables in the same directory, all will be well because all that gets stored is the name of the database container.

However, when you have a database container that is NOT in the same directory as its tables you are laying yourself open to potential problems. We created a table in our working directory (*C:\VFP60\CH07*) and attached it to a database that resided in the *C:\TEMP* directory. The backlink added to the table was:

```
..\..\TEMP\TESTDBC.DBC
```

After moving this database container to the *C:\WINDOWS\TEMP* directory, any attempt to open the table resulted in a '*cannot resolve backlink*' error and the option to either locate the missing DBC, delete the link and free the table (with all the dire consequences for long field names that this entails) or to cancel. Being optimists we chose to locate the database container and were given a dialog to find it. Unfortunately having found our DBC and selected it, we were immediately confronted with Error 110 informing us that the "*File must be opened exclusively*" Not very helpful!

Fixing the backlink for a table

So what can be done? Fortunately the structure of the DBF Header is listed in the Help file (see the "*Table File Structure*" topic for more details) and Visual FoxPro provides us with some neat low level file handling functions which allow us to open a file and read and write to it at the byte level. So we can just write in the new location for the DBC and all will be well. The only question is where to write it?

You will see from the Help file that the size of the table header is actually determined by the formula:

32 + (nFields * 32) +264 bytes

Where *nFields* is the number of fields in the table, which we could get using **FCOUNT()** – if we could only open the table! (There is also a **HEADER()** – a useful little function that actually tells us how big the table header is. Unfortunately it also requires that we be able to open the table.) But if we could open the table, we wouldn't need to fix the backlink either.

The backlink itself is held as the last 263 bytes of the table header. However, the only certain way of getting those vital 263 bytes is to try and read the maximum possible number of bytes that could ever be in a table header. (Trying to read beyond the end of file does not generate an error in a low level read, it just stops at the end of file marker.) Visual FoxPro is limited to 255 fields per record so we need, using the formula above, to read in 8,456 bytes. This is well within the new upper limit of 16,777,184 characters per character string or memory variable so all is well.

Fortunately the field records section of the header always ends with a string of 13 "NULL" characters (*ASCII Character 0*) followed by a "Carriage Return" (*ASCII Character 13*). So if we locate this string within the block we have read from the table, we will have the start of the backlink. The following function uses this technique to read the backlink information from a table (when only the table file name is passed) or to write a new backlink string (pass both the file name and the new backlink):

```
************************************************************************
* Program....: BackLink.prg
* Compiler...: Visual FoxPro 06.00.8492.00 for Windows
* Abstract...: Sets/Returns Backlink Information from a table
* ...........: Pass both DBF File name (including extension) only to
* ...........: to return backlink, also pass new backlink string to
* ...........: write a new backlink
************************************************************************
LPARAMETERS tcTable, tcDBCPath
LOCAL lnParms, lnHnd, lnHdrStart, lnHdrSize, lcBackLink, lcNewLink
lnParms = PCOUNT()
*** Check that the file exists
IF ! FILE( tcTable )
   ERROR "9000: Cannot locate file " + tcTable
   RETURN .F.
ENDIF
*** Open the file at low level - Read Only if just reading info
lnHnd = FOPEN( tcTable, IIF( lnParms > 1, 2, 0) )
*** Check file is open
IF lnHnd > 0
   *** Backlink is last 263 bytes of the header so calculate position
   *** Max header size is (32 + ( 255 * 32 ) + 264) = 8456 Bytes
   lcStr = FREAD( lnHnd, 8456 )
   *** Field records end with 13 NULLS + "CR"
   lcFieldEnd = REPLICATE( CHR(0), 13 ) + CHR(13)
   lnHeaderStart = AT( lcFieldEnd, lcStr ) + 13
   *** Move file pointer to header start position
   FSEEK( lnHnd, lnHeaderStart )
   *** Read backlink
   lcBackLink = UPPER( ALLTRIM( STRTRAN( FGETS( lnHnd, 263 ), CHR(0) ) ) )
   *** If we are writing a new backlink
   IF lnParms > 1
      *** Get the path (max 263 characters!)
      tcDBCPath = LEFT(tcDBCPath,263)
      *** Pad it out to the full length with NULLS
      lcNewLink = PADR( ALLTRIM( LOWER( tcDBCPath ) ), 263, CHR(0) )
      *** Go to start of Backlink
      FSEEK( lnHnd, lnHeaderStart )
```

```
      *** Write the new backlink information
      FWRITE( lnHnd, lcNewLink )
      *** Set the new backlink as the return value
      lcBackLink = tcDbcPath
   ENDIF
   *** Close the file
   FCLOSE(lnHnd)
ELSE
   ERROR "9000: Unable to open table file"
   lcBackLink = ""
ENDIF
*** Return the backlink
RETURN lcBackLink
```

What happens to views when I move the database container?

The good news is that moving a database container has no effect on views. Views are stored as SQL statements inside the database container and, although they reference the DBC by name, they do not hold any path information. So there is no need to worry about them if you move a DBC from one location to another (*phew!*).

Renaming a database container

Renaming a database container presents a different set of problems. This time, both tables and views are affected. Tables will be affected because of the backlink they hold - which will end up pointing to something that no longer exists. However, this is relatively easy to fix, as we have already seen, and can easily be automated. In this case, though, Views *will* be affected because Visual FoxPro very helpfully includes the name of the DBC as part of the query that is stored. Here is part of the output for a query (generated by the *GENDBC.PRG* utility that ships with Visual FoxPro, and which can be found in the *VFP\Tools* sub-directory):

```
FUNCTION MakeView_TESTVIEW
***************** View setup for TESTVIEW ***************
CREATE SQL VIEW "TESTVIEW" ;
   AS SELECT Optutil.config, Optutil.type, Optutil.classname FROM
testdbc!optutil

DBSetProp('TESTVIEW', 'View', 'Tables', 'testdbc!optutil')

* Props for the TESTVIEW.config field.
DBSetProp('TESTVIEW.config', 'Field', 'KeyField', .T.)
DBSetProp('TESTVIEW.config', 'Field', 'Updatable', .F.)
DBSetProp('TESTVIEW.config', 'Field', 'UpdateName', 'testdbc!optutil.config')
DBSetProp('TESTVIEW.config', 'Field', 'DataType', "C(20)")
* Props for the TESTVIEW.type field.
DBSetProp('TESTVIEW.type', 'Field', 'UpdateName', 'testdbc!optutil.type')
* Props for the TESTVIEW.classname field.
DBSetProp('TESTVIEW.classname', 'Field', 'UpdateName',
'testdbc!optutil.classname')
ENDFUNC
```

Notice that the database container is prepended to the table name on every occasion - not just in the actual ꜱᴇʟᴇᴄᴛ line but also as part of each field's "*updatename*" property. This is, no doubt, very helpful when working with multiple database containers but is a royal pain when you need to rename your one and only DBC. Unfortunately we have not been able to find a good solution to this problem. The only thing we can suggest is that if you use Views, you should avoid renaming your DBC if at all possible.

If you absolutely **must** rename the DBC, then the safest solution is to run *GENDBC.PRG* before you rename it and extract all of the view definitions into a separate program file that you can then edit to update all occurrences of the old name with the new. Once you have renamed your DBC simply delete all of the views and run your edited program to re-create them in the newly renamed database.

Note: The SQL code to generate a view is stored in the *"properties"* field of each *"View"* record in the database container. Although it is stored as object code, the names of fields and tables are visible as plain text. We have seen suggestions that involve hacking this properties field directly to replace the DBC name but cannot advocate this practice! In our testing it proved to be a thoroughly unreliable method which more often than not rendered the view both unusable and unable to be edited. Using *GENDBC* may be less glamorous, but it is a lot safer!

Managing referential integrity in Visual FoxPro

The term *"referential integrity"*, usually just abbreviated to *"RI"*, means ensuring that the records contained in related tables are consistent. In other words that every child record (at any level) has a corresponding parent, and that any action that changes the key value used to identify a parent is reflected in all of its children. The objective is to ensure that 'orphan' records can never get into, or be left in place in, a table.

Visual FoxPro introduced built-in RI rules in Version 3.0. They are implemented by using the persistent relationships between tables defined in the database container and triggers on the tables to ensure that changes to key values in tables are handled according to rules that you define. The standard RI builder allows for three kinds of rule as follows:

- *Ignore*: The default setting for all actions, no RI is enforced and any update to any table is allowed to proceed - exactly as in earlier versions of FoxPro
- *Cascade:* Changes to the key value in the parent table are automatically reflected in the corresponding foreign keys in all of the child tables to maintain the relationships
- *Restrict:* Changes which would result in a violation of RI are prohibited

Setting up RI in Visual FoxPro is quite straightforward and the RI builder handles all of the work for you. **Figure 7.3**, below, shows the set-up in progress for a simple relational structure involving four tables (We have used the tables from the VFP Samples *"TestData"* database to illustrate this section). So far the following rules have been established:

Table 7.4 *Typical RI Rule set-up*

Parent Table	Child Table	Action	Rule
Customer	Orders	Insert	Ignore
Customer	Orders	Update	Cascade
Customer	Orders	Delete	Restrict
Orders	OrdItems	Insert	Restrict
Orders	OrdItems	Update	Cascade
Orders	OrdItems	Delete	Restrict

The consequences of these rules are that a user can always add a new customer (*Ignore Customer Insert*), but cannot delete a customer who has orders on file (*Restrict Customer Delete*) and any change to a customer's key will update the corresponding order keys (*Cascade Customer Update*). For the orders table the rules are that an order item may only be inserted against a valid order (*Restrict Order Insert*), that no order may be deleted while it has items associated with it (*Restrict Order Delete*) and that any changes to an order's key value will be reflected in all of the items to which it refers (*Cascade Order Update*).

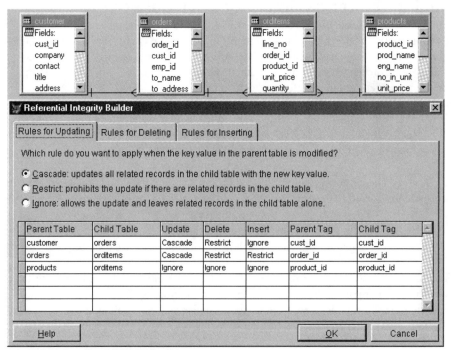

Figure 7.3 *Using the VFP RI builder*

Limitations of the generated RI Code

Unfortunately the implementation in Visual FoxPro is not very efficient - generating RI rules for a lot of tables results in an enormous amount of classical *'xBase-style'* procedural code being added to the Stored Procedures in your database container. The rules defined in the example above resulted in 636 lines of code in 12 separate procedures. Each table has its own named procedure for each trigger generated - thus in the example above procedures are generated named:

```
PROCEDURE __RI_DELETE_customer
PROCEDURE __RI_DELETE_orders
PROCEDURE __RI_INSERT_orditems
procedure __RI_UPDATE_customer
procedure __RI_UPDATE_orders
procedure __RI_UPDATE_orditems
```

(Note the inconsistency in capitalization of the 'PROCEDURE' key word!) Adding more tables and more rules increases the amount of code. Moreover this code is not well commented, and in early versions, contained several bugs which could cause it to fail under certain conditions - at least one of which has persisted through into the latest version of Visual FoxPro.

The following code is taken directly from the stored procedures generated by VFP V6.0 (Build 8492) for the example shown above:

```
procedure RIDELETE
local llRetVal
llRetVal=.t.
  IF (ISRLOCKED() and !deleted()) OR !RLOCK()
    llRetVal=.F.
  ELSE
    IF !deleted()
      DELETE
      IF CURSORGETPROP('BUFFERING') > 1
        =TABLEUPDATE()
      ENDIF
      llRetVal=pnerror=0
    ENDIF not already deleted
  ENDIF
  UNLOCK RECORD (RECNO())
RETURN llRetVal
```

You will notice that the italicized line of code is incorrectly placed, and should be outside of the IF !DELETED() block. As it stands, the return value from this code may be incorrect (depending on the value of '*pnerror*' at the time) if the record being tested is already marked for deletion.

Apart from this specific bug, and despite the criticisms leveled at the mechanism for generating the RI code, the code actually works well when used with tables that are structured in the way that was expected. It is certainly easier to use the RI builder than to try and write your own code! There is, however, one additional caution to bear in mind when using the RI builder.

Using compound keys in relationships
When generating the RI code for the tables in the example, this warning was displayed:

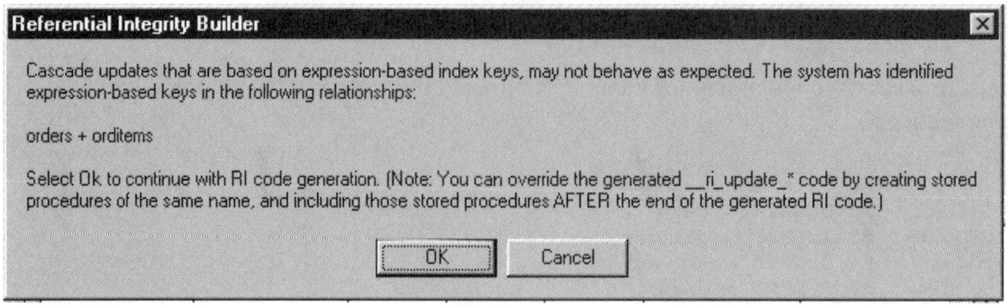

Referential Integrity Builder   ☒

Cascade updates that are based on expression-based index keys, may not behave as expected. The system has identified expression-based keys in the following relationships:

orders + orditems

Select Ok to continue with RI code generation. (Note: You can override the generated __ri_update_* code by creating stored procedures of the same name, and including those stored procedures AFTER the end of the generated RI code.)

    OK   Cancel

Figure 7.4 Warning!

What on earth does this mean? Clearly it is a serious warning or Visual FoxPro would not generate it! The answer is that the regular index used as the target for the persistent relationship between the Orders and OrdItems table is actually based on a compound key comprising the foreign key to the Orders Table plus the Item Number. The index expression in question is the one used on the child table *orditems*, which is actually "`order_id+STR(line_no,5,0)`". (This was set up so that when items are displayed they will appear in line number order. Not really an unreasonable thing to do!) However any attempt to insert or change a record in the child table (*orditems*), will cause a 'Trigger Failed' error.

The problem is that any rule set up on this table which needs to refer to the parent table will use, as a key for the `SEEK()`, the concatenated field values from the child table. This will, obviously, always fail since the key to the parent table (*'orders'*) is merely the first part of the concatenated key in the child. As the warning says, you can (fairly easily) edit the generated code so that the correct key value is used in these situations.

The following extract shows the problem:

```
PROCEDURE   __RI_UPDATE_orditems
*** Other code here ***
*** Then we get the old and new values for the child table
SELECT (lcChildWkArea)
*** Here is where the error arises!!!
lcChildID=ORDER_ID+STR(LINE_NO,5,0)
lcOldChildID=oldval("ORDER_ID+STR(LINE_NO,5,0)")
*** Other code here ***
*** If the values have changed, we have a problem!!!
IF lcChildID<>lcOldChildID
  pcParentDBF=dbf(lcParentWkArea)
  *** And here is where it all goes wrong

  llRetVal=SEEK(lcChildID,lcParentWkArea)


  *** And here is where the actual error is generated
  IF NOT llRetVal
    DO rierror with -1,"Insert restrict rule violated.",",","
    IF _triggerlevel=1
      DO riend WITH llRetVal
    ENDIF at the end of the highest trigger level
  ENDIF this value was changed
```

Since the key for the Child ID is hard-coded when the RI code is generated, the actual edit required is very simple - just delete the concatenation. Unfortunately your changes will only hold good as long as you do not re-generate the RI code.

The real answer to this problem, however, is very simple. *Just don't do it*! As we have already suggested, surrogate keys should always be used to relate tables so that you have an unambiguous method of joining two tables together. In addition to their other virtues, they also ensure that you never need to use compound keys in order to enforce RI.

What about other RI options?

The native builder handles only three possible alternatives when enforcing RI- *Cascade, Restrict and Delete* - and makes the assumption that 'orphan' records are always a "bad thing". In practice this is not necessarily the case (providing that you design for that contingency!) and there is at least one case in which an *'Adopt'* option would be useful. Consider the situation when a salesman, who is responsible for a group of customers and hence for their orders, leaves the company. Naturally we need to indicate that that salesman's ID is no longer valid as the salesman responsible for those customers and we need to assign a new person. But what about orders the salesman actually took while working for the company?

If we simply delete the salesman, an RI "Restrict" rule would disallow the delete because there are "child" records for that key. What is really needed is a variant on the deletion rule that says:

"If the parent record is being deleted, and a valid key is supplied assign any existing child records to the specified key."

This is not yet available in Visual FoxPro, but a trigger that enforces such a rule would be easy enough to create, the pseudo code is simply:

```
Check to see if any records exist referencing the key to be deleted
If none, allow the delete and exit
If a new, valid, key has been specified
  Change all existing child records to the new key
  Delete the original parent record
  Exit
```

Want more details on RI?

For more details on the subject of RI in Visual FoxPro and an example of a complete SQL-based alternative to the native RI code, we can do no better than refer you to Chapter 6 of the excellent *"Effective Techniques for Application Development with Visual FoxPro 6.0,"* by Jim Booth and Steve Sawyer (Hentzenwerke Publishing, 1998).

Using triggers and rules in Visual FoxPro

First we need some definitions. Triggers and rules can only be implemented for tables that are part of a database container to allow the developer to handle issues relating to data integrity. Triggers only fire when data is actually written to the physical table - so they *cannot* be used for checking values as they are entered into a buffered table. There are actually two sets of rules available - Field Rules and Table rules. Both field level and table level (or more accurately, '*Row Level*') rules can reference or modify any single field, or combination of fields in the current row. Rules are fired whenever the object to which they refer loses focus - whether the table is buffered or not - and so *can* be used for validating data as it is entered.

So what's the practical difference between a 'trigger' and a 'rule'?

A trigger, as implemented in Visual FoxPro, is a test that is applied whenever the database detects a change being written to one of its tables. There are, therefore, three types of triggers - one for each of the types of change that can occur (*Insert, Update and Delete*). The essence of a trigger is that the expression which calls it must return a logical value indicating whether the change should be allowed to proceed or not. This is simplest if the trigger itself always returns a logical value, so if a trigger returns a value of `.F.` an error is raised (Error #1539 - '*Trigger Failed*') and the change is not committed to the underlying table. Triggers cannot be used to change values in the record that has caused them to fire, but they can be used to make changes in other tables. A very common use of triggers is, therefore, for the creation of audit logs! (By the way, if you are wondering why this restriction exists, just consider what would happen if you could change the current row in code that was called whenever changes in the current row were detected!).

Like triggers, calls to rules must also return a logical value; but unlike triggers, they *can* make changes to the data in the row to which they refer. Also, since they do fire for buffered tables, rules can be used for performing validation directly in an application's UI thereby avoiding the necessity of writing code directly in the interface. A rule can also be used to modify fields that are not part of the UI (for example a "last changed" date, or a user id field). In practice the only difference between Field and Table rules is *when* they are fired.

Both triggers and rules apply (like any other stored procedure) whether the table in question is opened in an application or just in a Browse window. The differences between Triggers and Rules can be summarized like this:

Table 7.5 *Differences between Triggers and Rules*

Item	Fires	Capability
Field Rule	When field loses focus	Can reference or modify any field in the record
Table Rule	When the record pointer moves	Can reference or modify any field in the record
Trigger	When data is saved to disk	Cannot modify data in the record that fired the trigger

Why, when adding a trigger to a table, does VFP sometimes reject it?

Normally this indicates that the data that you have in your table already conflicts with the rule you are trying to apply.(You will sometimes see a similar problem when trying to add a candidate index to a populated table.) When you alter a table to add a trigger or rule, Visual FoxPro applies that test to all existing records - if the data in an existing record fails the rule, then you will get this error. The only solution is to correct the data before re-applying the rule.

Check the logic in your rules carefully

Another possible reason for errors when applying rules or triggers is faulty logic on the part of the developer. You need to be careful when defining rules to ensure you do not inadvertently throw Visual FoxPro into an endless loop. This can easily happen when using a rule to change the data because the change causes the **same** rule to fire again. For example, the following field rule will cause a "*Do Nesting Level*" error:

```
IF !EMPTY(ALLTRIM(clicmpy)) AND NOT ALLTRIM(PROPER(clicmpy))== ALLTRIM(clicmpy)
   *** Force the format to UPPER case! (This is a nonsense rule!)
   REPLACE clicmpy WITH UPPER(clicmpy)
ENDIF
```

The reason is that it can simply never succeed! The test actually states that if the field is not in **PROPER()** format, change it to **UPPER()**. Therefore the first time this rule fires, Visual FoxPro is locked into an endless loop where it finds the field is in the wrong format. It then changes the format to another format that fires the rule again, but the field is still in the wrong format, so it changes it again ... and so on *ad infinitum*! The following rule **WILL** work as expected:

```
IF !EMPTY(ALLTRIM(clicmpy)) AND NOT ALLTRIM(PROPER(clicmpy))== ALLTRIM(clicmpy)
   *** Force the format to PROPER case
   REPLACE clicmpy WITH PROPER(clicmpy)
ENDIF
```

Can I temporarily disable a trigger or rule then?

Certainly. The easiest way to do this is to include a test for an application level flag, (i.e. either a variable that is 'public' to the application, or a property on an application object) in the code that the trigger or rule implements. We would suggest using a variable because you may also want to do this outside of an application and it is easier to create a public variable from the command line than to have to instantiate your application object every time you want to use a table. The following code, placed in the stored procedure and called by a trigger will simply return a value of .**T**. when the specified variable is not found:

```
IF VARTYPE( glDisableRules ) = "L" AND ! EMPTY( glDisableRules )
   RETURN .T.
ENDIF
```

One question you may be asking yourself is why would anyone want to disable triggers or rules - after having gone to all the trouble of setting them up? It may be that if you are doing a bulk data load, or a block **REPLACE**, the penalty of validating each row individually would slow things down too much - especially when the changes have already been pre-validated before being applied. If this is a feature of your application it may actually be better to add a separate stored procedure to test whether rules should be applied or not and call it from every trigger or rule. Thus:

```
FUNCTION ApplyRules
LOCAL llRetVal
STORE .T. TO llRetVal
*** Test for presence of the disabling variable
IF VARTYPE( glDisableRules ) = "L" AND ! EMPTY( glDisableRules )
  llRetVal = .F.
ENDIF
RETURN llRetVal
```

Every trigger or rule function would then begin:

```
FUNCTION SomeTrigger
IF ! ApplyRules()
  RETURN .T.
ENDIF
*** Actual trigger code here
```

It is imperative that your triggers and rules return a logical .T. when their code is not being executed, otherwise a 'Trigger Failed' error will be generated.

How do I actually create my trigger and rule procedures?

The actual code, assuming you need more than a simple one-line rule, for triggers and rules is best stored in the database container as a Stored Procedure. This is not an absolute requirement, since Visual FoxPro would find a procedure even if it were not in the database container (providing that the necessary file had been established with a "`Set Procedure To`" command). However, since the procedure might be needed at any time the table that calls it is used, it makes more sense to leave it in the database container so that it is available whenever, and however, the table is used.

So the question remains - how do you create the actual code? There are (as usual in Visual FoxPro) two options. You can do it interactively using either the *Edit Stored Procedures* option when modifying the database or by simply issuing `MODIFY PROCEDURES` from the command window. You can also write (and test!) your code in a stand-alone program file and add it to the stored procedures programmatically using `APPEND PROCEDURES FROM <filename>`. Either way you must first have opened, and made current, the relevant database.

Gotcha with the Append Procedures command

There is one thing to bear in mind when using the Append Procedures command. The Help file comments on this command are literally accurate in respect of what the `OVERWRITE` clause for this command actually does. The Help file states that the `OVERWRITE` clause:

Specifies that the current stored procedures in the database are overwritten by those in the text file.

This does **NOT** mean that "*any procedure with the same name will be overwritten*", it means exactly what it says. **ALL** procedures currently in your database container are deleted and replaced by whatever is in the source file that you specify. We strongly recommend that you consign the OverWrite clause of this command to the trash bin right now.

But if I am updating a procedure without "overwrite", doesn't that mean I end up with two?

Indeed it does. If you already have a procedure in the database container named 'mytestproc' and then append a new version of the same procedure, you will have two procedures named 'mytestproc' in the database container. Fortunately, the newly appended procedure will be at the end of the file and thus will always be the version that VFP actually compiles, and uses. While it may look messy, it will work correctly. However, you should not really leave the database container in this state and as soon as possible you should get access to it and delete any redundant procedures.

An alternative approach is to always maintain stored procedures as a *complete* set of replacement procedures in an external file and then use the OverWrite clause of APPEND PROCEDURES to force the total replacement of all procedures. If you practice watertight version control you may feel confident enough to do this on a working application. (In which case, to paraphrase Rudyard Kipling, "*You're a braver man than I am, Gunga-Din*".)

How do I add a trigger to a table?

As with the code in the trigger procedure, this can be done either interactively in the table designer by inserting the appropriate expression in the "*Table*" tab of the dialog, or programmatically using the CREATE TRIGGER command. Remember that the calling expression must evaluate to a logical value, and it is preferable that a call to a stored procedure should return a logical value. Either way you will require exclusive access to the table.

So when should I use a trigger?

The answer, as always, is that it depends on your requirements. Triggers are normally used for either (and sometimes both) of two reasons. First, to maintain referential integrity (RI) - and this is how Visual FoxPro implements the code generated by the RI builder. Second, to create audit trails by tracking changes to a table. Remember that a trigger only fires when changes to a physical table are made and so are of no relevance when working with buffered data.

It is worth noting that within a trigger, the restriction that the GetFldState() and OldVal() functions can *only* be used on tables that have buffering enabled does not apply. Both functions will work without error, even on un-buffered tables, which is extremely useful when creating audit trails inside triggers.

A working example using triggers

The sample code for this chapter includes a small database ('*Auditlog'*) and a simple form ('*FrmAudit"*) which illustrates how triggers can be used to build an audit log. The form can be run stand-alone directly from the command line using the DO FORM command. The tables have been constructed as follows (the fields prefixed with a '#' are the primary keys):

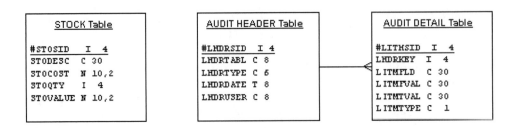

Figure 7.5 *Audit Logging Tables*

Triggers on the "Stock" table add data to the audit tables whenever a change is committed, however only the items which are actually changed get written during an update (all items are, by definition, changed when doing either an insert or delete). Other stored procedures are used to implement a standard "*newid*" function for generating primary keys, and also to implement a field rule for calculating the value of a stock item when both a quantity and a cost are supplied.

The audit logging functionality is handled by the "*BildLog*" function consisting of three parts. Firstly, because the function will use a transaction, it ensures that all of the supporting tables (including the PK generation table) are available and in the correct state. We cannot change the buffering mode of a table inside a transaction, so the normal PK generation routine (which will open the table and set BufferMode = 1) would cause an error unless the table is already open.

The next part of the trigger begins a transaction and inserts the table name and action (which are passed as parameters to the trigger) plus the current date, time and user id into the log header table. This insert is then committed before any further action is taken.

Finally, but still within the transaction, the insert to the audit details table is handled. A major issue with audit logging is to prevent the log tables from getting too large - which can be a real problem with high activity tables. The code here only writes the fields which have actually changed when an Update is taking place - though the entire record must be written for all Inserts and Deletes - which helps minimize the size of the tables.

The sample form, although simple, is fully functional and allows for adding, deleting and editing of the "Stock" table on page one and uses a view, constructed from the audit log tables, to review the history of changes to the table on page two. **Figure 7.6** shows the two pages of the form.

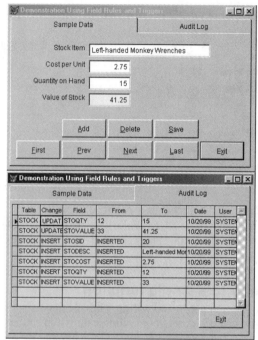

Figure 7.6 *Audit Log Demonstration form*

And when should I use a rule?

Rules are most commonly used for validation of data and, since they DO fire on buffered data, can be used to handle "*pre-save*" validation. By pre-save validation we mean checking that the data that has been entered or modified will not, *of itself*, cause an insert or update to fail. Whether you use a Field Rule or a Table Rule will depend on when you want the rule to fire (see **Table 7.5** for details).

Another common use for rules is for maintaining calculated (or dependent) fields within a record. Despite the fact that the rules for normalizing data to third normal form state that a row should not contain fields which are derived solely from other fields in the same row, there are many occasions when the inclusion of such fields is beneficial. Usually this is when tables are likely to get large and the overhead of re-calculating dependent values every time a form, report or other query is run becomes unacceptable. (In other words, "*de-normalizing for performance*"). Such a de-normalization carries with it the problem of ensuring that calculated fields are correctly maintained - but a simple rule, entered as a Field Rule, will ensure that things cannot get out of synchronization.

For example, consider the situation where a table is used to record details of the lines on an invoice. Typically you will have fields for Sale Price and Quantity Ordered. To display each line's value, without actually storing the calculated data, requires code in the UI control's *Valid* or *LostFocus* methods to re-calculate the value. By including a value field in the table, you can use a rule instead and simply bind a (Read-Only) control to that field. Here is an example of such a rule which would be called by both the Sale Price, and the Quantity Ordered fields:

```
FUNCTION CheckLineVal
IF NVL(SalePrice, 0) # 0 AND NVL(QtyOrdered, 0) # 0
  IF LineValue # SalePrice * QtyOrdered
    REPLACE LineValue WITH (SalePrice * QtyOrdered)
  ENDIF
ELSE
  IF NVL( LineValue, 0 ) # 0
    REPLACE LineValue WITH 0
  ENDIF
ENDIF
RETURN .T.
```

We need to call it from both fields to ensure that whichever is changed, the value is correctly updated. Note that we also check for and handle NULL values. A very similar rule is used on the "Stock" table in the "AuditLog" example for this chapter to calculate the value of stock held.

Must a trigger or rule always refer to a single function?

The only requirement is that the *expression* that you use to call a trigger or rule must always evaluate to a logical value. Providing that you can construct your calling expression so that Visual FoxPro can evaluate it to a logical value, there is no restriction on the number of functions that may be called. The following expressions are perfectly valid as either a trigger or a rule:

```
Field Rule: SalePrice # 0 AND CheckLineVal()
Message: "Sale Price cannot be $0.00. To raise a credit, enter Price less than
$0.00"

Field Rule: QtyOrdered > 0 AND CheckLineVal()
Message: "Quantity cannot be 0. To raise a credit, enter Price less than $0.00"
```

Using triggers and rules does, however, impose an overhead on the process of making changes and committing data to tables. The more complex your rules, the longer your navigation and save routines will take to execute. As always there is a trade-off between increased functionality and performance. The level that is acceptable in any situation can really only be determined by trial and error in the context of your application's requirements.

Chapter 8
Data Buffering and
Transactions

"The first faults are theirs that commit them, the second theirs that permit them." (Old English Proverb)

The whole topic of using data buffering and transactions in Visual FoxPro is an intrinsically confusing one - which is not helped by the choice of terminology associated with the functionality. This chapter seeks to de-mystify the issues surrounding buffering and transactions and shows how you can use the tools Visual FoxPro provides to manage data most effectively.

Using data buffering

Where are we coming from?
As stated in the introduction to this chapter, working with data buffering in Visual FoxPro seems to cause a lot of confusion. We feel this is largely due to the rather confusing implementation of buffering, and the somewhat odd (by accepted standards) nomenclature associated with the topic.

For example, to set buffering for a Visual FoxPro *DBF* file (which is a table) we have to use the heavily overloaded *CURSOR*SETPROP() function. Why not a separate, unambiguous, 'SetBufferMode()' function? While to confirm a pending transaction, the command is END TRANSACTION. Why not 'COMMIT' as in every other database language - a choice which is even more peculiar since the standard 'ROLLBACK' command **is** used to undo a transaction?

Furthermore, perhaps because of the way in which Visual FoxPro implements record (as opposed to 'Page') locking, the issue of controlling the placing and releasing of locks is apparently inextricably bound up with buffering. For example, in order to enable row buffering, which only operates on a single record, SET MULTILOCKS must be ON - but according to the Help file this setting merely determines Visual FoxPro's ability to lock *multiple* records in the same table - and it is scoped to the current data session anyway. This does not seem very logical and it is not really surprising that we get confused by it all.

What do we mean by 'buffering' anyway?
The principle is actually very simple. The concept of buffering is that when you make changes to data, those changes are not written directly to the source table, instead they go into a 'holding area' (the '*Buffer*') until such time as you instruct Visual FoxPro to either save them to permanent storage or discard them. **Figure 8.1** illustrates the concept. This holding area is what you actually 'see' in Visual FoxPro when using a buffered table and is, in reality, an

updateable cursor based on the source table. All changes are made to this cursor and are only written to the underlying table when the appropriate "update" command is issued.

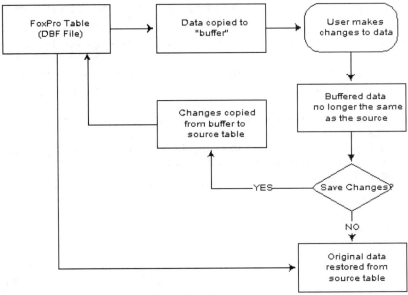

Figure 8.1 *Data buffering conceptualized*

Buffering strategies

Tables can be used with three different "*Buffering Strategies*". The first option is not to use buffering at all.

This was the only option in all versions of FoxPro prior to Visual FoxPro Version 3.0 and it is still the default behavior for Visual FoxPro tables today. This mode can be explicitly set using CURSORSETPROP('Buffering') with a parameter of "1". Any changes made are written directly and immediately to the underlying table. There is no '*undo*' capability unless it is programmed explicitly - by using SCATTER and GATHER for example.

The second option is for "*Row*" buffering which is set using CURSORSETPROP('Buffering') with a parameter of either "2" or "3". Changes are not sent to the underlying table unless one of two things happens. Either an explicit *TableUpdate()* or *TableRevert()* command is issued in the code, or the record pointer is moved in the underlying table. Any movement of the record pointer, however it is initiated for a table which is in row buffered mode, always causes an '*implicit*' *TableUpdate()*.

The third option is for "*Table*" buffering which is set using CURSORSETPROP('Buffering') with a parameter of either "4" or "5". In this mode changes are never sent 'automatically' to the underlying table, an explicit *TableUpdate()* command must always be used to send changes in the buffer to the underlying table, or *TableRevert()* to cancel changes. Attempting to close a table-buffered table while it still has uncommitted changes caused Visual FoxPro to generate an error in Version 3.0 but this behavior was changed in later versions so that pending changes are simply lost. There is no error, and no warning that changes are about to be lost, the buffered table is just closed.

Locking strategies

Closely allied with buffering is the question of "*locking*". Visual FoxPro always needs to lock the physical record in a table while changes are being made to its contents, and there are two possible strategies.

Firstly, a record can be locked as soon as a user starts making changes. (The lock is actually placed as soon as a valid key press is detected.) This is '*Pessimistic Locking*' and it prevents any other user from making or saving changes to that record until the current user has completed their changes and released the record by either committing or reverting their changes.

Secondly Visual FoxPro can attempt to lock a record only when changes are sent to the table. This is '*Optimistic Locking*' and means that even though a user is making changes to data, the record remains available to other users who could also make, and possibly save, changes to the same record while the first user is still working it.

Buffering modes

The buffer "*mode*" for a table is, therefore, the specific combination of the Buffering and Locking strategies. There are a total of five buffering modes for a table as illustrated by **Table 8.1.**

Table 8.1 Visual FoxPro Buffering Modes

Mode	Locking	Buffering	Comment
1	Pessimistic	None	The only option for FP2.x, default for VFP, tables
2	Pessimistic	Row	Lock placed by KeyPress Event. Record pointer movement forces save
3	Optimistic	Row	Lock placed by TableUpdate(). Record pointer movement forces save
4	Pessimistic	Table	Lock placed by KeyPress Event. Save must be initiated explicitly
5	Optimistic	Table	Lock placed by TableUpdate(). Save must be initiated explicitly

When working with Visual FoxPro we must be careful to distinguish between the individual *strategies* which we are setting for Buffering and Locking and the *buffering mode* which results from the combination of them. Unfortunately, as we shall see, Visual FoxPro itself is less careful about this distinction.

What does all this mean when creating data-bound forms?

This is where things start to get a little more complex (and not only because of the nomenclature). Let us consider the 'normal' situation where tables are added to form by the native dataenvironment. The form has a property named 'Buffermode' that has three possible settings:

- 0 None (default)
- 1 Pessimistic
- 2 Optimistic

Notice that these actually refer to the options for the *locking* strategy and have nothing to do with buffering at all! In fact the form will determine the *buffering* strategy for its tables all by itself, based upon their usage.

The sample code includes two forms '*DemOne*' (**Figure 8.2**) and '*DemTwo*' (**Figure 8.3**) which, when initialized, display the values for the Form's Buffermode property and the buffering mode of each table in the labeled textboxes. (The form's Buffermode can only be set at *design* time, so open the form and change the *BufferMode*, then run it to see the results for the different settings.) Both forms use the same two tables, which have a one-to-many relationship, but they display the 'many' side of the relationship in different ways. The first uses a grid, while the second simply shows individual fields directly on the form.

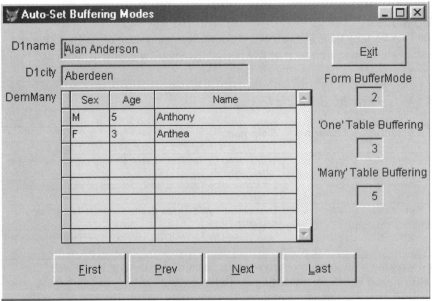

Figure 8.2 Auto-set buffer mode when a grid is present on the form

Notice that when the 'many' table is displayed in a grid it is opened, by the form, in table buffered mode. However, if the 'many' table is merely displaying single fields, then the buffering for the table will be the same as for the 'one' table for all settings of the Form's *Buffermode* property.

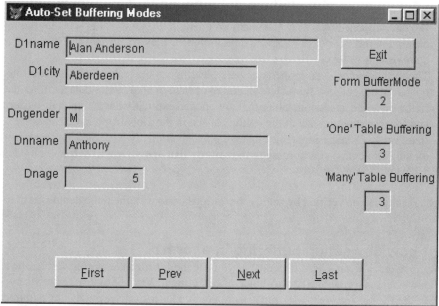

***Figure 8.3** Auto-set buffer mode with no grid*

If you run through all the options for the form's *Buffermode* property, you will have noticed that even with the form's *BufferMode* property set to *0-(None)* the cursor created by Visual FoxPro is still opened in *row buffered* mode when the tables are opened by the form's dataenvironment. "No buffering" apparently means "Row Buffering" to a form!

However, this is **NOT** the case when tables are opened directly with a USE command. Form *'DemThree'* is identical to *'DemOne'* except that instead of using the form's dataenvironment to open the tables they are opened explicitly in the *Load* method. In this situation the form's *Buffermode* property has no impact whatsoever, and the tables are opened according to settings in the *'Locking and Buffering'* section on the 'Data' tab of the Options dialog. This dialog really <u>does</u> set the buffer mode. It has five options which correspond to the five modes defined in **Table 8.1** above and which use the same numeric identifiers as the `CursorSetProp()` function.

However, the settings specified in the Options Dialog only apply to the *default* datasession. If the form is running a private datasession, then tables opened with the `USE` command will be set to whatever mode is specified for that datasession and this, by default, will be for no buffering at all.

Are you confused yet?

We certainly are! As far as we can tell, the situation is actually as follows:

- For tables opened by a Form's dataenvironment, it does not matter whether the form is running in the *Default* or a *Private* datasession. Tables are *always* buffered to at least *Optimistic Row* level.
- The form's *BufferMode* property actually determines the locking strategy, **not** the buffer mode, but *only* for tables which are opened by that form's dataenvironment.
- In the default datasession, tables that are opened explicitly have both their buffering and locking strategies set to the option chosen in the global Options Dialog.
- In a Private DataSession, tables that are opened explicitly have their buffering and locking strategies set according to the settings that apply for that datasession (Default = "No buffering").

These results can be verified by setting the various options in the three demonstration forms.

So just how do I set up buffering in a form?

The short answer, as always, is 'it depends'. If you use the form's dataenvironment to open tables then you can normally leave the choice of buffering to Visual FoxPro. Otherwise you can simply use the `CursorSetProp()` function in your code to set up each table as required. Either way you need to be aware of the consequences so that you can code your update routines appropriately.

Using BufferModeOverride

The dataenvironment class provides a property for each table (or, more accurately, '*cursor*') named "*BufferModeOverride*". This will set the buffer mode for that table (and only that table) to one of its six options - yes, that's right, **six** options, not five - as follows:

- 0 None
- 1 (Default) Use form Setting
- 2 Pessimistic row buffering
- 3 Optimistic row buffering
- 4 Pessimistic table buffering
- 5 Optimistic table buffering

Firstly notice that while the numbers 2 through 5 match the parameters for CursorSetProp() and are the same as those available through the Options dialog, the value required for setting "no buffering" is now 0 instead of 1. This is yet another inconsistency in the set up for buffering!

Secondly notice that the default value for this property is "1 - Use Form Setting". The form 'setting' referred to is, of course, the "*BufferMode*" property which, as we have seen, is actually for choosing the locking strategy to be applied. There is **no** form setting for controlling buffering!

Having said that, setting the *BufferModeOverride* property *will* ensure that the table is opened using the buffer mode that you specify. At least this property **is** correctly named, it overrides everything else and forces the table into the specified buffer mode in all situations.

Using CursorSetProp()

Irrespective of how a table is opened, you can always use the `CursorSetProp()` function to change the buffer mode of a table. However, if you are not using the form's dataenvironment to open your tables, then you have two options depending on whether your forms use the Default DataSession or a Private DataSession. In the first case you can simply set the required mode in the Options dialog and forget about it. All tables will always be opened with that setting and you will always know where you are.

If you use a Private DataSession then you need to do two things. Firstly you must ensure that the environment is set up to support buffering. A number of environment settings are scoped to the datasession and you may need to change the default behavior of some, or all of the following (see the *SET DATASESSION* topic in the help file for a full list of settings affected):

• SET MULTILOCKS	Must be set to ON to enable buffering, Default is OFF
• SET DELETED	Default is OFF
• SET DATABASE	"No database" is set by default in a Private DataSession
• SET EXCLUSIVE	Default is OFF for a Private DataSession
• SET LOCK	Default is OFF
• SET COLLATE	Default is 'MACHINE'
• SET EXACT	Default is OFF

Secondly you need to explicitly set the buffer mode of each table using the `CursorSetProp()` function with the appropriate parameter because the settings in the Options Dialog do not apply to private datasessions.

So what mode of buffering should I use in my forms?

To us the answer is simple. You should *always* use table buffering with an optimistic locking strategy (i.e. Buffer Mode 5). The reason is simply that, with the exception of building an index, there is nothing you can do in any other mode that *cannot* be done in this mode. While row buffering can be useful in development, we do not believe it has any place in a working application.There are just too many ways in which the implicit *TableUpdate()* (caused by moving the record pointer) can be triggered, and not all of them are under our direct control. For example, the `KeyMatch()` function is defined in the Help file as;

Searches an index tag or index file for an index key

Seems harmless enough - surely searching an index file cannot cause any problems. But a note (in the Remarks section right at the end of the topic) also states that:

KEYMATCH( ) returns the record pointer to the record on which it was originally positioned before KEYMATCH( ) was issued.

Hang on right there! Surely '**returns** the record pointer' implies that it **moves** the record pointer - which indeed it does. The consequence is that if you are using row buffering and want to check for a duplicate key by using `KeyMatch()`, you will immediately commit any pending change. (Of course in Version 6.0 or later you can always use *IndexSeek()* instead.) However, the same issue arises with many of the commands and functions that operate on a table - especially the older ones that were introduced into FoxPro before the days of buffering (e.g. `CALCULATE`, `SUM` and `AVERAGE`).

The fact that you have a table set up for table buffering does not prevent you from treating the table as if it were actually row buffered. Both the TableUpdate() and TableRevert() functions have the ability to act solely on the current row. The only practical difference, therefore, is that that no update will happen unless you explicitly call TableUpdate(). This may mean that you have to write a little more code, but it does prevent a lot of problems.

Changing the buffer mode of a table

We said, at the start of the last section, that you can always use `CursorSetProp()` to set or change the buffering mode of a table. This is true, but if the table is already table buffered, it may not be so simple because changing the buffering state will force Visual FoxPro to check the state of any existing buffers.

If the table is Row Buffered and has uncommitted changes, Visual FoxPro simply commits the changes and allows the change of mode. However, if the target is table buffered, and you try to change its buffer mode while there are uncommitted changes, Visual FoxPro complains and raises Error 1545 ("*Table buffer for alias "name" contains uncommitted changes*"). This is a problem because you cannot index a table while it is table buffered, so the only way to create an index on such a table is to switch, temporarily, to row buffering. Of course, the solution is simple enough - just ensure there are no changes pending before you try to change the buffer mode. But how can you do that?

IsChanged() - another function that FoxPro forgot?

Visual FoxPro provides two native functions that can be used to check the status of the buffers - `GetFldState()` and `GetNextModified()`. However, the first of these works only on the current row of a table and the second can only be used when Table Buffering is in effect. It seems to us that what is missing is a single function that will work in all situations and let you know whether there are changes pending in a table buffer. Here is our attempt at writing such a function:

```
***********************************************************************
* Program....: IsChanged.prg
* Compiler...: Visual FoxPro 06.00.8492.00 for Windows
* Abstract...: Returns a logical value indicating whether a table has
* ...........: pending changes, whatever the buffer mode employed
***********************************************************************
LPARAMETERS tcTable
LOCAL lcTable, lnBuffMode, lnRecNo, llRetVal, lcFldState
```

```
*** Check the parameter, assume current alias if nothing passed
lcTable = IIF( VARTYPE(tcTable) # "C" OR EMPTY( tcTable ), ;
                ALIAS(), ALLTRIM( UPPER( tcTable )))

*** Check that the specified table name is used as an alias
IF EMPTY( lcTable ) OR ! USED( JUSTSTEM( lcTable) )

    *** We have an error - probably a developer error, so use an Error to
report it!
    ERROR "9000: IsChanged() requires that the alias of an open table be" +
CHR(13) ;
        + "passed, or that the current work area should contain an" +
CHR(13) ;
        + "open table"
    RETURN .F.
ENDIF

*** Check the buffering status
lnBuffMode = CURSORGETPROP( 'Buffering', lcTable )

*** If no buffering, just return .F.
IF lnBuffMode = 1
    RETURN .F.
ENDIF

*** Now deal with the two buffer modes
IF INLIST( lnBuffMode, 2, 3 )

    *** If Row Buffered, use GetFldState()
    lcFldState = NVL( GETFLDSTATE( -1, lcTable ), "")

    *** If lcFldState contains anything but 1's then something has changed
    *** All 3's indicates an empty, appended record, but that is still a
change!
    *** Use CHRTRAN to strip out 1's - and just see if anything is left.
    llRetVal = !EMPTY( CHRTRAN( lcFldState, "1", "") )
ELSE

    *** Find the record number of the first changed record.
    *** Appended records will have a record number which is negative
    *** so we must check for a return value of "NOT EQUAL TO 0",
    *** rather than simply "GREATER THAN 0"
    llRetVal = ( GETNEXTMODIFIED( 0, lcTable ) # 0 )
ENDIF
RETURN lLRetVal
```

Essentially all that this function does is determine the type of buffering employed and use the appropriate native function to see if there are any changes. There are, however, a couple of assumptions here. Firstly, the function sees a newly appended, but totally unedited, row as "a change". This is reasonable since the only objective is determining whether the table has changed, not whether the change should be saved or not. Secondly, for tables using buffering modes of 4 or 5, no indication is given of how many changes there may be or whether the "current row" has actually changed. Again, given the objective this is reasonable.

It would be perfectly possible to amend the code to address these issues (perhaps by returning a numeric value indicating different conditions rather than a simple 'yes/no'). In our view, however, that might make the function too specific to qualify as a candidate for a generic procedure file which is where we would want to place the function.

Gotcha! when appending records with default values

There is, however, one potential problem to watch out for when using a routine such as this one. If you are adding a new record to a table which supplies a default value for one or more fields, you will get a "*false positive*" return when testing an otherwise unchanged record. This is because Visual FoxPro inserts a default value after the record is appended and therefore is seen by the functions that test fields as 'changed'. Fortunately there is a solution - the SETFLDSTATE() function can be used to clear the changed status of a specific field.

There is one limitation! SetFldState() uses the same numeric values as are returned by the GetFldState() function, so that values of 1 or 2 relate to edited records, while 3 and 4 relate to appended records. You cannot use SetFldState() to change the status of the *record*, only of individual fields. Thus you cannot tell VFP that a record being edited is suddenly a newly appended record by changing the status of all of its fields to "3", or that an appended record actually being edited by changing its fields to state "2". The following code shows what happens:

```
*** Open Table, add a record and check status
USE demone
CURSORSETPROP( 'Buffering', 5)
APPEND BLANK
? GETFLDSTATE( -1 )    && Returns "3433"
```

Remember, GetFldState(-1) always includes the status of the record's *Deleted* flag as the first item in its return string. So the return value here actually indicates that the *first* field in the table has changed (as expected, since it is the *SID* field and has a default value specified).

```
*** Now try and change the field state for the Key field
*** To 'UnEdited'
? SETFLDSTATE( 1, 1 )
```

This immediately generates Error 11, "*Function argument value, type, or count is invalid*" because the record is **not** being edited, it is an appended record. However, the following:

```
*** Change the field state for the Key field
*** To 'UnChanged'
? SETFLDSTATE( 1, 3 )  && Returns .T.
? GETFLDSTATE( -1 )    && Now returns "3333"
```

is perfectly acceptable, and *IsChanged()* will now return only the consequences of user initiated actions and will not see the changes arising from the use of default values. The obvious place to put such code is in a hook method called from the one that actually adds the new record. Such a method could use *IsChanged()* to determine if any default values were supplied and use *SetFldState()* to reset the record's field state.

Gotcha! Using GetFldState() when a table is at EOF()

One word of caution about using `GetFldState()` (which is not mentioned in the VFP Help Files). If the table you are testing happens to be at EOF(), the function will return a NULL value instead of the expected data type. You must ensure that you handle this situation properly by always using the NVL() function to convert any null return back to an empty string when using the "-1" parameter like this:

```
lcFldState = NVL( GetFldState(-1), "" )
```

or, if testing a specific field, to convert back into the expected numeric data type:

```
lcFldState = NVL( GetFldState("name"), 0 )
```

If you fail to do so, then any code which tests the return value will fail because of the way in which NULLS are propagated.

> *Interpreting NULL values: We find that the best way to think about a null value is to translate it as "I don't know." When viewed in this light the behavior of NULL values is clear - the answer to any question about the status of something whose value is "I don't know" is always going to be "I don't know!" Thus:*

llTestVal = .NULL.
*** Is llTestVal Empty?
? EMPTY(llTestVal) && Answer: .F. ('I don't know' is NOT a value defined as 'Empty')
*** Is llTestVal greater than 0
? llTestVal > 0   && Answer: .NULL. ('I don't know')
*** Is the name either Dave or Fred?
? INLIST(llTestVal, "Dave", "Fred") && Answer: .NULL. ('I don't know')

Using TableUpdate() and TableRevert()

When working with buffered data, two functions are absolutely vital - namely *TableUpdate()* and *TableRevert()*. These are the basic means by which you control the transfer of data between the Visual FoxPro buffers and the underlying data source. *TableUpdate()* takes pending changes from the buffers and commits them to the underlying table while *TableRevert()* refreshes the buffers by re-reading the data from the underlying data source. Successful completion of either function results in a *'clean'* buffer meaning that, as far as Visual FoxPro is concerned, the buffers and the underlying data source are synchronized.

Managing the scope of updates

Since Visual FoxPro supports both Row and Table buffering, both of the data transfer functions can operate either on the *'current record only'* or on *'all changed records.'* The first parameter that is passed to either function determines the scope and, alas, we have another source of possible confusion right here. The functions operate in slightly different ways and use different return values.

In Version 3.0 of Visual FoxPro, both *TableUpdate()* and *TableRevert()* would accept only a logical parameter to determine the scope of the change that they managed. Passing a value of .T. meant that all pending changes were to be actioned, while .F. restricted operations to the current row only, irrespective of the buffer mode in force.

TableRevert() returns the *number of rows* which were reverted and cannot really 'fail' unless there is a physical problem, like losing a network connection. In a row buffered table, or when specifying the scope as .F., the return value will, therefore, always be 1.

TableUpdate() always returns a logical value indicating whether the specified update succeeded, irrespective of the scope. In other words a return value of .T. indicates that all records in the scope have been successfully updated. However, when you use a logical parameter to determine the scope and the update fails for any reason, no error is generated and the function returns a value of .F. leaving the record pointer at the record which failed.

If you are updating a single record this is quite straightforward, but if you are updating multiple records in a table, and one record cannot be updated, it means that any further updates have not been tested. So, after resolving the conflict for the record that failed, there is no guarantee that re-submitting the update will not fail on the very next record. This can be a problem!

The behavior of *TableUpdate()* was, therefore, changed in Version 5 to accept *either* a logical or a numeric parameter for the scope, where 0 is equivalent to using .F. and 1 to using .T. The new behavior, which can only be specified by passing "2" as the scope parameter, specifically addresses the issues of updating multiple records.

When using table buffering, calling *TableUpdate()* with a scope parameter of "2" attempts to update all records which have pending changes. However, if a record cannot be updated, instead of stopping the function logs the record number which failed to an array (which you can specify as the fourth parameter) and continues trying to update any other changed records. The function will still return .F. if **any** record fails to update, but it will also have at least *tried* to update all available records. The output array contains a list of the record numbers that failed to update.

TableUpdate()'s second (force) parameter

One major difference between the syntax for *TableUpdate()* and *TableRevert()* is that the former can take an extra, logical, parameter in the second position in the parameter list. This controls the way in which the update behaves whenever a conflict is encountered.

By default, Visual FoxPro will reject an update whenever a conflict between the buffered data and the underlying data is detected (see the next section for a full discussion of conflict detection and resolution). By specifying a logical ".T." as the second parameter you can force an update to be accepted even in situations where it would otherwise fail. Naturally, this is not something that you would wish to do by default but there are, as we shall see later, situations where this behavior is not only desirable but also essential.

Specifying the table to be updated or reverted

Both *TableUpdate()* and *TableRevert()* operate on one table at a time. Their default behavior is that, unless specifically directed otherwise, they will act on the table in the currently selected work area. If no table is open in this work area, you get an error (*Error #13: Alias is not found*). Both, however, can act on any open table available in the current datasession and can accept either an *ALIAS* name (third parameter for *TableUpdate()*, second for *TableRevert()*) or a work area number.

We do not recommend the use of work area numbers in this, or any, situation where you are specifying a table other than the currently selected one. As far as we can see this functionality is included only for backward compatibility and has no place in the VFP environment. There are two reasons for avoiding the use of work area numbers. Firstly, they make your code dependent upon specific tables being opened in specific work areas - which is a major limitation if things change! Secondly you do not actually have any control over where VFP opens tables, cursors or views when you use a Form's DataEnvironment anyway. So relying on the work area number, rather than the alias, is a very risky strategy and is unnecessary.

The only time we recommend using the work area number is when saving the current work area by storing the return value of the SELECT() function. Using the work area number in this case ensures that should the current work area actually be empty, or the table it contains be closed during whatever operation you are doing, you can still return to it without error.

Conclusion

There is a lot of functionality and flexibility hidden away inside *TableUpdate()* and *TableRevert()*. When using buffering, you do need to be aware of exactly what the various combinations of their parameters can provide and to ensure that you are using the correct combination to meet your needs. While *TableRevert()* is pretty straightforward, *TableUpdate()* is more complex and so **Table 8.2** below provides a summary of what the various "practical" combinations of parameters for *TableUpdate()* will do.

Table 8.2 *TableUpdate() options*

Parameters				
Scope	Force	Table	Output	Action
0 or .F.	.F.			Attempt to update the current row only of current alias.
0 or .F.	.T.			Force update of the current row only of current alias.
0 or .F.	.F./.T.	Alias		Attempt/Force update of current row only of specified alias.
1 or .T.	.F.			Attempt update of all available rows of current alias. Stop on Failure.
1 or .T.	.T.			Force update of all available rows of current alias.
1 or .T.	.F./.T.	Alias		Attempt/Force update of all available rows of specified alias. Stop on Failure.
2	.F.	Alias	Array	Attempt all to update all available rows of specified alias. Note failures but do not stop.
2	.T.			Force update all available rows of current/specified alias.
2	.F./.T.	Alias	Array	Attempt/Force update of all available rows of specified alias. Note failures but do not stop.

How can I handle 'save' and 'undo' functionality generically?

It seems to us that many developers write this functionality directly into interface objects over and over again. The rationale is usually that 'each form has different requirements' - but is this really true? We are not so sure. The actual process of updating or reverting a table is always the same. The only issues are *when* you do it, which is determined by the validation processes, and *what* you do when something goes wrong. These are both serious issues and are indeed dependent on the situation, but neither affect the process of actually updating or reverting a table!

Reduced to the basics, therefore, the only real problem arises when you need to handle several tables at once because *TableUpdate()* and *TableRevert()* both expect to be passed a single table name on which to operate. The pseudo code for a generic 'Save' method therefore looks something like this:

```
Receive Alias of all tables to update as a comma separated list
For each table in the list
   Check buffering status
   Issue the appropriate variant of TableUpdate()
   Build a list of any errors
Return the result
```

While for a generic 'Undo' method the code is very similar indeed:

```
Receive Alias of all tables to revert as a comma separated list
For each table in the list
   Check buffering status
   Issue the appropriate variant of TableRevert()
```

```
Return the result
```

We have already discussed a function for retrieving an item from a comma separated list (see *GetItem()* in Chapter 2) so the only real issue is where should the code go? There are two basic options. Firstly, the code could be implemented as part of a "data handling" class which could simply be added to forms that require the functionality. Secondly, the necessary methods can be included as part of a "Data-Aware" Form class. We have chosen to illustrate the form class approach because the vast majority of Visual FoxPro applications are essentially form based. The occasions on which a separate data object would be necessary are, therefore, exceptions rather than the rule.

The design of the form class

In order to implement Save and Undo functionality for a form, we first need to set up our form class to provide the necessary methods. We have chosen to provide a set of template methods in our 'Root' form class (*xFrm* in *RootClas.vcx*) which will manage the Save process by implementing a Hook pattern.

The *SaveForm* method is the controller for the process and is the method which code in an instance of a form based on this class would call to actually attempt a "save". The *SaveForm* method first makes a call to the *BeforeSave* method. Any instance-specific code that needs to be called immediately before the actual save (e.g. pre-save validation) will be placed here. If this method returns .T., the *DataSave* method is then called, which is where the actual save will be attempted, and depending on the result, either the *AfterSave* or the *AfterFailSave* method is called to handle any instance-specific post-save processing.

A similar set of methods handles the Revert process, but since a *TableRevert()* cannot really "fail" we need only a single *AfterRevert* method.

The SaveForm method

The actual code used in the *SaveForm* and *RevertForm* methods is in fact identical, with the exception of the names of the methods to be called. It would, therefore, be possible to call a common, 'overloaded', handler method with a parameter indicating whether "Save" or "Revert" action is required. However, we do not really like this approach because it makes maintenance more difficult and does not really provide any tangible benefit. After all, only one type of action will ever be called at any time!

```
*** This method wraps the call to the DataSave  method
*** and includes calls to the Before and After Hooks
LPARAMETERS tcTables
LOCAL lcTables, llOk
WITH ThisForm

   *** If nothing is passed, assume all tables!
   lcTables = IIF(VARTYPE( tcTables ) # "C" OR EMPTY( tcTables ), .GetAllUsed(),
tcTables )
   IF ! EMPTY(lcTables)

     *** Call Instance-Level "Before" Hook
     llOk = .BeforeSave(lcTables)
```

```
*** If BeforeSave fails, code to handle the failure must be placed there
IF llOk

   *** Before was OK, so call main Save
   llOk = .DataSave( lcTables )
   IF llOk

      *** All saved, so call the Instance-Level "After" Hook
      .AfterSave( lcTables )
   ELSE

      *** Save failed, so call alternate Instance-Level "After" Hook
      .AfterFailSave( lcTables )
   ENDIF
ENDIF
ELSE

   *** No tables in use, just return .T.
   llOk = .T.
ENDIF
ENDWITH
RETURN llOk
```

The result of this approach is that we can now code the *DataSave* method specifically to handle the actual call to *TableUpdate()* because we have provided alternate locations for any instance specific code in either *Before* or *After* methods and because we also have coded the Revert functionality into its own set of methods.

A moot point is whether these "wrapper" methods should also issue a form level refresh. On the whole we prefer not to have it do so, since the type of refresh required may depend on the results of the save and so should be handled by instance specific code in either the *AfterSave* or *AfterFailSave* as appropriate. You may, of course, choose to do it differently.

The DataSave method

The actual code in this method is identical to that in *DataRevert* with the exception that the latter calls *TableRevert()*. Again these two methods could have been combined into a single method, but the reasons for not doing so are the same.

Although not yet discussed in this chapter, you will note that we are using a transaction here. We will have more to say about the whole issue of transactions later, but for now just accept that we are using one to ensure that multiple table updates or reverts either succeed, or fail, as a block - just as if we were really dealing with a single table:

```
LPARAMETERS tcTables
LOCAL llRetVal, lnCnt, lcToDo, lnBuffMode

WITH ThisForm

   *** Initialise Return Value to .T.
   llRetVal = .T.

   *** Start a transaction
   BEGIN TRANSACTION

   *** Loop through all tables
```

```
lnCnt = 0
DO WHILE .T.

  *** Retrieve table name
  lnCnt = lnCnt + 1
  lcToDo = .GetItem( tcTables, lnCnt )

  *** NULL return indicates end of the string
  IF ISNULL( lcToDo )
    EXIT
  ENDIF

  *** Check buffer mode of each
  lnBuffMode = .GetBufferMode( lcToDo )

  *** Issue the correct update command and "AND" the result
  DO CASE
    CASE INLIST( lnBuffMode, 2, 3 )

      *** We are Row Buffered
      llRetVal = llRetVal AND TABLEUPDATE( 0, .F., lcToDo )
    CASE INLIST( lnBuffMode, 4, 5 )

      *** We are Table Buffered
      llRetVal = llRetVal AND TABLEUPDATE( 1, .F., lcToDo )
    OTHERWISE

      *** No Buffering at all - so do nothing
  ENDCASE
ENDDO

*** Commit or Revert the transaction
IF llRetVal

  *** Everything was just fine
  END TRANSACTION
ELSE

  *** Something went wrong
  ROLLBACK
ENDIF
ENDWITH

*** Return Status
RETURN llRetVal
```

Using the new form class

The sample form DemSave.scx illustrates how the form class described can be used. We have created two new button classes (*xCmdStdDisableSave* and *xCmdStdDisableUndo*) based on our self-disabling button class which just call the form's *SaveForm* or *RevertForm* custom methods from their *OnClick* methods. Since these classes are intended solely for use with a form that has these methods, there is no code to check that the method actually exists! In fact we might have added these buttons directly to the form class itself but have not done so because we can never be sure that we will *always* want both buttons. (Remember - you cannot delete an object that is defined by the parent class in either a sub-class or an instance.) This follows from our assertion (see Chapter 3) that if the functionality is not in the **"MUST"** category, it doesn't belong in the class!

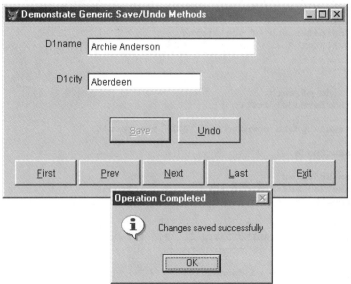

Figure 8.4 *A form using the Generic Save/Undo methods*

In this example, the *AfterSave*, *AfterFailSave* and *AfterRevert* methods simply display an appropriate message before calling a form level refresh. To test this form out simply start two instances of VFP and open the *demone* table in the second instance. After running the form in the first instance, make and save a change to the table in the second and then make and save a change to the same record in the form.

Detecting and resolving conflicts

In the preceding sections, we have seen how to detect changes in a table and how to attempt to update a buffered table, so the next issue is to ensure that the proposed change is not going to cause an update conflict when saved. One of the inherent problems with using optimistic locking in a multi-user environment is that it is possible for more than one user to make changes to the same record at the same time.

You may wonder why such a thing would ever be possible - surely two users could not be updating the same record at the time? In practice there are lots of scenarios where this can legitimately happen. Consider the situation in a Sales Order processing system. When an order is placed for an item, the current "available stock" must be adjusted to reflect the reduction. If two customers, being handled by two operators simultaneously, include the same item on their orders there is a good chance that a conflict will arise. Obviously this cannot happen if the system uses pessimistic locking but that has other, usually undesirable, consequences. In this scenario, the second operator who tried to access the item in question would receive a message that the record was in use by someone else and would not be able to make changes - not much help! Moreover pessimistic locking can only be used when a Visual FoxPro table is used directly as the data source - you cannot pessimistically lock a view of any sort.

When using buffering, Visual FoxPro makes a copy of all data as it is retrieved from the physical table and, when an update is requested, compares this copy with the current state of the data. If there are no changes, the update is allowed, otherwise the appropriate update conflict error (#1585 for Views, #1595 for tables) is generated. **Figure 8.5** illustrates, schematically, how this works and how an update conflict is detected.

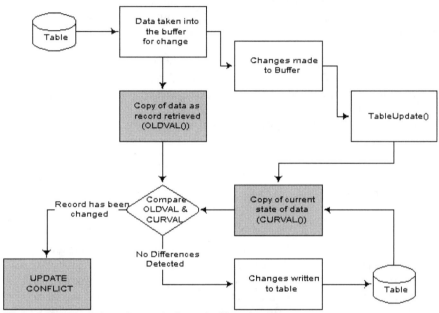

Figure 8.5 *Update schematic for a buffered table*

The role of OldVal() and CurVal()

The basis of all conflict detection lies in two native functions, "*OLDVAL()*" and "*CURVAL()*", which access the intermediate cursors created by Visual FoxPro when using buffered data. As their names imply, `OLDVAL()` retrieves the value of a field as it was when the user last read the data from the source, while `CURVAL()` retrieves the current state of the data in the source table. Both of these functions operate at the field level and, although both can accept an expression that evaluates to a list of fields, they are best used to retrieve field values singly to avoid the problem of resolving different data types.

There is one *gotcha!* with using `CURVAL()` to check the status of a view. Visual FoxPro actually maintains an additional level of buffering for a view which, unless the view is refreshed immediately before checking a field's value, may cause `CURVAL()` to return the wrong answer. We will have more to say about the `Refresh()` function, and its use, in the section on Views.

So how do I actually detect conflicts?

Before getting into the discussion of how to detect a conflict, let us be clear about what Visual FoxPro's definition of a conflict is. As intimated earlier, Visual FoxPro makes two copies of a record whenever a user accesses data. One copy is made available as the editable cursor and is where a user makes changes. The other is retained in its original state. Before allowing an update to proceed, Visual FoxPro compares this original cursor with the data currently stored on disk. A conflict occurs when these two versions of the data do not match exactly, and there are two ways in which that can happen. The first, and most obvious, is because the current user makes changes to a record and tries to save those changes *after* someone else has already changed and saved the same record. The second is a little less obvious and arises when a user does **NOT** make any changes but tries to "save" a record that another user **HAS** changed. Visual FoxPro will still see this as a conflict because the **OLDVAL()** and **CURVAL()** values are in fact different. This is best handled by not actually doing a **TableUpdate()** unless the current user really has made changes which is precisely why the *IsChanged()* function is so useful. It allows you to determine whether a **TableUpdate()** is necessary and to use code like this in your save routines:

```
llRetVal = .T.
IF IsChanged()
   llRetVal = TABLEUPDATE()
ENDIF
RETURN llRetVal
```

So, having avoided the possibility of conflicts when the current user has not made any changes by simply not trying to commit the record, there are basically two strategies you can adopt to detect conflicts. The first we call the '*Suck It and See*' approach. This simply means that you do not try and detect potential conflicts but just trap the result of a **TableUpdate()** command and, when it fails, take steps to find out why.

The second is the '*Belt and Braces*' approach in which you check each changed field and resolve conflicts before attempting to update the underlying table. While this looks more defensive, and therefore 'better', there is actually a hidden problem with it. In the amount of time that it takes (albeit very small) to check all changed fields against their current values, another user may succeed in changing the very record you are checking. So, unless you also explicitly lock the record before starting to check values, the actual update could still fail. Since we really want to avoid explicitly placing locks, you need to incorporate exactly the same check of the result of the **TableUpdate()** command, and provide the same handling for failure that you need in the much simpler just 'suck it and see' strategy!

Therefore, unless you have an overriding reason for pre-validating changes, we strongly recommend that you let Visual FoxPro detect conflicts and just trap for and handle such errors as they arise. However whichever strategy you choose, you will still need some means of finding which fields in a given record have changed, so that you can get the appropriate values from **CurVal()** and **OldVal()**. The following function, *GetUserChanges()*, returns a comma separated list of fields which have been changed by the current user:

```
**********************************************************************
* Program....: GetUserChanges.prg
* Compiler...: Visual FoxPro 06.00.8492.00 for Windows
* Abstract...: Returns a comma separated list of fields that have been changed
* ...........: by the user in the current row of the specified table
**********************************************************************
LPARAMETERS tcTable
LOCAL lcTable, lcRetVal, lnBuffMode, lcFldState, lnCnt, lcStatus
*** Check the parameter, assume current alias if nothing passed
lcTable = IIF( VARTYPE(tcTable) # "C" OR EMPTY( tcTable ), ;
            ALIAS(), ALLTRIM( UPPER( tcTable )))
*** Check that the specified table name is used as an alias
IF EMPTY( lcTable ) OR ! USED( JUSTSTEM( lcTable) )
  *** Error - probably a developer error, so use an Error to report it!
  ERROR "9000: GetUserChanges() requires the alias of an open table" ;
        + CHR(13) + "be passed, or that the current work area should " ;
        + "contain an" + CHR(13) + "open table"
  RETURN .F.
ENDIF
lcRetVal = ''
*** Check the buffering status
lnBuffMode = CURSORGETPROP( 'Buffering', lcTable )
IF lnBuffMode = 1
  *** Not buffered, so can be no 'pending changes'
  RETURN lcRetVal
ENDIF
*** If we get this far, we have a buffered record which MAY have changes
*** So check for fields that have changed values
lcFldState = NVL( GETFLDSTATE( -1, lcTable ), "")
IF EMPTY( CHRTRAN( lcFldState, '1', ''))
  *** Nothing but '1', therefore nothing has changed
  RETURN lcRetVal
ENDIF
*** So, we HAVE got at least one changed field! But we need to handle the
*** DELETED flag indicator first. We can use "DELETED()" as the field name
here!
IF ! INLIST( LEFT( lcFldState, 1), "1", "3" )
  lcRetVal = "DELETED()"
ENDIF
*** Now Get Rid of the Deleted Flag indicator
lcFldState = SUBSTR( lcFldState, 2 )
*** Get the field names for changed fields
FOR lnCnt = 1 TO FCOUNT()
  *** Loop through the fields
  lcStatus = SUBSTR( lcFldState, lnCnt, 1 )
  IF INLIST( lcStatus, "2", "4" )
    lcRetVal = lcRetVal + IIF( ! EMPTY( lcRetVal ), ",", "") + FIELD( lnCnt )
  ENDIF
NEXT
*** Return the list of changed fields
RETURN lcRetVal
```

Notice that we use the native **DELETED**() function as a field name in this function. Both **CurVal**() and **OldVal**() will accept this as a valid "field name" (returning a logical value indicating whether the field was deleted in the underlying table) so we can actually check for deletions as well as changes.

Having got a list of fields that have changed, we can use a function like *GetItem()* (one of our generic procedures, described in Chapter 2) to retrieve the individual field names if necessary. The original and current values for each changed field can then be retrieved and compared to determine where conflicts occur. The sample program *ListFields.prg* illustrates how this works, and lists on the screen the actual value, `CurVal()` and `OldVal()` for changes made to one of the demonstration tables. Here is the code:

```
************************************************************************
* Program....: ListFields.prg
* Compiler...: Visual FoxPro 06.00.8492.00 for Windows
* Abstract...: Illustrate use of GetUserChanges(), GetItem(), CurVal() and
OldVal()
************************************************************************
LOCAL lcChgFlds, lnCnt, lcCurFld

*** Open the Procedure file
SET PROC TO CH08 ADDITIVE

*** Open a Table and buffer it
USE demone
CURSORSETPROP("Buffering", 5, 'demone')

*** Make some changes
REPLACE d1Name WITH "William", d1City WITH "WallHouse"

*** Get list of changed fields
lcChgFlds = GetUserChanges( 'demone' )

*** Display Results
lnCnt = 0
DO WHILE .T.

    *** Retrieve field name
    lnCnt = lnCnt + 1
    lcCurFld = GETITEM( lcChgFlds, lnCnt )

    *** NULL return indicates end of the string
    IF ISNULL( lcCurFld )
        EXIT
    ENDIF

    *** Show field name
    ? "Field Name: " + CHR(9)
    ?? lcCurFld

    *** Show current Value
    ? "Actual Field Value      " + CHR(9)
    ?? &lcCurFld

    *** Current Disk Value
    ? "CURVAL() Value       " + CHR(9)
    ?? CURVAL( lcCurFld, 'demone' )

    *** Original Value
    ? "OLDVAL() Value       " + CHR(9)
    ?? OLDVAL( lcCurFld, 'demone' )
ENDDO
```

```
*** Lose changes
TABLEREVERT( .T., 'demone')
CLOSE TABLES ALL
```

OK then, having detected an update conflict, what can I do about it?

There are four basic strategies for handling update conflicts. You can choose one, or combine more than one in an application depending on the actual situation:

[1] The Current User Always Wins: This strategy is appropriate only in those situations in which the user who is actually trying to save is one whose data is assumed to be the most accurate. Typically this would be implemented on the basis of the ID of the user who is actually doing the save and would implement a business rule that certain people's information is of more value than others.

An example might be in a TeleSales application where an operator talking to the customer could have override rights to contact information for the customer (on the basis that the person actually *talking* to the customer is most likely to be able to get the correct details). Conflicts could arise in this situation when an administrator is updating a customer's details from data on file or last order, while an operator is getting new details directly from the customer.

The implementation of this strategy in Visual FoxPro is very simple indeed. Simply set the "*FORCE*" (second) parameter in the `TableUpdate()` function to ".*T.*" and re-submit the update.

[2] The Current User Always Loses: This is the exact reverse of the above situation. The current user is only allowed to save changes providing that no other user has made changes. Again this would normally be implemented on the basis of a User's ID and would reflect the probability that this particular user is likely to be working from "historical", rather than "current", information.

The implementation in Visual FoxPro is also very simple. The current user's changes are reverted, the source data is re-queried, and the user has to make any changes still required all over again. This is probably the strategy that is most often adopted - but usually on an across-the-board basis!

[3] The Current User Sometimes Wins: This strategy is the most complex of the four to implement but is actually quite common. The underlying principle is that when an update conflict occurs, you determine whether any of the fields that the current user has changed will affect the changes that were made by the other user. If not, the current user's record is updated automatically (using the `CURVAL()` values) so that the cause of the conflict is negated and the update is then re-submitted. However, because you cannot change the values returned by `OldVal()`, you need to force this second update.

Incidentally, this strategy also addresses the issue of how to handle a 'false positive' update conflict. This occurs when there is a discrepancy between the values on disk and those in the current user's buffer, but the current user's changes do not actually conflict with any of the changes made. Clearly this situation is not really a conflict but does need to be handled.

While not trivial, the implementation in Visual FoxPro is relatively easy. First, the CURVAL() function is used to determine how to update the current user's buffer so that it will not overwrite changes made by another user. Then the update is applied using the FORCE (second) parameter in the TableUpdate() to tell Visual FoxPro to ignore the conflict that will arise because OldVal() and CurVal() do not correspond.

[4] The Current User Decides: This is the "Catch All" scenario. The conflict does not fall under any recognizable business rule so the only solution is to ask the user whose save action has triggered the conflict what they wish to do about it. The underlying idea here is that you present the user who has triggered the conflict with a list of values - the one they just entered, the value that was in the table (i.e. that which they have just changed) and the value that is now in the table (i.e. that to which someone else has changed the original value). The user can then decide whether to force or revert their own changes.

The basic tools for implementing this strategy have already been discussed in the preceding section. All that is required is to determine which fields actually conflict and to present them to the user in such a way that the user can decide on a field by field basis what to do about the conflicts. In practice, this strategy is usually combined with Strategy [3] above so that the user is only presented with a list of fields where there is actually a conflict in the fields they have themselves modified.

Conflict resolution sounds fine in theory, how does it work in practice?

There are many ways of implementing conflict resolution. The most appropriate method will depend upon your application's requirements. However, in order to illustrate how you *might* implement it we have created a class named "*UpdRes*" (in the *UpdRes.vcx* library). This consists of a form, which has methods to create and populate a local cursor with the three required values for all fields causing a conflict. It implements a combination of the "Current User Sometimes Wins" and the "Current User Decides" strategies (**Figure 8.6**).

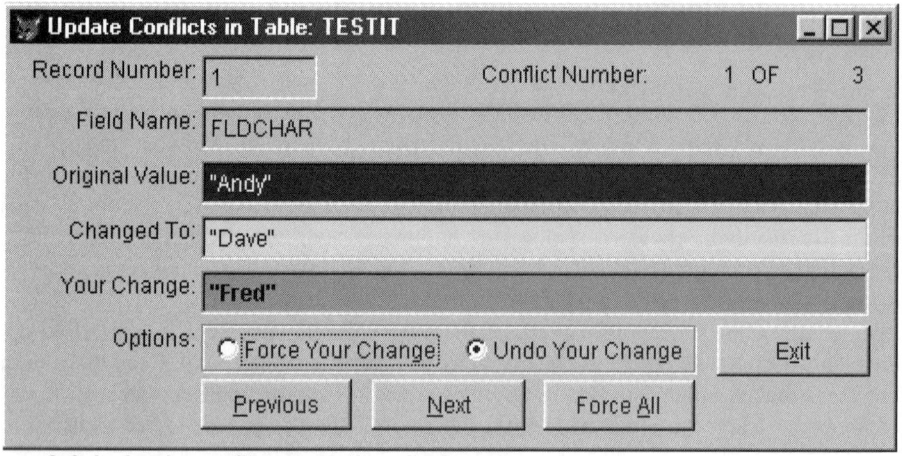

Figure 8.6 A simple conflict resolution display class

The form shows the user how many conflicts have been detected and displays, for each conflicting field, the values from OLDVAL(), CURVAL() and the current buffer. By default, all conflicts are flagged for resolution by reverting the current user's change and a simple option group allows the user to override the existing change on a field by field basis. An additional refinement is the "FORCE ALL" option which sets all conflicts to be resolved using the current user's values. When the user is satisfied, clicking on the exit button will apply the changes as specified to the table.

The Init method

The class is set up as a modal form and expects to receive two parameters - the DataSession number of the form which has called it, and the name of the table in that datasession which has caused the conflict. The code here simply sets the form into the correct datasession and then calls the *SetUpForm* and *CheckUpdates* methods:

```
LPARAMETERS tnDSID, tcTable
LOCAL llRetVal
WITH ThisForm

    *** Set this form to the passed in DataSession
    .DataSessionID = tnDSID

    *** Ceate cursor and bind fields to it
    .SetUpForm()

    *** Run the CheckUpdates() method for the specified table
    llRetVal = .CheckUpdates( tcTable )
    RETURN llRetVal
ENDWITH
```

The *CheckUpdates* method returns a logical value indicating whether there actually are any conflicts requiring user intervention and, because this value is returned from the Class *Init* method, will prevent the class from being instantiated when there are no conflicts that cannot be resolved programmatically. The calling code for this class must, therefore, take this possibility into account.

The SetUpForm method

This is extremely simple and merely creates the local cursor and sets the form controls to use this cursor as their controlsource. This needs to be done either in the *Init*, or in a method called from the *Init*, because we need to get the form into the correct datasession before creating the cursor. Since the required DataSession ID is passed as a parameter, we cannot access it in any method before the Form's own *Init*:

```
WITH ThisForm

    *** Create a local cursor for storing conflicts
    CREATE CURSOR curcflix ( ;
        cfxRecNum  C (  8), ;   && Conflict Number
        cfxFldNam  C (200), ;   && Field Name
        cfxOldVal  C (200), ;   && Original Value
        cfxCurVal  C (200), ;   && Current Value on disk
```

```
      cfxUsrVal  C (200), ;    && Change in the buffer
      cfxForcit  N ( 1) )      && User defined action

  *** Bind The Controls to it
  .TxtRecNum.ControlSource = "curcflix.cfxRecNum"
  .txtFldNam.ControlSource = "curcflix.cfxFldNam"
  .txtOrgVal.ControlSource = "curcflix.cfxOldVal"
  .txtCurVal.ControlSource = "curcflix.cfxCurVal"
  .txtNewVal.ControlSource = "curcflix.cfxUsrVal"
  .OptUsrChoice.ControlSource = "curcflix.cfxforcit"
  .Refresh()
ENDWITH
RETURN .T.
```

The CheckUpdates method

This is where some of the real work of the class is done. The first part of the code is concerned with ensuring that the correct table is available, selected and then determines what buffering it is using:

```
LPARAMETERS tuTable
LOCAL llRetval, lnBuffMode, lcTable, lnOldArea, lnNextRec, lnRows

*** Check Parameters
IF EMPTY(tuTable)
    *** Nothing passed, use current table
    lcTable = ALLTRIM( ALIAS() )
    IF EMPTY( lcTable )

        *** No table
        RETURN .F.
    ENDIF
ELSE
    DO CASE
        CASE TYPE( "tuTable" ) = "C"

            *** Assume Character string is the Required Alias
            lcTable = ALLTRIM( tuTable)
        CASE TYPE( "tuTable" ) = "N"

            *** Get the Alias for the specified work area
            lcTable = ALIAS( tuTable )
        OTHERWISE

            *** Invalid parameter - exit with error
            RETURN .F.
    ENDCASE
ENDIF

*** Check BufferMode
llRetVal = .T.
lnBuffMode = CURSORGETPROP( 'Buffering', lcTable )
IF lnBuffMode < 2

    *** If Table is not buffered just return
    RETURN .F.
ELSE
```

```
   *** Save current work area and select required table
   lnOldArea =  SELECT()
   SELECT (lcTable)
ENDIF
```

The next part of the method depends upon the mode of buffering that is being used. If Table Buffering is in force, the *CheckRec* method is called once for each row in which changes have been detected in order to populate the conflict cursor if necessary. If Row buffering is used, only a single call is necessary.

```
*** Need to handle Row Buffering and Table Buffering differently
WITH ThisForm

  *** Set form Caption and store target table to a Form property
  *** For use in the DoUpdates() method
  .caption = "Update Conflicts in Table: " + lcTable
  .cTarget = ALIAS()

  *** Check buffering mode
  IF lnBuffMode < 4

      *** Row Buffering
      llRetVal = .ChkRec( RECNO(), lcTable )
  ELSE

      *** Table Buffering - need to find all modified records
      lnNextRec = 0
      DO WHILE .T.
          lnNextRec = GETNEXTMODIFIED( lnNextRec )
          IF lnNextRec = 0
              EXIT
          ENDIF

          *** Try and update the record
          llRetVal = .ChkRec( lnNextRec, lcTable )
          IF ! llRetVal

              *** If failed, exit
              EXIT
          ENDIF
      ENDDO
  ENDIF
ENDIF
```

The final section of code merely checks the record count of the conflict cursor to see if anything needs to be done by the user. If not, a forced `TableUpdate()` is done on all records to clear the buffer:

```
*** Check the Conflict Cursor
IF RECCOUNT( "curcflix") = 0

  *** There are no unresolvable conflicts so just force the update
  *** By returning .F. to the Init() we prevent the object instantiating
  *** and the user will see nothing!
  llRetVal = ! TableUpdate( .T., .T. )
```

```
  ELSE
    GO TOP IN curcflix
  ENDIF
ENDWITH

*** Tidy Up
SELECT (lnOldArea)
RETURN llRetVal
```

The ChkRec method

This method is called once for each row that needs to be validated and is where the decision is made as to whether user intervention is required or not. For rows where a conflict cannot be resolved programmatically, a record for each field that requires user intervention is inserted into the conflict cursor:

```
LPARAMETERS tnRecNum, tcTable
LOCAL lnCnt, luCurVal, luOldVal, lnRows, llRetVal, lcFldList, lcFldName,
luUsrVal

*** Force the correct record to be current
SELECT (tcTable)
IF RECNO() # tnRecNum
    GOTO tnRecNum
ENDIF

*** Get the list of fields changed by the Current User
lcFldList = ""
lcFldList = ThisForm.GetUserChanges( tcTable )

*** Scan through the fields
FOR lnCnt = 1 TO FCOUNT()
    lcFldName = FIELD( lnCnt )
    luCurVal = CURVAL( FIELD( lnCnt ))
    luOldVal = OLDVAL( FIELD( lnCnt ))
    luUsrVal = EVAL( FIELD( lnCnt ))

    *** Will this field cause a conflict?
    IF luCurVal == luOldVal

        *** No Changes have been made to the field
        *** So no problem will arise
        LOOP
    ENDIF

    *** Changes have been made to the field
    IF ! FIELD( lnCnt ) $ lcFldList

        *** But The curent user has not modified the field
        *** So we can just update it from CurVal()
        REPLACE (FIELD(lnCnt)) WITH luCurVal
    ELSE

        *** Something has changed!  The question is WHAT?
        IF EVAL( FIELD(lnCnt) ) == luCurval
```

```
            *** User has not actually changed anything
            LOOP
      ELSE

            *** This is a conflict that we cannot resolve programmatically
            *** So add it to the Conflict Cursor
            WITH ThisForm
                INSERT INTO curcflix ;
                    ( cfxRecNum, ;
                      cfxFldNam, ;
                      cfxOldVal, ;
                      cfxCurVal, ;
                      cfxUsrVal, ;
                      cfxForcit ) ;
                    VALUES ;
                    ( .ExpToStr(RECNO()), ;
                      lcFldName, ;
                      .ExpToStr(luOldVal), ;
                      .ExpToStr(luCurVal), ;
                      .ExpToStr(luUsrVal), ;
                      2 )
                ENDWITH
         ENDIF
    ENDIF
NEXT
```

For each field in the record, this method reads the current user's buffered value, the
`OldVal()` and `Curval()` values and passes them through a logic check as follows:

```
IF the user has not changed this field, and the Old and Current values are
identical,
    ignore this field
ELSE
  IF the user has not changed the field, but the Old and Current values are
different,
      update the buffer directly with the Current Value
   ELSE
    IF the user has changed the field, but the value in the buffer is already
identical
        to the Current Value, ignore this change
     ELSE
        This really IS a conflict, so insert a row into the conflicts cursor
```

Note that this method uses the *GetUserChanges* function discussed above, although,
because this is a class, the code has been added (unchanged) as a method. The same logic
applies to the apparent duplication of the *ExpToStr* and *StrToExp* functions (which we
introduced in Chapter 2) as methods. This class depends upon the data being handled in a
specific way and must not rely on anything outside of itself. If we were to rely on these
functions being available in a procedure file, we would be breaking the encapsulation of the
class and leaving ourselves open to potential problems if the external procedures were to be
modified.

To see this class in action simply run the *ShowConf.prg* program included in the sample
code for this chapter. This program creates two instances of a simple data form (see **Figure
8.7**). Make some changes to one instance of the form then, *without clicking SAVE*, switch to

the other instance and make and SAVE some more changes. Clicking SAVE in the first form will now invoke the conflict resolution screen always assuming that the changes you made in the other instance have caused one or more conflicts.

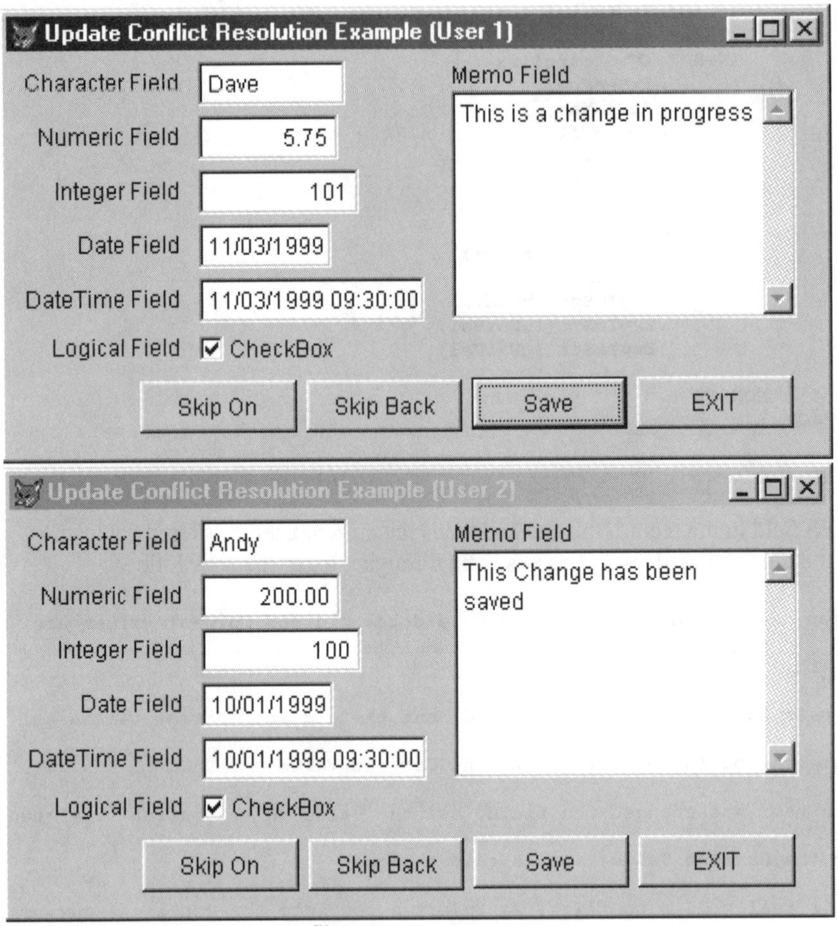

Figure 8.7 *Forcing update conflicts*

The code invoking the conflict resolution screen is contained (for the purposes of this demonstration) in the click method of the *Save* button of the form. Very little code is required, as follows:

```
*** Select the main table
SELECT (Thisform.PrimaryTable)

*** Try and update
llOk = TABLEUPDATE()

*** If update fails, create the conflict resolution object
IF ! llOk
```

```
oUpd = CREATEOBJECT( 'updres', ThisForm.DataSessionID, ALIAS() )

*** If the object exists there IS a real conflict, show the form
IF TYPE( 'oUpd' ) = "O" AND ! ISNULL( oUpd )
  oUpd.Show()
  ENDIF
ENDIF
```

Remember - the way the conflict resolution class is constructed ensures that the object only persists when a conflict that cannot be resolved programmatically is detected. This approach ensures that the user only sees a conflict when there really is one that needs positive intervention - everything else is handled transparently.

Using transactions

A transaction in Visual FoxPro provides an extra layer of buffering which can span changes to multiple tables (as opposed to "normal" buffering which is table-specific). There are, however, no options for controlling this additional layer. For any one transaction it is either "all or nothing," although you can nest transactions up to five levels deep and such nested transactions are unwound on a "*Last-In, First Out*" basis. The primary function of a transaction is to ensure that when changes to several tables are dependent on each other's success, no changes are made to any table unless all associated table updates can also be made.

A Transaction is initiated with a "`Begin Transaction`" command and is terminated by either an "`End Transaction`" ('Commit') or "`RollBack`" command. However, these are separate commands and do not constitute a '*Control Structure*' (like `IF...ELSE...ENDIF` or `DO CASE...ENDCASE`). There is no requirement for the closing command to be in the same method (or even the same program) as the initiating command, the only rule is that each `Begin Transaction` command is properly ended somewhere. However, it is certainly easier to read and maintain your code when your transaction management code is kept in one place.

Restrictions and limitations

Visual FoxPro controls and manages transactions through the DBC, therefore free tables cannot participate in a transaction, although a single transaction **may** include tables from multiple databases.

While a transaction is active, all records (from all tables) that are participating in the transaction are fully locked – you cannot either read from, or write to, these records! For this reason it is imperative that, in multi-user applications, transactions are only active for as short a time as possible.

Finally, commands that change the state of a table (as opposed to its data) cannot be used inside a transaction. A full list of these can be found in the Help file under the "*Begin Transaction*" topic. Note especially that the *CursorSetProp()* and *TableRevert()* functions are not supported while a transaction is active.

When do I need a transaction?

The only time that you really need to use a transaction is when handling data that, although stored in different tables, is interdependent. For example, in an inventory management application you would not actually want to update the free stock of an item if the order line for that item could not be saved for some reason. Although quite separate, these two actions are clearly inter-related and should be handled as if they really were a single operation. Thus, if the order can be placed, the stock must be updated but if the order cannot be placed, then the stock should not be updated.

It is perfectly possible to write code that achieves the necessary result (and many systems written in earlier versions of FoxPro have such code) but it is not a trivial exercise. A transaction gives us the ability to handle all of the issues with some very simple code like this:

```
BEGIN TRANSACTION
LOCAL 11Ok
11Ok = TABLEUPDATE ( 2, .F., "OrderLines", laFailed )
IF 11OK

   *** Lines were updated OK, now do the stock
   11Ok = TABLEUPDATE ( 2, .F., "FreeStock", laFailed )
ELSE

   *** Handle Order Item update errors here
ENDIF
IF 11OK

   *** All OK, so commit the changes
   END TRANSACTION
ELSE

   *** Something failed, so undo everything
   ROLLBACK
ENDIF
```

What effect does rollback have on my data?

The short answer here is none! The objective of a transaction is to ensure that either all changes get committed, or none do. It follows therefore that in the event of a failed transaction, the tables should be in precisely the same state as they were before the transaction was initiated. Rollback is not the same as a TableRevert() and it does not change the initial state of any data. However, if you have made changes to data *inside* the transaction, then any such changes will be undone as part of the rollback. The following code can be run from the command line to see how this works:

```
USE demone
CURSORSETPROP ( 'Buffering', 5 )
BEGIN TRANSACTION
BROWSE
REPLACE ALL d1city WITH "London"
```

Note that this *does* in fact change all the data. There are no restrictions on changing data inside a transaction, although you cannot change the state of a table (its Buffering Mode, Indexes and so on). You can even use *TableUpdate()* to "confirm" the changes:

```
? TABLEUPDATE ( 2, .F., 'demone' )
```

will apparently confirm the changes as shown by the fact that a SQL Select can now 'see' the change:

```
SELECT DISTINCT dlCity FROM demone INTO CURSOR cur_city NOFILTER
```

now gives you a single row with 'London' as the only city. However, although updated, the changes are still not "*committed*" and can still be reversed by rolling back the transaction:

```
ROLLBACK
SELECT DISTINCT dlCity FROM demone INTO CURSOR cur_city NOFILTER
```

Re-running the query returns the original list of cities as if nothing had happened.

Hey, does that mean I can use a transaction to enable SQL to see 'pending' changes?

The short answer is YES! A SQL query normally gets its data from the underlying table, so you cannot use SQL to check something that a user has entered, or changed, in a buffered table until the change has been saved using a *TableUpdate()*. However, Visual FoxPro always checks data which is cached in the transaction buffer before resorting to that stored on disk for queries on tables involved in transactions. So, by wrapping the *TableUpdate()* in a transaction, you can 'temporarily' update a table, run your SQL, and then roll back the changes.

There is, of course, a cost here (after all nothing is really free!). You must always remember that a transaction locks other users out of the records involved - so the golden rule when using a transaction is always to keep it active for as short a time as possible. We would not recommend using this technique for large amounts of data or complex queries, but it can be very effective when used for single table operations (like summing a set of values displayed in an editing grid).

How does a transaction impact on FoxPro's locking mechanisms?

At the simplest level, the answer is that a transaction has little effect on the way that Visual FoxPro handles the placing of locks. In other words, any time that a lock is called for either implicitly or explicitly, it will be placed. Many Visual FoxPro commands call for an "implicit" lock. (A full list of these commands, together with the type of lock they place, can be found in the Programmer's Guide, Chapter 17 "*Programming for Shared Access.*") Whenever one of these commands is used within a transaction, Visual FoxPro releases the lock it places on termination of the transaction.

Locks which are placed explicitly (using **RLOCK()** or **FLOCK()**) are respected by transactions and must, therefore, also be released explicitly by the appropriate **UNLOCK** command. However, we must say that we generally find little use for explicit locking in Visual FoxPro. If you are using buffered tables and transactions (and why would you not be?), the best and safest way to handle locking inside a transaction is to let Visual FoxPro do it for you.

Gotcha! Automatic locks not always released in Visual FoxPro Version 5.0

One word of caution if you are using Version 5.0 – there is a bug that can cause problems if you use commands which place automatic File Locks within a transaction. These locks are NOT released when the transaction terminates. The following code shows the problem:

```
*** Open a table
  USE <table>

*** Set Table Buffering
  CURSORSETPROP( 'Buffering', 5 )

*** Begin a Transaction
  BEGIN TRANSACTION

*** Use a command which calls for a file lock
  REPLACE ALL <field> WITH <testval> FOR <condition>

*** Check Locking Status
  ? ISFLOCKED()    && .F.

*** Update the Table
  ? TABLEUPDATE(.T.)    && .T.

*** Check Locking Status
  ? ISFLOCKED()    && .T.

*** Complete the Transaction
  END TRANSACTION

*** Check Locking Status - file is STILL locked
  ? ISFLOCKED()    && .T.
```

This can, in a multi-user environment, be a major problem when you need to do block updates on tables involved in one-to-many relationships. Fortunately, there is a simple work-around by using a SCAN...ENDSCAN with an explicit replace for the appropriate rows instead of a REPLACE ALL. Even more fortunately, this problem **has** been fixed in later versions of Visual FoxPro.

Can I use multiple transactions simultaneously?

Yes, currently transactions can be nested up to five levels deep and the TXNLEVEL() function can be used to determine the number of open transactions. However, nested transactions are always released on a Last-In First-Out basis so the logic needs to be constructed carefully to avoid inadvertently closing the wrong one - especially if the controlling code is contained in more than one method (or procedure). Providing that the sequencing is properly handled, it is no more difficult to use multiple transactions than to use a single one.

Multiple transactions are used when updating tables that form logical groups but which need not all be treated as a single unit. Since we cannot control events inside a transaction at any greater level of granularity than the transaction itself, the only way to handle such cases is by nesting the sub-group transactions inside a main or "wrapper" transaction. For example, consider adding a new customer and that customer's first order to a typical set of tables.

Clearly we do not want to add records to the Order Header table unless we have successfully added the new customer's first. This is the classic situation in which we would use a transaction. However, we would not want to add the order details if the order header could not be saved. This too implies a transaction, but should we reject both the customer and the order header just because we cannot update a detail line? In some situations the answer may well be yes, but in most cases we would really want the addition of the customer to 'stick' even if the order could not be added. A single transaction is not enough, but a pair of nested transactions will meet the bill very well as illustrated below:

```
*** Start the outermost ('Wrapper') transaction
BEGIN TRANSACTION

*** Update the Customer table first
llTx1 = TableUpdate( 1, .F., 'customer' )
IF llTx1

   *** Customer table updated successfully
   *** Start the second, 'inner' transaction for Orders
   BEGIN TRANSACTION
   llTx2 = TableUpdate( 1, .F., 'orderheader' )
   IF llTx2

      *** Orders Updated, now try details
      llTx2 = TableUpdate( 2, .F., 'orderdetails' )
      IF llTx2

         *** Both Order tables updated successfully
         *** So commit the orders transaction
         END TRANSACTION
      ELSE

         *** Order Detail update failed
         *** Roll back entire orders transaction
         ROLLBACK
      ENDIF
   ELSE

      *** Order Header update failed - no point in trying details
      ROLLBACK
   ENDIF

   *** But the customer update had already succeeded, so commit
   END TRANSACTION
ELSE

   *** Customer update failed - no point in proceeding
   ROLLBACK

ENDIF
```

This code may look a little strange at first sight but does emphasize the point that **BEGIN...END TRANSACTION** does not constitute a control structure. Notice that there are two starting commands, one for each transaction and two 'Commit' commands, one for the customer table and one for the *pair* of order tables. However there are *three* rollback commands. One for the outer transaction but *two* for the inner transaction to cater to the fact that either table involved might fail.

The logic gets a little more tricky as more tables are involved but the principles remain the same. However, when many tables are involved, or if you are writing generic routines to handle an indeterminate number of tables at each level, it will probably be necessary to break the transactions up into separate methods to handle Update, Commit and Rollback functions and to use the *TXNLEVEL()* function to keep track of the number of transactions. (Remember that Visual FoxPro is limited to five simultaneous transactions.)

Some things to watch for when using buffering in applications

Cannot use OLDVAL() to revert a field under table buffering

You may have wondered, when reading the discussion of conflict resolution earlier in this chapter, why we did not make use of the *OLDVAL()* function to cancel a user's changes in the same way that we used the value returned by *CURVAL()* to clear conflicts in different fields. The answer is simply that we cannot do it this way when using any form of table buffering if the field is used in either a Primary or Candidate index without getting a "Uniqueness of index <name> is violated" error. This is an acknowledged bug in all versions of Visual FoxPro and, since the work-around offered by Microsoft is to use the *TableRevert()* function instead, it seems unlikely to us that it will ever be fixed.

However, this does not seem to be an entirely satisfactory solution because *TableRevert()* cannot operate at anything other than "Row" level and so undoing a change to a key field **without** losing any other changes in the same record requires a little more thought. The best solution that we have found is to make use of the SCATTER NAME command to create an object whose properties are named the same as the fields in the table. The values assigned to the object's properties are the current values from the record buffer and we can change the property values using a simple assignment. The following program illustrates both the problem and the solution:

```
*********************************************************************
* Program....: ShoOVal.prg
* Compiler...: Visual FoxPro 06.00.8492.00 for Windows
* Abstract...: Illustrates problem with using OldVal() to revert field
* ..........: which is used in a Candidate key
* ..........: Ref: MS Knowledgebase PSS ID Number: Q157405
*********************************************************************
*** Create and populate a sample table
CREATE TABLE sample ( Field1 C(5) UNIQUE, Field2 N(2) )
INSERT INTO sample ( Field1, Field2 ) VALUES ( "one  ", 1 )
INSERT INTO sample ( Field1, Field2 ) VALUES ( "two  ", 2 )
INSERT INTO sample ( Field1, Field2 ) VALUES ( "three", 3 )

*** Force into Table Buffered mode
SET MULTILOCK ON
CURSORSETPROP( "Buffering", 5 )

*** FIRST THE PROBLEM
*** Change key field
GO TOP
REPLACE field1 WITH "four", field2 WITH 4
SKIP
SKIP -1

*** Revert value using OldVal()
REPLACE field1 WITH OLDVAL( "Field1" )
```

```
SKIP
SKIP -1

*** You now get a "Uniqueness of index FIELD1 is violated" error message
*** Click IGNORE and revert the table - loses changes in all fields!
TableRevert(.T.)

*** NOW THE SOLUTION
*** Repeat the Replace
GO TOP
REPLACE field1 WITH "four", field2 WITH 4
SKIP
SKIP -1

*** Scatter the fields to an Object
SCATTER NAME loReverter

*** Revert the Key Field value
loReverter.Field1 = OLDVAL( 'Field1' )

*** Revert the row in the table
TableRevert(.F.)

*** Gather values back
GATHER NAME loReverter
SKIP
SKIP-1

*** NOTE: No error, and the change in Field2 is retained
*** Confirm the reversion
TableUpdate(1)
BROW NOWAIT
```

At the time of writing, the behavior outlined above was rather erratic when a character string was used as the candidate key. For example, if you REPLACE field1 WITH "seven" *you do not get an error at all! However, there is nothing magical about the string "seven" as several other values were found that did not cause an error, but we could not discern a pattern in, or formulate any logical explanation for, the observed behavior.*

Gotcha! Row buffering and commands that move the record pointer

We noted earlier that changes to a record in a row buffered table are automatically committed by Visual FoxPro whenever the record pointer for that table is moved. This is implicit in the design of Row Buffering and is entirely desirable. What is not so desirable is that it is not always obvious that a specific command is actually going to move the record pointer and this can lead to unexpected results. For example, it is predictable that issuing a SEEK or a SKIP command is going to move the record pointer and therefore we would not normally allow such a command to be executed without first checking the buffer mode and, if row buffering is in force, checking for uncommitted changes.

Similarly you would expect that using a GOTO command would also move the record pointer if the specified record was not already selected. However, GOTO *always* moves the record pointer, even if you use the GOTO RECNO() form of the command (which keeps the record pointer on the same record) and so will always attempt to commit pending changes under row buffering.

In fact, any command which can take either an explicit record number or has a Scope (FOR or WHILE) clause is going to cause the record pointer to move and is, therefore, a likely cause of problems when used in conjunction with Row Buffering. There are many such commands in Visual FoxPro including the obvious like SUM, AVERAGE and CALCULATE as well as some less obvious ones like COPY TO ARRAY and UNLOCK.

This last is particularly sneaky. What it means is that if you are using explicit locking with a row buffered table, then unlocking a record is directly equivalent to issuing a *TableUpdate()* and you immediately lose the ability to undo changes. We are not sure whether this was really the intended behavior (though we can guess!) but it does underline the points made earlier in the chapter. First, there is no real place for row buffering in an application, and second, the best way to handle locking when using buffering is to allow Visual FoxPro to do it.

Chapter 9
Views in Particular, SQL in General

"There are many paths to the top of the mountain, but the view is always the same."
(Chinese Proverb)

The preceding two chapters have concentrated mainly on the management and use of tables in Visual FoxPro but there is much, much more that can be done by branching out into the world of SQL in general, and Views in particular. Since we are concentrating on Visual FoxPro, this chapter deals mainly with Local Views and does not address the subject of Offline or Remote views in any detail. We hope you will still find enough nuggets here to keep you interested.

Visual FoxPro views

The sample code for this chapter includes a separate database (*CH09.DBC*) which contains the local tables and views used in the examples for this section. We have not included any specific examples that use remote views (if only because we cannot guarantee that you will have a suitable data source set up on your machine) but where appropriate we have indicated any significant differences between local and remote views.

What exactly is a view?

The Visual FoxPro Help file defines a view in the following terms:

"A customized virtual table definition that can be local, remote, or parameterized. Views reference one or more tables, or other views. They can be updated, and they can reference remote tables."

The key word here is '*definition*' because a view is actually a SQL query that is stored within a database container but, unlike a simple Query (.*QPR*) file, a view is represented visually in the database container as if it actually were a table. It can, for all practical purposes, be treated as if it really were a table (i.e. to open a view, you simply use it, and it can also be added to the dataenvironment of a form at design time). There are at least three major benefits to be gained from using views.

First, because a view does not actually store any data persistently, it requires no permanent disk storage space. However, because the definition is stored, the view can be re-created any time it is required without the need to re-define the SQL. Second, unlike a cursor created directly by a SQL Query, a view is always updateable and can, if required, also be defined to update the table, or tables, on which it is based. Third, a view can be based upon local (VFP) tables, or can use tables from a remote data source (using ODBC and a '*Connection*') and can even use other views as the source for its data - or any combination of the above.

How do I create a view?

Visual FoxPro allows a view to be created in two ways, either visually (using the View Designer) or programmatically with the `CREATE SQL VIEW` command. For full details on using the View Designer, see *Chapter 8: Creating Views* in the Programmer's Guide. (However, remember that, like all the designers, the View Designer does have some limitations and certain types of views really do need to be created in code.) Whichever method you use, the process entails four steps:

- Define the fields which the view will contain and the table(s) from which those fields are to be selected

- Specify any join conditions, filters or parameters required

- Define the update mechanism and criteria (if the view is to be used to update its source tables)

- Name and save the view to a database container

One big benefit of using the view designer to create views is that it hides the complexity of the code required and, while the code is not actually difficult, there can be an awful lot of it (even for a simple view) as the following example shows. Here is the SQL for a simple, but updateable, one-table view that lists Company Names by city for a given country as shown in the View Designer:

```
SELECT DISTINCT Clients.clisid, Clients.clicmpy, Clients.clicity;
 FROM ch09!clients;
 WHERE Clients.clictry = ?cCountry;
 ORDER BY Clients.clicity, Clients.clicmpy
```

While here is the code required to create the same view programmatically:

```
CREATE SQL VIEW "CPYBYCITY" ;
   AS SELECT DISTINCT Clients.clisid, Clients.clicmpy, Clients.clicity ;
   FROM ch09!clients ;
   WHERE Clients.clictry = ?cCountry ;
   ORDER BY Clients.clicity, Clients.clicmpy

DBSetProp('CPYBYCITY', 'View', 'UpdateType', 1)
DBSetProp('CPYBYCITY', 'View', 'WhereType', 3)
DBSetProp('CPYBYCITY', 'View', 'FetchMemo', .T.)
DBSetProp('CPYBYCITY', 'View', 'SendUpdates', .T.)
DBSetProp('CPYBYCITY', 'View', 'UseMemoSize', 255)
DBSetProp('CPYBYCITY', 'View', 'FetchSize', 100)
DBSetProp('CPYBYCITY', 'View', 'MaxRecords', -1)
DBSetProp('CPYBYCITY', 'View', 'Tables', 'ch09!clients')
DBSetProp('CPYBYCITY', 'View', 'Prepared', .F.)
DBSetProp('CPYBYCITY', 'View', 'CompareMemo', .T.)
DBSetProp('CPYBYCITY', 'View', 'FetchAsNeeded', .F.)
```

```
DBSetProp('CPYBYCITY', 'View', 'FetchSize', 100)
DBSetProp('CPYBYCITY', 'View', 'ParameterList', "cCountry,'C'")
DBSetProp('CPYBYCITY', 'View', 'Comment', "")
DBSetProp('CPYBYCITY', 'View', 'BatchUpdateCount', 1)
DBSetProp('CPYBYCITY', 'View', 'ShareConnection', .F.)
DBSetProp('CPYBYCITY.clisid', 'Field', 'KeyField', .T.)
DBSetProp('CPYBYCITY.clisid', 'Field', 'Updatable', .F.)
DBSetProp('CPYBYCITY.clisid', 'Field', 'UpdateName', 'ch09!clients.clisid')
DBSetProp('CPYBYCITY.clisid', 'Field', 'DataType', "I")
DBSetProp('CPYBYCITY.clicmpy', 'Field', 'KeyField', .F.)
DBSetProp('CPYBYCITY.clicmpy', 'Field', 'Updatable', .T.)
DBSetProp('CPYBYCITY.clicmpy', 'Field', 'UpdateName', 'ch09!clients.clicmpy')
DBSetProp('CPYBYCITY.clicmpy', 'Field', 'DataType', "C(40)")
DBSetProp('CPYBYCITY.clicity', 'Field', 'KeyField', .F.)
DBSetProp('CPYBYCITY.clicity', 'Field', 'Updatable', .T.)
DBSetProp('CPYBYCITY.clicity', 'Field', 'UpdateName', 'ch09!clients.clicity')
DBSetProp('CPYBYCITY.clicity', 'Field', 'DataType', "C(15)")
```

First, it must be said that it is not really as bad as it looks! Many of the *View* level settings defined here are the default values and only need to be specified when you need something set up differently. Having said that, it still remains a non-trivial exercise (just getting all of the statements correctly typed is difficult enough!). So how can we simplify things a bit? Well, Visual FoxPro includes a very useful little tool named *GENDBC.PRG* that creates a program to re-generate a database container (You will find it in the ..\VFP60\TOOLS\GENDBC\ sub-directory). Views are, as stated above, stored in a database container. So why not let Visual FoxPro do all the hard work?

Simply create a temporary (empty) database container and define your view in it. Run *GENDBC* and you have a program file that not only documents your view, but can be run to re-create the view in your actual database container. More importantly there are, as we said, some limitations to what the designer can handle. One such limitation involves creating views that join multiple tables related to a common parent, but not to each other. The join clauses produced by the designer cannot really handle this situation and the only way to ensure the correct results is to create such views in code. Using the designer to do most of the work, and simply editing the join conditions in a *PRG* file, is the easiest way to create complex views.

One word of caution! If you do create views programmatically, be sure that you do not then inadvertently try to modify them in the view designer because you may end up with a view that no longer does what it is meant to. We strongly recommend naming such views differently to distinguish them from views that can be safely modified in the designer. To modify a programmatically created view, simply edit the program that creates it and re-run it.

When should I use a view instead of a table?

Actually you never need to use a table again! You can **always** use a view, even if that view is simply an exact copy of a single table. We will cover this point later in the chapter (see the section on *Scalability*). However, there are certainly some occasions when we think that a view should be used rather than using tables directly.

The first, and probably the most obvious, is when creating reports that require data from related tables. While the Visual FoxPro Report Writer is quite a flexible tool, it is not (in our opinion) easy to use when trying to work with multiple tables. A single view can reduce a complex relational structure to a "flat file" which is easily handled by the report writer, making the task of setting up reports that use grouped data much easier.

Another, perhaps less obvious use is that some controls, like grids and list or combo boxes, often need to use look-up tables to display descriptions associated with code fields. Creating an updateable view to combine the descriptions along with the 'real' data provides a simple and efficient way of handling such tasks. Chapter 6 (*Grids: The Misunderstood Controls*) includes an example which uses a view for precisely this purpose - a view, used as the *RecordSource* for the grid, includes a description field from a lookup table, and all fields *except* the description are updateable.

Views also provide a mechanism for accessing data in older versions of FoxPro without needing to convert the source data. If you try to add a FoxPro 2.x table to a Visual FoxPro database container, the tables become unusable by the 2.x application. In cases where you need to access the same table in both FoxPro 2.x and Visual FoxPro, a view provides the solution. Although the view must be stored within a DBC, the tables that it uses do not have to be.

This ability is, of course, not limited to FoxPro tables. A view can be defined to retrieve data from *any* data source into Visual FoxPro, providing that an ODBC connection to that data source can be established. Once the data has been pulled into a view it can be manipulated in exactly the same way as if it were native Visual FoxPro data. By making such a "*Remote*" view updateable, any changes made in Visual FoxPro can be submitted to the original data source.

The final occasion to use a view is when you need to obtain a sub-set of data. In this situation, creating a parameterized view is often better than simply setting a filter. In fact, when dealing with grids it is always better because grids cannot make use of Rushmore to optimize filters. For more details on using views in grids, see Chapter 6.

Hang on! What is a parameterized view?

Ah! Did we not mention this? A view does not always have to include all data from a table, nor do you always have to specify the exact filter condition at design time. Instead you can define a view which includes a filter condition which will be based on a parameter supplied at run time - hence the term '*Parameterized View*'.

A parameterized view is defined by including a filter condition that refers to a variable name, property or field in an open table which has been prefixed with a "?" as follows:

```
WHERE Clients.clicity = ?city_to_view ;
```

When the view is opened or re-queried, Visual FoxPro will look for the named variable and, if it finds it will simply apply the condition as specified to the SQL statement which populates the view. A simple parameterized view is included in the samples for this chapter (see *lv_CpyByCity* in CH09.dbc). If the named parameter is not found when the view is opened, or re-queried, a dialog box which requests a value for the parameter is displayed - like this:

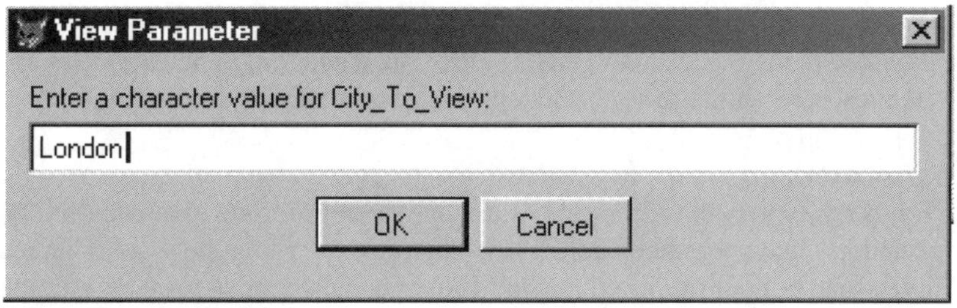

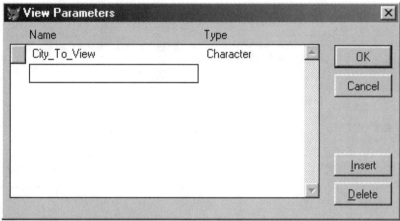

Figure 9.1 View Parameter Dialog

Defining view parameters

Notice that the prompt begins '*Enter a character value...*'. How does Visual FoxPro know that *City_To_View* is a character string? The answer is that it doesn't! This particular view was created in the view designer and, when using the designer, there is an option on the '**Query**' pad of the system menu ('*View parameters*') which allows you to define the names and data types of any parameters you specify in the definition for the view.

Figure 9.2 View Parameter Definition

If you are going to make use of the view parameters dialog in an application, and you define those views in the designer, always define your parameters explicitly in this dialog. (We would suggest that you use very descriptive names too!) If you do not define the parameter, then the dialog displayed to the user will **not** include the type of value expected and will simply state "*Enter a value for City_To_View*". (To do the same thing when defining a view in code merely requires (yet another) call to the *DBSETPROP()* function).

However, in our opinion, simply using the default dialog is not a good thing to do in an application for three reasons. First, Visual FoxPro does not validate the entry the user types into the dialog (even when you pre-define the parameter and its data type), and you cannot validate that entry before it is applied either. So if the parameter is invalid, you will simply get an error. Second, the dialog itself is not really very user-friendly. After all, what is the average user going to make of something that is asking for a 'View Parameter'? Finally, if you are using multiple parameters then, because Visual FoxPro can accept only one parameter at a time, the user will be presented with a series of dialogs one after another (very ugly).

Using parameterized views in a form

The solution is really very simple - just ensure that the appropriate parameter has been defined, is in scope and has been populated before opening or re-querying the view. There are many ways of doing this, but our preferred method is to create properties for view parameters at the Form level and then to transfer the values from those properties into the appropriate variables in whatever method is querying the view. This has two benefits. First, it ensures that the current values used by the view are available to the entire form. Second, it allows us to validate the parameters before they are passed to the view.

To enable a user to specify the necessary parameters, we must provide the user with an appropriate means for entering the parameters. This might be a pop-up form or some sort of selection control on the form itself. Most importantly, we can also get multiple parameters in one operation if necessary. A form that gives an example of such a mechanism is included in the sample code for this chapter (*VuParams.scx*).

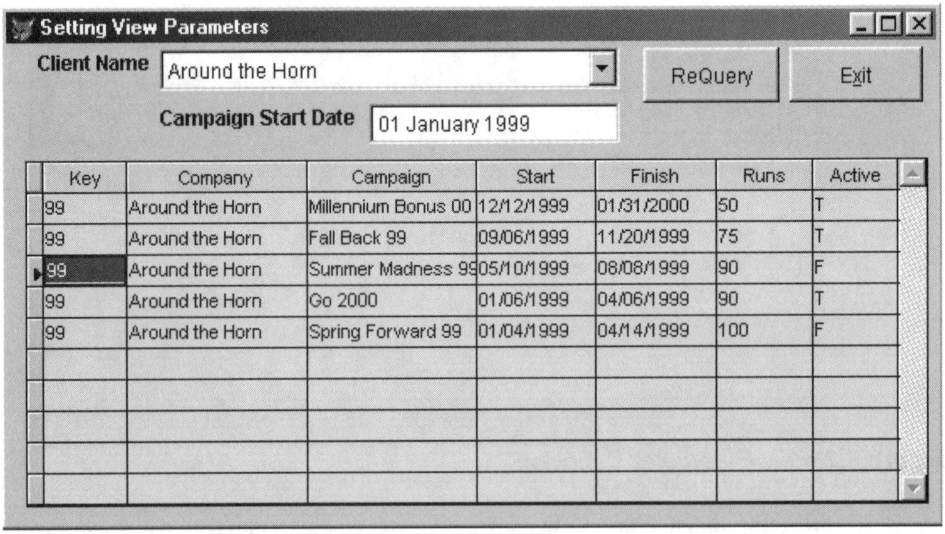
Setting View Parameters
Client Name
Around the Horn
ReQuery
Exit
Campaign Start Date
01 January 1999
Key
Company
Campaign
Start
Finish
Runs
Active
99
Around the Horn
Millennium Bonus 00
12/12/1999
01/31/2000
50
T
99
Around the Horn
Fall Back 99
09/06/1999
11/20/1999
75
T
99
Around the Horn
Summer Madness 99
05/10/1999
08/08/1999
90
F
99
Around the Horn
Go 2000
01/06/1999
04/06/1999
90
T
99
Around the Horn
Spring Forward 99
01/04/1999
04/14/1999
100
F

***Figure 9.3** Using a Parameterized View in a form*

This form uses a view (*lv_adcampanes*) that joins three tables, which are related as shown in **Figure 9.4** and accepts two parameters, one for the "Client Name" and the other for a "Start Date."

Figure 9.4 *Tables for View lv_AdCampanes*

The view has been added to the dataenvironment of the form with its **NODATAONLOAD** property set to .T. Since the "*Clients*" table is used both in the view and as the **RowSource** for the combo box, it has had its **BufferModeOverride** property set to none to disable buffering on that table (even though, in this example, the view is not updateable). The form has two custom properties to store the results of the user's selections. The "*ReQuery*" button has code in its *Click* method to ensure that these properties contain values and to transfer them to the defined parameters for the view before calling the **REQUERY()** function.

How do I control the contents of a view when it is opened?
The default behavior of any view (local or remote) is that whenever the view is first opened, it populates itself by executing the SQL that defines it. This applies whether you open the view explicitly with a **USE** command in code (or from the command window) or implicitly by adding it to the dataenvironment of a form. However, this may not always be the behavior that you want, especially when dealing with parameterized views or with any view, local or remote, that accesses large tables.

To prevent a view from loading all of its data, you must specify the **NODATA** option when opening it. In code, the key word is added to the end of the normal **USE** command like this:

```
USE lv_CpyByCity NODATA
```

However, in a Form's dataenvironment the cursor for the view has a *NoDataOnLoad* property that is set, by default, to .**F**. Setting this property to .**T**. ensures that you do not get the '*Enter value for xxx*' dialog when you initialize the form.

Whichever way you open your view, the result is the same: you get a view consisting of all the defined fields but no records. In a form, this allows bound controls to be initialized properly even when there is no actual data for them to display. However, unless you subsequently (typically in the *Init* method or a method called from the *Init*) populate the view, any controls bound to it will be disabled when the form is displayed. Visual FoxPro provides two functions which operate on views to control the way in which they obtain their data, **REQUERY()** and **REFRESH()**.

What is the difference between REQUERY() and REFRESH()
The **REQUERY()** function is used to populate a view which has been opened with no data. It is also used to update the contents of a parameterized view whenever the parameter has changed. When a view is requeried, the SQL defining the view is executed and the appropriate data set is retrieved. The function returns either 1 (indicating that the query succeeded) or 0 (if the query failed). However, note that the return value does *NOT* tell you if any records were

retrieved, merely if the SQL was executed properly. To get the number of matching records you still need to use _**TALLY** as the following code shows:

```
USE lv_cpybycity NODATA
City_to_view = 'London'
? REQUERY()      && Returns 1
? _TALLY         && Returns 6
City_to_view = 'Peterborough'
? REQUERY()      && Returns 1
? _TALLY         && Returns 0
```

The **REFRESH()** function has an entirely different purpose. It updates the contents of an existing view to reflect any changes to the underlying data since the view was last requeried. By default, only the current record is refreshed, although the function allows you specify the number of records, and the range for those records (based on an offset from the current record) that will be updated. However, **REFRESH()** does not re-query the data, even in a parameterized view for which the parameter has changed, as illustrated here:

```
USE lv_cpybycity NODATA
City_to_view = 'London'
? REQUERY()      && Returns 1
? _TALLY         && Returns 6
? clicity        && Returns 'London'
City_to_view = 'Peterborough'
? REFRESH()      && Returns 1
? clicity        && Returns 'London'
```

If **REFRESH()** simply ignores the changed parameter, what is the use of it? The answer is that because a view is always created locally on the client machine, and is exclusive to the current user, changes to the underlying table can be made which are not reflected in the view. This is easily seen if you open a view and then go to the underlying table and make a change directly. The view itself will not change but if you then try and make a change to the view and save it you will get an update conflict. Even worse, reverting the change in the view will still not give you the current value from the table - merely that which was originally in the view. The only way to get the view updated is to call a **REFRESH()**.

This is because the view has its own buffer, independent of that for the underlying table. It is not really an issue if you re-query a view each time the user wants to access a new data set. A **REQUERY()** always populates the view afresh. However, if you have a situation where several records are retrieved into a view and a user may make changes to any of them, it's best to ensure that as each record is selected, the view is refreshed. This ensures that what the user actually sees reflects the current state of the underlying table.

Why do changes made in a view sometimes not get into the underlying table?

This can happen when you are working with an updateable local view which is based on a table which was already open and buffered when the view was opened. The problem occurs because you then have two "layers" of buffering in force, but the view only knows about one of them. The standard behavior of Visual FoxPro when working with a local view is to open the underlying table with no buffering when the view is first queried. It does not matter to Visual FoxPro whether the view is opened from the command line, in a program or through the dataenvironment of a form.

This behavior ensures that when a *TableUpdate()* is called for the view (which *always* uses optimistic buffering), the changes to the underlying table are immediately committed. However, if the table is itself buffered, all that gets updated is the table's buffer and another *TableUpdate()* is required to ensure the changes are saved. To avoid this problem, do not explicitly open the table (or tables) on which the view is based. In other words when using a view in a form, do **not** add the source tables for the view to the form's dataenvironment. (If you absolutely must do so, then set the *buffermodeoverride* property for these tables to ensure that they are opened with no buffering.)

There is, of course, another situation in which the problem can arise. This is when you are using the *Default* datasession and have more than one form open. Obviously, since different forms may use tables in different ways, there is no reliable way of knowing that tables used by a view in one form have not already been opened in another form without explicitly testing for each table. If a table has been opened, and buffered, by another form what can you do about it? You cannot simply change the table's buffer mode. (That would affect the other form also.) You could modify your update commands to force an explicit *TableUpdate()* on the underlying table, but that seems (to us anyway) to defeat one of the main benefits of using a view - which is that it allows you to use data from multiple tables and treat it as if there were really only a single table involved.

The solution to this dilemma is to ensure that you use Private DataSessions for the forms that use updateable views. By using a private datasession you effectively force Visual FoxPro to open the underlying tables afresh (analogous to doing a USE..AGAIN on the table) and then there can be no ambiguity about the buffering state. In fact we would go further and say that, as a general rule, you really should not mix updateable views and the tables on which they are based in the same datasession. Either use views for everything (remember, you can create a view which is simply a direct 'copy' of the table) or use the tables directly!

Why would I want to create a view that is simply a copy of an existing table?

There are three reasons for doing this. The first, as discussed in the preceding section, is to avoid having to mix tables and views in the same form. The second is when the actual data is contained in an older version of FoxPro and is used by another application written in that version, which would prevent you from simply upgrading the tables to Visual FoxPro format. The third, and in our opinion the most important, is when you are creating a scaleable application.

What do you mean by a 'scaleable' application?

A scaleable application is one which is written to enable the source of the data to be changed from Visual FoxPro tables to some other data source - typically a back end server like SQL Server or Oracle. One of the biggest advantages of using views is that the *same* view definition can be used to access either local (i.e. Visual FoxPro) tables or remote (i.e. back end) data. The only practical difference between a local and a remote view is that the latter requires a "connection" to be defined in order to enable the data source to be queried. In all other respects the behavior of a local and a remote view is identical and the commands to manipulate them are the same.

This means that you can build, test and run an application entirely in Visual FoxPro. You can also, at a later date, redefine the views from "*local*" to "*remote*" and have your application run from a different data source without changing any of the code. (This assumes, of course, that the table names and their structures are the same in both Visual FoxPro and the back end database.)

Sounds cool! How do I do that?

In principle it is very simple – use views instead of tables. However, it is not just a question of substituting views for tables. There are many issues to consider because, when working with views, you really are working with a remote data source. A view-based application should, therefore, be modeled on a proper client/server architecture. So, having designed your application to use views that are based on local Visual FoxPro tables, you no longer need to use tables directly in the application. This gives you a working application that can later be switched over to use a different data source without requiring any code modification because once a view has been populated it does not matter to Visual FoxPro whether it is based on local or remote data. So how would you actually convert an application from local views to remote views? There are two possible solutions, assuming that table names and structures are identical in both Visual FoxPro and the remote data source.

One way is to create three database containers. The first contains the local Visual FoxPro tables and the second contains only the local views based on the tables in the first. The third contains the equivalent remote views (and the relevant connection information). This allows you to keep the names of both the Local and Remote views the same. Within the application, you provide a mechanism for specifying which of the View-based database containers is to be used. (This could be done by reading from an *INI* file or a registry setting.) By simply changing this database pointer, the application switches from using local to remote views and requires no additional code whatsoever.

This is the most flexible approach because it retains the possibility of running against either local or remote data. It also requires more set up and maintenance to ensure that the Local and Remote views are always synchronized with the tables. As with everything, there is a trade-off here.

The second way is actually to convert local views into remote views. This is best done by creating, as before, multiple database containers – although in this case we require only two (one for the local tables and one for views). To convert the views from local to remote, you first generate the code for the local views (using *GenDbc.prg*) as a program. This program can then be modified to redefine the views as remote views. The modified program is then run to generate a new database container including only remote views.

Although simpler to maintain, this is essentially a one-way operation because you lose the ability to run against local data when the views are re-defined. The approach will, as always, depend upon the specific needs of the application.

Converting local views into remote views programmatically

The following code shows how little the definition for a local view needs to be modified to turn it into a remote view. As you can see, apart from specifying the connection and the name of the database, there is actually no difference:

```
LOCAL:  CREATE SQL VIEW "CUSTOMERS" ;
           AS SELECT * FROM Vfpdata!customers

REMOTE: CREATE SQL VIEW " CUSTOMERS" ;
           REMOTE CONNECT "SQL7" ;
           AS SELECT * FROM dbo.Customers Customers
```

In fact, the rest of the code required to create either the Local or the Remote view is, again with the exception of the database name, identical - so, for example the Keyfield ("*customerid*") definitions look like this:

```
LOCAL
* Props for the CUSTOMERS.customerid field.
DBSetProp('CUSTOMERS.customerid', 'Field', 'KeyField', .T.)
DBSetProp('CUSTOMERS.customerid', 'Field', 'Updatable', .F.)
DBSetProp('CUSTOMERS.customerid', 'Field', 'UpdateName',
'vfpdata!customers.customerid')
DBSetProp('CUSTOMERS.customerid', 'Field', 'DataType', "C(5)")


REMOTE
* Props for the CUSTOMERS.customerid field.
DBSetProp('CUSTOMERS.customerid', 'Field', 'KeyField', .T.)
DBSetProp('CUSTOMERS.customerid', 'Field', 'Updatable', .F.)
DBSetProp('CUSTOMERS.customerid', 'Field', 'UpdateName',
'dbo.customers.customerid')
DBSetProp('CUSTOMERS.customerid', 'Field', 'DataType', "C(5)")
```

While the code for creating the connection is also very simple indeed and looks like this:

```
CREATE CONNECTION SQL7 ;
    DATASOURCE "SQL7 Northwind" ;
    USERID "xxxxxx" ;
    PASSWORD "yyyyyy"


**** Connection properties
DBSetProp('SQL7', 'Connection', 'Asynchronous', .F.)
DBSetProp('SQL7', 'Connection', 'BatchMode', .T.)
DBSetProp('SQL7', 'Connection', 'Comment', '')
DBSetProp('SQL7', 'Connection', 'DispLogin', 1)
DBSetProp('SQL7', 'Connection', 'ConnectTimeOut', 15)
DBSetProp('SQL7', 'Connection', 'DispWarnings', .F.)
DBSetProp('SQL7', 'Connection', 'IdleTimeOut', 0)
DBSetProp('SQL7', 'Connection', 'QueryTimeOut', 0)
DBSetProp('SQL7', 'Connection', 'Transactions', 1)
DBSetProp('SQL7', 'Connection', 'Database', '')
```

It is unlikely that in a production environment you would leave all of these settings at their defaults (which is what we see here), but the amount of modification required is very limited.

Of course, there is a whole raft of issues associated with actually designing and building a truly scaleable application. While that is definitely outside the scope of **this** book, the *mechanics* of scaling a view-based application are, as we have seen, really quite straightforward.

What is the best way to index a view?

Since a view is actually created by an SQL statement, it does not have any indexes of its own. However, since a view is always created locally and is exclusive to the current user, creating indexes for views is not, of itself, problematic (providing that you remember to turn off table buffering when creating the index). See *"How to index a buffered table"* in Chapter 7 for more information on this topic. The only question is whether it is better to create the index before, or after, populating the view.

To some extent this depends on the amount of data that you expect to bring down into the view and where that data is being retrieved. For example, to download some 90 records from a local SQL Server installation into a view and build indexes on two fields, we obtained the following results:

```
Open View and Populate = 0.042 secs
Index Populated View   = 0.003 secs
Total Time             = 0.045 secs

Open View and Index    = 0.033 secs
Populate Indexed View  = 0.016 secs
Total Time             = 0.049 secs
```

As you can see there is little practical difference here. The exact same processes, from the equivalent local Visual FoxPro table, yielded the following results:

```
Open View and Populate = 0.011 secs
Index Populated View   = 0.003 secs
Total Time             = 0.014 secs

Open View and Index    = 0.006 secs
Populate Indexed View  = 0.008 secs
Total Time             = 0.014 secs
```

The results here show even less difference. Using larger tables, running over a network or having a machine with different hardware and setup are all going to influence the actual timing. However in general, it seems reasonable to suppose that you should build indexes after the view has been populated. After all, indexing a view is always a purely local function, which cannot be said for the actual population of the view. In our little example, it is clear that retrieving the data takes longer than creating the indexes. When using views that are sub-sets of data, this is usually going to be the case, so the quicker the required data can be retrieved, the better. Adding indexes before populating the view imposes an overhead on this process and can generally be left until later.

More on using views

Views are extremely useful, whether you are building an application which is to be run entirely in Visual FoxPro, or is to be scaleable, or is just to be run against a remote data source. However, they do require a little more thought and some additional care in use. This section lists some additional things that we have found when working with views in general.

Using a default value to open a parameterized view

Earlier in this chapter, we said that when using a parameterized view, it is best to ensure that the view is opened with either an explicit NODATA clause or by setting the NODATAONLOAD property to .T. However, this approach means that opening a view actually requires two queries to be sent to the data source. The first query retrieves the structure of the view, and the second query populates it. This is unlikely to cause significant delays when working with a local view, even on a relatively slow network. However, as soon as we begin to think about remote views, another factor comes into play. In order to maximize performance, we do not want to send multiple queries to the back end. The question is – how can we avoid having to retrieve all available data (which might be an awful lot!) and also avoid the dreaded '*Enter a value for xxx*' dialog when a form using a parameterized view is initialized?

In fact, Visual FoxPro only requires the parameter on two occasions. First, when a view is opened for the very first time and second whenever a view is re-queried. At any other time, the parameter is irrelevant because you already have the view populated. Therefore, there is no need to make the parameter available globally, providing that it is initialized in whatever method is actually going to call the REQUERY() function. The solution is, therefore, to explicitly define a default value parameter in the *OpenTables()* method of the dataenvironment. However, this is not as simple as it might seem at first. The example form, *DefParam.SCX*, in the code which accompanies this chapter, uses a parameterized view (*lv_cpybycity*) and initializes it to retrieve data for '*London*' by including the following in the *OpenTables()* method of the dataenvironment:

```
City_to_view = "London"
DODEFAULT()
NODEFAULT
```

Notice that both the DoDefault() and the NoDefault are required here because of the way the interaction between the *OpenTables* method and its associated *BeforeOpenTables* event is implemented in Visual FoxPro - it looks a bit odd, but it works!

Using a view again

We have mentioned already that for all practical purposes, you can regard a view as a table. This should mean that you can issue a USE <name> AGAIN command for a view, and indeed you can do so. However, there is one difference between re-using views and using tables or cursors with the AGAIN keyword. When a view is used AGAIN, Visual FoxPro creates a pointer to the original view rather than creating a completely new, or '*disconnected*', cursor for it. The consequence is that if you change the content of the original view, the content of the alternate alias also changes. To be honest, we are not sure if this is a good thing or a bad thing, but either way it does seem to be a limitation to the usefulness of the USE <view> AGAIN option.

It is worth noting that, for REMOTE views only, there is also a `NOREQUERY` option that can be used with the `USE <view> AGAIN` command to prevent Visual FoxPro from re-loading the data for the view from the back end server.

Using dates as view parameters

Unfortunately, at the time of writing, there is a bug in Visual FoxPro Version 6.0 (SP3), associated with the setting of `strictDate`, which affects the use of dates as parameters for views. When a setting for `STRICTDATE` other than 0 is specified, there is no simple way to enter a date parameter through the default dialog. The only format that will be accepted is the unambiguous: `1999,01,01` but although this will be accepted without error, it will still not give the correct result when the query executes.

This is yet another reason for not using the default dialog to gather parameters for views. However, the workaround is fairly simple; just set `STRICTDATE` to 0 before opening or re-querying a view using date parameters and the view will then accept parameters in the normal date format. The sample code for this chapter includes a parameterized view (*lv_campanelist*) that requires a date. The following snippets show the result of various ways of supplying the parameter:

```
SET STRICTDATE TO 1
USE lv_campanelist
*** Enter in dialog: {12/12/1999}
    *** Result: Syntax error!
*** Enter in dialog: 12/12/1999
    *** Result: Error 2032: Ambiguous Date/DateTime constant
*** Enter in dialog: 1999,12,12
    *** Result: View is populated with ALL data irrespective of the value
entered

SET STRICTDATE TO 0
USE lv_campanelist
*** Enter in dialog: 12/12/99
    *** Result: View is correctly populated with data
```

Of course, if you are initializing your parameters in code, there is no need to alter `STRICTDATE` at all. Although you must still ensure that dates passed as parameters are unambiguous, that is easily done using either the *DATE(yyyy,mm,dd)* function or the *{^yyyy-mm-dd}* form to specify the value.

Creating views involving multiple look-up tables *(Example: LkUpQry.prg)*

We mentioned earlier in this chapter that the View Designer has some limitations when it comes to building views. Perhaps the most serious of these is that the designer always generates queries using the 'nested join' syntax which simply cannot deal with queries involving certain types of relationship. This is clearly seen when you try to build a view that includes tables linked to the same parent table, but not related directly to each other. Typically such linkages arise in the context of look-up tables. Consider the following schema:

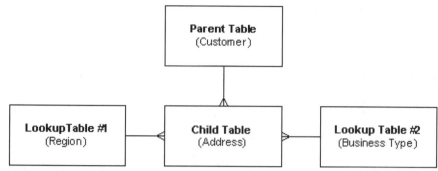

Figure 9.5 *View Parameter Dialog*

In this design, the parent table (*Customer*) has a single child table (*Address*) which is used to store the various locations at which a given customer carries on his business. Each address record contains two foreign keys, in addition to that of its parent, which link into lookup tables for '*Region*' and '*Business Type*'. Clearly, there is no direct relation between these two lookups, but it is easy to see why it would be necessary to be able to include the relevant descriptions in a view that provides details of a customer.

Figure 9.6 shows the view designer set-up for creating a view of these tables using the join conditions offered by the designer as default.

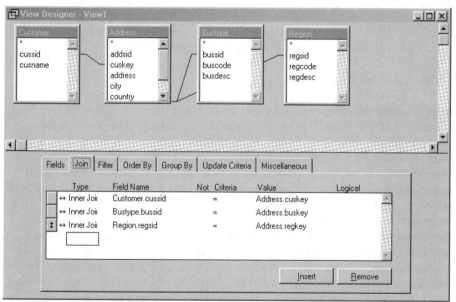

Figure 9.6 *View designer for a view involving lookup tables*

This produces the following query:

```
SELECT Customer.cusname, Address.address, Address.city, ;
       Bustype.busdesc, Region.regdesc;
  FROM  ch09!customer INNER JOIN ch09!address;
    INNER JOIN ch09!bustype;
    INNER JOIN ch09!region ;
   ON   Region.regsid = Address.regkey ;
   ON   Bustype.bussid = Address.buskey ;
   ON   Customer.cussid = Address.cuskey;
 ORDER BY Customer.cusname, Address.city
```

This first joins Address to Customer, then joins business type and finally region. Looks reasonable enough, doesn't it? However the results of running this query look a little peculiar (**Figure 9.7**):

Cusname	Address	City	Busdesc	Regdesc
Dewey, Cheetam and Howe	4029 Greenlands	Amherst,NY	Civil/Criminal Law	British Isles (UK & Eire)
Dewey, Cheetam and Howe	4029 Greenlands	Amherst,NY	Accountancy/Financial Advice	British Isles (UK & Eire)
Dewey, Cheetam and Howe	4823 Main Street	Boston, MA	Civil/Criminal Law	British Isles (UK & Eire)
Dewey, Cheetam and Howe	4823 Main Street	Boston, MA	Real Estate/Property Mgt	British Isles (UK & Eire)
Doolittle & Dalley	14 Connor Street	Dublin	Real Estate/Property Mgt	British Isles (UK & Eire)
Doolittle & Dalley	12 Someplace Crescent	London	Real Estate/Property Mgt	British Isles (UK & Eire)
Doolittle & Dalley	1233 Rue St Garde	Paris	Real Estate/Property Mgt	British Isles (UK & Eire)
Letcher and Scorer	789 Crosslands Drive	Quebec	Software Development	British Isles (UK & Eire)
Letcher and Scorer	789 Crosslands Drive	Quebec	Management/General Consultancy	British Isles (UK & Eire)
Letcher and Scorer	3444 Longshore Boulevard	Victoria	Software Development	British Isles (UK & Eire)
Letcher and Scorer	3444 Longshore Boulevard	Victoria	Management/General Consultancy	British Isles (UK & Eire)

Figure 9.7 *Query results*

As you can see, all customers are, apparently, in the same region. Even worse, when we attempt to save this view, an "Error 1806" message appears stating that:

"SQL: Column regkey is not found"

Maybe we need the keys in the result set to make this work? But no, adding the key fields does not help either. Maybe we need to specify Outer Joins instead of Inner joins for the lookup table? Again the answer is no. Finally, in desperation, let's try adding the tables in a different order. First add Address and the two lookup tables. Build the query and run it. Everything looks just fine! Now add in the customer table and join it. Re-run the query and now, instead of only one region, we get only one customer (and the error when we try and save the view is that "*Column cuskey is not found*").

The problem is that this type of query simply cannot be resolved in a single pass using the "nested join" syntax generated by the visual designer. To do it, we need to construct **two** queries - and this is why the View Designer cannot do it for us.

The 'visual' solution is first to join the Address table to its lookup tables (including the customer key) and save the resulting view definition. Next, join the customer table to this view. (Remember a view can include other views in its definition.) The views *lv_AddLkup* and *lv_CustAddress* in the sample code for this chapter show the intermediate and final results of this approach (**Figure 9.8**):

Cusname	Address	City	Busdesc	Regdesc
Dewey, Cheetam and Howe	4029 Greenlands	Amherst,NY	Accountancy/Financial Advice	Northern USA
Dewey, Cheetam and Howe	4029 Greenlands	Amherst,NY	Civil/Criminal Law	Northern USA
Dewey, Cheetam and Howe	4823 Main Street	Boston, MA	Civil/Criminal Law	Northern USA
Dewey, Cheetam and Howe	4823 Main Street	Boston, MA	Real Estate/Property Mgt	Northern USA
Doolittle & Dalley	14 Connor Street	Dublin	Real Estate/Property Mgt	British Isles (UK & Eire)
Doolittle & Dalley	12 Someplace Crescent	London	Real Estate/Property Mgt	British Isles (UK & Eire)
Doolittle & Dalley	1233 Rue St Garde	Paris	Real Estate/Property Mgt	Northern Europe
Letcher and Scorer	789 Crosslands Drive	Quebec	Management/General Consultancy	Canada
Letcher and Scorer	789 Crosslands Drive	Quebec	Software Development	Canada
Letcher and Scorer	3444 Longshore Boulevard	Victoria	Management/General Consultancy	Canada
Letcher and Scorer	3444 Longshore Boulevard	Victoria	Software Development	Canada

Figure 9.8 The correct result at last!

This will give the correct results and, while it is a rather long-winded approach, is the only way we know of to correctly resolve the problem using the view designer. Of course the solution is easily handled if you create the view definition in code. You can either use the standard SQL syntax as follows:

```
*** Standard Query Syntax
SELECT CU.cusname, AD.address, AD.city, BU.busdesc, RG.regdesc;
  FROM customer CU, address AD, bustype BU, region RG;
 WHERE AD.cuskey = CU.cussid ;
   AND BU.bussid = AD.buskey;
   AND RG.regsid = AD.regkey;
 ORDER BY cusname, city
```

or, if you prefer to use the ANSI 92 format, you can use 'sequential' joins, like this:

```
SELECT CU.cusname, AD.address, AD.city, BU.busdesc, RG.regdesc;
  FROM customer CU JOIN address AD ON AD.cuskey = CU.cussid ;
   JOIN bustype BU ON BU.bussid = AD.buskey ;
   JOIN region RG ON RG.regsid = AD.regkey ;
 ORDER BY cusname, city
```

These queries are included in *LkUpQry.prg* in the sample code, but if you want to use the nested join syntax, we are afraid you are on your own! While it may be possible, in certain situations, to get queries of this type to work using the nested join syntax, it is not worth the effort (unless you really like crossword puzzles). There are simpler, more reliable ways of handling the problem. Whichever approach you take, you will probably end up coding such views yourself rather than using the View Designer.

Creating parameterized views that require lists of parameters

Another major limitation of the view designer is that it cannot create a parameterized view that will correctly accept a list of parameters. In fact, the situation is even worse because although you can code such a parameterized view, you cannot specify the parameters through the dialog in a way that is meaningful to the SQL engine. The only solution that we have been able to find (to date) is to hand code the view and use macro substitution for the parameter. The SQL looks like this:

```
CREATE SQL VIEW lvCityList AS ;
  SELECT clicmpy, clicity, cliphon ;
    FROM clients ;
  WHERE INLIST( clicity, &?city_list )
```

When you open (USE) the view that this code creates, things look promising - the default dialog pops up asking for a value for '*city_list*'. So enter a list, but how? Well, the INLIST() function expects the values to be separated by commas, and each value has to be in quotation marks, so something like this should be just fine:

```
'London','Berlin','Stuttgart'
```

Clicking the dialog's "OK" button after entering this string, immediately raises Error 1231 ("*Missing operand*"). In fact *ANY* value that you enter causes this error and (obviously) the query does not populate the view. However, if you specify the same list of values and store them to the view parameter first, like this:

```
city_list = "'London','Berlin','Stuttgart'"
```

the view will function as required. To be perfectly honest, we are not sure why the dialog cannot be used to populate the parameter in this scenario, but clearly there is a problem with the way in which the entry from the default dialog is interpreted when the SQL is executed. The solution, if you require this functionality, is simply to avoid the View Designer and eschew (yet again) the default dialog for gathering parameters for the query.

A final word about the view designer
Let us repeat the warning we gave earlier about using the view designer. If you are using views you created in code, we strongly recommend that you name them differently from those that you create in the designer in order to avoid inadvertently modifying such a view visually. If you try and do so, the chances are that you will destroy your view completely because the designer will re-write the definition using the nested join syntax, which as we have already seen, may not be appropriate.

So is the designer really of any use? Yes, of course it is. For one thing it is much easier, even for a view that you know you will really have to code by hand, to use the designer to collect the relevant tables, get the selected field list, basic join conditions, filters and update criteria. Use the designer to create the view, but copy the SQL it produces into your own program file at the same time. Then use GenDBC.prg to get all the associated set-up code for the view and add that to your creation program too. Finally, edit the actual SQL to remove the nested joins and re-generate the view "correctly."

SQL in Visual FoxPro
Whether you are building database applications or middle-tier components, or are looking for a front end to a remote database, perhaps the most important reason for using Visual FoxPro is its integrated SQL engine. Many tools can use SQL, but few have the combination of a native database, embedded SQL Engine and GUI programming which makes Visual FoxPro so

flexible and powerful. In this section we will cover some of the things that we have learned (often the hard way) about using SQL. The sample code for this chapter includes a separate database (*SQLSAMP.DBC*) which contains the tables used in the examples for this section.

Joining tables *(Example ExJoins.prg)*

One of the most welcome changes in Visual FoxPro was the introduction, in Visual FoxPro 5.0, of support for a full set of joins. This effectively removed, for most developers, the necessity of fighting with the rather unwieldy (not to say downright persnickety) UNION command that previously had been the only way to manage anything other than a simple 'Inner Join'. We will, therefore, begin our discussion of using SQL with a brief review of the various join types that are available and the syntax for implementing them before we move on to other matters.

Table 9.1 (below) lists the four types of join that can be specified in SQL statements in Visual FoxPro. The basic syntax that must be used in all cases is:

```
SELECT <fields> FROM <table1> <JOIN TYPE> <table2> ON <condition>
```

Where <JOIN TYPE> may be any of those listed in the first column of the table:

Table 9.1 SQL Join Types in Visual FoxPro

Join Type	Includes in the result set
Inner Join	Only those records whose keys match in both tables
Left Outer Join	All records from the first table plus matching records from the second
Right Outer Join	Matching records from the first table plus all records from the second
Full Join	All records from both tables irrespective of whether any matches exist

The program *ExJoins.prg* runs the same simple query against the same pair of tables four times, using a different join condition each time. The actual results are shown in **Figure 9.9**, and the number of rows returned by each type of query was:

```
Full Join (top left):            14 Rows
Inner Join (bottom left):         9 Rows
Right Outer Join (top right):    10 Rows
Left Outer Join (bottom right): 13 Rows
```

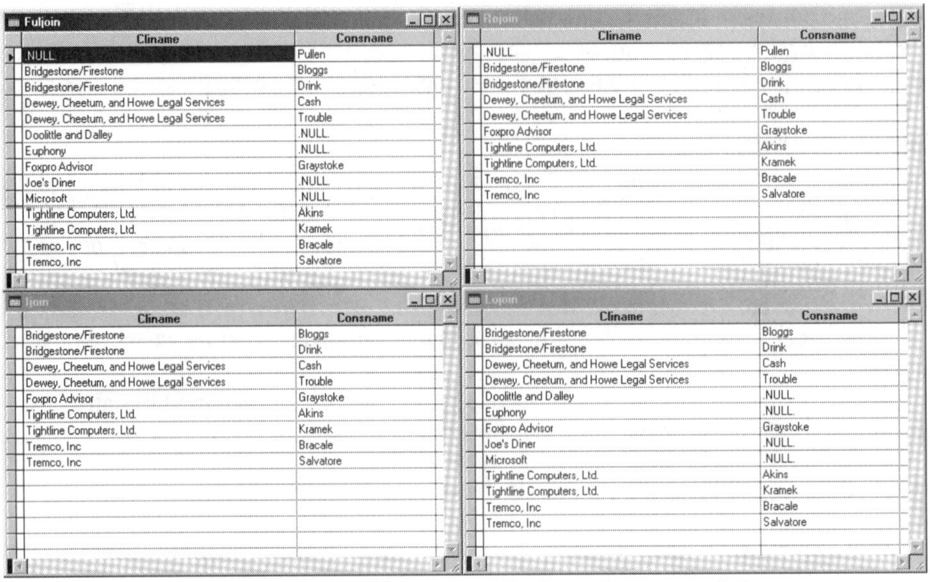

Figure 9.9 Different joins produce different results from the same data

Notice that with every condition, except the Inner Join, there is at least one row that contains a NULL value in at least one column. This is something that needs to be accounted for in code (or forms) which rely on either Outer or Full joins. As we have already mentioned, NULL values propagate themselves in Visual FoxPro and can cause unexpected results if their occurrence is not handled properly.

Constructing SQL queries

While there are usually at least two ways of doing things in Visual FoxPro, in this case there are three! You may use the 'standard' SQL syntax which uses a WHERE clause to specify both joins and filter conditions, or you can use the newer "ANSI 92" syntax which implements joins using the JOIN...ON clause and uses a WHERE clause to specify additional filters. The ANSI 92 syntax has two ways of specifying joins, either "sequential" or "nested" and they each have their advantages and disadvantages.

The following query uses standard SQL syntax to perform an inner join on three tables where the client name begins with the letter "D" and order the result:

```
SELECT CL.cliname, CO.consname, CO.confname, PH.phnnum, CO.conemail;
  FROM sqlcli CL, sqlcon CO, sqlpho PH ;
 WHERE CL.clisid = CO.clikey ;
   AND CO.consid = PH.conkey ;
   AND CL.cliname = "D" ;
 ORDER BY cliname, consname
```

Notice that there is no clear distinction between "join" and "filter" conditions. The equivalent query using "*sequential join*" syntax is a little clearer since the joins and their conditions are separated from the filter condition:

```
SELECT CL.cliname, CO.consname, CO.confname, PH.phnnum, CO.conemail ;
   FROM sqlcli CL ;
      INNER JOIN sqlcon CO ON CL.clisid = CO.clikey ;
      INNER JOIN sqlpho PH ON CO.consid = PH.conkey ;
   WHERE CL.cliname = "D" ;
   ORDER BY cliname, consname
```

The "*nested join*" format makes it even easier to separate the joins from their conditions. It is important to note that in this syntax, the joins and their conditions are processed from the outside in. Thus, in the following query, the first join to be processed adds the '*sqlcon*' table using the *last* '**on**' condition; the next to be processed adds '*sqlpho*' using the second-to-last '**on**' condition. Any additional joins would be processed in the same manner:

```
SELECT CL.cliname, CO.consname, CO.confname, PH.phnnum, CO.conemail;
   FROM sqlcli CL ;
      INNER JOIN sqlcon CO ;
         INNER JOIN sqlpho PH ;
         ON CO.consid = PH.conkey ;
      ON CL.clisid = CO.clikey;
   WHERE CL.cliname = "D";
   ORDER BY cliname, consname
```

Remember that all three of these queries actually produce the same results - the choice of style, in this case at least, is merely one of personal preference. However, while the style may not matter, the order in which you specify the joins definitely does matter as soon as you use either the nested, or the sequential join format. Changing the order in which the joins are specified can alter the result, and even prevent the query from running at all. (Reversing the sequence in the second illustration causes an '*Alias CO is not found*' error because the '*sqlcon*' table has not yet been joined to the query.) The standard syntax has the advantage in this respect because all necessary tables are specified first. The order in which the joins are listed does not affect the result, and you can even mix joins and filters without adversely affecting the outcome.

While the nested style is used to generate the SQL produced by the Visual FoxPro View and Query designers, we have already seen that there are some types of relationships that cannot easily be handled by this format. As far as we know, there are no conditions that the nested style can handle that the sequential style cannot and this is, therefore, our preferred style.

There is, however, one limitation to the implementation of the ANSI 92 syntax in Visual FoxPro. It is restricted to a maximum of nine joins. Now it may be just coincidence that Visual FoxPro also has a limit of nine UNIONs in a single SELECT statement. Or could it be that the way the syntax is actually implemented is by doing a union 'behind the scenes'? Either way, this limits the maximum number of tables that can be addressed to ten, but it is a limitation that, as far as we can determine, applies only if you use the join-based syntax.

How to Check the results of a query *(Example ChkQry.prg)*
How can we tell whether a SQL query has actually returned anything? After all, the query statement itself does not generate a return value. The answer is that there are several ways and

each has its advantages and disadvantages. Which one you actually use will depend on the type of query that you are running and the destination to which the output is directed.

Using Reccount()

Perhaps the most obvious thing to check is the record count of the output table or cursor. Visual FoxPro has a standard function, *RECCOUNT('AliasName')*, that returns the number of records in the specified record set without even having to select the work area (although the normal result of running a SQL query is to change work areas anyway). However, this is not an infallible guide for a number of reasons:

- RECCOUNT() always returns the number of physical records in a table, cursor or view. In other words it ignores the setting of the deleted flag on a record. The only time that RECCOUNT() changes is when a new record is added to the table or when the table is packed to remove deleted records.

- If the result of a query is a filtered view of the original data, RECCOUNT() returns the number of records in the underlying table (or cursor, or view) that has been queried. This particular problem can be avoided by forcing Visual FoxPro to always create a physical cursor for a query by including the NOFILTER clause.

- RECCOUNT() gets its information from the header of the table and does not actually perform a count of the number of records in the result set. While this is unlikely to be *wrong*, it may not give you the information that you need in every situation. For example, if you have records that contain only NULL values – is this really a valid result for a query?

- RECCOUNT() is only applicable if the output destination for the query is a cursor or table. If you are creating an array it is useless.

Using _TALLY

The second method for determining whether a query has returned anything is to use the system variable _TALLY. However, while it is certainly true that _TALLY will tell you how many records were returned by a query, it is important to remember that _TALLY is also set by a number of other commands. We are, once again, indebted to the tireless Tamar Granor and Ted Roche, and the '*Hackers Guide,*' for determining the definitive list of such commands:

Append From	Average	Blank	Calculate	Copy To
Copy To Array	Count	Delete	Delete-SQL	Export
Index	Pack	Recall	Reindex	Replace
Replace From Array	Select-SQL	Sort	Sum	Update-SQL

_TALLY does report the number of rows returned, irrespective of the output destination, but we must stress that it is only really reliable if tested immediately after the SQL query has been executed. Relying on it retaining its value is not safe and so, if you think you will need to know later what a particular query returned, always store the value to a variable immediately.

Two other cautions about using **_TALLY**. First, it will only tell you the number of records that qualified for inclusion in the result set. It does not mean that all records contain valid values. Second, if you are executing a query that includes a **COUNT()**, remember that such queries always return at least one record – even when the result is zero.

Using SELECT COUNT()

This is definitely the most reliable way of getting the number of records in a table or cursor. Moreover, there are two distinct ways of counting the records. By using **SELECT COUNT(*)**, you get the number of records irrespective of their contents (i.e. it is identical to **_TALLY**); but by specifying a particular field to count, you limit the result to include only those records where the specified field is not **NULL**.

However, like **RECCOUNT()**, this can only be used when a query directs its output to a physical cursor or table. If the result is a filtered view, the only way to use **SELECT COUNT()** is against the underlying table - and the result is, therefore, useless.

The test program (*ChkQry.prg*) shows the result of using **RECCOUNT()**, **_TALLY** and **SELECT COUNT()** in different situations. First, for a query involving an outer join that returns some records with **NULL** values. Second, by running the same query twice – once when it creates a filtered view and again to produce a physical cursor.

***Table 9.2** RECCOUNT(), _TALLY and SELECT COUNT() can differ!*

Query	Reccount()	_Tally	Count(*)	Count(<field>)
Outer Join - 13 Records, 4 with Nulls	13	13	13	9
Query produces a Filtered View (2 Records Qualify)	9	2	9	9
Repeat last query into a physical cursor (2 Records)	2	2	2	2

How to extend a SQL generated cursor

While SQL is normally thought of as providing a method for extracting data from an existing table or set of tables, it is perfectly possible to rename, or even create and populate, columns in a generated cursor. The method for doing so depends upon what you want as a result. The following sections illustrate some of the techniques that can be used to address different issues.

Defining new columns

The standard method for defining a new column is to include a constant value of the appropriate data type in the fields clause of a SELECT statement and use the 'AS' keyword to define a name for the column.

> *Note: In fact Visual FoxPro does not require the inclusion of the 'AS' keyword at all, nor do most back-end servers. In fact, some older versions of servers do not support the 'AS' keyword at all and including it in a query sent to such a back end causes an 'Invalid Column Name' error. Fortunately, the standard now seems to be that, even when not required, including 'AS' does not cause an error. There is no doubt that it does improve the readability of a query and its use is, we feel, amply justified on these grounds alone.*

The only possible *gotcha!* here is that when you specify the constants for the new columns you must ensure that you define large enough values for them to hold the data. For example, defining a new character column as "`SPACE(1)`" will do exactly that – create a column of type character with a width of one character. Similarly a column defined as "`0.0`" will create a numeric column whose definition is N (3,1), while simply specifying "`0`", rather than creating an integer data type, creates a numeric column of dimensions (1,0). Of course, for those data types (Currency, Date, DateTime and Logical) which are pre-defined, there is no issue. A full list of the standard data types and their appropriate initializing constants is given in **Table 9.3** below.

Table 9.3 Constants for initializing new columns

Data Type Required	Initialize With...
Character	SPACE(n)
Numeric	As many zeroes as needed, include decimal point if required
Currency	Either $0 or NTOM(0)
Logical	.T. or .F. as appropriate
Date	{} or a Date
DateTime	{/:} or DTOT({}) or a DateTime()
Other Data Types	Unconditionally join a cursor (or table) with just required field(s) and a single blank record

Adding a non standard data type

While you can define a constant value for all the basic data types supported by Visual FoxPro, there are no "constant" values for some of the other data types (e.g. memo, integer, float, double etc). The best solution that we know of is to create a dummy cursor which consists of a field (or fields) of the desired type and has a single record in it. This cursor can then be joined to the other tables used in a query and the result set will include an empty field of the appropriate type as illustrated below for Memo and Integer fields:

```
CREATE CURSOR memodummy ( memofield M(4), intfield I(4) )
APPEND BLANK IN memodummy

SELECT SQLCLI.*, MEMODUMMY.memofield AS CliNotes, MEMODUMMY.intfield AS CliInt
;
  FROM sqlcli ;
    JOIN memodummy ON 1=1;
  INTO CURSOR CurMemTest
```

Notice that, because we are using the JOIN...ON syntax, we must specify an ON condition. In this case we wish every record in the output set to have the extra fields, so we have specified a condition that always evaluates to TRUE. (Why not just use "=.T."? In case we need to communicate with a back end server that does not support logical fields. Any SQL engine will interpret "WHERE 1=1" as TRUE and "WHERE 0=1" as FALSE). Using the standard SQL syntax, no such trickery is needed and the equivalent SELECT is simply:

```
SELECT SQLCLI.*, MEMODUMMY.memofield AS CliNotes, MEMODUMMY.intfield AS CliInt
;
    FROM sqlcli, memodummy ;
    INTO CURSOR memtest
```

Making a SQL generated cursor updateable

If you are adding empty fields to a SQL generated cursor, it is presumably because you want to insert some values into them. However, the cursor generated as the result of a SQL query is always Read-Only. The simplest way to make such a cursor updateable is to issue a USE DBF('cursor alias') AGAIN. But this will only work as long the cursor is not merely a filtered view of the underlying data. Adding a NOFILTER clause to a SQL ensures that Visual FoxPro must create a physical cursor for the result set and not merely generate a filtered view. The following example creates an updateable cursor containing both fields from the source table and a new column:

```
SELECT SQLCLI.*, SPACE(12) AS NewField ;
    FROM sqlcli ;
    INTO CURSOR junk NOFILTER

USE DBF('junk') AGAIN IN 0 ALIAS UpdCur
USE IN junk
SELECT updCur
```

Concatenating character fields *(Example: concat.prg)*

Unfortunately, there is no easy way to concatenate character fields in a SQL Query. In reports, you can use commas to trim fields that need to be concatenated (and semi colons to add line breaks) but that will not work in a query. The nearest that Visual FoxPro has to an "operator" to concatenate two strings is the minus sign ("-"). However, this merely trims trailing spaces from the first field and appends the entire second field (untrimmed) to the result. Thus, given two fields defined as Character (10), the result will be as follows:

```
F1 => "Fred      "
F2 => "Smith     "
(F1-F2) => "FredSmith      "
```

which is not exactly what we would normally want. The only realistic alternative is to use explicit trimming functions around the fields to be concatenated and to include any necessary punctuation or spaces explicitly in the SELECT. So to generate a normal looking name field from the two fields above we would need to do one of the following:

```
SELECT ( ALLTRIM(F1) + " " + ALLTRIM(F2) ) AS FullName
SELECT ( ALLTRIM(F2) + ", " + ALLTRIM(F1) ) AS SortName
```

Not very elegant, but effective. There is, however, one *gotcha!* lying in wait here. If one of the fields is **NULL**, the concatenated result is also **NULL**. We are at a loss to explain this behavior. After all, trying to concatenate a character field with a **NULL** normally raises a "data type mismatch" error. We cannot see why merely adding an **ALLTRIM()** should change this behavior, but it does, and it can be very tricky to debug when it happens. The following program creates a result set that should contain a formatted string consisting of company name and a contact name:

```
********************************************************************
* Program....: ConCat.prg
* Compiler...: Visual FoxPro 06.00.8492.00 for Windows
* Abstract...: Illustrate the problem of concatenating character strings
* ..........: When one or other contains NULL values
********************************************************************

*** Generate a cursor containing NULL values for consname
SELECT CL.cliname, CO.consname ;
  FROM sqlcli CL ;
    LEFT OUTER JOIN sqlcon CO ;
    ON CO.clikey = CL.clisid ;
    ORDER BY cliname, consname ;
  INTO CURSOR lojoin

*** Create a Formatted output
SELECT ( ALLTRIM( cliname ) + " CONTACT: " + ALLTRIM( consname ) ) ;
  FROM lojoin ;
  INTO CURSOR Formatted NOFILTER
```

The result set from the first query looks like this:

Cliname	Consname
Bridgestone/Firestone	Bloggs
Bridgestone/Firestone	Drink
Dewey, Cheetum, and Howe Legal Services	Cash
Dewey, Cheetum, and Howe Legal Services	Trouble
Doolittle and Dalley	.NULL.
Euphony	.NULL.
Foxpro Advisor	Graystoke
Joe's Diner	.NULL.
Microsoft	.NULL.
Tightline Computers, Ltd.	Akins
Tightline Computers, Ltd.	Kramek
Tremco, Inc	Bracale
Tremco, Inc	Salvatore

Figure 9.10 *Intermediate result set*

But the second looks like this:

Formatted
Bridgestone/Firestone CONTACT: Bloggs
Bridgestone/Firestone CONTACT: Drink
Dewey, Cheetum, and Howe Legal Services CONTACT: Cash
Dewey, Cheetum, and Howe Legal Services CONTACT: Trouble
.NULL.
.NULL.
Foxpro Advisor CONTACT: Graystoke
.NULL.
.NULL.
Tightline Computers, Ltd. CONTACT: Akins
Tightline Computers, Ltd. CONTACT: Kramek
Tremco, Inc CONTACT: Bracale
Tremco, Inc CONTACT: Salvatore

Figure 9.11 *Final result set - complete with NULL values*

Notice that the **NULL** values have propagated through into the final result set! This is yet another example of how important it has become, in Visual FoxPro, to be aware of the possibility of **NULL** values appearing as the result of using Outer Joins. Fortunately, the solution is fairly simple. We only need to modify the second select to substitute an empty character string if either value is **NULL**, and the **NVL()** function does this for us:

```
*** Create a Formatted output
SELECT ( ALLTRIM( NVL(cliname,"") ) + " CONTACT: " ;
       + ALLTRIM( NVL( consname,"") ) ) ) ;
  FROM lojoin ;
  INTO CURSOR Formatted NOFILTER
```

This modified version will, at least, ensure that we see all of the company names, which is precisely why we used a left outer join in the first place.

Performing calculations *(Example: SQLCalc.prg)*
We often need to perform calculations on data that we extract using queries, so the question arises as to whether it is better to do such calculations as part of the query or to post-process the result set and do the calculations outside. There is no hard and fast answer but, if the calculation is relatively simple, and the data set to be processed is not too large, the overhead on the query should not be significant. The problem with post processing a query is that you will need to make the result set read/write, so there are actually three steps involved - the initial query, creating the read/write cursor and the process itself. The only real solution is to try it both ways in each case and see which works best in your particular situation.

Performing calculations in the query is not difficult, although you need to remember a couple of basic rules. First, the field that will store the result of the calculation should be named and formatted appropriately. Second, you cannot refer to a calculated field in either the field list or filter conditions. Any such reference will generate an error. The following **SELECT** clause is, therefore, invalid:

```
SELECT SUM( invamt ) AS totalinv, ;
       SUM( invpaid ) AS totalpaid, ;
       (totalinv - totalpaid) AS invbal ;
```

Conditionally including fields in a result set

The Visual FoxPro *Immediate IF* function (IIF()) can be used in a query to conditionally extract data from either of two fields into a single field. However, there is an overhead associated with this and the significance of that overhead will depend upon the nature of the condition and the number of records to be processed because the test will be applied to every record. As with performing calculations, the only way to tell if this is going to be a problem is to test thoroughly on realistic volumes of data.

The syntax for using it is exactly as you would expect. The following SELECT gets the content of one or other of two fields, depending on the value of a third:

```
SELECT IIF(type = "Residential", ResidenceCode, BusinessCode ) AS Type
```

Converting fields from one data type to another *(Example: SQLConv.prg)*

A very common requirement is to extract data from a database in some other format, usually as text for transferring to another application. Visual FoxPro has always provided a number of functions that can handle the conversion from various data types to their character string equivalents (STR(), DTOC() and so on). These can be used in queries to convert data from its original type into the appropriate character string.

Visual FoxPro Version 6.0 added new functionality to the TRANSFORM() function so that if used on an expression, WITHOUT specifying any formatting codes, a default conversion of the data to its string equivalent is performed. This greatly simplifies the task of converting data into character strings and is a welcome change indeed. For full details of this function's capabilities (and limitations) see the online Help File, but the basic functionality for creating a cursor which contains only character data from a table can now be provided very easily as follows:

```
*** Extract raw Customer/Invoice Information
SELECT  TRANSFORM( CL.cliname ) AS cliname, ;
        TRANSFORM( IN.invdate ) AS invdate, ;
        TRANSFORM( IN.invamt  ) AS invamt, ;
        TRANSFORM( IN.invpaid ) AS payment, ;
        TRANSFORM( invamt - invpaid ) AS invbal ;
   FROM sqlcli CL ;
     JOIN sqlinv IN ON IN.clikey = CL.clisid ;
   ORDER BY cliname ;
   INTO CURSOR curNumeric
```

Notice that the TRANSFORM() has converted the values to integers and formatted the field sizes accordingly which produces a cursor with the following structure:

```
CLINAME    Character   40
INVDATE    Character    8
INVAMT     Character    3
PAYMENT    Character    3
```

```
INVBAL       Character    1
```

Unfortunately it is *WRONG!* This is a common *gotcha!* that can trip you up whenever you allow Visual FoxPro to determine the size of a field which is created in a result set. Visual FoxPro *always* bases the field sizing on the first value it retrieves and then dumps all other data into the same field - in this case truncating the data to make it fit. So we have actually lost data here because the first invoice processed happened to have a balance of 0.00 which, after being transformed, results in a single character "0", in turn determining the width of the generated column. The very next record should have a balance of 622.00, but it now shows up as "6."

Similarly, if we wanted to convert the data into, say, currency format we could simply wrap an **NTOM()** function around each expression. But this would produce a cursor with the following structure:

```
CLINAME      Character    40
INVDATE      Character    8
INVAMT       Character    7
PAYMENT      Character    7
INVBAL       Character    5
```

This time the "invbal" field gets sized to 5 characters because that is the length required to store the first value that is calculated (now a transformed currency value "*£0.00*") and, once again we lose data in any other record where the balance exceeds "£9.99."

The obvious solution is to provide the appropriate formatting for the **TRANSFORM()** function; but in fact, in a SQL, query the **PADL()** function is the better option for two reasons. Like **TRANSFORM()**, it will convert any of the standard data types to their character equivalents. More importantly, it allows you to define the size of the resulting string and forces Visual FoxPro to size its generated column accordingly. So if we re-write the SQL above as follows:

```
*** Use PADL() instead of transform to get the 'right' results
SELECT   PADL( CL.cliname, 40 ) AS cliname, ;
         PADL( IN.invdate, 10 ) AS invdate, ;
         PADL( IN.invamt,  10 ) AS invamt, ;
         PADL( IN.invpaid, 10 ) AS payment, ;
         PADL( invamt - invpaid, 10 ) AS invbal ;
   FROM sqlcli CL ;
     JOIN sqlinv IN ON IN.clikey = CL.clisid ;
   ORDER BY cliname ;
   INTO CURSOR curCorrect
```

We get a cursor whose structure is appropriate for the task in hand:

```
CLINAME      Character    40
INVDATE      Character    10
INVAMT       Character    10
PAYMENT      Character    10
INVBAL       Character    10
```

> *Of course, there are many other ways of converting data into a text file. One that we really like (although it is only useful for files that are required in SDF format) is to make use of the new* STRTOFILE() *function in conjunction with the VFP application object's* DataToClip *method as follows:*

*** *Open a table*
USE <table>
*** *Copy contents to clipboard*
_cliptext = _VFP.DataToClip()
*** *Create a text file*
STRTOFILE(_cliptext, '<output file name>')

How to check your query's optimization *(Example: SQLShow.prg)*

The Visual FoxPro SYS(3054) function enables the nearest equivalent that we have to a "showplan" tool for checking the optimization of a query. While it is somewhat limited (for example its only display option is direct to the current output window), it can provide you with a lot of very useful information about the way Visual FoxPro sees your queries. The quickest way to get the output of SYS(3054) into a usable form is to use SET ALTERNATE to echo all screen output to a file of your choosing, as follows:

```
SET ALTERNATE TO showplan.txt
SET ALTERNATE ON
```

If you are running a program, you can also suppress the on-screen output using SET CONSOLE OFF (but this has no effect if you are just executing code from the command window). When finished, cancel the echoing of the output using:

```
SET ALTERNATE OFF
SET ALTERNATE TO
```

The SYS(3054) function has two levels of display determined by the parameter passed in the function call. The first level (parameter = 1) shows the utilization of indexes on tables and indicates the Rushmore Optimization for each table involved in the query as either None, Partial or Full. The following program (*SQLShow.prg*) shows how it works:

```
**********************************************************************
* Program....: SQLShow.prg
* Compiler...: Visual FoxPro 06.00.8492.00 for Windows
* Abstract...: Illustrate the use of VFP ShowPlan reporting
*■■■■■■■■■■■■■■■■■■■■■■■■■■■■■■■■■■■■■■■■■■■■■■■■■■■■■■■■■■■■■■■■■■■■■■■■

*** Enable Showplan reporting
SYS(3054,1)    && Actually returns "1" indicating Level 1 reporting is enabled

*** Disable screen and direct output to file
SET CONSOLE OFF
SET ALTERNATE TO showplan.txt
SET ALTERNATE ON
*** We need deleted ON to see the results
```

```
lcOldDel = SET( 'DELETED')
SET DELETED ON

*** Execute the query
SELECT CL.cliname, CO.consname ;
  FROM sqlcli CL ;
    JOIN sqlcon CO ON CO.clikey = CL.clisid ;
    ORDER BY cliname, consname ;
  INTO CURSOR ijoin

*** Restore settings
SET CONSOLE ON
SET ALTERNATE OFF
SET ALTERNATE TO
SET DELETED &lcOldDel

*** Turn off showplan reporting
SYS(3054,0)
```

This produces the following (unformatted) output in *showplan.txt*:

```
Using index tag Isdel to rushmore optimize table cl
Rushmore optimization level for table cl: full

Using index tag Isdel to rushmore optimize table co
Rushmore optimization level for table co: full
```

The second level (parameter = 11) shows both the index utilization for the table and also for any joins involved in the query. Using this option, the above query produces the following output:

```
Using index tag Isdel to rushmore optimize table cl
Rushmore optimization level for table cl: full

Using index tag Isdel to rushmore optimize table co
Rushmore optimization level for table co: full

Joining table cl and table co using index tag clikey
```

This tells us is that we have a "fully optimized" query. Both tables have an index on *DELETED()* and we are running with **DELETED = ON** (see the next section for more details on the role of **DELETED**), so the individual tables are both Rushmore optimizable. In addition, there is an existing index on the field used in the join condition. However, if we were to add a filter condition to the query (for example: **WHERE** consname = "A" **AND** confname = "B"), the results would now look like this:

```
Using index  tag Isdel to rushmore optimize  table cl
Rushmore optimization level for   table cl: full

Using index  tag Consname  to rushmore optimize  table co
Using index  tag Isdel to rushmore optimize  table co
Rushmore optimization level for   table co: partial

Joining table co and table cl using index  tag Clisid
```

Notice that the table '*co*' is now only partially optimized because, although there is an index on '*consname*' that can be used for the first part of the filter condition, there is no corresponding index that can be used for the second.

Things get a little more complex when more than two tables are involved, but the information is still very revealing. Consider the following query (the actual results don't matter for now):

```
SELECT CL.cliname, CO.consname,  PH.phnnum, SI.Invdate ;
  FROM sqlcli CL ;
    JOIN sqlcon CO ON CO.clikey = CL.clisid;
    JOIN sqlpho PH ON PH.conkey = CO.consid;
    JOIN  sqlinv SI ON SI.clikey = CL.clisid ;
  ORDER BY cliname, consname ;
  INTO CURSOR ijoin
```

When this is executed, showplan gives us the following report:

```
Using index tag Isdel to rushmore optimize table cl
Rushmore optimization level for table cl: full

Using index tag Isdel to rushmore optimize table co
Rushmore optimization level for table co: full

Using index tag Isdel to rushmore optimize table ph
Rushmore optimization level for table ph : full

Using index tag Isdel to rushmore optimize table si
Rushmore optimization level for table si: full

Joining table cl and table si using index tag Clikey
Joining intermediate result and table co using index tag Clikey
Joining intermediate result and table ph using index tag Conkey
```

The first few lines are similar to what we have been seeing already, but it is the join information we are really interested in. We can now see the sequence that Visual FoxPro is actually using to join the tables. In this case, it first joins '*SI*' (invoices) to '*CL*' (clients) and then adds '*CO*' (contacts) and finally '*PH*' (phone numbers). Normally you can safely allow Visual FoxPro to determine how best to join the tables, but just occasionally it will get it wrong (or at least, join them in a way that does not give you the results that you wanted). In these situations, we can use the additional 'FORCE' keyword in the FROM clause to ensure that Visual FoxPro runs the query exactly as we defined it. For example, amending the example query to force the join sequence:

```
SELECT CL.cliname, CO.consname,  PH.phnnum, SI.Invdate ;
  FROM FORCE sqlcli CL ;
    JOIN sqlcon CO ON CO.clikey = CL.clisid;
    JOIN sqlpho PH ON PH.conkey = CO.consid;
    JOIN  sqlinv SI ON SI.clikey = CL.clisid ;
  ORDER BY cliname, consname ;
  INTO CURSOR ijoin
```

produces the following results from showplan, and confirms that Visual FoxPro has indeed done what we asked for:

```
Using index tag Isdel to rushmore optimize table cl
Rushmore optimization level for table cl: full
Using index tag Isdel to rushmore optimize table co
Rushmore optimization level for table co: full
Joining table cl and table co using index tag Clikey

Rushmore optimization level for intermediate result: none
Using index tag Isdel to rushmore optimize table ph
Rushmore optimization level for table ph: full
Joining intermediate result and table ph using index tag Conkey

Rushmore optimization level for intermediate result: none
Using index tag Isdel to rushmore optimize table si
Rushmore optimization level for table si: full
Joining intermediate result and table si using index tag Clikey
```

So when should we actually use showplan? The glib answer is, of course, always! However, in practice it should be the first thing you check in two situations:

- When you find yourself wondering why a query is taking longer than expected

- When a query returns unexpected results

The effect of DELETED() on SQL

This is perhaps one of the least understood aspects of Visual FoxPro's SQL engine. While the details of the way in which Rushmore optimization actually works are still a closely guarded secret, the essential fact is that Rushmore relies on indexes in order to speed up the selection of data. The most significant factor is the way in which it handles records marked for deletion.

When you run Visual FoxPro with deleted set to **ON,** you are telling it to ignore any record which is marked for deletion, but how is it to find out which records are marked for deletion? The answer is that, unless you have an index that specifically includes those records, it has to check each and every record individually - even if you have no records marked for deletion. This is a comparatively slow operation and is probably the single most common cause of poor SQL performance in applications. The solution is simple, include a specific index on DELETED().

Running with deleted set **OFF** avoids the need for an index on DELETED(), but means that you may have to explicitly include an additional filter in your queries (i.e. **WHERE** ! DELETED()) if your tables can contain deleted records. However, this will result in only 'partial' optimization of your queries and may give you a worse performance than using an index on DELETED(), and setting DELETED = ON, even though you never have any deleted records.

However, creating an index on DELETED() is not, itself, the universal panacea - especially when large tables are involved. This is because whenever you access a table, (whether with an explicit USE command, or through a query) Visual FoxPro looks for, and loads into memory, the index on DELETED(). If you are running over a network this can be a long job for very large

tables and, in such circumstances, it is usually better not to have an index on DELETED().
Unfortunately there are no hard and fast rules about this, and the only real advice we can offer
is to try things out in your own environment to determine the optimum combination of indexes
and the setting of DELETED.

So what indexes should I create?
Unfortunately there are no 'easy' answers to this question. As you will have realized from the
preceding sections, the role of indexes on tables is crucial when we are considering SQL in
Visual FoxPro. While it is impossible to be absolutely prescriptive about this, there are a few
basic guidelines, but be prepared to amend them as a result of testing things with your own
data in your own operational environment.

The first one is that you should always create an index on the primary key field of your
tables - even if this is not defined as a "primary key" in your database. If you are not already
using surrogate keys (and why not?) you should still create an index on whatever field, or
combinations of fields, uniquely identify a record. If nothing else you will need this in order to
be able to join the table efficiently in queries.

Secondly, consider creating an index on DELETED(). While this will undoubtedly speed up
queries when you run Visual FoxPro with DELETED = ON, it may have an undesirable impact on
performance in other areas (e.g. loading forms), especially if your tables are very large. As
always, test in your own environment.

Thirdly, create indexes for any fields on which you will normally be conducting searches,
or setting filters. This will allow Rushmore to optimize both table joins and filter conditions
properly and will vastly improve the performance of your queries. Remember that the index
expression should exactly match the one that you will use in specifying the search or filter
condition. So, if you are adding an index on 'surname', but will normally be filtering for
"UPPER(surname)," then create the index on "UPPER(surname)" also.

*The presence of indexes whose keys are not defined in exactly the
same terms that are used when querying the tables is probably the
second most common cause of poor performance in SQL, but is one
that is easily picked up by using showplan. You will know that you have fallen foul
of this when you see a result showing partial optimization for a query that should
return full optimization because you know that there IS an index on the field in
question.*

Fourthly, avoid creating conditional indexes (i.e. those which use 'FOR <condition>') or
indexes based on inequality (i.e. those which use a 'NOT <condition>'). Rushmore cannot use
indexes of either type and simply ignores them. If you need them for other reasons, then create
both the required index and a simple index on the field. (This, too, is easily detected using
showplan.)

Finally, avoid inverting your tables. Your initial reaction to this question may be that it
would be safest to simply create an index on every field in the table – after all you never know
what you may want to search on do you? This is, however, usually a bad move, especially in
tables which have high levels of activity (whether Inserts, Updates or Deletions) because you
are forcing Visual FoxPro to maintain a large number of indexes with every transaction on the

table. This can significantly affect performance and, as always, there is a trade-off between performance in one area and performance in another.

Which is better for updating tables, SQL or native FoxPro commands?

This is a complex question and the answer depends on the type of update and the nature of the table. The best solution also varies depending on whether you are adding new records or updating existing data.

SQL INSERT vs APPEND

Generally speaking **SQL INSERT** will give better performance because it requires only a single update of any indexes associated with the table. When adding records to a table, Visual FoxPro has to update the table header and update any indexes with new values based on what has been added. Using **INSERT** is more efficient because it requires only one operation. The new record and its values are added simultaneously and the indexes updated.

However, in order to achieve this you must have all information available when the insert is performed and this is not always possible (e.g. when adding blank records through a data entry form). In this situation, especially if tables are buffered, it makes little practical difference how you actually add the record.

SQL UPDATE/DELETE vs REPLACE/DELETE

The answer here depends on how many records need to be updated. For single record updates, especially where the record is already selected and immediately available, we would tend to stick with the **REPLACE/DELETE** commands. In fact, even when the required record is not immediately available, it is usually better to use a **SEEK** and **REPLACE/DELETE** strategy rather than the SQL equivalent. The reason is simply that the SQL commands require a **WHERE** clause and must check the entire table (or at least the indexes) to ensure that there is not more than one record being specified. Conversely the default scope for the native Visual FoxPro commands is always the current record (i.e. **NEXT 1**) and so, for single record updates or deletions, it is usually quicker.

When we have to update multiple records, the situation is different. Both **REPLACE** and **DELETE** can take a conditional scope (i.e. **FOR <condition>**). This puts them into the same category as the SQL commands with their **WHERE** clause and the same rules will apply. Providing that the condition is optimizable, Visual FoxPro will use Rushmore in both situations and the difference will be insignificant. However, when the condition is not optimizable, the SQL commands will usually give a slightly better performance. The answer, as always, is to test individual cases and decide on their merits.

Conclusion

The whole question of using SQL in Visual FoxPro, whether directly or in views, is dependent upon so many factors that it is very difficult to be prescriptive about any aspect of it. The golden rule is to plan your table structures and indexes properly and to test, test and re-test your solutions in as many different ways as possible. Use **SYS(3054)** to confirm that what you expect is what is really happening, and be prepared for a few surprises when you do.

Chapter 10
Non-Visual Classes

"Delight at having understood a very abstract and obscure system leads most people to believe in the truth of what it demonstrates." (Aphorisms "Notebook J" by G. C. Lichtenberg)

The ability to define our own classes in Visual FoxPro is one of the most powerful features of the language. It allows us to create tools that can be re-used in a wide variety of circumstances and, because they are created as classes, also allows us to extend or modify their standard behaviors when requirements change in specific applications. That we can also create classes in code opens up a whole new realm of possibilities for developing standard approaches to common problems. In this chapter we explore some of the non-visual classes which we have developed to make our lives easier when writing Visual FoxPro applications. While not designed specifically as 'framework' classes, much of the functionality described in these classes would typically fall into the scope of an application framework.

How can I make use of INI files? *(Example: INIMAINT.SCX)*

While there is an increasing tendency to use the Windows Registry for storing data which relates to an application, the older *INI* file still offers several advantages for the application developer. First, it is simply a text file that can be stored locally on a client machine to hold user-specific information. This is a major benefit because it makes it easy to manipulate - whether you do so programmatically or with any available text editor. Second, because it can be located in an application's home directory, it is easy to remove if the application has to be removed from a machine, and is easy to replace if it inadvertently gets deleted. Third, it is possible to instruct even a novice user in how to correct errors or add new items to an INI file if necessary - even over the telephone if necessary.

While the registry provides a good home for information that is required 'system-wide' because it is automatically available to Windows applications, it is neither developer, nor user-friendly. It is tricky, not to say dangerous, to manipulate programmatically and uninstalling an application completely is much more difficult when entries have to be located in, and deleted from, the registry. Furthermore we would be very nervous about giving an experienced user (let alone a novice) access to their machine's registry - and the prospect of coaching a user, by telephone, to edit the registry is one which frankly, we find terrifying! Finally, if the information to be stored is purely application specific, and is accessed by nothing except the application, we can see no reason for **not** storing it with the application.

Overview

The *INI* File manager is a class that is designed to provide a seamless handling of .*INI* files (or any other text-based file that respects the *INI* file format). An *INI* file is a structured text file ("*STF*") which consists of a series of Section Headings (there must always be at least one of these) delimited with "*[ ]*" and then Item and Value pairings which include an "=". All data is held as character strings in *INI* files and, although there is a limitation of 64k on the size of an *INI* file, most applications are unlikely to get anywhere near this. A typical file might look something like:

```
Name: SYSTEM.INI

[SYSTEM]
NAME=SomeSystem
COPYRIGHT=Tightline Computers Ltd

[CONSTANTS]
STANDARDRATE=17.50
CONCESSIONRATE=15.00
UTILITYRATE=8.50
```

The key purpose of an *INI* file is to provide a means of storing information required by an application without having to resort to using a data table. Since an *INI* file is a simple text file, the information in it can be updated or amended by an end user using any text editor.

Windows provides a number of API functions that can access and write to *INI* files, but like all such functions, they are relatively complex. The manager is an example of a "Wrapper Class" which provides basic management functions for *INI* files, while also offering a more developer friendly interface to these API functions.

The *INI* file manager exposes six methods in its public interface, which are described in detail below. It is designed to be instantiated as a system level object – although it could be created as a transient object if required or as a component of an "Application Object". Almost all functionality in the *INI* File Manager is internal, the exceptions are that it requires some Visual FoxPro functions which, prior to Version 6.0 were only available in the FoxTools library. If this class is to be used with an earlier version of Visual FoxPro, a modification will be needed to the "*ChkFileName()*" method to load the library if it is not already present in memory.

Initializing the manager

There are two ways of creating the manager object. You can either load the class definition as a procedure file (which would be the best approach if the manager is to be created as a transient object), or you can run the program directly and create the manager as a global object. (This will create the reference to the manager as a PUBLIC variable but does not load the file into memory as a procedure.)

Whichever way is used, the initialization process takes an optional parameter which is the name of the *INI* file to be used as the default file by the manager. Internal checking processes will format this name into a fully qualified file name with the default extension "INI" and the default path of the current drive and directory. However, specific paths or other extensions will be respected if supplied.

Table 10.1 Creating the INI file manager object

Creating the Manager as a global object	Creating the Manager as a transient object
RELEASE goIniMgr	DO iniproc WITH <inifile>
PUBLIC goIniMgr	RELEASE goIniMgr
SET PROCEDURE TO iniproc ADDITIVE	
GoIniMgr = CREATEOBJECT('iniproc', <inifile>)	

If the file passed as the default file cannot be located on the specified path or on the default path, it will be created with a single section that is named the same as the file. Thus the setup command:

```
goIniMgr = CREATEOBJECT( 'inimgr', 'c:\testing\nosuch.txt')
```

will result (given the appropriate permissions and file creation rights) in the creation of a file named "*NOSUCH.TXT*" in the "*C:\TESTING*" directory containing simply the section header "*[NOSUCH]*" because, as noted in the introduction, an *INI* file always requires at least one header section.

The nocreate option

The class can accept a second, logical, parameter that is used to determine whether a new *INI* file should be created if a specified file is not found. The setting, initialized at start up, is held in a protected property and when explicitly set to .T., prevents the *INI* File Manager from attempting to create a file when the requested file is not found. Thus:

```
goIniMgr = CREATEOBJECT( 'inimgr', 'c:\testing\nosuch.txt', .T.)
```

will still instantiate the manager object and set the default file property, but it does **not** create the requested file if it does not already exist.

The default file

The *INI* Manager maintains an internal collection of file names that it recognizes and also keeps one of these files registered as the default file. When any read or write method is called, data will be read from or written to the default file, unless a specific file is passed as part of the instruction. The purpose of the default file is simply to avoid the necessity of having to keep passing and validating the file name of the same *INI* file since, normally, applications will use only a single *INI* file.

However, the *INI* Manager has the capability to query a specific file without actually changing the default setting (for example to read a specific value from a System *INI* or *STF* file) and to change whichever file is registered as default at any time.

File registration

The *INI* Manager uses an internal registration procedure to ensure that all file names passed to it are properly qualified with full path and extension. If no path is passed, the current working drive and directory are assumed, and if no extension is included the file is assumed to have an '.INI' extension. Although defaults are assigned to replace missing items of data, the *INI* manager will respect any path or extension information that is passed to it.

The public interface

The *INI* Manager public interface is extremely simple. There are only six methods that can be accessed and the manager has no exposed properties at all. The individual methods, and examples of how they may be used, are discussed in the following sections.

GetIniFile()

The *GetIniFile()* method takes no parameters and simply returns the name of whichever file the *INI* Manager is currently defining as the default file. If no file is registered, *GetIniFile()* returns an empty character string.

Examples:

This method can be called as part of a test to ensure that a file is registered:

```
IF EMPTY( goIniMgr.GetIniFile() )
    *** No INI File is defined
ENDIF
```

Alternatively the fully qualified file name of the current default file can be retrieved into a variable, or the return value can be used in a **REPLACE** or **UPDATE** statement. The following command simply displays the name of the currently registered *INI* file on screen:

```
? goIniMgr.GetIniFile()
```

SetIniFile()

The *SetIniFile()* method is used to set a specific *INI* file as the default target for Read/Write operations or to create a new *INI* file and set it as the default for future use. The method takes a single parameter – the name of a file – and sets that file as the new Default File for use by the Manager object. The return value is numeric as and will have one of three possible values:

- -1 Error in Input Parameters
- 0 Unable to Register the File
- 1 Specified File is Set as Default

If the file whose name is supplied does not exist on the specified (or default) path, the *INI* Manager will create the file and assign it a single section named the same as the file name, and make the new file the Default file.

Examples:
To set the standard Windows 'WIN.INI' file as the default file:

```
lnSuccess = goIniMgr.SetIniFile( 'C:\WINDOWS\WIN.INI' )
```

To set an *INI* file in the current working directory as the default file:

```
lnSuccess = goIniMgr.SetIniFile( 'eusys' )
```

To create a new file using *INI* file format in a specific location and set it as default:

```
lnSuccess = goIniMgr.SetIniFile( 'G:\DEV\SYSTEM\WORK.STF' )
```

GetValue(<Section>, <Item> [,<file>])

The *GetValue()* method returns the value stored for a specified item from the specified section of a file which observes the standard *INI* file format. The method takes two mandatory parameters (the name of the Section, and the name of the Item) and an optional third (the file to use). If the third parameter is omitted, the current default file is assumed.

The return value will always be of type character and will either be the specified value or an empty string. This method does not return an error value under any circumstances. Thus if either the Section or the Item name do not exist, or if the combination of Section and Item is invalid, an empty string is all is that is returned. Similarly if a parameter is omitted or invalid, an empty string is returned.

Examples:
To retrieve the value from the current default file of the 'Name' item in the 'System' section:

```
lcName = goIniMgr.GetValue( 'SYSTEM', 'NAME' )
```

To retrieve the name of the ODBC driver set up for reading FoxPro tables to the clipboard:

```
_ClipText = goinimgr.getvalue( 'FOXPRO FILES', 'DRIVER32',
'c:\windows\odbc.ini' )
```

 Note: Retrieving a value from a file other than the default file does not change the default file setting. The only way to change the default file setting is through the SetIniFile() method.

SetValue(<Section>, <Item>, <Value> [,<file>])

The *SetValue()* method writes the specified value to the Item and Section specified. If either the Section or Item do not already exist in the specified file, the appropriate entries are created otherwise existing values are simply overwritten. All of the parameters, including the value, must be passed as character strings but parameters are not case sensitive. The usual rules governing character strings apply, and FoxPro conversion functions may be embedded in the method call as normal.

SetValue() returns a numeric value as one of:

- -1 Error in Input Parameters

-    0 Unable to write to the specified file

-    1 Value Written successfully

Examples:
To set the value of the DATE Item in the System Section of the default file:

```
lnSuccess = goIniMgr.SetValue( 'SYSTEM', 'DATE', DMY(DATE()) )
```

To create a new Item in the system section of the default file:

```
lnSuccess = goIniMgr.SetValue( 'SYSTEM', 'newitem', 'newvalue' )
```

To create a new Section and Item in the default file:

```
IF goIniMgr.SetValue( 'NewSection', 'NewItem', 'somevalue' ) > 0
   *** Entries written successfully
ENDIF
```

Note: SetValue() will NOT create a new file if the specified file does not already exist or if there is no default file registered. In these situations the return value will always be 0.

ReadIniFile(<@ArrayName> [,<file>])

The *ReadIniFile()* method reads an entire *INI* file into a two-column array (which must be created in the calling routine and passed by *reference*). The array will always be correctly dimensioned for the values that are found in the *INI* file. The first column of the array contains the names of Section headings (including their '*[]*' delimiters) or Items, while the second column contains the delimiting symbols '*[]*' for Section headings or the actual values for Items.

ReadIniFile() returns a numeric value indicating the number of valid lines which were read into the target array. If no file name is passed as a parameter, the default file is assumed.

Example:
To read the entire contents of the default file into the array `laData`:

```
LOCAL ARRAY laData[1]
IF goIniMgr.ReadIniFile( @laData ) > 0
   *** At least one row found
ELSE
   *** No data returned
ENDIF
```

The contents of `laData` will look something like this:

```
laData[1,1]    [SYSTEM]
laData[1,2]    []
laData[2,1]    NAME
laData[2,2]    Test System
laData[3,1]    DATE
laData[3,2]    01/10/1998
```

WriteIniFile(<@ArrayName> [,<file>])

The *WriteIniFile()* method writes the contents of a two-column array (which must be created in the calling routine and passed by reference) to the specified *INI* File. The first column of the array must contain the names of the Section headings (no '*[]*' delimiters should be used) or the Items, while the second column must contain the delimiting symbols '*[]*' for Section headers and the actual values for Items.

The array must be ordered so that the first Element is always a Section name (i.e. has the second element set to "*[]*"). Subsequent rows of the array are treated as Item/Value pairs that belong to that section until a new Section Header row is encountered.

If a Section Name is not found, a new section is automatically created in the *INI* file, and if an Item name is not found, the item will be added to the parent section.

WriteIniFile() returns a numeric value indicating the number of valid lines which were written to the target file. If no file name is passed as a parameter, the default file is assumed, and if the file specified cannot be found or written to, a value of 0 is returned.

Example:
To write an *INI* File from an array:

```
LOCAL ARRAY laData[4,2]
laData[1,1] = "SYSTEM"
laData[1,2] = "[]"
laData[2,1] = "NAME"
laData[2,2] = "Test System"
laData[3,1] = "NewSection"
laData[3,2] = "[]"
laData[4,1] = "Version"
laData[4,2] = "   1.0G"
IF goIniMgr.WriteIniFile( @laData ) > 0
  *** Data was written successfully
ENDIF
```

The *INI* file will then look like:

```
[SYSTEM]
NAME=Test System
[NEWSECTION]
Version=1.0G
```

Using the INI file manager

The most obvious use for the *INI* file manager is for retrieving and updating system constants, stored in an external text file from within an application. The whole structure of the manager is designed specifically to simplify this process in a typical application environment where a single *INI* file is used to store all relevant data by making that file the default for all operations. However, both the *GetValue()* and *SetValue()* methods provide the capability to address files other than the default file when necessary.

The second main use for the *INI* file manager is to assist in the maintenance of application *INI* files. The *ReadIniFile()* and *WriteIniFile()* methods are designed to transfer a block of information between a FoxPro Array and an *INI* file. Probably the simplest way of handling this is to create a table (or cursor) with two columns which correspond to the required array structure and to use FoxPro's *SQL SELECT...INTO ARRAY* and *SQL INSERT INTO .... FROM ARRAY* to get data into something which can be used in a Form. The sample code accompanying this chapter includes a form ("*INIMAINT.SCX*") which uses a cursor to maintain the entries for an *INI* file.

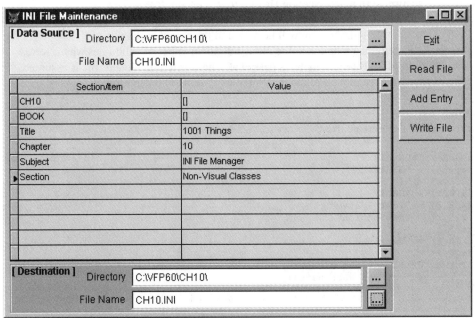

Figure 10.1 *Simple maintenance form for INI files*

While by no means comprehensive in its error handling, this example shows how to use the *INI* File Manager to read and write an *INI* file. The form provides for reading from either an existing *INI* file, creating a completely new one or reading data from a Visual FoxPro table. In this example the manager is created as a global object (*goIniMgr*) in the form's *Load* method.

Reading the data from the specified source into the form's cursor is handled by the custom *ReadFile()* method as follows:

```
LOCAL ARRAY laTfer[1,2]
LOCAL lcSceFile, lcOldFile
WITH ThisForm
   *** Check the source file, clear cursor if a new file is being created
   IF .chkSource() > 0
     IF EMPTY( ALLTRIM( .txtFName.Value ) )
        *** Creating a new file - just return
        ZAP IN curIniFile
        .RefreshForm()
        RETURN
     ENDIF
   ELSE
     *** Source file check failed!
     RETURN
   ENDIF

   *** Specified source is OK, so gather full path and file name
   lcSceFile = ALLTRIM( ADDBS( .txtDir.Value )) + ALLTRIM( .txtFName.Value )
   IF JUSTEXT( lcSceFile ) = "DBF"
     *** It's a table, so just read it into an array
     SELECT heading, item FROM (lcSceFile) ORDER BY sortorder INTO ARRAY laTfer
   ELSE
     *** It's an INI File (maybe). So read it
     goIniMgr.ReadIniFile( @laTfer, lcSceFile )
   ENDIF
   *** Clear Cursor and Copy results in
   ZAP IN curIniFile
   INSERT INTO curIniFile FROM ARRAY laTfer
   *** Strip off heading "[]" - they will be re-written anyway
   REPLACE ALL heading WITH CHRTRAN( heading, '[]','') IN curIniFile
   .RefreshForm()
ENDWITH
```

Writing the data out from the cursor is handled in the custom *WriteFile()* method as follows:

```
LOCAL ARRAY laTfer[1,2]
LOCAL lcOldFile, lcDestFile
WITH ThisForm
   *** Must have a destination
   IF EMPTY( .txtDestFName.Value )
     MESSAGEBOX( 'An output file must be specified!', 16, 'Unable to Continue')
     .txtDestFName.SetFocus()
     RETURN
   ENDIF
   *** We have a destination
   lcDestFile = ALLTRIM(ADDBS(.txtDestDir.Value)) + ALLTRIM(.txtDestFName.Value)
   *** Delete the File if it already exists
   IF ! FILE( lcDestFile )
     DELETE FILE (lcDestFile)
   ENDIF
   *** Now create a new, empty file ready for writing to
   *** We need to do this to ensure that deletions get made properly
   lnHnd = FCREATE( lcDestFile )
```

```
IF lnHnd < 0
  MESSAGEBOX( 'Unable to create new file ' + CHR(13) ;
                      + lcDestFile, 16, 'Cannot Contuinue')
  RETURN
ELSE
  FCLOSE(lnHnd)
ENDIF
*** Now write the new file - ignore empty "heading" fields
SELECT * FROM curinifile WHERE ! EMPTY(heading) INTO ARRAY laTfer
WITH goIniMgr
  *** Write file contents
  .WriteIniFile( @laTfer, lcDestFile )
ENDWITH
*** Clear Cursor
ZAP IN curIniFile
.RefreshForm()
ENDWITH
```

How to select a different work area, OOP style! (*Example:*

ChgArea.prg)

One of the most frequently written snippets of code, in almost any application, looks
something like this:

```
*** Save Current work area
lnSelect = SELECT()

*** Select Required Area
IF ! USED( <Alias> )
  USE <table> IN 0 AGAIN ALIAS <Alias>
ENDIF
SELECT <New Work Area>

*** Do Something There
...
<commands>
...
*** Return to original work area
SELECT (lnSelect)
```

Now, admittedly, this is not really very difficult, but it or some variant is repeated many
times in an application. We really should be able to do better than this now that we have all the
power of Object Orientation behind us and indeed we can.

Overview

The *SelAlias* class is designed to accept the alias name of a table as a parameter and switch to
that table's work area. If the table is not open it will open the table for us. More importantly it
will 'remember' that it opened the table and will, by default, close it when it is destroyed. The
class provides support for an additional parameter which can be used to specify an alias name
when it is necessary to open a table with an alias other than the real name of the table.

The class has no exposed properties or methods and does all of its work in its *Init* and *Destroy* methods. By creating an object based on this class, and scoping it as LOCAL, we need never write code like that shown above again.

A word on creating the selector object

A selector object may be created in the usual way by first loading the procedure file into memory and then using the *CreateObject()* function whenever an instance is needed. However, Version 6.0 of Visual FoxPro introduced an alternative method, using the *NewObject()* function, which allows you to specify the class library from which a class should be instantiated as a parameter. While it is marginally slower, it does mean that you do not need to load and retain procedure files in memory and is useful when you need to create an object 'on the fly', like this one. The syntax for both methods is given below. (Note that with *NewObject()*, if the class is not a visual class library, Visual FoxPro expects both a '*module or program*' name as the second parameter **and** either an *application name* or an *empty string* or a *NULL* value as the third.)

```
*** Using CreateObject()
SET PROCEDURE TO selalias ADDITIVE
loSel = CREATEOBJECT( 'xSelAlias', <Alias>, [|<Table Name>])

*** Using NewObject()
loSel = NEWOBJECT( 'xSelAlias', 'selalias.prg', NULL, <Alias>, [|<Table Name>])
```

One word of caution – if you use multiple instances of this class in the same procedure or method to open tables, either ensure that all objects are created from the same work area or that they are released in the reverse order to that in which they were instantiated. If you do not do this you could end up in a work area that was selected as a result of opening a table but which is now empty.

How the selector class is constructed

As mentioned in the overview this class has no exposed properties or methods and does all of its work in its *Init* or *Destroy* methods. Internally it uses three protected properties to record:

- the work area in which it was instantiated

- the alias of the table it is managing

- whether the table was already open on instantiation

The selector class *Init* method

The *Init* method does four things. First it checks the parameters. An alias name is the minimum that must be passed, and in the absence of the optional second parameter – the table name, it assumes that the table is named the same as the alias. If passed, the table name may include an extension and may also include a path. (Notice the use of ASSERT in this part of the method. The objective here is to warn developers of errors that may arise in the calling syntax without impacting the run time code.)

```
PROCEDURE INIT( tcAlias, tcTable )
    LOCAL llRetVal
    *** No Alias Passed - Bail Out
    IF ! VARTYPE( tcAlias ) = "C"
      ASSERT .F. MESSAGE "Must Pass an Alias Name to Work Area Selector"
      RETURN .F.
    ENDIF
    tcAlias = UPPER( ALLTRIM( tcAlias ))
    IF VARTYPE( tcTable ) # "C" OR EMPTY( tcTable )
      tcTable = tcAlias
    ELSE
      tcTable = UPPER( ALLTRIM( tcTable ))
    ENDIF
```

Next, it checks the currently selected alias. If this is already the required alias, it simply returns a value of .F. and the object is not instantiated. The reason is simply that if the table is already open and selected, there is nothing for the object to do anyway:

```
    *** If already in correct work area - do nothing
    IF UPPER(ALLTRIM( ALIAS() )) == tcAlias
      RETURN .F.
    ENDIF
```

Then it determines whether the required alias is already in use and, if not, tries to open the table under the specified alias. If it succeeds it sets its '*lWasOpen*' property to .F. This allows the same table to be opened more than once under different aliases. If the table cannot be opened, a value of .F. will be returned and the object will not be instantiated. (NOTE: A "production" version of this class should also check that the file exists, and that it is a valid Visual FoxPro table, before attempting to open it with a USE command. Such code has already been covered elsewhere and has been deliberately omitted from this class to keep it as simple as possible. See the *ISDBF()* function in Chapter 7, "How to compare the structures of two tables" for one solution.)

```
    *** If Specified Alias not open - Open it
    IF ! USED( tcAlias )
      USE (tcTable) AGAIN IN 0 ALIAS (tcAlias) SHARED
      *** And Check!
      llRetVal = USED( tcAlias )
      *** If Forced Open, Note the fact
      IF llRetVal
        This.lWasOpen = .F.
      ENDIF
    ELSE
      llRetVal = .T.
    ENDIF
```

Finally it stores the currently selected work area number and the alias name to its '*nOldarea*' and '*cAlias*' properties and switches to the required work area. The object is, therefore, only instantiated when everything has worked as expected:

```
    *** IF OK, save current work area and
    *** Now Move to the specified Work Area
```

```
    IF llRetVal
      This.nOldArea = SELECT()
      SELECT (tcAlias)
      This.cAlias = tcAlias
    ENDIF
    *** Return Status
    RETURN llRetVal
  ENDPROC
```

The selector class *Destroy* method
The Destroy method handles the tidying up of the environment. If the selector opened the table, it is closed – otherwise it is left open. The work area in which the object was instantiated is then selected and the object released:

```
PROCEDURE DESTROY
  WITH This
    *** If table opened by this object, close it
    IF ! .lWasOpen
      USE IN (This.cAlias)
    ENDIF
    *** Restore Previous work area
    IF ! EMPTY( .nOldArea )
      SELECT ( .nOldArea )
    ENDIF
  ENDWITH
ENDPROC
```

Using the selector class
The class is intended to be used to instantiate a local object in a procedure or method whenever it is necessary to change work areas. The example program (*ChgArea.prg*) shows how it may be used:

```
*************************************************************************
* Program....: ChgArea.prg
* Compiler...: Visual FoxPro 06.00.8492.00 for Windows
* Abstract...: Illustrate the use of the SELALIAS class for controlling
* ..........: and changing Work Areas. Output results to screen
*************************************************************************
*** Make sure we are all closed up
CLEAR
CLOSE TABLES ALL
*** Open Clients table
USE sqlcli ORDER 1 IN 0
? 'Using Selector with Just an Alias'
? '================================='
?
? "USE sqlcli ORDER 1 IN 0"
? "Area:"+PADL(SELECT(),2)+" Using Table "+JUSTSTEM(DBF())+" as Alias "+ALIAS()
?
*** Create a Client Selection Object
loSelCli = NEWOBJECT( 'xSelAlias', 'SelAlias.prg', NULL, 'SqlCli' )
? "loSelCli = NEWOBJECT( 'xSelAlias', 'SelAlias.prg', NULL, 'SqlCli' )"
```

```
? "Area:"+PADL(SELECT(),2)+" Using Table "+JUSTSTEM(DBF())+" as Alias "+ALIAS()
?
*** Open Invoices Table (temporarily)
loSelInv = NEWOBJECT( 'xSelAlias', 'SelAlias.prg', NULL, 'SqlInv' )
? "loSelInv = NEWOBJECT( 'xSelAlias', 'SelAlias.prg', NULL, 'SqlInv' )"
? "Area:"+PADL(SELECT(),2)+" Using Table "+JUSTSTEM(DBF())+" as Alias "+ALIAS()
?
*** Now close the Invoices table by releasing the object
RELEASE loSelInv
? "RELEASE loSelInv"
? "USED( 'SqlInv' ) => "+IIF( USED( 'SqlInv' ), "Still In Use", "Not Open" )
?
*** Now releaswe the Client table object
RELEASE loSelCli
? "RELEASE loSelCli"
? "USED( 'SqlCli' ) => "+IIF( USED( 'SqlCli' ), "Still In Use", "Not Open" )
?
? "Area:"+PADL(SELECT(),2)+" Using Table "+JUSTSTEM(DBF())+" as Alias "+ALIAS()
?
? "Press a key to clear the screen and continue..."
INKEY(0, 'hm' )
CLEAR

? 'Using Selector to create an Alias'
? '================================='
?
? "Area:"+PADL(SELECT(),2)+" Using Table "+JUSTSTEM(DBF())+" as Alias "+ALIAS()
?
*** Open Clients Again under new Alias
loSelCli = NEWOBJECT( 'xSelAlias', 'SelAlias.prg', NULL, 'Clients', 'SqlCli' )
? "loSelCli = NEWOBJECT('xSelAlias', 'SelAlias.prg', NULL, 'Clients',
'SqlCli')"
? "Area:"+PADL(SELECT(),2)+" Using Table "+JUSTSTEM(DBF())+" as Alias "+ALIAS()
?
*** Open Invoices Table (temporarily)
loSelInv = NEWOBJECT( 'xSelAlias', 'SelAlias.prg', NULL, 'Invoices', 'SqlInv' )
? "loSelInv = NEWOBJECT('xSelAlias','SelAlias.prg', NULL, 'Invoices',
'SqlInv')"
? "Area:"+PADL(SELECT(),2)+" Using Table "+JUSTSTEM(DBF())+" as Alias "+ALIAS()
?
*** Now close the Invoices table by releasing the object
RELEASE loSelInv
? "RELEASE loSelInv"
? "USED( 'Invoices' ) => "+IIF( USED( 'Invoices' ), "Still In Use", "Not Open"
)
?
*** Now release the Client table object
RELEASE loSelCli
? "RELEASE loSelCli"
? "USED( 'Clients' ) => "+IIF( USED( 'Clients' ), "Still In Use", "Not Open" )
?
? "Area:"+PADL(SELECT(),2)+" Using Table "+JUSTSTEM(DBF())+" as Alias "+ALIAS()
?
? "Press a key to clear the screen and finish..."
INKEY(0, 'hm' )
CLEAR
```

How can I manage paths in a form's dataenvironment?

The form's dataenvironment provides many benefits including the facility to auto-open and close tables, to set the buffering of individual tables and, at design time, to use drag and drop to create data bound controls on a form. However, there is one perennial problem with using the form's dataenvironment - the way in which it handles the issue of paths for the tables it contains is, to say the least, convoluted.

Every cursor created in the dataenvironment has two properties that are involved with the table name and path information, namely '*Database*' and '*CursorSource*'. However, they are used differently depending on whether the table in question is free or bound to a database container. The actual way in which information gets stored depends upon the location of the tables *at design time* according to the following rules:

Table 10.2 *Cursor properties that determine the location of source data*

Table Type and Location	Database	CursorSource
Bound Table, DBC on current drive	Relative Path and File Name of DBC	The name of the table in the DBC
Bound Table, DBC on different drive	Absolute Path and File Name of DBC	The name of the table in the DBC
Free Table on current drive	Relative Path and File Name of DBF	Empty
Free Table on different drive	Absolute Path and File Name of DBF	Empty

The following examples show the results of adding a table to the DE of a form while running a VFP session with drive "*G:*"set as the default drive and "*\VFP60*" as the current directory:

[1] Free Table on a different drive

```
Alias     = "messageb"
Database  = ""
CursorSource  = e:\vfp50\common\libs\messageb.dbf
```

[2] Free table in subdirectory of current working directory (G:\VFP60\)

```
Alias     = "customer"
Database  = ""
CursorSource  = data\customer.dbf
```

[3] Table from a DBC on a different drive

```
Alias     = "demone"
Database  = c:\vfp60\ch08\ch08.dbc
CursorSource  = "demone"
```

[4] Table from a DBC on the same drive but NOT a subdirectory of working directory (G:\VFP60\)

```
Alias     = "clients"
```

```
Database = ..\samples\data\testdata.dbc
CursorSource = "clients"
```

[5] Table from a DBC in subdirectory of current working directory (G:\VFP60\)

```
Alias    = "clients"
Database = data\testdata.dbc
CursorSource = "clients"
```

At run time Visual FoxPro will always try and use the information saved with the cursor first, but if the file cannot be found at the specified location, it will continue to search all available paths.

The 'no code' solution!

The easy answer to this issue is, therefore, to keep all tables (free or bound) and database containers in the same directory and to make sure it is defined as a sub-directory of your development directory. This ensures that Visual FoxPro only ever stores the relative path for tables. (See examples 2 and 5 above.)

When you distribute your application, ensure that a subdirectory (named the same as the one used during development) is created under the application's home directory and that all data files are installed there. However, there are many times when this solution is just not possible, most obviously when the application is being run on client machines but using shared data stored on a server. So what can we do about it?

The hard-coded solution!

A form's native dataenvironment cannot be sub-classed (although we can, of course, create our own dataenvironment classes in code). This means that there is no way of writing code into a form class at design time to handle the resolution of paths, because such code would have to be placed into the dataenvironment *BeforeOpenTables* method. (Why *BeforeOpenTables*? Because the *OpenTables* method creates the cursor objects and then calls *BeforeOpenTables* after the objects are created but before the information in them is used to actually open the tables.) So one approach is to add some code to the *BeforeOpenTables* method of every form to set the paths for the contained tables as necessary. This will work, but seems rather an '*old-fashioned*' way of doing it. Apart from anything else it would make maintaining an application with a lot of forms a major undertaking. There must be a better way!

The data-driven object solution!

If we cannot sub-class the native dataenvironment, perhaps we could create our own class to handle the work, and simply limit the code that has to be added to each instance of a form class to a single line? Indeed we can do just that, and if we use a table to hold path information we can also greatly simplify the task of maintaining the application. Such a solution is presented in the next section of this chapter.

The data path manager class

The data path manager class is designed to be instantiated as a transient object in the *BeforeOpenTables* method of a Form dataenvironment. It's function is to scan through all of the member objects of the dataenvironment and, for each cursor object that it finds, perform a look up in a separate 'system' table which defines the paths to be used for its tables at run time. While we still need to add code to the *BeforeOpenTables* method of the dataenvironment in every form that we create, we only need to add one line. The code executed is contained in a single class and uses a single table of pre-defined structure. Maintenance is, therefore, a minor matter when you adopt this strategy.

The path management table

The first component that we need in order to implement the strategy outlined above is the lookup table that will hold the information we wish Visual FoxPro to use at run time. This table has been (imaginatively) named 'datapath.dbf' and although we have included it in the project's database container we would normally recommend that it be used as a free table. The structure is as follows:

```
Structure For: C:\VFP60\CH10\DATAPATH.DBF
=============================================
DBC  : CH10.DBC
CDX  : DATAPATH.CDX

Associated Indexes
==================
   *** PRIMARY KEY: CTABLE: UPPER(CTABLE)
   ISDEL: DELETED()

Field Details
=============
   CTABLE    C ( 20,0 )  NOT NULL  && Table Name - either DBC Name or DBF File
name
   SET_PATH  C ( 60,0 )  NOT NULL  && Drive and Path
   SET_DBC   C ( 20,0 )  NOT NULL  && DBC Name (Bound Tables only)
   SET_TABLE C ( 20,0 )  NOT NULL  && Name of table in DBC (Bound Tables)
                                   && File name and extension (Free Tables)
```

To speed searches the table is indexed on the table name field and has an index on *DELETED()*. Since this table would probably be set up locally on a client machine (to handle individual's drive mappings), the issue of bringing down large indexes on *DELETED()* over the network is not likely to arise. We have our example table populated as illustrated in **Figure 10.2** below:

Ctable	Set_path	Set_dbc	Set_table
SQLCLI	F:\TEMP\	CH10.DBC	SQLCLI
SQLCON	F:\TEMP\	CH10.DBC	SQLCON
SQLINV	F:\TEMP\	CH10.DBC	SQLINV
SQLPHO	F:\TEMP\	CH10.DBC	SQLPHO
INIFILE	F:\TEMP\		INIFILE.DBF

Figure 10.2 Data path mapping table

The path management class (*Example: chgpaths.scx*)

The actual class, like the work area selector, does its work directly in the *Init* method, or methods called from *Init,* and has no exposed methods or properties. This means that, when instantiated, the object automatically carries out its function and can then be released. The class defines two protected properties for its internal use, an array to hold object references to the dataenvironment cursors and a property to store the reference to the calling dataenvironment object itself.

The principle behind its operation is that it receives a reference to the calling dataenvironment (as a parameter) and validates that the reference is both a valid object and actually relates to an object whose base class is 'dataenvironment.' The calling DE is then parsed to get a reference to each cursor object, which is stored to the internal array. Having opened the lookup table the final step is to retrieve each cursor's reference in turn and determine the name of the table on which it is based (uses *JUSTSTEM()* to return the name from the *CursorSource* property).

The table name is then looked up in the mapping table and depending on the data found (if any) the Database and CursorSource properties are updated. The actual code used is:

```
*******************************************************************
* Program....: DPathMgr.prg
* Compiler...: Visual FoxPro 06.00.8492.00 for Windows
* Abstract...: Uses lookup table to get correct paths for tables
* ..........: at run time, set the paths in DE Cursor Object
* ..........: Call from BeforeOpenTables Method of a Form DE
* ..........: Expects a reference to the DE to be passed - can use
NEWOBJECT():
* ..........: loPathSet = NEWOBJECT( 'dPathMgr', 'dpathmgr.prg', NULL, THIS )
*******************************************************************

DEFINE CLASS DPathMgr AS relation
   *** Define Protected Properties ***

   *** Array for list of Cursors
   PROTECTED aCursors[1]
   aCursors[1] = NULL

   *** Object Reference to the DE
   PROTECTED oDe
   oDe = NULL
```

The *Init* method is used to control the processing and first checks the parameter passed to ensure that it is a reference to a dataenvironment object. Next it calls the *GetTables* method and, if any tables are found, calls *OpenRefTable* to open the lookup table. Finally it calls the *SetPaths* method to actually check each cursor and see if a new path has been defined for it:

```
PROCEDURE Init( toDe )
   LOCAL lnCursors

   *** Check the parameter
   IF VARTYPE( toDe ) = "O"

      *** Have a valid Object reference
```

```
      This.oDe = toDe
      IF LOWER( This.oDE.BaseClass ) # "dataenvironment"

        *** But it's not a DE!
        ASSERT .F. MESSAGE "DPathMgr Class Requires a reference to the " ;
                     + CHR(13) + "DataEnvironment Object which calls it."
        RETURN .F.
      ENDIF
    ELSE

      *** Whoops - Not even an Object
      RETURN .F.
    ENDIF

    *** How many cursors are there?
    lnCursors = This.GetTables()
    IF lnCursors < 1

      *** Nothing to do - so just return OK
      RETURN
    ENDIF

    *** Check for DataPath Table and open it if necessary
    IF ! This.OpenRefTable()
      *** Cannot find the reference table
      RETURN .F.
    ENDIF

    *** Set the paths for the Cursors
    This.SetPaths( lnCursors )
    RETURN
ENDPROC
```

The *OpenRefTable* explicitly tries to open the DataPath table. This could, if necessary, be parameterized but we cannot see any great immediate benefit for doing so (rather the opposite in fact). There may conceivably be situations in which multiple mapping tables would be required by an application and it would then be entirely appropriate to pass a parameter for the table to use. However, by doing so you lose one of the main benefits of this approach, which is that the code to be inserted into the *BeforeOpenTables* of forms would no longer be the same for every form:

```
PROTECTED PROCEDURE openreftable

   *** Open up the Reference table
   IF ! USED('DataPath')
     USE datapath AGAIN IN 0 SHARED NOUPDATE
   ENDIF
   RETURN USED( 'DataPath' )
ENDPROC
```

The *GetTables* method uses the stored object reference to the calling dataenvironment to populate an array with all member objects. This is then scanned and references to cursor objects are stored to the array property. The method returns the number of cursors that it found:

```
PROTECTED PROCEDURE GetTables
  LOCAL ARRAY laObj[1]
  LOCAL lnObjCnt, lnCnt, loObj, lnRows, lcObjName

  *** Get a list of all objects in the DE
  lnObjCnt = AMEMBERS( laObj, This.oDe, 2)

  *** Scan the list
  lnRows = 0
  FOR lnCnt = 1 TO lnObjCnt

    *** Check if this object is actually a Cursor
    loObj = EVAL( "This.oDe." + laObj[lnCnt] )
    IF loObj.BaseClass = "Cursor"

      *** It is, so save its reference to the internal array
      *** Add a new row to the cursors array
      lnRows = lnRows + 1
      DIMENSION This.aCursors[ lnRows, 1]
      This.aCursors[lnRows] = loObj
    ENDIF
  NEXT

  *** Return Number of Cursors
  RETURN lnRows
ENDPROC
```

The *SetPaths* method is where the lookup into the mapping table is done and the results are used to reset each cursor's *Database* and *CursorSource* properties accordingly. If there is no entry in the lookup table, the cursor's properties are not changed in any way:

```
PROTECTED PROCEDURE SetPaths( tnCursors )
  LOCAL lnCnt, loObj, lcTable

  *** Scan the list
  FOR lnCnt = 1 TO tnCursors

    *** Retrieve the Object Reference from the array
    loObj = This.aCursors[lnCnt]

    *** Find the Table Name
    lcTable = UPPER( JUSTSTEM( loObj.CursorSource ))

    *** Look up the name in the reference table which lists
    *** where the data should be taken from
    IF SEEK( lcTable, "datapath", "ctable")

      *** We have a reference for this table!
      IF ! EMPTY( set_dbc )

        *** We have a bound table
        loObj.Database  = ALLTRIM( datapath.set_path ) ;
                      + ALLTRIM( DataPath.set_dbc )
        loObj.CursorSource = ALLTRIM(DataPath.set_table)
      ELSE

        *** Must be a free table
```

```
            loObj.Database =  ""
            loObj.CursorSource  = ALLTRIM( datapath.set_path ) ;
                              + ALLTRIM( DataPath.set_table )
        ENDIF
      ENDIF
    NEXT
  ENDPROC

ENDDEFINE
```

Using the data path manager

The sample form *ChgPaths.SCX* uses the data path manager to change the paths of the tables that have been added to its dataenvironment. To experiment with this, simply copy the *CH10.DBC* (and all the tables) to an alternate location and change the SET_PATH field in the copy of the *DataPath* table that remains in the original location. The only code that has been added to the form's dataenvironment is the single line in the *BeforeOpenTables* method, as follows:

```
NEWOBJECT( 'dpathmgr', 'dpathmgr.prg', NULL, THIS )
```

which instantiates the data path manager object and passes it a reference to the dataenvironment.

As shown in **Figure 10.3**, the original setup for each table in the form dataenvironment is derived from the local tables in the C:\VFP60\CH10 directory. **Figure 10.4** shows the result of running the form and, as expected, the tables in the form are being drawn from a completely different drive and directory.

Properties - chgpaths.scx
Cursor1
All
Data
Methods
Layout
Other
sqlcli
Alias sqlcli
BufferModeOverride 1
Comment (None)
CursorSource sqlcli
Database c:\vfp60\ch10\ch10.dbc
chgpaths.scx
sqlcli
Fields:
clisid
cliname
Indexes:
isdel
cliname

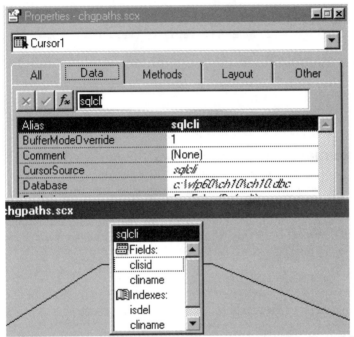

Figure 10.3 *Setup for the SQLCLI tables in the example form DE*

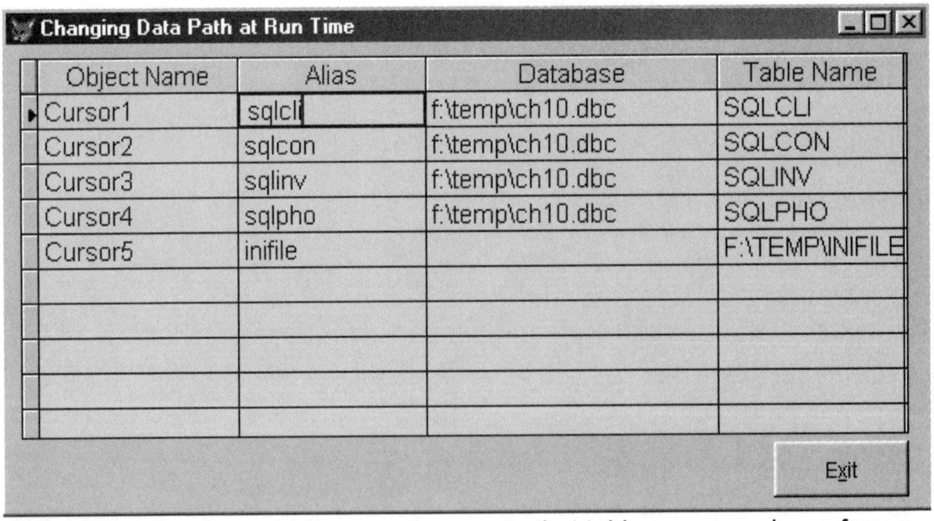

Changing Data Path at Run Time
Object Name
Alias
Database
Table Name
Cursor1 sqlcli f:\temp\ch10.dbc SQLCLI
Cursor2 sqlcon f:\temp\ch10.dbc SQLCON
Cursor3 sqlinv f:\temp\ch10.dbc SQLINV
Cursor4 sqlpho f:\temp\ch10.dbc SQLPHO
Cursor5 inifile F:\TEMP\INIFILE
Exit

Figure 10.4 *The example form running – note that tables are now drawn from a different source*

How can I manage forms and toolbars in my application?

There are probably as many answers to this question as there are developers writing applications using Visual FoxPro. A key part of any application framework is the mechanism for managing forms and all frameworks include a "Form Manager" of some sort. The mechanism for implementing it will depend on your framework but there are certain basic tasks that any such manager object *must* perform:

- Instantiation of forms (whether SCX or VCX based)

- Tracking which form (and which instance of a form) is currently active

- Ensuring that the appropriate toolbar is available

- Adding and removing forms to its own list of active forms as they are initialized or released

Of course there are many other functions that *could* be performed by the form manager (for example, adding/removing items to the Window list or 'cascading' forms as they are initialized) but the four listed above constitute the basic functionality which the class must provide.

In order to implement a form manager, it is necessary to create a '*managed*' subclass, for both Forms and Toolbars so that the additional code to interact with the manager can be isolated. The following sections present the code for these classes and for a form manager class that will handle all the basic tasks described above. This class has been designed to be instantiated as a 'global' object, which isn't the only way to do it, but is the simplest to illustrate. We could also have implemented the necessary methods as part of a broader 'application manager' class or even handled the instantiation and referencing of the form manager indirectly through an application object.

The managed form class

Forms intended to work with the form manager belong to a special class ('*xFrmStdManaged*' in *GenForms.vcx*). In addition to some necessary code in the *Init*, *Activate* and *Destroy* methods, three custom properties and two methods are required for interaction with the Form Manager as follows:

Table 10.3 *Custom properties and methods for the managed form class*

Name	PEM	Purpose
cInsName	Property	Instance name, assigned by the form manager when form initialized
cTbrName	Property	Name of the toolbar used by the form (if any)
lOneInstance	Property	When .T. prevents Form Mgr from creating multiple instances of the form
ReportAction	Method	Call manager's FormAction method
CheckFrmMgr	Method	Returns an object reference to the form manager

The custom properties

- The *cInsName* property is used to store the instance name assigned by the form manager, to a form when it is initialized. The form manager stores both the form name and the assigned instance name in its internal collection. This caters for multiple instances of a form by providing the form manager a means for uniquely identifying each instance of a particular form.

- The *cTbrName* is populated at design time with the name of the toolbar class associated with the form. This property will be read by the form manager at run time to determine which, if any, toolbars are needed and to ensure that when a particular form is activated, the correct toolbar is displayed.

- The *lOneInstance* property may be set to indicate to the form manager that the form is single instance only. When the form manager is instructed to instantiate a form which already exists in its collection, it will simply restore and activate the existing form if this property is set.

Form class *ReportAction* method

This method provides the "single point of contact" between the form and the form manager. It can be called by any form method that passes a parameter indicating the type of action required from the form manager (in our example, this would be either '**ACTIVATE**' or '**DESTROY**'):

```
LPARAMETERS tcAction
LOCAL loFrmMgr

*** Check parameter
IF VARTYPE( tcAction ) # "C"
    ASSERT .F. MESSAGE "Form's ReportAction method must be called with a
required action"
    RETURN
ENDIF
*** Now handle the call to the Form Manager
WITH ThisForm
    *** Get a Reference to the form Manager
    loFrmMgr = .CheckFrmMgr()
    IF VARTYPE( loFrmMgr ) = "O"
        *** Tell Form Manager to make this the active form
        loFrmMgr.FormAction( tcAction, .cInsName )
    ELSE
        *** No form Manager, so nothing special required
    ENDIF
ENDWITH
```

The responsibility for checking for the existence of the form manager is passed to the *CheckFrmMgr* method, which returns either the appropriate object reference or a **NULL** value. If a valid reference is returned, the method then calls the manager's *FormAction* method and passes *both* the required action *and* the form's instance name to provide an unambiguous reference for the form manager.

Form class *Init* method

The form class *Init* method expects to receive either a parameter object containing a property named *cInsName* or a character string which is the name to be stored to its *cInsName* property:

```
LPARAMETERS tuParam
*** Class method expects the Instance Name to be passed
*** either as 'cInsName' in a parameter object or as a string.
*** Could actually test here but what the heck! Live dangerously!
*** (In fact the test should be done in either the instance or the subclass)
IF VARTYPE( tuParam ) = "O"
   *** Store cInsName property to form property
   ThisForm.cInsName = tuParam.cInsName
   RETURN .T.
ENDIF
*** If not an object, is it a string?
IF VARTYPE( tuParam ) = "C"
   *** Store what is passed to form property
   ThisForm.cInsName = tuParam
   RETURN .T.
ELSE
   *** We have something seriously wrong here!
   ASSERT .F. ;
      MESSAGE "The form class used requires that an instance name" + CHR(13) ;
           + "be generated by form manager and passed to the form."  + CHR(13) ;
           + "Aborting form initialisation"
   RETURN .T.
ENDIF
```

This does mean that any instance of the form that requires additional parameters must extract, from its own list of parameters, the form manager generated instance name and pass that back to the class as follows:

```
LPARAMETERS toParams
*** Extract Instance name from the parameter object
IF VARTYPE( toParams ) = 'O' AND PEMSTATUS( toParams, 'cInsName', 5 )
   *** Pass Instance Name up to parent class method
   DODEFAULT( toParams.cInsName )
   IF toParams.nParamCount > 0
      *** Extract additional parameters named as "tuParm1" through "tuParmn"
   ENDIF
ELSE
   *** No Instance Name specified
   *** Take whatever action is appropriate at the time
ENDIF
*** Do whatever else is needed here
```

One major benefit of using a parameter object like this, as we discussed in Chapter 2, is that it allows you to use 'named' parameters which simplifies the code needed to read the passed in values.

Form class *Activate, Release* and *QueryUnload* methods

In addition, the class includes two lines of code in both the *Activate* and *Release* methods to initiate communication with the form manager. The code, in each case, calls the *ReportAction* method and passes the name of the method which is executing:

```
ThisForm.ReportAction( JUSTEXT( PROGRAM() ))
DODEFAULT()
```

Finally, the *QueryUnLoad* method of this class includes an explicit call to the *Release* method to ensure that however the user exits from the form, the Form Manager is notified. (This is because *QueryUnLoad* normally bypasses the Release method. The next event common to both *Release* and *QueryUnload* is *Destroy*, and this is too late for the Form Manager.)

The managed toolbar class

The use of toolbars in an application is difficult to address generically. Whether you use different toolbars for different forms, or use a single toolbar and enable/disable options as necessary will affect the design details. However, whichever approach you take, the toolbar will need to interact with your forms. Since the Form Manager controls the forms, it seems entirely reasonable that it should also look after the toolbars, which must, therefore, be designed accordingly. Our managed abstract toolbar class ("*xTbrStdManaged*" in GenClass.vcx) has been set up as follows.

First, the toolbar's *ControlBox* property has been set to .F. thereby ensuring that a user cannot inadvertently close a toolbar (now the responsibility of the form manger) and the toolbar has been given a Private DataSession. Three custom methods have been added and some code added to the native *Activate* method of the class as follows.

The toolbar class *Activate* method

The issue addressed here is to ensure that whenever a toolbar is activated, it will synchronize itself with whatever form is currently active on the screen. A toolbar's *Activate* method is called whenever the toolbar is shown, and since the form manager will handle toolbars by calling their *Show* and *Hide* methods we can use this to call the method that will synchronize the toolbar's settings with the current form:

```
*** Synchronize Toolbar to currently active form
*** Activate is called from Show() so will always fire
*** When Form Manager calls the Toolbar.Show()
This.SetDataSession()
```

The toolbar class *SetDataSession* method

When called, this method will either set the toolbar to the same datasession as the currently active form and then call the toolbar's custom *SynchWithForm* method. If no form is active, it simply calls the custom *SetDisabled* method:

```
LOCAL loForm
*** Get reference to active form
IF TYPE( "_Screen.ActiveForm" ) = "O" AND ! ISNULL( _Screen.ActiveForm )
   *** Get Reference to Active Form
   loForm = _Screen.ActiveForm
   *** Force Datasession to the same one
   This.DataSessionID = loForm.DataSessionID
   *** Call synchronisation method to handle toolbar settings
   This.SynchWithForm( loForm )
ELSE
   *** No form, so disable the toolbar!
   *** Note: This should never happen because the form manager should
   *** always be handling the visibility of the toolbar
   This.SetDisAbled()
ENDIF
```

The toolbar class *SynchWithForm* method

This is simply a template method to be completed in a concrete class. It is called by the custom *SetDataSession* method when an active form is found and is where you would handle any synchronization details (enabling/disabling buttons and so on). It receives, as a parameter, a reference to the currently active form.

The toolbar class *SetDisabled* method

This method provides default behavior to disable all controls on the toolbar when no active form is found. This should *never* happen when running under form manager control, but the behavior is provided for anyway.

The form manager class

The form manager class illustrated here has a very simple public interface. There are only three custom methods ('*DoForm*', '*FormAction*' and '*ReleaseAll*'). The *DoForm* method is intended to be called explicitly in code and is responsible for creating forms and their associated toolbars. The *FormAction* method is called automatically from the *Activate* and *Destroy* methods in the managed form class but could easily be extended to handle other actions if needed. The *ReleaseAll* method is designed to be called from the shutdown process but could also be called from a 'Close All Forms' menu item. This class is designed to work together with the Managed Form and Managed Toolbar classes described in the preceding sections. The actual code is discussed in the following sections.

Form manager definition and *Init* method

The class defines two arrays and four properties, all of which are protected as follows:

Table 10.4 *Custom properties and methods for the form manager form class*

Name	PEM	Purpose
aFmList	Array Property	The Forms Collection
aTbList	Array Property	The Toolbars Collection
nFmCount	Property	Number of forms contained in the Forms Collection
nTbCount	Property	Number of toolbars contained in the toolbars Collection
nFmIndex	Property	Index to the currently active form in the Forms Collection
nTbIndex	Property	Index to the currently active toolbar in the Toolbar Collection

The *Init* method simply initializes these properties:

```
DEFINE CLASS xFrmMgr AS RELATION
  PROTECTED ARRAY aFmList[1,4], aTbList[1,3]
  PROTECTED nFmIndex, nFmCount, nTbCount, nTbIndex

  FUNCTION Init
    WITH This
      *** Initialise Properties
      .aFmList = ""     && Form Collection
      .nFmCount = 0     && Managed Form Count
      .nFmIndex = 0     && Index into the Collection for current form
      .aTbList = ""     && Toolbar Collection
      .nTbCount = 0     && Toolbar Count
      .nTBIndex = 0     && Index into the Collection for current toolbar
    ENDWITH
  ENDFUNC
```

The form manager *DoForm* method

This custom method is where the form manager creates forms and any associated toolbars. It is the largest single method in the class but does not really lend itself to further decomposition. The method allows for up to three parameters to be passed in, but we would normally expect to pass a single parameter object. The only reason for this structure is to simplify calling the method directly from a menu item.

The first two parameters are used for the name and method to be used for instantiating the form. When calling an *SCX* only the form name need be passed, unless there are additional parameters, because the default value for the second will be .F. - which will invoke the DO FORM mechanism. If the form is to be instantiated from a class, the second parameter must always be passed explicitly as .T.

The first thing this method does is to check the parameters and generate (using SYS(2015)) a valid character string which will be used for both the object reference to the form and its "instance" name:

```
*****************************************************************
*** xFrmMgr::DoForm( tcFmName, tlIsClass, tuParm1, tuParm2, tuParm3 )
*** Exposed Method to Run a Form
*** Provision for 3 params, but normally would expect only 1 (as
*** A parameter object)
*****************************************************************
```

```
FUNCTION DoForm ( tcFmName, tlIsClass, tuParm1, tuParm2, tuParm3 )
LOCAL lnFormParams, lcFmName, loFmRef, lnFmIdx, llRetVal, lnCnt
  WITH This
    *** Check Parameters
    IF VARTYPE( tcFmName ) # "C"
      *** Form name is not supplied!
      ASSERT .F. MESSAGE ;
         "Name of a Form, or a Form Class," + CHR(13) ;
         + "Must be passed to Form Manager DoForm()"
      RETURN .F.
    ENDIF
    *** Set Return Flag
    llRetVal = .T.
    *** Form Name and Type must be present, how many form params?
    lnFormParams = PCOUNT() - 2
```

The next thing is to check whether the form has already been instantiated and, if so, whether the form has been defined as 'single instance'. The way the manager handles such forms is to simply re-activate the existing instance, set the toolbar (if any) and exit:

```
    *** Check to see if we have this Form already?
    .nFmIndex = .FmIdx(tcFmName)

    *** If we have it, is it single instance
    IF .nFmIndex > 0

      *** Get a reference to the form and see if we can
      *** have multiple instances of it.
      loFmRef = .aFmList[.nFmIndex, 1]
      WITH loFmRef

        *** Check to see if the form is single-instance
        IF .lOneInstance
          *** Restore form if minimised
          IF .WindowState > 0
             .WindowState  = 0
          ENDIF

          *** Force to top
          .AlwaysOnTop = .T.

          *** Activate the form
          .Activate()

          *** Cancel Force To Top
          .AlwaysOnTop = .F.

          *** Sort out Toolbars, pass the toolbar name (if any)
          .SetToolBar( .aFmList[.nFmIndex, 4])
          *** And Exit right now
          RETURN llRetVal
        ENDIF
      ENDWITH
    ENDIF
```

If the form is not already instantiated, or if it is but is not single instance, then a new form is required. First we generate the object reference and instance name, and then construct a parameter object for the form:

```
*** Either first run of the form, or a new instance is required
*** Create the parameter object
*** Generate an Instance Name and Object Reference
STORE SYS(2015) TO lcFmName, loFmRef

*** Create the Parameter Object
oParams = NEWOBJECT( "xParam", "genclass.vcx" )
WITH oParams

  *** First the Instance Name
  .AddProperty( 'cInsName', lcFmName )

  *** Add a property count
  .AddProperty( 'nParamCount', lnFormParams )

  *** Add any additional parameters to be passed to the form
  IF lnFormParams > 0
    FOR lnCnt = 1 TO lnFormParams
      lcPName = "tuParm" + ALLTRIM(STR(lnCnt))
      .AddProperty( lcPName, &lcPName )
    NEXT

  ENDIF
ENDWITH
```

Finally we can create the form itself. The *tlIsClass* parameter is used to decide whether the required form is an *SCX* file or a class and to instantiate the form appropriately:

```
*** Instantiate the form
IF tlIsClass

  *** Create as a class
  loFmRef = CREATEOBJECT( tcFmName, oParams )
ELSE

  *** Run as a Form using NAME and LINKED clauses
  DO FORM (tcFmName) NAME loFmRef WITH oParams LINKED
ENDIF

*** Update the Collection with the new form details
IF VARTYPE( loFmRef ) = "O"

  *** YEP - got a form, so increment form count and populate the collection
  .nFmCount = .nFmCount + 1
  DIMENSION .aFmList[.nFmCount, 4]
  .aFmList[.nFmCount, 1] = loFmRef          && Object Reference
  .aFmList[.nFmCount, 2] = lcFmName          && Instance Name
  .aFmList[.nFmCount, 3] = tcFmName          && Form Name
  .aFmList[.nFmCount, 4] = UPPER( ALLTRIM ( loFmRef.cTbrName ))   && Toolbar
to use

  *** Make this the Active Form
```

```
    .nFmIndex = .nFmCount

    *** Show the new form
    loFmRef.Show()
ELSE
    *** Form Initialisation failed for some reason
    llRetVal = .F.
ENDIF
```

After creating the form we check to ensure that the form really did get created, and then we populate the Forms collection with the relevant information. The last thing to do is to handle display of the toolbars, which is done by calling the *DoToolBar* method:

```
    *** Finally sort out the toolbar requirement
    IF llRetVal
      .DoToolBar( .aFmList[.nFmCount, 4] )
    ENDIF
    RETURN llRetVal
  ENDWITH
ENDFUNC
```

The form manager *DoToolbar* method
This method is called only when a new form, or a new instance of a form, is created. Its function is to update the Toolbar collection if the new form requires a toolbar. This may involve incrementing the count of an existing toolbar or creating a new toolbar. The same method handles both contingencies:

```
*****************************************************************
*** xFrmMgr::DoToolBar( tcTbName )
*** Protected method to create or set the named toolbar active
*** Called when creating a form
*****************************************************************
PROTECTED FUNCTION DoToolBar( tcTbName )
  WITH This
    LOCAL lnTbIdx

    *** Do we need a toolbar at all?
    IF EMPTY( tcTbName )
      *** No ToolBar Required, hide all
      .SetToolBar( "" )
      RETURN
    ENDIF

    *** Check to see if we have the toolbar already
    lnTbIdx = .TbIdx( tcTbName )
    IF lnTbIdx > 0

      *** We already have this one, so activate it
      *** And increment its counter by one
      .aTbList[ lnTbIdx, 2] = .aTbList[ lnTbIdx, 2] + 1

    ELSE

      *** We need to create it and add it to the collection
```

```
      .nTbCount = .nTbCount + 1
      DIMENSION .aTbList[ .nTBCount, 3]
      .aTbList[ .nTbCount, 1] = CREATEOBJECT( tcTbName )     && Object Ref
      .aTbList[ .nTbCount, 2] = 1                            && Toolbar Counter
      .aTbList[ .nTbCount, 3] = UPPER( ALLTRIM( tcTbName )) && Toolbar Name
   ENDIF

   *** Make the toolbar the active one
   .nTbIndex = .nTbCount
   .SetToolBar( .aTbList[ .nTbCount, 3] )
  ENDWITH
ENDFUNC
```

This method calls the *SetToolBar* method to sort out the display of toolbars and passes either the name of the required toolbar (if there is one) or an empty string. The latter causes the *SetToolBar* method to hide all existing toolbars.

The form manager *FormAction* method

This method is called from a form to request action from the form manager. Two parameters are expected, the first is the action required and the second is the instance name of the form that is requesting action. The managed form class calls this method whenever a form is activated or released to notify the manager of a change in status, passing the name of the calling method as the first parameter. The action taken depends on the call and additional actions could easily be provided for here:

```
*****************************************************************
*** xFrmMgr::FormAction( tcAction, tcInsName )
*** Exposed method for handling form requests
*****************************************************************
FUNCTION FormAction( tcAction, tcInsName )
  WITH This
    LOCAL lnFmIndex
    *** Do we have this form?
    lnFmIndex  = 0
    lnFmIndex  = .FmIdx(tcInsName)

    *** If we have it
    IF lnFmIndex > 0
      DO CASE

        CASE UPPER( tcAction ) = "ACTIVATE"
          *** Make this the Active form
          .nFmIndex = lnFmIndex
          .SetToolBar( .aFmList[.nFmIndex, 4])

        CASE UPPER( tcAction ) = "RELEASE"
          *** Clear the form from the collection
          .nFmIndex = lnFmIndex
          .ClearForm( .aFmList[.nFmIndex, 1] )

        OTHERWISE
          ASSERT .F. ;
          MESSAGE "Action: " + tcAction + " passed to Form Mgr " ;
              + CHR(13) + "But is not recognised"
          RETURN .F.
```

```
      ENDCASE
    ELSE
      *** Form was not started by Form Manager
      *** Nothing to do about it
    ENDIF
    RETURN
  ENDWITH
ENDFUNC
```

The form manager *ReleaseAll* method

As implied by the name, the last of the main methods simply releases all forms and toolbars that the form manager has in its collections. This is normally called from the shutdown process but may also be used to provide a 'Clear All' option in a menu:

```
****************************************************************
*** xFrmMgr::ReleaseAll
*** Exposed method for releasing ALL forms held by the Form Manager
*** Used when closing an application with forms still open
****************************************************************
FUNCTION ReleaseAll
  WITH THIS
    LOCAL loFmRef, loTbRef
    .nFmIndex = .nFmCount
    *** Release All forms
    DO WHILE .nFmIndex > 0
      *** Check we still have a form object
      loFmRef = .aFmList[.nFmIndex, 1]

      IF VARTYPE( loFmRef ) = "O"
        *** Release It
        loFmRef.Release()
      ENDIF
      .nFmIndex = .nFmIndex - 1
    ENDDO

    *** Re-Initialise Forms Collection
    DIMENSION .aFmList[1,4]
    .nFmCount = 0
    .nFmIndex = 0
    .aFmList = ""

    *** Release all Toolbars
    .nTbIndex = .nTbCount
    DO WHILE .nTbIndex > 0
      *** Check we still have a toolbar object
      loTbRef = .aTbList[.nTbIndex, 1]
      IF VARTYPE( loTbRef ) = "O"
        *** Release It
        loTbRef.Release()
      ENDIF
      .nTbIndex = .nTbIndex - 1
    ENDDO
    *** Re-Initialise Toolbar Collection
    DIMENSION .aTbList[1,3]
    .nTbCount = 0
    .nTbIndex = 0
```

```
    .aTbList = ""
    RETURN .T.
  ENDWITH
ENDFUNC
```

The form manager *ShowForms* and *HideForms* methods

These two additional custom methods are exposed in the form manager to provide a
mechanism for hiding and re-displaying all visible forms. This is useful if you are running a
report to preview and do not wish any existing forms to interfere with the visibility of the
report. The methods are essentially the same and loop through the form collection setting the
visible property of all forms. The hide method finishes by calling *SetToolBar* with an empty
string to remove any existing toolbars. The show method calls the *Show* method of the last
form that was active to restore it and its associated toolbar:

```
*************************************************************
*** xFrmMgr::HideForms
*** Exposed method to hide all forms held by the Form Manager
*** Used When running Print Preview with multiple forms open
*************************************************************
FUNCTION HideForms
  WITH This
    LOCAL nIndex, loFmRef
    nIndex = .nFmCount

    *** Hide All forms
    DO WHILE nIndex > 0
      *** Check we still have a form object
      loFmRef = .aFmList[nIndex, 1]
      IF VARTYPE( loFmRef ) = "O"
        *** Hide It
        loFmRef.Visible = .F.
      ENDIF
      nIndex = nIndex - 1
    ENDDO
    *** Hide all toolbars
    .SetToolBar( "" )
  ENDWITH
ENDFUNC


*************************************************************
*** xFrmMgr::ShowForms
*** Exposed method to show all forms held by the Form Manager
*** Used when closing Print Preview with multiple forms open
*************************************************************
FUNCTION ShowForms
  WITH This
    LOCAL nIndex, loFmRef
    nIndex = 0
    *** Show All forms
    DO WHILE nIndex < .nFmCount
      nIndex = nIndex + 1
      *** Check we still have a form object
      loFmRef = .aFmList[nIndex, 1]
      IF VARTYPE( loFmRef ) = "O"
```

```
      *** Show it
      loFmRef.Visible = .T.
    ENDIF
  ENDDO

    *** Restore the last active Form
    .aFmList[ .nFmIndex, 1].Show()
  ENDWITH
ENDFUNC
```

The form manager *ClearForm* method

This protected custom method removes a form and its associated toolbar from the forms and
toolbars collections. It is called from the *FormAction* method when a form notifies the
manager that it is being released:

```
***************************************************************
*** xFrmMgr::ClearForm( toFmRef )
*** Protected method to Remove a Form from the collection
***************************************************************
PROTECTED FUNCTION ClearForm(toFmRef)
  WITH This

    *** Cancel if not an Object
    IF Type('toFmRef') # "O" OR ISNULL(toFmRef)
      RETURN .F.
    ENDIF

    *** Check For an associated Toolbar
    lcTbName = .aFmList[.nFmIndex, 4]
    IF ! EMPTY( lcTbName )
      .ClearToolBar( lcTbName )
    ENDIF

    *** Clear the Form Collection Entry
    .nFmCount = .nFmCount - 1
    IF .nFmCount < 1

      *** Re-Initialise the Array if this was the last form
      DIMENSION .aFmList[1,4]
      .nFmCount = 0
      .nFmIndex = 0
      .aFmList  = ""
    ELSE

      *** Just Re-Dimension it
      =ADEL(.aFmList, .nFmIndex )
      DIMENSION .aFmList[.nFmCount ,4]
    ENDIF

    *** Re-Set the index = form count
    *** (The next form activation will re-set it anyway)
    .nFmIndex = .nFmCount
  ENDWITH
ENDFUNC
```

The form manager *FmIdx* method

This protected custom method is called with either an object reference to a form or the instance name of a form and searches the form collection to find and return the correct index into the collection for that form:

```
*****************************************************************
*** xFrmMgr::FmIdx( tuFmRef )
*** Scan the Forms Collection for the Reference which may
*** be either an object reference to a form or an instance name
*** Returns the ROW number if found
*****************************************************************
PROTECTED FUNCTION FmIdx(tuFmRef)
  WITH This
    LOCAL lnElem, lnIdx
    lnIdx = 0
    IF ! ISNULL(tuFmRef) AND .nFmCount > 0
      SET EXACT ON
      *** Scan the array
      IF TYPE("tuFmRef") = "O"
        lnElem = ASCAN(.aFmList, tuFmRef.cInsName)
      ELSE
        lnElem = ASCAN(.aFmList, tuFmRef)
      ENDIF
      *** Calculate the Row Number
      IF lnElem > 0
        lnIdx = ASUBSCRIPT(.aFmList, lnElem, 1)
      ENDIF
      SET EXACT OFF
    ENDIF
    RETURN lnIdx
  ENDWITH
ENDFUNC
```

The form manager *TbIdx* method

This protected custom method performs the same function for toolbars as the *fmIdx* method does for forms. It returns the index number of a toolbar in the toolbar collection. However, because this method is always called in the context of a known form, it always expects the *name* of the toolbar to be passed as a parameter. (The toolbar name is stored in the fourth column of the form collection.)

```
*****************************************************************
*** xFrmMgr::TbIdx( tcTbName )
*** Scan the Toolbar Collection for the Reference which will
*** be the name of the required Toolbar
*** Returns the ROW number if found
*****************************************************************
PROTECTED FUNCTION TbIdx(tcTbName)
  WITH This
    LOCAL lnElem, lnIdx
    lnIdx = 0
    *** Check we have a name, and at least one toolbar registered
    IF ! EMPTY(tcTbName) AND .nTbCount > 0
      SET EXACT ON
```

```
    *** Scan the array
    lnElem = ASCAN(.aTbList, tcTbName)
    *** Calculate the Row Number
    IF lnElem > 0
      lnIdx = ASUBSCRIPT(.aTbList, lnElem, 1)
    ENDIF
    SET EXACT OFF
  ENDIF
  *** Return the relevant Row Number
  RETURN lnIdx
ENDWITH
ENDFUNC
```

The form manager *SetToolbar* method

This protected custom method is responsible for controlling the display of toolbars on the screen. It expects to receive either the name of a toolbar or an empty string, as a parameter. The method simply loops through the toolbar collection and hides all toolbars except the one specified. If nothing is specified, all toolbars are hidden:

```
*****************************************************************
*** xFrmMgr::SetToolBar( tcTbrName )
*** Protected method to make the named toolbar active
*** Passing an empty string hides all toolbars
*** Called when activating a form
*****************************************************************
PROTECTED FUNCTION SetToolBar( tcTbName )
  WITH This
    LOCAL lnCnt
    *** Loop through the toolbar collection and hide all but the required one
    FOR lnCnt = 1 TO .nTBCount
      DO CASE

        CASE EMPTY( .aTbList[ lnCnt, 3 ] )
          *** No toolbars defined - Do Nothing
          *** Needed to avoid comparing to an empty string!

        CASE EMPTY( tcTbName )
          *** No Toolbar required, so hide it
          .aTbList[lnCnt, 1].Hide()

        CASE tcTbName == .aTbList[ lnCnt, 3 ]
          *** We want this one, so show it
          .aTbList[lnCnt, 1].Show()

        OTHERWISE
          *** Don't want this one, so hide it
          .aTbList[lnCnt, 1].Hide()
      ENDCASE
    NEXT
  ENDWITH
ENDFUNC
```

The form manager *ClearToolbar* method

This protected custom method corresponds to the *ClearForm* method and removes a toolbar from the form manager's toolbar collection. However because toolbars are only instantiated once, removing a form that has an associated toolbar does not necessarily mean that the toolbar should be released. Other forms may still require it. This method handles both situations by just decrementing the counter (held in column two of the toolbar collection) unless it falls below 1. In that situation the toolbar is released and the entire row is deleted from the collection:

```
**************************************************************
*** xFrmMgr::ClearToolBar( tcTbrName )
*** Protected method to make the named toolbar active
*** Passing an empty string hides all toolbars
*** Called when activating a form
**************************************************************
PROTECTED FUNCTION ClearToolBar( tcTbName )
  WITH This
    LOCAL lnIdx
    *** Find the row in the Toolbar Collection
    lnIdx = 0
    lnIdx = .TbIdx( tcTbName )

    IF lnIdx = 0
      *** This toolbar is not registered anyway
      RETURN
    ENDIF

    *** Decrement the counter
    .aTbList[ lnIdx, 2] = .aTbList[ lnIdx, 2] - 1
    IF .aTbList[ lnIdx, 2] = 0
      *** No Other Reference, so release the Toolbar
      .aTbList[ lnIdx, 1].Release()
      .nTbCount = .nTbCount - 1

      IF .nTbCount < 1
        *** Re-Initialise the Array if this was the last one
        DIMENSION .aTbList[1,3]
        .nTbCount = 0
        .nTbIndex = 0
        .aTbList  = ""
      ELSE
        *** Just Re-Dimension it
        =ADEL(.aTbList, lnIdx )
        DIMENSION .aTbList[.nTbCount , 3]
      ENDIF
    ENDIF
  ENDWITH
ENDFUNC
```

Using the form manager *(Example: FmgrTest.prg)*

As stated in the introduction to this section, the form manager class is designed to be instantiated as a global object. This has been done to avoid the necessity of the manager passing a reference to itself to every form created – with all the potential pitfalls for garbage collection that this would imply. The result is that the managed form class has to know how to check for the presence of the form manager and this is handled in that class by the *CheckFrmMgr* method. We accept that this may be seen as the 'wrong' way of doing things but take the view that "simpler is better" in this case. Adopting a different method would only require a change to a single method in the form class and we feel that the benefits of simplicity outweigh the loss of flexibility for this type of manager object.

The sample program instantiates a form manager object and uses it to create three pairs of forms. Each pair consists of the same form defined as both a SCX and as Class. One pair has no toolbar, one pair requires a 'button' toolbar and the third uses a 'combo box' toolbar. The basic code is:

```
SET CLASSLIB TO genclass, fmgrtest ADDITIVE
RELEASE goFrmMgr
PUBLIC goFrmMgr

*** Create the Form Manager Object
goFrmMgr = newobject('xFrmMgr', 'formmgr.prg', NULL)

*** Now run some forms as both Class and SCX
*** With and Without Toolbars.
*** Note that the Class-based forms require a logical .T. as parameter 2
goFrmMgr.Doform('btnbarfm')
goFrmMgr.Doform('btnbarfm',.T.)

goFrmMgr.Doform('cbobarfm')
goFrmMgr.Doform('cbobarfm',.T.)

goFrmMgr.Doform('notbarfm')
goFrmMgr.Doform('notbarfm',.T.)
```

The actual code also staggers the forms on screen so as to present the appearance illustrated in **Figure 10.5** below:

Figure 10.5 Running multiple forms under the Form Manager

As different forms get focus they are brought to the top and their associated toolbar is activated, as shown by the following illustrations:

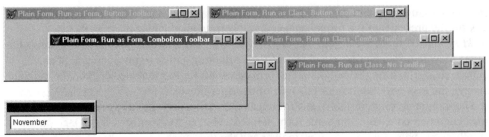

Figure 10.6 *SCX form with associated toolbar*

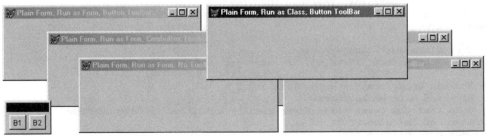

Figure 10.7 *VCX form with associated toolbar*

The form's behavior can also be tested by calling the form manager's *HideForms* and *ShowForms* methods directly:

```
GoFrmMgr.HideForms()  and   goFrmMgr.ShowForms()
```

Forms can also be released by clicking their close button and re-instantiated as necessary. To release all forms, call the form manager's ReleaseAll() method:

```
goFrmMgr.ReleaseAll()
```

How can I track and handle errors?

Probably the most comprehensive treatment of error handling strategy in Visual FoxPro is Doug Hennig's excellent paper, *"Error Handling in Visual FoxPro,"* which is available for download, complete with sample code, from his web site at www.stonefield.com. There is little point here in reiterating what Doug says, and the best advice we can offer is that if you need a complete error handling scheme, go get this paper and study it.

So what can we offer here instead? Well, we suspect that, in practice, most **applications** (as opposed to tools or utilities) do not actually try, or even need, to *handle* errors. This is because most of the errors that will arise in an application are likely to be code errors (i.e. errors in logic), with data consistency errors running a close second. The priorities in these situations are, therefore, to protect data integrity, inform the user that something has gone wrong and close the application down gracefully and safely. What we really need for this situation is something that will record what happened and provide as much information as possible about the state of the system when the error occurred.

Since Visual FoxPro is a database, it does not seem unreasonable to think that this sort of information should be recorded in a table, so that the information could be used to generate reports, record fixes and so on. What we are really talking about, therefore, is 'error recording' rather than 'error handling!' Of course, we still have to rely on Visual FoxPro's error handler to tell us when something has gone wrong. Not every error that Visual FoxPro detects will necessitate shutting down the application so there is still some *handling* element about it all - though perhaps not as much as you might think.

Classifying Visual FoxPro's errors

Visual FoxPro's default error handler provides for over 700 recognized errors, but they are not really categorized in any useful fashion. To try and make better use of the standard errors provided we have created a table (*'errmsg.dbf'*) containing all Visual FoxPro's standard error numbers and their associated text. Included in this table are three additional fields for "*Category*", "*Type*" and "*Action*" to give us the following structure:

```
ERRNUM        N  (   4)
ERRCAT        C  (  20)
ERRTYPE       C  (  20)
ERRACTION     C  (  10)
ERRTEXT       C  ( 200)
```

We classified the errors into one of the five categories listed below.

- Design Time Errors: These are things that can only occur during development of an application and which we would not, therefore, expect to encounter at any other time. These are mainly either compilation or '*In Use*' errors. Example: Error 1169: "*Project file is read-only.*"

- Developer Errors: Items in this category arise through errors in the code or logic. Many of these will be caught in testing and they arise from carelessness, fatigue, insufficiently defensive code or invalid assumptions on the part of the developer. Fixing these errors will invariably require changes to the source code. Example: Error 1127: "*You must use a logical expression with a FOR or WHILE clause.*"

- Run Time Errors: This category includes things that would be hard to catch at design time and which may not even be caught in testing. Most of these are related to missing or invalid files or to operations that may succeed in a development environment but which can fail at run time. As with developer errors, fixes will usually require changes to the source code. Example: Error 109 "*Record is in use by another user.*"

- System Errors: These are things that are not normally caused directly by errors in the source code but arise because of system environment or resource issues. The majority of these can really only be handled by shutting down the application. Example: Error 1986 "*GDI memory is low, close one or more windows and try again.*"

- <u>User Errors:</u> Only 11 out of the 700 standard errors could really be ascribed to this category. These are errors that we would normally expect to occur only as the result of some user action. Most should be capable of resolution without needing to close the application down, although it is unlikely that a generic solution could be devised to handle them. Example: Error 1523 *"Execution was canceled by the user."*

However, the problem is that some errors may well arise for different reasons. For example Error 1152 *"Cannot access the selected table."* could be caused by the network connection being lost (a *'system'* error), but also because the table used as the rowsource for a combo or list box has been closed too soon (either a *'developer'* or a *'run time'* error).

For each error we added a standard action which would either be to close down the entire application, abort the current process or to resolve the error. Note that these are not solutions, merely an indication of the expected severity of the error!

The error message text in this table is simply the standard message that Visual FoxPro generates. These are rarely 'user-friendly' and we would suggest replacing the standard messages with something more appropriate for your situation. (But this is definitely an 'exercise for the reader.')

Finally, where possible, we assigned each error a *'Type'* related to the situation in which it is most likely to be occur, for example *'SQL,'* *'Print,'* *'Index'* or *'Table.'* Only about half the errors could be assigned in this way, and not all these assignments are necessarily exclusive, but we felt it was a useful exercise nevertheless.

Logging errors (*Example: TrackErr.prg, ErrorLog.prg*)

There are three issues to address when creating an error-logging program. First, what should be logged? The short answer is *'as much as possible'*! It is easy to disregard superfluous information in an error log, but it is usually very difficult, if not impossible, to re-create the exact conditions in which an error occurred. The more information that you can gather about what happened, at the time it happens, the easier it will be resolve the problem.

Second, where should the log be stored? There is no generic answer to this question, but the solution we prefer is to include an entry in the application's INI file. This should define both the name and location of the error log and only needs to be read once when the application is started (see the INI File Manager topic, in this chapter, for details). The result can be stored to either a global variable or to a property of the application object, for use later. One key benefit of doing it this way is that it does allow each user to set up a local error log if necessary. (especially useful for developers and testers) without compromising your ability to maintain a centralized error log for the application as a whole.

The third issue is how should the error log be created? There are two basic options and each has some merit. We could use a table and write a record for each error directly to it. The obvious benefit of this approach is that it lends itself to analysis and reporting, and details of solutions and fixes can even be stored in the same table. The snag is that, especially in a large system, there is always the danger of running into conflicts when trying to access the table. Each record will, of necessity, involve a large amount of data and the last thing that you want to happen when trying to record an error is to raise another one!

Alternatively we could simply generate a text file with the details of each error, and in a table, record a summary of that error together with a reference to the output file. On the whole we like this approach better because it is the most flexible and keeps the size of the error log table to a minimum. One particularly neat idea we have seen was that whenever an error file was generated, it was automatically E-Mailed to the Development Team Leader.

Our error logging class, which is defined as a non-visual class (*'ErrorLog.prg'*), adopts the second approach and uses a table to record summary information and an auto generated text file to record details of the error and system state. Note that we have made no attempt to handle the situation in which an error in the error handling routines occurs. Not only is handling such an error a complex problem in its own right, it is far beyond the scope of this particular class to cover. The following sections discuss the main elements of the class.

The "errorlog" table

This table is used by the error logging class to record summary information about each error that occurs, and has the following structure:

```
LOGSID       Integer    4    && Error ID Number
LOGDTIME     DateTime   8    && Date/Time Stamp
LOGERRNUM    Integer    4    && VFP Error Number
LOGERRPROG   Character 60    && Program in which Error Occurred
LOGERRLINE   Integer    4    && Line Number in which Error Occurred
LOGERRUSER   Character 20    && User ID
LOGERRTXT    Character 60    && Error Log Path/FileName
```

A unique ID is generated for each error that is recorded in this table. This ID is then used as part of the name of the text file that records the details of the error to provide an easy means of cross-referencing.

Using the error-logging class *(Example: Errorlog.prg)*

This class is based on the Visual FoxPro *"Formset"* base class so that it can be given a private datasession. (The *FormCount* and *Visible* properties have been protected and set to 0, and .F., respectively). When the class is instantiated, it opens the Error Log and Error Message tables (with no buffering) in its private datasession and determines the path to which the log file should be written and the name of the application. We normally instantiate the error logging object at application start-up and assign it a global reference:

```
RELEASE goErrorLog
PUBLIC goErrorLog
goErrorLog = NEWOBJECT( 'xErrLog', 'errorlog.prg', NULL )
```

The class has only one exposed custom method, the *"LogError"* method and two exposed custom properties, *cNextAction* and *cUserMsg*.

Visual FoxPro's ON ERROR setting is then pointed to a simple wrapper program that will receive the DataSession, Program and Line Number in which the error occurred and call the *LogError* method, passing the parameters through, like this:

```
ON ERROR DO TrackErr WITH SET("DATASESSION"), PROGRAM(), LINENO()
```

The error-logging object inserts a record into the error log table and writes the detailed information to a text file. It then populates its exposed properties with the message and next action from the customized error message table. The wrapper program then reads these properties and the appropriate action is taken. The benefit of this approach is that it separates the logging process from that of communicating directly with the user and allows us to use the error logging class in situations where simply displaying a message box directly would not be appropriate.

The *TrackErr.prg* program typically looks something like this:

```
***********************************************************************
* Program....: TrackErr.prg
* Compiler...: Visual FoxPro 06.00.8492.00 for Windows
* Abstract...: Program called by ON ERROR to log Error Details
* ..........: ON ERROR DO TrackErr WITH SET("DATASESSION"), PROGRAM(),
LINENO()
***********************************************************************
LPARAMETERS tnDSID, tcProgram, tnLineNo
LOCAL lcNextAction, lcUserMsg

IF VARTYPE( goErrorLog ) = "O"
  *** Call Logging Method
  goErrorLog.LogError( tnDSID, tcProgram, tnLineNo )
  *** Now check the results
  lcNextAction = goErrorLog.cNextAction      && Next Action Required
  lcUserMsg    = goErrorLog.cUserMsg         && User Mesage Text

  *** Take Whatever Action is appropriate
  *** Typically this would be to display a Message for the user
  *** And either Re-Try or Close Down
  MESSAGEBOX( lcUserMsg, 16, "Application Error" )
ELSE
  MESSAGEBOX( "Error Logging is not Available", 16, "System Error" )
ENDIF
```

The text file created consists of a header and six detail sections as follows:

```
******** NEW ERROR: 12/22/99 09:50:44 AM ******************
Error : 1925: Unknown member TXTOUTPUT.
        at line 29 in FRMCHGPATHS.SETFORM
Source Code: ThisForm.txtOutPut.Value = ""

User  : TLC HOME # andykr
================================================================
Category: Developer
Type:
Action:    Endproc
***********************************************************************
[1] *** Memory dump: LIST MEMORY
[2] *** Data Dump
[3] *** Calling Chain
[4] *** Clipboard contents
[5] *** Object dump: LIST OBJECTS
[6] *** Data Session status: LIST STATUS
```

The program *TestErr.prg*, included in the sample code for this chapter, sets up the error-logging object and then generates an error.

How can I simplify getting messages to my users?

Visual FoxPro provides us with two built in mechanisms for communicating with our users. First, there is the **WAIT WINDOW** command, which is most suitable for handling status and information messages. Second, is the **MESSAGEBOX()** function, which provides for various formats of a modal form containing text and requires some action from the user. Both are quite useable and, while the various optional settings for the **Messagebox()** function are not easy to remember, it seems unnecessary to try and "re-invent the wheel" when it comes to message handling by devising a replacement for these two native tools.

However, one thing that we ought to consider (especially in the context of **COM** components, *n-tier* architecture and multiple 'front-end' applications) is that we would really like to avoid coding explicit calls to functions like **MESSAGEBOX()** and **WAIT WINDOW**. After all, both of these functions assume that you are running in an environment in which the concept of a 'window' means something and this may not always be the case.

We also want to remove the actual message text from our program code by extracting it into a table. This not only allows us to re-use messages but also helps keep messages consistent in our applications – so we don't ask the user to 'Confirm Changes' in one place and 'Save Changes' in another. It also makes changing the actual message text easier and, if you need to handle multiple languages, is the only practical way to do so. The following sections outline the construction and use of our table-driven message handling class.

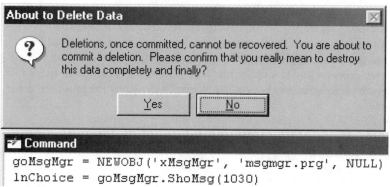

Figure 10.8 *Simple message handler class*

The standard message table *(Example: Msgtable.dbf)*

This table is used to store all of the relevant information for the user interface messages that we create. It is defined as a free table which, since it is always read-only at run time, we build into the **EXE**. In this case we are trading the benefits of having the table as part of a DBC for speed of access at run time. The structure of the table is very simple:

```
MSGNUM  I (   4,0 )  NOT NULL   && Message ID (Candidate Key)
MSGTYP  C (   1,0 )  NOT NULL   && Display Type Required
MSGTIT  C (  60,0 )  NOT NULL   && Title for MessageBox, Text for Wait
Window/Status
MSGBTN  N (   1,0 )  NOT NULL   && Button to set as default (For MessageBox only)
MSGTXT  M (   4,0 )  NOT NULL   && Message Text (For Messagebox Only)
```

A single (candidate) key is defined on the `MsgNum` field to provide a quick search capability by message number. Note that we have used a memo field for storing the actual message text, so that both the text and the layout of each message can be pre-defined.

We have defined a limited number of standard message types, which we use to pre-define the way in which a message is actually displayed, as follows:

Table 10.5 *Standard Message Type Definitions*

Code	Type	Style	Display Type
E	Error Dialog	Stop Icon with default 'OK' Button only	16
W	Warning Dialog	Exclamation Icon with 'OK' and 'Cancel' buttons	49
I	Information Dialog	Information Icon with default 'OK' Button only	64
C	Confirmation Dialog	Question Icon with 'Yes' and 'No' Buttons	36
X	Centered Window	Wait Window, centered on screen	99
Y	Default Window	Wait Window, top right corner of screen	98
Z	Status Bar	Sets text on default Status Bar	97

The message handling class *(Example:* M*sgmgr.prg)*

This class, like the Error Logging class described in the previous section, is based on a FormSet so it may have its own Private DataSession. The class is set up so that it need be instantiated only once as part of the application start up. Its *Init* method stores its own datasession to a protected property and sets up the message table in that datasession (which helps to ensure that the message table does not get inadvertently closed by the actions of other objects):

```
****************************************************************
* Program....: MsgMgr.prg
* Compiler...: Visual FoxPro 06.00.8492.00 for Windows
* Abstract...: Class Definition for Message Handler
****************************************************************
DEFINE CLASS xMsgMgr AS FORMSET
  PROTECTED FormCount, Visible, DataSession, nDSId
  FormCount   = 0        && Don't allow any forms
  Visible     = .F.      && Keep the Formset invisible
  DataSession = 2        && In a Private Datasession
  nDSId       = 1        && Default DS to 1

  PROCEDURE Init
    WITH This
      *** Open up the message table
      IF ! USED('msgtable')
        USE msgtable IN 0 AGAIN SHARED ALIAS msgtable
```

```
      ENDIF
      *** Save Message Handler's DataSession
      .nDSId = .DataSessionID
    ENDWITH
  ENDPROC
```

The class also has a single exposed custom method (*ShoMsg*) which expects to receive the ID Number of a message in the standard message table as a parameter. Having checked that the parameter is numeric, this method saves the current datasession and changes into the message handler's private datasession:

```
PROCEDURE ShoMsg( tnMsgNum )
  LOCAL lnOrigDS, lnRetVal
  WITH This
    *** Message Number must be numeric
    IF VARTYPE( tnMsgNum ) # "N"
      ERROR "9000: A valid numeric parameter must be passed to ShoMsg()"
      *** Return Error Indicator
      RETURN -1
    ENDIF
    *** Switch to Mesage Handler's DS
    lnOrigDS = SET("DATASESSION")
    SET DATASESSION TO (.nDSId )
    *** Locate Required Message Details
    IF SEEK( tnMsgNum, 'msgtable', 'msgnum' )
      *** Call Appropriate Handler for this message based on Type
      lnRetVal = .GetMsgStyle()
    ELSE
      *** Message Number not Valid
      ERROR "9000: Message Number " + ALLTRIM(STR( tnMsgNum )) + " Not
Recognised"
      *** Return Error Indicator
      lnRetVal = 0
    ENDIF
    *** Restore Original DS and Return
    SET DATASESSION TO (lnOrigDS)
    RETURN lnRetVal
  ENDWITH
ENDPROC
```

If the passed in message number is not found, the handler simply returns an error code (0), otherwise the record pointer is left pointing at the correct message and the protected *GetMsgStyle* custom method is called to pass the actual display of the message to the correct method, as follows:

```
****************************************************************
*** MsgMgr::GetMsgStyle() - Check Message Type and call appropriate handler
****************************************************************
PROTECTED PROCEDURE GetMsgStyle
  *** Check the current message type and call correct handler with
  *** any necessary parameters
  LOCAL lcMsgTyp, lnRetVal
  lcMsgTyp = msgtable.msgtyp
  DO CASE
    CASE lcMsgTyp = "E"
```

```
      *** Standard Error = "STOP" + "OK" button
      lnRetVal = .DoMsgBox( 16 )
    CASE lcMsgTyp = "W"
      *** Standard Warning = "EXCLAMATION" + "OK/Cancel" button
      lnRetVal = .DoMsgBox( 49 )
    CASE lcMsgTyp = "I"
      *** Standard Information = "INFO" + OK Button
      lnRetVal = .DoMsgBox( 64 )
    CASE lcMsgTyp = "C"
      *** Standard Confirmation = "QUESTION" + Yes/No Options
      lnRetVal = .DoMsgBox( 36 )
    CASE lcMsgTyp = "X"
      *** Wait Window Centered on screen
      lnRetVal = .DoWait(.T.)
    CASE lcMsgTyp = "Y"
      *** Wait Window at Top Right
      lnRetVal = .DoWait()
    CASE lcMsgTyp = "Z"
      *** Status Bar Message
      lnRetVal = .DoStat()
    OTHERWISE
      *** No Display Required - Return Success
      lnRetVal = 1
  ENDCASE
  *** Return Display Type
  RETURN lnRetVal
ENDPROC
```

The actual message displays are, with the exception of calculating the position for the centered 'wait window,' quite straightforward:

```
***********************************************************************
*** MsgMgr::DoMsgBox( tnParam ) - Call Message Box to display message
*** Return Button used to close Message Box
***********************************************************************
PROTECTED PROCEDURE DoMsgBox( tnParam )
  LOCAL lnRetVal, lcTxt, lcTit
  *** Get Message and Title from table
  lcTxt = ALLTRIM( msgtable.msgtxt )
  lcTit = ALLTRIM( msgtable.msgtit )
  *** Set Default Button - Store in Table as 1, 2 or 3
  IF ! EMPTY(msgtable.msgbtn)
    lnParam = tnParam + ((msgtable.msgbtn - 1) * 256)
  ELSE
    lnParam = tnParam
  ENDIF
  lnRetVal = MESSAGEBOX( lcTxt, lnParam, lcTit )
  RETURN lnRetVal
ENDPROC

***********************************************************************
*** MsgMgr::DoWait( tlCenter ) - Display Wait Window Message
*** No Specific Return Value
***********************************************************************
PROTECTED PROCEDURE DoWait( tlCenter )
  LOCAL lcTxt
  *** Get Message from table
```

```
   lcTxt = ALLTRIM( msgtable.msgtit )
   IF tlCenter
      LOCAL lnTexLen, lnRows, lnAvgChar, lcDispText, lnCnt, lcLine, lnCol, lnRow
      *** Calculate the size of the message
      SET MEMOWIDTH TO 80
      _MLINE = 0
      lnTexLen = 0
      lnRows = MEMLINES(lcTxt)
      *** Calculate the text size for positioning
      lnAvgChar = FONTMETRIC( 6, 'Arial', 8) / ;
                  FONTMETRIC( 6, _SCREEN.FontName, _SCREEN.FontSize )
      lcDispText = ''
      *** Find longest row of text in the message
      FOR lnCnt = 1 TO lnRows
         lcLine = ' ' + MLINE( lcTxt, 1, _MLINE) + ' '
         lcDispText = IIF(! EMPTY( lcDispText ), CHR(13), "") + lcDispText +
lcLine
         lnTexLen = MAX( TXTWIDTH(lcLine,'MS Sans Serif',8,'B')+4, lnTexLen)   && 4
is border
      NEXT
      *** Work out position for window based on longest row
      lnCol = INT((SCOLS() - lnTexLen * lnAvgChar )/2)
      lnRow = INT((SROWS() - lnRows)/2)
      *** Show Window centered
      WAIT WINDOW lcDispText AT lnRow, lnCol NOWAIT
   ELSE
      *** Simple Wait Window at Top/Right
      WAIT WINDOW lcTxt NOWAIT
   ENDIF
   *** Return 'Success'
   RETURN 1
ENDPROC


********************************************************************
*** MsgMgr::DoStat() - Display Status Bar Message
*** No Specific Return Value
********************************************************************
PROTECTED PROCEDURE DoStat()
   LOCAL lcTxt
   *** Get Message from table
   lcTxt = ALLTRIM( msgtable.msgtit )
   SET MESSAGE TO lcTxt
   *** Return 'Success'
   RETURN 1
ENDPROC
```

Using the message handler

Once the message-handling object is created, all that is needed to display a message is to call the *ShoMsg* method and pass the number of the required message. The sample code for this chapter includes a message table that defines one of each type of message. To test the handler, simply create the object and call a message:

```
goMsgMgr = NEWOBJECT('xMsgMgr', 'msgmgr.prg', NULL)
lnChoice = goMsgMgr.ShoMsg(1030)
```

The message handler will always return the identifying code for the button pressed to close a message box, or a numeric '1' for all other messages displayed.

Conclusion

We hope that the examples in this chapter have given you some useful ideas and are sure that you will be able to think of many other ways to use the power and flexibility of non-visual classes.

Chapter 11
Forms and Other Visual Classes

"Form and function are a unity, two sides of one coin. In order to enhance function, appropriate form must exist or be created." ("Rolfing: The Integration of Human Structions," by Ida P. Rolf).

Your application may implement logic that is more complex than rocket science, but if the interface is user-surly, no one will ever know or care. The most important thing to the people who will be using your application is whether or not it makes their job easier to do. Software that causes more work, or makes someone's working life more difficult, is bad software, no matter how you slice it. In this chapter, we will share some classes with you that will not only make life easier for your end-users but will also make life easier for you as you develop it.

How do I make my forms fill the entire screen regardless of the screen resolution? *(Example: CH11.VCX::FrmMaximize and Maximize.scx)*

If the application you are building is *sovereign*, (i.e. an application intended to be used exclusively by a user, as opposed to merely sharing a portion of the user's screen with other applications) you will probably want the forms to maximize themselves when instantiated, regardless of the screen resolution a particular user has set.

To do this you will need to calculate the ratio by which the current screen resolution differs from the standard (which should always be 640 x 480 anyway!) for which your forms are designed. This ratio can then be applied to all forms and their controls to resize everything without changing relative proportions. This is best accomplished by adding a *ResizeControls* method to the form class and calling it from the form's *Init* method, after first re-sizing the form itself, like so:

```
LOCAL loControl
WITH Thisform
  *** Determine the ratio needed to maximize the form
  *** depending on screen resolution and store it to form properties
  .WidthRatio = SYSMETRIC( 1 ) / 640
  .HeightRatio = SYSMETRIC( 2 ) / 480
  *** If resolution is higher than 640 x 480, reposition
  *** and maximize the form
  IF .WidthRatio > 1
    .Top = 0
    .Left = 0
    .Width = .Width * .WidthRatio
    .Height = .Height * .HeightRatio
    *** And resize each control contained in the form
```

```
      FOR EACH loControl IN .Controls
        .ResizeControls( loControl )
      ENDFOR
   ENDIF
ENDWITH
```

Note that we are using the native *SysMetric()* function to determine the current screen resolution and then calculate both the horizontal and vertical ratios. These ratios are saved as form properties and used immediately to re-size the form itself. We then loop through each of the objects in the form's *Controls* collection, calling the *ResizeControls* method, and passing an object reference to the control for each one.

The *ResizeControls* method must take different action depending on whether the object that it receives is a simple control or another container with more controls. To handle this situation the method has to be able to drill down into containers by calling itself recursively. The first task, however, is to set the *Top*, *Left*, *Height* and *Width* properties for the passed control if it has these properties. (Your first thought may well be that surely *all* visual controls have these properties? Not so, Pageframes, for example, do not actually have *Height* and *Width*, instead they have *PageHeight* and *PageWidth* properties.)

```
LPARAMETERS toControl
LOCAL loPage, loControl, loColumn, lnColumnWidths[1], lnCol

IF PEMSTATUS( toControl, 'Width', 5 )
  toControl.Width = toControl.Width * Thisform.WidthRatio
ENDIF
IF PEMSTATUS( toControl, 'Height', 5 )
  toControl.Height = toControl.Height * Thisform.HeightRatio
ENDIF
IF PEMSTATUS( toControl, 'Top', 5 )
  toControl.Top = toControl.Top * Thisform.HeightRatio
ENDIF
IF PEMSTATUS( toControl, 'Left', 5 )
  toControl.Left = toControl.Left * Thisform.HeightRatio
ENDIF
```

Next, we need to resize the font for the current control. If this happens to be a grid, it is a special case and must be handled separately because changing the font of a grid resets the column widths of the grid. Before modifying a grid, we must save all the column widths so that we can restore them afterward:

```
IF UPPER( ALLTRIM( toControl.Baseclass ) ) = 'GRID'
  DIMENSION lnColumnWidths[toControl.ColumnCount]
  FOR lnCol = 1 TO toControl.ColumnCount
    lnColumnWidths[lnCol] = toControl.Columns[lnCol].Width
  ENDFOR
  toControl.Fontsize = INT( toControl.FontSize * Thisform.WidthRatio )
  FOR lnCol = 1 TO toControl.ColumnCount
    toControl.Columns[lnCol].Width = lnColumnWidths[lnCol]
  ENDFOR
ELSE
  IF PEMSTATUS( toControl, 'Fontsize', 5 )
    toControl.Fontsize = INT( toControl.FontSize * Thisform.WidthRatio )
```

```
   ENDIF
ENDIF
```

Next, we must determine if we have an object that contains other objects. When this is the case, we must call the *ResizeControls* method recursively and pass it a reference to each of the contained objects. The following code does this when the current object is a pageframe, page, container, commandgroup, or optiongroup.

```
DO CASE
  CASE UPPER( toControl.BaseClass ) = 'PAGEFRAME'
    FOR EACH loPage IN toControl.Pages
      Thisform.ResizeControls( loPage )
    ENDFOR

  CASE INLIST( UPPER( toControl.BaseClass ), 'PAGE', 'CONTAINER' )
    FOR EACH loControl IN toControl.Controls
      Thisform.ResizeControls( loControl )
    ENDFOR

  CASE INLIST( UPPER( ALLTRIM( toControl.BaseClass ) ), ;
    'COMMANDGROUP', 'OPTIONGROUP' )
    LOCAL lnButton
    FOR lnButton = 1 TO toControl.ButtonCount
      ThisForm.resizeControls( toControl.Buttons[lnButton] )
    ENDFOR
```

Finally, we must handle the special cases. If the current object is a grid, we must set its *RowHeight* and *HeaderHeight* properties. We must also iterate through its columns collection and set the *Width* of each column contained in the grid:

```
  CASE UPPER( toControl.BaseClass ) = 'GRID'
    WITH toControl
      .RowHeight    = .RowHeight * Thisform.HeightRatio
      .HeaderHeight = .HeaderHeight * Thisform.HeightRatio
      FOR EACH loColumn IN .Columns
        loColumn.Width = loColumn.Width * Thisform.WidthRatio
      ENDFOR
    ENDWITH
```

But if the current object is either a combo or list box, we must recalculate and reset its *ColumnWidths*:

```
  CASE INLIST( UPPER( toControl.BaseClass ), 'COMBOBOX', 'LISTBOX' )
    LOCAL lnCol, lnStart, lnEnd, lnLen, lcColumnWidths
    WITH toControl
      IF .ColumnCount < 2
        .ColumnWidths = ALLTRIM( STR( .Width ) )
      ELSE
        lcColumnWidths = ''
        lnStart = 1
        FOR lnCol = 1 TO .ColumnCount - 1
          lnEnd = AT( ',', .ColumnWidths, lnCol )
          lnLen = lnEnd - lnStart
```

```
        lcColumnWidths = lcColumnWidths + ;
          IIF( EMPTY( lcColumnWidths ), '', ',' ) + ;
                ALLTRIM( STR( VAL (SUBSTR( .ColumnWidths, lnStart, lnLen ) ) ;
                * Thisform.WidthRatio ) )
          lnStart = lnEnd + 1
        ENDFOR
        lnLen = LEN( .ColumnWidths ) - lnStart + 1
        lcColumnWidths = lcColumnWidths + ',' + ;
          ALLTRIM( STR( VAL (SUBSTR( .ColumnWidths, lnStart, lnLen ) ) ;
          * Thisform.WidthRatio ) )
        .ColumnWidths = lcColumnWidths
    ENDIF
  ENDWITH

  OTHERWISE
      *** There is no otherwise...I think we got all cases
ENDCASE
```

How do I create resizable forms? *(Example: CH11.VCX::cusResizer and*
Resize.scx)

The self-maximizing form class discussed above is a special case of a re-sizable form, in that it
is a once-only operation, but the basic principles are the same. Each time the form is resized,
we need to calculate the ratio by which the form's height and width have changed relative to its
original dimensions and then apply that ratio to each control on the form to retain the same
relative size and positions at all times.

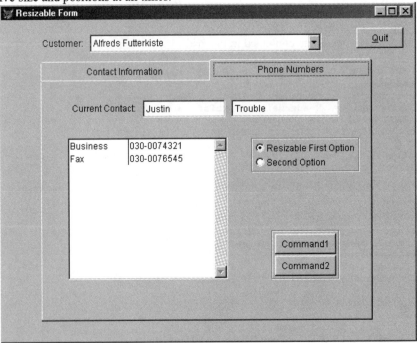

Figure 11.1 Resizable form - as instantiated with original dimensions

The best way to handle this is to create a class that will do the necessary calculations and simply add it to each form that needs to be made resizable. The foundation classes that ship with Visual FoxPro version 6.0 actually include such a resizer class. However, while it may be adequate for simple forms, with a few basic controls, it is rather limited and does not handle more complex controls like grids, combos or list boxes properly. Nor does it even attempt to resize or reposition OptionGroups or CommandGroups. As a result, in our opinion it does not merit much attention.

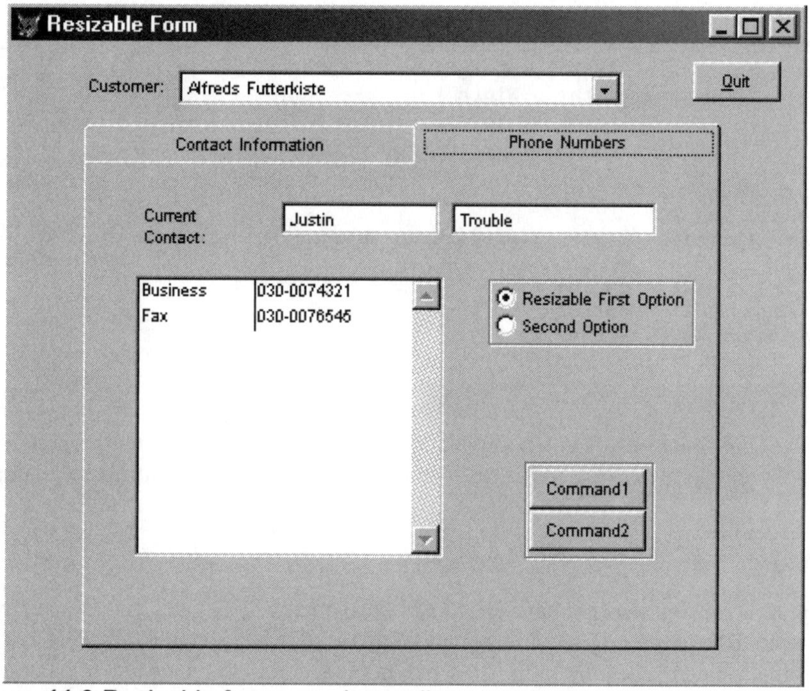

Figure 11.2 *Resizable form - made smaller*

To provide maximum flexibility, we have created a *Resizer* class that *will* handle all these requirements properly. The object based on this class must be added to the form or form class in its *Init* method because it needs to save the original dimensions of all form controls when it is instantiated. Clearly, we must ensure that all form controls have been instantiated before the resizer's *Init* method runs so we use code like this in the form's *Init* method:

```
IF DODEFAULT()
  This.AddObject( 'Resizer', 'cusResizer' )
ENDIF
```

As stated above, the key to making the class function property is first to save all the relevant visual orientation properties for each object on the form. In Visual FoxPro 6.0, we can make use of each form control's *AddProperty* method to save this information within the object itself. Thus, when the resizer object is instantiated, its *SaveOriginalDimensions* method processes the form's controls collection, drilling down into all containers (similar to the *frmMaximize* class presented above). This method creates the properties required to save *Height, Width, PageHeight, ColumnWidths* and so on. Obviously, the object's base class determines which properties are added via *AddProperty*. This code, in the resizer's *Init* method, invokes its custom *SaveOriginalDimensions* method like so:

```
LOCAL loControl

WITH Thisform

   *** Save form dimensions at instantiation
   .AddProperty( 'nOriginalHeight', .Height )
   .AddProperty( 'nOriginalWidth', .Width )

   *** Set a minimun Width and Height to avoid errors later
   .MinWidth = .Width / 2
   .MinHeight = .Height / 2

   *** Now save the relevant visual properties (height, width, columnwidths,
etc)
   *** of all the controls on the form
   FOR EACH loControl IN .Controls
     This.SaveOriginalDimensions( loControl )
   ENDFOR
ENDWITH
```

SaveOriginalDimensions drills down into all containers, adding the required properties and initializing them with the correct values as it spins through the form's controls collection:

```
LPARAMETERS toControl
LOCAL loPage, loControl, loColumn, lnCol
```

Obviously, if the object does not have an *AddProperty* method, we can't use it to add the properties required to save the original dimensions. If this is the case, we bail out. This may cause some anomalies later when the form is resized, but it is certainly preferable to having a fatal error:

```
IF ! PEMSTATUS( toControl, 'AddProperty', 5 )
   RETURN
ENDIF
```

Next we check for the usual properties: *Height, Width, Top* and *Left*. If they are valid properties for the current object, we add the required properties to the object and save its original dimensions:

```
IF PEMSTATUS( toControl, 'Width', 5 )
   toControl.AddProperty( 'nOriginalWidth', toControl.Width )
ENDIF
IF PEMSTATUS( toControl, 'Height', 5 )
   toControl.AddProperty( 'nOriginalHeight', toControl.Height )
ENDIF
IF PEMSTATUS( toControl, 'Top', 5 )
```

```
  toControl.AddProperty( 'nOriginalTop', toControl.Top )
ENDIF
IF PEMSTATUS( toControl, 'Left', 5 )
  toControl.AddProperty( 'nOriginalLeft', toControl.Left )
ENDIF
IF PEMSTATUS( toControl, 'Fontsize', 5 )
  toControl.AddProperty( 'nOriginalFontSize', toControl.FontSize )
ENDIF
```

Next we check to see if the current object is a container. If it is and it contains other objects, we will have to pass them to this method recursively:

```
DO CASE
  CASE UPPER( toControl.BaseClass ) = 'PAGEFRAME'
    FOR EACH loPage IN toControl.Pages
      This.SaveOriginalDimensions( loPage )
    ENDFOR

  CASE INLIST( UPPER( toControl.BaseClass ), 'PAGE', 'CONTAINER' )
    FOR EACH loControl IN toControl.Controls
      This.SaveOriginalDimensions( loControl )
    ENDFOR

  CASE INLIST( UPPER( ALLTRIM( toControl.BaseClass ) ), 'COMMANDGROUP',
'OPTIONGROUP' )
    LOCAL lnButton
    FOR lnButton = 1 TO toControl.ButtonCount
      This.SaveOriginalDimensions( toControl.Buttons[lnButton] )
    ENDFOR
```

We can also handle the special cases here. For example, grids have *RowHeight* and *HeaderHeight* properties that need to be saved and we need to save the original widths of all of its contained columns. Combo and List boxes also require special handling to save the original *ColumnWidths:*

```
  CASE UPPER( toControl.BaseClass ) = 'GRID'
    WITH toControl
      .AddProperty( 'nOriginalRowHeight', .RowHeight )
      .AddProperty( 'nOriginalHeaderHeight', .HeaderHeight )
      .AddProperty( 'nOriginalColumnWidths[1]' )
      DIMENSION .nOriginalColumnWidths[ .ColumnCount ]
      FOR lnCol = 1 TO .ColumnCount
        .nOriginalColumnWidths[lnCol] = .Columns[lnCol].Width
      ENDFOR
    ENDWITH

  CASE INLIST( UPPER( toControl.BaseClass ), 'COMBOBOX', 'LISTBOX' )
    WITH toControl
      .AddProperty( 'nOriginalColumnWidths', .ColumnWidths )
    ENDWITH

  OTHERWISE
    *** There is no otherwise...I think we got all cases
ENDCASE
```

Having saved all the original values, we need to ensure that the resizer is invoked whenever the form is resized. A single line of code in the form's *Resize* method is all that is needed:

```
Thisform.cusResizer.AdjustControls()
```

The custom *AdjustControls* method loops through the form's controls collection in much the same way as the *SaveOriginalDimensions* method. In this case, however, the method invokes the *ResizeControls* method to resize and reposition the controls using the form's current width divided by its original width as the factor by which its contained controls are made wider or narrower.

The sample form Resize.SCX shows how the class can be used to handle resizing a reasonably complex form. However, a word of caution is in order here. This class will not cope with objects that are added at run time using delayed instantiation. This is simply because the set up assumes that all objects exist before the resizer itself is instantiated. If you need to use delayed instantiation in a resizable form, call the resizer's *SaveOriginalDimensions* method explicitly with a reference to the newly added object and then immediately invoke the *ResizeControls* method.

Certain other classes that we introduced earlier in this book would also require modification to function properly in a resizable form. For example, when used in a resizable form the expanding edit box introduced in Chapter 4 requires that its *SaveOriginalDimensions* method be called each time it is expanded. Since its size and position changes whenever the form is resized, it is not enough to store this information once when the edit box is instantiated.

How do I search for particular records? *(Example: SearchDemo.scx and Srch.scx)*

The ability to find a specific record based on some sort of search criterion is a very common requirement. We have created a generic 'pop-up' form (*Srch.scx*) which can be used to search for a match on any field in a given table. You just need to be sure that any form that calls it, does so with the following parameters in the order in which they are listed.

Table 11.1 Parameters passed to the search form

Parameter Name	Parameter Description
ToParent	Object reference to the calling form
TcAlias	Alias in which to perform the search
TcField	Field in which to search for a match
TcAction	Action to take when a match is found

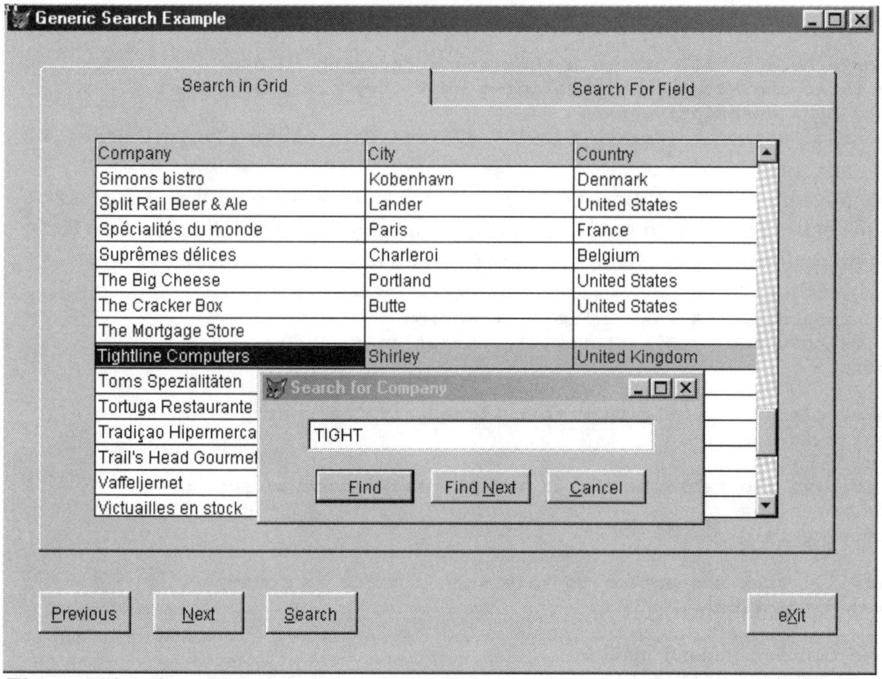

Figure 11.3 *Generic search form in action*

Each object on the calling form must be capable of registering itself with this form as the current object. This is required because when the user clicks on the 'search' button, the button becomes the form's *ActiveControl*. However, we want to search on the field bound to the control that was the *ActiveControl* prior to clicking on the search button, so we need some way of identifying it. All we need to achieve this functionality is a custom form property called *oActiveControl* and the following code in the *LostFocus* method of our data aware controls:

```
IF PEMSTATUS( Thisform, 'oActiveControl', 5 )
  Thisform.oActiveControl = This
ENDIF
```

The search form is instantiated with this code in the calling form's custom *Search* method. Notice that the search form is only instantiated if the calling form does not have a reference to one that already exists:

```
*** First see if we already have a search form available
IF VARTYPE( Thisform.oChild ) = 'O'

  *** If we have one, just set the field to search
  Thisform.oChild.cField  = JUSTEXT( This.oActiveControl.ControlSource )
  Thisform.oChild.Activate()
ELSE
  DO FORM Srch WITH This, This.cPrimaryTable, ;
    JUSTEXT( This.oActiveControl.ControlSource ), ;
    'This.oParent.oActiveControl.SetFocus()'
```

```
ENDIF

*** This works because all controls that are referenced in code
*** have a three character prefix defining what they are ( e.g., txt )
*** followed by a descriptive name
Thisform.oChild.Caption = 'Search for ' + SUBSTR( This.oActiveControl.Name, 4 )
```

The search form saves the parameters it receives to custom form properties so they are available to the entire form. It also sends a reference to itself back to the calling form so that the calling form is able to release the search form (if it still exists) when it is released:

```
LPARAMETERS toParent, tcAlias, tcField, tcAction
IF DODEFAULT( toParent, tcAlias, tcField, tcAction )
  WITH Thisform

    *** Save reference to the form that kicked off the search
    .oParent = toParent

    *** Also save the table to search and the field name to search
    .cAlias = tcAlias
    .cField = tcField

    *** Finally, save the action to take when a match is found
    .cAction = tcAction

    *** Save Current record number
    .nRecNo = RECNO( .cAlias )

    *** Give the parent form a reference to the search form
    *** So when we close the parent form we also close the search form
    .oParent.oChild = This
  ENDWITH
ENDIF
```

The search form has three custom methods, one for each of the command buttons. The *Find* method searches for the first match on the specified field to the value typed into the textbox like so:

```
LOCAL lnSelect, lcField, luValue, lcAction

*** Save current work area
lnSelect = SELECT()
WITH ThisForm
```

If the field contains character data, we want to force the value in the textbox to uppercase. This is easily accomplished by placing a ! in its format property in the property sheet. Therefore, there is no need to perform this task in code:

```
  luValue = IIF( VARTYPE( .txtSearchString.Value ) = 'C', ;
    ALLTRIM( .txtSearchString.Value ), .txtSearchString.Value )
  SELECT ( .cAlias )
```

We then check for an index tag on the specified field using our handy dandy *IsTag()* function. If we have a tag, we will use SEEK to find a match. Otherwise, we have to use LOCATE:

```
IF IsTag( .cField )
  SEEK luValue ORDER TAG ( .cField ) IN ( .cAlias )
ELSE
  lcField = .cField
  IF VARTYPE( EVAL( .cAlias + '.' + lcField ) ) = 'C'
    LOCATE FOR UPPER( &lcField ) = luValue
  ELSE
    LOCATE FOR &lcField  = luValue
  ENDIF
ENDIF
```

If a match is found, we perform the next action that was passed to the form's *Init* method and save the record number of the current record. Otherwise, we display a message to let the user know that no match was found and restore the record pointer to where it was before we started the search:

```
*** If a match was found, perform the next action
IF FOUND()

  *** Save record number of matching record
  .nRecNo = RECNO( .cAlias )
  SELECT ( lnSelect )
  lcAction = .cAction
  &lcAction
ELSE
  WAIT WINDOW 'No Match Found!' NOWAIT

  *** Restore Record Pointer
  GOTO .nRecNo IN (.cAlias )
  SELECT ( lnSelect )
ENDIF
ENDWITH
```

The code in the *FindNext* method is very similar to the code in the *Find* method. Unfortunately, we must use LOCATE in the *FindNext* method because SEEK always finds the first match and always starts from the top of the file. The is the code that finds the next record, if there is one:

```
*** If we are on the last record found, skip to the next record
SKIP

*** Must use LOCATE to Find next because seek always starts
*** at the top and finds the first match
lcField = .cField
luValue = IIF( VARTYPE( .txtSearchString.Value ) = 'C', ;
  ALLTRIM( .txtSearchString.Value ), .txtSearchString.Value )
IF VARTYPE( EVAL( .cAlias + '.' + lcField ) ) = 'C'
  LOCATE FOR UPPER( &lcField ) = luValue REST
ELSE
  LOCATE FOR &lcField  = luValue REST
```

```
ENDIF
```

The code in the search form's custom *Cancel* method cancels the search, repositions the record pointer, and closes the search form like so:

```
WITH Thisform
  GOTO .nRecNo IN ( .cAlias )
  .Release()
ENDWITH
```

Some of the most important code resides in the *Destroy* method of each form. If the search form did not have this code in its *Destroy* method:

```
IF TYPE( 'Thisform.oParent.Name' ) = 'C'
  Thisform.oParent.oChild = .NULL.
ENDIF
```

it would refuse to go away when the user clicked on the CANCEL button because the form that called it would still be pointing to it. In this case, the reference held by the calling form is known as a *dangling reference*. The reference that the search form has to the calling form (This.oParent) cleans up after itself automatically, so it is less troublesome. When the search form is released, the reference it holds to the calling form is released too. This code in the calling form's *Destroy* method makes certain that when it dies, it takes the search form with it:

```
*** Release the Search form if it is still open
IF VARTYPE( Thisform.oChild ) # 'X'
  Thisform.oChild.Release()
ENDIF
```

How do I build SQL on the fly? *(Example: FilterDemo.scx and BuildFilter.scx)*

Many excellent third-party tools are available and provide this functionality as well as the ability to create, modify, and print reports over the output of user-generated SQL. It is not our intention to re-invent the wheel here. If the requirements of your application for end-user generated SQL are complex, clearly the solution is one of these very fine products. Having said that, there are occasions when it is necessary to present the end-user with a means of building a very simple filter condition that can be applied to a single table. In this case, the third-party tool may provide a lot more functionality than you require. BuildFilter.scx is a simple filter builder and is provided with the sample code for this chapter. It builds the filter condition for a single alias. With slight modification and the addition of a pageframe, this form can easily be modified to join two tables (or more) prior to building the filter.

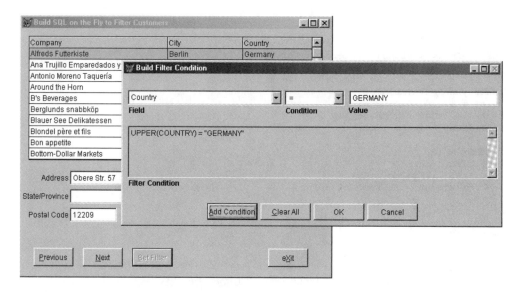

Figure 11.4 *Generic form to build filter condition*

Call BuildFilter.scx using this syntax:

```
DO FORM BUILDFILTER WITH '<ALIAS>' TO lcSQLString
```

You can then use the returned filter condition to run a SQL query like this:

```
SELECT * FROM <alias> WHERE &lcSQLstring INTO CURSOR Temp NOFILTER
```

or to set a filter on the specified alias like this:

```
SELECT <alias>
SET FILTER TO ( lcSQLstring )
```

The *BuildFilter* form expects to receive a table alias as a parameter and stores it to the custom *cAlias* property in order to make it available to the entire form. The custom *SetForm* method is then invoked to populate the custom *aFieldNames* array property that is used as the *RowSource* for the drop down list of field names pictured above. After ensuring that the specified alias is available, the *SetForm* method uses the **AFIELDS()** function to create laFields, a local array containing the names of the fields in the passed alias. Since we do not want to allow the user to include memo fields in any filter condition, we scan the laFields array to remove all memo fields like so:

```
LOCAL lnFieldCnt, laFields[1], lnCnt, lcCaption, lnArrayLen
WITH Thisform

  *** Make sure alias is available
  IF !USED( .cAlias )
    USE ( .cAlias ) IN 0
```

```
  ENDIF

  *** Get all the field names in the passed alias
  lnFieldCnt = AFIELDS( laFields, .cAlias )

  *** Don't include memo fields in the field list
  lnArrayLen = lnFieldCnt
  lnCnt = 1
  DO WHILE lnCnt <= lnArrayLen
    IF lnCnt > lnFieldCnt
      EXIT
    ENDIF
    IF TYPE( .cAlias + "." + laFields[ lnCnt, 1 ] ) = "M"
      =ADEL( laFields,lnCnt )
      lnFieldCnt = lnFieldCnt - 1
    ELSE
      lnCnt = lnCnt + 1
    ENDIF
  ENDDO
```

After the memo fields have been removed, the array, *ThisForm.aFieldNames*, is built using the remaining elements in the laFields array. *Thisform.aFieldNames* contains two columns. The first column contains the field's caption if the passed alias is a table or view in the current dbc and the caption property for the field is not empty. If the passed alias is a free table or its caption is empty, the first column of the array contains the name of the field. The second column of the array always contains the field name:

```
  DIMENSION .aFieldNames[ lnFieldCnt,2 ]
  FOR lnCnt = 1 TO lnFieldCnt
    lcCaption = ""
    IF !EMPTY( DBC() ) AND ( INDBC( .cAlias, 'TABLE' ) ;
      OR INDBC( .cAlias, 'VIEW' ) )
      lcCaption = PADR( DBGetProp( .cAlias + "." + laFields[ lnCnt, 1 ], ;
        'FIELD', 'CAPTION' ), 40 )
    ENDIF
    IF EMPTY( lcCaption )
      lcCaption = PADR( laFields[ lnCnt, 1 ], 40 )
    ENDIF
    .aFieldNames[ lnCnt, 1 ] = lcCaption
    .aFieldNames[ lnCnt, 2 ] = PADR( laFields[ lnCnt, 1 ], 40 )
  ENDFOR
  .cboFieldNames.Requery()
  .cboFieldNames.ListIndex = 1
ENDWITH
```

It is the form's custom *BuildFilter* method that adds the current condition to the filter. It is invoked each time the ADD CONDITION button is clicked:

```
LOCAL lcCondition
WITH Thisform
  IF TYPE( .cAlias + '.' + ALLTRIM( .cboFieldNames.Value ) ) = 'C'
    lcCondition = 'UPPER(' + ALLTRIM( .cboFieldNames.Value ) + ') ' + ;
      ALLTRIM( Thisform.cboConditions.Value ) + ' '
  ELSE
    lcCondition = ALLTRIM( .cboFieldNames.Value ) + ' ' + ;
```

```
        ALLTRIM( Thisform.cboConditions.Value ) + ' '
ENDIF

*** Add the quotation marks if the field type is character
IF TYPE( .cAlias + '.' + ALLTRIM( .cboFieldNames.Value ) ) = 'C'
   lcCondition = lcCondition + CHR( 34 ) + ;
     UPPER( ALLTRIM( .txtValues.Value ) ) + CHR( 34 )
ELSE
   lcCondition = lcCondition + ALLTRIM( .txtValues.Value )
ENDIF

*** If there are multiple conditions and them together
.cFilter = IIF( EMPTY( .cFilter ), lcCondition, .cFilter + ;
   ' AND ' + lcCondition )
ENDWITH
Thisform.edtFilter.Refresh()
```

There is no validation performed on the values entered for the filter condition. This is something that you will definitely want to add if you use this little form as the basis of a SQL generator in your production application. This could be accomplished by adding a *ValidateCondition* method to the form. This method would be called by the *BuildCondition* method and return a logical true if the text box contains a value appropriate for the data type of the field selected in the drop down list. Our *Str2Exp* function introduced in Chapter 2 would help to accomplish this goal.

How can I simulate the Command Window in my executable? *(Example: Command.scx)*

Occasionally you may find it necessary to walk an end-user of your production application through a simple operation such as browsing a specific table. You may think that your users need a copy of Visual FoxPro in order to do this. Not true! With a simple form, a couple of lines of code and a little macro expansion, you can easily create a command window simulator to help you accomplish this task.

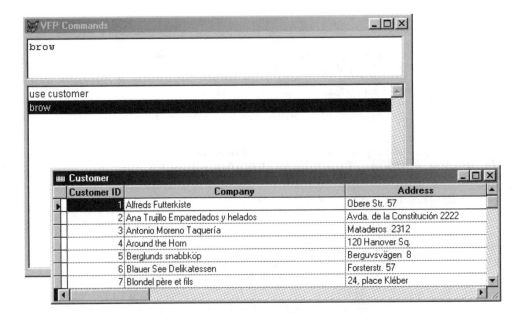

Figure 11.5 *Simulated Command Window for your executable*

The Command Window form consists of an edit box and a list box. The form's custom *ExecuteCmd* method is invoked whenever the user types a command into the edit box and presses the **ENTER** key. The command is also added to the list box using this code in the edit box's *KeyPress* method:

```
*** IF <ENTER> Key is pressed, execute the command
IF nKeyCode = 13

  *** Make sure there is a command to execute
  IF !EMPTY( This.Value )
    WITH Thisform

      *** Add the command to the command history list
      .lstHistory.AddItem( ALLTRIM( This.Value ) )

      *** Execute the command
      .ExecuteCmd( ALLTRIM( This.Value ) )
    ENDWITH

    *** Clear the edit box
    This.Value = ''
    This.SelStart = 0
  ENDIF
  *** Don't put a carriage return in the edit box!
  NODEFAULT
ENDIF
```

A command may also be selected for execution by highlighting it in the list box and pressing ENTER or double-clicking on it. The list box's *dblClick* method has code to display the current command in the edit box and invoke the form's *ExecuteCmd* method. The command is executed, via macro substitution, in this method:

```
LPARAMETERS tcCommand

*** Direct output to _screen
ACTIVATE SCREEN

*** Execute command
&tcCommand

*** Re-activate this form
ACTIVATE WINDOW FrmCommand
```

If the command is invalid or has been typed incorrectly, the form's *Error* method displays the error message. This is all that is required to provide your executable with basic command window functionality.

Wrappers for common Visual FoxPro functions *(Example: CH11.VCX::cntGetFile and CH11.VCX::cntGetDir)*

We find there are certain Visual FoxPro functions that we use over and over again in our applications. `GetFile()` and `GetDir()` are two that immediately spring to mind. `GetFile()` is especially troublesome because it accepts so many parameters. We can never remember all of them and have to go to the Help file each time we invoke the function. Creating a little wrapper class for it has two major benefits. First, it provides our end-users with a consistent interface whenever they must select a file or directory. Secondly, we no longer have to refer to the Help file each time we need to use the `GetFile()` function. All of its parameters are now properties of the container class and they are well documented.

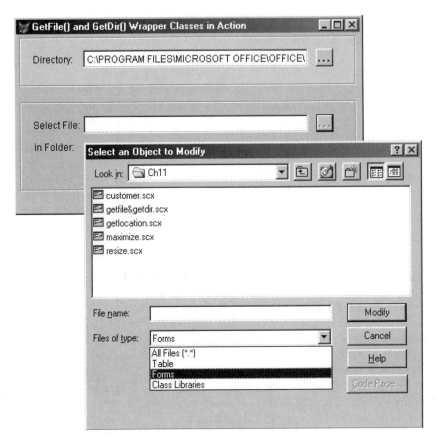

Figure 11.6 *Wrapper classes for GetFile() and GetDir() in action*

CntGetFile is the container class used to wrap the `GetFile()` function. It consists of two text boxes and a command button. The first text box contains the name of the file returned by the function. The second text box contains path. The command button is used to invoke the `GetFile()` function with the appropriate parameters. The following table lists the custom properties used for parameters accepted by `GetFile()`

Table 11.2 cntGetFile custom properties used as parameters to GetFile()

Property	Explanation
cFileExtensions	Specifies the extensions of the files displayed in the list box when 'All Files' is not selected. When "Tables" is chosen from the Files of Type list, all files with a .dbf extension are displayed. When "Forms" is chosen from the Files of Type list, all files with .scx and .vcx extensions are displayed.
cText	Text for the directory list in the Open dialog box
cTitleBarCaption	Title bar caption for the GetFile() dialog box
nButtonType	0: OK and Cancel buttons. 1: OK, New and Cancel buttons 2: OK, None and Cancel buttons "Untitled" is returned with the path specified in the Open dialog box if nButtonType is 1 and the user chooses the New button
cOpenButtonCaption	Caption for the OK button

To use the class, just drop it on the form, set all or none of the properties specified above, and you are finished. The fully qualified file name returned from the `GetFile()` function is stored in the container's custom *cFileName* property.

CntGetDir wraps the native `GetDir()` function and operates in a very similar fashion. The parameters accepted by the function are custom properties of the container and the function's return value is stored in its custom *cPath* property.

Presentation classes

A stock of standard presentation classes will make your life as a developer much easier. These presentation classes are generally composite classes that you have "canned" because they perform common tasks that are required in many different parts of the application. These presentation classes tend to be application specific. For example, a visual customer header or order header class will speed development of all forms that display customer or order information. Not only do presentation classes such as these enable you to develop applications more quickly, they also give the application a consistent look and feel that will be appreciated by your end-users.

Although presentation classes tend to be application specific, we have a few that we use across many applications.

Postal code lookup class *(Example: CH11.VCX::cntAddress and GetLocation.scx)*

Generally speaking, the fewer times the end-user has to touch the keyboard, the better your application will run. When you can find ways to reduce the amount of information that must be entered, you can reduce the number of mistakes made during the data entry process. This is why lookup classes like the one presented in this section are so useful. The entry of address information lends itself to this kind of implementation because postal code lists are readily available from a variety of sources.

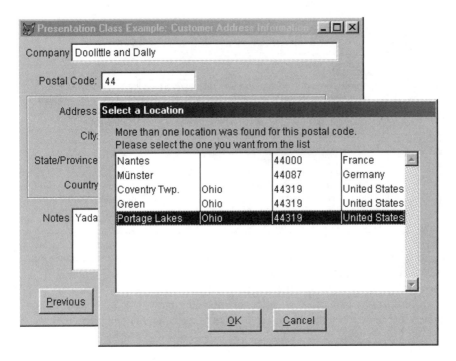

Figure 11.7 *Postal Code lookup form called from presentation class*

When the postal code or zip code lookup table is used to populate a set of address fields, all of the relevant information (city, province or state and country if necessary) is copied from the lookup table. That is, the address information is not normalized out of the table containing it. The postal code lookup table is only used to populate the required fields with the correct information if it is found. Typically, postal code lists are purchased from and maintained by a third party. Changing such tables locally is not a good idea because there is no guarantee that the next update won't clobber these changes.

The popup form is called from the custom *FindCity* method of the *cntAddress* presentation class. The address container looks like this and can be dropped on any form that needs to display an address:

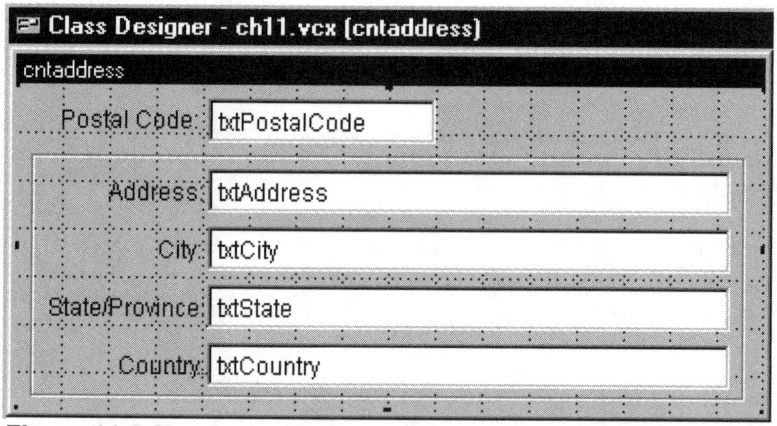

Figure 11.8 *Standard address container class*

Our address container and associated lookup form expect to have a parameterized view present called lv_PostalCode. This view contains city, state and country information by postal code and has the following structure:

Table 11.3 *Structure of lv_PostalCode parameterized view*

Field Name	Data Type	Description
City	Character	City Name
Sp_Name	Character	State/Province/Region Name
PostalCode	Character	Postal Code
Ctry_Name	Character	Country Name
Pc_Key	Integer	Postal Code Primary Key

The view parameter, vp_PostalCode, determines how the view is populated. So if you want to use this container class and its associated lookup form, you have two choices. You can create the lv_PostalCode parameterized view from your lookup table(s) as described above. Or you can modify to container class and the lookup form to use the structure of your particular postal code lookup table. The result is a class that can be used wherever you need to display or lookup address information in your application.

The address container class has one custom property called *lPostalCodeChanged*. This property is set to false when *txtPostalCode* gets focus. It is set to true in the text box's *InterActiveChange* method. This is done so we have some way of knowing, in the container's *FindCity* method, whether the user actually typed something into the postal code text box. *FindCity* is invoked when the postal code text box loses focus. Clearly, if the user made no changes to the contents of the textbox, we do not want to search for the postal code and populate the text boxes in the container:

```
LOCAL vp_PostalCode, loLocation, lnTop, lnLeft

*** Check to see if the user changed the postal code
```

```
*** If nothing was changed, we do not want to do anything
IF ! This.lPostalCodeChanged
  RETURN
ENDIF

*** Get all the records in the lookup table for this postal code
vp_PostalCode = ALLTRIM( This.txtPostalCode.Value )
REQUERY( 'lv_PostalCode' )
```

If the view contains more than a single record, we must present the user with a popup form from which he can select one entry. We use the OBJTOCLIENT function to pass the top and left co-ordinates to the popup form so that it can position itself nicely under the postal code text box:

```
*** If more than one match found, pop up the city/state selection screen
IF RECCOUNT( 'lv_PostalCode' ) > 1

  *** Get co-ordinates at which to pop up the form
  *** Make it pretty so it pops up right under the textbox
  lnTop = OBJTOCLIENT( This.txtAddress, 1 ) + This.txtAddress.Height + ;
    Thisform.Top
  lnLeft = OBJTOCLIENT( This.txtAddress, 2 ) + Thisform.Left
```

The popup form is modal. It must be if we expect to get a return value from the form using the following syntax. We pass the form the view parameter and the coordinates at which it should position itself. The modal form returns an object that contains the record details of which item was selected, if one was selected in the lookup form:

```
DO FORM GetLocation WITH vp_PostalCode, lnTop, lnLeft TO loLocation

  *** Now we check loLocation to see what the modal form returned
  WITH This

    *** Since we are storing address info in the customer record
    *** we want to make sure we do not clobber anything that was entered
    *** that is NOT in the postal code lookup
    IF !EMPTY( loLocation.PostalCode )
      .txtPostalCode.Value = loLocation.PostalCode
    ENDIF
    IF !EMPTY( loLocation.City )
      .txtCity.Value = loLocation.City
    ENDIF
    IF !EMPTY( loLocation.StateProv )
      .txtState.Value = loLocation.StateProv
    ENDIF
    IF !EMPTY( loLocation.Country )
      .txtCountry.Value = loLocation.Country
    ENDIF
  ENDWITH
ELSE
```

If there is either one matching record or no matching records, we do not want to pop up the city selection form. We merely want to populate the text boxes with the information in the lookup table. If you wanted to allow the user to add a new entry to the lookup table, you could call the appropriate maintenance form from here if the view contains no records:

```
WITH This
  IF !EMPTY( lv_PostalCode.PostalCode )
    .txtPostalCode.Value = lv_PostalCode.PostalCode
  ENDIF
  IF !EMPTY( lv_PostalCode.City )
    .txtCity.Value = lv_PostalCode.City
  ENDIF
  IF !EMPTY( lv_PostalCode.Sp_Name )
    .txtState.Value = lv_PostalCode.sp_name
  ENDIF
  IF !EMPTY( lv_PostalCode.Ctry_Name )
    .txtCountry.Value = lv_PostalCode.Ctry_name
  ENDIF
ENDWITH
ENDIF
```

The Location Selection form uses the parameters passed to its *Init* method to position itself appropriately and populate its list box. The object that returns the selected information is populated in its *Unload* method.

Generic log-in form *(Example: LogIn.scx)*

Almost every application requires a user to log-in, whether as part of a security model or simply to record the current user's name (so we know who to blame when things go wrong!). This little form uses a view that lists all current user names and their associated passwords and checks that the entered values are valid. If all is well, the form returns the current user name, otherwise it returns an empty string.

Note that it doesn't matter how you actually store your user information, providing that you can create a view called lv_UserList with two fields (named *UserName* and *Password*) containing a list of valid Log-In Names and their associated Passwords for use by this form.

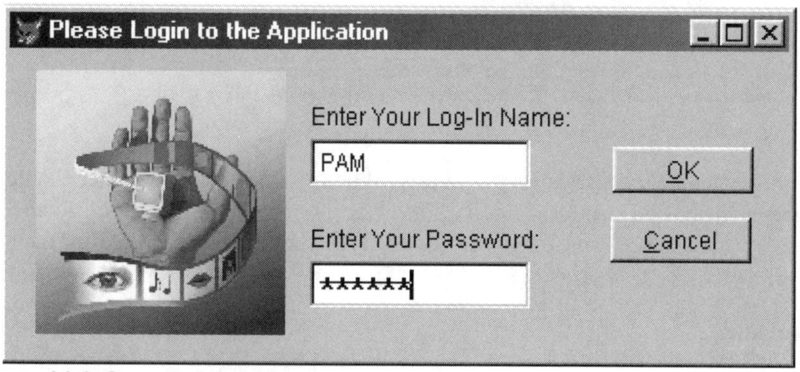

Figure 11.9 *Generic log-in form*

Log-in form construction

The log-in form is very simple indeed and has three custom properties and three custom methods, as follows:

Table 11.4 *Log-in form properties and methods*

PEM	Type	Description
cUserName	Property	User Log-In name, returned after successful log-in
nAttempts	Property	Records number of failed attempts at logging in
nMaxAttempts	Property	Determine the number of tries a user is allowed before shut-down
Cancel	Method	Closes Log-In Form and returns an Empty String
ValidateUserName	Method	Check User Name is in the current list of valid users
ValidatePassword	Method	Check Password is correct for the given user name

When the form is instantiated, focus is set to the User Name entry field. The *Valid* method of this field allows for the user to use the "cancel" button to close the form but otherwise will not allow focus to leave the field unless the form's *ValidateUserName* method returns .т. This form has been set up so that both User Name and Password entry are case sensitive (although you may prefer a different approach). The *ValidateUserName* method is very simple and merely checks to see if what has been entered by the user matches an entry in the form's *lv_userlist* view as follows:

```
SELECT lv_UserList
*** Get an exact match only!
LOCATE FOR ALLTRIM( lv_UserList.UserName ) == ALLTRIM(
Thisform.txtUserName.Value  )
IF !FOUND()
   *** User name is not valid
   Thisform.txtUserName.Value = ''
   MESSAGEBOX( 'We do not recognize you. Please re-enter your name', ;
               16, 'Invalid user name' )
   RETURN .F.
ELSE
   *** User Name is Valid - save it to the form property
   Thisform.cUserName = ALLTRIM( Thisform.txtUserName.Value  )
ENDIF
```

The password entry field behaves very similarly, although since this is only accessible once a valid user name has been entered, the *ValidatePassword* method merely checks the currently selected record to see if the password supplied matches the one required for the user name:

```
SELECT lv_UserList
IF ALLTRIM( lv_UserList.Password ) == ALLTRIM( Thisform.txtPassword.Value  )
   *** Everything is just peachy keen
ELSE
   *** Password was incorrect!
   Thisform.txtPassword.Value = ''
   *** Increment Attempt Counter
```

```
Thisform.nAttempts = Thisform.nAttempts + 1
*** Check that we have not reached the maximum allowed attempts
IF Thisform.nAttempts = Thisform.nMaxAttempts
   *** Still No good - throw user out!
   MESSAGEBOX( 'You obviously do not remember your password. Good-bye!', ;
              16, 'Too Many Bad Login Attempts' )
   Thisform.Cancel()
ELSE
   *** Allow another try
   MESSAGEBOX( 'Invalid password. Please re-enter.', 16, 'Invalid Password' )
   RETURN .F.
ENDIF
ENDIF
```

The number of attempts that a user is allowed to make is controlled by the *nMaxAttempts* property, which is set to 3 by default.

Using the log-in form

The form is defined as a modal form so that it can be executed in the start-up routine of an application using the DO FORM <name> TO <variable> syntax. The action taken after the log-in form is run will, obviously, depend on the result and code similar to the following can be used in the start up program for the application:

```
CLEAR ALL
CLEAR
DO FORM login TO lcUserId
IF EMPTY( lcUserID )
   *** Log-In Failed
   QUIT
ENDIF
*** Log - In was succesful carry on
```

The lookup text box class *(Example: CH11.VCX::txtlookup and Contacts.SCX)*

It is often possible to handle the lookup and display of information on a form merely by setting a relation into the lookup table. If, however, the lookup table does not have an appropriate index tag to use in a relation, you need another way to do this. This is when it is useful to have a text box that can perform a lookup and then display the result. The lookup text box class, used to display the contact type in the Contacts.scx form pictured below, allows you to handle this task by merely setting a few properties.

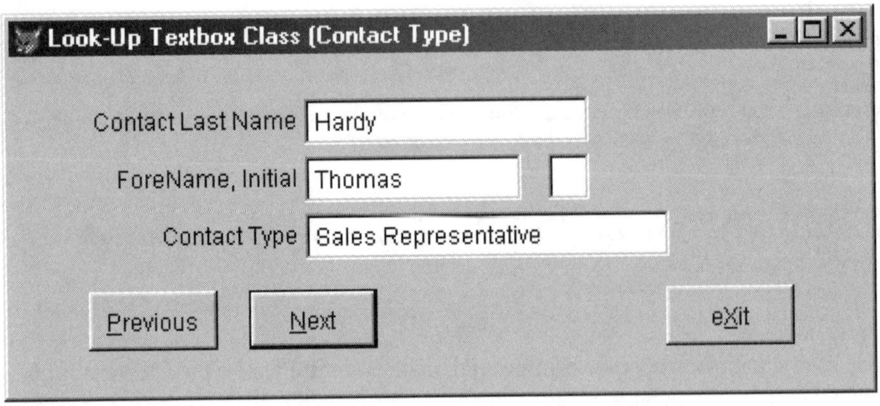

Figure 11.10 *Lookup text box class in use*

The text box is designed to be used unbound and instead uses the table and field specified in its *cControlSource* property to determine the value it should be taking as its *ControlSource*.

Table 11.5 *Custom properties for the lookup text box class*

Property	Description
cAlias	Alias name of the table to be searched
cControlSource	Table and Field which contains the key value to use in the lookup
cRetField	Field from the search table whose value is to be returned
cSchField	Field from the search table in which the key is to be looked up
cTagToUse	Name of the index tag to use in the lookup (Optional)

Initializing the lookup text box

When the text box is initialized, it sets its *Value* to the contents of the specified field by evaluating its *cControlSource* property in its *Init* method as follows:

```
DODEFAULT()
*** Copy-in control source
IF EMPTY(This.ControlSource) AND !EMPTY(This.cControlSource)
  This.Value = EVAL(This.cControlSource)
ENDIF
```

Updating the lookup

A custom method (*UpdateVal*) is called from the native *Refresh* method to handle the actual lookup as follows:

```
LOCAL lcRetFld, luSchVal, lcSchFld, luRetVal
*** If table has been specified, add it to the Search and Return Field names
IF !EMPTY(THIS.cAlias)
  lcRetFld = This.cAlias + '.' + This.cRetField
  lcSchFld = This.cAlias + '.' + This.cSchField
ELSE
  lcRetFld = This.cRetField
  lcSchFld = This.cSchField
ENDIF
*** Get the current key value
luSchVal = EVAL(This.cControlSource)

IF ! EMPTY(luSchVal)
  *** Do LookUp - using index if one has been specified
  IF EMPTY(This.cTagToUse)
    luRetVal = LOOKUP(&lcRetFld, luSchVal, &lcSchFld)
  ELSE
    luRetVal = LOOKUP(&lcRetFld, luSchVal, &lcSchFld, This.cTagToUse)
  ENDIF
ELSE
  luRetVal = " "
ENDIF
*** Update Display
IF ! EMPTY( luRetVal )
  This.Value = luRetVal
ELSE
  This.Value = ""
ENDIF
```

Using the lookup text box class

Since the basis on which the class operates is that it is always unbound, it can only be used as a read-only "display" control. Moreover it cannot be used inside a grid because there would be no way for the control to determine, for anything other than the current row, what should be displayed. Given these limitations, the class is still useful for those occasions when it is necessary to display the result of a lookup in an interactive environment. All you need to do is set its custom *cControlSource* to the name of the field that contains the foreign key from the lookup table. In our sample form, this is Contact.ct_key. Put the name of the lookup table into its custom *cAlias* property. *CSchField* and *cRetField* properties must contain the names of the fields in the lookup table that contain the key value and the descriptive text to display. If the lookup table is indexed on this key value, place the name of this tag in the control's custom *cTagToUse* property.

Conclusion

A stock of generic presentation classes will give you a big productivity boost because you can use them over and over again. Not only will they help you produce applications more quickly, they will also help to reduce the number of bugs you have to fix because they get tested each time you use them. We hope that this chapter has given you a few classes you can use immediately as well as some ideas for creating new classes that are even more useful.

Chapter 12
Developer Productivity Tools

"In an industrial society which confuses work and productivity, the necessity of producing has always been an enemy of the desire to create." ("The Revolution of Everyday Life" by Raoul Vaneigem)

The tools included in this chapter were developed to make our lives as developers simpler. None of these would normally be available (or even useful) in an application, ut all are permanent members of our development toolkits. Having said that, none of these tools is really finished. There is always something more that could be added and we hope that you, like us, will enjoy adding your own touches.

Form/class library editor *(Example: ClasEdit.prg)*

As you are probably aware, the formats of the Visual FoxPro Form (*SCX*) file and Class Library (*VCX*) file are identical. Both are actually Visual FoxPro tables and the only differences are in the way that certain fields are used and that an *SCX* file can only contain the object details for a single form, whereas a class library can contain many classes. Since they are both tables we can 'hack' them by simply using the file directly as a table and opening the table in a browse window. However, this is not easy to do because, with the exception of the first three fields (*Platform*, *UniqueID* and *Timstamp*), all the information is held in memo fields. So we have created a form to display the information contained in either a SCX or a VCX file more easily (**Figure 12.1** below).

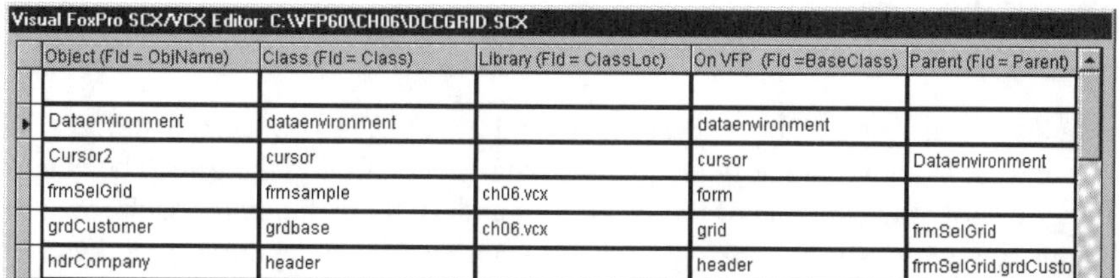

Figure 12.1 SCX/VCX editor

Why do we need this? How often have you wanted to be able to change the class on which some object contained in a form is based or to be able to redefine the parent class library for a class? If you are anything like us, it is something we often want to do and there is no other simple way of doing it than by directly editing the relevant SCX or VCX file. The most important fields in the files are listed in **Table 12.1** below:

Table 12.1 Main fields in a SCX/VCX file

FieldName	Used For
CLASS	Contains the class on which the object is based
CLASSLOC	If the class is not a base class, the field contains the VCX file name containing the class definition. If the class is a base class, the field is empty.
BASECLASS	Contains the name of the base class for this object
OBJNAME	Contains the object's Instance Name
PARENT	Contains the name of the object's immediate container
PROPERTIES	Contains a list of all the object's properties and their values that are not merely left at default values
PROTECTED	Contains a list of the object's protected members
METHODS	Contains the object's method/event code
OBJCODE	Contains the compiled version of the event code in binary format
OLE	Contains binary data used by OLE controls
OLE2	Contains binary data used by OLE controls
RESERVED1	Contains 'Class' if this record is the start of a class definition, otherwise empty
RESERVED2	Logical true (.T.) if the class is OLEPUBLIC, otherwise logical false (.F.)
RESERVED3	Lists all User-defined members. Prefix "*" is a Method, "^" is an Array, otherwise it's a Property
RESERVED4	Relative path and file name of the bitmap for a custom class icon
RESERVED5	Relative path and file name for a custom Project Manager or Class Browser class icon
RESERVED6	ScaleMode of the class, Pixels or Foxels
RESERVED7	Description of the class
RESERVED8	#Include File name

Of all these fields, we are most likely to want to amend the *OBJNAME*, *CLASS* and *CLASSLOC* fields and these are the three fields that we have placed first in the grid. The edit regions below the grid show the contents of the Properties and Methods fields for each row in the file and although you *could* edit property settings, or even method code, directly in these windows we prefer to work through the property sheet. (We have not found any problems doing it directly, but it doesn't feel safe somehow!)

One useful feature of the form is that we can enter one line commands directly into the 'Run' box and execute them. As the illustration shows, this is useful for handling global changes to items inside a form or class library.

Using the SCX/VCX editor

To run the editor we use a simple wrapper program, named *clasedit.prg* (which is included with the sample code for this chapter). This simply runs the form inside a loop as long as a new SCX or VCX file is selected from the dialog. As soon as no selection is made, the loop exits and releases everything. Each time the editor is closed the SCX or VCX file is re-compiled to ensure any changes that have been made are properly saved.

```
************************************************************************
* Program....: ClasEdit.prg
* Compiler...: Visual FoxPro 06.00.8492.00 for Windows
* Abstract...: Runs the SCX/VCX Editor inside a loop until no file
*...........: is selected in the GetFile() Dialog
************************************************************************
LOCAL lcSceFile
CLEAR
CLEAR ALL
CLOSE ALL
*** Close any open libraries
SET CLASSLIB TO
*** And SCX/VCX Files
IF USED('vcxedit')
  USE IN vcxedit
ENDIF
*** Initialise the control variable
DO WHILE .T.
  *** Get Source File Name
  lcSceFile = GETFILE( 'SCX;VCX' )
  IF EMPTY(lcSceFile)
    EXIT
  ENDIF
  *** Open Source file and set buffer mode to Optimistic Table
  USE (lcSceFile) IN 0 ALIAS vcxedit EXCLUSIVE
  CURSORSETPROP( 'Buffering', 5 )
  *** Run the form
  DO FORM ClasEdit WITH lcSceFile
  READ EVENTS
  *** Compile the SCX/VCX File
  IF JUSTEXT( lcSceFile ) = "SCX"
    COMPILE FORM (lcSceFile)
  ELSE
    COMPILE CLASSLIB (lcSceFile)
  ENDIF
ENDDO
```

Form Inspector *(Example: InspFprm.scx and ShoCode.scx)*

This simple little tool provides the ability to inspect a form and all of its objects while that form is actually running. There are several ways to do this, but we like this one because it is simple, easy to use and allows us to get a 'quick and dirty' look at what a form is doing when we are running it in development mode. It also allows us to set or change properties of the form, or any object on the form, interactively.

The form is designed to accept an object reference to an active form and to display information about that form in its pageframe. Typically we use it by setting an On Key Label command like this:

```
ON KEY LABEL CTRL+F9 DO FORM inspForm WITH _Screen.ActiveForm
```

The table information page

When activated, the "Table Information" page is displayed The list box on this page shows any tables that are used by the target form. (If the form does not use any tables, the only entry in this list box will be 'No Tables Used.') Selecting a table in the list populates the associated fields showing the status of that table and the grid which shows the current record details.

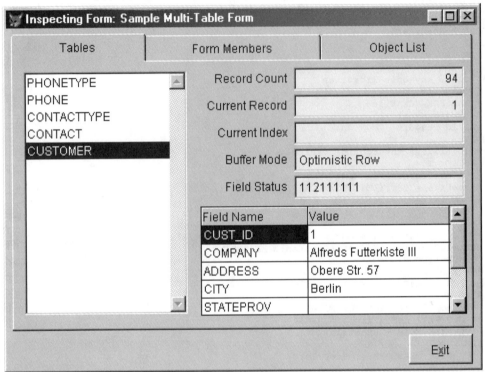

Figure 12.2 Form Inspector - table information page

The form information page

The second page of the form contains a list box which is populated when the form is initialized, using the native **AMEMBERS()** function, with all properties, events, methods and any objects from the target form.

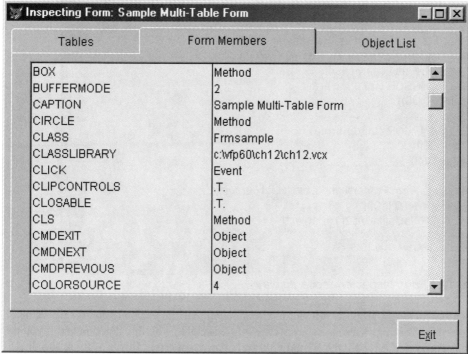

Figure 12.3 *Form Inspector - form information page*

   Double-clicking a method or event in this list brings forward a modal window containing any code associated with that method in the form (Note: only code which has been added directly to the form is viewable in this way, inherited code will not be seen here):

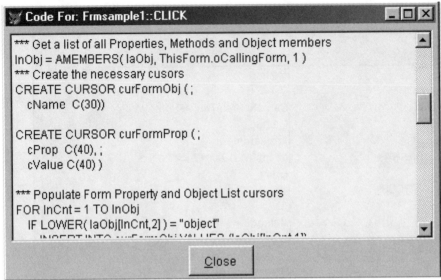

Figure 12.4 Form Inspector - code display

Double-clicking a property brings forward a dialog that allows you to change the value of that property. (Warning: There is no error checking associated with this function and if you try to set a property that is read-only, Visual FoxPro will raise an error. This is a 'quick and dirty' tool!)

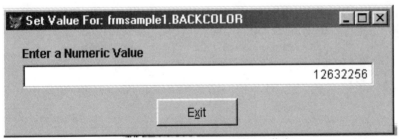

Figure 12.5 Form Inspector - property setting dialog

Finally, double-clicking an object populates the third page of the form with the properties, events, methods and any contained objects for that object.

The object list page

The third page is used to display details of any object on the form. As with the form list, double-clicking on a method or event displays any code associated with that method and double-clicking on a Property brings forward the setting dialog. Note that method code is retrieved using the `GetPem()` function and there appears to be a bug in this function in Version 6.0 so it will not retrieve code that exists in methods of a "page." Code in any object on a page, or in methods of the pageframe, is retrieved correctly, but methods of the page always show as empty even when they do have code at the instance level.

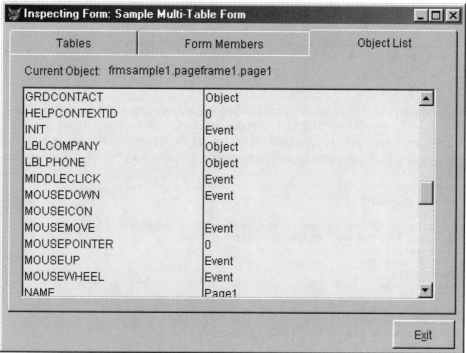

Figure 12.6 Form Inspector - object information page

Double-clicking on an object in this list box re-populates the list with the details of that object and updates the 'Current Object' line on the page. **Right-clicking** in the list box selects the parent of the current object (if there is one) and makes it possible to walk up and down the object hierarchy.

Construction of the inspection form

The *Init* and *SetUpForm* methods
The *Init* method is used to receive and store the object reference to the form to be inspected to a form property. It then forces the inspection form into the calling form's datasession and sets its caption to include the caption of the calling form. Finally it calls the custom *SetUpForm* method:

```
LPARAMETERS toSceForm

IF VARTYPE( toSceForm ) # "O"
    *** Not passed a form object
    RETURN .F.
ENDIF
```

```
WITH ThisForm
    *** Save reference to Calling Form
    .oCallingForm = toSceForm
    *** Set DataSession to same as the Calling Form
    .DataSessionID = .oCallingForm.DataSessionID
    *** Set Up Caption
    This.Caption = "Inspecting Form: " + .oCallingForm.Caption
    *** Set Up this form
    .SetUpForm()
ENDWITH
```

The *SetUpForm* method is primarily responsible for populating the list box on Page One of the inspection form with a list of the tables being used by the calling form. It then calls the custom *UpdFormProps* method to populate the list box on the "Form Members" page before returning control to the form's initialization process. The actual code in the *SetUpForm* method is:

```
LOCAL ARRAY laTables[1]
LOCAL lnTables
*** Get a list of tables in use in the calling form's DataSession
lnTables = AUSED( laTables, ThisForm.DataSessionId )
*** Build a cursor for all open tables
CREATE CURSOR curAlias ( ;
    cTable C(30), ;
    nArea  I( 4) )
IF lnTables > 0
    INSERT INTO curAlias FROM ARRAY laTables
ELSE
    INSERT INTO curAlias VALUES ('No Tables Used', 0 )
ENDIF

*** Set Up the Tables List Box
WITH ThisForm.pgfMembers.Page1.lstTables
    .RowSourceType = 6
    .RowSource     = "curalias.cTable, nArea"
    .ReQuery()
    .ListIndex     = 1
ENDWITH

*** Get the Form Properties
ThisForm.UpdFormProps()
```

The *UpdTable* method

This custom method is called from the *Activate* method of the 'Tables' page and is responsible for populating the status fields, and the grid on that page, with the details for the currently selected table. The method is also called from the *InterActiveChange* method of the list box on page one so that the details are kept synchronized with the currently selected table.

```
LOCAL lcTable, lcMode, lnMode, lnSelect, lcSafety, lcField, lcFVal
WITH ThisForm
    *** Lock the screen while updating
    .LockScreen = .T.
```

```
WITH .pgfMembers.page1
  lcTable = ALLTRIM(.lstTables.Value)

  *** If no tables used
  IF lcTable == 'No Tables Used'
      ThisForm.LockScreen = .F.
      RETURN
  ENDIF

  *** Record Count & Record Number
  .txtRecCount.Value = RECCOUNT( lcTable )
  .txtCurRecNo.Value = IIF( EOF(lcTable), "At EOF()", RECNO( lcTable ))

  *** Current Index Tag & Key Expression
  .txtCurTag.Value = ORDER( lcTable )

  *** Buffer Mode
  lcMode = ""
  lnMode = CURSORGETPROP( 'Buffering', lcTable )
  lcMode = IIF( lnMode = 1, 'No Buffering', lcMode)
  lcMode = IIF( lnMode = 2, 'Pessimistic Row', lcMode)
  lcMode = IIF( lnMode = 3, 'Optimistic Row', lcMode)
  lcMode = IIF( lnMode = 4, 'Pessimistic Table', lcMode)
  lcMode = IIF( lnMode = 5, 'Optimistic Row', lcMode)
  .txtBufMode.Value = lcMode

  *** Field Status
  IF lnMode > 1
    .txtFldState.Value = NVL( GETFLDSTATE( -1, lcTable ), "At EOF()")
  ELSE
    .txtFldState.Value = ""
  ENDIF
ENDWITH

*** Current Record Details
lnSelect = SELECT()
IF USED( 'currec' )
  lcSafety = SET("SAFETY")
  SET SAFETY OFF
  ZAP IN currec
  SET SAFETY &lcSafety
ELSE
  CREATE CURSOR curRec ( ;
    cField C (40), ;
    cValue C (60) )
ENDIF
SELECT (lcTable)

*** Get the record Details
FOR lnCnt = 1 TO FCOUNT()
  lcField = FIELD( lnCnt )
  lcFVal = TRANSFORM( &lcField )
  INSERT INTO currec VALUES (lcField, lcFVal)
NEXT
SELECT (lnSelect)

*** Populate and update the Grid
WITH ThisForm.pgfMembers.Page1.grdCurRec
  .RecordSource = "currec"
```

```
  GO TOP IN currec
  .SetFocus()
ENDWITH

*** Release the screen
.LockScreen = .F.
ENDWITH
```

The *UpdFormProps* method

This custom method simply gets the list of form members by using the native **AMEMBERS**() function. Details are written out to a local cursor. The only tricky items here are that certain properties are not directly recoverable, either because they are actually collections (e.g. 'Controls') or because they are themselves object references which only have values within the calling form (e.g. 'ActiveControl'). These are specifically excluded and the keyword *'Reference'* is inserted so they will not cause problems later on:

```
LOCAL ARRAY laObj[1]
LOCAL lnObj, lnCnt, lcProp, lcPName, lcPVal
WITH ThisForm
  *** Lock Screen while updating display
  .LockScreen = .T.
  *** Get a list of all Properties, Methods and Object members
  lnObj = AMEMBERS( laObj, ThisForm.oCallingForm, 1 )
  *** Create the necessary cusors
  IF USED( 'curFormProp' )
     USE IN curformprop
  ENDIF
  CREATE CURSOR curFormProp ( ;
     cProp  C(40), ;
     cValue C(40) )

  *** Populate Form Property and Object List cursors
  FOR lnCnt = 1 TO lnObj
    IF LOWER( laObj[lnCnt,2] ) = "object"
      INSERT INTO curFormProp VALUES (laObj[lnCnt,1], "Object")
    ELSE
      lcProp = LOWER( laObj[lnCnt,2] )
      IF lcProp = "property"
        lcPName = LOWER(laObj[lnCnt,1])
        *** Ignore properties that return Object References/Collections
        IF lcPName=='columns' OR lcPName=='pages' OR lcPName=='controls' ;
            OR lcPName == 'buttons' OR lcPName == 'objects' ;
            OR lcPName == 'parent' OR lcPName == 'activecontrol' ;
            OR lcPName == 'activeform'
          INSERT INTO curFormProp VALUES (laObj[lnCnt,1], 'Reference')
          LOOP
        ENDIF

        *** Otherwise get the current Value
        lcPVal = TRANSFORM( EVAL("ThisForm.oCallingForm."+laObj[lnCnt,1]) )
        INSERT INTO curFormProp VALUES (laObj[lnCnt,1], lcPVal)
      ELSE
        INSERT INTO curFormProp VALUES (laObj[lnCnt,1], laObj[lnCnt,2])
      ENDIF
    ENDIF
```

```
NEXT

*** Set up the Form Property ListBox on Page 2
WITH ThisForm.pgfMembers.page2.lstFormProps
   .RowSourceType = 6
   .RowSource     = "curFormProp.cProp, cValue"
   .ReQuery()
   .ListIndex     = 1
ENDWITH

*** Unlock the screen
.LockScreen = .F.
ENDWITH
```

The *UpdObjProps* method

This custom method is essentially the same as the *UpdFormProps* method above except that it updates the inspection form's 'current object' reference and retrieves the PEMs for whatever object this reference is currently pointing to. The information is displayed in the list box on page three of the inspection form:

```
LPARAMETERS tlSetForm
LOCAL ARRAY laObj[1]
LOCAL loFormObj, lnObj, lnCnt, lcProp, lcPName, lcPVal

WITH ThisForm
  *** Freeze Screen while updating
  .LockScreen = .T.
  IF ! tlSetForm
    *** Update the Current Object Reference
    loFormObj = EVAL( "This.oCurobj." ;
                    + ThisForm.pgfMembers.page3.lstObjProps.Value )
    *** Save Current Object Ref
    .oCurObj = loFormObj
  ELSE
    loFormObj = .oCurObj
  ENDIF
  lnObj = AMEMBERS( laObj, loFormObj, 1 )

  *** Create local cursor
  IF USED('curobjlist')
    USE IN curObjList
  ENDIF
  CREATE CURSOR curObjList ( ;
     cProp   C(40), ;
     cValue  C(40) )

  *** Populate Property List cursor
  FOR lnCnt = 1 TO lnObj
    lcProp = LOWER( laObj[lnCnt,2] )
    IF lcProp = "property"
      lcPName = LOWER(laObj[lnCnt,1])
      *** Ignore properties that return Object References/Collections
      IF lcPName == 'columns' OR lcPName == 'pages' OR lcPName == 'controls' ;
          OR lcPName == 'buttons' OR lcPName == 'objects' ;
          OR lcPName == 'parent' OR lcPName == 'activecontrol' ;
```

```
         OR lcPName == 'activeform'
         INSERT INTO curObjList VALUES (laObj[lnCnt,1], 'Reference')
         LOOP
      ENDIF

      *** Otherwise get the current Value
      lcPVal = GETPEM( loFormObj, laObj[lnCnt,1] )
      INSERT INTO curObjList VALUES (laObj[lnCnt,1], TRANSFORM( lcPVal ))
   ELSE
      INSERT INTO curObjList VALUES (laObj[lnCnt,1], laObj[lnCnt,2])
   ENDIF
NEXT

*** Set up the Object Property ListBox on Page 3
WITH .pgfMembers.page3.lstObjProps
  .RowSourceType = 6
  .RowSource     = "curObjList.cProp, cValue"
  .ReQuery()
  .ListIndex     = 1
ENDWITH

*** Update Current Control
.pgfMembers.page3.txtCurObj.Value = SYS(1272, .oCurObj )

*** Unlock Screen
.LockScreen = .F.
ENDWITH
```

The list box behaviors

The only other significant code in the inspection form is in the *DoubleClick* method of the list boxes on both pages two and three and additionally in the *RightClick* method of the list box on page three. The *RightClick* code is very simple and merely determines whether the currently selected object has a parent and, if so, makes that object the current object before calling the form's *UpdObjProps* method as follows:

```
WITH ThisForm
    *** Check for Parent
    IF TYPE("ThisForm.oCurObj.Parent" ) = "O"
        *** Make Parent Current
        .oCurObj = .oCurObj.Parent
        .updObjProps(.T.)
    ELSE
        *** Do Nothing
        MESSAGEBOX( "Current Object Has No Parent", 16, "Cannot Step Back" )
    ENDIF
ENDWITH
```

The code in the *DoubleClick* methods is a little more complex and uses the current record in the cursor to which the list box is bound to determine what action is required. The code for both list boxes is essentially the same and looks like this:

```
LOCAL lcStr, loCurObj, lcProperty, lcType
WITH ThisForm
```

```
DO CASE
  CASE INLIST( curObjList.cValue, 'Method', 'Event' )
    *** And we have an object
    IF VARTYPE( ThisForm.oCurObj ) = "O"
      *** Get any Code in the method
      lcStr = GetPem( ThisForm.oCurObj, ALLTRIM(curObjList.cProp) )
      IF EMPTY(lcStr)
        lcStr = "No Code at this level"
      ENDIF
      *** Show the code Window
      DO FORM shoCode WITH lcStr, ;
              ThisForm.oCurObj.Name + "::" + ALLTRIM(curObjList.cProp)
    ENDIF

  CASE curObjList.cValue = "Object"
    *** Get New Object PEMS
    .UpdObjProps(.F.)

  CASE curObjList.cValue # "Reference"
    *** Must be a property - Get its current value
    loCurObj = EVAL( "ThisForm.oCurObj." + ALLTRIM( curObjList.cProp) )
    *** And name
    lcProperty = SYS(1272,ThisForm.oCurObj) + "." + ALLTRIM(curObjList.cProp)
    *** And Data Type
    lcType = TYPE( "loCurObj" )
    *** Get new value
    DO FORM SetProp WITH lcProperty, lcType, loCurObj TO luNewVal
    *** Update the Property
    lcProperty = "ThisForm.oCurObj." + ALLTRIM( curObjList.cProp)
    &lcProperty = luNewVal
    *** Update the display
    .UpdObjProps(.T.)

  OTHERWISE
    *** Ignore it!
ENDCASE
ENDWITH
```

Our industrial strength grid builder *(Example: gridbuild.vcx::gridbuild)*

When you take our super duper, industrial strength grid builder for a test drive, you will probably be struck by its close similarity to the native Visual FoxPro grid builder. This resemblance is no accident. Microsoft ships the source code for its wizards and builders with Visual FoxPro version 6.0. So if you require special functionality from a builder, you no longer have to re-invent the wheel. You can customize the Visual FoxPro's very own builders. We are especially grateful to Doug Hennig for sharing with us his initial work on the grid builder. It made the development of this variant of the builder much easier.

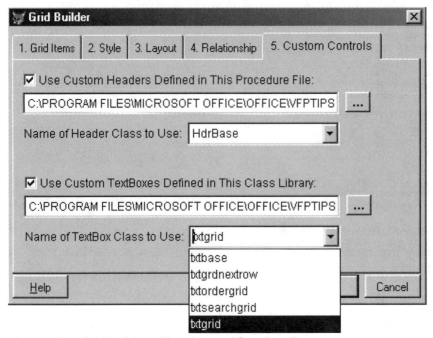

Figure 12.7 *Grid builder with enhanced functionality*

In order to use our improved builder, you first need to register it by running GridBuildReg.prg included with the sample code for this chapter. This program adds a new record to Builder.dbf in the Visual FoxPro wizards subdirectory. Builder.app uses this table to determine which builder program to run.

Now you will need to rebuild the GridBuild.pjx, the project that contains our industrial strength grid builder and is included with the sample code for this chapter. If you have not already done so, you must unzip the source code for the builders which is supplied with Visual FoxPro 6.0. You will find it in HOME() + '\TOOLS\XSOURCE\XSOURCE.ZIP'. Unzipping the file using the default settings creates a directory structure that starts at HOME()+'\TOOLS\VFPSOURCE' and spans several levels. After you have unzipped the source code, follow these steps to install the industrial strength grid builder:

1. Copy the files GridBuild.pjx and GridBuild.pjt from the directory containing the sample code for this chapter to HOME()+'\TOOLS\VFPSOURCE\BUILDERS.'

2. Copy the files GridMain.prg, GridBuild.vcx and GridBuild.vct from the directory containing the sample code for this chapter to the HOME()+'\TOOLS\VFPSOURCE\BUILDERS\GRIDBLDR' folder.

3. Now you are ready to rebuild the project. Build GridBuild.App and when it is finished, move the app to the HOME()+'\WIZARDS' directory.

From now on your grid builder will have new and improved functionality. If you reinstall Visual FoxPro or apply a service pack that overwrites Builder.dbf, all you need to do is rerun GridBuildReg.prg to re-register GridBuild.app as the default grid builder.

So why did we need an improved grid builder? The native Visual FoxPro grid builder has the following shortcomings:

- It does not size bound columns correctly, i.e. based on the width of their *ControlSource*

- It does not name bound columns and their contained controls appropriately for the column's *ControlSource*

- There is no way to tell it to use custom classes

This version of the builder addresses all three of these issues but, after struggling to get our enhancements working, we began to wonder if it might not have been easier to write our own builder from scratch. It was very nice of Microsoft to give us access to the source code for these builders. It would have been even nicer if they had commented and debugged it! For example, we found several bugs in the native builder, especially when we began removing columns from the grid.

We eventually discovered that the builder code could not handle removals if the columns had names other than the default "column1", "column2", etc. We also discovered that the native grid builder expected all the headers to have their default names in order to handle them without blowing up!

Since we wanted to touch as little of the original code as possible, we renamed the columns and headers to their default names in the *Load* method of our custom GridBuild class. For this reason, if you invoke the builder and use the CANCEL button to exit, you will find that all your column and header names have been reset to their Visual FoxPro default names. This is easy to fix. Just invoke the builder and exit by pressing the OK button.

Most of the native grid builder's functionality can be found in the GridBldr class of GridBldr.vcx. Just in case new functionality is added to this class in future versions of Visual FoxPro, we decided to subclass it and modify our subclass. You will find the code that provides the enhanced functionality in the class GridBuild.vcx::GridBuild.

Resizing grid columns properly

Fortunately, we did not have to bang our heads against the keyboard to figure this one out. Most of the work had already been done by Doug Hennig and presented at the Third Annual Southern California Visual FoxPro Conference in August, 1999. What he discovered was that the grid builder already had a method called *SetColWidth* to perform the necessary calculations and resize the columns. However, the builder was passing the wrong value to the method! After much digging and experimenting, we discovered that Visual FoxPro was adding new columns to the grid with a default width of 75 pixels in its *ResetColumns* method. That method then performed the following check in order to decide whether or not to size the new column correctly with respect to the bound field:

```
*- don't reset the width if the user already changed it
IF wbaTemp[m.wbi,1] # wbaCols[m.wbi,1] AND wbaCols[m.wbi,1] # 0
  wbaTemp[m.wbi,1] = wbaCols[m.wbi,1]
ENDIF
```

Since wbaCols[m.wbi, 1] holds the current *ColumnWidth* of the column being processed by the grid builder, it was never equal to zero and the *ColumnWidth* was never resized properly. All we had to do was initialize the *ColumnWidth* for newly added columns to zero and they were resized properly.

Renaming columns and their controls appropriately

We added a method called, strangely enough, *RenameControls* to our GridBuild class to handle this task. This method is called from the *Click* method of the builder's OK button and renames the columns and its contained controls based on the name of the field to which the column is bound. This method also replaces base class headers and base class text boxes with your custom classes if a custom class has been specified of the "Custom Controls" page of the builder.

```
LOCAL lnRows, lnCnt, lcField, loColumn, lcHeader, loHeader, ;
  lnCtl, lnControls, lacontrols[ 1, 2 ], lnCount, lcCaption

*** If no columns defined, bail out now
IF wbaControl[ 1 ].ColumnCount = -1
  RETURN
ENDIF
lnRows = ALEN( wbaCols, 1 )
```

Next, we loop through the builder's wbaCols array to rename each column to reflect the name of the field to which it is bound. The builder stores the current column name in column seven of its wbaCols array. The name of the field to which it is bound is stored in column two. The builder maintains one row in the array for each column in the grid:

```
FOR lnCnt = 1 TO lnRows
  lcField = wbaCols[ lnCnt, 2 ]
  IF NOT EMPTY( lcField )

    *** Get the default name of the column
    loColumn = EVALUATE( 'wbaControl[1].' + wbaCols[ lnCnt, 7 ] )

    *** Rename the column and header according to the field name
    loColumn.Name = 'col' + lcField
    wbaCols[ lnCnt, 7 ] = loColumn.Name
```

This code removes base class headers and replaces them with our custom headers if this option was specified on the fifth page of the builder. It then renames the header in a manner consistent with the column in which it resides. Note that, when adding custom headers to the grid column, we must first remove all controls contained in the column because the column expects its header to be the first control in its controls collection. If it isn't, the resulting grid will not function properly. After the custom header is added to the column, the rest of the controls are re-added:

```
IF ThisFormSet.Form1.Pageframe1.Page5.chkCustomHeaders.Value = .T. AND ;
   !EMPTY( Thisformset.cHeaderClass )

   *** Now remove all the base class headers and add custom headers
   *** We have to remove all the objects in the column so that
   *** the newly added custom header is controls[1]
   lnControls = loColumn.ControlCount
   lnCount = 0
   FOR lnCtl = 1 TO lnControls
      IF UPPER( loColumn.Controls[ 1 ].BaseClass ) = 'HEADER'

         *** Save the header's caption before removing it
         lcCaption = loColumn.Controls[ 1 ].Caption
         loColumn.RemoveObject( loColumn.Controls[ 1 ].Name )
      ELSE

         *** Save information about the other controls in the column
         *** before removing them

         lnCount = lnCount + 1
         DIMENSION laControls[ lnCount, 2 ]
         laControls[ lnCount, 1 ] = loColumn.Controls[ 1 ].Name
         laControls[ lnCount, 2 ] = loColumn.Controls[ 1 ].Class
         loColumn.RemoveObject( loColumn.Controls[ 1 ].Name )
      ENDIF
   ENDFOR

   *** Add the custom header
   loColumn.AddObject( 'hdr' + lcField, Thisformset.cHeaderClass )

   *** Make sure to set the caption
   loColumn.Controls[ 1 ].Caption = lcCaption

   *** Add back the other column controls
   FOR lnCtl = 1 TO lnCount
      loColumn.AddObject( laControls[ lnCtl, 1 ], laControls[ lnCtl, 2 ] )
   ENDFOR
ELSE

   *** If we are not using custom headers, just rename it
   loColumn.Controls[ 1 ].Name = 'hdr' + lcField
ENDIF
```

The method also replaces the native text boxes and renames them. The code that does this is very similar to the code presented above.

The Custom Controls page of the grid builder

Adding this page to the grid builder was probably the easiest part of enhancing it. It was also the most fun because we got to use two really cool functions that are new to Visual FoxPro 6.0: FILETOSTR() and ALINES(). These functions enabled us to populate the combo box from which a custom header class can be selected. Since custom headers cannot be defined visually and must be defined and stored in a program file, these two functions greatly simplified the job of parsing out the names of the classes from within the program file. Here is our cool code from the *Valid* method of the text box containing the name of the procedure file to use:

```
LOCAL lcProcFile, lcStr, laLines[ 1 ], lnLines, lnCnt, lcClass, lnLen

IF EMPTY( ThisformSet.cProcFile )
  RETURN
ENDIF
lcProcFile = Thisformset.cProcFile

*** Now populate the combo with the names
*** of the custom classes in the procedure file
This.Parent.cboHeaderClass.Clear()
lcStr = FILETOSTR( lcProcFile )
lnLines = ALINES( laLines, lcStr )
FOR lnCnt = 1 TO lnLines
  IF 'DEFINE CLASS' $ UPPER( laLines[ lnCnt ] )
    lnLen = AT( ' AS', UPPER( laLines[ lnCnt ] ) ) - 13
    lcClass = ALLTRIM( SUBSTR( laLines[ lnCnt ], 13, lnLen ) )
    This.Parent.cboHeaderClass.AddItem( lcClass )
  ENDIF
ENDFOR
This.Parent.cboHeaderClass.ListIndex = 1

*** Make sure custom header class is available
IF !EMPTY( lcProcFile )
  IF lcProcFile $ SET( 'PROCEDURE' )
  ELSE
    lcProcFile = '"' + lcProcFile + '"'
    SET PROCEDURE TO &lcProcFile ADDITIVE
  ENDIF
ENDIF
```

Adding method code to grid columns

In Chapter 6, we presented a grid class with multiline headers. Using the class is very
expensive because a lot of code has to be added to the instance in order for it to function
properly. In order to make it easier to implement, we added a little code to our grid builder so
it would add the required code to the grid columns at design time. This code, in the builder's
OK button, eliminated the need to manually add code to each column's *Moved* and *Resize*
method:

```
*** OK, now see if we are using a dynamic multi-line header grid
*** If so, prompt the user to see if code should be written into the
*** column's moved and resize methods
IF LOWER( wbaControl[1].class ) = 'grdmlheaders'
  IF MESSAGEBOX( 'Do you want to add the required code' + chr( 13 ) + ;
    'to the grid columns to keep' + chr( 13 ) + ;
    'the multi-line headers positioned correctly?';
    , 4 + 32, 'Add code Now?' ) = 6
    FOR EACH loColumn IN wbaControl[1].columns
      loColumn.WriteMethod('Moved', 'Column::Moved()' + CHR( 13 ) + ;
        'This.Parent.RefreshHeaders()' + CHR( 13 ) + ;
        'NODEFAULT' )
      loColumn.WriteMethod('Resize', 'Column::Moved()' + CHR( 13 ) + ;
        'This.Parent.RefreshHeaders()' + CHR( 13 ) + ;
        'NODEFAULT' )
    ENDFOR
```

```
    ENDIF
ENDIF
```

If you should happen to experience any little quirks when using our grid builder, keep in mind that they are more likely to be quirks of the native Visual FoxPro grid builder. The only time we have experienced anything out of the ordinary is when we have repeatedly added, removed and re-ordered columns in a single builder session. It is possible that you may too. If you are able to track down the reasons for these anomalies by examining GridBldr.vcx::GridBldr (the native grid builder), please e-mail us with the solution. One look at the source code, and you will understand why we had neither time nor patience to investigate further.

Class cataloger *(Example: vcxlist.scx)*

The purpose of *VCXList* is to read the contents of a specified project file and to build a table which contains the details of all of the visual classes used in that project. It is extremely simple to use, just invoke the form, select the project and hit the 'Go' button.

A new table will be created in the home directory of the project, named **vcxlist.dbf** with the following structure:

```
CCLASLIB  C ( 60,0 )  && Class library name
CCLASNAME C ( 35,0 )  && Class Name
CBASECLAS C ( 25,0 )  && VFP Base Class
CPARENT   C ( 50,0 )  && Parent Class library and name
CDESC     C (150,0 )  && Class Description
```

This table is also used by our "MC.PRG" utility (see below).

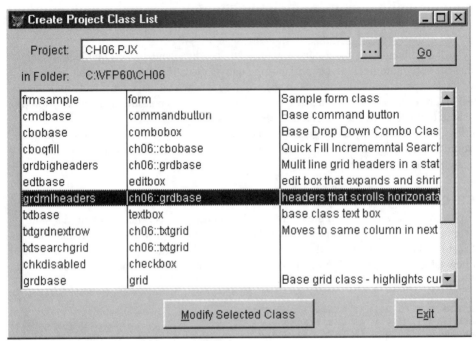

Figure 12.8 *Class Cataloger - vcxlist.scx*

While you have this form open, you can also open the class designer for any class by simply selecting the class in the list box and clicking on the "Modify Selected Class" button.

What *VCXList* does

This form does all of its work in the custom *SetUp* method. First, the method reads the name of the selected project and changes the default directory to that of the project. If a table named **vcxlist.dbf** is found, it is opened exclusively and cleared. Otherwise, a new table is created in the project home directory. This table needs to be located there because all the paths stored in the project file are relative to the project home directory. If this is not also the default directory, then opening class libraries can be problematic.

The project file is then opened as a DBF and a local array is populated from the **NAME** field of the project for all entries whose **TYPE = "V"** (Visual Class Library). Then for each class library identified, the native **AVCXCLASSES()** function is used to retrieve the details of the classes it contains and to insert the data into the table.

Finally the list box is populated (by the custom *Updlist* method) and the form is ready for immediate use to provide quick access to any class used in the project. While this is quite useful in its own right, the real purpose of this utility is to create the *vcxlist* table.

A wrapper for 'modify class' *(Example:mc.prg)*

This little program was originally devised by Steven Black when we were all working on a very large project in early 1999. The problem we faced was that there were a large number of class libraries and remembering which library held which class was difficult. The purpose of MC.PRG is to simplify the task of opening a specific class for modification by using a table to store the necessary details of all classes. This incarnation of the program makes use of the `vcxlist.dbf` table, which was described in the preceding section.

To open the class designer, just call *MC*, as a function with the name of the required class:

```
MC( <class name> )
```

You can even specify a method to modify so that when the designer opens, that method's code window will be opened for editing.

```
MC( <class name>, <method name> )
```

Here is the code for the program:

```
************************************************************************
* Program....: MC.PRG
* Compiler...: Visual FoxPro 06.00.8492.00 for Windows
* Abstract...: This program was originally devised and written by Steven Black
* ..........: while we were all working together on a major project in early
1999.
* ..........: We would like to acknowledge this, and all Steven's
contributions,
* ..........: and to thank him for his willingness to share his ingenuity
* ..........: and knowledge with the rest of us.
* Syntax.....: MC( <classname>[,<methodname>]) or
* ..........: DO MC WITH <classname>[,<methodname>]
*■■■■■■■■■■■■■■■■■■■■■■■■■■■■■■■■■■■■■■■■■■■■■■■■■■■■■■■■■■■■■■■■■■■■■■■■■■■
LPARAMETERS tcClass, tcMethod
LOCAL lcClass, lnSelect, lcOrigDir, lcOldError, lcLoc, lcMethod

*** Must pass a class name at least!
IF VARTYPE( tcClass ) # "C" OR EMPTY( tcClass )
   RETURN
ELSE
   *** Get the Class name
   lcClass = LOWER( ALLTRIM( tcClass ))
ENDIF

*** Save Current Work Area
lnSelect= SELECT()

*** Open VCXList Table
IF ! USED("VcxList")
   *** Disable Error handling temporarily
   lcOldError = ON("ERROR")
   ON ERROR *
   lcLoc = ""
   *** Locate the VCXList Table to use
   lcLoc = LOCFILE( "VCXList", "DBF", "Where is" )
   *** Restore Error handling and check result
   ON ERROR &lcOldError
   IF ! EMPTY( lcLoc ) AND 'vcxlist' $ LOWER( lcLoc )
      *** OK - Open the Table
      USE (lcLoc) AGAIN SHARED IN 0
```

```
   ELSE
       *** Not located - Abort
       WAIT WINDOW "Cannot locate VCXList.DBF - Aborting"
       RETURN
   ENDIF
ENDIF
*** Select VCXList
SELECT VCXList

*** Make VCXList Location current default because the
*** classlibs are saved with paths which are relative
*** to the project's location (and hence to VCXList)!
lcOrigDir = FULLPATH( CURDIR() )
SET DEFAULT TO JUSTPATH( DBF() )

*** Did we get a method name too?
IF VARTYPE(tcMethod) = "C" AND ! EMPTY( tcMethod)
   lcMethod= " Method " + tcMethod
ELSE
   lcMethod= ''
ENDIF

*** Find the Required Class
LOCATE FOR ALLTRIM(cclasname) == lcClass
IF FOUND()
   *** Show the VCX name
   WAIT WINDOW 'Opening Class Libray: ' + ALLTRIM(cClasLib) NOWAIT
   MODI CLASS (ALLTRIM(cClasName)) of (ALLTRIM(cClasLib)) &lcMethod NOWAIT
ELSE
   WAIT WINDOW "Class " + lcClass + " Not Found" NOWAIT
ENDIF

*** Restore Original Location and Work Area
SET DEFAULT TO (lcOrigDir)
SELECT (lnSelect)
```

The code itself is quite straightforward. The only thing to note is the use of the LOCFILE() function to find the vcxlist.dbf table. As far as we can tell, it's an entirely undocumented feature of LOCFILE() that when used to locate a file, the file path is added automatically to the current VFP search path. (This is true in all versions of Visual FoxPro.)

This means that once you have identified where the table is located, the directory is added to your current search path and all subsequent calls to *MC* will find the table. Of course, if you are working on several projects this could be a problem, and you may prefer to replace LOCFILE() with a simple GETFILE() which does **not** alter your search path. However we feel that since most of us work on only one project at a time, adding the location of vcxlist.dbf to the search path is a useful time-saver.

A form/class library documentation utility *(Example:genscode.scx)*

One of the many things that changed with the introduction of Visual FoxPro Version 3.0 was that it became more difficult to visualize the code for forms. This is because instead of producing a program file for a screen, all code was stored in memo fields in the table that defines the form. A similar strategy was also adopted for class libraries. The documentation wizard included with Visual FoxPro, and the 'code export' option provided with the class browser are both useful. However, we still felt the need for a simple utility to document all properties and methods of a form, and for documenting either a single class, or an entire class library. *Genscode.SCX* is the result.

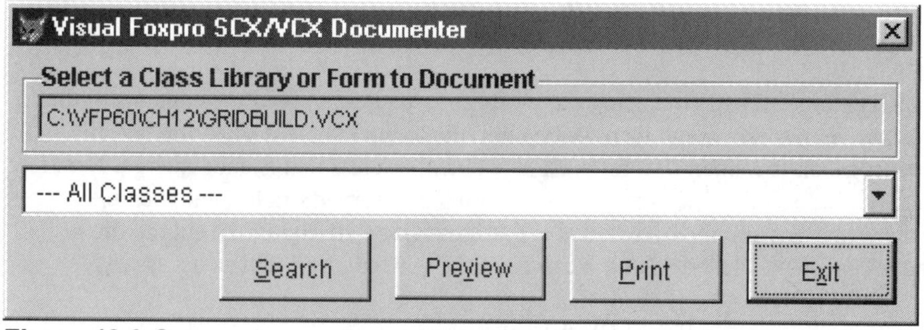

Figure 12.9 Genscode.scx: Form/VCX Documenter

When a form, or class library is selected and either the "Preview" or "Print" button is clicked, the form's custom *WriteCode* method is called to produce the output as a text file which is either opened for on screen viewing or sent directly to the printer. The text file is not saved by default so if you need to create a permanent record, use the preview option and use the standard "Save As" menu option to save the file under a new name. Here is the code that actually produces the documentation, which is contained in the *WriteCode* method.

First we define some constants and open the source and destination files:

```
***************************************************************************
*** Genscode::WriteCode() Method
***************************************************************************
LOCAL ARRAY laText[1]
LOCAL lcSource, lcTarget, lnFno, lnOldMemo, lnNumLine, lnCnt, lcText,
lcClassName

*** Announce
WAIT WINDOW NOWAIT 'Generating Source Code...'

*** Print property constants
#DEFINE CRLF CHR(13)+CHR(10)
#DEFINE LOC_USER '***** USER DEFINED *****' + CRLF
#DEFINE LOC_PROP '***** PROPERTIES *****' + CRLF
#DEFINE LOC_METH '***** METHODS *****' + CRLF
#DEFINE LOC_LINE REPLICATE('=',SET('MEMOWIDTH'))

*** Extract source file name
lcSource = THISFORM.txtSource.Value
lcTarget = THISFORM.cOutputName

*** Ensure target file does not exist
IF FILE(lcTarget)
  DELETE FILE (lcTarget)
ENDIF

*** Open target file for writing
lnFno = FCREATE(lcTarget)
```

```
*** Write header info
lcText = 'SOURCE FILE: ' +UPPER(ALLTRIM(lcSource))
FPUTS(lnFno,lcText)
FPUTS(lnFno,LOC_LINE)
lcText = 'Documented: '+TTOC(DATETIME()) + CRLF
FPUTS(lnFno,lcText)
```

The actual details are gathered using the ALINES() function to read the contents of the memo fields into a local array, and then written out line by line to the destination text file. A standard header block is written first for each new object or class that is encountered. Next any User-defined properties or methods are written (from the Reserved3 field), and then the content of the properties and methods fields are written. Once the end of the source file is reached, the output file is closed so that it can either be viewed or printed as necessary.

```
*** Write details (by looping thru VCX)
SELECT vcx
SCAN
  *** Ignore font info / old versions etc.
  IF EMPTY(timestamp) OR DELETED()
    LOOP
  ENDIF

  *** Get Class Name
  lcClassName = ALLTRIM(objname)
  IF Thisform.cboSelectClass.ListIndex > 1
    *** Ignore classes unless required
    IF ! (UPPER(ALLTRIM(lcClassName)) == ;
          UPPER(ALLTRIM(Thisform.cboSelectClass.DisplayValue)))
      LOOP
    ENDIF
  ENDIF

  *** Object header
  FPUTS(lnFno,PADR('Name ',17,'.')        + ' ' + UPPER(ALLTRIM(objname)) )
  FPUTS(lnFno,PADR('Class ',17,'.')       + ' ' + UPPER(ALLTRIM(class)) )
  FPUTS(lnFno,PADR('Parent ',17,'.')      + ' ' + UPPER(ALLTRIM(parent)) )
  FPUTS(lnFno,PADR('Base Class ',17,'.')  + ' ' + UPPER(ALLTRIM(baseclass)) )
  FPUTS(lnFno,PADR('Description ',17,'.') + ' ' + UPPER(ALLTRIM(reserved7)) +
CRLF)
  *** User defined items
  IF !EMPTY(reserved3)
    DIMENSION laText[1]
    laText = ""
    lnNumLine = ALINES( laText, reserved3)
    FPUTS(lnFno,LOC_USER)
    FOR lnCnt = 1 TO lnNumLine
      lcText = laText[ lnCnt ]
      DO CASE
        CASE ISBLANK(lcText)
          lcText = ''
        CASE LEFT(lcText,1) = '*'
          lcText = 'Method: ' + SUBSTR(lcText,2)
        OTHERWISE
          lcText = 'Property: ' + lcText
```

```
      ENDCASE
      IF !EMPTY(lcText)
        FPUTS(lnFno,lcText)
      ENDIF
    NEXT
    FPUTS(lnFno, LOC_LINE + CRLF)
  ENDIF

  *** Properties
  IF !EMPTY(properties)
    DIMENSION laText[1]
    laText = ""
    lnNumLine = ALINES( laText, properties)
    FPUTS(lnFno,LOC_PROP)
    FOR lnCnt = 1 TO lnNumLine
      lcText = laText[ lnCnt ]
      FPUTS(lnFno,lcText)
    NEXT
    FPUTS(lnFno, LOC_LINE + CRLF)
  ENDIF

  *** Methods
  IF !EMPTY(methods)
    DIMENSION laText[1]
    laText = ""
    lnNumLine = ALINES( laText, methods)
    FPUTS(lnFno,LOC_METH)
    FOR lnCnt = 1 TO lnNumLine
      lcText = laText[ lnCnt ]
      DO CASE
        CASE UPPER(LEFT(lcText,9)) = 'PROCEDURE'
          lcText = '*** '+UPPER(ALLTRIM(SUBSTR(lcText,10))) + ' METHOD'
        CASE UPPER(LEFT(lcText,7)) = 'ENDPROC'
          lcText = LOC_LINE + CRLF
        CASE ISBLANK(lcText)
          lcText = ''
      ENDCASE
      IF !EMPTY(lcText)
        FPUTS(lnFno,lcText)
      ENDIF
    NEXT
  ENDIF
ENDSCAN

*** Tidy-up - close output file
FCLOSE(lnFno)

*** Clear messages
WAIT CLEAR
```

Share.prg - a class browser add-in

This very useful tool was created by Steven Black and is available for free download from his web site at *www.stevenblack.com*. Its function is to take a single class and copy it into a new class library. However, not only does it extract the specified class, it will also determine and copy all the classes in the specified class' inheritance hierarchy to the new library.. The result is that your new library will contain all of the classes necessary to use the selected class without the necessity for supplying a full set of class libraries.

Figure 12.10 (below) shows the result of using this utility to extract all of the classes required for a complex composite class in an *'appclass'* library. As you can see, the new VCX has included the entire class hierarchies for all the controls used, even though they are actually defined in several different libraries:

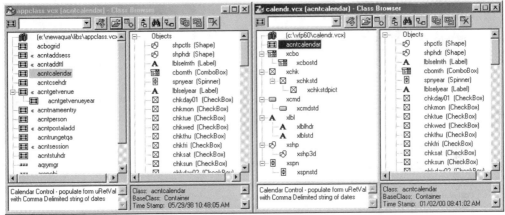

Figure 12.10 *Results produced by the Share.prg Class Browser add-In*

In order to use this utility you first need to register the program as a Class Browser add-in. To do so, first copy the *share.prg* program to the same directory in which `browser.app` and `browser.dbf` reside (normally the VFP home directory). Next, open the Class Browser to create the system object reference to the browser ("*_oBrowser*") and from the command window call the browser's *'AddIn'* method as follows:

```
_oBrowser.AddIn( "Class Extractor", "share.prg" )
```

That's all that there is to it. Now you can open any class library in the browser and when you bring up the right-click menu, the "Class Extractor" will be available through the "Add-Ins" option. (Remember, the Class Browser has two different short-cut menus depending on where you click. The Add-Ins option is on the main Browser shortcut menu and is not available on the Class menu that appears when you right-click in either of the main detail windows.) It is hard to overestimate the usefulness of this little tool and even if you do not use the class browser for anything else, this should definitely be part of your standard toolkit.

A kinder finder *(Example: Finder.scx)*

Have you ever needed to know all the places within an application that a particular table was used? Or how about all the forms that contain an instance of a specific class? Our kinder finder makes this a very easy job indeed. All you need to do is enter the search string and select the directory to search. The form then populates the file types combo box with the valid file types found in the specified directory. The "Files to Search" and "Field Names to Search" lists are populated appropriately when a new file type is selected. After selecting one or more files and specifying at least one field to search, press the GO button, and the form displays the results on the next page.

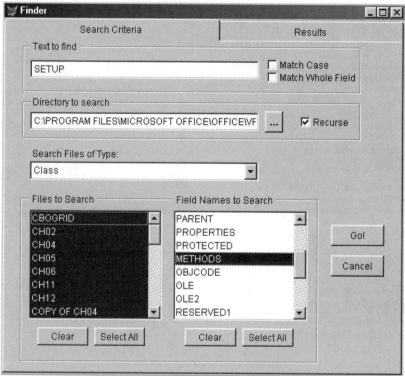

Figure 12.11 *Finder.scx: Searching for all classes that have a setup method*

The directories to search are placed into the form's custom *aDirectories* property by its custom *SetDirectories* method. It also repopulates the combo and list boxes by calling the form's custom *GetFileTypes* method:

```
IF ! EMPTY ( .cDirectory )

  *** Check out the file types in the selected directory
  *** Add what is available to the combo box of file types
  .GetFileTypes( .cDirectory )

  *** See if we need to recurse through the selected directory
  IF .lRecurse
    .GetChildDirectories( .cDirectory )
  ENDIF
ENDIF
```

This code in the custom *GetChildDirectories* method fills the array with the fully qualified path of all subdirectories in the tree:

```
LPARAMETERS tcDirectory

LOCAL lnDirCnt, laDirs[1], lnCnt, lnLen
IF ! ( tcDirectory == Thisform.cDirectory )

   *** add the current directory to the list if it isn't the root
   lnLen = ALEN( Thisform.aDirectories ) + 1
   DIMENSION Thisform.aDirectories[ lnLen ]
   Thisform.aDirectories [ lnLen ] = tcDirectory

   *** see if we must add any new file types
   Thisform.GetFileTypes( tcDirectory )
ENDIF

*** Now see if we have any directories under the current directory
lnDirCnt = ADIR( laDirs, tcDirectory + '*.*', 'D' )
IF lnDirCnt > 1
  FOR lnCnt = 1 TO lnDirCnt
    IF LEFT( laDirs[ lnCnt, 1 ], 1 ) # '.'

      *** Make sure we have a directory and not a file
      IF DIRECTORY( tcDirectory + laDirs[ lnCnt, 1 ] )
        Thisform.GetChildDirectories( tcDirectory + laDirs[ lnCnt, 1 ] + '\')
      ENDIF
    ENDIF
  ENDFOR
ENDIF
```

The *GetFileTypes* method uses the entries in the table FinderTypes.dbf to determine which file types should be included in the combo box. It examines the extension of each file in the specified directory and adds it to the form's *aFileTypes* array if it can be found in FinderTypes.dbf and is not yet a member of the array:

```
LOCAL lnFileCount, laFiles[ 1 ], lnFile, lcExtension, lnSelect, lnLen

lnSelect = SELECT()
lnFileCount = ADIR( laFiles, tcDirectory + '*.*' )
IF lnFileCount > 0
  FOR lnFile = 1 TO lnFileCount
    lcExtension = UPPER( ALLTRIM( JUSTEXT( laFiles[ lnFile, 1 ] ) ) )

    *** See if this is a 'legal' file extention
    SELECT FinderTypes
    LOCATE FOR ALLTRIM( FinderTypes.cExtension ) == lcExtension
    IF ! FOUND()
      LOOP
    ENDIF

    *** Legal entension...see if we already have it in the array
    IF ASCAN( Thisform.aFileTypes, FinderTypes.cAbbr ) = 0

      *** If this is the first file type found,
      *** replace the '(none)' entry that the combo was initialized with
      lnLen = ALEN( Thisform.aFileTypes, 1 )
      IF lnLen = 1 AND Thisform.aFileTypes[ 1, 1 ] = ' (None) '
      ELSE
        lnLen = lnLen + 1
```

```
         DIMENSION Thisform.aFileTypes[ lnLen, 2 ]
      ENDIF

      *** Add this file type to the list
      Thisform.aFileTypes[ lnLen, 1 ] = FinderTypes.cAbbr
      Thisform.aFileTypes[ lnLen, 2 ] = FinderTypes.cExtension
   ENDIF
  ENDFOR
ENDIF

SELECT ( lnSelect )
```

Each time a selection is made in the combo box, the form's *GetFileNames* method is invoked to repopulate the list box of files to search:

```
LOCAL lnfile, lnFileCnt, lnDirCnt, lnDir, laFiles[1], lnTotalFiles, lcFileType

lnTotalFiles = 0

*** If we only have '(none)' as a file type, do nothing
IF EMPTY( Thisform.cFileType )
   RETURN
ELSE
   lcFileType = UPPER( ALLTRIM( Thisform.cFileType ) )
ENDIF

lnDirCnt = ALEN( Thisform.aDirectories )
FOR lnDir = 1 TO lnDirCnt

   *** Get all the files in the current direcotry
   lnFileCnt = ADIR( laFiles, Thisform.aDirectories[ lnDir ] + '*.*' )

   *** Loop through the files and add the ones of the correct type to the array
   *** Column 1 is the file name and column 2 is the directory it is located in
   FOR lnFile = 1 TO lnFileCnt
     IF UPPER( ALLTRIM( JUSTEXT( laFiles[ lnFile, 1 ] ) ) ) == lcFileType
        lnTotalFiles = lnTotalFiles + 1
        DIMENSION Thisform.aFileNames[ lnTotalFiles, 2 ]
        Thisform.aFileNames[ lnTotalFiles, 1 ] = JUSTSTEM( laFiles[ lnFile, 1 ] )
        Thisform.aFileNames[ lnTotalFiles, 2 ] = Thisform.aDirectories[ lnDir ]
     ENDIF
   ENDFOR
ENDFOR

*** Sort the file names
ASORT( Thisform.aFileNames, 1 )
```

The form's *GetFieldNames* method is then used to repopulate the fields to search list box:

```
LOCAL lcExtension, lnSelect, lnFld, lnFldCnt, lcFile, laFields[ 1 ]

lnSelect = SELECT()
lcExtension = UPPER( ALLTRIM( Thisform.cFileType ) )

*** See what kind of file we have
SELECT FinderTypes
LOCATE FOR ALLTRIM( FinderTypes.cExtension ) == lcExtension
```

```
IF FOUND()

  *** It's a text file so we can't select any fields
  IF FinderTypes.lIsText
    DIMENSION ThisForm.aFieldNames[ 1 ]
    Thisform.aFieldNames [ 1 ] = ''
  ELSE

    *** It's some standard structure like a pjx, scx, vcx etc.
    *** Get its structure into the aFieldNames array and refresh the list box
    IF FinderTypes.lStatic
      lcFile = ALLTRIM( Thisform.aFileNames[ 1, 1 ] )
      SELECT 0
      USE ( Thisform.aFileNames[ 1, 2 ] + lcFile + '.' + lcExtension ) ;
        AGAIN NOUPDATE
      lnFldCnt = AFIELDS( laFields )
      USE
      DIMENSION Thisform.aFieldNames[ lnFldCnt ]
      FOR lnFld = 1 TO lnFldCnt
        Thisform.aFieldNames[ lnFld ] = laFields[ lnFld, 1 ]
      ENDFOR
    ELSE

      *** The selected file type is dbf
      Thisform.GetDBFFields()
    ENDIF
  ENDIF
ENDIF

SELECT ( lnSelect )
```

The form's custom *Search* method spins through each selected file, looking for a match on the specified search string in the selected fields. When a match is found, a record is inserted into a cursor so that the search results can be displayed in the grid on the second page.

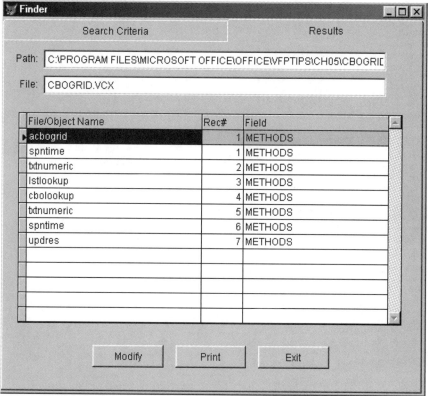

Figure 12.12 Search results: a list of all classes that have a setup method

Most of the work is accomplished in the custom *SearchTextFile* method if the chosen file is a text file and in the custom *SearchTable* method if it is a form, class or other table based entity. Clicking on the **MODIFY** button allows you to edit the form, class, report, etc. right from the results page.

Conclusion

As stated in the introduction to this Chapter, these tools are intended for Developers to use and are not offered as 'complete and production ready'. Please don't be offended if you discover a bug and feel free to alter or extend any of these tools to suit yourselves. We would love to hear of any major problems you find, and of any new directions that these examples may suggest to you.

Chapter 13
Miscellaneous Things

"There are three roads to ruin; women, gambling and technicians. The most pleasant is with women, the quickest is with gambling, but the surest is with technicians." (Georges Pompidou, French president. Quoted in "Sunday Telegraph," London, 26 May 1968).

This chapter contains an assortment of useful tips and utilities that do not really belong in any one place but which may be useful in their own right from time to time. Enjoy!

Using the Visual FoxPro debugger

The Visual FoxPro debugger, in the form that was first introduced in Version 5.0, is a very powerful set of tools which can be of enormous value when testing your code. However, it is also quite a complex tool and can take some getting used to.

Features of the debugger windows

Each of the windows available in the debugger has some interesting feature that may not be obvious. Here are some of the things that we have gleaned about them:

Locals Window

- You can change the value of a local variable or property by clicking in the values column of the window and typing in a new value. Such changes will be retained as long as the variable or property remains in scope
- Right-clicking brings up a shortcut menu which allows you to toggle the visibility status, and hence the clarity of the display, of :
  - **Public** Variables declared with the PUBLIC keyword
  - **Local** Variables declared with the LOCAL keyword
  - **Standard** All variables in the scope of the procedure named by "Locals for"
  - **Objects** Object references
- You can drill down into an object or array by clicking on the "+" sign in the window
- The Locals Window can be invoked programmatically with ACTIVATE WINDOW LOCALS

Watch Window

- You can change the value of a local variable or property by clicking in the values column of the window and typing in a new value. Such changes will be retained as long as the variable or property remains in scope
- You can drill down into an object or array by clicking on the "+" sign in the window

- You can drag expressions to and from the Command Window and the 'Watch' entry line
- You can drag expressions from the trace window directly into the 'Watch' entry line
- Shortcut references like *This* and *ThisForm* can be used in Watch expressions
- To see the name of whichever object is under the mouse pointer at any time include the following in the list of Watch expressions: "`SYS(1272, SYS(1270))`"
- The watch window can be activated programmatically with `ACTIVATE WINDOW WATCH`

Trace Window

- In addition to the 'Resume' (green triangle) and 'Cancel' (Red circle) options, the debugger provides four movement options when tracing code as follows:
  - **Step Into**: Execute current line of code only
  - **Step Over**: Disables trace while executing a subroutine, or call to a method or user-defined function
  - **Step Out**: Resumes execution of the current procedure or method but suspends again when the procedure/method is completed
  - **Run to Cursor**: Resumes execution from the current line and suspends when the line containing the cursor is reached
- Hovering the mouse pointer over a variable or property reference displays a tooltip window showing the current value for that item. You can limit what is evaluated by highlighting text in the trace window. One use for this is verifying that an object is really an object by stripping off a method call. For example, hovering the mouse over "*oObj.Init()*" will not display anything, but if you highlight only "*oObj,*" you will get a tooltip showing "*Object.*" Another use is to get the value of items enclosed in quotes; selecting the "*toObj.Name*" from "`CASE TYPE("toObj.Name") =`" will display the value of the name property in the tooltip.
- **Set Next Statement** option: When you are in trace mode, you can jump blocks of code, or re-execute code, simply by moving the mouse cursor to the required row and choosing 'Set Next Statement' from the 'Debug' menu (Keyboard: "`ALT D + N`"). Whereas the 'Run to Cursor' option temporarily disables tracing but still runs the code, 'Set Next Statement' moves directly to the specified location without executing any intervening code at all.
- Code can be copied from the trace window and pasted into the command window or to a temporary program and executed independently either as a block or by highlighting lines and executing them directly.
- You can highlight and drag text directly from the trace into the watch window.
- The Trace window can be activated programmatically with `ACTIVATE WINDOW TRACE`.

Debugout Window

- Any valid FoxPro expression preceded with the command DEBUGOUT is evaluated and echoed to the debug output window. All of the following are valid: DEBUGOUT "Hello World", DEBUGOUT DATE(), DEBUGOUT 22/7.
- DEBUGOUT output can be enabled programmatically using SET DEBUGOUT TO <file> [ADDITIVE] and disabled with SET DEBUGOUT TO.
- ASSERT messages, and any events that are being tracked in the event tracker, are also echoed to the DebugOut destination (i.e. to file or window or both).
- To track custom methods or native methods that are not available in the event tracker, include DEBUGOUT PROGRAM() statements. (Note: Such statements do not even need to be removed. If the output window is not available because it is not open or because the program is being executed under a run time environment, all DebugOut commands are simply ignored.)
- The DebugOut window can be activated programmatically with ACTIVATE WINDOW "Debug Output."

CallStack Window

- Enabling "Show Call Stack Order" places a sequential number alongside each program in the Call Stack window indicating the order in which they are executing. For some reason, control of this function has been named 'Ordinal Position' in the pop-up menu which appears when you right-click in the Call Stack window.
- Enabling the 'Call Stack' Indicator displays a black triangle in the border of both the Call Stack and Trace windows whenever you are viewing a program other than the one that is currently executing. In the Call Stack window this triangle indicates which program you are viewing, while in the Trace window it indicates the line, in that program, which is executing.

Configuring the debugger

The set-up for the debugger is controlled through the Options dialog, where it has its own tab. The settings are all stored (as with all other options controlled by this dialog) in the Windows registry.

Which frame to use?

The debugger can be run in either its own 'frame,' which makes it a separate application, or within the FoxPro 'frame,' in which case it becomes a set of individual windows which are available from the tools menu and which float over the desktop. The main benefits of using the debug frame are that it doesn't take precious screen space away from whatever you are running, all of the debugger windows are contained in a single top level window and are readily accessible and the "Fix" option works. The main drawback to using the debug frame is that if you have code in *LostFocus* or *Deactivate* events, that code will get fired when you switch to and from the debugger and may interfere with whatever you are trying to debug.

Setting up the debugger windows

The debugger's default configuration options can be found in the Visual FoxPro Options dialog (accessible from the Tools pad of the main menu) where they have their own tab. However, the interface for this page is non-standard and it is not immediately obvious that the items available for configuration depend on which window is specified by the option button in the 'Specify Window' section, as follows:

Table 13.1 Debug window set-up options

Window	Options
Call Stack	Font and Colors Call Stack Order Call Stack Current Line Indicator Call Stack Indicator
Locals	Font and Colors
Output	Font and Colors Log output to file (specify default file)
Trace	Font and Colors Show line numbers Trace between breakpoints Pause between line execution
Watch	Font and Colors

The significance of 'trace between breaks'

Note that for the Call Stack window to be available in the debugger, you need "Trace between break points" to be set ON but this option is, helpfully, located under the "Trace Window" options. However, unless you are actively inspecting the Call Stack, we strongly recommend that you keep this window closed. It is the slowest debugger window to refresh while stepping through code.

In fact the setting of "Trace between breaks" is the main factor in determining the impact of keeping the debugger open while running code. We prefer to leave it turned off by default, only setting it from the shortcut menu in the debugger when needed.

Close debug windows that you do not need!

The more debug windows you have open, the greater the impact on your code's execution time. It is worth noting that, when running the debugger in "debug frame", you do not actually need to have *any* of the individual debugger windows open, so long as the frame itself is active. If you have defined and enabled any required breakpoints, (including those defined in the Watch Window) the breakpoints will still fire as expected. This means that you can run your code with the absolute minimum of slowdown.

Setting breakpoints

Visual FoxPro allows for four types of breakpoints as shown in the following table. The main difference is that the breakpoints based on a location halt execution before the line of code executes, while those based on expressions take effect after the line of code has executed.

Table 13.2 *Types of breakpoints*

Breakpoint Type	Takes Effect
At Location	Immediately <u>before</u> the line of code is executed
At Location If expression is true	Immediately <u>before</u> the line of code is executed if condition is met
When expression is true	Immediately <u>after</u> the line of code that caused expression to become true
When expression is changed	Immediately <u>after</u> the line of code that caused expression to change

There are many ways of setting breakpoints in the debugger. Here are some that we find most useful:

- Right-click on a line of code while editing method code in the form or class designer or in a PRG and choose "Set Breakpoint" (applies to Version 6.0 with service pack 3). This sets a 'break at location' breakpoint.
- In the trace window, you can select any line of code, then right-click - Run To Cursor. This is a quickie breakpoint that's very useful for, for example, stopping after a loop terminates or at some other immediate juncture without setting a permanent breakpoint.
- In the trace window, click on the margin beside a line of code. This sets a 'break at location' breakpoint and displays a red dot in the margin to indicate the breakpoint. Double-click on the same line again, to clear the breakpoint.
- In the watch window click in the margin beside any watched expression. This sets a 'when the expression changes' breakpoint, and displays a red dot in the margin to indicate the breakpoint.
- From the debugger tools menu choose 'Breakpoints' to bring up a dialog where you can set any of the different breakpoint types explicitly. However, as far as we know, this is also, the *only* place in which you can set the PASS COUNT option for an 'at location' breakpoint. This is a useful one to remember if you want to set a breakpoint inside a loop but not have it executed until a specific number of iterations of the loop have occurred.
- Add an explicit "SET STEP ON" anywhere in any code. This will unconditionally suspend execution and display the debugger with the trace window open.

When running the debugger in its own frame, an additional dialog shows all currently defined breakpoints and allows you to selectively enable/disable them. Note that the 'Clear All' button not only disables all breakpoints, it also clears them from history.

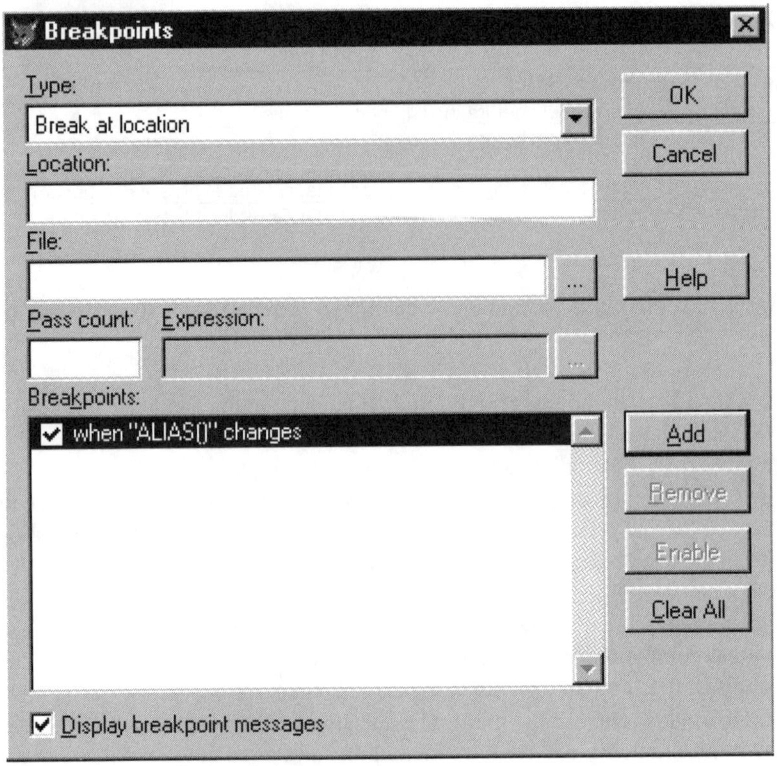

Figure 13.1 *BreakPoint dialog*

Despite the Help File stating that **"CTRL+B"** will display this dialog in either Debug or FoxPro frame, this dialog does not seem to be available when running the debugger in FoxPro Frame.

Useful breakpoint expressions
Often the most difficult decision is how to get Visual FoxPro to break at precisely the point that you want, without having to add explicit code to whatever you are testing. Here are a couple of suggestions we have found useful:

Use a "time based" breakpoint
Quite often we want to examine the state of our objects immediately after some user interaction - like immediately after a message box or other modal dialog. Enter a watch expression like this:

```
MINUTE( DATETIME() )
```

and set a breakpoint on it. Then run your test code and wait at the appropriate dialog until the minute changes before exiting from the dialog. The breakpoint will immediately halt execution and allow you to examine the state of the system. The same expression can also be used to halt large (or endless!) loops.

Use the program function

To set a breakpoint that will fire whenever a specified program or method is executed use an expression like:

```
"checkmethod" $ LOWER( PROGRAM() )
```

This will switch from .F. to .T. whenever "*checkmethod*" starts executing and by setting a 'when expression changes' breakpoint you can halt execution right at the start of the code block. This can, and should, be made very specific - especially when you want to break on a call to a native VFP method which may exist in many objects. For example, the following breakpoint will only interrupt when the *Click* method of an object named '*cmdnext*' begins to execute:

```
"cmdnext.click" $ LOWER( PROGRAM() )
```

while the following line will break in when any method of the same '*cmdnext*' object executes:

```
"cmdnext" $ LOWER( PROGRAM() )
```

Limiting breakpoints to changes

One of the problems with using a 'when expression changes' breakpoint is that Visual FoxPro will regard the watched expression as changed when whatever is being monitored comes into, or goes out of, scope. To avoid this and limit breaks to those occasions on which the value has *really* changed, use an IIF() function to return a constant from the watch expression unless the value has really changed. For example, the following expression will interrupt program execution whenever a variable named '*lnCnt*' is in scope and changes to or from a value of "*3*," but otherwise will be totally ignored:

```
IIF(TYPE("lnCnt")="N" AND lncnt = 3, .T., .F.)
```

Similarly the return value from a SET("DATASESSION") test can be used to ensure that when debugging with multiple datasessions open, only the correct one is being tracked by the debugger. Thus setting a breakpoint on a watch expression like this:

```
IIF( SET("DATASESSION") # 1, ALIAS(), "WRONG DS")
```

will break only when the currently selected ALIAS() changes in a data session **except** the Visual FoxPro default datasession (i.e. DataSession = 1).

How do I ensure that my custom methods fire when I expect them to?
One of the biggest problems that we all encounter when working with objects is that it is not always obvious when events fire. The purpose of the Event Tracker, which is built into the debugger, is to allow you to follow the sequence in which Visual FoxPro's native events fire. By enabling Event Tracking you can direct Visual FoxPro to echo the name of events and methods as they fire, to either the debug output window or to a text file. However, you cannot track all of Visual FoxPro's native events and methods and there is no provision at all for tracking custom methods. So if you need to track exactly what is being executed, you must either use the coverage logger or include code to create a log file into your classes.

Fortunately, the introduction of the *STRTOFILE()* function in Version 6.0 makes this very simple indeed. A single line of code is all that is needed, as follows:

```
STRTOFILE( PROGRAM() + CHR(10) + CHR(13), '<log file name>', .T. )
```

This will output the name of the currently executing method or procedure to the specified file. The final parameter ensures that the text is added to the target file if it already exists, otherwise *STRTOFILE()* would simply overwrite the log file.

We have used this technique to monitor exactly what code in a compiled application actually gets executed during 'user testing.' In order to do this selectively, we wrap the line of code that writes the log file in a test for a system variable (read from the application's *INI* file at start-up). Thereafter simply changing the setting in the INI file allows us to turn run time logging on and off.

Writing code for ease of debugging and maintenance
There have been many pages of good advice written to try convince programmers that they should adopt good defensive practices, use proper, standardized naming conventions and plan their code before writing it. Alas, all too often we still see things that make us wonder whether some programmers are even remotely bothered about being able to test, debug and even maintain their code. Here are some of our thoughts, for what they are worth, on writing better code.

Use a variable/property naming convention
There has been much debate in the FoxPro community over the years about such topics as whether the "m." prefix is a good thing to use or whether the standard Microsoft convention should be adopted for naming variables in all situations. We don't think that it matters too much what the details of your naming convention actually are, so long as you are consistent in its application. Why so?

The reason is that Visual FoxPro is a weakly typed language. In other words, it does not enforce data typing for its properties or variables. This means that without specific testing, you cannot be sure what type of data a variable actually holds because a variable derives its type from its data and changes to reflect whatever data it is given. This is, paradoxically, both one of Visual FoxPro's strengths, and also one of its great weaknesses.

It is a strength because it allows us to define a variable anywhere that we need one (without having to formally declare it) simply by assigning a value to a reference. This makes the programming language very flexible and easy to use.

It is a weakness for two reasons. First it means that there need not be a single place in a method, procedure or function where all the variables used are declared. This can lead to the same variable name being re-declared at different places within the code. Another consequence is that minor typographic errors cause errors at run time because what is actually a misspelled variable name is accepted by the compiler as a new variable declaration. Second, it means that even when a variable has been explicitly declared, named and initialized with a specific data type, the mere act of assigning data of an inappropriate type will not generate an error. The variable simply changes to accommodate the data.

To address the first issue, we strongly recommend you make a habit of declaring any variables that you create in a specific part of the program (normally right at the very start). There is no easy way to avoid the second problem except to ensure that when data is assigned to a variable, that variable's name correctly indicates the data type. This may result in more variables being created and used but, in our opinion, this is a small price to pay for clarity and ease of maintenance.

While using a naming convention will not actually prevent errors, we find it tends to make it easier to keep things conceptually separate and so minimizes the chance of introducing error. Whether you extend your naming convention to include Objects, Fields and Files is really up to you, but these things are generally less immediately significant. We feel it is better to ensure that there is proper documentation for a database and its tables, and for exposed properties and methods of classes.

Keep procedures and methods as short as possible

This may sound obvious, but less code means fewer bugs. More importantly it is easier to both manage the code and understand the logic when dealing with clearly focussed methods or procedures. As a general rule a method should handle one, and only one, specific piece of functionality. (Adopting this principle also makes it easier to name methods!) The greater the degree by which a method is overloaded, the more difficult it is to maintain and the greater the risk of something going wrong.

Use "return" statements in method and procedure code

Like most Visual FoxPro programmers we tend to be a little sloppy in our use of Return statements, especially when we are not actually returning a value explicitly. Most of the time this is not a problem. The FoxPro compiler is smart enough to accept that when it runs out of code in one place, it should return to the bit of code that started it off and it will implement an 'implicit' RETURN for us. However, this can cause problems when debugging code, especially in situations where the last line to be executed is either a function call or a call to another method. By adding the explicit RETURN statement, you have an opportunity to stop within the calling method when tracing code in the debugger.

Use asserts to help catch errors at development time

Asserts are extremely valuable to the developer because they allow us to handle problems differently at development and at run time without actually having to change any code. This is because Visual FoxPro will only execute a line of code that begins with an **'ASSERT'** statement if the code is running in development mode and **SET ASSERTS** is **ON**. In any other situation the line is treated as if it were a comment and does not interfere with program execution.

One common use of **ASSERT** is to warn developers (and testers) when something has not behaved as expected. The objective here is to provide additional information when testing in development. The following code snippet shows how this might be done:

```
luSomeVar = SomeProcessResult()
IF VARTYPE( luSomeVar ) # "C"
  ASSERT .F. MESSAGE 'SomeProcessResult has failed to return a Character String'
  RETURN .F.
ENDIF
```

The error message will only ever be displayed when **SET ASSERTS** is on and the process fails to return a character string. In all other situations, if the process fails to return a character string, the code will simply return a logical .F. and continue its normal execution.

The second common use of Asserts is to check programming logic. This is slightly different from the first example in that the test, in this case, will only be performed when **ASSERTS** are enabled and so at run time the test will not even be attempted:

```
ASSERT PCOUNT() # 3 MESSAGE "Expected 3 parameters, received " +
PADL(PCOUNT(),2)
```

Keep processing and logic separate

One of the easiest ways of simplifying your code is to ensure that you do not mix up processing and logic. As an example of what we mean, consider the following code that was taken, as shown here, from an actual application:

```
IF cheknam(alltrim(table2.legal_name ))== cheknam(alltrim(;
thisform.pageframe1.page1.text1.value)) AND NOT cheknam(alltrim(;
table2.legal_name)) == cheknam(alltrim(curval('legal_name','BUYER'))
```

This may look very cool - but how on earth is one supposed to interpret and debug something like this? In fact, if you check this line of code carefully you will discover that there is actually a missing parenthesis! How *should* the statements have been written? Well maybe something like this would have been a little clearer:

```
*** Do all ChekNam() functions first
lcSceName = ChekNam( ALLTRIM( table2.legal_name ))
lcInpName = ChekNam( ALLTRIM( ThisForm.PageFrame1.Page1.Text1.value ))
lcLegName = ChekNam( ALLTRIM( CURVAL( 'legal_name', 'BUYER')))

*** Now do the test!
IF lcSceName == lcInpName AND NOT lcSceName == lcLegName
```

Why do we think this is better? There are three reasons:

- The calls to the *ChekNam()* function are handled separately. We can therefore check, (in the debugger even if we did not want to place checking code in the program) that the return values are really what we expect.
- We can actually reduce the number of calls that we make to the *ChekNam* function. The test requires that the value that we called *lcSceName* be used twice, so the original code has to make two calls to the function, passing the same value each time.
- We now have separated the program logic from the processing carried out by the *ChekNam()* function. This means that even without knowing what the *ChekNam()* function does, we can at least see what the IF statement is actually testing and can validate the results in the debugger.

Working with datasessions

We have not covered the use of datasessions specifically in any other part of the book - mainly because we could not decide whether the topic was related to data or to forms. Here are a few tips and tricks for using datasessions.

How do I share datasessions between forms?

It is actually very easy to get a form (or report) to use the private datasession of the object that called it. Simply set the child object's *DataSession* property to "1 - Default Data Session". This works because of the way Visual FoxPro interprets the term '*Default*' in this context and it isn't what you might reasonably expect!

When you first start Visual FoxPro and open the "DataSession Window", you will notice that the current datasession is "*Default(1)*". Setting a form's datasession property to "*1 - Default Data Session*" would seem likely to ensure that the form uses the same DataSession number 1 that VFP refers to as Default. Alas this is not necessarily true! In this context the term 'Default' really means that the form does **NOT** create a private datasession for itself but just uses whatever datasession is current *when it is instantiated*. This is why a form whose datasession property is left at "*1 -Default Data Session*" shares the data session of the form that launches it.

If a form uses its own dataenvironment to AutoOpen/AutoClose tables, only those tables that are actually opened by the child form will be closed. In other words, if the child form requires a table which is already open in the parent form's datasession, Visual FoxPro is smart enough to recognize that fact and will not re-open such tables when the child form is instantiated, or close them when the child form is released.

One thing to note is that if you allow a form to share in the private datasession of another, when you release the child form the Visual FoxPro Current DataSession name will change to '*Unknown(n)*', where 'n' is the datasession number of the form which originally created the datasession. However, this does not appear to cause Visual FoxPro any problem although it can be a little disconcerting when you first notice it happen. The reason appears to be that although Visual FoxPro is capable of re-naming the datasession to the current owner when the child form is instantiated, it does not know how to re-name it when that form is released and so simply leaves it as '*Unknown*'.

How do I change datasessions?

Despite the information to the contrary in the Help File, a form's *DataSessionID* property is actually read-write at run time. You can, therefore, force a form to run in a specific datasession by setting its *DataSessionID* property directly in code. However, if you have any bound controls on your form, changing the form's data session after they have been bound will cause you serious problems. The degree of severity will depend on the control in question. A grid will simply lose its *RecordSource* and go irrevocably blank. A list box whose *RowSource* is taken from a table will cause an *'Unable to Access Selected Table'* error and will disappear, while a combo box will simply go blank. Interestingly, re-connecting the form to the correct datasession will restore things to normal in the case of both list and combo boxes, though not for grids. The moral of this story is that if you need to change a form's datasession, do it in the form's LOAD before any controls have been instantiated, and do not allow the form's dataenvironment to AutoOpen tables.

There may, however, be occasions in which you will need to manipulate an object's *DataSessionID* property. For example, toolbars are often required to switch themselves into the datasession of the currently active form. (Our "managed" toolbar class in Chapter 10 has such code and this is not a problem because such generic toolbars do not have data bound controls.)

For objects that do not have a *DataSessionID* property, you must use the SET DATASESSION command to change the global datasession. This may be required for a global object (e.g. an Application Object) that is created in the Visual FoxPro default data session, but which may need access to tables opened by a form in a private datasession. Providing that you first save the current datasession and restore it immediately afterwards, this should not cause problems, even when other objects with data bound controls are present. The following code snippet shows how:

```
*** Save Current DS
lnDSID = SET( "DATASESSION" )
*** Change Datasession
SET DATASESSION TO <new session number>
*** Do whatever is needed and then revert
SET DATASESSION TO (lnDSId)
```

How do I get a list of all active datasessions? *(Example: getallds.prg)*

There is no native way to get a list of all active datasessions programmatically, but since we would normally only be interested in the datasessions being used by forms, we can use the *_Screen.Forms* collection to determine which are active. The following function does precisely this and populates an array (which is passed by reference) with the datasession number and the owning object name. The function returns the number of active datasessions that it finds:

```
*********************************************************************
* Program....: GetAllDS.prg
* Compiler...: Visual FoxPro 06.00.8492.00 for Windows
* Abstract...: Populate array with all open datasessions
* ...........: Pass target array by reference to this function
* ...........:      DIMENSION aDSList[1]
* ...........:      lnNumSess = GetAllDs( @aDSList )
*********************************************************************
LPARAMETERS taSessions
EXTERNAL ARRAY taSessions
LOCAL lnCurDatasession, lnSessions
*** Initialize Counter
lnSessions = 0
*** Loop through Forms Collection
FOR EACH oForm IN _SCREEN.FORMS
   *** Have we got this session already?
   IF ASCAN( taSessions, oForm.DatasessionID) = 0
      *** If not, add it to the array
      lnSessions = lnSessions + 1
      DIMENSION taSessions[lnSessions,2]
      taSessions[lnSessions,1] = oForm.DatasessionID
      taSessions[lnSessions,2] = oForm.Name
   ENDIF
NEXT
*** Return the number of sessions
RETURN lnSessions
```

Miscellaneous items

The remainder of this chapter is a collection of things that we haven't specifically included elsewhere. There is no particular link between them, but they are worth mentioning, even if only as a reminder.

What is the event sequence when a form is instantiated or destroyed?

As is often the case with Visual FoxPro, the answer is that 'it depends.' In this case it depends upon whether the form is being instantiated from a *SCX* file using 'DO FORM' or from a VCX file using CREATEOBJECT() or NEWOBJECT(). Instantiating the form as a class is the simplest, and here is the sequence of events:

```
FORM.LOAD
  INIT for each control
```

```
FORM.INIT
FORM.SHOW
FORM.ACTIVATE
FORM.REFRESH
  WHEN for 1ˢᵗ control in Taborder
  GOTFOCUS for 1ˢᵗ Control in Taborder (if it has one)
```

The basic start-up sequence is, therefore, given by the acronym "*L.I.S.A.R.*". By default, the individual controls on the form are instantiated in the order in which they were added to the class in the designer. However by using the '*Bring to Front*' and '*Send to Back*' options, you can alter the sequence in which controls are instantiated. (Although it really shouldn't matter in what order things are instantiated. Creating classes that rely on controls being instantiated in a particular order is not, in our opinion, good design!)

Releasing a form class is essentially the reverse of the initialization process. The *Release* method provides the means to programmatically initiate the process, while the *QueryUnload* method is called when a user clicks on the 'window close' button in a form. Neither calls the other unless you specifically add code to make them do so, but both call the form's *Destroy* method:

```
FORM.RELEASE or FORM.QUERYUNLOAD
FORM.DESTROY
  DESTROY for each control (in reverse order)
FORM.UNLOAD
```

This means that if you require code to be executed irrespective of whether the user closes a form by clicking on a command button (which calls *Release*) or the 'window close' button (which calls *QueryUnload*), then that code must be placed in the form's *Destroy* method.

In the case of a form created from a SCX, the basic sequence of form events is the same, but the presence of the native DataEnvironment complicates the issue. Notice that the dataenvironment *OpenTables* method is the first method called (it fires *BeforeOpenTables*) – even before the form's *Load* method is called. After the form *Load* method has completed successfully, the cursors are initialized. This ensures that when the form's controls are instantiated, those that are bound to data will be able to do so properly:

```
DATAENVIRONMENT.OPENTABLES
DATAENVIRONMENT.BEFOREOPENTABLES
FORM.LOAD
  INIT for each cursor in the DataEnvironment
DATAENVIRONMENT.INIT
  INIT for each control in the form
FORM.INIT
FORM.SHOW
FORM.ACTIVATE
FORM.REFRESH
  WHEN for 1ˢᵗ control in Taborder
  GOTFOCUS for 1ˢᵗ Control in Taborder (if it has one)
```

The release process is, as far as the form itself is concerned, identical to that above. Notice that the DataEnvironment is not actually destroyed until *after* the form has been unloaded from memory:

```
FORM.RELEASE or FORM.QUERYUNLOAD
FORM.DESTROY
  DESTROY for each control (in reverse order)
FORM.UNLOAD
DATAENVIRONMENT.AFTERCLOSETABLES
DATAENVIRONMENT.DESTROY
  DESTROY for each Cursor in the DE (in reverse order)
```

How do I get a reference to a form's parent form?

There are a couple of ways of doing this, the most obvious being simply to have the parent form pass a reference to itself when calling the child form - thus:

```
DO FORM <child form> WITH This
```

However this does require that the child form's *Init* method must be set up to receive the object reference as a parameter and then store it to a form property. Interestingly the object pointed to by Visual FoxPro's *_Screen.ActiveForm* property does not change when a new form is instantiated until that form's *Init* method has completed successfully. (This makes sense when you remember that returning a logical .F. from either the *Load* or *Init* methods will prevent the new form from instantiating.)

Therefore to get a reference to the calling form, there is no need to pass anything at all. Simply store *_Screen.ActiveForm* to a property in either the *Load* or *Init* method of the child form. Normally we would place this sort of code in the *Load* method (to leave the *Init* free for handling parameters) like this:

```
IF TYPE("_Screen.ActiveForm.Name") # "U"
  ThisForm.oCalledBy = _Screen.ActiveForm
ENDIF
```

Note that we cannot reliably use the **VARTYPE()** function here because it will fail if there is no active form.

How do I get a list of all objects on a form?

The Visual FoxPro Form object has a collection named "*Controls*" and an associated counter property ("*ControlCount*") holds a reference to every object on the form. However, this collection only holds references to objects that are *DIRECTLY* contained by the form. So, for example, it will not include objects that are on a page, inside a pageframe on the form. All it will have is the reference to the pageframe. To get a list of all objects, we will therefore need to 'drill down' into each container that is encountered.

Fortunately every Visual FoxPro container class has a collection (and associated counter) which holds references to the objects that the container owns. Unfortunately, these collections are not all named the same as the following table indicates:

Table 13.3 *Container class collections*

Base Class	Collection	Counter Property
_Screen	Forms	FormCount
_Screen	Controls	ControlCount
Formset	Forms	FormCount
Form	Controls	ControlCount
Toolbar	Controls	ControlCount
PageFrame	Pages	PageCount
Page	Controls	ControlCount
Grid	Columns	ColumnCount
Column	Controls	ControlCount
Container	Controls	ControlCount
Custom	Controls	ControlCount
Control	Controls	ControlCount

This variation in naming makes writing a routine that will drill down through a form a little more difficult because we must test the baseclass of each container that we encounter in order to ascertain what its collection property is called. The sample form *LogCtrls.Scx* has a recursive custom method (*GetControls*) and a custom array property (*aAllControls*) which is used as the collection for all controls and is populated by the custom *AddToCollection* method. Finally, a custom *RegisterControls* method is used to initialize the array property and to start the drill down process by calling the *GetControls* method with a reference to the form itself. Here is the code for the *RegisterControls* method:

```
*** LogCtrls::RegisterControls Method
*** Initialises Form Collection and Calls the recursive GetControls()
WITH ThisForm
    *** Clear the current list (if any)
    DIMENSION .aAllControls[1,3]
    .aAllControls = ""
    *** Start the Drill-Down with the Form Object itself
    .GetControls( This )
ENDWITH
```

The *GetControls* method is a little more complex. The first thing it does is to create a local reference to the object passed to it as a parameter (note that it will use the Form itself if nothing is passed). Next it calls the *AddToCollection* method to add the object to the collection and then stores the object's base class into another local variable for use later:

```
*** LogCtrls::GetControls Method
*** Drills down through form and populates the custom collection array
LPARAMETERS toStartObj
LOCAL loRef, lnCnt, lnControls, loObj

*** Get ref to parent or to form, by default
loRef = IIF( TYPE('toStartObj')='O', toStartObj, THISFORM )
*** Add This object to the collection
ThisForm.AddToCollection( loRef )
```

```
*** Get the Base Class of the current object
lcClass = LOWER(ALLTRIM(loRef.BaseClass))
```

Next we need to determine what sort of object we are dealing with in the current iteration. First we check to see whether we are dealing with one of the classes which use something other than a 'controls' collection. If so we call the *GetControls* method recursively while looping through that object's collection:

```
*** Now Process the current object
DO CASE
  CASE lcClass = 'pageframe'
    FOR lnCnt = 1 TO loRef.PageCount
      *** Call this method for each page
      THISFORM.GetControls( loRef.Pages[lnCnt] )
    NEXT

  CASE lcClass = 'grid'
    FOR lnCnt = 1 TO loRef.ColumnCount
      *** Call this method for each column
      THISFORM.GetControls( loRef.Columns[lnCnt] )
    NEXT

  CASE lcClass = 'formset'
    FOR lnCnt = 1 TO loRef.FormCount
      *** Call this method for each form
      THISFORM.GetControls( loRef.Forms[lnCnt] )
    NEXT
```

Any other container class will be using a "Controls" collection so we can process them all in a single case statement. (Notice that we check, using an exact comparison, for the '*page*' base class. This is to avoid falling foul of Visual FoxPro's slightly idiosyncratic string comparison which would return .т. if we simply included '*page*' in the list, but the object was a '*pageframe*'.)

If the current object is a container, this code loops through its *controls* collection. Again we check the base class of each object that we encounter and, if it is another container, call the *GetControls* method recursively passing a reference to the object. However, if it is not a container, a reference to it is passed to the *AddToCollection* method so that it can be logged:

```
*** OK, is it an object which has a controls collection?
  CASE INLIST( lcClass, 'form', 'container', 'column', 'custom', 'control' ) ;
          OR lcClass == 'page'
    *** If so, loop through its collection
    FOR lnCnt = 1 TO loRef.ControlCount
      *** Get a reference to the current object
      loObj = loRef.Controls[lnCnt]
      IF INLIST( loObj.BaseClass, 'Container', 'Pageframe', 'Grid', 'Custom',
'Control' )
        *** Call this method recursively if it is a contained container
        ThisForm.GetControls( loObj )
      ELSE
        *** Just add the object to the collection
        ThisForm.AddToCollection( loObj )
      ENDIF
```

```
NEXT
```

If the current object does not trigger any of the conditions in this case statement, it is not a container and has already been logged so we can safely ignore it and exit from this level of recursion:

```
OTHERWISE
    *** Nothing more to do at this level
ENDCASE

*** Just return
RETURN
```

The only other code is that which actually adds an object to the form's 'aAllControls' collection. This is very simple indeed because it receives a direct reference to the object that it has to log as a parameter from the *GetControls* method:

```
LPARAMETERS toObj
LOCAL loRef
IF VARTYPE( toObj ) # "O"
    *** If not an object, just return
    RETURN
ELSE
    *** Get Local Reference
    loRef = toObj
ENDIF
```

After checking that the parameter is indeed an object, the next task is to determine how many items have already been logged:

```
WITH ThisForm
    *** Get number of rows already in collection
    lnControls = ALEN( .aAllControls, 1 )
  *** If 1 row - is it populated?
    IF lnControls = 1
        lnControls = IIF( EMPTY( .aAllControls[1,1]), 0, 1 )
    ENDIF
    *** Increment the counter
    lnControls = lnControls + 1
```

A new row is then added to the collection and the elements of the collection populated:

```
    *** Add a row to the array
    DIMENSION .aAllControls[ lnControls, 3]
    *** Populate the new row
    .aAllControls[ lnControls, 1] = loRef.Name           && Object Name
    .aAllControls[ lnControls, 2] = loRef                && Object Reference
    .aAllControls[ lnControls, 3] = SYS(1272, loRef )    && Object Hierarchy
ENDWITH
*** Just Return
```

RETURN

There are many situations in which it is useful to be able to loop through all controls on a form. While this code is specifically written to populate a collection array, with the exception of the two calls to the *AddToCollection* method, the code is completely generic and could be used anytime it's necessary to drill down through a form. Furthermore, since the *GetControls* method is called with an object reference, it does not have to start with the form. It can just start with whatever object reference it is passed.

How can I set focus to the first control in the tab order?

One answer to this question is that you could use code similar to that given in the preceding section to drill down through a container (i.e. the form, or a page in a form) to find the contained object that has its *TabIndex* property set to 1. Then simply set focus to that object and exit.

Alternatively when using forms with multiple pages, rather than repeatedly executing this drill down code, you might prefer to build a special collection (when the form is instantiated) to record for each page a reference to the object which is first in the Tab Order. Then all that would be needed would be to scan that collection for the required page and set focus to the specified object.

How do I return a value from a modal form?

Elsewhere, we have already discussed some techniques for passing parameters between objects of varying types. What we have not covered specifically anywhere else are the various techniques for getting values back from a modal form. The concept of "*returning a value*" is only meaningful when the form returning the value is modal because the implicit requirement is that some process must be interrupted, or suspended, until the required value is returned. Only by using a modal form can you ensure that:

- The process cannot continue until the value is available
- The value is returned to the correct place in the calling code.

There are essentially three ways of getting a value back from a modal form, but one of them works only for forms which are run as SCX files, one works with forms that are instantiated from VCX files and one works irrespective of how the form is created. Remember that, although we are talking about returning 'a value', this 'value' could be a parameter object containing multiple items (see *Chapter 2 "Functions and Procedures"* for more information on creating and using parameter objects).

Returning a value from a form

The actual mechanism for returning a value from a form is quite straightforward. You simply place a RETURN <value> command as the last line of code in the form's *UNLOAD* method. This is the last form method to be executed before a form is released and so it is a perfectly logical place for the return statement. However, there is one little catch. If the value that you wish to return is coming from a control on the form, by the time the form's Unload method runs all controls have been released, so the values that they held will no longer be available. To get around this problem you must ensure that any control values you wish to return are saved to form properties no later than in the Form's *Destroy* method. (See the section earlier in this chapter for details of the event sequence when a form is instantiated or destroyed.)

Hiding a modal form

One way of getting access to values that are contained within a modal form is simply to hide the form instead of releasing it. When a modal form is hidden, whichever form was active immediately prior to the modal form being instantiated becomes the active form once again. In other words, the form that *called* the modal form is re-activated. Providing that you have, within the calling form, a valid reference to the modal form you can access any exposed properties of the form, or of its contained controls. This approach will work irrespective of the way in which the form is instantiated.

The following code snippet shows how this might be done for a form instantiated directly from a class:

```
*** Instantiate a modal form
oFm = NEWOBJECT( 'modalform', 'formclasses' )
*** Show the form and ensure that it is modal
oFm.Show(1)
*** When form is 'released' it is actually hidden!
*** Access the Modal form's properties directly
ThisForm.SomeProperty = oFm.ModalFormProperty
*** Release the modal form when done
oFm.Release()
```

While for a form that is created from an SCX file, the following code is equivalent:

```
*** Instantiate the modal form
DO FORM modalform NAME oFm LINKED
*** When the modal form is "released" it is actually hidden!
*** The NAME 'oFm' can now be used to access it directly:
ThisForm.SomeProperty = oFm.ModalFormProperty
*** Release the modal form when done by releasing the "linked name"
RELEASE oFm
```

Using do form <name> to <variable>

For modal forms that have been created as SCX files and which are run using the DO FORM command, there is a specific syntax you use to save a value which is returned from the form, as follows:

```
DO FORM modalform TO luRetVal
```

When the modal form is released, whatever was returned from the form's *Unload* method will be saved to the variable 'luRetVal'. Note that this variable does not need to have been previously declared and will be created as needed. However, if the called form does not contain a RETURN statement in its *Unload* method, the variable will NOT be created. So, in our opinion, it is much safer to always explicitly declare the return variable, and initialize it, rather than just relying on there being a return statement.

Returning a value from a form instantiated directly from a class

The problem in this situation is that there is no way to return both the object reference *AND* a return value from either the `CreateObject` or `NewObject` functions. Since both must return a reference to the new object we have to find another way of getting a value back. The solution is to pass a parameter object to the form that can then be returned by the modal form when it is released.

The form class must be set up to receive, and store to a property, the parameter object that is passed to it. (Normally we would also have the class *Init* method call its *Show* method directly to make the form visible immediately on instantiation.). This object must be populated with the relevant properties while the form is active and returned to the calling method (or procedure) from the modal form's *Unload* method. The code to instantiate the modal form would look like this:

```
*** Create the Parameter object
oParamObj  = CREATEOBJECT( 'parameterobject' )
*** Instantiate the modal form
oModalForm = CREATEOBJECT( 'modalformclass', oParamObj )
*** Check the returned object properties
IF oParamObj.FormWasOK
  *** Do whatever
ELSE
  *** Do something else
ENDIF
```

How do I change the mouse pointer in a form while a process is running?

As usual, the basic answer is very simple. All visual controls have a *MousePointer* property that determines the shape of the mouse cursor when the cursor is positioned over a control. However, because each control has its own setting for controlling the mouse pointer there is no single property or method to control the *MousePointer* property for all controls on a form at once.

The standard way to change all the values of a property for all objects on a form is to use the form's *SETALL* method. The following code sets the mouse pointer for all controls on a form to the 'hourglass':

```
WITH ThisForm
  *** Set the form's own mouse pointer
  .MousePointer = 11
  *** Now all contained objects
  .SetAll( 'MousePointer', 11 )
ENDWITH
```

To restore to the default setting, simply repeat this code with a value of 0 instead of 11. However, this does rely on all controls on the form using the same *MousePointer* property setting at all times. If you already have different *MousePointer* property settings for different classes of control, the only alternative is to loop through all controls on a form and save each control's current *MousePointer* property and set it explicitly to the required value. (You can use code similar to that shown in the "*How do I get a list of all objects on a form?*" section of this chapter.). To restore the mouse pointer you would simply have to repeat the process and read the saved value. We feel this is a fairly unusual scenario and would normally expect to find all controls using their 'default' (*MousePointer = 0*) setting.

So far, so good! Unfortunately there is an exception to everything that we have said above when a grid is involved. While a grid does have a *MousePointer* property, we are not quite sure why. In Version 6.0, anyway, it does not seem to behave the same way as other controls and only affects the display when the mouse is over an area of the grid which does not contain any data. No matter what the grid's *MousePointer* property is set to, moving the mouse over the populated portion of the grid always displays the "I" beam cursor.

The best solution that we can come up with is to add a transparent *SHAPE* object to cover the grid (except for the scrollbars). The result is that it is actually the shape object's *MousePointer* that the user sees when they move their mouse pointer over the grid. Of course if the grid is not Read-Only, we must provide some mechanism for detecting a click on the shape and transferring it to the relevant portion of the grid. Fortunately some new functions in Version 6.0 can help us out here. The sample code includes a form ("*ChgMPtr.scx*") which shows how this works. Here is the code from the Click method of the shape that overlays the grid:

```
*** We need to know the name of the grid
WITH ThisForm.grdVatrates

   *** Use AMOUSEOBJ() to get details of the mouse position
   LOCAL ARRAY laList[1]
   AMOUSEOBJ( laList, 1 )

   *** X and Y co-ordinates are in Rows 3 and 4
   lnX = laList[3]
   lnY = laList[4]

   *** Initialise some variables
   lnGObj = 0
   lnGrow = 0
   lnGCol = 0

   *** Use GRIDHITTEST() to get Grid Row/Col under the mouse
   llStat = .GridHitTest(lnX, lnY, @lnGobj, @lnGRow, @lnGCol)

   *** Send Shape behind the grid
   This.ZORDER(1)

   *** Activate the correct cell in the grid
   .ActivateCell( lnGRow, lnGCol)
   .SetFocus()

ENDWITH
```

This code determines where in the shape the click occurred and translates that position into the corresponding row and column of the grid. We then drop the shape behind the grid and activate the correct cell. The only trick is that we need to restore the shape to its 'On Top' position when the grid loses focus, but the Grid has no *LostFocus* method! So we have to add code to the grid's *Valid* method instead, and call the grid's own *ZOrder* method to send the grid 'To Bottom' thereby restoring the shape object to its original position over the grid.

How can I create a 'global' property for my application?

In Visual FoxPro, properties are scoped to objects so it is not really possible for a property to be "global" in the same way that a memory variable can. The best we can do is to define the property as belonging to an object whose scope is global. Given this approach we have a couple of options.

First we could simply create an object of the required class and associate its reference with a Public variable, like this:

```
RELEASE goGlobalObject
PUBLIC goGlobalObject
goGlobalObject = NEWOBJECT( <class>, <classlibrary> )
```

Anything in the application now has access to '*goGlobalObject*' and hence to all of its properties and methods. This is how an 'Application Object' (sometimes known as a '*god*' object) is usually created. Of course if the object is created in the startup program of the application, there is no need to explicitly declare its reference as 'Public', providing that it is not explicitly declared as 'Local'. Any private variable created in the startup program is effectively 'public' to the application anyway.

With the introduction into the language (in Version 6.0) of the *AddProperty* method, an intriguing alternative to creating a global object was opened up. The Visual FoxPro "_Screen" object is actually a ready-made global object and since it has an *AddProperty* method of its own, we can simply add any properties that we require globally directly to the screen object as follows:

```
_Screen.AddProperty( 'cCurrentUser', '' )
```

But wait, we hear you cry, what happened if you run your application with the screen turned off? Actually it makes no difference at all. The _Screen object is still available even if you do not show it and you can still access its properties and methods – including any custom properties or those of added objects – at any time.

How can I 'browse' an array? *(Example ArToCurs.prg)*

One of Visual FoxPro's minor irritants is that there is no good way to actually see the contents of an array. There are, of course, several ways of getting at an array. You can use the debugger to expand and drill down through an array or you can list it to screen, or to a text file, but none of them are entirely satisfactory. After all, we can create an array from a cursor using SQL by simply issuing a command like this:

```
SELECT <fields> FROM <table> INTO ARRAY <name>
```

What we cannot do is the opposite – turn an array back into a cursor so that we can browse it, or view it in a form or whatever else we may need at the time. The *ArToCurs* function does the job for us by taking a reference to an array, and optionally a cursor name, and building a cursor from the contents of the array.

There is a caveat for the code as presented here. This function will not handle arrays containing object references. It would not be difficult to amend the code so that it did (maybe by getting the *name* of the object), but this function was not intended for that purpose so it is not written that way. The return value is the number of rows in the cursor that was created. Here is the code:

```
*******************************************************************
* Program....: ArToCurs.prg
* Compiler...: Visual FoxPro 06.00.8492.00 for Windows
* Abstract...: Accepts an array and converts it into a cursor
*******************************************************************
LPARAMETERS taSceArray, tcCursorName
LOCAL ARRAY laStru[1]
LOCAL lnRows, lnCols, lnCnt, lcColNum, lnColSize, lcInstr
EXTERNAL ARRAY taSceArray

*** Check that we have an array as a parameter
*** NB Cannot use VarType() here in case array does NOT exist!
IF TYPE( "taSceArray[1]" ) = "U"
  ASSERT .F. MESSAGE "Must pass a valid Array to ArToCurs()"
  RETURN
ENDIF

*** Default Cursor Name to "arraycur" if nothing passed
lcCursor = IIF( VARTYPE( tcCursorName ) = "C" AND ! EMPTY( tcCursorName ), ;
             ALLTRIM( LOWER( tcCursorName )), "arraycur" )

*** Determine the size of the array
lnRows = ALEN(taSceArray,1)
lnCols = MAX( ALEN(taSceArray,2), 1 )
DIMENSION laStru(lnCols, 4)

*** Create the structure array
lcInstr = ""
FOR lnCnt = 1 TO lnCols
  *** Name Columns with the Data Type + Zero Padded number
  lcColNum = PADL( lnCnt, 5, "0" )
  laStru[ lnCnt, 1 ] = VARTYPE( taSceArray[ 1, lnCnt] ) + lcColNum
  laStru[ lnCnt, 2 ] = "C"                 && Data Type
  *** Determine Maximum Column width needed
  lnColSize = 1
  FOR lnRowCnt = 1 TO lnRows
    lnColSize = MAX( lnColSize, LEN( TRANSFORM( taSceArray[lnRowCnt, lnCnt] )))
  NEXT
  laStru[ lnCnt, 3 ] = lnColSize           && Col Width
  laStru[ lnCnt, 4 ] = 0                    && No Decimals
  *** Add the field to the Insert String
  IF ! EMPTY( lcInstr )
    lcInStr = lcInstr + ","
  ENDIF
  IF lnCols > 1
    lcInStr = lcInstr+"TRANSFORM(taSceArray[lnCnt,"+ALLTRIM(STR(lnCnt))+"])"
```

```
  ELSE
    lcInStr = lcInstr+"TRANSFORM(taSceArray[lnCnt"+"])"
  ENDIF
NEXT

*** Create the cursor from the structure array
CREATE CURSOR (lcCursor) FROM ARRAY laStru

*** Populate the cursor
FOR lnCnt = 1 TO lnRows
  INSERT INTO (lcCursor) VALUES ( &lcInStr )
NEXT
GO TOP IN (lcCursor)

*** Return Number of records
RETURN RECCOUNT( lcCursor )
```

Windows API Calls

There are an awful lot of these and they are, alas, not well documented for Visual FoxPro users. Here are some Visual FoxPro functions which use API calls that we have found useful. Although presented here as stand-alone functions, normally we would collect these sort of functions into either a procedure file, or as methods of a class. The benefit of using a visual class (e.g. a '*custom*' class) is that when these functions are needed, an object based on the class can simply be added directly to the form that needs it.

One of the biggest problems for most Visual FoxPro developers when beginning to work with the Windows API is that the functions rely heavily on defined constants. But it is not always easy to determine where these constants actually come from, or even what they are. Gary DeWitt has gleaned, and very generously made available to everyone, over 4000 Windows constants as Visual FoxPro "#DEFINE" statements. A copy of his file ('*windows.h*') is included with the sample code for this chapter.

How do I find the file associated with a file type? *(Example: findexec.prg)*

This little function is useful because it tells you *where* the executable file associated with a given file extension is located. For any file extension that has a specific Windows association, the return value consists of the full path and file name to the executable program. This can then be manipulated using the native Visual FoxPro functions (JUSTPATH() , JUSTFNAME() etc) to extract whatever information you really need.

Note that the API function that we are using here (*FindExecutable()*) can accept a specific path and file name, but the file must exist. So, to be absolutely certain, we have opted to create a temporary file, with the required extension, in the current working directory and use that file to determine the result. However, this means that passing any of the Windows executable extensions (i.e. 'COM', 'BAT' or 'EXE'), which are not associated to specific applications, will simply return the location of this temporary file. This is not a problem, since the whole purpose of the function is to determine where the executable program which runs a non-executable file type is located:

```
******************************************************************
* Program....: FindExec.prg
```

```
* Compiler...: Visual FoxPro 06.00.8492.00 for Windows
* Abstract...: Returns the full path and file name of the windows exe
* ...........: which is associated with the specified function
*************************************************************************
LPARAMETERS tcExt
LOCAL lcRetVal, lcFileExt, lcFileName, lnFileHandle, lcDirectory, lcResBuff
STORE "" TO lcRetVal, lcFileExt, lcFileName, lcDirectory
*** Check that an extension is passed
IF VARTYPE( tcExt ) # "C" OR EMPTY( tcExt )
  ERROR "9000: Must pass a file extension to FindExec()"
  RETURN lcRetVal
ELSE
  lcFileExt = UPPER( ALLTRIM( tcExt ))
ENDIF

*** This function MUST have a file of the requisite type
*** So create one right here (just temporary)!
lcFileName = "DUMMY." + lcFileExt
lnFileHandle = FCREATE( lcFileName )
IF lnFileHandle < 1
  *** Cannot create file
  ERROR "9000: Unable to create file.  FindExec() must stop" ;
      + CHR(13) + "Check that you have the necessary rights for file creation"
  RETURN lcRetVal
ENDIF
FCLOSE( lnFileHandle )

*** Create the return value buffer and declare the API Function
lcResBuff = SPACE(128)
DECLARE INTEGER FindExecutable IN SHELL32 ;
        STRING @cFileName, ;
        STRING @cDirectory, ;
        STRING @cBuffer

*** Now call it with filename and directory
lnRetVal = FindExecutable( @lcFileName, @lcDirectory, @lcResBuff)

*** Check the return value
lcMsgTxt = ""
DO CASE
  CASE lnRetVal = 0
    lcMsgTxt = "Out of memory or resources"
  CASE lnRetVal = 2
    lcMsgTxt = "Specified file not found"
  CASE lnRetVal = 3
    lcMsgTxt = "Specified path not found"
  CASE lnRetVal = 11
    lcMsgTxt = "Invalid EXE format"
  CASE lnRetVal = 31
    lcMsgTxt = "No association for file type " + lcFileExt
  OTHERWISE
    *** We got something back
    *** String is Null-terminated in the result buffer so:
    lcRetVal = LEFT(lcResBuff, AT(CHR(0), lcResBuff) - 1)
ENDCASE

*** Delete the dummy file we created.
DELETE FILE (lcFileName)
```

```
*** Display Results and return
IF ! EMPTY( lcMsgTxt )
  MESSAGEBOX( lcMsgTxt, 16, "FindExec Failed" )
ENDIF
RETURN lcRetVal
```

How can I open a file using Windows file associations? *(Example: runfile.prg)*

This is remarkably simple using the *ShellExecute()* function. This function either opens or prints the specified file (which can either be an executable file or a document). Here is the code:

```
**********************************************************************
* Program....: RunFile.prg
* Compiler...: Visual FoxPro 06.00.8492.00 for Windows
* Abstract...: Open or Print a named file/document using windows association
**********************************************************************
LPARAMETERS tcDocName, tlPrint
LOCAL lnRetVal, lnShow, lcAction
*** Check Parameters
IF VARTYPE( tcDocName ) # "C" OR EMPTY(tcDocName)
    WAIT WINDOW "Must Pass a valid document name and extension" NOWAIT
    RETURN
ENDIF
*** Must have an Extension too
IF EMPTY( JUSTEXT( tcDocName ))
  WAIT WINDOW "Must Pass a valid document name and extension" NOWAIT
  RETURN
ENDIF

*** Check action, if tlPrint = .T., the "Print" otherwise "Open"
lcAction = IIF( tlPrint, "Print", "Open" )
lnShow   = IIF( tlPrint, 0, 5 )

*** Declare API function
DECLARE INTEGER ShellExecute IN Shell32.dll ;
  LONG HWnd, ;
  STRING cAction, ;
  STRING cFileName, ;
  STRING cParameters, ;
  STRING cPath, ;
  INTEGER nShowWindow

*** Now execute it
lnRetVal = ShellExecute( 0, lcAction, tcDocName, "", "", lnShow)

RETURN
```

Note that we have set this function up to accept a fully qualified path and file name as a single parameter. In fact you could use it equally well by splitting the parameter into file name and path and passing them separately as the *cFileName* and *cPath* parameters.

The *nShowWindow* value is set to 5 (i.e. '*Show*' the application) when opening a document, and to 0 (hide the application) when printing a document. (The full range of values can be found in the *WinUser.h* file under the "*ShowWindow() Commands*" heading.)

How can I get the user's Windows log-in name? *(Example: getlogin.prg)*

There is actually a purely VFP way of getting this information by using the *SYS(0)* function which returns the machine name and current user log-in name. The return value is a single string and uses the "#" symbol to separate the machine name from the user name. So one possible solution is to use:

```
lcCurrentUser = ALLTRIM( SUBSTR( SYS(0), AT('#', SYS(0))+1))
```

However there is also a *GetUserName()* function which will return the same information and which can be wrapped as a simple, user defined function as follows:

```
***************************************************
* Program....: GetLogIn.prg
* Compiler...: Visual FoxPro 06.00.8492.00 for Windows
* Abstract...: Get Windows Log-In Name
***************************************************
LOCAL lcUserName, lcRetVal

*** Declare API Function
DECLARE GetUserName IN Win32Api ;
    STRING @cString, ;
    INTEGER @nBuffer

*** Initialise the buffers
lcUserName = SPACE(50)

*** Get the Login Name
GetUserName( @lcUserName, LEN(lcUserName) )

*** String is Null-terminated in the result buffer so:
lcRetVal = LEFT(lcUserName, AT(CHR(0), lcUserName) - 1)

*** Return Login ID
RETURN lcRetVal
```

How can I get directory information? *(Example: windir.prg)*

The Windows API contains several functions that can be used to get directory information. Some are also available from within Visual FoxPro (e.g. changing the current directory) while others are not (e.g. finding the *Windows* or *System* directories). The following program collects several of these functions together and uses a numeric index to determine the action required as follows:

Table 13.4 API directory functions

Index	Action
1	Returns the full path to the Windows System Directory.
2	Returns the full path to the Windows Home Directory.
3	Returns the full path to the current working directory. (Equivalent to "CD" in Visual FoxPro).
4	Accepts additional parameter which is either a relative path, or a fully qualified path, and makes that the current working directory. Returns either the fully qualified current directory or an error message if the specified directory does not exist.
5	Accepts additional parameter which is either a relative path, or a fully qualified path, and creates the directory. Returns either 'Created' or 'Failed'.
6	Accepts additional parameter which is either a relative path, or a fully qualified path, and deletes the directory. Returns either 'Removed' or 'Failed'.

It is worth noting that these functions will handle either UNC or conventional drive identifiers with equal facility that may make them useful in some situations. Here is the code:

```
**********************************************************************
* Program....: WinDir.prg
* Compiler...: Visual FoxPro 06.00.8492.00 for Windows
* Abstract...: Windows API Directory Functions
* ..........: Calling Options
* ..........: 1  -> Return Windows System Directory
* ..........: 2  -> Return Windows Directory
* ..........: 3  -> Return Current Working Directory
* ..........: 4, <path> -> Set Working Directory (Accepts Relative Path)
* ..........: 5, <path> -> Create Named Directory (Accepts Relative Path)
* ..........: 6, <path> -> Remove Named Directory (Accepts Relative Path)
**********************************************************************
LPARAMETERS tnWhich, tcDirName
LOCAL lcSysDir, lnBuffer, lnDirLen, lcRetVal
*** Initialize the buffers
lcSysDir = REPLICATE(CHR(0),255)
lnBuffer = 255
*** Execute Appropriate call
Do CASE
    CASE tnWhich = 1
        *** Windows system directory
        DECLARE INTEGER GetSystemDirectory IN Win32API ;
            STRING @cBuffer, ;
            INTEGER nSize
        *** Call the function
        lnDirLen = GetSystemDirectory( @lcSysDir, lnBuffer )
        lcRetVal = LEFT( lcSysDir, lnDirLen )

    CASE tnWhich = 2
        *** Windows system directory
        DECLARE INTEGER GetWindowsDirectory IN Win32API ;
            STRING @cBuffer, ;
            INTEGER nSize
        *** Call the function
        lnDirLen = GetWindowsDirectory( @lcSysDir, lnBuffer )
        lcRetVal = LEFT( lcSysDir, lnDirLen )
```

```
CASE tnWhich = 3
    *** Current working directory
    DECLARE INTEGER GetCurrentDirectory IN Win32API ;
        INTEGER nSize, ;
        STRING @cBuffer
    *** Call the function
    lnDirLen = GetCurrentDirectory( lnBuffer, @lcSysDir )
    lcRetVal = LEFT( lcSysDir, lnDirLen )

CASE tnWhich = 4
    *** Set Default Directory
    DECLARE INTEGER SetCurrentDirectory IN WIN32API ;
        STRING cNewDir
    *** Call the function, return name if OK, empty string if not
    lcRetVal = IIF( SetCurrentDirectory( tcDirName) = 1, tcDirName, ;
                                         "Directory does not exist")

CASE tnWhich = 5
    *** Create Directory
    DECLARE INTEGER CreateDirectory IN WIN32API ;
        STRING cNewDir, ;
        STRING cAttrib
    *** Call the function
    lnSuccess = CreateDirectory ( tcDirName, "")
    lcRetVal = IIF( lnSuccess = 1, "Created", "Failed" )

CASE tnWhich = 6
    *** Remove Directory
    DECLARE INTEGER RemoveDirectory IN WIN32API ;
        STRING cKillDir
    *** Call the function
    lnSuccess = RemoveDirectory( tcDirName)
    lcRetVal = IIF( lnSuccess = 1, "Removed", "Failed" )

OTHERWISE
    *** Unknown Parameter
    lcRetVal = ""
ENDCASE
*** Return the directory location
RETURN lcRetVal
```

Note that the "remove directory" option will only operate if the target directory is empty of all files.

How can I get the number of colors available? *(Example: wincols.prg)*

The number of colors can be calculated from the number of color bits that are allocated for each pixel. This is one (of many) values that can be obtained using the *GetDeviceCaps()* function. However, in order to determine where to get its values, this function needs to be passed the context id (which is obtained from the *GetDC()* function) to get which we need the Windows "*WHnd*" handle. This can be obtained either by using the FoxTools library like this:

```
SET LIBRARY TO FoxTools.fll ADDITIVE
```

```
lnHWND = _WHTOHWND( _WMainWind() )
```

or, as here, the API function *GetActiveWindow()* can be used to return the handle to the main FoxPro window:

```
**********************************************************************
* Program....: WinCols.prg
* Compiler...: Visual FoxPro 06.00.8492.00 for Windows
* Abstract...: Returns the number of colors available
**********************************************************************
LOCAL lnHWND, lnBitsPixel, lnDeviceContext

*** Declare API Functions
DECLARE INTEGER GetActiveWindow IN WIN32API

DECLARE INTEGER GetDC IN Win32Api ;
            INTEGER nWHnd

DECLARE INTEGER GetDeviceCaps IN Win32Api ;
            INTEGER nDeviceContext, ;
            INTEGER nValueToGet

*** Get the Windows Handle for the Active Window
lnHWND = GetActiveWindow()

*** First get the device context for the current window
lnDeviceContext = GetDC( lnHWND )

*** Then get number of color bits per pixel
lnBitsPixel = GetDeviceCaps( lnDeviceContext, 12)

*** Return Result
RETURN (2 ^ lnBitsPixel)
```

How do I get the values for Windows color settings? *(Example: getwcol.prg)*

There are two parts involved in this process. Firs we need to retrieve the color setting for the required Windows item from Windows itself. (There is an API function that will do this.) Then we convert that value into the red, green and blue components that we can use within Visual FoxPro. (Although, if all you are doing is setting a color property, then Visual FoxPro can use the Windows Color Number directly and the conversion is not necessary.) Here is the function:

```
**********************************************************************
* Program....: GetWCol.prg
* Compiler...: Visual FoxPro 06.00.8492.00 for Windows
* Abstract...: Returns the Red, Green, and Blue color values for a
* ..........: given numbered Windows Object Color
**********************************************************************
LPARAMETERS tnObjectNumber
*** Check Parameter
IF VARTYPE( tnObjectNumber ) # "N" OR ! BETWEEN( tnObjectNumber, 0, 28)
    WAIT WINDOW "Must pass windows color number between 0 and 28" NOWAIT
    RETURN
```

```
ENDIF

*** Get the required color setting
DECLARE INTEGER GetSysColor IN Win32API ;
              INTEGER nObject
lnWinCol = GetSysColor(tnObjectNumber)

*** Convert to RGB Values
lnSq256 = 256 ^ 2
lnRedGrn = MOD( lnWinCol, lnSq256 )

*** Now get the individual components
lcBlue   = TRANSFORM( INT( lnWinCol/lnSq256 ) )
lcGreen  = TRANSFORM( INT( lnRedGrn/256) )
lcRed    = TRANSFORM( MOD( lnRedGrn,256) )

*** Return RGB string
RETURN (lcRed + "," + lcGreen + "," + lcBlue)
```

This function requires a numeric constant that identifies a Windows element. These are all defined in the "*Windows.h*" file included with the sample code for this chapter, but some of the key ones are listed here for convenience.

Table 13.5 Constants for Windows element colors

Constant	Windows Element Color
1	Background (Windows Desktop)
2	Title Bar (Active Window)
3	Title Bar (Inactive Window)
5	Window Background
9	Title Bar Caption Text (Active Window)
19	Title Bar Caption Text (Inactive Window)
13	Highlighted Item Background
14	Highlighted Item Text
17	Command Button
18	Command Button Text

How do I change the cursor? *(Example: ChgCursor.prg)*

You can easily customize your cursors using the Windows API. For example, you can replace the standard static hourglass with an animated hourglass that rotates, just by issuing this function call:

```
ChgCursor( FULLPATH( 'HourGlas.ani' ), 32514 )
```

Note that the *ChgCursor()* function takes two parameters. The first is file name that is to be used for the cursor – in the example above this is one of the Windows standard "animated" cursor files. The second parameter is a constant which defines which cursor type (i.e. I-beam, hand, hourglass) will be replaced with the new file. These constants can be found in Windows.h and a list of them is also included in ChgCursor.prg itself.

One good use for this function is to change the standard I-beam cursor to an arrow when you want to use a grid that is either read-only, or looks like a list box, using a single line of code (as opposed to the methodology we outlined earlier in this chapter):

```
ChgCursor( FULLPATH( 'Arrow_m.cur' ), 32513 )
```

Just be aware that if you do, *all* of your I-beam cursor will be replaced by the arrow. This includes any text boxes that may be on the form so make sure that the change only applies when the mouse is over the grid. Here is the program we use to change the cursor:

```
**********************************************************************
* Program....: ChgCursor.prg
* Compiler...: Visual FoxPro 06.00.8492.00 for Windows
* Abstract...: Changes the specified cursor to the specified .cur or .ani file
**********************************************************************
LPARAMETERS tcCursorFile, tnCursorType
LOCAL lcNewCursor

ASSERT VARTYPE( tcCursorFile ) = 'C' ;
  MESSAGE 'Must Pass a File Name to ChgCursor.Prg'
ASSERT VARTYPE( tnCursorType ) = 'N' ;
  MESSAGE 'Must Pass a Numeric Cursor Type to ChgCursor.Prg'

IF INLIST( JUSTEXT( tcCursorFile ), 'CUR', 'ANI' )
  IF FILE( tcCursorFile )
    DECLARE INTEGER LoadCursorFromFile in Win32Api String
    DECLARE SetSystemCursor in Win32Api Integer, Integer

    lcNewCursor = LoadCursorFromFile( tcCursorFile )
    SetSystemCursor( lcNewCursor, tnCursorType )
  ENDIF
ENDIF
```

How do I customize my beeps? *(Example: MsgBeep.Prg)*

If you look at system sounds in the Windows control panel, you will notice that different sounds are defined for different types of events. It is a very simple matter to use these settings to play sounds that are consistent with other Windows application when you display a message box in Visual FoxPro. It is even more convenient because the MESSAGEBOX icon constants are identical to those used to identify the associated sounds in the Windows API. To play the sound associated with critical stop set up in the Windows control panel, all you need to do is this:

```
MsgBeep( 16 )
```

The program used to wrap this API function is very simple indeed:

```
**********************************************************************
* Program....: MsgBeep.prg
* Compiler...: Visual FoxPro 06.00.8492.00 for Windows
* Abstract...: Play the specified system sound as a beep
```

```
*               Note that the beep constants correspond to the MESSAGEBOX Icon
constants
**********************************************************************
LPARAMETERS tnBeep

DECLARE INTEGER MessageBeep IN Win32API INTEGER
MessageBeep( tnBeep )
```

How do I find out if a specific application is running? *(Example:*
IsRunning.prg)
As you read through the Window API Help, you may run into the `FindWindow` function and
think that you can use this to find out if a particular application is running. Unfortunately, this
function requires you to know the exact caption displayed in the application window's title bar.
Sometimes this is impossible. For example, when a document is being edited in Microsoft
Word, the Word window's caption contains the name of the document being edited. Because it
is generally not possible for your Visual FoxPro application to know these details, we cannot
use the *FindWindow()* function to determine whether Word is running. To solve this problem,
our *IsRunning()* function makes use of the Windows API `GetWindowText` function.

IsRunning() is an overloaded function. If called with no parameters, it returns a parameter
object that contains an array property. This array contains the names of all the running
applications. If a partial string such as 'Microsoft Word' is passed, it returns a logical true if the
application is running. If you wanted to expand upon its functionality, you could modify it to
return a two-dimensional array and populate the second column of the array with the
application's window handle:

```
**********************************************************************
* Program....: IsRunning.prg
* Compiler...: Visual FoxPro 06.00.8492.00 for Windows
* Abstract...: When passed a string (i.e., 'Microsoft Word'), return .T.
* ..........: if the application is running. When invoked with no parameters,
*...........: returns a parameter object whose array lists all running
*...........: applications
**********************************************************************
FUNCTION IsRunning
LPARAMETERS luApplication

LOCAL luRetVal, lnFoxHwnd, lnWindow, lnWhich, lcText, ;
  lnLen, laApps[1], lnAppCnt

*** Declare necessary Windows API functions

DECLARE INTEGER GetActiveWindow IN Win32Api

DECLARE INTEGER GetWindow IN Win32Api ;
  INTEGER lnWindow, ;
  INTEGER lnWhich

DECLARE INTEGER GetWindowText IN Win32Api ;
  INTEGER lnWindow, ;
  STRING  @lcText, ;
  INTEGER lnLen
```

```
DECLARE INTEGER IsWindowVisible IN Win32Api ;
  INTEGER lnWindow

lnAppCnt = 0

*** Get the HWND (handle) to the main FoxPro window
lnFoxHwnd = GetActiveWindow()
IF lnFoxHwnd = 0
  MESSAGEBOX( 'Invalid return value from GetActiveWindow', 16, 'Fatal Error' )
  RETURN
ENDIF


***  Loop through all the running applications
lnWindow = GetWindow( lnFoxHwnd, 0 )
DO WHILE lnWindow # 0

  *** Make sure we do not have the Visual Foxpro window
  IF lnWindow # lnFoxHwnd
    IF GetWindow( lnWindow, 4 ) = 0 AND IsWindowVisible( lnWindow ) # 0
      lcText = SPACE( 254 )
      lnLen  = GetWindowText( lnWindow, @lcText, LEN( lcText ) )

      *** If the function was passed an Application Name, check for a match
      *** Otherwise, Add this to the array
      IF lnLen > 0
        IF VARTYPE( luApplication ) = 'L'
          lnAppCnt = lnAppCnt + 1
          DIMENSION laApps[ lnAppCnt ]
          laApps[ lnAppCnt ] = LEFT( lcText, lnLen )
        ELSE
          IF UPPER( ALLTRIM( luApplication ) ) $ UPPER( ALLTRIM( lcText ) )
            RETURN .T.
          ENDIF
        ENDIF
      ENDIF
    ENDIF
  ENDIF

  *** See if there is another running application
  lnWindow = GetWindow( lnWindow, 2 )
ENDDO

*** Either we haven't found a match for the passed application name
*** or we are returning an array of all running applications
IF VARTYPE( luApplication ) = 'L'
  SET CLASSLIB TO Ch13 ADDITIVE
  luRetVal = CREATEOBJECT( 'xParameters', @laApps )
ELSE
  luRetVal = .F.
ENDIF

RETURN luRetVal
```

To see *IsRunning()* in action, just type DO DemoIsRunning in the command window (after you have downloaded and unzipped the sample code, of course!) to view a cursor which lists all running applications.

Using the DECLARE command

You will have realized from the preceding sections that the key to accessing the Windows API is the Visual FoxPro DECLARE command. This command registers a function which is defined in a Windows *Dynamic Linked Library* (.*DLL* file) and makes it available to Visual FoxPro as if it actually were a native function. You can think of DLLs as the Windows equivalent of the familiar Visual FoxPro procedure files but, unlike a procedure file, the functions contained in a DLL must be registered individually before they can be accessed.

The basic syntax and usage of DECLARE is explained reasonably clearly in the online Help files, and even more clearly in the "*Hacker's Guide to Visual FoxPro 6.0,*" but there are a few points that are worth emphasizing when working with API functions:

- The function name is actually case sensitive! This is most unusual in Visual FoxPro and is therefore worth mentioning here. If you receive an error that states "Cannot find entry point…." then almost certainly you have the case for the function name wrong..
- Not only is the function name case sensitive but in some cases the actual function name may not be the same as that which is stated. (This is because there may be different functions for different character sets. Thus the API "*MessageBox*" function is actually two functions – "*MessageBoxA*" which works with single-byte character sets and "*MessageBoxW*" for unicode character sets. However, you do not normally need to worry about this since, if Visual FoxPro cannot find the function specified, it will append an "A" and try again.)
- There is no such file as '*WIN32API.DLL*" despite the fact that you will often see functions being declared in this library. It is actually a 'shortcut' that instructs Visual FoxPro to search a pre-defined list of files including: *Kernel32.dll*, *Gdi32.dll*, *User32.dll*, *Mpr.dll*, and *Advapi32.dll*.
- When declaring a function, you can specify a local alias for that function by including the 'AS' keyword in the declaration. This can be useful because while the actual function name is case sensitive, the local alias (being known only to Visual FoxPro) is not.

How do I check what API functions are loaded?

The native DISPLAY STATUS report includes, at the very end, a list of all declared DLL functions together with the actual file in which the function is located as illustrated:

Declared DLLs:

GetActiveWindow	C:\WINDOWS\SYSTEM\USER32.DLL
GetSystemDirectory	C:\WINDOWS\SYSTEM\KERNEL32.DLL
GetWindow	C:\WINDOWS\SYSTEM\USER32.DLL
GetWindowText	C:\WINDOWS\SYSTEM\USER32.DLL
IsWindowVisible	C:\WINDOWS\SYSTEM\USER32.DLL

How do I release an API function?

Unfortunately, there is no way to release a single API function once it has been declared. Issuing either a CLEAR DLLS or a CLEAR ALL will release all declared functions but in this case at least, it really is "all or nothing!"

Chapter 14
Project Management

"After one look at this planet any visitor from outer space would say 'I WANT TO SEE THE MANAGER.' " ("The Adding Machine" by William Burroughs)

FoxPro developers have been using the Project Manager to manage files since the introduction of FoxPro 2.0. This chapter will discuss some Project Manager tricks in Visual FoxPro.

The Project Manager has been an important tool to Visual FoxPro developers over the years. It allows developers to organize all the files that are included for an application. It provides an easy mechanism to modify any of these files and to compile all the source code included in the project, as well as build APP files, EXEs, and DLLs. The release of Visual FoxPro 6.0 Service Pack 3 also allows developers to build multi-threaded COM objects.

The Project Manager is the VFP interface to the project metadata file. The project metadata file is a VFP free table that ends with the PJX extension and a memo file that has the PJT extension. These files combine information about each file that is tracked in the project. The project metadata files contain one record per file and a reference pointer to each file. Information like the version number, author name and address, whether the source code is included in the executable for debug reasons, and whether the executable is encrypted is also tracked in the project file.

What happens when building an executable?

The building of a project entails many steps. First, all the files referenced in the code are verified to be in the project. If they are not in the project, the build process searches them out in all directories already referenced in the project (via files already in the project) and adds them. If they are not found, the developer is prompted to manually locate them. Each file is compiled if the source has been updated since the last build, the databases' stored procedures are compiled, and menu code is generated and compiled. The rest of the process depends on the choice of build type selected.

> There are several Build options available in Visual FoxPro 6.0, Service Pack 3 (the latest update from Microsoft as of the writing of this book). We note the version of VFP since Service Pack 3 introduced the newest build option, the multi-threaded COM server DLL. The build dialog was changed to reflect this new option and clarify exactly what the other build options are used for.

The rebuild project build option tells VFP to step through the previously described process. There is no further action performed. This is by far the fastest of the build options.

The application build option performs the actions that are done for a rebuild, and then merges all the source files marked for inclusion into an application (.APP) style of executable file. This is a full executable file in Visual FoxPro, but it requires Visual FoxPro to be executed directly. It can be called from another VFP executable that is already running within the run time environment.

The Win32 executable / COM server (.exe) build option performs all the actions that are done for the application executable. Then the app file goes through a metamorphic process that adds the needed boot code to make it a Windows executable that calls the needed run- time DLL files, adds the icon and the .exe version information. The executable generated will require the VFP run-time files (Vfp6r.dll and Vfp6rXXX.dll (XXX denotes the specific language version)) to run outside of the VFP development environment. A Type Library file is generated if there are OLE Public classes in the project.

The single-threaded COM server (.DLL) build option and the multi-threaded COM server (.DLL) options build full COM objects and the needed Type Library (.TLB) files after going through the rebuild process. The Type Library file is generated in the same directory as the DLL. These projects also need to have classes marked as OLE Public. The multi-threaded DLL requires a special run-time file called VFP6T.DLL. All servers that are built are added to the Server page of the Project Information dialog.

How to use the project options to your advantage

The Project Information dialog presents developers with key details about the project and the files that are part of the project.

The first page is the Project tab. This form allows the developer to enter in their address information. This information is stored in generated code for menus. Other than that, it is only documentation for the project. Back in the 2.x days, the project information was also stored in the generated screen code. More importantly, this page gives developers access to key settings for the build process.

How do you use a project's Debug Info setting?

The Debug Info setting is critical in two situations. The first is when debugging an application and tracing through code. If the code was not compiled with the Debug Info on (checked), then you get a "Source is out of date" message in the Trace Window. This can be truly aggravating when you are ten levels deep in the call stack and you hit a program that was compiled without the debug code. We hate when that happens!

It is critical to note that a file is not compiled unless the Recompile All is checked when doing the build or the file was modified since the last build. Checking on the Debug Code option does not guarantee that all files will have source compiled in. The only time is when the Rebuild All is marked. The second situation that is critical is when you are building the final shipping version of the application.

There is a significant difference in executable size between the Debug Code being checked on and off. We recommend checking this option off when building the code to be shipped with the release. The size could be more than 10 times bigger with code included. We had one case of an .exe being 50 megabytes with source code included for debugging and just over 4 megabytes without it. Sending code with Debug Code set on ships the source code in the executable. This is how the Trace Window can display each line being executed. Note that the customer or another developer will have access to this code if it is shipped to the production arena.

How do you use a project's Encrypted setting?

This brings us to the Encrypted setting. Don't you just love how this all flows together? The Encrypted setting causes the generated executable to be encrypted so other developers cannot get access to the source code inside of the executable. It is pretty useless in the author's mind since there are third party tools that will decompile an executable. Naturally, these third party tools allow you to stamp a key so another copy of the product cannot decompile it. This is rather like blackmailing you to buy the product isn't it? On the other hand, the tool has some excellent use when someone loses the source code or the original developer skips town so it might be worth buying. Encrypted executables also cannot be compressed when zipped up based on the encryption scheme used internally. This author would love if Microsoft would allow the developer to enter a key when encrypting the executable to circumvent third-party tools and truly make it a valuable setting.

The Last Built text box displays the date and time the last build was completed – a useful reminder of when you last compiled the application. The projecthook setting is tackled in Chapter 15, Project Objects and ProjectHooks.

How do you set a custom icon for an executable?

This is a two-step process. The first is to assign the `_screen.Icon` property to the icon file in the main start up program. The second is to use the Project Information dialog to attach the icon to the project. What happens during the project build with this icon? Well, it is physically stored into the executable. This gives Windows the ability to display your custom application icon instead of the cute fox icon. We say the cute icon, since we actually had a customer once note that they did not want us to replace the "cute" foxhead with some other icon for their application <g>.

> *The icon file (.ico) can store multiple copies of the icon image. Each of these images is a different resolution. It is important to edit both images since Windows uses a 16 x 16 pixel image for application windows and the 32 x 32 pixel image for displaying a larger view in applications like Windows Explorer.*

We recommend getting one of the icon editing tools so you can either create your own icons or modify icons that you purchase. It is very important to use an icon editor that can edit both images. We use the Microsoft Imagedit.exe applet that shipped with VFP 5.0. When an icon is opened you are typically asked which of the images you want to edit. You should be able to select either the EGA/VGA 16 Color image (32x32) or the Small Icon 16 Color image (16x16). If one of the images is missing from the icon file, we do a "select all" on the image that does exist, and copy it to the clipboard. We open up the other image in the icon file and paste the clipboard contents to the image editor. The second image will either be expanded or shrunk. We like the automatic adjustment option that ImageEdit provides when expanding or shrinking the graphic to fit the new size.

The proper use of icons can polish up an application and give it a more professional appearance. One of the easiest ways to build up a good collection of icons is to purchase several third-party image/icon CD-ROMs. There is plenty of useless icons on these CDs, but one good icon is easily worth the price of the entire CD when you consider how much time you can spend creating your own.

How do you manage files in the Project Manager?

The Project Information Files tab allows you to sort via the ListView that contains the list of files. This means that developers can sort the list of files by the file type, the file name, last modified, whether it is included and the code page. Double-clicking on the "headers" will cause the column to be sorted. This dialog also allows you to toggle if the file is included or excluded from the application or executable builds. The included files show an "X" and the excluded files display an empty box. If the box is gray filled, that indicates the main file for the project. Files that maintain a code page can also be updated to the native code page. This is important for developers building applications that run outside of their native language and/or code pages.

How do you manage Servers from the Project Manager?

The Project Information Servers tab lists the classes in the project, both in Visual Class Libraries and program files (via **DEFINE CLASS** code) that are marked *OLEPublic*. Each class that is available as a server is listed in the list box on the left side of the page. As you scroll down the list, the Class Name, Class Library, description, help file, and help context id change for that specific class. Settings can be made to indicate if the Automation Server is single-threaded, multi-threaded, or cannot be created at all through the Instancing option.

This is an important setting from a performance perspective. Single-threaded servers need an instance for each and every reference to the class. Only one process can be called at a time to that instance. This was a problem prior to Service Pack 3 when two processes needed to access separate methods in a server as only one could be handled at a time. If this is a performance issue, the multi-threaded server can step in and handle both calls with one instance. Type Library information is also displayed on this dialog.

How do you set the project's object description?

Creating technical documentation has always been a low priority for most developers we know. It is not one of the fun things we do in our job. Each file that is tracked in the project has an optional description that can be filled in. This particular feature of the Project Manager is very useful in a team environment so all developers can understand what the file accomplishes or which features it supports. It can also be helpful in one-person shops to remind the developer what the purpose of the file is.

The description can be accessed via the Project Manager's shortcut menu (right-click menu) or the main menu Project|Edit Description... option. This option displays the Edit Description dialog (see **Figure 14.1**). Enter in the text that describes the file and save it by pressing the OK button. Naturally, pressing the Cancel button will revert the changes you just typed in.

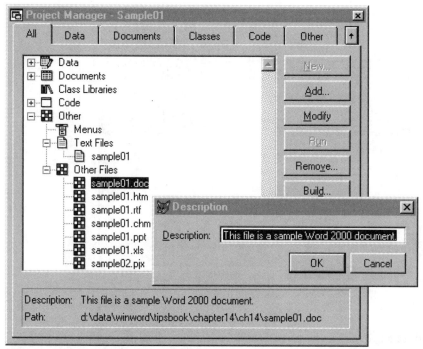

Figure 14.1 *Using the file description to describe the file's purpose in the application can help you and your teammates understand what it is for without opening the file up.*

Several files retain the description inside the file source code metadata, others are saved in the project's metadata. The descriptions entered in the Project Manager are retained in the class definitions (not the same for class libraries), databases, contained tables and the view definitions. If the descriptions are added/changed via the Class, Database, Table, or View Designer, they are stored in the source metadata and displayed in the Project Manager. The rest of the descriptions are stored directly in the project file. This is important to know if you ever have a project file corrupted. (Yes it does happen, although less frequently than in the 2.x days.) If you do not keep solid backups of the project files and have one corrupted, you will lose the descriptions during the rebuild of a new project.

How to set the executable version information
The Visual FoxPro 6.0 Project Manager stores the latest version information that is set up through the Build Dialog (see **Figure 14.2**). This information is used by the build process and stored in the resulting executable (.EXE). It should be noted that it is not stored in the application (.APP) file if that is the type of executable you generate.

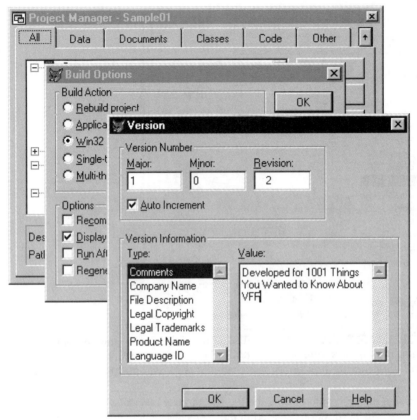

Figure 14.2 *Using the Build Options dialog to get the Version dialog, VFP developers can store information directly into the resulting executable. Some of this information can be seen in tools like Windows Explorer.*

This version information can be extracted via the new native function **AFILEVERSION**. If for some reason you are using VFP 5.0, you will need to use the **GetFileVersion** function that is available in FoxTools.fll. There are some differences in the calling of the functions and the information in the array of each function, so if you use VFP 5.0, consult the Help file.

In VFP 6, **AFILEVERSION** function returns a zero if the file specified in the second parameter is not found. If the file is found, the array is created with 15 elements. **Table 14.1** contains the information that would be seen by executing a **LIST MEMO** in the Command Window:

```
?AGETFILEVERSION(laEXEDetails, "Sample01.exe")
```

Table 14.1 *– Sample output from AGETFILEVERSION of the Sample01.exe*

Array Position	Contents	Sample Values
1	Comment	"Developed for 1001 Things You Wanted to Know About VFP"
2	Company Name	"Kirtland Associates"
3	File Description	"Cool Application"
4	File Version	"1.0.1"
5	Internal Name	"sample01"
6	Legal Copyright	"January 2000"
7	Legal Trademark	"Sample Trademark"
8	Original File Name	"sample01.exe"
9	Private Build	""
10	Product Name	"Sample.exe"
11	Product Version	"1.0.1"
12	Special Build	""
13	OLE Self Registration	""
14	Language	"English (United States)"
15	Translation Code	"040904e4"

The `AFILEVERSION` function can be used to determine the version details in more than just VFP executables; it can also be used to get version specifics on other Windows executables. Therefore if you run the following code, you will get 9.0.2719 echoed to the screen for the initial version of Excel 2000:

```
AGETFILEVERSION(laEXEDetails, ;
             "C:\Program Files\Microsoft Office\Office\EXCEL.EXE")
?laExeDetails[4]
```

So what is the use of this feature? We use it to display the version information in both our standard splash screen and on the application's About window.

What are the advantages of including the Config.fpw in the project?

The Config.fpw file allows Visual FoxPro developers control over the VFP environment settings. Adding the file to the project allows for easy editing of the settings for the application. Marking it included in the project will incorporate the configuration into the executable. VFP automatically uses this file to make any configuration changes as the application is starting. If the file is not marked as included in the project, it needs to be distributed separately with the executable.

This is a sample Config.fpw file that can be included in the project. The settings inside this file would cause VFP to start up without the main screen being displayed and the FoxUser file in the system directory under the application root directory to be used as the apps resource file:

```
* Application starts with VFP Frame off
screen  = off
resource = system\foxuser.dbf
```

Including the file in the executable will eliminate the need for the install process having to load a configuration file and then assigning it through the usual mechanisms. In the past we might have included to a - c parameter on the command line within a shortcut for the application. If the user double-clicked on the executable in Windows Explorer, the settings were never made because the configuration file was never loaded. The other mechanism is the FOXPROWCFG DOS environment variable, but this forces the support staff or the user to make sure this is set up on each machine that the executable is run on. The other disadvantage of using the DOS environment setting is that it is the default configuration file for all loaded VFP applications. We like to have more control for each application, thus assigning a specific configuration file for each released system.

How can we include non-VFP objects in the project?

VFP developers are familiar with the different file types that are tracked in a standard VFP project like forms, reports, labels, visual class libraries, programs, APIs, applications, menus, text files, databases, and free tables. Did you know that you could include files from your favorite word processor, spreadsheet, graphics package or other application?

There are several non-VFP files we like to include in the project manager for all applications we develop. If you have the Project Manager configured to open the file when double-clicked, it works just like Windows Explorer and will fire up the associated program and open the file. We like to include these non-VFP file types in the Other Files category in the Project Manager since it shows the file extension. One of the issues with this technique is the default file type for this category is a bitmap (.bmp;.msk) and the rest of the file types in the list are graphical. You need to select the "All Files" option and pick the file you want added to the project.

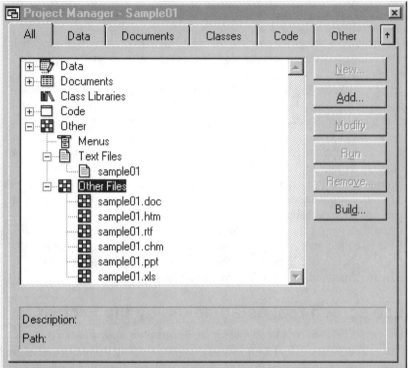

Figure 14.3 *Project Manager with non-VFP files included in the project*

There are a couple of noteworthy items to mention with this functionality. If you do not exclude these files, they will be built into the executable generated during the build process. They are included by default when you add them in. This can be beneficial if you want them shipped with the end product and do not want to send them as a separate file. The negative side of the coin is that these files will add the full byte size of the file to your executable. These bloated files can lead to slower loading executables and the need for more memory to run the application.

The first of the files we like to have as part of the project is a ReadMe.txt file. This file includes any details that the development staff needs to include for the users to read after they load the latest revision of the application. This file has a list of new features, bug fixes, and outstanding issues for the version we are releasing. This gives the user base a starting point to understand what they need to review and the development staff a way to track a history of what was worked on for the release and what still needs to be completed before we ship.

The second type of file we typically include are word processing files. There are several documents used for project management and development within the life cycle of a project. These include proposals, functional specifications, change control orders, priority listings and OLE Automation documents. Adding these files to a project can save the time required to find the directory within the word processor each time one of these documents needs to be modified. It would also be prudent to mention that these files should be closely managed outside of the project as well, since they are important to the success of the project.

Help files can be included whether they are the older HLP format or the newer compiled HTML format (CHM). This gives the project developers access to the generated Help file without firing up the application.

HTML files can be modified using the native VFP editor, but there are better tools that modify this file type. If you have the HTM extension assigned to a tool like FrontPage or Hot Metal, or defaulting to a browser like Netscape Navigator or Internet Explorer, these files will be opened outside of Visual FoxPro.

Even though project files are native to Visual FoxPro, they can be added to a project as an Other File. Sounds kind of strange, doesn't it? Double-clicking on this file will open the project in its own instance of the Project Manager. If the architecture you have selected has one main executable and several applications that are run from the main executable you can set up the controlling project and have the "app" projects available from within it.

There is virtually no limit to the number of external files that are part of the project file, only the 2 gigabyte file size limit on the project metadata table. The only requirement is that the file added must have a registered file extension that is associated with a program. We encourage you to leverage this functionality when you find it appropriate.

How to reduce screen real estate taken by the Project Manager

Docking functionality is usually associated with toolbars. Many new VFP developers have not been introduced to the docking capability of the VFP Project Manager because they see it as a form on the desktop. The Project Manager can be a full size form or can be shrunk to a toolbar-like existence. This can be toggled by clicking on the arrow command button to the right of the tabs.

The Project Manager gets docked only when it is dragged to the top toolbar/menu area of the development environment or by double-clicking the Project Manager *TitleBar* (also known as the form *Caption*). The only way to close a docked project is by using the File|Close menu option. You can also undock the project to close it via the close button.

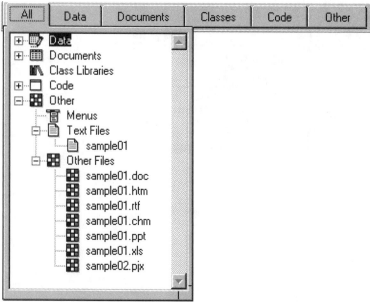

Figure 14.4 *This is what the Project Manager looks like when it is docked to a toolbar and one of the pages are accessed by clicking on the page tab*

How to tear off tabs from the Project Manager

Tear off tabs have nothing to do with your favorite canned cold beverage. Well it might if you have some old fashioned cans, but when it comes to Visual FoxPro, tear off tabs have to do with the Project Manager that has been reduced to its toolbar-like state. Click on the page of your choice, and then drag the page tab off the toolbar. This will leave the tab on the desktop.

Once the tab has been torn off the toolbar, you can drag it anywhere you want on the VFP desktop. VFP remembers where you left the project when it is closed, but for some reason it does not save the state of the pages torn off. Grabbing the lower right corner of the tab allows you to size it just like a regular sizable window. Dragging any of the sides cannot do this – it must be the corner. Closing and reopening the project reattaches the tabs that were previously torn off. Clicking on the pushpin will toggle the pushpin. This should lock where the tab is, so you cannot drag it anywhere until it is again toggled "out". In VFP 6.0 with Service Pack 3 applied, the pushpin has no effect on the drag capability.

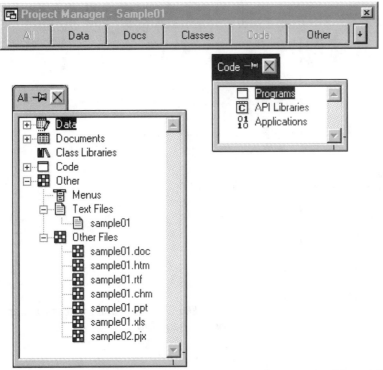

Figure 14.5 *Here is this chapter's sample project with the All and Code pages torn off*

You can expand the Project Manager to full size even with the tabs torn off. The pages that are torn off are disabled and remain torn off. You can return the tabs back to the Project Manager in either expanded or reduced size by dragging them back, but you can only tear them off when the Project Manager is in the reduced state.

What problems exist when opening a database in the project?

One thing we learned early and often is that the project automatically opens any databases that have their hierarchy expanded on the Data or All tabs the first time either tab is given focus. If the project was closed when the Data tab had focus, it will open up any databases that are expanded when the project is opened.

The databases are opened exclusively or in shared mode, based on the environment setting of SET EXCLUSIVE. This can be critical if developing in a team situation that does not use some form of source code control with copies of the same project with different names. This author has struggled through this with his team until he instituted a projecthook class that SET EXCLUSIVE OFF when the project opens. This way, everyone on the team can play in the same sandbox without locking out access to the databases. If one developer gets exclusive use of the database and another opens the data tab, the Project Manager tries to get the different details out of the database but cannot read the database. It goes into "slow motion" mode and slowly draws the TreeView with just the nodes native to VFP. No tables, views, connections, or stored procedures are displayed. Another problem with this mode is that nobody else can build an application since the Project Manager needs exclusive use of the database to recompile the stored procedures. We are not sure why this is necessary since they are compiled each time they are saved after an edit session.

If the database is opened via the Project Manager, it cannot be closed with the CLOSE DATABASES ALL command. The command effectively does a SET DATABASE TO, which makes no database the current database. The only way to close databases opened via the Project Manager is to select the database and press the Project Manager's close button or close the project.

Project dragging and dropping tricks

Many developers are surprised to find out that the Project Manager is a drag-n-drop client and server. This means that files can be dragged to the Project Manager from many sources including other projects and from outside of Visual FoxPro.

What happens when dragging from one project to another?

Dragging files between two different projects creates a reference in the second project for that file. If there is a description for the file, this description is also added to the second project, even for files that don't store the description in the file itself. If the file is a program set as the main program of the originating project, VFP will prompt you with a question that asks if you want to make the file the main program in the second project. You do not need to be on the same page in each project. The file is naturally added to the correct category based on the file extension.

How do I drag objects from a project to a designer?

Dragging files from the project to a form or class designer can save time during development. Many project objects can be dragged to the Form or Class Designer. The dropped objects are instantiated in the designer.

Dragging a field from a database contained table, view or free table to a form or class will instantiate the associated class for the data type. The advantage of this feature is that it creates a bound object in the class without the use of a dataenvironment. Many developers we have instructed over the years feel they need to first drop on a class and then set the *ControlSource*. While the manual setting of the *ControlSource* works, it requires developers to perform an extra step. The other advantage of this technique is that it incorporates the IntelliDrop capability seen when you perform this operation from the dataenvironment. This way the classes specified in advance are used instead of the VFP base classes.

Tables dragged to a form or class will instantiate a grid. If you right-click and drag, you are presented with the option of the grid class (or other class you have set for the Multiple setting in the Field Mapping in the Tool|Options).

If you want a specific class dropped on another container class, you can select it in the Project Manager and drag it to the container class. This does not bind the object like the drag operation of a table field. This allows you to override the IntelliDrop settings that are pre-mapped.

We expected that an icon dropped on a form might set the form Icon property and that dropping a graphic would generate an image object. They don't. Other objects not mentioned in this section cannot be dropped onto a form or container class.

What happens when dragging from project to program code?

In the same spirit described in the preceding section, you can drag and drop different project objects to code editors. The name of the object is displayed in the code window. For instance, if you drop a field name in the Command Window, you get the field name. Unfortunately you do not get the table.fieldname syntax. This works for every object type in the project except the stored procedure names. The only objects that carry over the file extension are the files in the "other" category.

What happens when dragging from Class Browser or Component Gallery to a project?

We tested a couple of other ideas with this capability by dragging files from the VFP Class Browser and its close cousin, the Component Gallery.

We expected that dragging classes from the Class Browser to the Project Manager would add the class. Unfortunately, this does not work. We dragged the icon in the upper left corner to the project, just like we have many times to another instance of the Class Browser. It plain does not work in the version of VFP 6.0 that we run, which is Service Pack 3.

Even more interesting is that performing the same tests in the Component Gallery proved successful. Pick the class in the Component Gallery and drag the icon in the upper left hand corner or the icon in the right pane and drag it to the Project Manager. If the file is a class, there is a dialog presented which is asking how you want to add the file to the project (see **Figure 14.6**). You have an option to add the existing class library or add a copy of the class to another class library. The file is added. Cool! Any file that can be added to a project can be dropped from the Component Gallery. Quickly adding common files to a project from your favorite catalog is a pretty powerful technique!

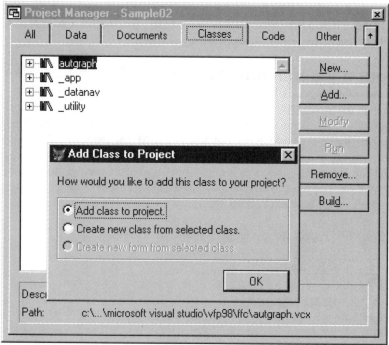

Figure 14.6 *Here is the Add Class to Project dialog that is presented when dropping files from the Component Gallery into a project*

What happens when dragging from a non-VFP application to a project?

Another cool capability is that files can be dragged onto the Project Manager from outside of VFP. The Project Manager is just one of many parts of VFP that were enabled for OLE Drop and Drag in VFP 6.0.

So how can I leverage this feature? Pop open Windows Explorer or your favorite replacement. If we drag and drop VFP specific files from Explorer to the Project Manager, they are added to the appropriate category. Non-VFP files are added to the "other" category. If we drag a shortcut from the desktop, we get a shortcut (.LNK) file added to the "other" category in the Project Manager.

How to take advantage of the project User field

Each of the Visual FoxPro metadata files contains a User field that is not used at all by VFP itself. It is designed to be used by developers for whatever purpose they see fit. This field is not exposed by the Project Manager interface but can be accessed by opening the project metadata as a table and browsing it.

We have not met many developers that use this functionality in the project file. One use that we have been thinking about lately is storing a last backed up date/time stamp in this field and hooking in a process that zips up all the files in the project to a compressed file via DynaZip. Unfortunately the current Files object does not expose this field to the developer at this time and the backup process will need to "hack" the project file.

How to go about documenting the project file

Until the projecthook was given to us in VFP 6.0, the only way to access the project information was to open up the project file as a table and process through the records. It is very important to remember that you should process through a copy of the original project file. This precaution is needed in case you make an accidental change to a field that confuses the Project Manager and disables the ability to open it.

Hacking the project file is not as big a deal as it might initially sound since the project file is well documented in what else, a project, which is in the `HOME()+"Filespec\"` directory. See **Table 14.2** for a list of projects for each of the releases.

Table 14.2 – List of the VFP project file layout specifications available

Project	Reports	VFP Releases
60Spec.pjx	60Pjx1.frx 60Pjx2.frx	VFP 6.0
50Spec.pjx	50Pjx1.frx 50Pjx2.frx	VFP 5.0
30Spec.pjx	30Pjx1.frx 30Pjx2.frx	VFP 3.0
26Spec.pjx	26Pjx1.frx 26Pjx2.frx	All VFP Release

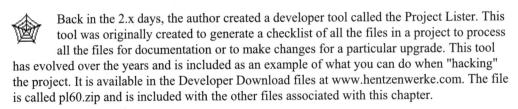

Back in the 2.x days, the author created a developer tool called the Project Lister. This tool was originally created to generate a checklist of all the files in a project to process all the files for documentation or to make changes for a particular upgrade. This tool has evolved over the years and is included as an example of what you can do when "hacking" the project. It is available in the Developer Download files at www.hentzenwerke.com. The file is called pl60.zip and is included with the other files associated with this chapter.

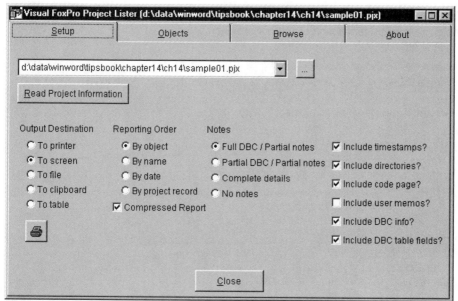

Figure 14.7 *This is the VFP Project Lister that is an example of "hacking" the VFP project file*

The Project Lister utility lists the different source objects that are in a specific VFP project. As noted, this tool was created to list each of the objects in the project as a checklist as an application was being developed. As time moved on, more and more features were added to give more details about each of the objects. Now the Project Lister is used to document the basics about projects developed and to determine what exactly is in projects we are looking to take over. The current incarnation not only plows through the different source code objects, but does a decent rudimentary job of documenting a database container as well. Please note that it will not give you the depth that something like the Stonefield Database Toolkit gives you, but it is useful.

Table 14.3 *Features that are included in the Project Lister*

Select project to document from an open project or one residing on disk
Configurable reports allow you to select what information appears
Configurable list of project objects allow you to select what object types appear on reports
Can browse the objects that will appear in output
Select from several reports (both large and compressed print) and different orders
Output to preview report, printed report, text file, Windows clipboard, or free table format
Requires VFP 6 because it incorporates some of the new Project Object properties, events, and methods

Conclusion

Visual FoxPro's Project Manager gives you a single location to manage all facets of project development and build creation. However with Visual FoxPro 6.0, the Project Manager is still only half the story. For readability's sake, the "rest of the story" on projects, project objects and project hooks are covered in the next chapter. Read on!

Chapter 15
Project Objects and
Projecthooks

"I have yet to see any problem, however complicated, which, when you looked at it in the right way, did not become still more complicated." (Paul Anderson writing in "New Scientist (London," 25 Sept. 1969)

This chapter will introduce the new ProjectHook and Project objects in VFP 6.0, and some uses of these important developer tools. We wrap up with an example that ties both the VFP ProjectHook and the Project Object in a utility known as the RAS Project Builder.

It is the author's opinion that the combination of the projecthook and project object was one of the single most exciting features in the release of Visual FoxPro 6.0. These two features expose the events of the Project Manager and extend a developer's ability to add to the Interactive Development Environment (IDE) of Visual FoxPro. The projecthook is a VFP base class that allows custom code to run in response to actions taken by the developer when using the Project Manager. The Project Object is a COM object that allows developers to perform actions that were previously regulated to "hacking" the project files (.PJX).

How to use ProjectHooks to catch a big fish

First we want to approach the new projecthook class. The projecthook can be subclassed and extended just like the other base classes in VFP. This class, when instantiated, hooks into different events that are triggered by the Project Manager. The projecthook is optionally instantiated when a project is opened. It is important to note that the projecthooks are not automatic; they require you to specify a projecthook class for each project.

Creating a projecthook class is as straightforward as creating any other class in Visual FoxPro. Using the CREATE CLASS command brings up the New Class dialog shown in **Figure 15.1**. You specify the class name, base it on the VFP projecthook (or another projecthook class you have created previously), and select the class library that you want to save the class.

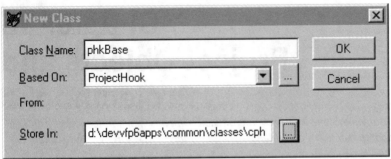

Figure 15.1 *The VFP New Class Dialog that demonstrates how to create a new projecthook class*

Once you click on the OK button the all-new projecthook will be available in the Class Designer. You can peruse the Property Sheet to see all the properties and methods that are available. There is a complete list of methods in **Table 15.1**.

Table 15.1 *This is a list of methods and their use for the projecthook class.*

Method	Use
AfterBuild	Allows developer to check number of errors found during the build action. This is also a great place to reset environment to settings saved before they were set in the *BeforeBuild* method.
BeforeBuild	Allows developers to stop a build based on conditions or desired parameters. Also a place to put code to prompt developers for possible settings and adjust environment for the build.
Destroy	Standard VFP *Destroy* method.
Error	Standard VFP *Error* method.
Init	Standard VFP *Init* method.
OLEDragDrop	Standard VFP *OLEDragDrop* method.
OLEDragOver	Standard VFP *OLEDragOver* method.
OLEGiveFeedBack	Standard VFP *OLEGiveFeedBack* method.
QueryAddFile	Fires when a new file of any type is added to the project. Code can be included to certify that the file can be added to the project. Includes logic that performs a NODEFAULT so the file is not added to the project.
QueryModifyFile	Fires when an existing file of any type is selected to be modified from the project. Code can be included that will certify that the file can be modified from the project. Includes logic that performs a NODEFAULT so the file is not modified through the project.
QueryRemoveFile	Fires when an existing file of any type is selected to be removed from the project. You can optionally delete the file from disk as well. Code can be included that will certify that the file can be removed from the project. Includes logic that performs a NODEFAULT so the file is not removed from the project.
QueryRunFile	Fires when an existing file of any type is selected to be run from the project. Code can be included that will certify that the file can be run from the project. Includes logic that performs a NODEFAULT so the file is not run from the project.

Once the projecthook is created it is simply designated as the project's projecthook via the Project Info dialog (see **Figure 15.2**). The option is on the Project page and is selected by checking the Project Class checkbox and proceeding through the Project Reference dialog (class selection dialog). You need to know that the class is a projecthook. If you do not select a projecthook, you will be punished with a message that says just that.

Once you successfully select the projecthook class, it is important to remember that you need to reopen a project so the projecthook is instantiated. The Project Manager is not capable of instantiating the class after it is designated unless you perform this action.

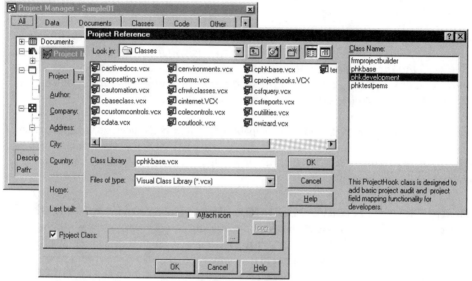

Figure 15.2 *The VFP projecthook selection dialog – it looks strangely similar to the Class Selection dialog presented by the VFP AGETCLASS function*

How to set up a global ProjectHook for all projects

Besides setting up a projecthook for an individual project, developers can have a projecthook as the default projecthook for all new projects that are created in the future. This is set up through the VFP Tools|Options dialog on the Projects page.

When a new project is created it is assigned the global projecthook. Almost sounds like we are taking up a cause to save the planet. But seriously, if you have a projecthook developed that is generic in nature, then this is your ticket.

What happens when a ProjectHook is lost or deleted?

So you are wondering what happens if you have a projecthook designated for the project and something goes bad. It happens. Someone goes in and innocently hacks the projecthook library and toasts the file. Or worse – someone intentionally changes some code hoping to add the greatest thing since sliced bread and makes it so the class no longer instantiates. Or what if the class is deleted from the class library? What happens with the project? Simple – the project does not open. I know you are thinking this is an ingenious security feature to unleash to stop the junior developers from getting into the project the day before release. Well, if they are as sharp as the developers we work with, they will open up the Help file or this book and see that the project can be opened without the projecthook. The MODIFY PROJECT command supports a NOPROJECTHOOK clause. Here is an example:

```
MODIFY PROJECT d:\devvfp6apps\bookproject\tips.pjx NOPROJECTHOOK
```

Rats, guess we'll have to still restrict the login of those junior developers the day before the release <g>.

> *If you create a new project that you think better of and decide to scrap it, VFP will prompt you with a message asking if you would like to remove the project files or retain them. If you set up a global projecthook and go through this scenario, you will not be prompted since VFP adds the projecthook class reference into the project file and it is no longer empty.*

So what can you do with this powerful capability? In reality, you can do almost anything your heart desires. Later in this chapter, there are several sections that detail implementations of our own ideas as well as ideas of other developers that we have incorporated into our projecthook.

What did Microsoft leave out of the first release of ProjectHooks?

What is missing? For one thing, a project *Activate* and *Deactivate* method would be very handy. We have these in a utility to control changes needed as the user selects a new project. You will see examples later in this chapter that change the Field Mapping settings in the registry when the project is opened. If you open several projects during a session in VFP, the last Field Mappings registered are used when you drop-n-drag fields from the dataenvironment to the form. If the projects are using separate class libraries, you will get a "cross-pollination" of class libraries in the projects. In our office, we have a subclass of the framework base classes for each project and several of our developers work on different projects each day. Since we use the projecthook described later in the chapter, the projects need to be exterminated of the "foreign classes" from other projects on a regular basis since developers who are intensely changing code tend to forget about the Field Mapping mix-ups.

There is one example of a projecthook that ships with Visual FoxPro 6.0. The example shows how you can leverage the different events and track the activity developers perform with the project by writing out an entry every time a file is modified or run or the project is open or built. This also allows the activity to be viewed when the project is closed. Not an overly sophisticated example, but it is efficient at demonstrating the power of these classes. This class and the example form can be found in the HOME(5)+"solution\tahoe\" directory. The files include the sample form called acttrack.scx/sct and the actual projecthook, which is called activity_tracker and resides in the project_hook.vcx.

How to access information in the Project and Files object

Project Object is built into Visual FoxPro and cannot be subclassed. It is a COM interface to the project file. In the past developers had to "hack" the project file by opening it up as a VFP free table via the USE command. The use of the SQL-Select command and the project opened as a free table is a powerful combination to extract information that is stored in the metadata. While some of these techniques are still useful, the project object reduces the need to "hack" the project metadata.

There is one difference in accessing the COM interface to the project from the standard way you might be accustomed to using. COM objects are instantiated via the CREATEOBJECT(), CREATEOBJECTEX(), or NEWOBJECT() functions. The project object is created for you any time a project is opened. The project object is created for each open project and is accessed via the _VFP application object. This object gives you access to several properties and methods to gain information about the project. Here is some code that accesses key information from the project:

```
WITH _vfp.ActiveProject
    ? .VersionNumber    && Displays next build version number
    ? .MainFile         && Displays name (and path) of main file
    .CleanUp()          && Packs the project metadata
ENDWITH
```

The files collection of the project object is how one gets access to the individual files within the project. There are a number of properties that are associated with each file. There are also behaviors that can be called to manipulate the files in the project. Here is some code that accesses key information from a file in the project:

```
WITH _vfp.ActiveProject
    ? .Files[1].Description  && Displays description of first file
    ? .Files[1].Modify()     && Modifies the first file in native designer
ENDWITH
```

Both the project and file object's properties can be set just like any other VFP object property through an assignment statement:

```
_vfp.ActiveProject.Files[1].Exclude = .T.
```

Through these two COM objects, we have almost complete control over all the files in our VFP projects.

How to use Project Objects in development

It is always nice to get plenty of theory and mumble-jumble of how things work, but there is nothing like having some real life examples to bring it all together. That is what this section will do. Most examples do the "list the files in a project" technique. While we find these examples valuable, they do not serve much use in our development environment.

How to build a basic Application Wizard

We will first demonstrate pieces of an application wizard where the project object and files object are leveraged. One example we developed that leverages both the Project object and the Files object is an Application Wizard. The concept is pretty simple. Process through all the mechanical steps we did for each new project development kickoff. Some of you might be asking why go through all this effort when VFP comes with an Application Wizard? The reason is simple – it does not support our framework and it did not meet the needs of our implementation architecture.

The process of manually building the initial project took a developer several hours to complete. Using the application wizard, it now takes all of ten minutes. Here are the basic steps involved:

1. Create the project directory and all needed/standard subdirectories

2. Subclass framework classes down to a customer level, then the project level

3. Generate the main program and compiler "faker" program

4. Generate the Config.fpw file

5. Copy over the starting menu template

6. Generate the framework database and associated tables

7. Add custom framework extension tables

8. Generate needed free tables

9. Subclass phkDevelopment projecthook for the project and set key properties

10. Populate the Field Mapping Option Utility table with needed records

11. Generate the Project file and populate with needed files

12. Do the initial Build the project

13. Send a message to developer to start doing some real work <g>

The code used to subclass the projecthook and change the *cFieldMappingCategory* property on the fly in step nine is demonstrated in **Listing 15.1**. This uses two techniques that might need some explanation. The first is the CREATE CLASS … NOWAIT. This command creates the class and displays it in the Class Designer, then continues on. The next bit of code uses some "builder" technology with the ASELOBJ command. This returns an array with an object reference to the projecthook in the Class Designer. A simple assignment statement and the projecthook is ready to roll by the standards in our shop. The second bit of explanation required are the KEYBOARD and DOEVENTS commands. The designer needs to be closed and Ctrl-W is the "save without asking me if I'm really sure" shortcut. Since this is all happening in code and since the keyboard buffer is a Windows event, the DOEVENTS was added to make Windows tell VFP to close the Class Designer at that moment – not to wait until later when it takes a breath.

Listing 15.1 Code needed to subclass the projecthook programmatically

```
LPARAMETERS tcProjectHook, tcProjectFieldMappingConfig

#define ccPROJECTHOOKSLIB       "k:\vfpaddon\rasprojecthooks\cProjectHooks"
#define ccPROJECTHOOKSBASELIB "k:\vfpaddon\rasprojecthooks\cPhkBase"
#define ccPROJECTHOOKSBASE      "phkDevelopment"

create class (tcProjectHook) of ccPROJECTHOOKSLIB ;
      as ccPROJECTHOOKSBASE from ccPROJECTHOOKSBASELIB nowait

* Set the class property for the projecthook cFieldMappingCategory property
aselobj(laProjectHookRef, 1)

if type("laProjectHookRef[1]") = "O"
   laProjectHookRef[1].cFieldMappingCategory = tcProjectFieldMappingConfig
endif

* Make sure the reference to the projecthook is released
release laProjectHookRef

* Handle the VFP Windows that open with no Resource File
if wexist("PROPERTIES")
   release window "Properties"
endif

if wexist("FORM CONTROLS")
   release window "FORM CONTROLS"
endif

* Close the newly created class opened in Class Designer
* The keystrokes are "buffered" until all classes are created
keyboard '{CTRL+W}'

* Added to close the class designers down
doevents()
```

Steps eleven and twelve are the workhorses when it comes to leveraging the project object and the file object. This is where the application's project gets created, populated, and initially built. As usual, there are some key issues to point out.

First are some missing "features" or properties within the project object. These are the author items like name, company and address. Hopefully these will show up in the next release of VFP. It would be nice to pre-populate these settings in the project when creating it.

The Files object *Add* method performs all the magic. The key to this method is to make sure you include the extension of the file you are adding. This is how VFP understands what file category to add it under in the Project Manager. The first major item is to create the project via the CREATE PROJECT command. Note that the project is created with the NOPROJECTHOOK option. This ensures that no hook is associated with the project until it is added later. It even overrides a global hook setting. Then add all the files that are needed. We found out the hard way that you need at least one file from every directory for each file type. For instance, if we have class libraries in the project's Libs directory and the framework's Libs directory, we need to add one file from each. This way the build of the project can find the rest of the files in the search path that it establishes from the previously added files. Any files called through the technique of indirect calls (via macro substitution or **EVAL()**) must also be added with direct calls to the *Add* method.

 The code **in Listing 15.2** is just a small part of the code we use in production. If you are interested in reading the whole program, it is available in the Developer Download files available at www.hentzenwerke.com as GenProjectFile.prg with the other examples from this chapter.

Listing 15.2 *Code used to generate the project, populate it with files and initially build the project to pull in the associated files*

```
LPARAMETERS tcProjPrefix, tcProjectDir, ;
            tcBusinessGroupDir, tcSystem, tcProjectHook

#DEFINE ccPROJECTHOOKSLIB  "k:\vfpaddon\rasprojecthooks\cProjectHooks.vcx"

CREATE PROJECT (lcProjectName) NOWAIT SAVE NOSHOW NOPROJECTHOOK

IF TYPE("_vfp.ActiveProject") = "O" AND !ISNULL(_vfp.ActiveProject) ;
   AND FILE(lcProjectName)

   ? "Project file created " + lcProjectName + " at " + TTOC(DATETIME())

   WITH _vfp.ActiveProject
      * Set some of the Build Version information
      .HomeDir             = tcProjectDir
      .AutoIncrement       = .T.
      .Debug               = .T.
      .VersionNumber       = "1.0.0"
      .VersionComments     = "Visual FoxPro Application"
      .VersionCompany      = "Kirtland Associates, Inc"
      .VersionDescription  = ""
      .VersionCopyright    = ALLTRIM(STR(YEAR(DATE())))
      .VersionTrademarks   = ""
      .VersionProduct      = ALLTRIM(tcSystem)
      .VersionLanguage     = "English"

      * RAS 05-Oct-1999 Added the projecthook connection.
      * They must be in this order, library first, class second
      * otherwise a dialog is displayed and the wizard crashes
      .ProjectHookLibrary = ccPROJECTHOOKSLIB
      .ProjectHookClass   = ALLTRIM(tcProjectHook)

      * The main program needs to be added first to become
      * the SET MAIN for the project
      lcFile = tcProjectDir + "programs\" + tcProjPrefix + "Main.prg"
      DO AddFileToProject WITH lcFile

      * Add database container
      lcFile = tcProjectDir + lcDatabaseDir + tcProjPrefix + ".dbc"
      DO AddFileToProject WITH lcFile

      * Add some free tables
      lcFile = tcProjectDir + "system\" + tcProjPrefix + "config.dbf"
```

```
      DO AddFileToProject WITH lcFile

      * Add the Stonefield Database Toolkit classes
      lcFile = "K:\VfpAddOn\Stonefield\SDT\Source\DbcxMgr.vcx"
      DO AddFileToProject WITH lcFile

      lcFile = "K:\VfpAddOn\Stonefield\SDT\Source\SDT.vcx"
      DO AddFileToProject WITH lcFile

      * RAS 27-Sep-1999 Added the Config.fpw template
      lcFile = tcProjectDir + "text\" + "Config.fpw"
      DO AddFileToProject WITH lcFile

      * Make sure the Config file is included
      _vfp.ActiveProject.Files("Config.fpw").Exclude = .F.

      * RAS 27-Sep-1999 Added the ReadMe.txt template
      lcFile = tcProjectDir + "text\" + "ReadMe.txt"
      DO AddFileToProject WITH lcFile

      * Make sure the Config file is included
      _vfp.ActiveProject.Files("ReadMe.txt").Exclude = .T.

      * Build the project using the Rebuild option to pull in
      * the rest of the project files
      llBuildResult = .Build(1)
      ? "The result from the build was: " + TRANSFORM(llBuildResult) + ;
         " at " + TTOC(DATETIME())
   ENDWITH
ELSE
   ? "Project file creation failed for " + lcProjectName + ;
      " at " + ttoc(datetime())
ENDIF


PROCEDURE AddFileToProject (tcFileName)

IF FILE(tcFileName)
   _vfp.ActiveProject.Files.Add(tcFileName)
   ? "Added file: " + tcFileName + " at " + TTOC(DATETIME())
ELSE
   ? "  Problem adding file " + tcFileName
ENDIF

RETURN

*: EOF :*
```

The project object *Build* method allows you to do any of the build options available to the developer via the project's Build Options dialog. We chose the rebuild project so the rest of the project files would be pulled in as needed and each file is compiled for the first time.

Overall this project was fun and it demonstrated the power of having an open interface to the development environment. It is also saving us time and money on each project we work on.

ProjectHook and Project Object tricks

We will use a real life, in production projecthook that has been in use by the author since the end of the VFP 6.0 beta. We will also demonstrate how the projecthook and project object can be used in conjunction with each other with a new tool called the RAS Project Builder.

How to enhance the base projecthook

There are several files that make up the CPhkBase class library. First is the phkBase class. This class is a direct subclass of the VFP projecthook. It is always good practice to build your own copy of the VFP classes so you have a basis for enhancements at one level of the class hierarchy. All other classes are subclassed from the phkBase class (see **Figure 15.3**). We added a few methods and properties at this level that we knew would be handy for all the projecthooks we developed (see **Table 15.2** and **Table 15.3**)

Table 15.2 *Methods added to our phkBase projecthook with a short description of their usage*

Method	Description
DeveloperMessage	Used to display a message to the developer. If lWaitMessage is True a WAIT WINDOW is displayed, otherwise the message is sent to the DEBUGOUT window.
GetPProp	Returns the value of the property sent as a parameter. This allows developers to access protected properties with a simple interface.
Release	Releases the instantiated object.
SetProjectObjReference	Used to set up the ProjectInfo property to the ActiveProject if one exists. Yes there is a possibility that a developer would instantiate a projecthook without a project.
ShellAdditionalInit	Used to extend the Init() method without having to override the Init() code in subclasses. Called from the Init() method.
zzAbout	Contains any documentation specific to the class.

Table 15.3 *Properties added to our phkBase projecthook with a short description of their usage*

Properties	Description
Builder	The program (prg) or visual class library/classname (vcx) that points to the builder for the class based in BUILDER.DBF.
BuilderX	The visual class that points to the BuilderB Builder for this class.
cVersion	The version number of the specific class.
lWaitMessage	Toggles the messaging between the developer mode WAIT WINDOWS or DEBUGOUT statements.
oProjectInfo	Contains an object reference to the project information.

The Builder and BuilderX properties are properties that the native VFP Builders will recognize. These hooks will come in handy if you create a projecthook builder class/program.

There are two other projecthook classes in the library. The first is phkTestPems. This class' purpose in life was to test out the property, events and methods provided by VFP. We used this class as part of the beta cycle to verify we were getting what Microsoft was advertising. There are no additional methods or properties. There is code in each of the VFP Event Methods that fires a message using the following code:

```
THIS.DeveloperMessage(PROGRAM())
```

The *lWaitMessage* property is set to true so when you run this code you get a `WAIT WINDOW` any time a hook is fired when some action is performed from the Project Manager. Not really useful, but it serves its purpose to test out the different events.

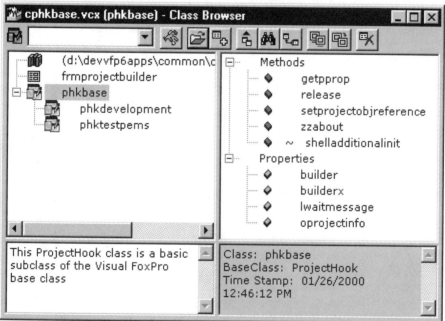

Figure 15.3 *CPhkBase class library that shows the class hierarchy for the projecthooks*

How to create a useful development projecthook

The last class, phkDevelopment, is the real meat and potatoes of the library. This is the base for all project specific projecthooks. This class provides some key functionality that many VFP developers have desired to be added to the native IDE. This is the true beauty of the projecthook extension. It allows us to add functionality to the development environment without having to wait for Microsoft to move our request to the top of the priority list. This concept of enhancing development makes VFP shine over other developer tools. Some of the features we implemented in phkDevelopment:

- Field Mapping Utility

- Cleaning out hard coded printer information in reports

- Project Audit (activity tracking)

- File Backup capability

- Displaying compiler/build messages to Status Bar or `WAIT WINDOW`

- Instantiating toolbar with button to call RAS Project Builder

- Changing the default directory to the project directory

- Adjusting the path custom to a project path

Each of these major features will be discussed in the following sections.

Table 15.4 *Methods added to our development projecthook with a short description of their usage*

Method	Description
cBuildMessageSetting_assign	Certifies that the proper assignments of the cBuildMessageSetting property are made.
cCleanReportPrinters_assign	Certifies that the proper assignments of the cCleanReportPrinters property are made.
ChangeToProjectDirectory	Changes the default directory to the project's home directory.
ChangeToProjectPath	Adds directories to the SET PATH that are needed by the project.
CleanReportPrinter	Will eliminate the hardcoded printer information in the Report metadata (.FRX) file.
FieldMappingDo	Called to process all the Field Mapping Checks, then runs the process.
FieldMappingPropertyCheck	Used to check all the developer settings for the Field Mapping properties of this ProjectHook.
FieldMappingSet	Used to set the Field Mapping settings to the registry.
FieldMappingTableClose	Used to close the Field Mapping Option Table.
FieldMappingTableOpen	Used to open the Field Mapping Option Table.
ModifyFileBackup	Used to create a .bak type file of the source code files that don't have this native behavior.
ProcessReportFiles	Called from the Build method to loop through the files and process any reports needed before building.
ProjectActivate	Fired by the classes *Init()* method to process items when the project is opened or activated.
ProjectAuditDo	Called to make appropriate checks then call the opening of the Project Audit table.
ProjectAuditSetSessionId	Initializes the cSessionId property for the Project Audit capability.
ProjectAuditTableClose	Used to close the Project Audit table.
ProjectAuditTableCreate	Used to generate the table used by the project audit functionality.
ProjectAuditTableOpen	Used to open the project's Audit Table.
ProjectAuditTableReindex	Used to rebuild the indexes for the project Audit Table.
ProjectAuditUpdate	Updates the project Audit Table.
ProjectBuilderToolBarinit	Instantiates the RAS Project Builder toolbar if it is the first project opened and the IUseProjectBuilderTb property is set to true.
ProjectBuilderToolBarinit	Releases the RAS Project Builder toolbar if it is the last project standing and the toolbar exists.

Table 15.5 *Properties added to our development projecthook with a short description of their usage*

Properties	Description
aErrorDetail[1,0]	A collection of details about the last error to occur during processing.
cBuildMessageSetting	Contains the message setting type, "S" statusbar (default) and "W" wait window.
cCaption	Contains the caption for the MessageBox().
cCleanReportPrinters	Contains the indicator if the reports in the project should have the printer information scrubbed from the metadata (.FRX). Settings include "C"lean, "V"iew, or "S"kip (default).
cDeveloper	Is used as an identifier for the projecthook. This is for internal use by the RAS Project Builder routine.
cFieldMappingCategory	Is used to set the field mapping data types to the settings for this category in the Field Mapping Option Table.
cFieldMappingTableAlias	Contains the ALIAS() used for the Field Mapping Option Table.
cFieldMappingTableDirectory	Contains the directory to the Field Mapping Table.
cFieldMappingTableName	Contains the table name of the Field Mapping Option Table.
cFieldMappingVfpCategory	Contains the default category to set all the field mapping data types to VFP base classes.
cOldNotify	Contains the old SET('NOTIFY') for reset later.
cOldStatusBar	Contains the old SET('STATUS BAR') for reset later.
cOldTalk	Contains the old SET('TALK') for reset later.
cOldTalkWin	Contains the old SET('TALK,1') for reset later.
cPathDirectories	Contains the additional directories that need to be in the SET PATH.
cPathDirectories	Contains the additional directories that need to be in the SET PATH.
cProjectAuditAlias	Contains the Project Audit Table alias set when the table is opened.
cProjectAuditDirectory	Contains the directory path for the Project Audit Table.
cProjectAuditTable	Contains the name of the table used to track project events.
cProjectBuilderGlobalVariable	Is the variable name that the Project Builder toolbar is instantiated as.
cProjectBuilderTbClass	Holds the name of the class that is the RAS Project Builder toolbar.
cProjectBuilderTbClassLib	Holds the name of the class library that the RAS Project Builder toolbar resides.
cSessionId	Contains the unique session id for the project. This is stored in the project's Audit Table to determine all the events that happened in a session.
lCreateBackupFile	When source code is modified, determines if the .bak type file is created that does not have this native behavior.
lFieldMappingActive	Is used to have the Field Mapping feature active to the ProjectHook.
lUseProjectAudit	Determines if the Project Audit capabilities are used for this current project.
lUseProjectBuilderTb	Determines if the RAS Project Builder toolbar is instantiated when this class is instantiated.
oRegistry	This property contains an object reference to the Registry Manipulation object.

How to have the projecthook set the current directory and path

Before the projecthook, every time we opened a new project we were forced to manually change the default VFP directory to the project's directory. This is done so individual forms can be run standalone and the SET PATH is correctly finding all the files necessary to run the features we are developing. The author typically hits a half dozen projects every day and this can become quite tedious.

Many developers created a program to set the path, the current directory and other environmental settings before opening the project with a **MODIFY PROJECT ...NOWAIT**. This is no longer needed since the projecthook can run the same type of code each time the project is opened. So what are the advantages between a program that does this and the projecthook instantiating? There are a number of advantages. First we don't need a custom program duplicated for each project since the code is written once in the highest-level projecthook class. Maintenance is minimized by the object-oriented design of the class. Next, there is no hardcoding paths in the program. The projecthook uses the project directory that is stored already in the project. Thirdly, I can use the VFP IDE to open projects and not worry about the entire list of project opening programs being in the existing VFP path and making sure we open the correct project. This is a problem since most developers name the opening project program identically across projects. So what directory are we in? Which project is going to open when I run SetPath.prg? With the projecthook designated for the project, we just hit the File menu and pick one of the last projects I worked on or jump to the Command Window and execute the **MODIFY PROJECT** line of code that is already there. Simple.

So what code is needed to have this advantage? Here are two methods extracted out of the phkDevelopment class which are called from the *ProjectActivate* method:

```
* phkDevelopment.ChangeToProjectDirectory()
* Set the default directory to the project's home
* directory so the generic pathing works
*  ie SET PATH TO data, forms, classes, graphics
IF TYPE("THIS.oProjectInfo") = "O" AND !ISNULL(THIS.oProjectInfo)
    IF !EMPTY(THIS.oProjectInfo.HomeDir)
        CD (THIS.oProjectInfo.HomeDir)
    ELSE
        THIS.DeveloperMessage("Project directory setting is empty...", .T.)
    ENDIF
ELSE
    * This should never happen, unless you manually
    * CREATEOBJECT() the class without a project.
    THIS.DeveloperMessage("Project reference not available", .T.)
ENDIF


* PhkDevelopment.ChangeToProjectPath()
LOCAL lcOldPath                        && Retain old SET PATH

IF !ISNULL(THIS.cPathDirectories) AND !EMPTY(THIS.cPathDirectories)
    IF VARTYPE(THIS.cPathDirectories) = "C"
        lcOldPath = SET("PATH")
        lcNewPath = THIS.cPathDirectories

        SET PATH TO &lcOldPath, &lcNewPath
    ELSE
        THIS.DeveloperMessage("Path Directory property is not character")
    ENDIF
ELSE
```

```
   * No special pathing requirements for this project
ENDIF
```

There is one drawback to this method. Since there is no Activate method for the project that we can hook into, this code is only run when we open the project. The RAS Project Builder tool discussed later in this chapter has a workaround for this issue.

How to programmatically control the VFP IntelliDrop settings

Visual FoxPro 5.0 introduced the IntelliDrop feature native to the development environment. When building forms and classes, you can drag and drop items from the dataenvironment, a project, or Database Designer and when you drop it in the designer, the specified class is used when creating the object. The big benefit to this is that you get to specify the classes instead of using the default VFP base classes. The IntelliDrop capability is managed via the Tool|Options dialog on the Field Mapping page. These settings are retained in the Windows Registry. You immediately see the benefits of this functionality. It is yet one more way to customize the development environment.

There are two big drawbacks of this implementation. The first is one that is immediately realized if you use different classes in different projects. This could be due to the fact that you have subclassed framework classes for each project, or it could be that different clients have source code from different frameworks.

The second is the fact that these settings are stored in the registry, which is machine specific. If you have multiple developers working on the same project, each has to go through the tedious process of setting the Field Mapping settings for the project. This is complicated by the fact that most developers are working on multiple projects. If you are having problems with a machine and want to jump over to another machine on the network, you have to go through and reset those settings for that machine.

This can be more than an aggravation. Fortunately, there is a solution that can be developed with a program or a projecthook. VFP guru John Petersen has shared a tool he developed called OptUtility. This is a simple form and table combination that stores different configurations for all the VFP base classes. It performs all the maintenance operations and writes directly to and from the registry to map these settings. You run the form, select the project grouping, and push a button to update the registry. This is a cool tool I use all the time. The one issue is that I need to remember to go push the button. This occasionally is overlooked and I get cross-pollination of class libraries in my different projects.

Table 15.6 *OptUtil.dbf free table which stores the Field Mapping information used in the IntelliDrop Manager portion of the phkDevelopment projecthook*

Field	Name	Type	Size	Description
1	Config	C	20, 0	This is the configuration name. We fill this in with a reference that is tied to represent the project.
2	Type	C	20, 0	This is the VFP base class object name.
3	ClassName	C	50, 0	This is the class name that is set in the registry for the VFP base class in the Field Mapping section.
4	ClassLoc	C	254, 0	This is the class library (with fullpath) where the class designated in the ClassName column resides.

The first time I saw VFP 6.0 and the projecthooks, I immediately saw the use of the projecthook to update the registry with the information mapped in the OptUtility table. Since the projecthook is instantiated when the project is opened, we could hook into the initialization process and run code to map classes to the registry. The code for this is found in **Listing 15.3**. This eliminated the need to remember to run the OptUtility each time. The drawback of this is that there is no project *Activate* method available, so if you jump projects, or open another project, you will get the new mapping and have the same potential problems as forgetting to run the mapping utility.

Listing 15.3 *This code is found in the FieldMappingSet method of the phkDevelopment projecthook. This code maps the IntelliDrop settings to the Windows' Registry based on the grouping selected.*

```
* Registry roots (ripped off from VFP98\ffc\Registry.h)
#DEFINE HKEY_CLASSES_ROOT         -2147483648  && BITSET(0,31)
#DEFINE HKEY_CURRENT_USER         -2147483647  && BITSET(0,31)+1
#DEFINE HKEY_LOCAL_MACHINE        -2147483646  && BITSET(0,31)+2
#DEFINE HKEY_USERS                -2147483645  && BITSET(0,31)+3

LOCAL lcIntellidropKey       && VFP Registry Options Key for Intellidrop
LOCAL lnOldSelect            && Save the old workarea

* Only process the registry entries if Registry object instantiated
IF !ISNULL(THIS.oRegistry)
    * Build the first part of the registry key for Intellidrop
    lcIntellidropKey = "Software\Microsoft\VisualFoxPro\" + ;
                    _VFP.VERSION +;
                    "\Options\Intellidrop\FieldTypes\"

    lnOldSelect     = SELECT()
    lcFieldMapAlias = THIS.cFieldMappingTableAlias

    * Get all the class settings for the project
    SELECT * ;
       FROM (lcFieldMapAlias) ;
       WHERE Config = ALLTRIM(THIS.cFieldMappingCategory) ;
       INTO CURSOR curSetReg

    lnRecords = _TALLY
```

```
   IF _TALLY = 0
      THIS.DeveloperMessage("No field mappping class records to " + ;
                            process for " + ;
                            ALLTRIM(THIS.cFieldMappingCategory))
   ELSE
      * Update the Registry
      SCAN
         * This is the Visual Class Library setting
         THIS.oRegistry.SetRegKey("ClassLocation", ;
                               ALLTRIM(curSetReg.ClassLoc),;
                               lcIntellidropKey + ALLTRIM(curSetReg.Type),;
                               HKEY_CURRENT_USER)
         * This is the actual class set for the base class
         THIS.oRegistry.SetRegKey("ClassName", ALLTRIM(curSetReg.ClassName),;
                               lcIntellidropKey + ALLTRIM(curSetReg.Type),;
                               HKEY_CURRENT_USER)
         THIS.DeveloperMessage(ALLTRIM(curSetReg.Type) + ;
                            " set to " + ;
                            ALLTRIM(curSetReg.ClassLoc) + "::" + ;
                            ALLTRIM(curSetReg.ClassName), ;
                            .T.)
      ENDSCAN
   ENDIF

   * Close the temp cursor
   USE IN curSetReg

   SELECT (lnOldSelect)
ELSE
   THIS.DeveloperMessage("Registry object is not instantiated")
ENDIF

* In case the messages are sent to the WAIT WINDOW
WAIT CLEAR
```

Frankly this feature can save a tremendous amount of time if you are constantly changing projects like we do. If you work on the same project all the time or only use one set of base classes for all your projects, this part of the projecthook will be pretty much useless. You can turn this feature off by setting the *lFieldMappingActive* property to .F..

How to remove the printer information from VFP reports

There have been plenty of writings in the various online forums and FoxPro publications about the report metadata retaining development printer information. This can cause a number of support problems in a production application if the client does not have the same printers.

There have been several developer solutions to this problem. Most are written as a program that scans the project file (.pjx), opens up the report metadata and then cleans out the Tag and Tag2 columns of the first record. Steve Sawyer passed along one of the better programs that performs this service. I have incorporated this code, along with Steve's enhancements, to selectively modify certain information in the Expr column of the first record in the report metadata.

The code to perform the scrubbing is located in the *CleanReportPrinter* method in the projecthook, which is called by the *ProcessReportFiles*. The *CleanReportPrinter* code cleans the printer specifics in one report file. As with all the features of the phkDevelopment, the feature can be turned on and off. This is accomplished with the *cCleanReportPrinters* property. There are several settings available. "Clean" will cause the scrubber to do the work, "View" will perform the **WAIT WINDOW** messages if the **ELSE** logic is uncommented (until a better implementation is made), and "Skip" will bypass the process all together.

Listing 15.4 *This code is found in the CleanReportPrinter method of the phkDevelopment projecthook. This code blanks out the Tag and Tag2 fields of the first record in the report metadata file. Selective details of the Expr column of the first record are also removed.*

```
* Reports have a nasty habit of saving printer information in the
* first record of the report metadata.  This routine selectively
* removes some of the hardcoded printer information so the users
* can use different printers than the development staff without problems.
LPARAMETERS tcFrx2Chk, tcAction

*? Still need to come up with alternative to the View report information

* Parameter Check
IF VARTYPE(tcAction) != "C" OR EMPTY(tcAction)
   This.DeveloperMessage("Report parameter was empty of incorrect data type")
   RETURN
ENDIF

IF VARTYPE(tcAction) != "C"
   tcAction = "VIEW"
ENDIF

* Move on to the business of the method
This.DeveloperMessage(PROPER(tcAction) + "ing Report: " + tcFrx2Chk, .T.)

* Check for the report to exist
IF FILE(tcFrx2Chk)
   USE (tcFrx2Chk) ALIAS curFrx2Chk EXCLUSIVE
ELSE
   This.DeveloperMessage(tcFrx2Chk + " does not exist.")
   RETURN
ENDIF

* Check if report opened okay (otherwise error handler just
* displayed a message and life moved on).
IF !USED("curFrx2Chk")
   RETURN
ENDIF

LOCATE

* Handle the Expression field
IF !EMPTY(curFrx2Chk.Expr)
   IF UPPER(tcAction) == "CLEAN"
      REPLACE curFrx2Chk.Expr WITH ;
            STRTRAN(curFrx2Chk.Expr, [DEVICE], [*DEVICE])
      REPLACE curFrx2Chk.Expr WITH ;
            STRTRAN(curFrx2Chk.Expr, [DRIVER], [*DRIVER])
```

```
      REPLACE curFrx2Chk.Expr WITH ;
              STRTRAN(curFrx2Chk.Expr, [OUTPUT], [*OUTPUT])
      REPLACE curFrx2Chk.Expr WITH ;
              STRTRAN(curFrx2Chk.Expr, [DEFAULT], [*DEFAULT])
      REPLACE curFrx2Chk.Expr WITH ;
              STRTRAN(curFrx2Chk.Expr, [PRINTQUALITY], [*PRINTQUALITY])
      REPLACE curFrx2Chk.Expr WITH ;
              STRTRAN(curFrx2Chk.Expr, [YRESOLUTION], [*YRESOLUTION])
      REPLACE curFrx2Chk.Expr WITH ;
              STRTRAN(curFrx2Chk.Expr, [TTOPTION], [*TTOPTION])
      REPLACE curFrx2Chk.Expr WITH ;
              STRTRAN(curFrx2Chk.Expr, [DUPLEX], [*DUPLEX])
      This.DeveloperMessage(tcFrx2Chk + " column Expr: cleaned", .T.)
   ELSE
      * This.DeveloperMessage(tcFrx2Chk + " column Expr: " + curFrx2Chk.Expr)
   ENDIF
ENDIF


* Handle the Tag field
IF !EMPTY(curFrx2Chk.TAG)
   IF UPPER(tcAction) == "CLEAN"
      REPLACE curFrx2Chk.TAG WITH SPACE(0)
      This.DeveloperMessage(tcFrx2Chk + " column Tag: cleaned", .T.)
   ELSE
      * This.DeveloperMessage(tcFrx2Chk + " column Tag: " + curFrx2Chk.Tag)
   ENDIF
ENDIF


* Handle the Tag2 field
IF !EMPTY(curFrx2Chk.Tag2)
   IF UPPER(tcAction) == "CLEAN"
      REPLACE curFrx2Chk.Tag2 WITH SPACE(0)
      This.DeveloperMessage(tcFrx2Chk + " column Tag2: cleaned", .T.)
   ELSE
      * This.DeveloperMessage(tcFrx2Chk + " column Tag2: " + curFrx2Chk.Tag2)
   ENDIF
ENDIF

* Now pack to be sure you don't get memo bloat
IF UPPER(tcAction) = "CLEAN"
   PACK
ENDIF

* Close the report (.frx)
IF USED([curFrx2Chk])
   USE IN curFrx2Chk
ENDIF

WAIT CLEAR

RETURN
```

This routine is called from the RAS Project Builder that is discussed later in this chapter. We don't recommend running this for every build since it is not necessary in the development environment unless you print to more than one printer in the office. This theory may not apply if the report was developed with a printer that differs from the Windows' default printer. On the other hand, it is highly recommended to perform this routine on the production build cycle before sending it to a client site.

How to track what is done within the Project Manager

Have you ever wondered how many times you altered a specific file or who was the last person who touched the critical class library? There are plenty of options when it comes to Source Control that will give you these statistics. VFP does work with source control providers that conform to the Source Control Application Programmer Interface (API). But what if you don't have these controls implemented in your office? What if you wanted to know how many times you opened a project or built the code? What can you do? One option is to implement what I call the "poor developer's project audit trail".

There are a number of methods that execute when Project Manager events are triggered. Each of these event methods has a call in it to the *ProjectAuditUpdate* method. Here is the code in the projecthook's *QueryModifyFile* method:

```
THIS.ProjectAuditUpdate("Modified File", toFile.Name + ;
                IIF(EMPTY(tcClassName),""," (" + tcClassName + ")"))
```

It is important to note that if this feature is not desired (as if <g>), you can toggle the *lUseProjectAudit* property to .F..

Listing 15.5 *This code is found in the ProjectAuditUpdate method of the phkDevelopment projecthook and inserts a row into a VFP free table specified by the cProjectAuditTable property*

```
LPARAMETER tcActivity, tcParameter

IF THIS.lUseProjectAudit
   IF PCOUNT() < 2 OR VARTYPE(tcParameter) != "C"
      tcParameter = ""
   ENDIF

   * Always check to see if the table is open because of the possiblility
   * of it being closed via a CLOSE TABLES or CLOSE DATA from the
   * Command Window
   IF !USED(THIS.cProjectAuditAlias)
      THIS.ProjectAuditTableOpen()
   ENDIF

   * See the ProjectAuditTableCreate() method for field list
   INSERT INTO (THIS.cProjectAuditAlias) ;
      VALUES (LOWER(JUSTPATH(THIS.oProjectInfo.Name)), ;
            JUSTFNAME(THIS.oProjectInfo.Name), ;
            tcActivity, ;
            tcParameter, ;
            THIS.cSessionId, ;
            DATETIME())
ENDIF
```

Now that all the event hooks are filling up the table, what can you do with them? Even if there is source code control in place, we like to see when the file was modified most recently on the server:

```
SELECT cProjFile AS cName, ;
       PADR(mFileName,60) AS cFile, ;
       cSessionId, ;
       MAX(tUpdated) ;
   FROM projectaudit ;
   WHERE cActivity = "Modified" ;
     AND "program1.prg" $ mFileName ;
   GROUP BY cProjFile, cFile ;
   INTO CURSOR curTemp
```

We can also see how many times a project was opened:

```
SELECT cProjFile AS cName, ;
       COUNT(*) AS nCount ;
   FROM projectaudit ;
   WHERE cActivity = "Opened" ;
   GROUP BY cProjFile ;
   INTO CURSOR curTemp
```

These are trivial examples of course, but the details are there in the table for your archival and developing SQL code is what we do for a living, so enjoy.

How to generate automatic backups of metadata

Visual FoxPro generates a backup file when a developer modifies a program file. The .bak file is generated when the modified program is saved. Not all VFP objects get this safety feature when modified. So is a developer left hanging? Obviously not, since we are writing about this topic in this chapter <g>. The phkDevelopment projecthook example leverages the *QueryModifyFile* method to call the custom *ModifyFileBackup* method. This code copies the metadata files before proceeding to the designer of choice. It should be noted that the file is copied even if the developer saves no changes from the designer.

The code in **Listing 15.6** was grabbed off the FoxWiki, which is located at www.Fox.Wikis.com. VFP guru Jim Booth posted it on this incredible knowledge base. This routine copies all the different metadata files to a separate file named the same but with a different extension. Just like the limitation of the program backup file, only one level of backup is retained.

Listing 15.6 This code is found in the ModifyFileBackup method of the phkDevelopment projecthook. This code copies the different metadata files to a backup file when they are modified.

```
LPARAMETERS toFile

* Only process if the project requires this functionality
IF THIS.lCreateBackupFile
   * Continue on and process the backup
```

```
ELSE
   RETURN
ENDIF

LOCAL lcFile                        && File metadata table
LOCAL lcFpt                         && Associated metadata memo file
LOCAL lcBak                         && Name of the backup for the table
LOCAL lcFptBak                      && Name of the backuo for the memo
LOCAL lcOldSafety                   && Save the setting to reset Safety

lcOldSafety = SET("SAFETY")
lcFile      = UPPER(toFile.Name)
lcBak       = SUBSTR(lcFile,1,LEN(lcFile)-3) + "SCT"

SET SAFETY OFF

* No need to handle the PRGs, DBFs since they get
* backed up natively
DO CASE
   CASE RIGHT(lcFile,3) = "SCX"
      lcFpt    = SUBSTR(lcFile,1,LEN(lcFile)-3) + "SCT"
      lcBak    = SUBSTR(lcFile,1,LEN(lcFile)-3) + "SXK"
      lcFptBak = SUBSTR(lcFile,1,LEN(lcFile)-3) + "STK"

   CASE RIGHT(lcFile,3) = "VCX"
      lcFpt    = SUBSTR(lcFile,1,LEN(lcFile)-3) + "VCT"
      lcBak    = SUBSTR(lcFile,1,LEN(lcFile)-3) + "VXK"
      lcFptBak = SUBSTR(lcFile,1,LEN(lcFile)-3) + "VTK"

   CASE RIGHT(lcFile,3) = "FRX"
      lcFpt    = SUBSTR(lcFile,1,LEN(lcFile)-3) + "FRT"
      lcBak    = SUBSTR(lcFile,1,LEN(lcFile)-3) + "FXK"
      lcFptBak = SUBSTR(lcFile,1,LEN(lcFile)-3) + "FTK"

   CASE RIGHT(lcFile,3) = "MNX"
      lcFpt    = SUBSTR(lcFile,1,LEN(lcFile)-3) + "MNT"
      lcBak    = SUBSTR(lcFile,1,LEN(lcFile)-3) + "MXK"
      lcFptBak = SUBSTR(lcFile,1,LEN(lcFile)-3) + "MTK"

   CASE RIGHT(lcFile,3) = "LBX"
      lcFpt    = SUBSTR(lcFile,1,LEN(lcFile)-3) + "LBT"
      lcBak    = SUBSTR(lcFile,1,LEN(lcFile)-3) + "LXK"
      lcFptBak = SUBSTR(lcFile,1,LEN(lcFile)-3) + "LTK"

   OTHERWISE
      SET SAFETY &lcOldSafety
      RETURN
ENDCASE

IF FILE(lcBak)
   ERASE FILE &lcBak
ENDIF

COPY FILE (lcFile) TO (lcBak)

IF NOT EMPTY(lcFpt)
   IF FILE(lcFptBak)
      ERASE FILE &lcFptBak
   ENDIF
```

```
   COPY FILE (lcFpt) TO (lcFptBak)
ENDIF

SET SAFETY &lcOldSafety

RETURN
```

RAS Project Builder

The RAS Project Builder (frmProjectBuilder in CPhkBase) is a combination of the VFP Project Build dialog, the Build Version dialog and the Project Information dialog. How many times have you made that last gold production build and find out that you forgot to set Debug Code off in the Project Information dialog resulting in a 50 megabyte executable on the 500 CDs that were just cut? This dialog brings all the compiler settings together so you can build the executable with all the information in front of you at one time.

It is important to note that there are several features in the RAS Project Builder (see **Figure15.4**) that work in conjunction with the RAS ProjectHook, but it is not required. In fact, there is no requirement for any projecthook at all. The only requirement is that one project (or more) must be open.

Features that are not available without the RAS ProjectHook are the Process Project Audit Trail checkbox, the Clean Printer Information from Reports checkbox and textbox, the Project Activate commandbutton, the Reset Field Mapping commandbutton and the Field Mapping page on the pageframe. The rest of the options are available for all projects.

So what does this product have to do with the projecthook section of this book? There are several code examples inside this tool that demonstrate the project object, the projecthooks, and the various properties, events and methods associated with them.

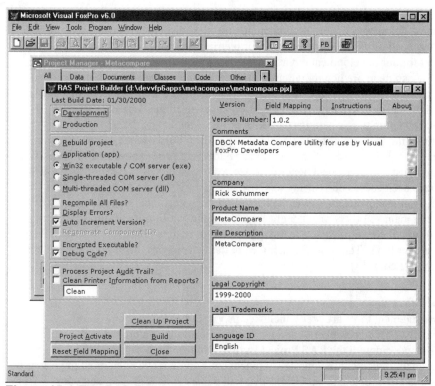

Figure 15.4 *The RAS Project Builder in action. Note the "PB" button added to the toolbar at the top of the screen. This button is instantiated when the phkDevelopment (or subclass) projecthook is instantiated.*

There are very few methods in the project object, but this utility leverages both of the important ones. The first is the project object's *Build* method. At first we used the BUILD command, but there are some features not supported by the command that are supported by the method. The Build method supports showing the build errors when the build is completed and it also handles support for regenerating component ids for the different COM server options. The second method used is the *Clean* method. This method packs the project metadata file. This option can be accessed on the VFP Project menu as well.

Several project object properties are accessed and demonstrated through this utility. All the version information that is sitting on the version page is accessed via the *VersionComment*, *VersionCompany*, *VersionCopyright*, *VersionDescription*, *VersionLanguage*, *VersionNumber*, *VersionProduct*, and *VersionTrademarks* properties. The ability to set on the Auto Increment Version is bound to the *AutoIncrement* property, the Encrypted Executable to the *Encrypted* property, and the Debug Code setting to the *Debug* property. The projecthook name and class are displayed on the About page and are accessed through the *ProjectHookClass* and *ProjectHookLibrary* properties. Same goes for the Source Code Provider via the *SCCProvider* property.

The Development/Production toggle option group is important to talk about as well. Production option defaults to the build to recompile all files, display errors, and sets up the reports to be scrubbed of possible development printer information. We determined that these settings are best for our development environment. The Production setting also does a SET STRICTDATE TO 1 so there are no ambiguous messages from user date entry in the production application. The Development setting does the reverse and does a SET STRICTDATE TO 2 so we are alerted to the Y2K issues that our code may have introduced inadvertently. The Development/Production toggle settings can be overridden by setting them through the interface after picking the type of build you want to perform. For instance, if you desire to not show errors and not clean the reports of possible development printer information for a production build, just click the checkboxes to reflect your wishes.

 We have been successfully using this tool since late 1999. It has naturally gone through some enhancements via the beta tester's suggestions. We are placing it in the public domain so others may benefit from this handy utility. It has no warranty in any way and was originally developed as a learning tool, but over time it has taken a life of its own like many developer tools. The source is included in the Developer Download files available at www.hentzenwerke.com.

Conclusion

The project management tools are pretty inclusive in Visual FoxPro. When you run into a limitation, you are likely to be able to build your own extension via a projecthook or another developer tool as we did with the RAS Project Builder. Hopefully this chapter brought you some useful code to implement in your development environment and even more importantly will inspire you to build tools and extensions that will enhance the VFP IDE and your development experience.

Chapter 16
Creating Reports

"It's the same each time with progress. First they ignore you, then they say you're mad, then dangerous, then there's a pause and then you can't find anyone who disagrees with you." (Tony Benn quoted in "The Observer," London, 6 Oct. 1991)

Visual FoxPro developers have not had a lot to cheer about since before the release of Visual FoxPro 3.0 when it comes to having a state of the art report designer. The reality of software development is that reports are crucial. Reports are used by our customers to analyze the terabytes of data that the applications track. These outputs may be used to simply remind the user of the boss's phone number, or to allow the CEO to decide on an important billion dollar merger. This is why the report creation process is so important and why VFP developers need a serious bag of tricks when leveraging the good ole Report Designer.

The primary focus of most database applications is to store important information that is critical to the people who use the systems. The next most critical functionality is the process of summarizing and reporting the information so it can be used by the business to make decisions based on the data that is tracked.

I have heard experienced developers say that the best way to create reports is hire someone who likes to do them. They flat out do not want to create reports. In the past we have heard developers say stuff like "I don't do data," but lately we are starting to hear the "I don't do reports" mantra. Data output is the goal of most applications. Some customers want elaborate output that might be used to publish a book or sales brochure, others just need a listing of the latest sales numbers to make sure goals are being met daily. Frankly, this author loves doing reports. Reports are the lifeblood of the customers we work for and we get great pleasure when the raw data is transformed into information that allows the customers to analyze their business.

The output from an application is a great place to start when designing a new application. When we sit down with a customer to start collecting requirements we initially ask what the goal of the system is for the customer. The next step is to define the reports and the output they need to generate and analyze. You might be asking, why start with the reports? The customer is stating the different entities and attributes as they discuss the outputs. These easily translate to data elements in the data model.

The real trick is making the VFP Report Designers twist and turn in the directions that the customers need. This chapter will tackle some basic and interesting techniques to help you generate some of the reports that customers demand.

It is important to note at this time that many of the tips presented in this chapter apply to both reports and labels. There are many similarities between the Report and Label Designer, almost as if they are the same code internally. We see two significant differences between the designers. The first is the New Label dialog presented for a new label that lists all the Avery Label formats available for selection. The second difference is the default way pages are defined within the File|Page Setup… dialog when new reports and labels are created. Reports default to printing to the printable page while labels default to printing to the whole page.

All the samples presented in this chapter can be found in the CH16.pjx project. All the report samples can be run from the Ch16Rpts form.

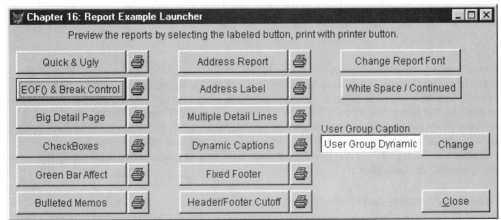

Figure 16.1 The Ch16Rpts form demonstrates all the samples and tips discussed throughout this chapter

Report Rule #1

The number one rule to getting successful reports in VFP is to let Visual FoxPro do what it does best, which is manipulate the data. Using proven techniques like SQL-Selects or even some old fashioned Xbase data commands like SCAN…ENDSCAN to process the data and create a cursor for the report to format is a best practice which has worked for years. This is the Keep It Simple Simon (KISS) methodology that we have employed to creating reports with the VFP Report Designer.

Formatting techniques

Billy Crystal's character Fernando on Saturday Night Live coined the phrase, "It is not how you feel, it is how you look, and I look marvelous." This cannot be said enough when it comes to reports. This is why we will tackle some of the "pretty" issues that have helped us over the years and may enhance the reports you generate.

How to speed printing with printer fonts

FoxPro developers moved into the world of Windows back in the 2.x days. One of the big advantages of the Windows version was the invention of graphical reports and the ability to easily have different fonts. With this newfound feature was a big trade-off. Graphical reports are much slower than their DOS counterparts. The reason for this is that the image is sent to the printer instead of the ASCII stream of the DOS reports. The same still holds true today in Visual FoxPro.

One way to speed up reports generated from the Report Designer is the use of printer specific fonts in the reports. So what fonts are best? This will depend on the printers your customers are using. For example, our customers for the most part have standardized on Hewlett Packard LaserJets. These printers have CG Times and Univers native. Many printer manufacturers are including True Type fonts in memory.

How to generate the "greenbar" effect *(Example: GreenBar.frx, GreenBar2.frx)*

The "greenbar" effect is a throwback to the paper that was used on the high-speed printers typically associated with big iron mainframes. The paper has alternating green and white bars to help the folks reading the report to follow the data across a wide sheet of paper.

Creating a facsimile of greenbar paper is as simple as printing shaded rectangle fields. In the Print When logic, place code similar to the following:

```
MOD(RECNO(),2) = 0
```

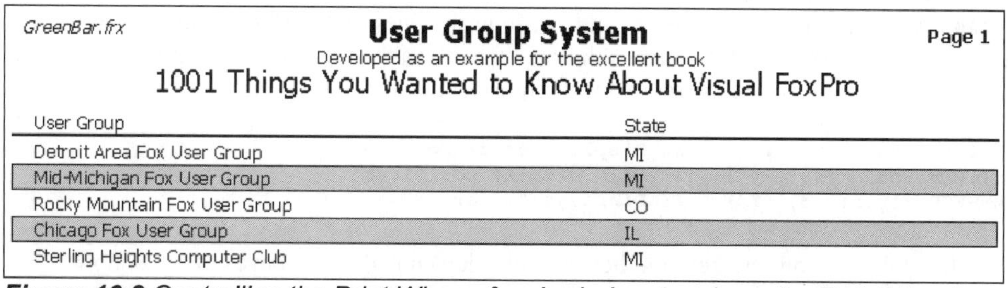
GreenBar.frx
User Group System
Page 1
Developed as an example for the excellent book
1001 Things You Wanted to Know About Visual FoxPro

User Group	State
Detroit Area Fox User Group	MI
Mid-Michigan Fox User Group	MI
Rocky Mountain Fox User Group	CO
Chicago Fox User Group	IL
Sterling Heights Computer Club	MI

***Figure 16.2** Controlling the Print When of a shaded rectangle on the Detail Band creates the Green Bar effect*

The `MOD()` function takes the first parameter, divides it by the second parameter and returns the remainder. In the code we have here, the Print When logic is true every other record so alternating records get a shaded background. Increase the second parameter to lower the frequency of the shading.

There is a second technique (demonstrated in the GreenBar2.frx sample) to have multiple detail lines in consecutive order to have shading. This technique follows the same premise with the shaded rectangle and uses the Print When that has code similar to this:

```
INLIST(MOD(RECNO(),6), 4, 5, 0)
```

The code sample will have the effect of printing three records without shading followed by three records with shading. The tip implementation is straightforward. First figure out how many detail lines you want shaded and double it. This number is the second parameter of the `MOD()` function. The rest of the parameters to the `INLIST()` function are the remainders that `MOD()` will return. You will need to make half of the remainders the parameters to the `INLIST()`. If you want the shading reversed, change the code in the Print When to:

```
INLIST(MOD(RECNO(),6), 1, 2, 3)
```

It works well if you remove the border of the shaded rectangle in this situation, otherwise you will have lines in between each detail line. Selecting the shaded rectangle and changing the Pen size to "none" via the Format menu can accomplish this.

From our experience, we recommend reducing the number of lines and rectangle boxes on the report because they are hard to work with since the placement on the report will differ between printers. It is best to test a simple example on the various customer printers before estimating development time for a report with lines and boxes all over the layout. It is also our experience that the shading can enhance the layout and make objects stand out.

How to generate CheckBoxes in reports *(Example: Checks.frx)*

How many customers are used to seeing .T. or .F. on a report for a logical field and how many of them understand the logical syntax? We are sure there are a few users who can answer yes to that, but how many developers want to explain what this means to a vice-president of General Motors?

To save a little face and having to write up a page of documentation so the Director of Human Resources can explain the .T. and .F. logical values to the VP of Human Resources, the developer comes up with a simple solution – transform the logical values into characters in the report expression. There are several techniques that work:

```
IIF(lVisited,"Y","N")       && Display Yes or No
IIF(lVisited, "Yes", "")    && Only display positives
TRANSFORM(lVisited, "Y")    && Displays "Y" or "N"
```

While these options are helpful, they are not spicy enough for the eyes of a VP. So we need to come up with another alternative. What really grinds into a seasoned developer is a statement like, "Gee, Microsoft Access reports have nice little checkboxes in the reports, just like my data entry form. Are you saying Visual FoxPro applications cannot do this"? Maybe I should have my Secretary kick open Access and have at it." As you might imagine, the solution is pretty easy when a challenge is set forth like this <g>.

Wingdings to the rescue! You use a technique much like the first line of code in the samples just discussed. Using the immediate-if (IIF), you print a character from the Wingdings character set instead of the default report font. So you ask, how the heck do I know the ASCII value of the Wingding that looks like ⊠? There is an applet that comes with all the Windows operating systems call the Character Map (see **Figure 16.3**).

Clicking on the character of choice will place it in the "Characters to copy area". The applet also shows the character's ASCII value in the lower right corner that can be used in combination of the ALT-key for developers with a preference of the keyboard. Jump back to VFP, and paste the character into the report expression dialog in the appropriate part of the IIF statement (see **Figure 16.4**). Change the font for the object to the Wingdings font and you are good as done. **Figure 16.5** shows the sample report in designer mode, **Figure 16.6** shows the report in preview mode.

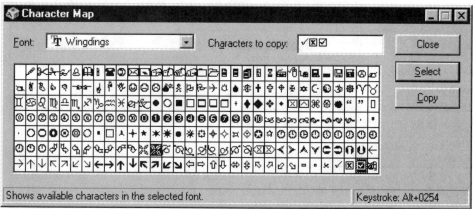

Figure 16.3 *The Windows Character Map applet is an excellent source of graphics to be used on reports (and forms) without the heaviness of a graphic file*

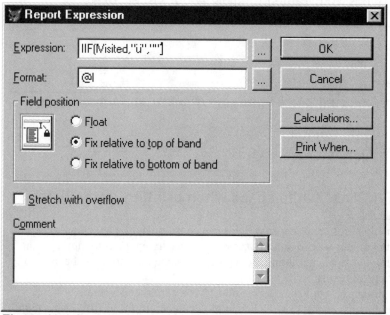

Figure 16.4 *Once you copy the character in Character Map, paste it into the report expression*

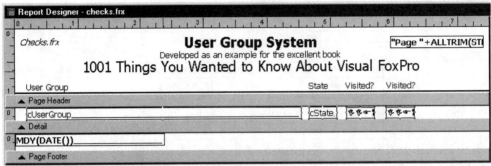

Figure 16.5 *After changing the font to Wingdings, it will make the code unreadable in the Report Designer. It is still readable in the Report Expression dialog.*

Checks.frx	**User Group System**		Page 1
	Developed as an example for the excellent book		
	1001 Things You Wanted to Know About Visual FoxPro		

User Group	State	Visited?	Visited?	Visited?
Detroit Area Fox User Group	MI	.T.	☒	✓
Mid-Michigan Fox User Group	MI	.F.		
Rocky Mountain Fox User Group	CO	.F.		
Chicago Fox User Group	IL	.T.	☒	✓
Sterling Heights Computer Club	MI	.T.	☒	✓

Figure 16.6 *The easy work with check boxes pays off with a professional looking report*

It should be noted for the record that this technique also works for data displayed in a grid and on forms.

How to reduce/increase white space when printing memo fields

(Example: WhiteSpace.frx/.prg)

The amount of information presented in memo fields can consume more paper than we would like. We have found the easiest way to reduce excess paper use in reports is to minimize the white space from memo fields when printing the report. The same technique can be used to double space long strings of text as well.

This tip is pretty straightforward since sizing objects is a common developer task when designing reports. The tip concentrates on the height of the object. In **Figure 16.7** we see the rightmost object shorter than the leftmost. This was accomplished by sizing the bottom upwards with the keyboard. You can use the mouse to do this or a combination of the Shift plus up or down arrow keys. The trick is to move the bottom of the object even with the line next to the object's expression.

> The sizing technique discussed in this section only works if you do not have Snap to Grid set for the report. If Snap to Grid is set on, the object will not make small incremental changes to the size of the object; rather it will make size changes in relation to the grid size set for the report.

Figure 16.7 *This is the designer mode of two fields on the WhiteSpace.frx report. The only difference is that the left one is "taller" and the right one was " shrunk up".*

The exact opposite, growing the height of the object from the VFP default, can give the benefit of extra white space to leave room for notes or enhance the readability of the report. The key to the extra white space is to not stretch it past the second line indicator (underline).

This same tip can be used for detail line white space as well. Just shrink up all the fields on the line and remove the white space between them and the band bar. This can save pages and pages from long reports. It may also mean the difference between printing a single page report and one that takes up just a couple of lines on the second page.

How to display a field in preview but not print mode *(Example: GreenBar.frx)*

Ever wanted to include comments to the end user on a report, but not have them show up on the final printed output? This little trick allows items to be seen in the preview mode of the report, but doesn't include them in the printed hard copy of the report.

This is accomplished by adding the following Print When condition to a report object:

```
NOT WEXIST("Printing...")
```

The chapter sample used is the GreenBar report. There is a note to send the report to the group president. It only shows up in the preview mode.

Another reason we can see this feature being useful is for reports that print secure information. For instance, take a manager's report that lists the salaries of the employees. Security access is given for the authorized users to run the report. If they accidentally print the report to a printer in a cubical area and then take a phone call, and forget that they printed the report, obvious problems can follow. The employees are likely to see it, and there would be trouble in paradise. To avoid printing the secure information at all, you can employ this technique to guard against potential problems.

How to minimize pain using lines and boxes *(Example: PeriodYtd.frx)*

We have said for as long as we have used the Windows versions of FoxPro and Visual FoxPro that the use of lines and boxes must be avoided if at all possible. The reason for this is straightforward, depending on the printer or printer drivers involved. The lines tend to have a mind of their own on where they want to print on a page. The will float around, sometimes by a few pixels, and sometimes by more. We like to refer to this problem as the "floating line syndrome". So what are you to do when asked by a customer to reproduce a form that looks more like graph paper than a report used to analyze a business? Just follow a few of the rules we have developed.

We have already stated rule number one, limit the use of lines. This does not mean go back to underlining headings with the minus sign. We use lines to underline our page headings and liberally use them to underline the Group Headers and Footers to differentiate detail blocks. These types of lines do not cause the pain we described in the previous paragraph. Proper use of pen width and pen style will enhance the reports.

Rule number two is to use the rectangle object when creating a box. We have inherited a number of reports that each contained a peculiar feature – the original developers used four lines (instead of a rectangle) to display a box. The first time you need to extend the box made with lines will be enough to turn your hair gray. Realigning each line is tedious work. If the report suffers from the "floating line syndrome," this will only be magnified with the different sides of the form floating away from each other.

Lastly, if a line is vertical and is used in several bands, draw one line across all the bands it is needed in. Never try to use a separate line in the group header, the detail band and the group footer. You will save hassles later when maintaining the report by drawing the one line across the bands. This way you will not have to worry about lining them up correctly or that the floating line problem will cause support issues. The other benefit is that the lines also stretch as the band stretches when the report is run.

How to use float to your advantage

The float functionality of the Report Designer is critical in formatting reports with fields that are printed below a multi-line memo.

The contents of a memo field often print more than one line. What happens to the objects that are to print after or below the memo field? If they are not marked to float or be fixed relative to the bottom of the band, they will print within (on top or underneath) the memo information. This is typically an undesired feature. Put the other objects below the stretchable field and mark them fixed relative to the bottom of the band or set the float property of the object. The band will adjust its height according to the contents of the memos during printing and the other items will always remain below the memos. If the memos are blank they will not be allotted space in the band and everything below will move up.

How to print bullet symbols with stretchable fields *(Example: BulletMemo.frx)*

Have you ever printed out the contents of a memo field or large character field and wanted to mark the beginning of it with a bullet mark? There is a problem when there is a report object that is stretchable and has text that wraps more than one line before the bulleted item. If there are no stretchable fields preceding the bulleted item you can just put a bullet marker next to the text (see **Figure 16.8**).

BulletMemo.frx
User Group System
Developed as an example for the excellent book
1001 Things You Wanted to Know About Visual FoxPro
Page 1
Detroit Area Fox User Group
DAFUG meets on the third Thursday of the month (except for July). The Royal Oak Public Library is located one mile west of I-75, one mile east of Woodward Avenue, and one mile north of I-696. Free parking is available in
President: Steve Sawyer
Secretary: Rick Schummer
Mid-Michigan Fox User Group
Meets the 3rd Saturday of each month from 9:30am-12:15pm. Informal discussions continuing afterwards at lunch.
The Rocky Mountain FoxPro User Group is headed by Doug Sherman.
FoxPro User and Developer Group of Chicago
Bill O'Connor leads the Chicago FoxPro Users and Developer Group.
Sterling Heights Computer Club

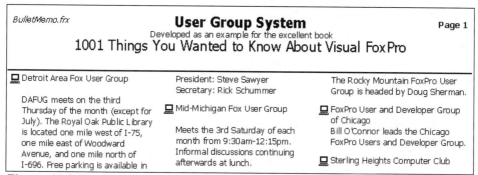

***Figure 16.8** This is an example that prints a bullet next to the start of a long text string that wraps to another line*

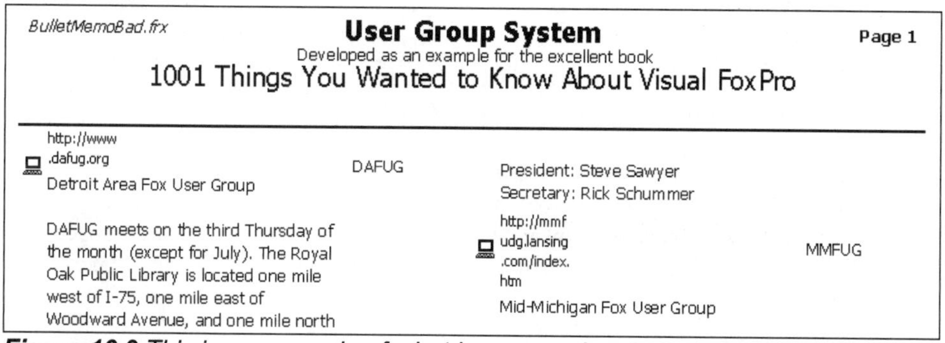

BulletMemoBad.frx
User Group System
Developed as an example for the excellent book
1001 Things You Wanted to Know About Visual FoxPro
Page 1
http://www.dafug.org
Detroit Area Fox User Group
DAFUG
DAFUG meets on the third Thursday of the month (except for July). The Royal Oak Public Library is located one mile west of I-75, one mile east of Woodward Avenue, and one mile north
President: Steve Sawyer
Secretary: Rick Schummer
http://mmfudg.lansing.com/index.htm
MMFUG
Mid-Michigan Fox User Group

***Figure 16.9** This is an example of what happens when bullets are not floating correctly with the associated text*

The solution presented is applicable to any report objects that need to be next to each other on a report when these objects are below another stretchable object. This problem is easily resolved. Create two separate field objects. The first is the bullet that can be a simple asterisk, or you can find a Wingding character or image file to fill this need. The second is a field object that prints a long character field. The example (BulletMemo.frx) uses the combination of a character field and a memo field separated by linefeeds. Make sure that both of these fields are set to float and that the report object used to print the lengthy text is set to Stretch with overflow. The bullet field must be wide enough to partially fit under the memo field. By overlapping the two report objects, the two will float together. Otherwise they will separate as demonstrated in **Figure 16.9**. Make sure that you also send the bullet field to back so the extra width does not impede the printing of the stretchable report object that prints the long text.

How to build a mailing address without gaps *(Example: Address.frx)*

We often see developers struggle to rid themselves of the gap displayed between address line one and the city, state and postal code. This is usually associated with the less frequently populated address line two. These gaps are typically not preferred by customers. In fact, this author once earned a development job because he knew a couple of techniques to rid the "blasted blank line" from a potential customer's important mailing labels.

The first technique uses the commonly known "Remove line if blank" feature that is available under the Print When dialog for each report object. This works fine for labels since there is typically no other object next to the address of the label. This is not always true in a report. The report may have an address on the left and details about the company on the right side of the report. If there are any details on the same line as address line two, you are in trouble because VFP cannot remove the line as it is not blank.

Address.frx	**User Group System** Developed as an example for the excellent book 1001 Things You Wanted to Know About Visual FoxPro	Page 1
Detroit Area Fox User Group (DAFUG) .T. PO Box 51954 Livonia, MI 48151-1954		Computer Geeks Made Up User Group (CGMUUG) .F. 1234567 Main Street Suite 23459 Anytown, MI 40000-0000

Figure 16.10 This is an example of two different addresses displayed without the "gap" left by an empty address line two on the DAFUG address

This is where the second technique comes in handy. The VFP Report Designer has two "special characters", the comma and semi-colon, that are handled differently in a report expression. The comma concatenates items together in the expression and includes a space in between them. If the concatenated expression is empty, it translates to a null string (SPACE(0)). It can be literally translated in code as:

```
IIF(EMPTY(<expression>), SPACE(0), SPACE(1)+ALLTRIM(<expression>)).
```

The semi-colon is literally converted into a carriage return and/or line feed. If the expression is empty the line is eliminated in the same fashion as when the "Remove line if blank" option is set. Another nice side benefit is that you can mix and match data types in this manner. VFP will handle the printing without forcing the developer to transform them to the character data type.

So how does one take advantage of these special characters? Here is the code used in the example displayed in **Figure 16.10**:

```
cUserGroup,"("+ ALLTRIM(cAbbr) + ")"; cAddress1; cAddress2; ALLTRIM(cCity) +
",", cState, SPACE(1),cPostalCode
```

This one line expression is used instead of four individual text report objects. The disadvantage of this technique is that you have only one font for the entire object.

How to use DBC field captions in reports *(Example: DynCaption.frx)*
The VFP Database Container allows you to enter Captions for each field in a table or view. Unfortunately the Report Designer does not take advantage of this feature in the same fashion as the Form Designer. You just get the field in a field report object when you drag a field from

the report dataenvironment. The field Caption is not placed on the report as it is on a form. The technique described in this section allows the reports to dynamically read the Database Container Captions via the `DBGETPROP()` function.

The technique is implemented using a field object since a report label object cannot be changed dynamically at run time. Instead of hard coding the column headers or field labels in the report, you can get the field Caption from the database container. In the field object enter an expression that is patterned after the following syntax:

```
DBGETPROP(<tablename.fieldname>, "FIELD", "CAPTION")
```

This gives developers optimum flexibility by making changes to the field captions in the database. If the user wants the report caption changed, just update the field caption in the database. The big drawback is slower performance since the report needs to access the database container each time the expression is evaluated. A benefit is that all reports that use this technique will have the same caption for the same field. Consistency is a good thing. You can also make changes to the column headers and field labels without the need to recompile the application or send an updated report file separately to reflect the requested change.

Band problems

This section of the report chapter has nothing to do with issues of the music industry, rather how to use the data grouping features of the VFP Report Writer to ease your report creation.

How to avoid orphaned headers and widowed footers *(Example: HdrFootCutoff.frx)*

A group header is orphaned when there are no detail lines printed between it and the end of the page. This happens when you have enough room at the end of a report page to print the group header, but not enough room to print the detail line. The group footer is widowed when there is not enough room between the last detail line and the end of the report page to print the group footer.

The orphaned group header is simple to correct since the VFP Report Designer has a built in mechanism to handle it. Here are the steps to implement this technique:

1. First go to the detail band and get the height of the band. Double-click on the detail bar to bring up the Detail dialog.

2. Copy the band height to the clipboard.

3. Proceed to the Data Grouping dialog (Report Menu, Data Grouping...) and select the group you are trying to prevent from being orphaned.

4. At the bottom of the page you will see a "Start group on new page when less than" spinner. Paste the detail height in this spinner. This value must be greater than the height of the detail band. We prefer to set this to the height of the detail band plus the group header height to ensure that we can fit at least one detail record and the group header.

The VFP Report designer checks after printing each group footer for the room left at the bottom of the page to see if it can fit the next group header. This page space calculation takes into account the group start space you entered in step 4 above. If there is room for both the group header and one detail line the header is printed.

There is no built in capability to handle the widowed footers, but fortunately there is a fairly simple solution:

1. Get the detail and group footer bands designed and working exactly the way you want them for the report.

2. At this time you need to expand the size of the detail line by the height of the group footer. You will be inserting a new object into the detail band.

3. Then create a field object in the group footer that is the height of the group footer. This object is going to be a dummy field that never prints so the width can be anything you want. We place some text in the expression like "Footer Placeholder, never printed". We create it in the footer band because it is sized to the full height of the band. This gives us the visual we need to size it correctly.

4. In the properties dialog for this dummy field object, make sure to go to the Print When dialog and set the "Remove line if blank", and place a .F. in the "Print only when expression is true" text box. This setting makes sure that this dummy field is never printed.

5. This object is moved to the detail band and placed at the bottom of the detail band. It should butt up against the lowest object in the detail band unless you want space between the detail bands in the printed report. Move the detail band bar up tight to this object after you have positioned it.

What this accomplishes is to fool Visual FoxPro into thinking the detail line needs more room than it really does. The VFP Report Designer now thinks it needs enough room for the actual detail, plus the group footer. If it does have enough room at the bottom of the page, it prints the detail and removes the footer placeholder. Now the footer fits nicely on the page when it is printed. If the faked out detail line does not fit, then it moves to the next page and the footer has the company of at least one detail line and is no longer widowed.

How to have second summary bands with EOF() *(Example: EOFBreakIt.frx)*

The native Report Designer provides Title and Summary bands to print out information at the beginning and end of the report. These bands provide the ability for a developer to put this summary information on its own page or include it in the flow of the report. What if you want some summary numbers to print after the last detail line, and then have a full summary page with report statistics on a separate page (ideal for the summary band)?

This is where a grouping on EOF() provides some added flexibility for the developer. It provides a group band footer that can be used for summary counts, sums, and the rest of the aggregate features built into the Report Designer. The built in summary band can then be used with the "New Page" option set to force the actual report summary to its own page. The summary band can then be used for the actual report summary with a different format or can serve as an executive summary.

How to create flexible control breaks *(Example: EOFBreakIt.frx/prg)*

Creating a report that can be used for different sort and control break criteria is challenging. Reusability is one of the goals of good software design, so can we have reusability with VFP reports? This section demonstrates one method to reuse reports by showing an easy workaround/trick that you might find helpful in eliminating the need for multiple reports that fundamentally have the same information.

 The EOFBreakIt program and corresponding report that comes with the chapter's Developer Download files available at www.hentzenwerke.com demonstrates this technique.

Build the report to meet the requirements of the customer. When there are grouping breaks, instead of using the field(s) as the expression, use a generic group name expression. In the example report we use the expression cBreakGroup.

The rest of the technique is implemented in SQL-Select code (or views if you have this preference) when preparing the data for the report. Each of the grouping expressions are dynamic fields that are created through the **AS** clause. The virtual fields are also used in the **ORDER BY** clause as well. This is how you get the report to print with dynamic control breaks. Here is some example code:

```
**** Run first version of the report ****
USE v_groupsbygroupcat

SELECT *, cCategory AS cBreakGroup ;
   FROM v_groupsbystate ;
   ORDER BY cBreakGroup ;
   INTO CURSOR curReport

* Publish the report if data
IF _TALLY > 0
   REPORT FORM EOFBreakit PREVIEW NOCONSOLE
ELSE
   MESSAGEBOX("No data to report!", 0+16, _screen.Caption)
ENDIF

**** Run second version of the same report ****
USE v_groupsbystate

SELECT *, cState AS cBreakGroup ;
   FROM v_groupsbystate ;
   ORDER BY cBreakGroup ;
   INTO CURSOR curReport

* Publish the report if data
IF _TALLY > 0
   REPORT FORM EOFBreakit PREVIEW NOCONSOLE
ELSE
   MESSAGEBOX("No data to report!", 0+16, _screen.Caption)
ENDIF
```

The first report instance prints the records grouped by category, the second instance is grouped by state. The key to getting this grouping set is the `<field expression> AS cBreakGroup`.

The cBreakGroup can also be a virtual field on the view as well. We use this technique quite a bit in our every day work since it reduces the number of reports to maintain in a large system. Quite often we see the commonality in the output long before the users do. This can be a huge time saver in most development projects.

How to build two (or more) sets of detail lines *(Example: PeriodYtd.frx)*

Developers have fine-tuned the skills of cranking out various kinds of reports that list details of one sort or another. One question that gets posted in online discussions on CompuServe, FoxForum.com, or the Universal Thread once in a while is "How do I print multiple sets of detail lines?" The question usually revolves around details from two different tables, each having their own unique data, yet need to be mixed together throughout the same report. The same technique can be used to solve the problem with two sets of details within one table.

The example we frequently see in our reporting is the need to print the details summary for a group of items for the current reporting period, directly followed by the year-to-date totals for each of these items. In this case the details are the same, but the items are repeated for each grouping.

As we stated in the opening of this chapter, let Visual FoxPro do what it does best by first crunching on the data. The steps will follow a pattern. The pattern will require a SQL-Select for each set of detail records. One of the fields in the SQL-Select will be a record type that will distinguish the detail band that it belongs to. Picking the data type and the value of this field is important since it is used to determine the order of the detail band. Each SQL-Select must have the same field names and exact size since the queries will be merged together with the `UNION` clause after the detail band queries are run.

The example outlined in the PeriodYtd.prg and listed in the code below answers the question "What are the sales of books by each user group for the last quarter of 1999 and for the entire year?"

```
SELECT cUserGroup, ;
       ySales AS ySalesReported, ;
       "P" AS cPeriodOrYTD, ;
       dPeriodEnd ;
   FROM ch16sales ;
   WHERE dPeriodEnd = {^1999-12-31} ;
   INTO CURSOR curPeriod

SELECT cUserGroup, ;
       SUM(ySales) AS ySalesReported, ;
       "Y" AS cPeriodOrYTD, ;
       {^1999-12-31} AS dPeriodEnd ;
   FROM ch16sales ;
   WHERE dPeriodEnd => {^1999-01-01} ;
     AND dPeriodEnd =< {^1999-12-31} ;
   GROUP BY cUserGroup ;
   INTO CURSOR curYTD

SELECT * ;
```

```
    FROM curPeriod ;
UNION ;
SELECT * ;
    FROM curYTD ;
    ORDER BY 3, 1 ;
    INTO CURSOR curReport

IF _TALLY > 0
    REPORT FORM PeriodYTD PREVIEW NOCONSOLE NOWAIT
ELSE
    MESSAGEBOX("No data to report!", 0+16, _screen.Caption)
ENDIF
```

The first query gets the last quarter sales. The second query pulls together the year-to-date numbers for each user group. The final SQL-Select merges the first two queries together and sorts the information by the detail record type (cPeriodOrYTD), followed by the user group name. The cursor in the example has 4 rows of data which produces 4 detail lines on the report.

Table 16.1 *The data in the cursor called curReport*

cUserGroup	ySalesReported	cPeriodOrYTD	dPeriodEnd
Detroit Area Fox User Group	750.0000	P	12/31/1999
Sterling Heights Computer Club	50.0000	P	12/31/1999
Detroit Area Fox User Group	2450.0000	Y	12/31/1999
Sterling Heights Computer Club	400.0000	Y	12/31/1999

The report layout is important as well. The key to the success of the report is to generate a group for the detail record type field. This is what generates the repeat mechanism that outputs the different detail lines.

There are many variations on this technique. If you are combining different data from different tables, the SQL-Selects become a bit more tedious to code. The result sets must match exactly field for field, both in size and data type. To ensure the results sets match, you may have to perform data conversions or insert columns in your SQL statements.

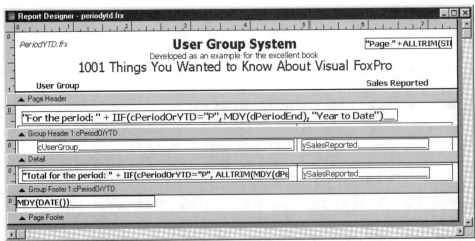

Figure 16.11 *The multi-detail report layout in the Report Designer – notice that each group of detail lines must have its own group band*

How to simulate a detail line longer than one page *(Example: DetBigPage.frx)*

There is a limitation with the VFP Report Designer with report band height. The maximum height of a single band is the length of the page (based on the printer driver it is designed with or printed on). This means that you cannot have a detail band span over one page. So what is a developer to do if the data in a record is too large to print on one page? Fortunately there is an easy workaround for this problem.

First you need to create a grouping on `RECNO()` in the report grouping dialog (Report | Data Grouping menu). You can optionally select the grouping on `RECNO()` to start on a new page with no problems. If you have other groupings in the report, make the `RECNO()` grouping the highest-level group (closest to the Detail Band). Close the grouping dialog to return to the Report Designer. The Page Header and Footer band heights should be set first. Make sure the Page Header band is set for "Constant band height".

The key to making this trick work is to utilize the three bands as the entire detail band. The three bands involved are the `RECNO()` Group Header, the VFP provided Detail Band and the `RECNO()` Group Footer. Each of the three bands can have the height of one full page (less the height of the page header and footer combined). This means that the details can be presented in 3 full pages instead of the one page limited by the Report Designer.

There are two additional options available. If you want a two page detail you must make the detail and either the `RECNO()` Group Header or Group Footer larger. How large you might ask? The detail band should be as big as you can fit on a page of paper, less the Page Header and Page Footer heights. It will differ based on the paper size and whether you are printing in Portrait or Landscape mode. If you want a three page detail you need to expand both the `RECNO()` Group Header and Footer to the full page size height.

> There is one situation where this trick will not work and that is the printing of memo fields that are set to stretch. A stretch of the Detail Band will cause the report to surpass the one page limit on a single band (which is the limitation that this trick works around).

At this point you are ready to layout the fields, labels and other objects on the report. All fields must be a fixed size. None of the objects can be set to float since the stretch is unavailable. You will need to size the long text fields that are expected to word wrap to be a fixed size. This should not be a large problem since you now have multiple pages to work with for the information.

How to fix the location of footer *(Example: FixFooter.frx)*

It has always been our focus to make reports look good and be as compact as possible, but from time to time we are requested to print additional white space. This particular section deals with a request for a fixed size of the header, detail, and footer combination.

The situation is as follows. A user wants to have the top ten employees of each sales group printed in sales performance order. Some sales groups may have 10 sales employees; others may have less than 10 employees. The head of the sales group does not want to play favorites and wants the same amount of space dedicated to each of the groups on the report, regardless of the number of people in the group.

This unique request requires "outside of the box" thinking. First you need to create a report variable. In the example we called this report variable nMaxRowsInGroup. This variable is defined to count the number of records via the Calculate option in the grouping. Initialize it to zero, mark it for release after the report and have it reset at the group level.

In the group footer put a field with the following expression:

```
REPLICATE(CHR(13), <nFixedRows> - nMaxRowsInGroup)
```

The `CHR(13)` is a carriage return. Make sure to mark the stretch with overflow for this `REPLICATE`d field. The carriage return adds a blank line to the stretchable field. The expression <nFixedRows> is the maximum number of rows you will be printing in the detail band. The example report has a hard coded value of 10. This does not need to be the case. You can preprocess the selected cursor with SQL-Select:

```
SELECT COUNT(cCategory) AS nCount ;
    FROM ch16ug ;
    GROUP BY cCategory ;
    INTO CURSOR curTemp

SELECT MAX(*) AS nFixedRows ;
    FROM curTemp ;
    INTO CURSOR curTemp2
```

In this example, the last query gives you the maximum number of rows that you will process with a report grouping. This value can be used as part of the REPLICATE() function to make the reports a bit more dynamic.

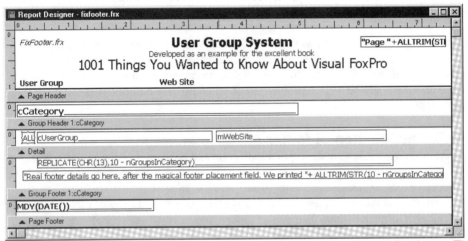

Figure 16.12 The fixed footer sample report is shown in the Report Designer. The key to the success of fixing the position of the group footer information is the use of the VFP REPLICATE() function in the group footer.

How to print "Continued" when detail overflows *(Example: WhiteSpace.frx/.prg)*

Ever have a request to print "Continued…" on the footer of a page when the group header/details print on one page and finish up on the next page? If you follow the Microsoft direction with KnowledgeBase article Q118560, you will be chasing a fox in the wrong direction. The technique described in the article does not work in all cases. In fact, of the techniques we have tried over the years, the second technique discussed in this section is not exactly perfect in our eyes, but the results are correct.

KnowledgeBase article Q118560, "How to Indicate Record Continues on Next Page of Report" should be called the "How to Rarely Print Continued." It suggests creating a report variable for the group with an Initial value of .F. and a Value To Store of .T., then conditioning the printing of "Continued…" at the bottom of the page on whether this variable is false. What happens is that when a new group starts, the variable is set to .F., and then set to .T. when the next record of the group is printed. If the next record after that goes on the next page, "Continued" doesn't get printed. Therefore, the only time "Continued" is printed is when the group header is printed without any details on the same page. If this is what you are looking for, then you have the simpler of the two solutions.

The better solution requires the use of a public memory variable. In our example, we'll call the variable glNewGroup. Before running the report, declare the public memory variable and initialize it to false. The memory variable is manipulated in a couple of functions. Naturally these functions must be in the call stack or available via the SET PROCEDURE command.

The variable glNewGroup is set to true each time a new group is encountered in the report. Calling a function, GroupHeaderOnExit in our example, from the group header's "Run Expression on Exit", does this. The glNewGroup variable is then set to false each time the group footer is encountered by calling another function, GroupFooterOnExit in our example, from the group footer's "Run Expression on Exit" . What this tells the Report Designer is that the group footer has been printed and the group header has not yet been printed, therefore there is no need to print the "Continued" message in the footer. Here are examples of the procedures needed:

```
FUNCTION GroupHeaderOnExit
glNewGroup = .T.
RETURN .T.

FUNCTION GroupFooterOnExit
glNewGroup = .F.
RETURN .T.
```

The Run Expression on Exit does not allow the assignment to be done directly. This is why we generate the functions. The final item needed is the message in the page footer. The expression used in the field object can be something like the following code:

```
IIF(glNewGroup,"Details continued on the next page...",SPACE(0))
```

Now the report only prints the "Continued" on the pages that have detail lines still to print before the group footer (even if blank) is printed.

Other report techniques

How to avoid hard coded printer problems

Reports are sometimes designed in a way that forces a developer to choose settings like portrait, landscape, duplex, or other printer specific settings. Often the choice is made based on the number of data fields that need to be printed in the detail lines. Some choices are made based on customer demands. These choices can accidentally get saved in the report and can cause problems with printing on customer printers.

The printer orientation is determined by the setting in the File|Page Setup dialog in Visual FoxPro when a report is being modified. You then enter the Print Setup dialog to select the orientation. Select the orientation that the report requires. This setting will stick with the report no matter what the orientation setting is for that printer (either in Windows or the VFP default printer set via a SYS(1037)). The key is to leave the Windows default printer selected before making the orientation selection. If another printer is selected, VFP will tie the setting of the printer to the report

There are some concerns with the Printer Setup dialog that need to be watched. One can get into trouble in the following scenario.

Let's say that you followed all our steps described above and everything worked great. Now call SYS(1037) and choose some other printer that is different from the Windows default printer. Now MODIFY REPORT, do not make any changes at all, but just hit CTRL+W to save the report. Visual FoxPro just saved the information about a specific development printer within your report, overwriting the original "default printer" settings. Now the report will print to that specific printer or use the attributes associated with that printer when printing the report to the client's printer. The difference between printers can be subtle or significant. If the development printer supports duplexing and the client's printer does not, instructions for the printing could have negative effects.

This is why one should always MODIFY REPORT while SYS(1037) (or File|Page Setup) is set to the default printer. See the chapter on ProjectHooks to see a technique that will scrub this hard coded report information from the FRX files.

How to use the Expression Builder for cursor fields not defined in the report's DataEnvironment

The Expression Builder apparently got smarter when used with the Report Designer between FoxPro 2.6 and Visual FoxPro. It has been proven time and time again that smarter is not always better. Back in the 2.6 days the Expression Builder would display all the fields in all the open tables. The VFP Expression Builder only displays the fields for tables included in the dataenvironment of the report. Plenty of developers don't utilize the dataenvironment but do leverage the Expression Builder.

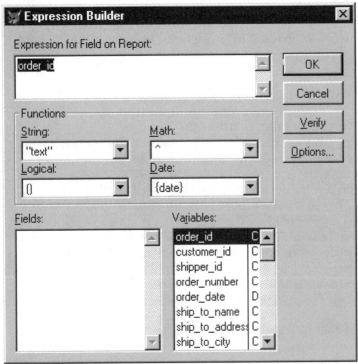

Figure 16.13 The Expression Builder with the Order table from TasTrade database fields scattered to memvars

The VFP Expression Builder (see **Figure 16.13**) is accessed via the Report Expression dialog. It displays the table fields on the left side of the dialog and the scoped variables on the right side of the dialog. The method to populate the variables side is simply open the table or view, or run some SQL-Select code to build a cursor, then make it the active work area. Execute the following code in the VFP Command Window:

```
SCATTER MEMVAR MEMO
```

The variables created are displayed in the list box in the bottom right corner of the Expression Builder. You can use these variables in the expression just like the fields from a table by double-clicking on the memory variable or by tabbing to the list and selecting the variable you want. One of the side advantages to this technique is the alias of the table is not included in the expression like it is when you select a field in the dialog. Hard coding the alias in the expression makes the report inflexible when it could be used with several different cursors.

How to get the label formats to be available

One of the frequent questions posed from VFP developers the first time they create labels is how they can preload the different standard label formats available on the market? There are more than 80 different Avery® layouts natively supported in Visual FoxPro.

The different Avery labels formats are stored in the registry (see **Figure 16.15**). If you want the layouts loaded, the easiest way is to run the VFP Label Wizard. It is one of the rare times we recommend running the Visual FoxPro Wizards. See **Figure 16.14** for the message that is displayed the first time the wizard is run.

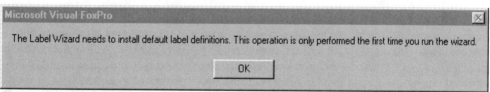

Figure 16.14 The first time you run the Label Wizard you are presented with a message window telling you that it is going to add the standard Avery label formats to those available in VFP

You can also add the formats to the registry by double-clicking on the file Labels.reg in the `HOME()+"Tools\AddLabel\"` directory in Window's Explorer. This runs the Registry Editor and loads the settings into the Registry. This is the same way that the Label Wizard loads the Registry.

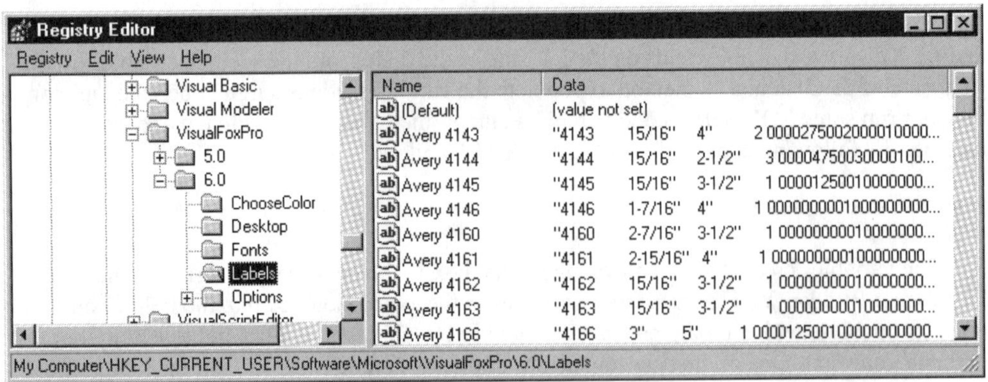

Figure 16.15 *The Avery label formats are stored in the Windows Registry*

Report Metadata Manipulation

The Visual FoxPro report source code is stored in ordinary VFP free tables with the FRX/FRT extensions. Since we all manipulate data for a living (well most of us do) it is only natural for us to want to hack into the metadata files. The key to "messing with the code" is to only perform these operations on backups. Never run a code hacker tool on the only copy of any report table (or any of the other metadata tables). It does not take very much to disable the Report Designer from opening a report. Once you understand this power and flexibility, and the layout of the report file, you can leverage this knowledge to build tools that ease your development experience.

How do you change fonts programmatically? *(Example: ChgFont.prg)*

Applications are distributed to customers who have a variety of tastes. One of the items that customers most like customized to their tastes is report layouts and fonts. While developers can make a good living changing and tweaking reports, there frequently is little time to handle this aspect of our jobs and these changes often become a lower priority.

The problem with the Report Designer when it comes to changing fonts is that you must pick not only the font, but the size, and if it is bold or italic for the report object. This means you must select objects that have the exact same font attributes, otherwise they all become the same. This is a very tedious process for reports that have a lot of different font sizes and styles. What if there was a way to speed up the process?

The report characteristics are stored in table format. The *FontName* is stored in the FontFace column of this table. The solution is to scan the table and replace the value of the column with a new *FontName*. Here is the core code of the ChgFont program:

```
USE (tcReportMetadata) EXCLUSIVE IN 0 ALIAS curFontChanger

SELECT curFontChanger

SCAN
   IF !EMPTY(FontFace)
      REPLACE FontFace WITH tcFontName IN curFontChanger
```

```
    ENDIF
ENDSCAN

USE IN curFontChanger
```

There are other situations like multiple fonts being used in the same report and you may only want to change specific ones, for example:

```
REPLACE ALL FontFace WITH "Arial" FOR FontSize = 10
```

There is a danger with this process that you need to be aware of. Different fonts have different font metrics. What this means is, different fonts have different heights, widths, shapes, sizes, and styles. This can have bad side affects if not used appropriately. If you are using a plain fixed size font like Courier New and decide to change to something like Goudy Stout, your label objects may get truncated since Visual FoxPro stores the pixel width of the text objects. The sizes in the development designers are not reflective of what you get when you run the report with a **REPORT FORM** command. If a font specified in a report is not loaded on the user's PC, Windows will substitute one that it feels closely represents the same attributes as the font you specified. Windows is not always good at this and the report may print differently than designed. On the other hand, if you are moving to fonts with similar font metrics you will save a lot of time and effort pleasing the customer.

How to convert paper sizes (Letter -> A4 Print) *(Example: Letter2A4.prg)*
Developers who have customers with more than one paper size standard, such as 8.5 x 11 and A4, will appreciate this section. We came across a program that converts the paper types for all reports in one directory. For those that do not, it will give you a little more insight into the guts of the report metadata. Developers who work natively in the A4 world and have customers that work with letter size paper can easily reverse engineer the process for their needs.

Listing 16.1 This code converts a report from Letter to A4 paper size

```
LOCAL lcOldSelect              && Saves of the current workarea
LOCAL lnCounter                && FOR loop counter
LOCAL laFRX                    && Array of reports

lcOldSelect = SELECT()

SELECT 0
=ADIR( laFRX, '*.FRX')

FOR lnCounter = 1 TO ALEN(laFRX, 1) STEP 1
   USE (laFRX[lnCounter, 1]) IN 0 EXCLUSIVE

   * Change the setting in the first record from Letter to A4
   REPLACE Expr WITH SUBSTR(Expr, 1, AT("PAPERSIZE", Expr) - 2) + ;
               "PAPERSIZE=9" + ;
               SUBSTR( Expr, AT("PAPERSIZE", Expr) + 12), ;
               Width WITH 77433.000

   LOCATE FOR TRIM(Expr) = 'DATE()'
```

```
   IF FOUND()
      REPLACE HPos WITH 1562.5, Width WITH 8854.167
   ENDIF

   LOCATE FOR TRIM(Expr) = '"Page "'

   IF FOUND()
      REPLACE HPos WITH 66250.000
   ENDIF

   LOCATE FOR TRIM(Expr) = "_PAGENO"

   IF FOUND()
      REPLACE HPos WITH 70416.667
   ENDIF

   USE
ENDFOR

SELECT (lcOldSelect)

RETURN
```

Conclusion

Reporting can be fun just because of the challenges we are faced with in the limitations of the Visual FoxPro Report Designer. We always figure that the paying customers will present yet another report they need that at first appears to be impossible within these limits. In reality, there have been very few reports that we could not accomplish using the tools VFP gives us. In the next chapter we will discuss some additional items in managing the reporting process.

Chapter 17
Managing Reports

"Report me and my cause aright." ("Hamlet" by William Shakespeare)

Using the Visual FoxPro Report Designer is only half the battle when generating reports for an application's users. While the battle with the Report Designer can be challenging, there is the other half of this process, which is managing the report creation, presentation and output. This chapter covers a number of tips on polishing the output, working with the report preview mode, debugging and a couple of reporting alternatives using native VFP capabilities and automation.

In the previous chapter we covered some tips and techniques on working directly with the Report Designer. This chapter has a slightly different focus in that most of the discussion centers on the `REPORT FORM` command or alternative mechanisms.

How to leverage reports and datasessions

Visual FoxPro reports default to the current datasession. Reports are also capable of running in their own private datasessions, just like forms. While this sounds like an intriguing feature to leverage at first, we find ourselves rarely using them (see the section "How to preview multiple reports at once").

The main reason we do not use the report's private datasession is that we generally use SQL-Select code to prepare the data for the report. If we use a report with a private datasession, we have to hard code the cursors in the dataenvironment, or we have to write code specifically for the report in the methods of the dataenvironment. Both of these scenarios have drawbacks in our opinion since the code is only useable in the report it is defined. The report becomes inflexible since it can only be used with the static cursors. The reports with hard-coded dataenvironments have little flexibility other than the ability to leverage parameterized views.

The alternative process we use is to set up the report cursors in a form with a private datasession. The SQL code that we use is typically generated from a number of user-defined criteria. The user-criteria are entered through the form's interface. Based on the combination of user-entered selections we dynamically build the SQL-Select(s) and generate the final cursor(s) that are used in the report. Since we already have a form to allow the user the entry of the criteria, why not take advantage of the form's private datasession? The code that can be generated (via macro substitutions) is much easier to work with in the form than it would be in a report dataenvironment method.

Since the report uses the default datasession (which really means the current datasession, not datasession 1) we can define the data specifically for a report via a custom report criteria form, or we can use the datasession of another form (like a data entry form) if the requirements demand it. This approach provides complete flexibility.

How to create a report template for a project *(Example:*
Untitled.frx)

One of the common complaints about Visual FoxPro is the lack of object-oriented reports. It would be cool to define a report and have the base features be inherited just like classes, but we have to settle for another old fashioned technique of having a report template. The described technique is nice in the fact that we can leverage some default behavior of Visual FoxPro.

What happens when you execute the following code in the command window?

```
CREATE REPORT
```

A new report is opened in the VFP Report Designer. At this moment the report is not named. (It shows up as Report N, where N is the sequence number of the report created for that VFP session.) You can only perform a Save As from the menu, not a Save to current file name. What happens when you execute the following code in the Command Window?

```
CREATE REPORT untitled
```

The exact same thing – a new unnamed report is opened in the VFP Report Designer and can only be saved with the Save As. So what is happening here? You might also be asking why anyone would want to add the unnecessary "untitled" to the command line? The key here is to leverage this native behavior of Visual FoxPro. First create a new report and save it with the name "untitled.frx". Now when VFP is asked to create a new report with the `CREATE REPORT untitled` command, it will open the "untitled.frx" template in the Report Designer as long as it can be found.

So how can we take advantage of this behavior? The first step is to create the report template. Each project may differ, but create the basics of the report so that it meets the customer's requirements. In the "untitled.frx" chapter example we include the system name and the page number in the header, the date in the footer, a grouping on `EOF()`, and set the default font for the report to Tahoma. In a production environment (or system) generic fields can be created for things like the application name, the natural language equivalent of the selection criteria, date, time, page numbers, report name, or a grouping on the `EOF()`. You can size the headers, footers, include default title pages, and anything else that your heart desires or that the customer demands.

Another technique we use all the time is to include the "untitled.frx" in a project. We save the template to the project report directory. This becomes the template for the entire project. When we have a new report to develop we just modify the "untitled" report from the Project Manager. This allows development teams to share the common template for the project and to have separate templates for different customers or even different projects for the same customer. We exclude the "untitled" report in the Project Manager so it is not included in any released executable. It is a report that the customers would never run so there is no need to release it.

One other point worth discussing is enhancing or modifying the template. Since the default behavior of Visual FoxPro is to save the new report with a different name, you will always need to Save As "untitled.frx". Because we are building reports from a static template instead of a dynamic class, any changes made to the template are not propagated to existing reports that were created with the templates.

How to print a range of pages *(Example Range.scx)*

Printing page ranges in the VFP Report Designer seems like an obvious tip, but it is one we frequently help other developers discover so we decided to include it in this chapter. The **RANGE** clause on the **REPORT FORM** command allows developers (and users) to specify the pages they want output to the printer, VFP desktop screen, or a file.

The following sample code provides a peek at a method of leveraging this feature in an application:

```
REPORT FORM (lcReportName) TO PRINTER NOCONSOLE ;
       RANGE (THISFORM.txtStartPage.Value), (THISFORM.txtEndPage.Value)
```

The range is ignored if the report is previewed. The start range cannot be less than 1, but the range end can be higher than the number of pages in the report. If your start range is more than the number of pages, you get one blank sheet of paper.

As the example code shows, the key is to allow the entry of the page range for the report. Add a couple of text box or spinner controls to a form to give the users a range to enter. Make sure the fields default to 1 for the starting page and something ridiculously high like 999 to make sure all the pages get printed if they do not touch select the range. This is a perfect feature to add to the your report criteria base form.

How to print 'Page x of y' on a report *(Example PageXofY.frx/scx)*

One of the more frequent questions asked by Visual FoxPro developers is how to get the number of pages that are in the report so they can print Page xx of yy on the report. Many document centric software packages like word processors have been able to do this for years. Many other Microsoft products like the Office suite have these capabilities, so why not Visual FoxPro? Well once again there is a process that we can run our reports through to get this answer.

Visual FoxPro stores the current page number in a system variable called **_PageNo**. At the end of the report the number of pages is stored in this variable. The most common solution proposed for this problem is to run the report twice, first:

```
PRIVATE pnTotalReportPages
pnTotalReportPages = 0
REPORT FORM <ReportFormName> NOCONSOLE
pnTotalReportPages = _PageNo
```

The scope of the memory variable (pnTotalReportPages in the example) should be **PRIVATE** since it will be used outside of the method/procedure that it is declared in when the report is created. Do not forget to initialize the **PRIVATE** memory variable that will contain the number of pages before running the report for the page counter phase. Otherwise you could have trouble with the report not running since this variable is likely used in the report. At this point the memory variable pnTotalReportPages contains the number of pages and you can use it the second time you run the report.

Figure 17.1The example report heading shows the Page x of y in the upper-right corner.

Here is an example of the page numbers being printed out on the report. It allows you to preview the report in design mode without having to set up the total pages variable in advance.

```
"Page " + ALLTRIM(STR(_PAGENO)) + ;
IIF(TYPE("pnTotalReportPages")="N"," of "+ALLTRIM(STR(pnTotalReportPages)),"")
```

As an alternative, the following line of code is used by many VFP developers to determine the number of pages in a report.:

```
REPORT FORM <ReportFormName> NOCONSOLE TO NUL
```

The biggest disadvantage of the Page xx of yy technique is that the report actually runs twice which can be time consuming for longer reports. The VFP report Printing dialog is also displayed twice when printing to the printer, once for the counting phase and once for the actual output of the report. When previewing a report, the dialog is displayed once for the counting phase. It is our experience that the end users find the performance hit outweighs the benefit of having this information, but the technique works well for those that see this as a must have.

How to allow users to select number of copies *(Example PageXofY.frx/scx)*

Application users love to generate reports and they love to distribute them to their various co-workers and bosses. Thus the requirement of printing a specified number of copies is a frequent system development request that requires a generic solution to be developed.

The solution is a plain **FOR** loop around a **REPORT FORM** since there is no built in clause for the **REPORT FORM**. An interface needs to be built that will support a user selecting the number of copies, unless there is a specific requirement that a fixed number of copies are generated.

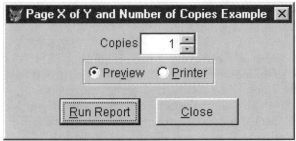

Figure 17.2 *The example form that allows users to enter between 1 and 999 copies of a report to the printer*

The sample code to handle this technique is found in the Run Report commandbutton. The preview output only requires one iteration through the report generation. We guess it might be fun to unleash a user-hostile interface to make the user preview the number of copies they select. We also suggest some appropriate questioning if there is going to be more than 20 or so copies made since we believe enough trees in the South American rainforest have met an untimely death:

```
IF THISFORM.opgOutput.Value = "Preview"
    lnNumberOfCopies = 1
    lcOutput         = "PREVIEW"
ELSE
    lnNumberOfCopies = THISFORM.spnCopies.Value
    lcOutput         = "TO PRINTER"
ENDIF

FOR lnCount = 1 TO lnNumberOfCopies
    REPORT FORM (lcReportName) &lcOutput NOCONSOLE
ENDFOR
```

The example spinner control is where the property settings are to restrict the number of copies from being less than 1 and greater than 999.

Another option to handle multiple copies is to use the **PROMPT** clause on the **REPORT FORM** command allowing the end user to select a number of copies if the printer driver supports this option. We have stayed away from the **PROMPT** clause because our users did not want the extra dialog displayed after the typical report criteria entry form in our applications. This method of selecting the number of copies hands over control to the Windows print driver to leverage the printer's ability to print copies without running the report multiple times. This is a more efficient way to get more than one copy to a printer.

How to find "Variable not found" errors in a report

VFP developers who have used the Report Designer at some point have run up against the "Variable <variable> not found" error message while testing their latest application executable. This message is aggravating since it is displayed without telling you where the expression is flawed in the report. This expression is sometimes difficult to find since there could be dozens of fields on the report. To compound this problem, the expression failure could be in the calculation of fields, calculation of report variables, or Print When conditions. Have you ever tracked down a bad expression in someone else's report in a line object's Print When? Condition. Trust us, it is not much fun.

Fortunately there is a technique that speeds up the tracking of these painful bugs. The key to a quick resolution is to suspend the program code after the final cursors are prepared. If this is not practical, prepare the data manually. Once the data is prepared, modify the report and preview it. The error will be displayed. After you close the report preview mode the Report Designer will display the expression field that the error is occurring. At this point you can make the correction, save the report and try again. Repeat until all bugs are eradicated.

How to avoid having a report disable the system menu

Ever had a report preview close down and the menu is disabled? There was a bug in VFP 5.0 that we are not sure is fixed in the latest version of VFP. This is one of those painful, intermittent, and hard to reproduce bugs that do not happen with all reports. The solution is not painful so it is worth mentioning at this time.

The steps that have been common to disabling the system menu are as follows:

1. Run a form for a report which contains the selection criteria.

2. Preview the needed report (via a commandbutton).

3. Close report using the preview window close button in the upper right hand corner.

4. Close the report criteria form.

At this point all menu items are disabled just like a modal form is running. If the user exits out of the report preview mode using the escape key or the exit commandbutton on the preview toolbar the menu items are not disabled. The workaround is to wrap the **REPORT FORM** command with a **PUSH MENU** and **POP MENU**.

```
PUSH MENU _msysmenu
REPORT FORM <ReportName> PREVIEW...
POP MENU _msysmenu
```

The menu push and pop does have some significant memory requirements, but the machine horsepower needed to run VFP 6.0 based applications can easily handle this.

How to collate pages from different reports

There are times when several completely different report layouts need to be collated or sequenced in the output. We have had customers who have legal documents that are regularly printed out on entirely different paper, but are considered part of a package. How can one get the Report Designer to print different reports to different pages of print, or entirely different layouts to be collating together?

The solution we have designed took some out of the box thinking. The basic design consists of using a driving report criteria selection form. This form has all the user selectable interface objects to determine the base record set. This form then "drives" the reports to print in sequence.

Once the user makes the criteria selection the report object goes into action. The sequence can be patterned in the following steps:

1. Queries are run to get the record set matching the user's selections.

2. Start loop through the initial query result.

3. Subquery for report one is made to get one or more records for the report based on the initial query

4. REPORT FORM <report 1>.

5. Subquery for report two is made to get one or more records for the report based on the initial query.

6. REPORT FORM <report 2>.

7. Keep repeating through all the reports.

8. Loop to step 3 until all records are processed.

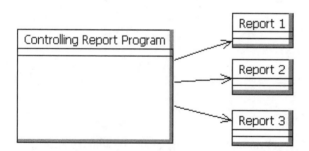

Figure 17.3 *This is the architecture used to call different reports in sequence when packaging and collating different report layouts*

At first the design looks like it is best suited for reports that do not print page numbers since each report will initialize the **_PAGENO** variable to 1 when the report is printing. There is a way to work around this limitation by creating a **PRIVATE** variable that keeps track of the report pages printed. Initialize the memory variable to 0 and after each report, add the value of **_PAGENO** to it. In our reports we typically use the following expression to print the page number on the report:

```
"Page "+ALLTRIM(STR(_PAGENO))
```

In the multi-report layout situation we need to add the private memory variable to the number of pages in the current report:

```
"Page " + ALLTRIM(STR(_PAGENO + ;
                      IIF(TYPE("pnAllPrevPages") = "N", pnAllPrevPages, 0)))
```

We recommend checking the type of the private memory variable so you can run the report standalone (without the calling form). If the report is run with the collating process, the variable will already be defined and the report will run fine. If you are just testing the report alone (i.e. Previewing from the Report Designer), checking the variable type will avoid a "Variable not found" error. Most reports do not require multiple layouts, but if the situation arises where you need them, at least you will have a starting point to begin.

How to display a custom 'Printing Dialog' *(Example Contacts.frx,*
ChangePrintingWindow.prg)

Over the years many developers have asked about changing the "Printing..." dialog displayed when a report is sent to a printer. One of the reasons many developers like to provide their own dialog is that the VFP dialog notes the report name that is being printed. **Figure 17.4** shows an example of this dialog. Does "timelistd.frx" have any meaning to an end user? These developers like to have more control over the display. Can it be done? Of course, otherwise why would we print a section in the chapter?

Figure 17.4 *The VFP printing dialog*

 First check out the program ChangePrintingWindow.prg available with the chapter's Developer Download files available at www.hentzenwerke.com. The program code can be found in **Listing 17.1**.

Listing 17.1 *This code displays a custom Printing dialog*

```
LPARAMETER tcTitle, tcIcon, tcText

* VFP Window name of default printing window
#DEFINE ccWIN_PRINTING "Printing..."

* Define the local variables
LOCAL lcFont
LOCAL lnSize
LOCAL lcStyle
LOCAL lnTitle
LOCAL lnLeftBorder
LOCAL lnTopBorder
LOCAL lnHeight
```

```
LOCAL lnWidth

* Only change the window if it exists
IF WEXIST(ccWIN_PRINTING)
   IF EMPTY(WPARENT(ccWIN_PRINTING))
      lcFont      = WFONT( 1, ccWIN_PRINTING )
      lnSize      = WFONT( 2, ccWIN_PRINTING )
      lcStyle     = WFONT( 3, ccWIN_PRINTING )
      lnHeight    = FONTMETRIC(6, lcFont, lnSize, lcStyle)
      lnWidth     = FONTMETRIC(4, lcFont, lnSize, lcStyle) + ;
                    FONTMETRIC(1, lcFont, lnSize, lcStyle)
      lnLeftBorder = SYSMETRIC(3) / lnHeight
      lnTitle     = (SYSMETRIC(9)+2) / lnWidth
      lnTopBorder = SYSMETRIC(4) / lnWidth

      DEFINE WINDOW CustomPrint ;
         FROM WLROW(ccWIN_PRINTING), WLCOL(ccWIN_PRINTING) ;
         SIZE WROWS(ccWIN_PRINTING) - lnTopBorder, ;
         WCOLS(ccWIN_PRINTING) - lnLeftBorder ;
         SYSTEM ;
         TITLE tcTitle ;
         MINIMIZE ZOOM FLOAT CLOSE ;
         ICON FILE (tcIcon) ;
         FONT lcFont, lnSize;
         STYLE lcStyle ;
         COLOR RGB(0, 0, 0, 192, 192, 192)

      DEFINE WINDOW CustomPrintReport ;
         FROM 0, 0 ;
         TO (WROWS(ccWIN_PRINTING) - lnTopBorder) / 3, ;
         WCOLS(ccWIN_PRINTING) - lnLeftBorder ;
         NONE ;
         FONT lcFont, lnSize;
         STYLE lcStyle ;
         COLOR RGB(0, 0, 0, 192, 192, 192) ;
         IN WINDOW CustomPrint

      ACTIVATE WINDOW CustomPrint
      ACTIVATE WINDOW ccWIN_PRINTING IN CustomPrint
      MOVE WINDOW ccWIN_PRINTING TO - (lnTopBorder + lnTitle), - lnLeftBorder
      ACTIVATE WINDOW CustomPrintReport
      @ 1, 1 SAY PADC(tcText, WCOLS("CustomPrintReport"))
   ENDIF
ENDIF

RETURN ""
```

The code is straight forward if you have developed in FoxPro 2.x. For those FoxPro developers who have started with the VFP generation, the code may not be straightforward. The program takes three parameters. The first is the form title, followed by the form icon, and finally a message to be displayed on the dialog. By using the **DEFINE WINDOW** command, we can create an old, FoxPro 2.x style form in memory. The **ACTIVATE WINDOW** command then makes the newly defined window visible and gives it focus. The **MOVE WINDOW** command is taking the existing VFP dialog and moving it off the visible screen so the new custom dialog is seen and is the only Printing dialog visible. The **@ 1, 1 SAY** displays the text defined on that line at row one and column one of that form.

The method of getting the custom dialog to be displayed requires a call directly from a report field to the ChangePrintingWindow procedure. The program determines whether the report is printing or previewing to see if the VFP dialog is active. We create a field on the report in the report title or header band. This new field is patterned after the following expression:

```
ChangePrintingWindow("Custom Printing","Print.ico","Printing Contacts...")
```

There are a couple of drawbacks to this approach. The first is the most compelling reason we typically stay with the standard dialog. The cancel commandbutton is not available. Therefore the user has no option to terminate the printing. This may be a feature in some cases when the report must run no matter what. The second is that the page numbers are not displayed as the report is generated. We can overcome this problem by adding a field in the report header that calls a custom method that displays the **_PageNo** variable on the custom form.

How to change the title of Print Preview window *(Example:*
Contacts.scx/frx)
Many developers do not want the standard Print Preview window in their applications because the title of the preview form displays the report file name.

The VFP **REPORT FORM** command has a **WINDOW** clause that allows developers to define a form that the report can be displayed in. The form definition properties are used by the report instead of the native VFP Preview Window. Here is a code example of how we use this technique:

```
LOCAL loReportForm
LOCAL lcClassPath
LOCAL lcReport

lcReport    = "Contacts"

* Create the form that the preview is run in and hide all other windows.
loReportForm = NEWOBJECT("frmPreview", "ch16.vcx")

HIDE WINDOWS ALL

* Make the window settings with your preferences
WITH loReportForm
   .Height = _screen.Height - 30
   .Width  = _screen.Width - 10
   .Name   = "loReportForm"
   .Caption = .Caption + " - " + lcReport

   KEYBOARD "{ctrl+f10}"
ENDWITH

REPORT FORM (lcReport) PREVIEW WINDOW loReportForm

* Release the forms and bring other windows back
loReportForm.Release()
```

```
SHOW WINDOWS ALL

RETURN
```

One of the problems encountered during the development of this technique was that the form *WindowState* property setting in the class does not matter. We set it to Maximized, but the form always comes up unmaximized. We tried setting it in the class, and we tried to set it in the code once the class was instantiated. Since neither of these settings worked we forced the **KEYBOARD** command to max the form.

 The form class that we use in the samples is called frmPreview and is in the Ch16.vcx class library included in the chapter's Developer Download files available at www.hentzenwerke.com.

The only properties set in this class that are not the default settings are the form's *AlwaysOnTop* and *Caption*. There is a second class that is subclassed from the frmPreview class called frmPreviewSDI. This is a Top-Level (also known as a Single Document Interface or SDI) form used for the same purpose, but for a SDI based application (see the "How to show a report preview as a Top-Level form" section in this chapter).

The **REPORT FORM** command makes the custom form *Visible* so there is no need to handle this in code. We hide all the other application windows just in case there are any *AlwaysOnTop* forms and restore them when the preview is completed.

How to show a report preview as a Top-Level form *(Example: ContactsSDI.scx/frx)*

Visual FoxPro 5.0 gave developers the capability to build top-level forms. These forms run outside of the VFP desktop. Visual FoxPro 6.0 introduced a new capability with the **IN WINDOW** clause for the **REPORT FORM** command to preview reports in a top-level form. This new feature allows developers who are constructing SDI applications to preview reports without exposing the VFP desktop.

This tip is building upon the solution described in the section "How to change the title of Print Preview window". You need to build a form class with the desired look and feel. This can be a VFP form class that is created with the Form Designer, or programmatically via the **DEFINE CLASS**. The key is to set the *ShowWindow* property to 2 - As Top-Level Form.

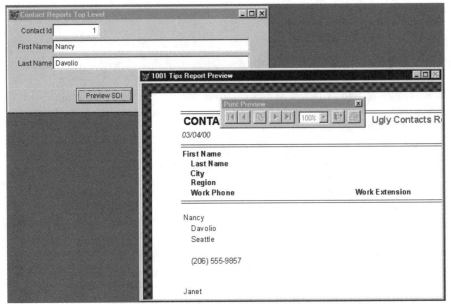

Figure 17.5 *Top-level data entry form and top-level report preview*

 The form class that we use in the samples is called frmPreviewSDI and is in the Ch16.vcx class library included in the chapters Developer Download files available at www.hentzenwerke.com. This class is a subclass of the frmPreview form; therefore look at some of the default properties set in this class as well.

The top-level report preview concept can be carried forward one more step by making the report preview form be a MDI (Multiple Document Interface) child form of another top-level form. The additional property that needs to be set to distinguish this is the *MDIForm* property. Set the *MDIForm* property to `.T.`. The advantage of this property is for developers who have an SDI application and have a main form that other MDI forms run inside. This gives the same look and feel of a standard VFP application, but more control over event/method handling of the main form that you do not have with the VFP _screen object.

We also want to note at this time that the VFP system menu and Command Window are disabled as if a modal form is running when you preview reports in a top-level form. Microsoft has stated that this behavior is by design. The root cause for this is that the report preview is in its own loop internally within Visual FoxPro and prevents other windows from functioning. This is documented in the Microsoft Knowledgebase article Q178384. The solution is to add a **NOWAIT** parameter to the call to the **REPORT FORM**. We are not sure that the ramifications are all that important since we never see the Command Window in a production application. The menu used in a SDI application is not the VFP system menu either, but we thought this was important to mention in case you are tripped up by this behavior.

How to preview multiple reports at once *(Example MultiReps.scx)*

One of the exciting advantages of Visual FoxPro is the ease of having multiple instances of a form. Users can compare the facts tracked about customer one in one form and customer two in another form within an application. Would this feature be nice with reporting as well? Absolutely!

The **REPORT FORM** command has this **NOWAIT** clause that has absolutely nothing to do with the **WAIT WINDOW**. It is designed to allow the code following the report call to execute and leaves the report available in the report preview window. To let users bring up multiple reports and let the preview window remain on screen using the following syntax:

```
REPORT FORM (ReportName) PREVIEW NOWAIT
```

This works fine unless you want to bring up another report preview of the same report. This may be the same report name but different query information, or the exact same report so the user can look at different pages. If the report name is the same but you want to choose a report for another query criteria you cannot use the same report name. (See the "How to get end users to modify report layouts" section of this chapter for a method of generating new report metadata files to work around this issue.)

> *The NOWAIT clause has an interesting side effect. Since the report is finished and other code runs after the* REPORT FORM, *it appears that the Preview mode of the report loses the dataenvironment or at least the cursor it is tied to. Clicking on the preview toolbar to move to page 2 or later brings up the VFP table open dialog. This is impractical in a production application. The workaround for this is to use a Private Datasession for the report.*

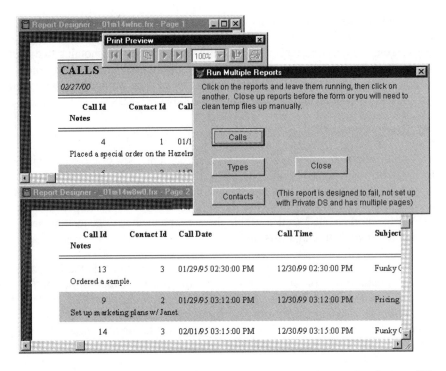

Figure 17.6 *This is an example of two of the same reports running in two different preview windows. Each report is positioned on a different page.*

If you do not need to run the same report you can run reports all day and all night in this fashion (provided they all have private datasessions) within the limits of memory and file handles.

How to remove printer info in production reports

There are plenty of gotchas in a product as complicated as Visual FoxPro. One of the better-known problems is the hard coded printer information that gets stored in the report metadata. The issue revolves around the printer used as the report is developed. Information specific to this printer is stored with the report and can cause confusion with a different printer driver used in the production application environment.

One example is developing reports with a printer that supports duplexing. If the customer's production environment has printers that do not support duplexing you could have problems printing the reports. The same thing could happen if the development printer has a higher resolution than the production printers.

The solution involves hacking the printer data out of the report metadata (FRX). The information is stored in the very first record of the report. The bottom line is that it is very safe to blank out both the TAG and TAG2 fields. The tricky part comes with the EXPR field. This field needs to be selectively modified. In EXPR you can specify the number of copies, the page orientation, the printer to use, and a few other things. We comment out the DEVICE,

DRIVER, OUTPUT, DEFAULT, PRINTQUALITY, YRESOLUTION, TTOPTION, and DUPLEX options for all reports by placing a "*" in front of each option in the EXPR field. The rest of the ones we have encountered (ORIENTATION, PAPERSIZE, COPIES) in our reports have not had a negative effect.

An automated solution to this problem is discussed in the Project Hooks chapter under a section called "How to remove the printer information from VFP reports".

How to allow end users to modify report layouts *(Example ModiReports.scx)*

We are sure that many developers have crossed paths with a client that is a strong enough user (or thinks they are) to open up the VFP Report Designer and create their own reports. This section will show you how you can expose the VFP Report Designer to the users at run time so they can not only modify existing reports, but can create new reports as well. The Report Designer is available at run time – you will not get the infamous "Feature not available" errors that you get with the other designers.

One of the keys to opening up the functionality is to keep the reports excluded in the project and ship them with the executable for installation on the client site. The report files are typically included in the project file and built into the distributed EXE or APP file. If users are going to modify the report, they must be excluded in the project so they are not built into the executable. These report source files are included in the setup/installation program. This way the users can modify the reports via a development version of Visual FoxPro or through the executable you have built for them.

The end users will need some strong technical knowledge of the VFP Report Designer at this point. This will likely require some training from the development staff or outside training classes. We can recommend that they buy a copy of this book to read the two chapters on reports to better understand some of the complexities and approaches to solving reporting problems. Seriously, the users will need a strong understanding of the database schema and the Report Designer to be able to use this functionality, but that was predetermined ahead of time when the users requested this adhoc capability.

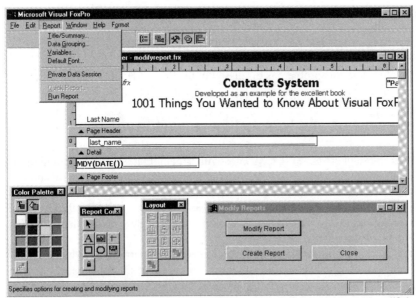

Figure 17.7 *Example run time executable with default settings modifying a report*

To create a new report you can take one of two approaches. The first is to do a plain and simple CREATE REPORT command. The example form (ModiReports.scx) has this code in the Create Report commandbutton Click method. The other option is to leverage the technique discussed in the section on "How to create a report template for a project" and to run code like:

```
CREATE REPORT untitled
```

This will bring up the report template called Untitled.frx or will just bring up the standard VFP default report layout if the Untitled.frx does not exist.

The Report Designers toolbars (Report Controls, Layout and Color Palette) states are stored in the application resource file (FoxUser.dbf) in rows with Id fields equal to "TTOOLBAR". The easiest way to guarantee that your app will have access to the needed toolbars is to create a clean resource file, set it as the resource file for the development environment, modify a report, open all the toolbars (via the View menu), and save the report. Save off the resource file for applications you plan to release with the report modification capability. This file will need to be shipped with your app.

Another method is to create a "View" menu pad named _msm_view. On this menu add a VFP bar. The bar number to be added is the _mvi_toolb. Having this menu option in your application will make the toolbars available.

Are there dangers in exposing this functionality? In a word, absolutely! The big concern is the extra support exposure with the customer. As cool as this feature is, we can say with confidence that the users will get themselves in trouble by breaking code and you will get the call for support. The tradeoff is well worth it though if you have good clients who are capable in this regard and can save you time and energy making those little tweaks here and there.

How to print a memo field with Rich Text Format *(Examples RtfReport1.frx, RtfReport2.frx, ReportsProc.prg)*

One of the cool advantages of a graphical report designer is the enhancement of fonts to make a report appear more palatable. One of the problems presented to developers is changing fonts within text in a field. The solution to this situation is to leverage the Rich Text Format (RTF) of documents. This text can be stored in a memo (or general) field within a table. This format can be printed on a VFP report using the Picture/ActiveX Bound Control that is similar in many ways to a form's OLEBoundControl.

There are two approaches we have worked with. The first option (demonstrated in the RTFReport1.frx example) is to store the RTF document in a general field. The general field can be directly output on a report by binding the field to the report control. It is well known that VFP general fields bloat to the point that they take more room than the original documents, therefore many developers have avoided them.

RtfReport.frx   **Contacts System**   Page 1
Developed as an example for the excellent book
1001 Things You Wanted to Know About Visual FoxPro

Example 1

Company is Kirtland Associates, Inc

Proves that we have a real life example of the DIFFERENT ✳℡Ω☞✳℡Ω formatting that can be saved in a Rich Text Format document.

This can be handy for storing templates of documents that are used to format reports.

Big Text
small text
Italic Text
Bolded Text

Example 2

Detroit Area FoxUser Group

DAFUG meets on the third Thursday of the month (except for July). The Royal Oak Public Library is located one mile west of I-75, one mile east of Woodward Avenue, and one mile north of I-696. Free parking is available in the Farmers Market lot just east of us across Troy Street. Metered parking is available in the city lot just to the west of us.

222 East Eleven Mile Rd.
Royal Oak, Michigan 48067

Admission to DAFUG meetings will be granted free to anyone for 1 (one) meeting. After that you must either join the group (at the low cost of $30 a year, $15 for a half year) or you will be asked to pay $5 per meeting you attend. The $5 will grant you admission but no other rights or privileges of membership.

Figure 17.8 *Multi-column report demonstrating output of the Rich Text Format documents stored in a VFP table*

The second approach (demonstrated in the RtfReport2.frx example) is to store the RTF documents in a memo file. Binding the report to a memo field that contains raw RTF code will just display the RTF code as text, not use the formatting characteristics. The solution is to copy the RTF code to a temporary file and append it to a temporary cursor in a general field. The report is then bound to the temporary general field in the temporary cursor. Putting the RTF document in a temporary cursor removes the permanent general field bloat since the cursor goes away when it is closed. The process is as follows:

1. Modify your application table so it contains a memo field called mRTFText to hold the raw RTF document.

2. Populate the table with the desired RTF documents.

3. Add the following code to your procedure file:

```
* ReportsProc.prg
#DEFINE ccRTFFILE    "temp.rtf"
```

```
* This procedure will save code in RTF Memo Field to an
* RTF Document file on disk, then append it to a temporary
* cursor in the a General Field
**********************
PROCEDURE AppendGenRTF
**********************
LPARAMETER tcMemoFieldName

LOCAL lcRTFTempDirectory
LOCAL lcRTFTempFile
LOCAL lcOldSelect
LOCAL lcOldSafety

lcRTFTempDirectory = ADDBS(SYS(2023))
lcRTFTempFile      = lcRTFTempDirectory + ccRTFFILE
lcOldSelect        = SELECT()
lcOldSafety        = SET("SAFETY")

 * Copy the current RTF memo to a file
SET SAFETY OFF
COPY MEMO (tcMemoFieldName) TO (lcRTFTempFile)

* Append to the temp cursor
IF !USED("curRTFGeneral")
   CREATE CURSOR curRTFGeneral (gRTF g)
ENDIF

SELECT curRTFGeneral
APPEND BLANK
APPEND GENERAL gRTF FROM (lcRTFTempFile) CLASS WORD.DOCUMENT LINK

SELECT (lcOldSelect)
RETURN .T.
ENDPROC

* This procedure will Blank out (remove) the RTF General Field
* and erase the temporary RTF file
**********************
PROCEDURE BlankGenRTF
**********************
LOCAL lcRTFTempDirectory
LOCAL lcRTFTempFile
LOCAL lcOldSelect
LOCAL lcOldSafety

IF !USED("curRTFGeneral")
   * Nothing to do
ELSE
   lcRTFTempDirectory = ADDBS(SYS(2023))
   lcRTFTempFile      = lcRTFTempDirectory + ccRTFFILE
   lcOldSelect        = SELECT()
   lcOldSafety        = SET("SAFETY")

   SELECT curRTFGeneral

   SET SAFETY OFF
   BLANK FIELDS gRTF
   ERASE (lcRTFTempFile)
```

```
    SELECT (lcOldSelect)
    SET SAFETY &lcOldSafety
ENDIF

RETURN .T.
ENDPROC
```

4. Create a report with a Picture/ActiveX Bound Control in the detail band and bind it to the gRTF Field.

5. Add a call to AppendGenRTF(<RTF Memo fieldname>) in the OnEntry() Event of the Detail Band of the report. This populates the general field from the memo field.

6. Add a call to BlankGenRTF () in the OnExit() Event of the Detail Band of the report. This removes the previously printed RTF document.

7. Making sure to SET PROCEDURE to ReportsProc ADDITIVE, run the report.

8. Each of your RTF documents is printed in the detail band of your report!

How to select the paper tray

If you're writing a report using the Report Designer, you can set up which tray to use (every time you print the report) by choosing File/Page Setup from the menu and then pushing the "Print Setup" commandbutton. There you can set which tray you want and it's saved with the report. You can also change it at runtime if you wish or have the user set the settings at runtime via SYS(1037).

If you're not using the Report Designer, then you must rely on the SYS(1037) setup. You can't really change the printer setup programmatically, but you can fake it. If you know the printer is called "HP LaserJet 4P" in the Control Panel Printers section and you want to choose the Manual Feed, you can do the following:

```
SET PRINTER TO NAME "HP LaserJet 4P"

IF PRTINFO(7) != 4       && If not set to manual feed
    KEYBOARD "{TAB}{TAB}{TAB}M{ENTER}"
    =SYS(1037)
ENDIF
```

This code instructs VFP to direct the printed output to a printer defined in Windows as "HP LaserJet 4P," then checks to see if the Manual Feed is not currently selected. If not, then it brings up the SYS(1037) dialog (Print Setup) and stuffs the keyboard buffer with the keystrokes necessary to choose Manual Feed from the Paper Source list. (We are assuming there isn't another paper source that begins with "M".) One of the problems is that this code is very specific to the printer driver and if the printer manufacturer changes the driver, you may find that the code is no longer working.

Other alternatives to the native Report Designer

As efficient as the Report Designer is, it is a bit clunky and has some limitations. Since we live in a component-based world, why not leverage some of the other options available to us? This section will address a couple of techniques we have used in our application development experience.

How to use OLE Automation to Word *(Example WordAuto1.prg, WordAuto2.prg)*

One of the oddest features we have ever seen in software history was a word processing add-in for Lotus 123 back in the mid-1980s. Developers love to try to stick a square peg through a round hole. There is no reason to try to push Visual FoxPro into becoming a word processor when there are a number of excellent ones already on the market. Word Automation via Visual Basic for Applications (VBA) allows developers to manipulate Microsoft Word and can be used to create reports.

 This section will attempt to demonstrate some basics on how to substitute Word for the Report Designer, not as a complete guide on manipulating Word. For more on this go to www.hentzenwerke.com and look for Tamar E. Granor and Della Martin's book. "Office Automation with Visual FoxPro."

The examples presented for this section show some basic concepts you need to implement when automating Word. The first is to get an object reference to Word itself with a call to `CREATEOBJECT("Word.Application")`.

Listing 17.2 *This code uses Automation to build a table in Word and then formats it*

```
* WordAuto2.prg
LOCAL loWord
LOCAL loDocument
LOCAL loRange
LOCAL loTable

#DEFINE ccCR  CHR(13)
#DEFINE ccTAB CHR(9)

OPEN DATABASE ch16
USE v_shortcontactlist IN 0
SELECT v_shortcontactlist

lnRecCount = RECCOUNT("v_shortcontactlist")

loWord       = CREATEOBJECT("Word.Application")
loWord.Visible = .T.

* Create a new document using the default template "Normal"
loDocument   = loWord.Documents.Add()
loRange      = loDocument.Range()

* Create a Word table with 1 extra row than data, and 3 columns
loTable = loWord.ActiveDocument.Tables.Add(loRange, lnRecCount + 1, 3)
```

```
WITH loTable
   WITH .Rows[1]
      .Cells[1].Range.InsertAfter("Name")
      .Cells[1].Range.Font.Name = "Tahoma"
      .Cells[2].Range.InsertAfter("Company")
      .Cells[2].Range.Font.Name = "Tahoma"
      .Cells[3].Range.InsertAfter("Email")
      .Cells[3].Range.Font.Name = "Tahoma"
      .Shading.Texture = 100
   ENDWITH

   SCAN
      WITH .Rows[RECNO()+1]
         .Cells[1].Range.InsertAfter(ALLTRIM(Last_Name) + ", " +
ALLTRIM(First_name))
         .Cells[1].Range.Font.Name = "Tahoma"
         .Cells[1].Range.Font.Size = 10
         .Cells[2].Range.InsertAfter(ALLTRIM(Company_Name))
         .Cells[2].Range.Font.Name = "Tahoma"
         .Cells[2].Range.Font.Size = 10
         .Cells[3].Range.InsertAfter(ALLTRIM(Email_Name))
         .Cells[3].Range.Font.Name = "Tahoma"
         .Cells[3].Range.Font.Size = 10
      ENDWITH
   ENDSCAN
ENDWITH

lcDirectory = FULLPATH(CURDIR())

loWord.ActiveDocument.SaveAs(lcDirectory + "ContList.doc")
loWord.Quit()

RELEASE loDocRange
RELEASE loTable
RELEASE loRange
RELEASE loDocument
RELEASE loWord

RETURN

*: EOF :*
```

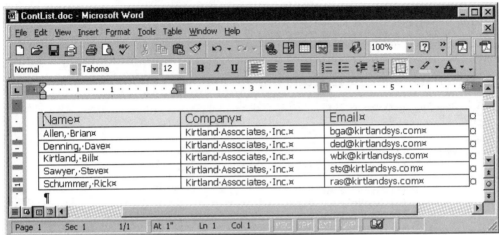

Figure 17.9 *Demonstration of VFP data being presented in Microsoft Word*

As was demonstrated in the samples, generating reports in Word can cause a developer to crank out quite a bit of code. It is a very manual process. One way to avoid this is to develop some Word templates (.DOT) files in advance. We have used bookmarks, which can be filled in with VFP data. The bookmarks are named placeholders inside a document template. The following code is a way to read the names of the bookmarks into an array:

```
lnCountMarks = loWord.ActiveDocument.Bookmarks.Count()

DIMENSION laMark(lnCountMarks)

FOR lnCount = 1 TO lnCountMarks
    laMark[lnCount] = loWord.ActiveDocument.BookMarks(lnCount).Name
ENDFOR
```

Once the bookmarks are determined from the template you can match them up with the data that needs to be inserted into the bookmark. This is handled with code as follows:

```
loWord.ActiveDocument.Bookmarks["City"].Select()
loWord.Selection.TypeText(lcCity)
```

The Select method highlights the entire bookmark and the TypeText method overwrites it with the text that is passed. One word of caution – each bookmark must be filled in with character data so you will need to translate it to the character type before stuffing it into the Word document.

How to output to other file types

The advancement of end user tools has allowed the application developer to concentrate on the non-reporting components of application development. More and more people are getting proficient with Microsoft Office tools like Word, Excel and Access. These tools have powerful graphing and report capabilities. There are also other tools like Lotus 123, Quattro Pro, and

Visio. VFP developers have a couple of ways to leverage these tools. The first one requires an understanding of Visual Basic for Applications (VBA) and writing code to automate products. Unfortunately this concept is only available for tools that have implemented VBA and have exposed an interface that can be manipulated via Automation. The second and more generic method is to export any of a number of different common file layouts so they can be imported into other tools.

There are many obvious benefits to leveraging these end user tools. The biggest is filling in features that are not native to Visual FoxPro. VFP cannot be the "do everything" tool that we might wish. We live in a component based development world today. This allows developers to add functionality to applications, regardless of the features Microsoft provides within VFP. The second advantage/benefit of using the tools users are experienced in is that they can create any output their heart desires, within the tool's boundary. This also allows them to reduce their financial investment in the custom software development cycle and allows software developers to focus on the parts of application development in which they excel.

There are two commands that can be used to create files native to other software packages. The **EXPORT** command generates different spreadsheet file formats. The second command, **COPY TO**, can generate all the files that the **EXPORT** command can and many others. It also has a few more clauses that give you more control over which fields are included in the exported file.

All this boils down to is the always desired, complete adhoc reporting capability that our users request for nearly every application we develop. The key to a successful implementation of adhoc reporting is abstracting the complexity of the data model. This is where the established views and queries can come in handy. Having these predefined removes the education of outer joins for the users. It can be a bit frustrating explaining a normalized database to users who more than understand the business, but have no idea about relational database theory.

This is why we provide an interface that allows users to select the type of data they want and export it out to a number of different file formats. The formats we most commonly work with are SDF, WK1, CVS, XL5, FOX2X (free table dbfs), and DELIMITED (comma and tab). This works best in conjunction with one of the commercial query tools or even a homegrown form that allows users to select specific data or the predefined views and queries.

How to create HTML and ASCII text output *(Example HTMLMerge.prg)*
FoxPro has had the **TEXTMERGE** feature to generate text files since its roots in DOS. Today, Visual FoxPro developers can leverage this powerful output capability to dynamically generate HTML pages and ASCII text files.

There are a few concepts you need to understand to get text merge output generated. The **SET TEXTMERGE** command needs to be called twice. The first call turns on the **TEXTMERGE** functionality. The second line opens up the file, which the output is directed:

```
SET TEXTMERGE ON
SET TEXTMERGE TO (tcFileName) ADDITIVE NOSHOW
```

The **ADDITIVE** clause on the **SET TEXTMERGE** command allows you to append output to an existing file, and **NOSHOW** is similar to the **NOCONSOLE** clause on the **REPORT FORM**, it removes the echo from the VFP desktop. The file is opened in the same manner as opening up a file using the VFP low-level file input and output command **FOPEN()**. The file handle is stored in the **_TEXT** system variable. This gives you the ability to also use low-level file IO commands to derive information as the file is being generated. In the sample listing, we use the **FSEEK()** function to determine the number of bytes in the file.

Listing 17.3 *This partial code listing generates HTML which can be viewed in a web browser*

```
* HTMLMerge.prg
LPARAMETER tcFileName

#DEFINE ccHTMLTEMPLATEHEAD   [TemplateHead.htm]

IF RECCOUNT() > 0
   * Copy template to the new file we are creating
   COPY FILE ccHTMLTEMPLATEHEAD TO (tcFileName)

   * Open new file and merge rest of text
   SET TEXTMERGE ON
   SET TEXTMERGE TO (tcFileName) ADDITIVE NOSHOW

   * Heading
   \<p align="center"><font face="Tahoma"><b>1001 Tips Contact List HTML Sample
   \\ </b></font>
   \<p></p>
   \<table border="0" width="900">

   * Create HTML row for all records in data set
   SCAN
      \  <tr>
      \    <td><font face="Tahoma" size=2>
      \\       <<ALLTRIM(last_name)+", " + ALLTRIM(first_name)>> </font></td>
      \    <td><font face="Tahoma" size=2> <<ALLTRIM(email_name)>> </font></td>
      \    <td><font face="Tahoma" size=2> <<ALLTRIM(company_name)>> </font></td>
      \    <td><font face="Tahoma" size=2> <<ALLTRIM(city)>> </font></td>
      \    <td><font face="Tahoma" size=2> <<state>> </font></td>
      \    <td><font face="Tahoma" size=2> <<postalcode>> </font></td>
      \  </tr>
   ENDSCAN

   * Wrap up the report footer
   \</table>
   \<p><font face="Tahoma" size="2">
   \<<DATETIME()>><br>
   \<<tcFileName>>

   * Get the number of bytes in the file
   lnFileSize = FSEEK(_text,0,2)        && Determine file size, assign to pnSize

   * Get the size of the file using the Low-Level file IO command
   \<br><<"The "+tcFileName+" is "+ALLTRIM(STR(lnFileSize))+" bytes long.">>
   \</font></p>
   \</body>
   \</html>

   * Close the file and turn off textmerge
```

```
      SET TEXTMERGE TO
      SET TEXTMERGE OFF
ENDIF
```

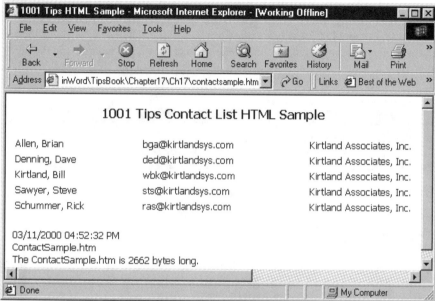

Figure 17.10 *Demonstration of VFP data being presented in a web browser*

In the sample listing we use a COPY FILE command to copy a file to the same file as we plan to generate using TEXTMERGE. Then we open the file with the ADDITIVE clause to append more information on to the file. Some of the readers may be asking why we would be doing this. What we have done in advance is create a HTML page in our favorite HTML editor. This allows us to create templates using the convenience of the What-You-See-Is-What-You-Get (almost) editor. This technique gives us a standard header, possible background image, and some font settings for all HTML pages generated. The same can be done for a common footer as well. This means that only the dynamic data needs to be coded and formatted.

There are a number of commercial products that assist in the generation of HTML output like Rick Strahl's "WebConnect". If you have simple needs the power of TEXTMERGE will get the job done with ease. The TEXTMERGE feature is also an alternative to the REPORT FORM ASCII. Although it does take more effort to format the output in code, you have far more control with the format when using TEXTMERGE instead of the ASCII option.

How to generate PDF output

The Adobe Acrobat Portable Document Format (PDF) has been gaining momentum as a standard format on the Web and as an exchange mechanism for formatted output. Generating output for the Web historically has required formatting output using HTML tags. The Acrobat Reader is available for free and PDF files can be viewed directly in the web browser via the

ActiveX control for Internet Explorer and an add-in for Netscape. It is also platform independent since it can be viewed in Windows or on the Macintosh. The Acrobat files are also compressed which is ideal for reports that need to be distributed.

VFP reports are generated as a PDF file by printing directly to the PDFWriter printer driver. This requires a full license of Adobe Acrobat, but the viewing of the output only requires Adobe Acrobat Reader, which is free. Once you print a report to the PDFWriter printer driver, you are prompted to provide a name for the PDF file. The file is based on the Adobe PostScript engine and the output is laid out exactly like the output would be in the VFP preview window or to a printer. You are still limited to the features of the VFP Report Designer, but the viewing and distribution of the report is enhanced.

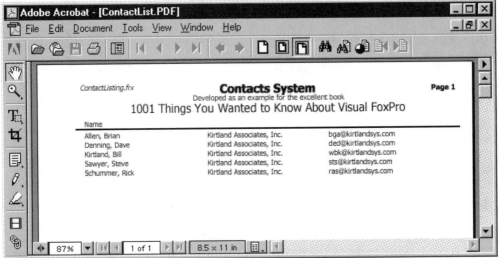

Figure 17.11 *This is a VFP report presented in Adobe Acrobat*

You can create PDF files from any program that can output to a printer. You can even combine Automation to Word (or another program) from VFP, then print this output to the PDFWriter printer driver.

Once the PDF file is created, it can be annotated with Adobe Exchange. This is another feature in the Adobe Acrobat product. How many times have you wished for the ability to search for text within a report? This is another big advantage of this technique – you can search for text inside the report output. It is pretty fast, even with big documents. Hotlinks to web sites are live and will fire up the default web browser when they are clicked on. These features make the reviewing of VFP reports interactive.

All the described features in this section require user interaction. If you want to generate reports to PDF format unattended, visit the West Wind web site (www.west-wind.com) to pick up the free wwPDF classes created by Rick Strahl.

How to review code from the report/label designer *(Example ReportWalkthru.prg, ReportWalkthru01.frx, cMeta.vcx)*

All report code that we generate in the VFP Report Designer is stored in a report metadata file (.frx). This is nothing more than a VFP free table. The problem posed by the metadata table is that one cannot easily read the information stored in rows and columns. We can browse the metadata tables, but this is not developer-friendly either. This section will present two techniques to reviewing and documenting the report code.

The preferred method of getting information out of the metadata tables is to query the information via SQL-Select statements. You will get a better understanding of the report metadata by hacking the report files. Always hack *copies* of the production source code. Hacking the report file is not as big a deal as it might initially sound since it is well documented in the project in the HOME()+"Filespec\" directory. Select the appropriate version of VFP (ie 60Spec.pjx) and preview the 60Frx1 and 60Frx2 reports. There is plenty of detail in these reports to get you on the way to building a report documenter. Naturally, since we are writing a chapter on reports and discussing techniques of reviewing code and documenting your reports, it would make sense to give an example.

Since the nice folks at Microsoft were kind enough to document the layout of the report file, we will not go into this in detail. However, there is one field in the file that is not documented and deserves some explanation. This is the TimeStamp field. The TimeStamp field is a 32-bit (numeric compressed) field that the FoxPro development team created to save on file space in the reports and label (as well as the projects, forms, visual class library) metadata. This field is used to determine if objects need to be recompiled and are updated whenever the object in the report or label is changed. The code to process the field into a format we normally read as date and time is provided in **Listing 17.4**. This code can be found in the CMeta.vcx class library as part of the chapter's Developer Download files available at www.hentzenwerke.com.

Listing 17.4 Converting the TimeStamp field in a FRX file is simple once you understand the algorithm to change it into a date and time format that we are used to reading

```
LPARAMETER tnTimeStamp, tcStyle

LOCAL lcRetVal                  &&  Requested data returned from procedure

IF TYPE('tnTimeStamp') != "N"   &&  Timestamp must be numeric
   WAIT WINDOW "Time stamp passed is not numeric"
   RETURN ""
ENDIF

IF tnTimeStamp = 0              &&  Timestamp is zero until built in project
   RETURN "Not built into App"
ENDIF

IF TYPE('tcStyle') != "C"       &&  Default return style to both date and time
   tcStyle = "DATETIME"
ENDIF
```

```
IF !INLIST(UPPER(tcStyle), "DATE", "TIME", "DATETIME")
   WAIT WINDOW "Style parameter must be DATE, TIME, or DATETIME"
   RETURN ""
ENDIF

lnYear   = ((tnTimeStamp/(2**25) + 1980))
lnMonth  = ((lnYear-INT(lnYear)     )*(2**25))/(2**21)
lnDay    = ((lnMonth-INT(lnMonth)   )*(2**21))/(2**16)

lnHour   = ((lnDay-INT(lnDay)       )*(2**16))/(2**11)
lnMinute = ((lnHour-INT(lnHour)     )*(2**11))/(2**05)

&& Multiply by two to correct truncation problem built in
&& to the creation algorithm (Source: Microsoft Tech Support)
lnSecond = ((lnMinute-INT(lnMinute))*(2**05))*2

lcRetVal = ""

IF "DATE" $ UPPER(tcStyle)
   lcRetVal = lcRetVal + RIGHT("0"+ALLTRIM(STR(INT(lnMonth))),2) + "/" + ;
                         RIGHT("0"+ALLTRIM(STR(INT(lnDay))),2)   + "/" + ;
                         RIGHT("0"+ALLTRIM(STR(INT(lnYear))),2)
ENDIF

IF "TIME" $ UPPER(tcStyle)
   lcRetVal = lcRetVal + IIF("DATE" $ UPPER(tcStyle), " ", "")
   lcRetVal = lcRetVal + RIGHT("0"+ALLTRIM(STR(INT(lnHour))),2)   + ":" + ;
                         RIGHT("0"+ALLTRIM(STR(INT(lnMinute))),2) + ":" + ;
                         RIGHT("0"+ALLTRIM(STR(INT(lnSecond))),2)
ENDIF

RETURN lcRetVal
```

 The code to process the metadata into output that can be reviewed can also be found in the ReportWalkThru.prg which is available as part of the chapter's Developer Download files available at www.hentzenwerke.com.

Here is the core of this code, which processes the report metadata and converts the date.

```
loMetaDecode = CREATEOBJECT("ctrMetaDecode")

* Create a table from the opened Report Form because the
* Methods memo will have some carriage returns inserted between
* different methods.
SELECT *, ;
       PADR(loMetaDecode.TimeStamp2Date(timestamp),18) AS cTimeStamp ;
   FROM FrxData ;
   WHERE !EMPTY(Expr) ;
   ORDER BY vpos, hpos ;
   INTO CURSOR FrxDataWT

REPORT FORM rptWT.frx NOCONSOLE PREVIEW
```

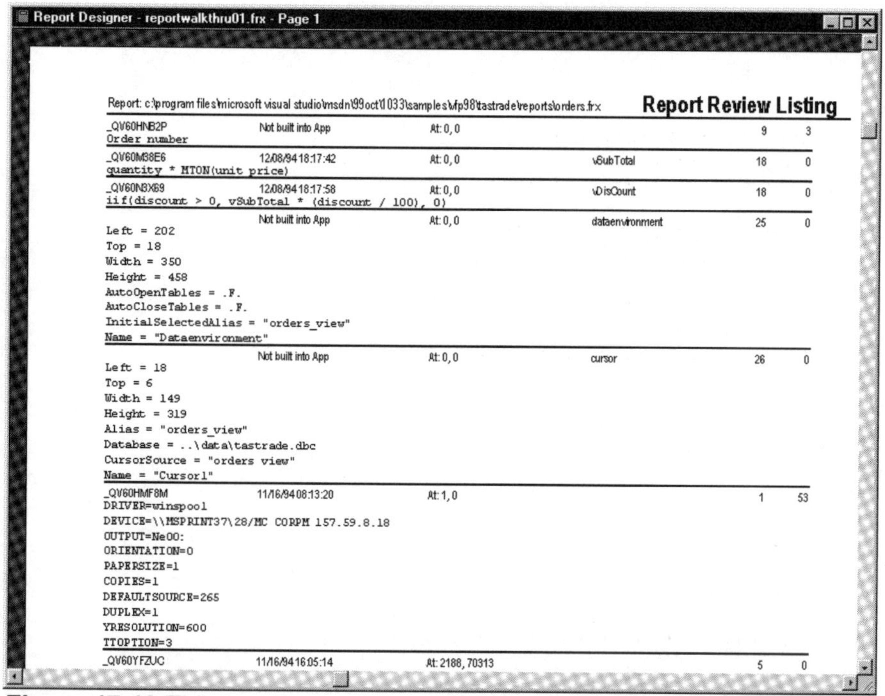

Figure 17.12 *This is an example report generated by the ReportWalkThru program*

As you can see, writing quick tools that provide output makes team reviews of reporting much easier than having developers examine each object expression via the VFP Report Designer.

Conclusion

It's true that the Visual FoxPro Report Designer has a number of annoying limitations. Hopefully the tips and techniques presented in this chapter will help your users get better presentation of the output they request. The techniques in this chapter are workarounds for many of the limitations, but they are also designed to allow you to make a more flexible reporting mechanism for users. Hopefully you found these useful.

Index